The Baptism of Christ
St John the Evangelist, Ardamine
Designed by Clayton & Bell, London, 1859

KEN HEMMINGWAY

# THE
# CHURCH *of*

# ✛ IRELAND

## *An illustrated history*

*Consultant editors*

DR CLAUDE COSTECALDE & PROF BRIAN WALKER

BOOKLINK

St Patrick. Detail of centre lancet of stained-glass
window at Holy Trinity Church, Ballycastle, Co. Antrim
Designed by Thomas Earley (1819–93) and made by
Earley & Powell of Dublin in 1868
DAVID LAWRENCE
© RCB ARCHIVE

# Contents

## The Province of Armagh 108

## The Province of Dublin 274

# FOREWORD

Although there is no corner of the entire island of Ireland that is not part of a Church of Ireland parish or diocese, the most distinctive feature of this Church is a strong sense of *family*. Culturally and demographically extremely diverse, and, like every family, not always without the occasional domestic disagreement, this sense of family is nevertheless utterly unmistakable whenever the Church of Ireland meets in General Synod, as happens in the spring of each year. The General Synod brings together bishops, clergy and laity over a number of days to pray, to plan and to legislate for the future of the Church, seeking always the guidance of the Holy Spirit for its deliberations.

One of the elements that unites the Church of Ireland as a family is the way we worship, using the liturgies of the Book of Common Prayer. This way of worshipping shapes much of the way we express our faith, and its particular language has influenced even our modes of thought. Indeed part of the preface to the traditional 1662 Book of Common Prayer says a great deal about the character of the Church of Ireland throughout its long history. It speaks (in its distinctive period English) of finding a middle way between 'too much stiffness in refusing, and of too much easiness in admitting any variation…' What is being said of liturgy might well be applied to many other aspects of the Church of Ireland's everyday life and witness. There is always the uneasy feeling that aggressive extremism will destroy far more than it can create. After a long period of revision and experimentation, the Church of Ireland produced a new version of the Book of Common Prayer early in the twenty-first century, providing not only the long familiar services in traditional language, but also liturgies in contemporary language, together with new and highly adaptable services for more informal styles of worship.

The Church of Ireland is also profoundly a biblical community. Central to our life as a Church is the witness of Holy Scripture, which we firmly proclaim as 'God breathed' and containing all things necessary for eternal salvation through faith in Jesus Christ. As part of this witness to the centrality of the Scriptures, we encourage a breadth of emphasis and understanding in relation to the faithful engagement of the people of God with these Scriptures.

Naturally and properly, a church that seeks to proclaim the Gospel in every age must also be open to the promptings of the Holy Spirit. Therefore, by way of example, the General Synod of 1990 agreed to the ordination of women to the priesthood and the episcopate, recognising that gifts of ministry and eligibility for ordained ministry are not confined to males alone. Since then, the Church of Ireland has profited immeasurably through the ordained ministry of many women throughout the island and – in 2013 – has broken new ground with the election of the first woman bishop for the Church of Ireland.

This book arose from a welcome initiative by the publisher who has produced illustrated histories of other Churches in Ireland. The volume comprises the work of many contributors with a diverse range of interests and approaches. Each tells the story of the Church of Ireland in his or her own way. In many respects, such diversity reflects the variety within the Church of Ireland itself. This book achieves the remarkable task of covering every parish or union/group of parishes, with illustrations of over two thirds of all the churches. The hundreds of illustrations by many skilled photographers, along with the information provided, reveal the precious built and cultural heritage throughout Ireland, north and south, for which church members remain responsible. At the same time, the modern presence of the church in every diocese is clearly demonstrated and we can see how these buildings continue to be used effectively, for the witness and communal sharing of the Christian faith in today's world.

Although history has moulded the Church in distinctive ways, as this book shows, we must embrace the future with hope and with confidence in God's providence as central for the Church of Ireland. Uncovering new ways of 'being the Church in a changing world' are an exciting and invigorating aspect of being part of the family of the Church of Ireland as the twenty-first century unfolds.

+Richard                                          +Michael
Archbishop of Armagh                    Archbishop of Dublin

Noah and the dove
St John the Evangelist, Ardamine
Designed by Clayton & Bell 1864
KEN HEMMINGWAY

# A History of the Church of Ireland

KENNETH MILNE

## Introduction

History is more than a chronicle of events. It brings 'added value' to a study of the past, seeking to interpret it in terms of *why* certain things happened and what those events themselves set in train, and how trends developed, sometimes quite surprisingly, and if so, why so?

Historians have to follow the twin paths enunciated by the *Manchester Guardian*'s legendary editor, CP Scott, that though comment is free, facts are sacred, but they may well find in the course of research that the evidence on which some 'facts' are based can be flimsy in the extreme. Furthermore, there are times when soundly based facts have been misused in the interests of propaganda so that their true significance has been misread. 'Spin' is by no means a new phenomenon: it has a long ancestry. Nor has it been the prerogative of secular politicians. Indeed, while the emergence in the Churches of a professional attitude to communications is to be welcomed, there is evidence aplenty of ecclesiastics spinning like mad. The invention of printing and the spread of literacy boosted a practice that had its roots in the distant past, but the claims and counter-claims that accompanied the spread of the Reformation in Europe gave rise to both sides in religious controversy appropriating 'truth' for their own purposes.

The study of the history of the Church of Ireland is a flourishing academic pursuit, as a glance at the catalogues of Irish, British and indeed American publishers over the last thirty years will confirm. The scholars, by no means all of them either Irish or Anglican, have found that the history of this Church provides them with a fruitful field of enquiry, bringing to their work the attitudes and skills of their art. In the process of their labours they have engaged in some de-mythologising, questioning some ancient and reassuring perceptions, the abandonment of which has, curiously enough, had a confidence-building effect on the psychology of many thoughtful members of that Church, rather than the reverse. Perhaps bearing out the scriptural adage (John 8.32) that 'the truth shall make you free.'

Some claims and counter-claims of many centuries have gradually been abandoned, but the Church of Ireland holds to its claim to be that part of the Christian Church that experienced the Reformation *in Ireland*. This position, of course, carries us into territory where the terms of reference are those of the theologian rather than the historian. Nonetheless, it is this self-perception of the Church of Ireland that accounts for the fact that the present text carries the reader back to the earliest days of Christianity on the island.

I did not know the true God; and I was taken to Ireland in captivity with so many thousand men, in accordance with our deserts, because we departed from God, and we kept not His precepts, and were not obedient to our priests, who admonished us for our salvation.

And the Lord brought down upon us 'the wrath of His indignation' and dispersed us among many nations, even to the end of the earth, where now my littleness is seen among foreigners. And there the Lord opened (to me) the sense of my unbelief, that, though late, I might remember my sins, and that I might return with my whole heart to the Lord my God, who had respect to my humiliation, and pitied my youth and ignorance, and took care of me before I knew Him, and before I had wisdom, or could discern between good and evil, and protected me and comforted me as a father does his son.

Wherefore I cannot keep silent …

From St Patrick's Confession

# The early Irish church

Among many of Ireland's unsung heroes must be numbered Palladius, sent by Pope Celestine I as 'the first bishop of the Irish', and whose thunder has been stolen by his successor, Patrick. Indeed, it seems that there were already some Christians in the country at the time of Palladius' mission. It is, however, Patrick, whose name is forever associated with the conversion of Ireland, and undeniably his achievements were considerable.

The second verse from St Patrick's Breastplate is illustrated in the bronze artwork by Oisin Kelly.
© THE ARTIST'S ESTATE
DOWN COUNTY MUSEUM

## Saint Patrick's mission

St Patrick
by Marion Le Broquy
ST PATRICK'S CATHEDRAL DUBLIN

Two documents have come down to us as authentically written by the saint himself: the Confession is a defence of his mission, and the Letter to Coroticus, in which he excommunicated a British chief whom Patrick held responsible for the enslavement and eventual murder of some of his Irish converts. Much of the tradition attaching to his life and ministry is the result of an accumulation of myths, which in many cases were used to promote his cult, not least by those political and Church leaders who had the ecclesiastical primacy of the See of Armagh in mind. Nonetheless, it can be stated with some certainty that he was a native of Roman Britain at a time when Roman control of that province was coming to an end, and that he was a Christian, son of a deacon and grandson of a priest. At the age of sixteen he was taken prisoner by Irish raiders on his father's estate (the whereabouts of which we cannot tell), and brought to Ireland where he endured six years of enslavement tending livestock in the north of the country.

He escaped, probably making his way back to Britain, and vividly describes his call to be the apostle of the Irish. Though declaring himself to be 'untutored', this may be undue modesty, and while the years between his escape and his eventual return to the land of his captivity are shrouded in mystery, and the subject of much scholarly (and heated) discussion based on the fragmentary nature of the evidence, he is considered by some to have received some theological training on the continent. The precise date of his return to Ireland, traditionally 432, is likewise much debated, but there is a general consensus that it was some time mid-fifth century. His travels seem to have been confined to the northern half of the island of Ireland where he claimed to have baptised, confirmed and ordained bishops, notwithstanding traditions elsewhere.

Slemish Mountain, County Antrim, where legend tells us Patrick spent six years tending livestock
JILL JENNINGS
SCENIC IRELAND

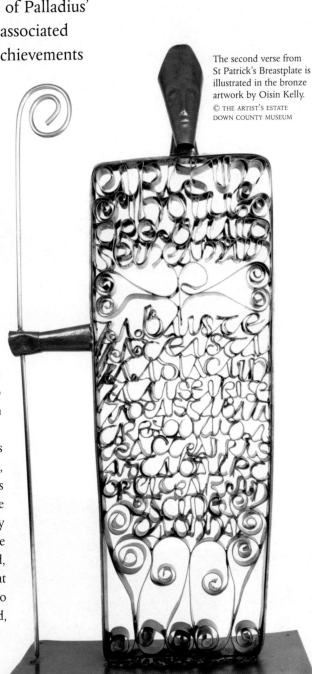

Imaginary reconstruction of life in a monastic settlement based on Nendrum Abbey, County Down. The tide mill, situated on Strangford Lough, is visible bottom left of this illustration.
© HMSO NIEA BUILT HERITAGE DOE

Devenish Island, County Fermanagh
SCENIC IRELAND

## Formation of the monasteries

The Church that he established is considered by some to have followed the British and continental model of territorial dioceses governed by bishops, more often than not based on towns. This, however, was a structure that owed much to the urban character of Roman society, whereas Irish society was not urban, and was based on allegiance to kings, sub-kings and aristocratic leaders, many of whom in the course of time were to give land to the Church, very often for the formation of monasteries; these came to be a prominent feature of the Irish Church, and were frequently under abbots drawn from the ruling family, who often claimed dynastic rights to the monastery. Until comparatively recently, it was widely held that the Irish Church was almost entirely monastic, but modern scholars dispute this, maintaining that bishops were not side-lined as had once been generally believed, but in fact exercised episcopal jurisdiction and were by no means confined to a subordinate role.

Gallarus Oratory, a single cell stone construction on Dingle Peninsula, County Kerry
GNU FREE DOCUMENTATION LICENCE

Tynan Cross, west County Armagh, AD 800–900, is almost all that remains of the monastery founded in the village of Tynan.
SCENIC IRELAND

The monasteries were of great importance, not only in the life of the Church, but for the wider society which they served: they provided hospitality for travellers, and often fostered and educated the sons of local families. But they bore little resemblance to the impressive religious houses that were so characteristic of medieval Europe. They may well have been splendidly situated, usually, of necessity, near a river that provided them with food, water and drainage, but rather than the stereotypical abbey or priory they were more like villages, surrounded by an earthen or stone embankment – groups of buildings, some little more than huts, though sometimes they possessed a striking feature such as a round tower (a kind of campanile) or a sculpted high cross. Prominent among the features of the monastic settlement was the church, often centrally situated, with its adjacent graveyard. Nendrum, County Down, is a fine example. The monks lived in cells of wood or stone, sometimes accommodating one, sometimes two or three. Needless to say, only those buildings constructed of stone have survived such as Gallarus Oratory, close to St Flannan's Cathedral in Killaloe, County Clare, a fine example of an early Irish Church building, while St Doulagh's, Balgriffin, County Dublin (diocese of Dublin) retains much of its early medieval character. To the north-east of the church is the baptistery also known as St Doulough's Well. It is an octagonal structure with a central water-filled basin, now without parallel in Ireland. The monks' cells survive most spectacularly on Skellig Michael (County Kerry). The community gathered for celebration of the Mass and the saying (or, perhaps, singing) of the daily round of offices. They also ate together, so there was a refectory with its attendant kitchen. The monastery

St Doulagh's, Balgriffin, County Dublin (diocese of Dublin)
RCB ARCHIVE

Postage stamp designed by R.J. King, commemorating the Annals of the Four Masters, 1944

was largely self-sufficient, drawing its produce from its fields and pastures, its garden and, of course, its river or the sea, as location dictated.

## The purpose and achievement of the monastery

The primary purpose of the monastery, and what had drawn the community there, was the *opus dei*, the worship of Almighty God, and all activities were directed towards the furtherance of that vocation. The education provided for the boys fostered by the community, who were part of the abbot's household, was to prepare them for the ministry of the Church: a grounding in Latin and in liturgical texts, the psalter in particular. The splendid artistic achievements of the monasteries, from the sixth to the ninth centuries, derived from the requirements of worship. Some of the illuminated manuscripts, regarded as among the most sumptuous gospel books in the world, were treated with particular honour, and even deemed to have great supernatural powers. This was the case with the psalter attributed to Colmcille, dated to the mid-sixth century, which reposes in the library of the Royal Irish Academy in Dublin. Known as the 'cathach' (battle-book) from its reputation as a talisman, the richly embossed leather satchel in which it was kept survives in the National Museum of Ireland. But by far the most splendid of such manuscripts is the Book of Kells, which may have been the work of the monks of Iona, in Scotland. It can be seen in the library of Trinity College, Dublin.

Similarly, the chalices and patens wrought in gold and silver were (exceptional, no doubt) examples of the sacred vessels used in the Mass. The Ardagh Chalice is a remarkable instance of how the cup could be embellished with designs that reflect those that similarly illuminated the vellum of the manuscripts.

By their very nature, it is the achievements in stone of the monks or of the craftsmen that they employed that have best survived and in many cases are still to be found in the precincts of Church of Ireland places of worship. The Irish high crosses, whose most distinctive feature is the ring where the horizontal arms join the vertical shaft, are well represented by those at St James's Church in Castledermot, County Kildare (diocese of Glendalough). Nearby stands a round tower, a feature that has become the emblem of the Irish Church (if not indeed of Celtic Ireland itself). These towers, while for the most part lacking the splendid

The Book of Durrow, written *c.* AD 680, is the first of the great series of richly decorated Gospel books of the early Irish church, followed by the Book of Kells in AD 790. The content of the Books of Durrow and Kells is similar, with the four gospels of Matthew, Mark, Luke and John making up the main body of the book. The Book of Kells now has 340 leaves written or illuminated on both sides.

This page from the Book of Kells illustrates the Temptations of Christ

The Cross of Cong was designed in the twelfth-century at the behest of King Turlough O'Connor, the last High King of Ireland. The ornamental cross was designed as a processional cross for use in the Abbey at Tuam but taken by Turlough O'Connor on his retirement to Cong.
NATIONAL MUSEUM OF IRELAND

A sculpture of an Irish monk and his cat Pangur Bán, by Imogen Stuart
O'FIACH LIBRARY AND ARCHIVE

sculptural decoration that so characterises the high crosses, are potent, indeed romantic, reminders of a civilisation that was renowned throughout Europe. The round tower at Glendalough, given its dramatic situation in the glen of the two lakes, is probably one of the most iconic images of Irish culture, familiar to every visitor to Ireland. Again, known in the Irish language as 'cloig-theach' ('bell-house'), its purpose was linked to the daily round of monastic offices, perhaps by a bell rung at each of the four windows by hand, or perhaps by rope. Some sixty of these structures remain, and apart from that at Castledermot splendid examples are to be found in proximity to St Canice's Cathedral, Kilkenny (diocese of Ossory) and St Brigid's Cathedral, Kildare (diocese of Kildare). Normally free-standing, they have on occasion been incorporated into later Church buildings, such as at Lusk and Swords (both in the county and diocese of Dublin).

## The missionary outreach of the Irish Church

This book is intended to present a picture of the Church of Ireland, so, by definition, it concerns itself with the whole island of Ireland. Yet it would be serious omission if no mention were to be made of the missionary outreach of the Irish Church, not least in the centuries which we have been considering so far. Irish missionaries exerted considerable influence on the character (and cultural life) of Christianity elsewhere in Europe, and seen most clearly in the monastic life of Britain and the continent. Reference has already been made to the strong possibility that one of the most famous of the illuminated manuscripts was, in fact, the work of scribes outside Ireland, most likely Iona. But these were Irish foundations.

Another cogent reason for mentioning, however briefly, the Irish who made their name abroad is that they account for so many of the names of saints to which Church of Ireland places of worship have been dedicated. There are, as the reader will shortly become aware, countless parishes that honour St Patrick and St Brigid. There are many but for whom less prominent names would have been virtually forgotten. St Fachtna (whose cathedral is at Rosscarbery, County Cork (diocese of Ross), St Fethlimidh (diocese of Kilmore) and many, many others. Their entitlement to be numbered among the saints of Ireland has in some measure been acknowledged by their inclusion in The Book of

At Kilmore, County Cavan, the Cathedral of St Feidhlimidh has an inserted twelfth-century Romanesque doorway. It was removed from an early monastery on Trinity Island in Lough Oughter. It is a four-order arch with chevron decoration. There are intertwined animals and interlaced ornament on the jambs.

## ◆ THE HIGH CROSS

Irish high crosses are internationally recognised icons of early medieval Ireland. High crosses can be either plain or decorated. They were usually found on early church sites and served a variety of functions including liturgical, ceremonial, and symbolic uses. They also served as markers for an area of sanctuary; as well as focal points for markets, which grew around church sites. The 'classic' Irish high crosses are located at Durrow Abbey, Kells, Clonmacnoise and Monasterboice. These high crosses are decorated with panels inscribed with biblical themes. It is believed that the sculpted panels were originally painted. On these decorated high crosses, the east face tends to show scenes from the Old Testament and the Book of Revelation; while the west face shows scenes from the New Testament. It is likely that the ring around the crosses may have had a structural function to strengthen the arms of the cross, although some interpret this as representing the cosmos.

Clonmacnoise High Cross from the east featuring scenes from the Old Testament

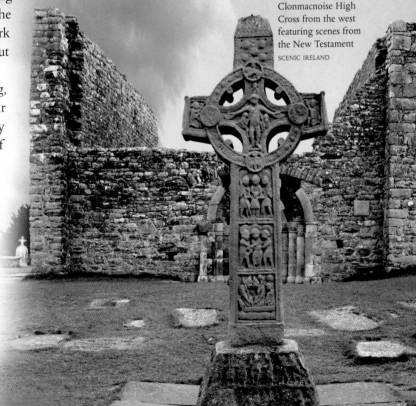

Clonmacnoise High Cross from the west featuring scenes from the New Testament
SCENIC IRELAND

Stained-glass window depicting
St Columbanus – The Abbazia St Columbano, Bobbio
GIFFORD SAVAGE
BANGOR ABBEY

Common Prayer (2004), 'to remind us of the continuing work of the Holy Spirit in the Church in all ages.'

Prominent in this roll of honour, however, are names unlikely to be overlooked. Most noteworthy among these (if only because of the great number of churches dedicated to him) is Colmcille (Columba), who established a monastery in his native Derry, but is especially renowned for the foundation of Iona off the west coast of Scotland, and who played a formative role in the spread of Christianity with an Irish character in much of northern Britain. Colmcille, with Patrick and Brigid, has the distinction of a feast day, with proper collect and readings, in the Book of Common Prayer. But others went even further afield. Comgall, founder of a community at Bangor, County Down (diocese of Down), from which Columbanus travelled to continental Europe, is still revered at Bobbio in northern Italy, and one of his companions, Gall, is commemorated by the Swiss town that bears his name. The rebuilding of the Church and its attendant centres of learning in the period following the disintegration of the Roman Empire owed much to those Irish scholars, such as John Scottus ('the Irishman', as the word then denoted) Eriugena, at the Carolingian court.

The key to Bangor Abbey found in a nearby stream in 1910 by James Wallace
GIFFORD SAVAGE
BANGOR ABBEY

In the last decade there have been major celebrations for St Columbanus in Bangor, Co. Down, and in Europe. A delegation from Bangor went to Bobbio, northern Italy, in November 2007. Deputy Lord Mayor of Bangor, Diane Peacocke, Alderman Marsden Fitzsimons and Signor Farinella in front of the monastery at Bobbio. The original monastery was founded in 614 by St Columbanus.
MARSDEN FITZSIMONS

# The Irish Church
# in the medieval period

The ninth century saw a major disruption of Irish society and of the Irish Church, with the increasing frequency of Viking raids. Beginning as spasmodic forays on the coast and later penetrating inland by river, these warriors were intent on plundering the settled communities that they encountered on their expeditions. The monasteries being, so to speak, sitting targets, offered provisions and treasures of one kind or another, and their surrounding populace provided a fertile source of captives and slaves.

## The effect of Viking raids on the Irish Church

By degrees these marauders from northern Europe formed settlements of their own, some of them, like Dublin, Limerick and Waterford, developing into important urban networks that came to have a significant role in the great Viking trading networks that encompassed much of England, Scotland and the Isle of Man. A Scandinavian kingdom of Dublin emerged, of mixed Irish and Norse ethnicity. The Battle of Clontarf (1014), which history books once portrayed as a decisive encounter whereby the Irish drove out the Norse invaders, is now regarded as essentially an attempt by the Irish king of Leinster, in alliance with the Viking settlers, to resist (successfully) an attempt by the high king, Brian Ború of Munster, to impose his suzerainty.

Ulster bore the brunt of early Viking raids as the Northmen moved from the coastal monasteries inland, up Strangford Lough (below), Lough Neagh and Lough Erne. It was further south that they built their seaport towns.
ESLER CRAWFORD PHOTOGRAPHY

It is clear that there was a Christian community in Dublin, most probably the result of missionary activity from England, and that its first bishop, Dunán (consecrated about 1028) owed canonical obedience to Canterbury. It was not until the synod of Kells-Mellifont (1152) that the See of Dublin was elevated to an archbishopric. According to the 'Black Book' of Christ Church, the Norse king of Dublin, Sitriuc, provided Bishop Dunán with the site for that cathedral in about the year 1030.

## Reform of the Irish Church

The synod of Kells-Mellifont, like its predecessor at Rathbreasil, sought to bring the governance of the Irish Church into greater conformity with European norms, not least by attempting to create a diocesan system whereby archbishops and bishops exercised effective episcopal authority. Much of the impetus for reform and the reordering of the Church derived from Malachy, bishop of Connor, subsequently archbishop of Armagh. The archbishop of Canterbury and indeed, the pope, lamented what they regarded as serious irregularities in the Irish Church, and Pope Gregory VII (1073–85) saw much that called for greater discipline – not, indeed, only in Ireland. The synods were part of that reforming movement.

A signal innovation on Malachy's part was the introduction to Ireland of the continental religious orders. On his way to Rome to request that each of the Irish archbishops should be granted the 'pallium', symbolic of papal recognition, he visited the Cistercian abbey at Clairveaux, becoming acquainted with Bernard, its founder. Impressed by its mode of religious life, he left four companions there with the intention that, in due course, they would form the nucleus of his foundation at Mellifont (1142), the first Cistercian house to be created in Ireland, and, indeed, the first religious house following the rule of a continental order to be established in the country. This was the first of many, which came to grief centuries later at the hands of Henry VIII in the sixteenth century, their ruins a familiar feature of the Irish landscape to this day, and a few continuing to be places of worship in the post-

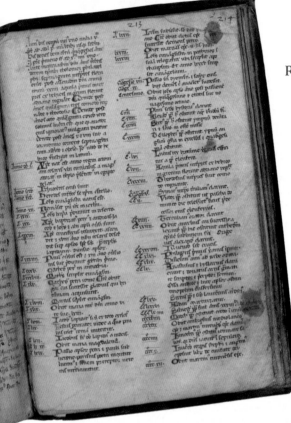

Folio from *Liber Niger* (the early 14th-century Black Book), associated with Henry de la Warre de Bristol, prior of Holy Trinity – commonly called Christ Church- who was prior in 1301. It contains documents in Latin and Norman-French relating to the Priory.

PARCHMENT. RCB LIBRARY, DUBLIN. CHRIST CHURCH CATHEDRAL ARCHIVES

The cathedral archives also contain *Liber Alba* (White Book), an early sixteenth-century century compilation by Thomas Fich (d. 1518) sub-prior. It contains copies of documents relating to the priory.

PARCHMENT. RCB LIBRARY, DUBLIN. CHRIST CHURCH CATHEDRAL ARCHIVES

Mellifont Abbey, County Louth, Ireland's first Cistercian Abbey founded in 1142 by St Malachy following a visit to a French Cistercian Abbey at Clairvaux

SCENIC IRELAND

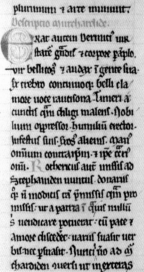

Reformation Church. Malachy also visited the Augustinian Canons at Arroaise in Flanders. He was inspired to introduce that pattern of the religious life to Ireland, and to his mind, the Augustinian canons were the ideal when a monastic community served a cathedral, the bishop being titular head, but a prior regulating the daily life of the house.

This was to provide the model whereby some of the Irish monasteries conformed to a more continental pattern of life, and when Laurence O'Toole, abbot of Glendalough, came to Dublin as its second archbishop, he made Christ Church a house of Augustinian canons. This was also to be the case at the Benedictine cathedral of the Holy Trinity, Downpatrick (diocese of Down). But despite the strenuous efforts towards reform made by some of its leaders, it was the alleged irregularities of the Irish Church that would provide the English crown with the opportunity to secure papal endorsement, indeed a papal directive, to intervene in Irish affairs.

Down Cathedral of the Holy Trinity in ruins pre-1790. Painting by Dr James Moore from a pencil drawing by Samuel Wooley

Dermot McMurrough, the King of Leinster, best known for bringing the Normans to Ireland. This illustration is from Geraldus Cambrensis, a Welsh priest who made two visits to Ireland soon after the Norman invasion and wrote two books completed in 1189. The books were largely propagandist with the intention of justifying the invasion by portraying the Irish as primitive and degenerate. In fact, McMurrough was honoured by Bernard of Clairvaux and was instrumental in the founding of at least three abbeys.

### The Anglo-Norman invasions

The pattern of the Norman conquest of England in 1066 differed from the subjugation of Ireland in 1169 in that the Irish conquest was to be a process that ebbed and flowed over many centuries. Nonetheless, the first coming of the Normans was of huge significance for Ireland and for the Irish Church. This was especially to be the case at the time of the Reformation, when the religious changes in England were imposed on Ireland. Thus, parts of the Irish Church were to be Anglicised many centuries before the efforts to make it Anglican.

Henry II of England came to Ireland in 1171, and remained for a year. His main purpose in coming was to ensure the fealty of those Norman lords, such as Robert FitzStephen and Richard de Clare (Strongbow) who, crossing from Wales, had taken much of the eastern part of the island. They had first come in 1169, with royal consent, at the invitation of Dermot McMurrough, King of Leinster, to support his struggle to maintain his kingdom in the face of the attacks of enemies that included the high king, Rory O'Connor. Henry was, for the most part, well received by both Normans and Irish: the former readily acknowledging their feudal obligations to him, and the latter similarly pledging their loyalty, though given the enormous gulf that existed between their understanding of kingship and Henry's, it is unlikely that they fully realised the implications of their submission.

The king was also received cordially by the leaders of the Church. This is scarcely to be wondered at as Henry, who had long considered extending his rule to Ireland, had secured from Pope Adrian IV (an

Daniel MacLise (1854) painted The Marriage of princess Aoife with Richard deClare set in the romanticised ruins of Waterford. As reward for Norman support in securing his position as King of Leinster McMurrough promised the hand of his daughter Aoife in marriage to Richard deClare (Strongbow) along with the kingdom of Leinster on his death.

An illustration of the tomb of Richard fitzGilbert de Clare, Lord of Strigoil, better known as Strongbow, lying in Christ Church Cathedral, Dublin. The monument is not in fact Strongbow as the original was lost in 1562 when the roof of the cathedral fell in. This early fifteenth-century effigy was introduced as a substitute soon afterwards. The smaller figure is a mystery.

LINEN HALL LIBRARY

Englishman) who had responded to the royal protestations that the Irish Church was in dire need of reform by issuing a letter, known as 'Laudabiliter' from its initial word. This letter authorised the conquest of Ireland in the interests of reforming the Irish Church. Mindful of that papal commission, Henry saw to it that a council of the Church was convened at Cashel with the consent of the archbishop and organised by two of the king's clergy. The pope's imprimatur was evident from the fact that the bishop of Lismore presided, as papal legate. Issuing from this council, or synod, was an agreement that the Irish Church should 'conform to the example of the Church of England', especially in such matters as marriage laws and tithes.

## English influence

The most effective way in which conformity to the ways of the English Church could be obtained was by the placing of Englishmen in leading ecclesiastical positions in Ireland, and inevitably this was the policy that was adopted. As early as 1217, it had been decreed that only Englishmen should be appointed either to bishoprics or cathedrals. Therefore, many years before the Protestant Reformation of the sixteenth century, key positions in the Irish Church were held by English clergy or clergy of English descent. Of course, there were parts of the country where such decrees had no force, and a constant preoccupation of the crown and its officers in Ireland had been the tendency of the ruling class to 'go native', in regions where Gaelic influence remained strong. Again and again laws were passed to arrest this trend, culminating in the Statute of Kilkenny (1377) that sought to prevent the further erosion of Norman ways by, amongst many other proscriptions, forbidding the appointment of the Irish to any ecclesiastical position in the English colony. Such edicts could be generally enforced in those parts of Ireland that were firmly under English rule, most of all in the Pale (the area around the city of Dublin), and in towns and cities elsewhere. Laurence O'Toole was the last Irishman to be appointed archbishop of Dublin, and from the fourteenth century all the senior positions at St Patrick's Cathedral were in English hands. Much the same situation came about in the monasteries and priories. In effect, there came to be two distinctive Churches in the Irish and English parts of the island.

As will become all too evident in the course of this chapter, Ireland's surviving architectural heritage is meagre as compared with that of most European countries, and, in particular, that of Britain. To some extent this can be explained by the relative poverty of the country. Alastair Rowan, in *The buildings of Ireland: North West Ulster*, made the point that, 'By European standards Churches in Ireland are simple affairs: very few that date from the middle ages are still in use for religious worship – most are nineteenth century', and, writing in 1979, he made the point that 'Ireland has never been a rich country and has little money for sustained elaborate building.' One might add that what buildings there were frequently suffered in the intermittent frontier

The Rock of Cashel
SCENIC IRELAND

The Rock of Cashel has been an important ecclesiastical and political site from at least the fourth century. In 1101, Muircheartach Ua Briain, King of Cashel, gave the Rock of Cashel to the Church. The site contains a number of medieval buildings including the round tower, Cormac's Chapel and the Gothic cathedral. In 1152, Cashel was acknowledged as one of the four archbishoprics of Ireland.

A Grotesque of a dog biting its tail found in the churchyard of St Cedma, Larne, previously an Augustinian Abbey, and now incorporated in the church wall

St Laurence O'Toole, the last Irishman to be appointed archbishop of Dublin for many centuries, depicted in stained glass in Christ Church Cathedral, Dublin

DAVID LAWRENCE © RCB ARCHIVE

Dublin Castle from Charles Brookings
*The City of Dublin 1728.*
Three parts of the medieval castle are
still visible.

wars that were characteristic of much of the medieval period. Such being the case, nothing remains from the medieval period of that most fragile and vulnerable of ecclesiastical ornamentation, the stained-glass window, and little survives to show us what frescoes there were on church walls.

The course of the political struggle against conquest and appropriation has dominated Irish history books until very recently, to the extent that little attention was paid to the more pacific aspects of life in the middle ages, or to the existence of the more colourful (if sometimes romanticised) pleasures of medieval life that in common with other European countries, Ireland, and in particular, urban Ireland, experienced. Since the coming of the Anglo-Normans in the late twelfth century, Dublin had been the centre of government, and Dublin Castle the nerve-centre of royal power, as, indeed, it remained until 1922. It is, therefore, in the settled area of Dublin and its environs (the Pale), that traces of medieval Church life are best preserved, though there are other important centres as well, notably Kilkenny and Limerick, places where the officers of the crown held sway.

Archbishop Henry of London
(1212–28) who began
construction of the present
Cathedral of St Patrick, Dublin
ST PATRICK'S CATHEDRAL

What has been attempted so far in this brief sketch is to provide some impression of the context in which the medieval Irish Church existed, and the examples that follow are not intended as a comprehensive inventory of what is to be seen by the visitor. They are merely intended to give some idea of what may be discovered, especially by enquirers who have some idea of what they are looking for.

## Christ Church and St Patrick's, Dublin

The two Dublin cathedrals, Christ Church and St Patrick's, are prime examples of the survival of medieval fabric and monuments. Though heavily restored in the nineteenth century, recent researches and explorations have revealed that to dismiss them as 'Victorian' is to do them less than justice. For instance, Professor Roger Stalley maintains that 'the nave of Christ Church represents the most distinguished piece of Gothic architecture in Ireland'. Likewise, that most striking architectural feature of St Patrick's, the great Minot Tower, is essentially medieval, as is the tower of St Audoen's, Cornmarket (diocese of Dublin), which claims to be the oldest of the parish Churches still open for public worship. St Audoen's is also the location of the Portlester Chapel, a splendidly preserved chantry chapel, endowed to ensure the perpetual saying of prayers for the Eustace family, and a solitary surviving example of an aspect of religious life in the middle ages whereby the trade

Floor tile in
St Patrick's
Cathedral, Dublin
DERMOTT DUNBAR
ST PATRICK'S CATHEDRAL

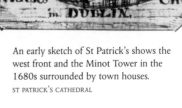

An early sketch of St Patrick's shows the
west front and the Minot Tower in the
1680s surrounded by town houses.
ST PATRICK'S CATHEDRAL

St Nicholas' Collegiate Church, Galway, as with many churches belonging to the Church of Ireland, has absorbed medieval culture and artefacts into the structure of the building.

Floor tile in
St Patrick's Cathedral, Dublin
DERMOTT DUNBAR
ST PATRICK'S CATHEDRAL

gilds and religious confraternities endowed chapels and chaplains. We can glimpse other vestiges of medieval life, such as dancers, musicians and fruit-gatherers in the stone carvings on the capitals of the north transept of Christ Church.

This may be an appropriate point at which to address the often-asked question as to why Dublin has two cathedrals in one diocese. (A related enquiry as to how both of them came to be places of Church of Ireland [Anglican] worship belongs further on.)

The Cathedral of the Holy Trinity, commonly called Christ Church, as has already been mentioned, was founded as a cathedral in about the year 1030, and soon became also a priory of Augustinian canons. St Patrick's, its origins possibly lying in a pre-Norman church outside the city walls dedicated to the saint, was in 1191 turned by Archbishop Cumin (Laurence O'Toole's successor as archbishop, and the first of many English holders of that office) into a collegiate church served by a community of clergy who were not a monastic community as generally understood. Cumin's successor, Henry of London, transformed the edifice into the largest Church building in Ireland and raised it to the status of a cathedral (which Cumin probably had it in mind to do). Why Cumin reconstituted St Patrick's we cannot tell, but a likely reason is that he preferred to have a cathedral chapter that was not, as was the case with Christ Church, a monastic community. Whatever the reason, Dublin had, until the disestablishment of the Church of Ireland, two diocesan cathedrals, which, from time to time, vied with each other for primacy.

Prominent features of both cathedrals are funerary monuments, testimony to the prestige of the political and merchant élites in city and Church. While none of these memorials rival the splendour of such later examples as the opulent seventeenth-century Boyle monument in St Patrick's, they are important, not only aesthetically, but for what they say to us about their time. The metal and stone tablets on the walls and floor of the north transept of Christ Church tell of such figures, though by far the best-known monument in Christ Church is that of 'Strongbow', the Norman leader, who is credited with having played some part in the Norman re-building of the cathedral, and who was buried somewhere within the walls. The fact that the effigy is no longer the original, but probably that of a fifteenth-century knight does nothing to disenchant the modern tourist, any more than it did the Dublin traders for whom 'Strongbow's tomb' was a well-known venue for ratifying their business transactions. In a land in which medieval artefacts, especially those remaining *in situ*, are few and far between, it is important to recognise the significance of the surviving medieval tiles in Christ Church, on whose designs those of the nineteenth-century restoration are based. Among the brass memorials at St Patrick's, most deserving of attention is that portraying Archbishop Richard Talbot, who is credited with establishing the cathedral's musical tradition, and is, therefore, depicted accompanied by groups of minor canons and boy choristers.

Medieval stone head that once surmounted the ancient arched doorway into the Cathedral of St Fin Barre in Cork
JOSEPH SALEH
ST FIN BARRE'S CATHEDRAL, CORK

Nineteenth century imitation of medieval two-colour tiles in Christ Church Cathedral Dublin
CHRIST CHURCH CATHEDRAL DUBLIN

A medieval tomb in St Canice's Cathedral, Kilkenny

St Nicholas' Collegiate Church, Galway
*c.* 1880
ST NICHOLAS, GALWAY

St Canice's Cathedral and round tower, Kilkenny

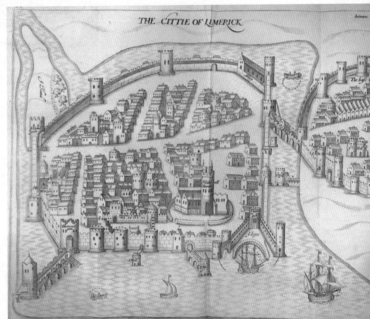

Limerick, 1590, with St Mary's Cathedral

Griffin and fish – symbols of good and evil from St Multose, Kinsale

## The Medieval Church beyond Dublin

Away from Dublin we can discover interesting traces of medieval life. St Canice's Cathedral, Kilkenny (diocese of Ossory) has many important features. Mention has already been made of the adjacent round tower, testimony to the site's ancient ecclesiastical past. Though it bears the hallmarks of repeated periods of damage, neglect and repair, St Canice's retains much of its medieval ambience. It is rich in monuments, some of the most striking dating from the middle ages, and bearing witness to the power of the Butlers, earls of Ormond, in the territory. A feature of St Mary's Cathedral, Limerick (diocese of Limerick), and unique among Irish cathedrals and churches, are the richly carved wooden misericords in the choir, recalling a time when the demands of the liturgy on the worshipper were somewhat mitigated by enabling him to have some repose while standing. As with the Butlers of Ormond, so also the O'Briens of Thomond are well represented by the monuments in St Mary's. St Brendan's Cathedral, Clonfert, County Galway (diocese of Killaloe and Clonfert) has one of the great treasures of Irish architecture in its wonderfully decorated twelfth-century doorway.

Nor have the ancient cathedrals a monopoly on features that well reward inspection. The Collegiate Church of St Nicholas, Galway (diocese of Tuam), which can hold its own with most Irish cathedrals, is a spacious medieval foundation, which has benefited greatly from the sensitive awareness on the part of its custodians of its possibilites, both liturgical and otherwise. St Mary's Collegiate Church in Youghal (diocese of Cork, Cloyne and Ross), is noted for the architecture of its fifteenth-century six-light east window, though the glass is much later, and displays the arms of the powerful Munster dynasty, the earls of Desmond. St Multose, Kinsale (also diocese of Cork, Cloyne and Ross) is another important building, which, despite restoration, is recognisably medieval in character.

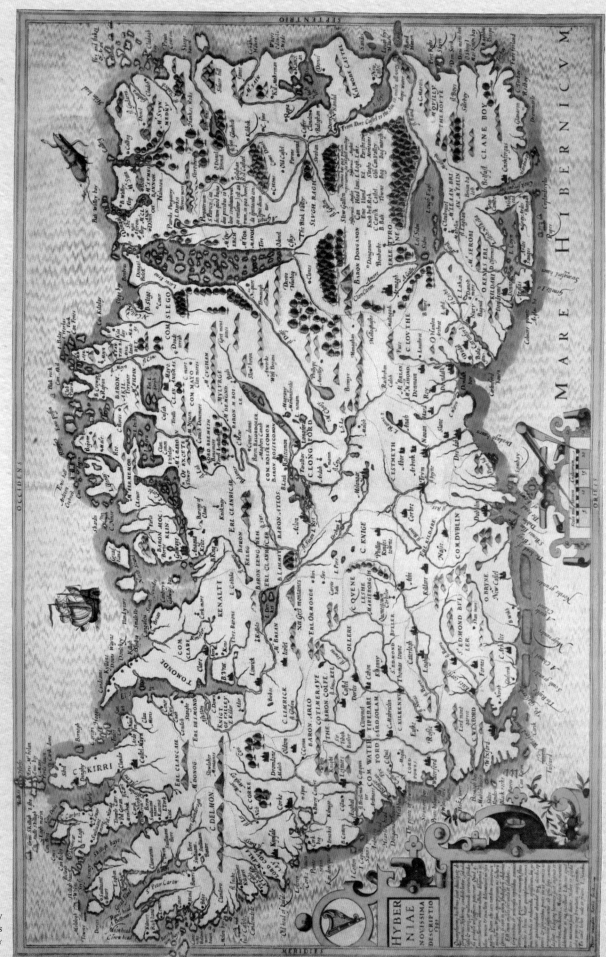

1591 map of Ireland by
Jodocus Hondius
LINEN HALL LIBRARY

# The Reformation

**W**hen its position as the 'Established Church of Ireland', that is, the country's state Church, was ended by act of parliament of 1869, a written constitution for the newly self-governing Church was required. This came into force in 1870, and, with some revisions, remains in force. 'The Preamble and Declaration' to the Constitution of the Church of Ireland maintains that, while preserving continuity with what went before, in terms of doctrine, liturgy and *modus operandi,* the Church of Ireland is in the Reformation tradition.

Indeed the Preamble and Declaration claims that it is 'the Ancient Catholic and Apostolic Church of Ireland'. While to modern ears that sounds exclusive, if not presumptuous, at least it makes it abundantly clear that the Church of Ireland does not see itself, and never has seen itself, as the creation of Henry VIII, or of the Irish Church Act of 1869 by which its link with the British state was broken. A leaflet published in 2002 by the Association for Promoting Christian Knowledge (a Church of Ireland publishing imprint), put it like this:

> The Church of Ireland is Catholic because it is in possession of a continuous tradition of faith and practice, based on the Scriptures and early traditions, enshrined in the Catholic creeds and apostolic ministry.
>
> The Church of Ireland is Protestant or Reformed, because it affirms 'its constant witness against all those innovations in doctrine and worship, whereby the Primitive Faith hath been from time to time defaced or overlaid.'

## A sense of identity

At the risk of labouring the point, it is important to stress that this perception of itself as being both Catholic and Protestant lies at the heart of the Church of Ireland's sense of identity, and goes a long way towards explaining its form of ordained ministry and its liturgical life. This needs to be understood if the buildings of the Church of Ireland and their ornaments that are so much part of that Church's heritage are to make sense to the observer. Therefore, the Protestant Reformation of the sixteenth century that convulsed so

The pulpit in Kilmacrennan church came from a Congregational chapel in Galway via a Jesuit church there. It is finely carved with gures from the Reformation.
LUCY ELLEN PHOTOGRAPHY

Norman arch, St Nicholas', Carrickfergus
DERMOTT DUNBAR

## ◆ MARTIN LUTHER AND THE REFORMATION

Martin Luther (1483–1546) is regarded as the founder of the German Reformation. He was born in Saxony and ordained a priest in 1507. On 31 October 1517, his protest against the sale of indulgences (material goods in exchange for remission of punishment for sin) was posted on the door of the church at Wittenberg. He refused to retract his objections both to the Vatican and to the Diet of Worms in Germany. His actions led to a schism and the emergence of a new Protestant movement. He is regarded as the founder of modern day Lutheranism and the Protestant revolution.

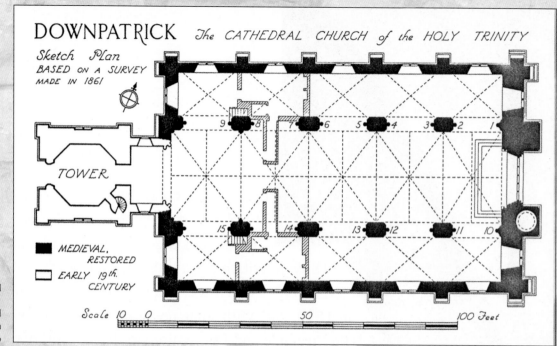

DOWNPATRICK *The CATHEDRAL CHURCH of the HOLY TRINITY*

*Sketch Plan*
BASED ON A SURVEY
MADE IN 1861

TOWER

■ MEDIEVAL,
RESTORED

□ EARLY 19th.
CENTURY

*Scale* 10  0        50        100 *feet*

Ground plan of Down Cathedral
based on a survey made in 1861
showing the original medieval
fabric of the church
HMSO

Carrickfergus in the sixteenth century. Both the Norman
Castle and St Nicholas' Church begun by John de
Courcy in the twelfth century are clearly visible.
BRITISH LIBRARY

much of Europe has a pivotal place in any discussion of the history of the Church of Ireland. While there was no Irish university, and no Irish printing press, Irish Churchmen and scholars were not untouched by the great revolution in learning that was taking place elsewhere in Europe, and which contributed so largely to the movement started by the Protestant reformers. However, the prevailing culture, particularly where Gaelic civilisation endured, had not given rise to that questioning of the teaching and practice of the Church that had so widely taken root elsewhere. But while there was no challenge to the papacy, and little or no demand for a reformation of the Church in Ireland, the country's position as a conquered (or part-conquered) land made it inevitable according to the politics of the time that her people would be expected to accept the religion of the ruler, as elsewhere in Europe.

A strong element in garnering support for the Reformation in England was the evident decline in standards that had beset the religious life as found in many of the monastic houses which, however it may have been exaggerated by those who coveted their property, provided the Crown with a pretext for the closure of monasteries and the appropriation of their assets. The Irish monasteries were generally in poor shape, but the mendicant orders were deeply rooted in the population, and were recently described by a historian as 'the most fragrant bloom among fetid vegetation'. This improvement was due in large measure to the influence of Observant friars, who had done much to encourage the orders to recapture the discipline of their vows. Perhaps the greatest fault where the larger Irish monasteries were concerned was a growing addiction to worldly ambition, most notably seen in

Circular panels of tiles in the nave of Christ Church
Cathedral Dublin. The tiles are nineteenth-century copies
of the medieval floor tiles.
CHRIST CHURCH CATHEDRAL, DUBLIN

According to Peter Harbison the early seventeenth-century Crucifixion reredos from the Galway Chapel of St Multose, Kinsale is perhaps the most vividly crowded and iconographically rich of all the Irish crucifixion scenes. It is now built into the interior south aisle.

ostentatious building programmes, in which they were encouraged by their lay patrons, often their relations, and frequently the lessees of monastic lands on most favourable terms. We need to bear in mind that such features of the post-Reformation Church as the lay possession of monastic lands and indeed the appointing of clergy to parishes by influential lay patrons were widespread. Likewise, given the poverty of so many parishes, 'pluralism', whereby priests not infrequently held several cures (and neglected some of them), was widespread pre-Reformation, and not by any means confined to the post-Reformation Church. Such practices were generally accepted by Rome. Admittedly, a chronic shortage of clergy combined with a low income from tithes in many places, would exacerbate the situation where the reformed Church was concerned.

## Imposition of the Reformation

The Reformation, therefore, was imposed on Ireland and lacked the support that Henry VIII was given in England by sections of the people, both learned and unlearned. Having said that, however, it is important to remember, what has already been alluded to in previous pages, that the English crown had exercised great influence on the Irish Church, especially in the Pale, since the early middle ages, so that many ecclesiastical positions, and most of the important ones, were held by Englishmen, who were by no means unused to taking their orders from England. Furthermore, and this is a point of considerable significance when attempting to account for the comparative ease with which initial changes were made, the Reformation was introduced in stages, and the earliest phase had to do with jurisdiction, that is to say, royal control of the Church, rather than with its doctrine. This is illustrated by the fact that Henry's title as 'Lord of Ireland', bestowed on the English crown by the pope in the twelfth century, was raised to 'king of Ireland' by act of parliament in 1541, and his new title was promulgated at Mass celebrated by the archbishop of Dublin at St Patrick's Cathedral. A complicating factor, however, was that Catholics of old-English descent saw Adrian IV's 'Laudabiliter' as their charter, so that English dominion over Ireland might be construed as dependent on a papal grant!

## ◆ 'SQUINT' WINDOWS

In 1175, the English Church Council ordered that lepers should not live among the healthy. In 1179, the Lateran Council at Rome decreed that leper communities should have their own priests, churches and cemeteries.

The 'Squint' or Leper's window at St Cedma's, Larne, formerly had a stone below it to allow infected persons to look into the church and hear the service. There was no glass in the window at that time. Above this window is a sandstone grotesque believed to represent St Cedma. Below is a carved rosette, unusually this rosette has three rows of petals rather than two.

LEFT: The 'Squint' window St Nicholas', Carrickfergus. The stained glass was a later addition.

In Ireland the introduction of leper hospitals roughly correlates with the Anglo-Norman conquest of AD 1169–71. Indeed, preliminary documentary research indicates that these institutions were largely founded and funded by Anglo-Norman settlers. Carrickfergus, County Antrim, had a leper hospital on the east suburb of the town dedicated to Saint Bridget. This was an ancient monastic foundation.

In the year 1536, the Irish parliament passed the Act of Supremacy, which decreed that Henry, his heirs and successors, were the heads of the Irish Church. Other legislation required that all office-holders in the state, whether lay or clerical, must assent to the royal supremacy over the Church, and that to reject it was high treason. While this parliament had little control over territory beyond the Pale, its laws were binding on the entire island, whether or not they could be immediately enforced. For the most part, the monasteries were suppressed without resistance and the monks now pensioned off. While the government ran into some opposition from both clergy and laity over the dissolution of the monasteries, in time this was overcome. However, strong pleading, especially from Dublin Corporation, that Christ Church Cathedral be spared, was successful, though it ceased to be an Augustinian priory, the existing prior and canons becoming the first dean and chapter! There was another priory of Augustinian canons (only five in number) at All Hallows, outside the city wall, and their house was given to Dublin Corporation. In the reign of Queen Elizabeth, it became the premises of Trinity College, founded to be 'mother of a university', and intended to further Reformation principles in Ireland. When King Henry took the opportunity to appoint a zealous reformer, George Browne, to the vacancy in the See of Dublin caused by the assassination of Archbishop Alen (for reasons not connected with religious matters), Christ Church, and many other places of worship, were to suffer the destruction of their sacred relics, including the *baculus Ihesu* (staff of Jesus), whose appeal to the faithful had brought many pilgrims, and consequent revenue, to the cathedral.

Trinity College, founded in 1592 by Royal Charter from Elizabeth I, from *The City of Dublin*, 1728 by Charles Brooking

The Book of Common Prayer
RCB LIBRARY

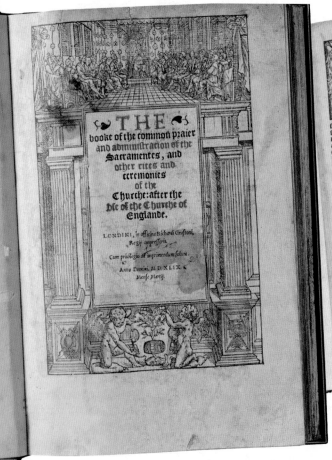

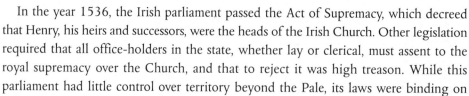

## The Book of Common Prayer

When in the course of time the doctrinal and liturgical changes of the Reformation were introduced, it was at Christ Church that the Book of Common Prayer was first used in Ireland, and it was these changes, largely brought in under Henry's successor, Edward VI, by means of the Prayer Books of 1549 and 1552 (the latter much more influenced by Reformation theology) that most disturbed both clergy and laity. To put it rather crudely: they could stomach 'Catholicism without the pope', which was, in a sense, what Henry VIII had imposed. The king himself had, after all, refuted many of Luther's teachings and was complicit in the martyrdom on the continent of William Tyndale (whose translation of the scriptures into English was to have such influence on the Authorised Version published under King James I's aegis). However, when it came to such matters as the doctrine of the Mass, the invocation of saints and devotion to sacred relics, their conflict of loyalties was strained to the limit.

The progress of the Reformation was by fits and starts, rather like the conquest of Ireland itself, but it never secured the adherence of the people of Ireland to anything like the extent that it did in other parts of the crown's domains. Many reasons for this have been put forward, and remain matters of intense discussion. But it can scarcely be denied that the fact that the progress of the Anglican Reformation went hand in glove with territorial conquest was a grave disadvantage, as was the crucial shortage of reforming clergy. Those clergy who promoted Reformation principles were in many cases English or of English descent, and were unable, until it was too late, to minister to Irish-speaking people. Nor should we overlook the role played by the counter-Reformation, and of the Jesuits in particular, whose vocation it was to recover such ground as had been lost by the papacy, Ireland being high on their agenda. The rather arresting comment that in Ireland the counter-Reformation preceded the Reformation has a grain of truth in it.

The Hamiltons' castle at Killyleagh, County Down, built on land formerly held by the MacCartan family, was tranferred to James Hamilton by King James I.
DUBLIN PENNY JOURNAL

## The Plantation of Ulster

Another Reformation tradition (Calvinism) was introduced into Ireland as a consequence of the plantation of Scots settlers in Ulster. Since bishops were not part of this tradition, it eventually produced the Presbyterian Church in Ireland, strongly resistant to Anglican attempts to make it conform. As we shall see, the Church of Ireland wished to see 'Dissenters' excluded, like Roman Catholics, from political life. For, while the Church of Ireland never secured the adherence of a majority of Irish people, nor, indeed of all Protestants, it held by law a privileged position, and, in accordance with the norms of the time, the powers of the state were deployed in its favour.

This provides the answer to a question that is commonly posed as to how it came about that so

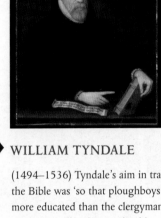

HERTFORD COLLEGE, OXFORD

### ◆ WILLIAM TYNDALE

(1494–1536) Tyndale's aim in translating the Bible was 'so that ploughboys should be more educated than the clergyman himself'. As this was illegal in England he travelled to Germany where he made the first English translation. The invention of the printing press allowed for wide distribution of his work. The New Testament was printed in English in 1526 and the Old Testament was available in England by 1530. However, Papal authorities had Tyndale arrested in Brussels where he was tried for heresy and burnt at the stake in 1536.

His translations drew directly from Hebrew and Greek texts and provided the basis for the King James Authorised Version of the Bible which is still widely appreciated today.

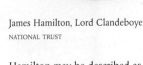

James Hamilton, Lord Clandeboye
NATIONAL TRUST

Hamilton may be described as the founder of modern Bangor. In 1617, he rebuilt the old church, of which nothing had survived save the fourteenth-century tower. A plain, rectangular building without chancel or transcepts, with two small windows at the east end. This church was attached to the east of the old tower, which had no steeple at that time.

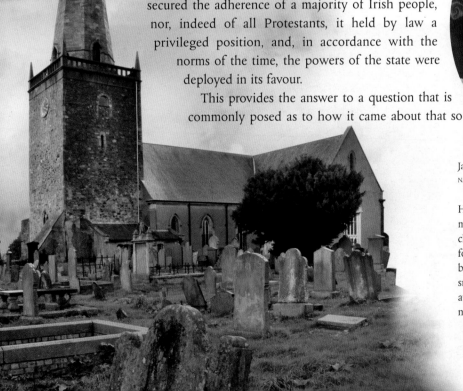

Bangor Abbey
DERMOTT DUNBAR

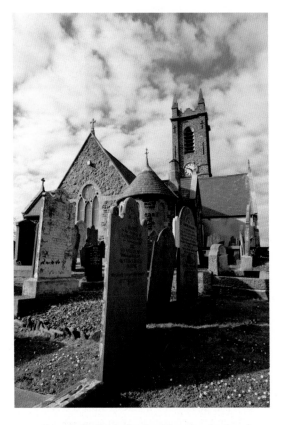

Donaghadee Parish Church, a Plantation church at the sea port where Hugh Montgomery arrived in Ulster from Scotland. Montgomery received land around Newtownards, Movilla and Greyabbey from James II. The church was rebuilt in 1626.
DERMOTT DUNBAR

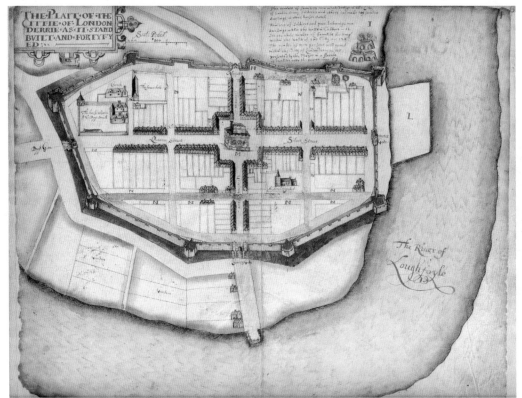

Raven's Plantation plan of Londonderry, the last walled city to be built in western Europe. St Columb's is clearly marked.

many of the ancient Church buildings of Ireland belong to the Church of Ireland. The answer, however strange it may seem to our ears today, is that since the days of Constantine in the fourth century, European states saw themselves as having a central role in the government of the Church, and this was very much the case when the Normans came to Ireland. Bishops, like earls and other nobility who were vassals of the crown, were required to pay homage to the king for their lands. This principle, that the crown should exercise authority over the property of the Church, was accepted both during and after the Reformation. Therefore, property that was in the possession of the Church at the time of the Reformation was retained by the reformed, Established Church of Ireland.

Ballinderry Middle Church stands east of Portmore, Lough Neagh. Puritan in style it is held to be one of the finest examples of a Plantation church in Ireland.
DERMOTT DUNBAR

# THE 1600s
## The Established Church of Ireland under threat

It was under Henry VIII's successors, Edward VI and Elizabeth I (leaving aside the short-lived attempt by Mary Tudor to restore papal authority) that the Reformation in England and inevitably in Ireland took a more decisively Protestant character.

While there had indeed been powerful figures in Henry's reign in both Church and state who were distinctly Protestant in their policies, Archbishop Browne of Dublin for instance, it had been possible for many of the Anglo-Irish, and indeed some Gaelic leaders in those parts of the country that remained largely autonomous, to accept the royal supremacy and the suppression of the monasteries with relative equanimity. However, doctrines encapsulated in the two editions of the Book of Common Prayer issued under Edward in 1549 and 1552 left little room for compromise, especially since these prayer books were made mandatory on all worshippers by Acts of Uniformity, imposing serious penalties on those 'recusants' who failed to conform. The 1552 book in particular, defined the Protestant character of the Reformation in these islands much more clearly than had previously been the case. The Prayer Book of 1549 had, for instance, included an order for 'The Supper of the Lorde and holy Communion, commonly called the Masse', while the book of 1552 of simply called the service 'The order of the ministracion of the Holy Communion'.

From this time, the blurring of the edges between traditional Roman Catholic teaching and practice and what was now required by law was increasingly impossible, and two clearly identifiable religious communities emerged. Indeed, for some who espoused reform the religious changes in England and Ireland were by no means far-reaching enough, and there was a growth in Protestant 'dissent' from the Established Church. The influence of those imbued with the teaching of John Calvin of Geneva was initially quite considerable in the formulation of doctrine in the Irish Reformation. But the changes in the Established Church fell far short of what many reformers required, not least in the crucial matter of the perpetuation of the office of bishop. Therefore, the Church of Ireland was to find itself the object of deep hostility from people who took their lead from either Rome or Geneva, and in the seventeenth century it was to experience great trauma at the hands of the adherents to both of these

A facsimile reprint of the 1549 edition of
The Book of Common Prayer
RCB LIBRARY

Seventeenth-century Communion silverware
from St Catherine's, Aldergrove, Co Antrim
DERMOTT DUNBAR

## JOHN CALVIN AND THE REFORMATION

John Calvin (1509–1564) was a prominent French reformer and theologian based in Geneva. He introduced a number of important reforming measures including the introduction of 'vernacular catechisms and liturgy' and new church government structures which were very important for Presbyterianism.

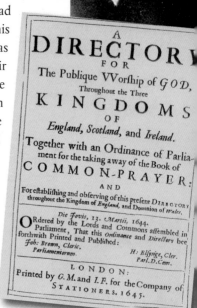

## ◆ ARCHBISHOP GEORGE BROWNE

George Browne (died *c.* 1558) was an English Augustinian friar appointed by Henry VIII to the vacant episcopal see of Dublin. He became the king's main instrument in his desire to establish the state church in the Kingdom of Ireland, declaring the King Supreme Head of the Church, renouncing the authority of the Pope. Under Edward VI he began the introduction of Protestant reforms: the Common Prayer Book was used from 1549.

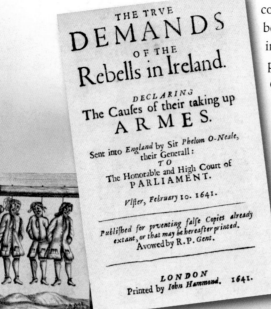

Dromore Cathedral was completely destroyed in 1641 and the new structure, of which small portions are still visible, was built by Bishop Jeremy Taylor.

In the rebellion of 1641 the church of St Cedma's, Larne was fortified against attack and many took refuge in the church.
DERMOTT DUNBAR

traditions. It could survive such rejection while retaining the support of crown and parliament, but was in dire straits when that support was lacking.

### Changes in the seventeenth century

The first attack on the prerogatives of the Church of Ireland came during the Cromwellian interregnum, mid-seventeenth century, when dissent of a particularly radical nature came to political and ecclesiastical power and overthrew both monarchy and episcopate. The second came scarcely two decades later, under the Roman Catholic James II. Civil war between parliament and crown in England that erupted in the 1640s spread to Ireland, the loyalty of the army in Ireland being divided between the two sides. The Irish situation was rendered more complex by the fact that since 1641 the military in Ireland had been engaged in the suppression of a large-scale uprising. This insurrection encompassed many parts of the island, but was particularly bitter in Ulster where Gaelic families vented their deep sense of grievance at the loss of their lands to the planters brought over from Scotland and England within living memory. Again, while the old Anglo-Irish and the Gaelic leaders shared a common religious faith, they reacted differently to the opportunities, as some of them saw it, presented by the internecine strife among the English. Cromwell's victory, and the imposition of his rule as 'lord protector' of Ireland, had vast implications for the Established Church, which in its episcopal character and modes of worship was scarcely less repellent to him than Roman Catholicism.

While not formally 'disestablished', the structures of the Church were dismantled, most drastically by the removal of the bishops (many of whom fled to England, where they lay low) and the replacement of the Book of Common Prayer, use of which was prohibited, by a 'Directory of Worship', that was in line with the more Puritan theological views of the new régime. The new rulers also favoured the Geneva Bible (produced by English scholars exiled to that city), rather than the Authorised Version of 1611, which, quite apart from its association with King James, drew heavily on yet another English language version, 'the Bishops' Bible', an Elizabethan response to the more explicitally Calvinist Geneva version. The Bishops' Bible was heavily drawn upon by the translators of the Authorised King James', eighty per cent of which used material first written by Tyndale.

In parts of Ireland, especially those centres of population where government was in control, Dublin in particular, places of public worship came under 'independent', or 'godly' ministers acceptable to the new political élite. Some of these came from England, others were Church of Ireland ministers who conformed. Cromwell planned a thorough audit of the performance and assets of the Church of Ireland with a view to ecclesiastical and educational reform, but the

# ◆ THE KING JAMES BIBLE

2011 marked 400 years since the King James Bible was first published. Of the many English translations of the Bible that have been produced, none has been as enduring and influential as the KJV.

A copy of the Bishop's Bible printed in London by Christopher Barker, 1588. The year 1588 saw the defeat of the Spanish Armada and it is thought that this bible was specially printed to commemorate this event. Barker was the father of Robert Barker who printed the first edition of the authorised King James Bible in 1611.
ST COLUMB'S CATHEDRAL, DERRY

As the reign of Elizabeth (1558–1603) was coming to a close, we find a draft for an Act of Parliament for a new version of the Bible: 'An act for the reducing of diversities of bibles now extant in the English tongue to one settled vulgar translated from the original.' The Bishop's Bible of 1568, although it may have eclipsed the Great Bible, was still rivalled by the Geneva Bible. Nothing ever became of this draft during the reign of Elizabeth, who died in 1603, and was succeeded by James 1, as the throne passed from the Tudors to the Stuarts. James was James VI of Scotland, and had been for thirty-seven years. He was born during the period between the Geneva and the Bishop's Bible.

The king rejoined that he:

'Could never yet see a Bible well translated in English; but I think that, of all, that of Geneva is the worst. I wish some special pains were taken for an uniform translation, which should be done by the best learned men in both Universities, then reviewed by the Bishops, presented to the Privy Council, lastly ratified by the Royal authority, to be read in the whole Church, and none other.'

Accordingly, a resolution came forth:

'That a translation be made of the whole Bible, as consonant as can be to the original Hebrew and Greek; and this to be set out and printed, without any marginal notes, and only to be used in all churches of England in time of divine service.'

Accordingly in 1604, forty-seven men began to work on the translation. The translators were organised into six groups, and met respectively at Westminster, Cambridge, and Oxford. Ten at Westminster were assigned Genesis through 2 Kings; seven had Romans through Jude. At Cambridge, eight worked on 1 Chronicles through Ecclesiastes, while seven others handled the Apocrypha. Oxford employed seven to translate Isaiah through Malachi; eight occupied themselves with the Gospels, Acts, and Revelation.

Based on *A Brief History of the King James Bible* by Dr Laurence M Vance

This is a first edition of the King James authorised version of the Bible, printed by Robert Barker in London, 1611. It was presented to St Columb's Cathedral by Dean Richard King, Dean of Derry 1921–46.
ST COLUMB'S CATHEDRAL, DERRY

Bellamont House, Cootehill, Co Cavan
Colonel Thomas Coote was granted the O'Reilly lands in Co. Cavan at the Act of Settlement in 1662. He married a Miss Hill from Hillsborough and founded the town of Coote Hill which by 1800 had become a prosperous linen town. Bellamont House, in Palladian style, was originally built in 1725 for his nephew Colonel Thomas Coote, Earl of Bellamont, a judge, by Sir Edward Lovett Pearce.
JOHN COOTE

Stuart Restoration occurred before anything much had been accomplished, and to this day Cromwell is generally remembered in the public mind in Ireland as a perpetrator of massacre and defiler of churches.

### Cromwell's legacy

St Multose, Kinsale
It was in this church that Prince Rupert proclaimed Charles II as King, after hearing the news that Cromwell had had King Charles I executed in London. Prince Rupert's fleet was at anchor in Kinsale harbour at the time.

What Cromwell did accomplish, however, through an ambitious plantation scheme, was a transfer of land from Catholic to Protestant hands whereby his political supporters and army personnel were rewarded for their services by land taken from his opponents, some of whom were compensated for their loss by grants of (usually poorer) lands in the province of Connacht. When in 1660 the Stuart dynasty in the person of Charles II was restored to the throne, some effort was made to redress great injustices that had resulted from the Cromwellian land settlement, for instance, the loss of land by supporters of the crown. But the satisfaction obtained by many of the dispossessed was minimal, and some gained nothing at all. Eventually most of Ireland's major land-owning families were Protestant, and, whatever their religious complexion when they first came into possession of their Irish estates, in due course were assimilated into the Church of Ireland. The result was that a religious minority held most Irish estates, differing in ecclesiastical affiliation from the great bulk of their tenants, who in many cases could claim that in times past the land had been theirs. Two strands therefore combined to characterise relations between Catholic and Protestant in Ireland: land and religion.

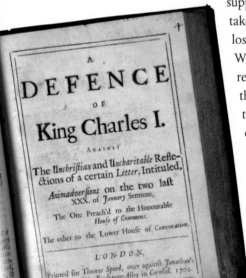

A
DEFENCE
OF
King Charles I.
AGAINST
The Unchristian and Uncharitable Reflections of a certain Letter, Intituled, *Animadversions* on the two last XXX. of *January* Sermons,
The One Preach'd to the Honourable House of Commons.
The other to the Lower House of Convocation.

LONDON,
Printed for *Thomas Speed*, over against *Jonathan's Coffee-House in Exchange-Alley in Cornhill*. 1702.

UNION THEOLOGICAL COLLEGE

To the surprise of many, and the disappointment of some, the Established Church of Ireland was, like the monarchy, restored to its former status in 1660 though some of the Church's financial losses proved irretrievable. While there were strong advocates of the cause of Protestant dissent, it is generally agreed by historians

that acceptance of the restoration of the Church of Ireland by the landed class (who dominated politics) or at least their acquiescence, was a symptom of a longing for a stable society, after generations of turmoil. One of the iconic images that remains in the memory of the Church of Ireland is the spectacle of the consecration of twelve bishops at St Patrick's Cathedral, Dublin, on 27 January 1661, and their subsequent solemn procession up the hill to Christ Church where a survivor of the *ancien régime*, Jeremy Taylor of the diocese of Dromore, preached to them of the essential nature to the Church of the episcopal order.

Ballinderry Middle Church, Co. Antrim
In 1664, Jeremy Taylor instructed that the church should be built. The roof timbers, pulpit and pews were removed from Portmore to furnish Ballinderry.

## Spiritual renewal of the Established Church

In spite of the disruption of the Cromwellian interlude, the fact remains that much was done to reform the Church of Ireland in the 1630s under the direction of Thomas Wentworth, Charles I's viceroy in Ireland, and subsequently after the Restoration of the Stuart monarchy in 1660. Jeremy Taylor was one of a number of outstanding scholar bishops who, both before and after the civil war, in addition to being deeply convinced that while the status of the Established Church of Ireland was fundamental to the nature of the state, were also alive to its spiritual and organisational shortcomings. Major efforts were made by Taylor and others to address what were perceived by some as serious deficiencies, both theological and administrative, in the Church's witness. Thomas Wentworth, earl of Strafford, lord deputy (viceroy) in Ireland of Charles I, in co-operation with Bishop Bramhall of Derry, who had come to Ireland with Wentworth, led the movement to bring about a spiritual renewal of the Established Church. 104 'articles of faith' of 1615 were replaced by the less Calvinistic thirty-nine Articles of the Church of England. Bramhall and Taylor energetically purged the Church of clergy that they considered excessively Presbyterian in outlook, and Taylor was vigorous in ejecting Presbyterian ministers from those parishes where they had taken up duty as an almost inevitable consequence of a shortage of Anglican clergy and an influx of ministers from Scotland. Archbishop Laud of Canterbury, a close associate of Wentworth (they were both to end their lives on the scaffold), looked with favour on this policy of regenerating the Church of Ireland. Laud was (fatally, for him) to be the target of English critics of what they saw as his ultra-monarchist and ritualistic policies, and the 1630s have been described as the 'Caroline' period in the Irish Church. But while that period is sometimes seen as 'high Church', this denotes its emphasis on Anglican principles rather than on the externals of worship. While public worship in the Church of Ireland is less constrained today by restrictive rules than it has been since Disestablishment, it is probably accurate to say that it is regarded as 'high' in theology and 'low' in externals. It has, indeed, been described as the last remnant in the Anglican Communion of the pre-Laudian Church!

Bishop Myler Magrath, who changed allegiance as expediency required and even managed to be both Church of Ireland Bishop of Clogher and Roman Catholic Bishop of Down and Connor. He married twice, had several children and died a wealthy man in 1622 at the age of 99. He is buried in a tomb in the medieval cathedral on the Rock of Cashel.

Sam Hutchison, *Spires, Towers and Pinnacles*

### ◆ BISHOP JEREMY TAYLOR 1613–67

Jeremy Taylor, was born in Cambridge in 1613. He attended Gonville and Caius College. Ordained around 1635, he served in Wales, until he went in 1658 to Portmore, Co. Antrim, as a chaplain to Viscount Conway. In 1661, he was consecrated as bishop of Down and Connor. He built several churches and restored Dromore cathedral. Many of his parishes had Presbyterian incumbents who refused to accept episcopacy and the Book of Common Prayer. They were replaced by episcopally ordained clergy.

While these actions caused controversy, he was widely regarded for his religious writings. With their emphasis on prayer, ritual and liturgy, in books such as a life of Christ, *The Great Exemplar* (1649) and *Rules and Exercises of Holy Living* (1652), he earned a high reputation, which as survived to this day. Many later readers, including Charles Wesley, a century later, have found these books of spiritual benefit. On his death in 1667, he was buried in Dromore Cathedral.

Stained-glass window from St John's, Malone, Belfast

The Cromwellian period reversed the procedures. Some of the parish clergy accepted the new dispensation, others left their posts, were dismissed, or were replaced by ministers more acceptable to the state. However, following the Restoration of the monarch and the Church of Ireland, with Bramhall now in the key position of archbishop of Armagh, and Taylor restored to the episcopate as bishop of Down and Connor, the policy of disciplining or removing dissenting occupants of parishes resumed with renewed vigour. 1662 saw the introduction of a new Book of Common Prayer (its forms of worship still authorised for use in the Church of Ireland), to be followed in 1666 by a new Act of Uniformity which made use of the 1662 Irish mandatory. Nor was Taylor simply an energetic administrator. His writings, in particular *The Rule and Exercises of Holy Living* and *The Rule and Exercises of Holy Dying* are still regarded as classics of Anglican devotion.

Another luminary of the period, Bishop William Bedell of Kilmore, put his hand to a neglected task, the translation of the scriptures into the Irish language. He fell victim to ill-health, exacerbated by hardships he endured during the 1641 rebellion, though in fact he had been locally held in high regard beyond his own community.

Bishop William Bedell of Kilmore
with translations

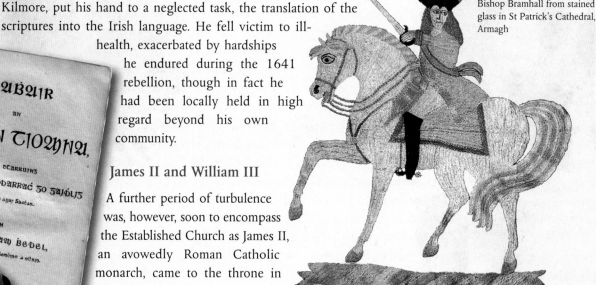

Bishop Bramhall from stained
glass in St Patrick's Cathedral,
Armagh

## James II and William III

A further period of turbulence was, however, soon to encompass the Established Church as James II, an avowedly Roman Catholic monarch, came to the throne in 1685. The Church of Ireland bishops gave him a guarded welcome: he was, after all, their legitimate king, but as it became increasingly clear to them that he intended to promote the interests of his co-religionists, so did opposition to his rule grow within the Church. Understandably, his Catholic subjects saw things differently, his policy opening to them those positions in public life previously restricted to his Protestant (that is to say, Anglican) subjects. Many Protestants were now dispossessed of office in the army, the courts of law and the borough corporations. No bishops were removed from office, but Roman Catholics were appointed to several vacancies. Nor were there any restrictions on Church of Ireland freedom of worship. Indeed, few Church buildings or cathedrals were disturbed, though a new (and Roman Catholic) dean of Christ Church, Dublin, Alexius Stafford, was appointed, his predecessor

Embroidered image from a Victorian Orange flag of William III, son-in-law to James II, by marriage to James's daughter Mary.
BELOW: Commemorative coin celebrating the accession of William and Mary to the throne
ARCHIVE OF THE ORANGE LODGE

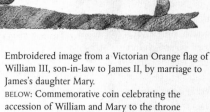

having taken flight to England and thereby forfeited his office. (Stafford was killed in 1691 at the Battle of Aughrim where he was a chaplain in the Jacobite army.)

Within a very short time, James, whose Roman Catholicism led to his overthrow in England, had taken flight to France, and his subsequent attempt, with the help of his ally Louis XIV, to retrieve his crown came to grief at the Battle of the Boyne in 1690, and William III, William of Orange, James's son-in-law, was installed as king. While William was a Calvinist, he had no compunction in accepting the Anglican established Church in both England and Ireland, and once again the Church of Ireland found its rights and prerogatives restored. Its leaders had, needless to say, been greatly shaken by the misfortunes that had afflicted them, whether under Cromwell or James, and were determined that there should be no recurrence of circumstances under which their constitutional role had been in peril, most particularly under James. From now on, strong efforts would be made to ensure that Roman Catholics (and Dissenters) were excluded from political life in Ireland, and what has come to be known as the period of Protestant (Anglican) Ascendancy began. It was to endure, in one form or another, for the best part of a century-and-a-half.

The first cathedral built after the Reformation was the Cathedral Church of St Columb, Derry, County Londonderry, completed in 1633.
ST COLUMB'S CATHEDRAL, LONDONDERRY

An Irish oak chair belonging to St George's Belfast. It is believed that King William sat in this chair to listen to a sermon on his way through Belfast in 1690.
DERMOTT DUNBAR

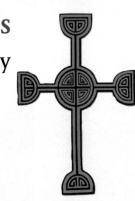

# THE 1700s
## Protestant Ascendancy

The 18th century saw the Church of Ireland reach the zenith of its political and ecclesiastical status in Ireland. This was the era of 'Protestant Ascendancy', a term that derived from the hegemony of the Protestant Establishment, but came to denote the Church of Ireland landed class who enjoyed that prestige and wielded that power. Yet it was a status that was in many ways precarious, as its leaders were only too well aware, and depended on the might of the state to secure its position.

St Anne's parish church opened in Donegall Street, Belfast in 1776.
FROM BENN'S *History of the Town of Belfast*, 1823

St Peter's Drogheda, 1749–52, Diocese of Armagh

'Not quite finished' in 1752 according to Mrs. Delany, and it is attributed to Hugh Darley. One of a number of modest classical churches of the 1740s including Clogher Cathedral (1744 – by James Martin) and Knockbreda (1737 – by Richard Castle). St Peter's has a Palladian façade of limestone ashlar, channelled on the ground floor; a broad eaves pediment is broken by a large central tower rising above it through two storeys. The pinnacled clock stage and needle spire date to the 1780s and are by Francis Johnston.

The interior is a big classical hall, galleried round three sides, supporting a long coved ceiling, the shallow chancel flanked by two fine wall monuments and is ornamented with wonderful late baroque plasterwork. The east window is pointed with switch-line tracery, an indication of Gothic survivalism or the first inklings of eighteenth-century Gothic.
MICHAEL O' NEILL

Georgian Dublin
The Parliament House Dublin, 1790, by James Malton

The Church of Ireland had survived the shocks of the Cromwellian and Jacobite episodes, and while the Treaty of Limerick (1691), which copper-fastened the Williamite victory had held out to the Catholics a hope of relative tolerance of their religion, such was not to be the case for generations to come. Yet the Established Church seldom felt secure and sought constant reassurance from the crown that its loyalty was properly appreciated, and, in return, its privileges confirmed.

## Penal laws

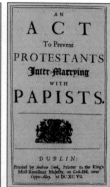

The Irish parliament, exclusively Protestant and overwhelmingly Anglican, set about enacting between 1697 and 1709 a raft of legislative measures, the 'popery laws', whose purpose was the exclusion of Catholics from public life and, where landed property, the source of social status, was concerned, their relegation to the rank of tenant rather than landlord. These 'penal laws', struck at the roots of the Roman Catholic Church by measures that banished religious orders and bishops (thereby seeking to eliminate the ordination of future clergy), prohibited Catholics from purchasing freehold land and deprived Catholic families of the rights of primogeniture by requiring that the estates of Catholic landlords should be divided among all sons rather than being inherited by the eldest. While this procedure was often evaded, sometimes with the connivance of Protestant neighbours, it constituted a further stage in the transference of the bulk of Irish land from Catholic to Protestant ownership.

However, the laws inhibiting Catholic clergy from exercising their ministry were frequently circumvented, though from time to time offenders were severely punished, even with death, and the threat of stringent enforcement remained. In time, however, those laws that attempted to prevent clergy from exercising their priestly functions came to be widely ignored, and the extirpation of Roman Catholicism from the land was soon to be deemed an unattainable objective. As a report to the Irish House of Lords on the state of popery in Ireland in 1730 made clear, Catholic religious houses were to be found in many parts of the country, even in the shadow of Dublin Castle, and bishops were exercising their episcopal powers widely, if largely clandestinely. Furthermore, Catholic schoolmasters abounded, often ignoring the law that required them to register with the Church of Ireland bishop, while the wealthier

'Mass in a Connemara Cabin'
Painting by Aloysius O'Kelly (1853–1936)

Catholics continued, despite the threat of dire penalties, to send their sons to the Catholic colleges on the continent to be educated for the priesthood.

In the course of the century, much of the penal legislation fell into desuetude, sometimes because of the sheer impracticability of enforcing it, sometimes because it was increasingly odious to those charged with enforcing it – bishops of the Established Church among them. But even such ecclesiastics as Dean Swift, who have come to be regarded as having impeccable philanthropic tendencies, seldom went so far as to deny the Protestant nature of the state. Sometimes the law was ignored because it had to a large extent achieved its purpose, since the main thrust of the penal laws, to secure political power in Church of Ireland hands and the proprietorship of Irish land in Church of Ireland families, had been largely accomplished. Nor did Protestant dissenters escape severe discrimination. A 'sacramental test act' of 1704 required that the holders of public office, whether nationally or at local level, at least in theory, must give evidence of having received Holy Communion according to the rites of the Established Church. Thus it was that dissenters could find themselves excluded from the councils of municipal corporations in largely Presbyterian areas of population.

With discrimination and general economic recession in Ireland many 'Dissenters' (Presbyterians) left Ireland for North America.

A Penal cross could be easily carried to celebrate mass in a secluded place during Penal times.
DIOCESE OF ELPHIN

Marie Angelique de la Cherois (1700–71) was born in Lisburn, Co. Antrim, the daughter of French Huguenot refugees, Daniel de la Cherois and Marie Angelique Crommelin. Her mother's family played an important role in introducing the manufacture of linen to Ulster. In 1685, Louis XIV of France revoked the Edict of Nantes which had guaranteed the right of the Huguenots to exist as a protestant minority in a catholic country. Faced with this repression, large numbers of Huguenots fled the country and it is reckoned that about 10,000 of these French refugees came to Ireland. Many settled in Dublin. Most eventually became members of the Church of Ireland.

## Irish society in the European context

It is of course vital to bear in mind that we are considering a period before modern ideas of democracy, even of majority, let alone minority, rights held sway. The social distinctions that were to be found in Ireland were not exceptional in Europe. Indeed the gulf between higher and lower clergy that was to be a feature of the Established Church here was far from being unknown elsewhere. What was extraordinary about the Irish situation was that landlord and tenant, prelate and peasant, worshipped at different altars, though all paid tithes towards the maintenance of the rector or vicar whose ministrations in most cases they eschewed. But *cujus regio, ejus religio*, still obtained, and, the crown being Protestant, so also must be those who wished to enjoy such political rights as then existed. We are still in the era of the *ancien régime*. Jacqueline Hill, the Maynooth historian, has well described the European context in which the Irish Protestant Ascendancy operated:

> In Ireland as elsewhere, issues of rights and liberties were discussed, in general, with little reference to the bulk of the population. Viewed from this perspective, it hardly signified that the majority was of a different religion and culture from the dominant élite … There was nothing unusual by contemporary standards about that.

Such is the background against which the very real achievements, both intellectual and material, of Protestant Ireland came into being: the shaping of Georgian Dublin, the laying out of provincial estates, the building of stately homes. Some Irish nationalists have, understandably, been ambiguous in their appreciation of such things. Nor should we forget the fierceness with which religious controversy was conducted, particularly in the early decades of the eighteenth century. Irish Protestants were well aware, and

### ◆ POWERSCOURT HOUSE AND GARDENS, WICKLOW

In 1603, Powerscourt Castle and lands were granted to an Englishman, Richard Wingfield. His descendants were to remain at Powerscourt for over 350 years.

Powerscourt was much altered in the eighteenth century. Richard Wingfield (1697–1751) commissioned the architect Richard Castle to remodel the house and grounds. He created a splendid mansion around the shell of the earlier castle. The north front was adapted to present a grand entrance in the Palladian manner, while the south and front faced the gardens and was initially only two storeys in height. An extra storey was added in 1787 and further major alterations were made in the late nineteenth century. The house contained some of the finest eighteenth century interiors in Ireland. A recent fire destroyed the interior of the building but the exterior has been faithfully rebuilt.

The gardens at Powerscourt were laid out in two main periods. When the house was rebuilt in the decade after 1731, the surrounding grounds were laid out in a series of formal rides and parkland to the north, with carefully planned gardens and terraces to the south.

SCENIC IRELAND

The Irish House of Commons
CAMPBELL COLLEGE BELFAST

constantly reminded by pamphleteers, of the pressures and persecutions which their co-religionists suffered abroad. It was only in the late 1700s that notions of 'tolerance' surfaced to any great extent (often, indeed, espoused by a minority of Church of Ireland bishops). Though even then, the prerogatives of the Established Church of Ireland were stressed as a bulwark, not only against popery, but also against the growth of unbelief in society, leading, it was feared, to an increase of profligacy among its leaders. In time, a growing sense of Irish identity developed among a minority of Protestants, led by 'patriots' (a term used to denote their dedication to Irish, even Catholic, interests) such as Henry Grattan. When the influence of the Enlightenment and the French Revolution spread to Ireland, their tenets were to be espoused by a leadership that was largely Protestant, and indeed, as with Lord Edward Fitzgerald, of aristocratic lineage.

## Clergy and people

The effectiveness of the ministry of the Established Church left much to be desired. At the Reformation, the pastoral responsibilities that had hitherto been discharged by the secular and religious clergy answerable to Rome, had, in law, been transferred to the newly established Church of Ireland, which struggled to provide adequate care even for those who were prepared to accept its ministry. Indeed, the pre-Reformation Church had found itself severely stretched as it attempted to provide pastoral care to the people, especially through the administration of the sacraments, particularly in those relatively sparsely populated areas that lay outside Dublin's control. Though, as has already been acknowledged, the mendicant orders worked strenuously to improve matters, the poverty of the people resulted in a high incidence of 'plurality', that is, of clergy who out of necessity held multiple cures in order to secure a livelihood. This inevitably resulted in widespread 'non-residence', that is to say, parishes without resident clergy, and for whom the rites of the Church were irregularly available. For people who sought the ministry of the clergy of the Established Church the situation was

*On the Irish Parliament*

Ye paltry underlings of state,

Ye senators who love to prate

Ye rascals of inferior note,

Who, for a dinner, sell a vote

Ye pack of pensionary peers,

Whose fingers itch for poets' ears

Ye bishops, far removed from saints,

Why all this rage? Why these complaints?

The point is plain; remove the clause;

Defend your liberties and laws.

Be sometimes to your country true;

Have once the public good in view;

Bravely despise champagne in court,

And choose to dine at home with port;

Let prelates by their good behaviour

Convince us they believe a saviour;

Nor sell what they so dearly bought –

Their country – now their own – for nought.

JONATHAN SWIFT 1733

1603–25 Bishop Bernard Adams, scholar of Trinity College, Oxford, doctor of divinity, minister and preacher found the palace at Limerick suitable and in good repair. The cathedral church of St Mary was also in good condition and the citizens bound to keep it in good repair.

*Diocese of Limerick* John Canon Begley 1927

The Bishop's Palace, Limerick

The Bishop's Palace, Limerick, is an early eighteenth-century adaptation/rebuilding in Palladian style of a medieval castellated town house, the only example in Limerick city of Palladian architecture in a domestic building and also the oldest of its kind standing in the Englishtown, Limerick. The Civic Trust now own and have restored the building.

LIMERICK CIVIC TRUST

exacerbated by a chronic shortage of clergy, so that plurality and non-residence came to be regarded as endemic. There is evidence that there were many faithful (and often impecunious) Church of Ireland clergy, but their existence has been somewhat masked by the prevalence of ambition and negligence among many others, particularly in the higher ranks.

While it was to the bishops that one would have looked to remedy the situation, they themselves were frequently non-resident, at least for long periods, preferring the amenities of Dublin (or sometimes London and Bath, for most of the more remunerative sees were given by the crown to Englishmen as part of that great web of patronage that lay at the heart of government and was the norm). Such episcopal failings were by no means peculiar to the bishops and other dignitaries of the Church of Ireland, and were common throughout Europe, but what made the Irish episcopate more vulnerable to criticism was its remoteness (in more senses than one) from the great majority of the population, and the fact that it drew its emoluments, often very considerable indeed, from lands to which its entitlement was often in dispute. In addition, it demanded tithes paid by a resentful population who, be they Roman Catholic or Dissenter, were also encumbered with contributing towards the support of the ministry of the Church to which they gave their fealty.

Knockbreda parish church, Newtownbreda, Belfast, 1737
DERMOTT DUNBAR

## Philanthropic figures

There were, however, distinguished and influential voices that were far from unaware of the ills of society. Perhaps Jonathan Swift, dean of St Patrick's, Dublin, 1713–45, is most famous of them all. While politically a firm believer in the concept of a 'Protestant Nation', he concerned himself not only with the ills of the state, but also with the sufferings of the poor, showing particular care (and generosity) for those who lived within the shadow of his deanery. Swift was but one of many philanthropists whose works of charity alleviated to some extent the terrible hardships endured by the great majority. Narcissus Marsh, provost of Trinity College, Dublin, and later archbishop of Dublin, not only espoused scholarship, but endeavoured to assist scholars less fortunate than himself by founding Ireland's first 'public' library. George Berkeley, bishop of Cloyne, was a philosopher and highly original thinker. Like Swift, Berkeley addressed what seemed to him to be the country's major economic woes, calling for the construction of roads and canals, and seeking to redress the impact of famine and poverty by founding a workhouse. Ahead of his time, Berkeley called for the removal of obstacles to the admission of Roman Catholics to Trinity College, though, as with Swift and other progressive thinkers of the day, he drew the line at undermining the

Dean Jonathan Swift 1667–1745
Born in Dublin, Swift became a prebendary of St Patrick's in 1699. In 1710, he became a Tory pamphleteer and dean of St Patrick's in 1713. He was a satirist and author. *Gulliver's Travels* is the best known of his books.

St Michael's Church, Trory, Co Fermanagh, 1778–88
Most churches, especially in the countryside, were simple rectangular buildings.
CLOGHER DIOCESE

James Malton's engraving of St Patrick's, Dublin, published 1793

The Georgian building of the Belfast Charitable Society was erected in 1774 and existed as Belfast's Poor House until the 1880s.

An Act of parliament gave the Society considerable power over the welfare of the town's citizens. As well as taking in the destitute, sick and poor, they administered the water supply, and exercised authority over town planning, policing and fire fighting. Children in the poor house were taught the skills of mechanised cotton spinning and weaving.

The Society was financed by contributions from the Churches, individuals and organisations such as the Ballast Board.

The House of Industry, Limerick, seen here on the extreme left of 'View of Limerick & Newtown Pery from the Watch House on the N Strand' by Henry Pelham, 1786.
Church of Ireland clergy were at the forefront of establishing the workhouse in Limerick with Roman Catholic clergy also consulted on how best to relieve the poor. In 1792, both Church of Ireland and Roman Catholic bishops were asked to help with financial contributions.
LIMERICK CITY LIBRARY

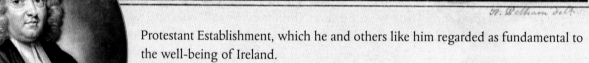

## ◆ GEORGE BERKELEY BISHOP OF CLOYNE

George Berkeley, Bishop of Cloyne, is considered one of the great philosophers of the early modern period. Indeed the author of his entry in the Cambridge Dictionary of Irish Biography (2009) states that 'Berkeley is unarguably Ireland's greatest philosopher, and his work is part of every undergraduate philosophy curriculum.'
Born in 1685, Berkeley was educated at Kilkenny College and Trinity College, Dublin. He was ordained into the Church of Ireland in 1721. He served as Dean of Derry from 1724 to 1734 when he became Bishop of Cloyne. He was responsible for a large volume of published work that dealt with a wide range of philosophical, political and social matters. He criticised the poor economic state of Ireland in the 1730s and put the leading question, 'Whose fault is it if poor Ireland still continues poor?' He also urged harmony between the Established Church and the Roman Catholic clergy. His main claim to fame relates to his philosophical publications. His most important works were *A New Theory of Vision* (1709) and *Principles of Human Knowledge* (1710). Berkeley is known for his metaphysical doctrine, a form of subjective realism.

Protestant Establishment, which he and others like him regarded as fundamental to the well-being of Ireland.

However, times were changing inexorably, and while it would be well into the nineteenth century before the state reached the conclusion that the Established Church was no longer vital to its well-being (and that, moreover, it constituted a fatal weakness), yet there came about a growing awareness on the part of British governments that the interests of the Irish Church and the British state did not

MARSH'S LIBRARY

## ◆ NARCISSUS MARSH

Narcissus Marsh, successively Provost of Trinity College and Archbishop of Dublin, built a public library in 1701. Marsh's Library, situated in St Patrick's Close, adjacent to St Patrick's Cathedral, Dublin, is the oldest public library in Ireland with a collection of over 25,000 books and 300 manuscripts..

*Ways & Means or Vox Populi!!*

# THE UNITED IRISHMEN AND THE '98 REBELLION

Formation of the Society of United Irishmen by Wolfe Tone, Samuel Nielson and Thomas Russell

Many of the key figures in the United Irishmen, Theobald Wolfe Tone, Thomas Russell, Lord Edward Fitzgerald and Robert Emmet, had a Church of Ireland background. Tone, baptised in St Mary's Parish Church Dublin, July 1763 is widely regarded as the founder of Irish Republicanism. He is known for his famous phrase to substitute the common name of Irishman for the denominational labels of 'Protestant, Catholic and Dissenter'.

A majority for the Union in the Irish parliament was partly obtained by bribery and the creation of peerages as this contemporary cartoon indicates.
LINEN HALL LIBRARY

necessarily coincide. Paradoxically, this happened in the wake of the Act of Union of 1800 whereby, dissatisfied, and indeed alarmed, at the ineffectiveness that the Irish parliament had shown in combating revolution and addressing Irish grievances, the kingdoms of Ireland and Great Britain were merged, the Irish parliament was abolished and, on 1 January 1801, the United Kingdom of Great Britain and Ireland came into being.

The political and social turmoil of the 1790s saw the formation of the Orange Association, later the Orange Order, in Co. Armagh. Blacker was an early leader in the Orange movement. He was a member of the Church of Ireland, as were most of its original members, although presbyterians soon joined. An early statement of the organisation, *c.* 1798, described it as 'an association of those who are attached to the religion of the Reformation, and will not admit into its brotherhood persons whom an intolerant spirit leads to persecute, injure, or upbraid any man on account of his religious opinions'.

Following his attempted uprising to overthrow British rule in Ireland in 1803, Robert Emmet was executed in front of St Catherine's parish church, Thomas Street, Dublin.

St Catherine's, from an engraving by James Malton, published 1797. He notes that the church 'is an exact copy from a design by Palladio, with some omissions, not to the advantage of the composition'.

William Blacker of Carrickblacker, Co. Armagh
DUBLIN UNIVERSITY MAGAZINE

# THE 1800s
## Reform and Reorganisation

The Act of Union of 1800 found general support among the leaders of the Established Church. For one thing, the fifth article of the Act appeared to secure the Church's constitutional position in perpetuity, for it stated:

> … that the Churches of England and Ireland, as now by law established, be united into one protestant episcopal Church, to be called 'the United Church of England and Ireland' and that the doctrine, worship, discipline and government of the said united Church shall be, and shall remain in full force for ever, as the same are now by law established for the Church of England.

As things turned out, the phrase 'for ever', turned out to mean seventy years!

Each century brought its particular challenges to the Established Church in Ireland, not least the nineteenth century, when, despite what had been guaranteed by the Union of the kingdoms of England and Ireland, the government of the newly-constituted United Kingdom of Great Britain and Ireland rapidly set about exercising its prerogatives where the United Church was concerned, and these were in many ways unpalatable for its Irish component. The state was motivated by several considerations. For one thing, the coming to power of a series of Whig (Liberal) governments at Westminster, imbued with zeal for major constitutional reforms. These included such major statutes as the great Reform Bills of 1832, which initiated a process whereby the franchise was gradually widened in both Britain and Ireland, and had implications for the Irish branch of the Church. English Non-conformists, sensitive to the plight of their Irish brethren, and, in some cases, sympathetic to the strivings for relief of Irish Roman Catholics, were a force to be reckoned with where the Liberals were concerned, and their commitment to the Established Anglican Church was less total than that of the Tories (Conservatives). Furthermore, British governments of all complexions faced an unprecedented and hugely powerful popular movement for 'Catholic emancipation' led by Daniel O'Connell.

Daniel O'Connell, the 'Liberator'
Painting by Catterson Smith, RHA, 1841–42
DUBLIN CITY COUNCIL/CIVIC PORTRAIT COLLECTION

Catholics felt cheated as their hopes of equality had been raised in the 1790s and remained unfulfilled after the Union.

Daniel O'Connell, the Kerry landowner and lawyer, brought together priests, the middle class and peasantry into one formidable agitation and his Catholic Association, founded in 1823, created a sophisticated local administrative network never before achieved by an Irish political organisation. This formidable display of Catholic power in Ireland persuaded Wellington's government to give way. In 1829, Catholics won their emancipation.

Later O'Connell called for a repeal of the Union – the return of a Dublin parliament. The Whigs adamantly refused but with O'Connell's support for the 1832 Reform Act they entered into alliance with him. In the 1840s, O'Connell returned to the cause of repeal.

JONATHAN BARDON *The Shorter Illustrated History of Ulster*

St George's, High Street, Belfast opened in 1816 as a Chapel of Ease for St Anne's due to the increase in population as the city industrialised.
DERMOTT DUNBAR

Arthur Wellesley was born in Dublin on 29 April 1769 and baptised the next day at St Peter's Church, Aungier Street. Son of the 1st earl of Mornington, and his wife, Anne, daughter of the 1st Viscount Dungannon, he was educated at Trim, Co. Meath, where his family estate was located, and Eton College. He entered the army and, after rapid promotion, was appointed in 1809 to command British forces in the Peninsular Campaign. Due to his successful leadership in this war, he was created the Duke of Wellington in 1814. In 1815, his army, of whom one third are estimated to have been been Irish soldiers, defeated Napolean at the Battle of Waterloo.

He became British prime minister in 1828. Immediately he was faced with Daniel O'Connell's success at the May parliamentary by election in Co. Clare. Thanks in part to his understanding of Irish politics and society, he persuaded the King to accept the catholic emancipation bill. He died in 1852. A memorial obelisk in his honour in Phoenix Park, Dublin, was completed in 1861.

RCB ARCHIVE

Cashel Palace was built in 1730 by Archbishop Theophilus Bolton. The decision was made by the Church to sell the property in 1959 and in May 1962 it opened as a luxury hotel. The palace's 28 acres of garden are in fact older than the house itself. These beautiful gardens surround the Rock of Cashel and the thirteenth century cathedral. The Bishop's Walk is a private path leading directly to the Rock of Cashel, built for the convenience of Archbishop Theophilus Bolton.

CASHEL PALACE HOTEL

## Government intervention

It was, however, a Tory government, reading the signs of the times, which opened membership of parliament to Roman Catholics by replacing an oath that was objectionable to Catholics with one to which they could subscribe with a clear conscience. Slowly but surely, Roman Catholics came to predominate among the one hundred members elected by Irish constituencies. The position of an Anglican state Church in Ireland increasingly appeared an anomaly. While the Church of Ireland still had strong political allies at court and in parliament, even in the eyes of its strongest allies (who clung to the belief that the established status of the Church of Ireland was vital for the welfare of that part of the United Kingdom), it was exposed to serious criticism on several grounds. Great inequalities of wealth existed, especially between bishops and many of the other clergy. Some diocesan bishops drew enormous incomes, partly from landed property, and partly from tithes, whereas great numbers of clergy survived on a fairly minimum income. The lack of pastoral care in many parts of the country was by no means a negligible factor in attracting criticism.

## The Church Temporalities Act

The Church Temporalities Act of 1833 was parliament's attempt to address these glaring anomalies. It was a wide-ranging statute that sought to remedy many weaknesses that, in the eyes even of its supporters, made the Church of Ireland vulnerable to the attacks of critics, some of whom were already talking in terms of 'disestablishment'. This drastic remedy was to come about several decades later, but not before the Church had undergone a radical restructuring. To those leaders of the Church of Ireland who resented state interference, the politicians replied that the assets of the Established Church were at the disposal of the state. The state, so to speak, had given, and the state could take away. There were leading Churchmen in England who perceived in what parliament was doing to their counterparts in Ireland a foretaste of what might happen to them. This was especially so among the Tractarians, a movement in the English Church, centred on the university of Oxford, that deplored state interference in matters spiritual, and sought to recapture the independence and liturgical life of the early Church (as they saw it), and for whom the passing of the Church Temporalities (Ireland) Act was a case of 'national apostasy', as they described it.

The ramifications of the Church Temporalities Act were considerable, but these can be summed up as bringing about a redistribution of the 'temporalities', or material assets, of the Church of Ireland. Two of the four archbishoprics were abolished, Tuam being subsumed into Armagh and Cashel into Dublin. Some dioceses were amalgamated, giving the diocesan pattern that to a large extent survives to this day. Fundamental to the provisions of the act was that the revenues of dioceses that were amalgamated and lost their separate bishop (as, for example, when Raphoe was joined to Derry, and Down to Dromore), went to the Irish

The organ, Chapel Royal
DERMOTT DUNBAR

The Chapel Royal in Dublin Castle was the official Church of Ireland chapel of the Household of the Lord Lieutenant of Ireland from 1814 until the creation of the Irish Free State in 1922. The creation of the new Irish State terminated the office of Lord Lieutenant and his British government régime in Ireland, which had been based in Dublin Castle.

Isaac Mann, Bishop of Cork 1772–88,
responsible for the building of the
Bishop's Palace, Cork

Thomas Carter, rector and prebend of
Ballymore and Dean of Tuam 1841
ANTHONY MALCOMSON

1864 Map of the Dioceses
RCB LIBRARY, DUBLIN

Glebe House, Churchill, Co. Donegal, 1828
Now owned by the Heritage Council

Rev James Pratt, Rector of Youghal,
County Cork by Hugh Douglas Hamilton
*c.* 1795

Church Commissioners. This was to all intents and purposes a new body that for the first time provided the Church with a central administration. It took over duties that had formerly been discharged by the Board of First Fruits, which owed its existence to Queen Anne. The queen had surrendered the right, taken over by the crown from the papacy at the Reformation, whereby the newly appointed clergy surrendered a portion of their first year's income, this money, thanks to the Queen's gesture, being put at the disposal of the Board. The new Commissioners' terms of reference were strictly confined to making loans for the building of churches and glebes (rectories). It was some comfort to those clergy who resented the changes brought about by the Church Temporalities Act that politicians had, with reluctance, conceded that the funds derived from it should continued to be used entirely for ecclesiastical purposes. This was not to be the case in the aftermath of the second great nineteenth-century statute affecting the Church of Ireland: the Irish Church Act of 1869.

The manner in which the government disposed of the assets of the Established Church under the Church Temporalities Act of 1833 brought home to the Church of Ireland in no uncertain terms the price that could be paid for its status as the state Church, though establishment had its compensations, among them the Church's entitlement to tithes, an issue that was to be at the root of much controversy and not a little rural violence in the 1830s.

## Tithes and taxes

In fact, it seemed that no sooner had the Established Church emerged from one crisis than it was at the centre of another. There had for many years been deep resentment on the part of those who were by law compelled to pay tithes for the upkeep of the clergy of the Church of Ireland, even, to some extent, on the part of its own members, but most particularly on the part of the members of other Churches who had in addition to sustain their own ministers.

The Emigrant Ship leaving Belfast, 1852
John Glen Wilson, 1827–62

Famine and evictions often left emigration as the only option. The ship set off down Belfast Lough from Clarendon Dock with a view of the 'Crystal Palace', (the white building behind the ship with the white sails) sited on Queen's Island. As a venue for firework displays, concerts and other entertainment, the island was popular until the Palace burned down in 1864.

The practice whereby Christians paid a 'tithe' or tenth of their income (generally much less than a tenth as time went on) had its roots in the early years of the Christian Church. Originally paid in kind as a proportion of the produce of the land, it had long since become a tax that was paid in coin. It was levied on the poorest as well as the richest, and bore especially heavily on the poorer tenants and peasantry. Because of the Church of Ireland's legal standing, the obligation to pay tithe was backed by the law of the land. While the local rector or his vicar was the main beneficiary, few of the clergy collected it personally, more often than not contracting with a 'tithe proctor', frequently a local farmer and quite possibly a Catholic. The commission that was the proctor's entitlement provided an incentive to extract the maximum due from the payer. Organised resistance to the payment of tithe developed sporadically throughout the country, north and south in the early decades of the nineteenth century, a time of agricultural depression and growing Catholic confidence in the wake of O'Connell's achievement of Catholic Emancipation. Presbyterians and other Dissenters, like Roman Catholics, chafed at the burden, and resentment over tithes was a major cause of the migration of more prosperous Presbyterians to the United States and Canada.

The withholding of tithes by those who would not, or often could not, pay resulted in a widespread campaign of protest. The clergy, or, more usually their tithe proctors, invoked the support of constabulary and military, resulting in arrests, confiscations and even evictions, and great numbers of court cases resulted. The term 'Tithe War' came into usage, as deep resentment against the clergy of the Established Church mounted. For their part, deprived of what was in many cases the main source of their income, clergy and their families underwent great hardship, even verging on

## ◆ FAMINE 1845–52

In 1845, Ireland millions of people were dependent on the potato as a staple food. Potato blight spread from the eastern seaboard of America in 1843 and throughout Europe by 1845 via the potato seed trade. The consequence was devastating and between starvation and emigration the population was decimated. Government measures proved completely inadequate. Catholic and Protestant churches in Britain and abroad collected funds to be distributed by their colleagues in Ireland.

Discovery of potato blight in Ireland
Painting by Daniel McLeod
NATIONAL FOLKLORE COLLECTION
UNIVERSITY COLLEGE DUBLIN

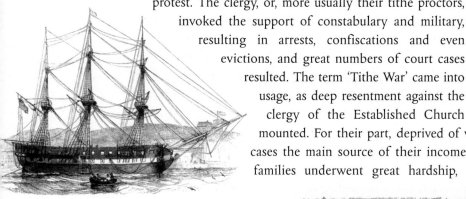

In 1847, an American warship the USS *Macedonian* arrived from New York with food aid.
ILLUSTRATED LONDON NEWS

Many Church of Ireland clergy played a key role in famine relief efforts during the Great Irish Famine. One such example was Rev. Dr Robert Traill, rector of Schull, Co. Cork, seen here in this illustration from the *Illustrated London News*, 20 February 1847. The artist, James Mahony, praised Traill, 'whose humanity at the present moment is beyond all praise'. He also described how he witnessed 'the efforts of the vicar's family to relieve the affliction around them; and we met his daughters reurning from their work of charity in the poorest portion of the town'. Dr Traill died of famine fever in April 1847. It has been estimated that 40 Church of Ireland clergy died of exhaustion or disease contracted in course of famine relief.

CONSOLATION FOR THE MILLION.—THE LOAF AND THE POTATO.

This cartoon of 1847, showing the potato, restored to health, hand in hand with cheap bread, reflected British attitude to the situation in Ireland and the speed at which they tried to dismiss the continuing severity of the famine.
LINEN HALL LIBRARY

President of the United States of America, Barack Obama and Canon Stephen Neill on the occasion of the President's visit to the town of Moneygall in Co. Offaly in 2011. In 1850, the President's ancestor, Fulmouth Kearney, son of the village shoemaker and a member of the Church of Ireland left Moneygall for Ross County, Ohio. He was one of millions of Irish people who emigrated to America in the nineteenth century. Canon Neill is rector of Templeharry church where members of the Kearney family were baptised.

PETE SOUZA, WHITE HOUSE, WASHINGTON

starvation, in many cases being brought relief by individuals among the Catholic community and their priests. The government attempted to alleviate the plight of the more destitute of the clergy by making available a loan of one million pounds (later turned into a grant) and by encouraging them to negotiate mutually acceptable terms with those on whom they depended for their income. But none reached the root of the problem, until parliament passed a number of statutes addressing the crisis, culminating in an act of 1838 whereby tithe became a rent-charge, payable by the landlords (who, doubtless, passed on at least a portion of the imposition to their tenants). But the clergy of the Established Church, and their tithe-proctors, were no longer in the line of fire.

Town dwellers were by no means immune from the financial demands of the Established Church. There was a plethora of local taxes, including the parish cess, and since the late seventeenth century, ministers' money, a tax for the support of the clergy of the Established Church in those urban areas not subject to tithe. While, as with tithe, there was some resentment at such impositions, at least those who paid, whether belonging to the Church of Ireland or not, could see some return for their money. Not only was the cess put to such ecclesiastical and charitable purposes as the upkeep of the church building and provision of the necessities for public worship, for poor relief and care of orphans, but was essential for such rudimentary public services as there were. For instance, it fell to the parishes to supply public lighting, paving, scavenging, and, most important in an age of open fires at home and workplace, fire-fighting equipment. The Church of Ireland parishes, particularly in Dublin, were major providers of local government. The responsibilities of lay parish officers for the maintenance of their church lay deep in the medieval period in Ireland as elsewhere, and were inherited by the post-Reformation Church. The range of these duties broadened considerably in the succeeding centuries, becoming ever more burdensome and inefficiently discharged until, mid-nineteenth century, the reshaping of municipal government in Ireland transferred them to the secular authorities who were in a better position to undertake them.

## Elementary education and pastoral care

Another countrywide issue of great importance to the Church occurred simultaneously: the question of universal elementary (what today is more generally termed primary) education. Here again, the Established Church had rights and prerogatives that it clung to in an increasingly

LISBURN MUSEUM

Alexander Turney Stewart, a member of the Church of Ireland from Lisburn, emigrated to America in 1818. He became one of the wealthiest citizens in New York thanks to the great success of his department stores. In 1863, Lisburn experienced a serious famine due to the American Civil War which prevented the export of cotton to Britain and Ireland, thus causing great suffering among the cotton workers of the town. Stewart chartered a boat, the *Mary Edison*, to bring food for the cotton workers. On Stewart's death his wife paid for the construction of the Episcopalian Cathedral of the Incarnation, Garden City, New York, in his memory.

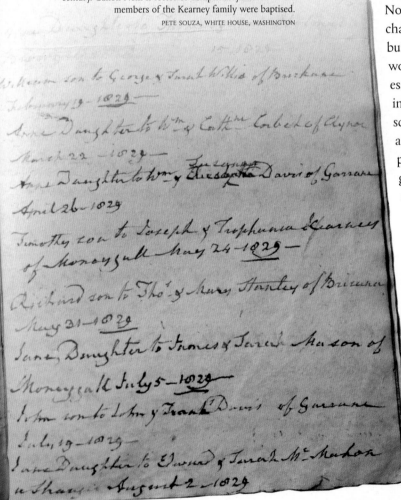

Templeharry Parish baptismal record for Timothy Kearney, ancestor of Barack Obama

TEMPLEHARRY PARISH CHURCH

unfavourable environment. Elsewhere in this volume, Susan Parkes writes of the part that the Church of Ireland had played, and had, indeed, been required by the state to play, since Reformation times. Suffice it to say here that the Church of Ireland's claims to monopolise the provision of state-funded elementary education were rebuffed when the (theoretically) non-denominational National Schools came into being. The response of the Established Church was to set up an alternative system, under the auspices of the Church Education Society, and for decades both systems existed in tandem, until the financial implications of Disestablishment in the 1870s compelled more and more parishes to put their schools under the national board. They were happy enough to do so because by then the Churches had achieved an ambition common to them all whereby National Schools became (what they remain to this day in the Republic) largely Church-related.

The constitutional challenges facing the Church of Ireland in this period must be dealt with in some detail, so relevant are they to its place in the life of the country. Nor can the strenuous efforts made by the Church to retain its prerogatives escape attention. There is, however, a danger that what might be termed the 'pastoral' aspect of the Church's performance can receive less attention than it deserves. The energies of the great majority of clergy were not devoted to the big political issues that have been outlined above. Day by day, public worship was conscientiously conducted, more especially Sunday by Sunday. People were baptised, confirmed, married, visited and buried. Pastoral care was exercised, frequently by dutiful pastors. Schools were provided, at both elementary and grammar school levels. And, especially in the nineteenth century, there was a great awakening of philanthropic awareness and activity.

In an age when state provision of what we now call 'social services' was minimal (though developing), the Churches, and not least the Established Church, were fortunate in the large numbers of energetic and caring members whose faith commitment moved them to give their time, talents and sometimes, even, their lives, for the sake of others. An account of this dimension to the life of the Established Church is to be found on other pages. Nor did such people confine their endeavours to their fellow members. In our more ecumenical age we may look with some reservations on the work of evangelical societies, some of which had connections with the Church of Ireland, and whose energies were directed towards the conversion

### ◆ VERE FOSTER PHILANTHROPIST

Vere Henry Louis Foster, 1819–1900, was a member of the Irish gentry whose family seat was at Glyde Court, Ardee, County Louth. Foster was educated at Eton and Oxford and after graduation entered the Foreign Office where his promising career as a diplomat was put aside in 1847 when he returned to Ireland. The rest of his life was dedicated to helping his countrymen. He devoted himself unselfishly to bettering the conditions of the poorer classes of Ireland believing that the only immediate remedy to Ireland's problems was emigration. Therefore he provided sound and accurate advice on work and wages in America and Canada; paid the passages of aspiring emigrants out of his own pocket and, when his own money ran out, borrowed from his brother. He opened subscription lists, encouraging all and sundry to contribute to his Irish Female Emigration Scheme, while his first-hand account of the conditions which emigrants endured as they travelled to the new world eventually led to changes in the law.

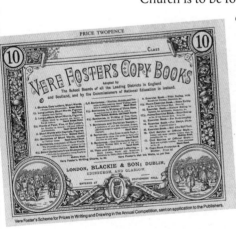

Vere Foster is mainly remembered for his copy books and his efforts to change the education system in Ireland.

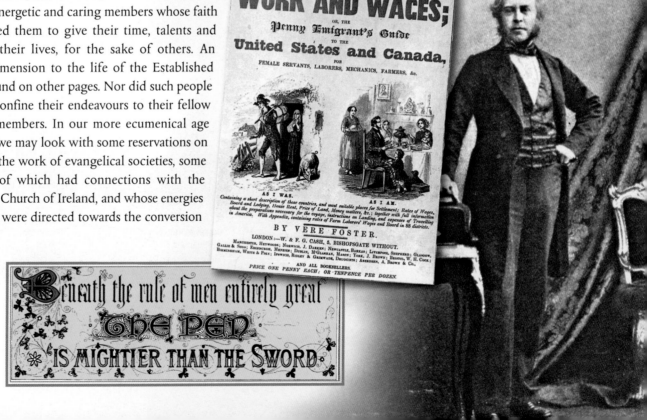

REAL UNION WITH IRELAND.

Having won Catholic Emancipation, O'Connell's aim was to bring about repeal of the Union. In 1840, he founded the National Repeal Association. The cartoon shows O'Connell advancing across the Irish Sea using the heads of Wellington and the Duke of Newcastle as stepping stones. He is holding out the head of the King's brother, the reactionary Duke of Cumberland. The Whigs, led by Lord Melbourne, are advancing towards Ireland stepping on the heads of the Irish Anglican bishops.

## ◆ LAND REFORM

The late nineteenth century witnessed a movement for major land reform, spearheaded by the Land League under Michael Davitt, and C.S. Parnell, himself a landowner, demanding what became known as the 3 Fs; fair rent, free sale, fixity of tenure. From 1870, various British governments introduced a series of Irish Land Acts. These measures gave new security to tenants. The Wyndham Land Purchase Act of 1903 set the conditions for the breakup of large estates and gradually devolved ownership of the land to tenants, finally resolving the Irish Land Question.

of others to that Church. Especially liable to be censured today are those who seemed to offer relief from hardship in return for religious conformity. It is not for historians to judge, but rather to seek to establish truth, whether of behaviour or motivation, and always to have in mind the differing mentalities of different times. As one Church of Ireland bishop complained (in the House of Lords, when, as happened fairly frequently, Church reform was being debated) the Church's performance in past years was being measured in accordance with 'modern' standards. Such may be termed 'special pleading', but something can be said in mitigation of attitudes that were accepted as the norm in perhaps less enlightened days. This holds good when we consider the overseas missionary work of the times, which is described elsewhere.

### Disestablishment

By the mid-nineteenth century, successive British governments had made it abundantly clear to the Established Church of Ireland that it was dependent on the pleasure of crown and parliament for how it deployed its temporalities. Church leaders might vigorously argue for the centrality of their established position to the very security of the state (by which they meant not only the maintenance of British rule in Ireland, but also the fact of the state as having a religious dimension). But the time had come when government believed otherwise, and the writing was on the wall so far as Church establishment in Ireland was concerned. With the coming to power of a Whig government headed by W.E. Gladstone, one of whose great objectives was

Castle Ward as painted by Mary Ward
NATIONAL TRUST NI

In Ireland in the second half of the nineteenth century the majority of landowners were members of the Church of Ireland. At the same time the majority of Protestant labourers, rural and industrial also belonged to the Church of Ireland. In rural Ireland there were relatively small numbers of Church of Ireland landowners, compared to much greater numbers of Church of Ireland small farmers and labourers, as found particularly in Ulster.

A 1900 view of Castle Bernard, home of the Earls of Bandon, near the town of Bandon, Co Cork.
NATIONAL LIBRARY OF IRELAND

to achieve the pacification of Ireland and the reconciliation of its people with the Union, the Church of Ireland was once more to find itself occupying a key role in political affairs.

The term 'Established Church' has occurred a great many times in the preceding pages, and it denotes the position of the Church of Ireland as the state Church. It may be appropriate at this stage to spell out more clearly what establishment entailed. For one thing it meant that the bishops of that Church had a role in parliament. Prior to the Union, Ireland had its own parliament, comprising the House of Lords and the House of Commons. The twenty-six Irish bishops (including the four archbishops) sat in the Lords, and therefore had a strong say in the framing of all parliamentary measures, not least those effecting the governance of the Church. They also had some influence in the House of Commons, because several bishops controlled 'pocket' boroughs, and had considerable influence on the selection of MPs for those constituencies. The other side of the coin was, of course, that the crown appointed all the bishops, and these appointments were part of the web of patronage by which crown and government sought to reward supporters and control parliament at a time when highly disciplined political parties such as we are familiar with today, were unknown. The crown also appointed to other high dignities in the Church, such as deans, though tended to leave the selection of these to the lord lieutenant (viceroy). This close influence of monarch and government on the appointment to ecclesiastical offices was not something dating from the time of Henry VIII, but was common throughout Europe. Indeed, even when the Roman Catholic monarchs Mary Tudor and James II reigned, they continued to make such appointments. James II, as already mentioned, installed a Roman Catholic Dean of Christ Church, Dublin, the previous occupant of the stall having fled. The exiled James II and his son, the 'Old Pretender', continued to appoint to Irish bishoprics despite the fact that their appointees had no hope of assuming office.

Not only did the Church of Ireland episcopate sit in parliament in Dublin (and continue to have representatives at Westminster after the Union), but by virtue of its established status, Church law was part and parcel of the law of the land. As we have seen, this gave the entitlement of clergy to tithes the force of law, and also obtained in matters concerning marriage and inheritance.

An unflattering portrait of Disraeli, Conservative Prime Minister 1868 and 1874–80, and the issue of Disestablishment

ANTHONY MALCOMSON

St Thomas' Rathlin Island
Painting by Lord Mark Kerr, 1833

Standing on a fine elevated site with panoramic views of the harbour and Church Bay is St Thomas' Parish Church which was erected sometime in the first quarter of the nineteenth century, probably in 1812. It occupies the site and retains the name of an earlier church, built in 1722, dedicated to Primate Thomas Lindsay of Armagh, and put up under the patronage of Bishop Hutchinson. From an early date in the eighteenth century the island parish was a vicarage attached to Ballintoy. However, in 1720 the holder of the small tithes, Rev. Dr Archibald Stewart gave up his interest, and the great tithes were acquired from Colonel Curry by the Board of Irish Trusts. Following on from this change, resources for the support of a clergyman were available and Rathlin Island was constituted a separate parish. Over the years, it was served by a series of rectors and curates, and has had close association with a few mainland parishes, being finally united with Ballintoy in 1963.

HECTOR McDONNELL

Holy Trinity, Glencraig, Craigavad, County Down, was constructed in 1857; the architect was Francis Farrell of Dublin.
DERMOTT DUNBAR

The Hon. and Rt Reverend Richard Ponsonby,
Bishop of Derry *c.* 1831–53 by Catterson Smith
ANTHONY MALCOMSON

Although regarded initially as a threat, it can be argued that disestablishment 'liberated' the Church of Ireland. Links between Church and state were broken. Episcopal appointments were no longer controlled by the crown. The Church achieved self-government in all matters of doctrine and organisation. National and local diocesan synods, with elected members and clergy, controlled Church policy. In most parishes episcopal and private patronage of clerical appointments was ended and local parochial nominators now played a key part in appointment of rectors.

## ◆ HOME RULE

In the 1880s the issue of Irish self-government again became a major focus of debate under Charles Stewart Parnell, founder of the Irish Parliamentary Party. Prime minister William Ewart Gladstone made two unsuccessful attempts to pass Home Rule in 1886 and 1893. Parnell's leadership ended when he was implicated in a controversial divorce scandal. Opinions divided and Parnell lost his North Kilkenny seat in an acrimonious by-election, December 1890.

THE TWO PARNELLS; OR, THE MAN BESIDE HIMSELF.
PARNELL THE PATRIOT AND PARNELL THE TRAITOR.

Gladstone recognised that the possession of such privileges by a Church that commanded the allegiance of a relatively small minority of the population was a cause of legitimate resentment on the part of Roman Catholics and Dissenters. He realised that here was one area in which he could bring about change in Ireland (he was yet to address even more contentious matters, such as land reform and home rule), while at the same time satisfying a large section of public opinion in Ireland and among his own supporters in Britain. The result of the census of population taken in 1861 highlighted the anomaly in a parliamentary democracy whereby a Church that had the allegiance of not more than one eighth of the people (and could not claim a majority in a single Irish county) possessed the prerogatives that went with establishment. In the face of strenuous opposition from the Conservative Party, the keenly felt displeasure of Queen Victoria and a position of non-cooperation on the part of the Church of Ireland, Gladstone saw his Irish Church Act through parliament in 1869. He is credited with having drafted much of this substantial statute himself. A staunch Anglican, he had no wish to damage what he conceived to be the best interests of the Church of Ireland. Indeed, he was confident that a disestablished Church would be a healthier one, and he envisaged a more creditable role for it when freed from privileges that attracted so much hostility in the country.

## The Representative Church Body and the General Synod

Under the terms of the Act, the Church was given time to organise itself for the new dispensation, which would come into force on 1 January 1871. From that date, the union of the Irish and English Churches (formed in 1801 by the Act of Union) was dissolved. The Church of Ireland was left in possession of all cathedrals, churches and church schools that were then in use, other lands and properties being transferred to Commissioners of Church Temporalities. These commissioners were required by law to use the funds thus raised for a number of purposes, including substantial allocations to

An alarmed Gladstone facing continuing problems in Ireland from *Pat*, Dublin 1881

St Patrick's College, Maynooth (the state-founded and partially state-funded seminary for training Roman Catholic priests) and the Presbyterian Church, in both cases to replace annual state grants that they had been accustomed to receive in the past. However, a major charge on the commissioners' funds was to secure the livelihoods of the serving clergy and their successors, and other church employees, and highly elaborate schemes were devised to do so. The necessary finance was given to a new body, the Representative Body of the Church of Ireland, which was, as it still is, the trustee for the Church, and whose initial funding was augmented by a generous response from the laity.

The minutiae of the Irish Church Act probably did not arouse much excitement on the part of the average members of the Church. However, the construction of a new scheme of governance did engage their attention. As prescribed by the act, the newly disestablished Church of Ireland was to be governed by a General Synod, and there was to be lay participation in this. A 'convention',

Maynooth College was founded in 1795 as the Royal College of St Patrick by the Irish Parliament, as a seminary for the education of Roman Catholic priests. Later it received a government grant, but following disestablishment both this grant and the *regum donum* given to presbyterian ministers were abolished. In 1966, the college was opened to lay students. Legislation in 1997 established the National University of Ireland, Maynooth as a totally separate body. Recently, the Centre for the Study of Irish Protestantism has been established at Maynooth. The centre seeks to explore Irish protestantism in the context of its social, cultural and historical dimensions.

ST PATRICK'S COLLEGE, MAYNOOTH

Charles Stewart Parnell

Charles Stewart Parnell was the Irish Nationalist parliamentary leader, 1880–90. Colonel Edward James Saunderson was the Irish Unionist parliamentary leader, 1885–1906. Both were members of the Church of Ireland.

itself including elected lay members, drew up a constitution for the Church, and a major cause of controversy during its proceedings was the question of what role the bishops should play in the General Synod. Even more controversial, and the occasion of sometimes frenzied debate, was the revision of the Book of Common Prayer. Now that the Church of Ireland was master of its own affairs, it was strongly held by some of its members that attention should be given to a consideration of how the Church should express its beliefs in worship. 'Protestant' and 'Catholic' perspectives were hotly debated by those who felt that the moment to emphasise Reformation principles was at hand, and others who feared lest the Church's claim to be an authentic part of Catholic Christendom was at stake. The Book that emerged in 1878 was generally regarded as having met the criteria of most members of the Church, whatever reservations or regrets they may have entertained. It was probably just as well for the Church of Ireland that the traumatic experience of disestablishment happened when it did, giving the Church some breathing space before it underwent further tremors in the early decades of the twentieth century when a reinvigorated Irish nationalism and an equally fervent unionist response tore Ireland apart.

Colonel Edward James Saunderson

At the west end of Christ Church Cathedral is a fully-integrated stone bridge, leading to the former Synod Hall, which was built on the site of St Michael's, a prebendal church of Christ Church, demolished by Street during his restoration of the cathedral. The Synod Hall (which incorporates the old St Michael's Tower), completed 1890, was formerly used for holding General Synods, and Diocesan Synods for Dublin, Glendalough and Kildare. It is now home to the *Dublinia* exhibition about medieval Dublin.

From *Dublin Sights*

Synod Hall, Dublin, completed 1890, now home to the exhibition *Dublinia*

A meeting of Synod with Archbishop Gregg in the chair *c.* 1957

St Anne's Cathedral, Belfast
Building work to replace old St Anne's began in 1899 at the turn
of the century. The cathedral was consecrated in June 1904.
Added in 2007 the Spire of Hope representing Christian
hope shining as light in the world rises 300 feet above
ground level. Placed where the central axis of the North-
South transcepts crosses the central East-West axis, the line
from the altar to the Great West doors.
SCENIC IRELAND

# THE 1900s
## A divided island

Acommon failing on the part of Church historians (at least until fairly recently) was to deal with their subject in isolation, often neglectful of the powerful external forces that helped shape ecclesiastical affairs. The Church of Ireland had, as we have already seen, been buffeted about by state policies for centuries. Indeed, how could an established Church fare otherwise in a community a majority of whom were increasingly conscious of a distinctive Irish identity and determined that this should find expression in political self-determination?

### The growth of Irish nationalism

The growth of Irish nationalism in the late nineteenth century, reaching its apogée in the early decades of the twentieth, brought about a situation of enormous consequence for the Church of Ireland as an institution and for its members as individual citizens.

Admittedly, while the link between the Church of Ireland and the British state ended on 31 December 1870, the perception of the former Established Church as part and parcel of the *ancien régime* remained. Facing into a period of intensifying nationalist feeling, there was considerable apprehension among the Church's leadership and its general membership that they might pay dearly for the part that it had played in the past as part of the British establishment, a part which could scarcely be denied.

The official voice of the Church was heard at the meeting of the General Synod in 1912, when the archbishop of Armagh, presiding, denounced the proposals for 'home rule' then on offer, which promised the devolution of some powers to a parliament in Dublin. The archbishop, while claiming that 'our Church knows no politics', proceeded to describe the third Home Rule bill that was before parliament at Westminster as 'a bill for the political annihilation of the Protestants of Ireland'. On 28 September 1912, 'Ulster Day', hundreds of thousands of Ulster Unionists publicly declared their determination to resist Home Rule by signing the 'Solemn League and Covenant', and the many clergy, including bishops, of the Church of Ireland who did so were, for the most part, accurately representing the sentiments of their parishioners. In the following January an Ulster Volunteer Force that would in time number 100,000 men came into being. Its nationalist counterpart in the south was not long in following.

Of course, while the great majority of Protestants were unionist in outlook, by no means all were. One prominent northern cleric, Rev. J.F. MacNeice, refused to sign the

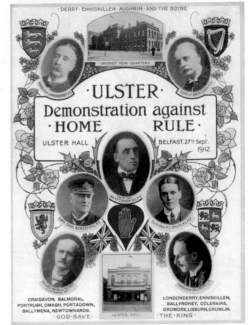

ORANGE ORDER

'Home Rule is Rome Rule' reflected Unionist religious fears which had been heightened the Vatican's 1908 Ne Temere decree on mixed marriages. Other concerns were that under Home Rule the industrial success of the north would be jeopardised and the links with the British crown would be undermined. Feelings ran so high that on Ulster Day, 28 September 1912, Ulstermen and women publicly declared their support for the Union by signing Ulster's Solemn League and Covenant.

Sir Edward Carson signing the Covenant in Belfast City Hall on Ulster Day
ORANGE ORDER

ST NICHOLAS, CARRICKFERGUS 1938

John Frederick MacNeice, pictured here *c.* 1935, was rector of
St Nicholas' Church, Carrickfergus, 1908–31, and eventually
Bishop of Down, Dromore and Connor, 1934–42. He made an
independent stand by refusing to sign the Ulster Covenant in
1912, because he believed that it condoned the use of force which
he feared could lead to violence and civil war.

In his monograph *Carrickfergus and its Contacts* MacNeice looked
back on this period:

> Where were the churches [in Ireland after November 1918]? It is a fair
> question, but a similar question may be asked – where were the
> churches when the Great War, which shattered the world began?
> It is probably true that the majorities in the countries that became
> belligerent, did not desire war. The majorities were not organised: the
> churches had not put sufficient emphasis on their message. The militant
> forces which represented minorities were organised … It was too late to
> work for peace when war had begun. On a smaller scale the same was
> true of Ireland. The lesson to all Churches from the Great War is to use
> the years of peace for their war against war, and that is the lesson to the
> Churches in Ireland from the dreadful years in which Ireland was a
> veritable hell.

MacNeice was committed to an ecumenical approach to
strengthening Irish Christianity. He denounced sectarian violence
in Belfast in 1935. A powerful advocate for social justice, he
appears to have been the first Anglican cleric to formally denounce
Nazi treatment of Jews.

FROM *Side by side in a small country*

Ulster Covenant because he believed it sanctioned physical force. Dr
Kathleen Lynn, numbered among the Dublin insurgents in 1916, was only
one of several participants whose background was in the Church of Ireland
and other Protestant churches. A remarkable fact, already alluded to, is that
Protestants, and not least members of the Church of Ireland, have
an honoured place in the Valhalla of Irish nationalism. The founder
of Irish republicanism, Theobald Wolfe Tone, came of Church of
Ireland stock, as did Thomas Addis Emmet and Robert Emmet. In
fact the United Irishmen, Ireland's prototype republican movement,
imbued with the principles of revolutionary France, was founded in
Belfast, and counted among its leaders north and south both
Anglicans and Presbyterians. Throughout the later nineteenth
century, the outstanding leader of Irish nationalism was Charles
Stuart Parnell, who carried the torch after Isaac Butt, both of whom
were Church of Ireland, as were leading members of the Young
Ireland movement two generations earlier such as Thomas Davis,
author of *A nation once again*.

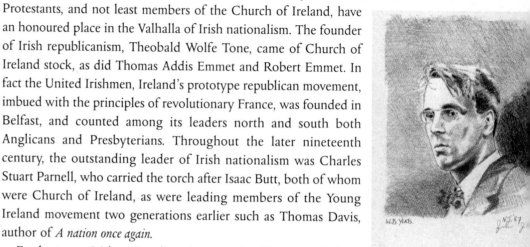

Furthermore, Irish nationalism drew much of its strength from
the cultural revival that blossomed towards the close of the nineteenth
century. This remarkable movement blended two literary streams: that of
the Gaelic world, expressed in the Irish language, and a flowering of Anglo-
Irish literature, whose vehicle was English. Douglas Hyde, one of the
founders of the Gaelic League, was dedicated to the revival of the Irish
language as the vernacular of the country. The literary movement culminated
in the foundation of the Abbey Theatre by WB Yeats and Lady Augusta
Gregory, both of whom, like Hyde, were members of the Church of Ireland,
as were playwrights such as J.M. Synge and Seán O'Casey who gave the
Abbey its international reputation.

The point in rehearsing this well-known list of names is to demonstrate
that independent Ireland's emerging identity, both political and cultural,
was much more complex than is sometimes supposed. Of course there was
another huge influence on Irish development, that of the Roman Catholic
Church, to which the great majority of people on the island gave their
allegiance, and whose teaching coloured much of the early legislation of
the newly created Irish Free State (now the Republic of Ireland). Indeed
the ideals of republicans, Celtic revivalists and the Vatican sometimes sat
uneasily together, but it would today be acknowledged that the influence,

William Butler Yeats, poet, w
the grandson of Rev. William
Butler Yeats, rector of Tullyli
J.M. Synge, playwright, was
grandson of Rev. Dr Robert
Traill, rector of Schull. C.S.
Lewis, writer, was the grands
of Rev. Thomas Hamilton,
rector of Dundela. Cecil Day
Lewis, British poet laureate,
born in Ballytubbert Rectory
son of Rev. Frank Day Lewis
The father of poet Louis
MacNeice, Rev. J.F. MacNeic
became Bishop of Down,
Dromore and Connor.

HURBERT DUNN

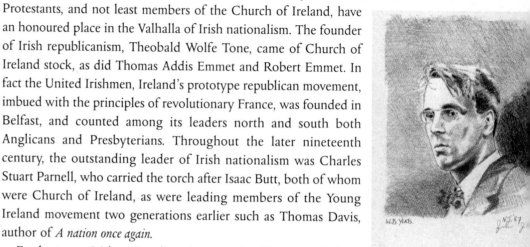

## ◆ WORLD WAR I 1914–18

When the First World War broke out Ireland seemed on the brink of civil war, with the
presence of armed members of the Ulster Volunteer Force and the Irish Volunteers..
However, both sets of men pledged themselves to the Allied cause. The Ulster Volunteer
Force formed the 36th Ulster Division, forever remembered for their slaughter at the
Somme in 1916 with the loss of 5,500 men. The 10th Irish Division suffered very
heavy losses at Gallipoli in 1915. Over 200,000 Irishmen fought in the war, in several
theatres and around 50,000 died.

The Battle of the Somme, 1916
Painting by J.P. Beadle
BELFAST CITY COUNCIL

even power, of the Roman Catholic Church was clear for all to see. Perhaps it is worth quoting words from Yeats' celebrated, some would say notorious, speech in the newly created Irish senate. When commenting on the aversion of some Protestants to legislation that would ban divorce and remarriage, he declaimed:

> I think it is tragic that within three years of this country gaining its independence we should be discussing a measure which a minority of this nation considers to be grossly oppressive. I am proud to consider myself a typical man of that minority. We against whom you have done this thing are no petty people. We are one of the great stocks of Europe. We are the people of Burke; we are the people of Grattan; we are the people of Swift, the people of Emmet, the people of Parnell. We have created most of the modern literature of this country. We have created the best of its political intelligence.

## Reaction to attempts of Gaelicisation

Yeats was scarcely the 'typical' member of the Protestant minority that he claimed to be: nor could his attitude to divorce be regarded as in conformity with the strongly enunciated position of the larger Protestant Churches at the time. Nonetheless, there were aspects of life in the Irish Free State that many Protestants found uncomfortable, and while most were spared the opprobrium that their most pessimistic spokespersons had forecast, in the turbulent years of the War of Independence from 1916 to 1922 some Protestant families suffered grievously from acts of terrorism, losing their lives or going in fear of doing so. The period of such attrition was short-lived, but there were some experiences that impinged disagreeably on everyday life. A great number of Protestants found uncongenial the attempted Gaelicisation of the new state, most obvious in its promotion of the Irish language through compulsion in schools and its introduction as an essential requirement in public examinations and for entry to the public service. Yet there was no unanimity, for in 1914 was founded 'Cumann Gaelach na hEaglaise: the Irish Guild of the Church', its purpose being to keep what it regarded as the spirit of the Ancient Celtic Church alive in the Church of Ireland, to extend the use of the Irish language in its services and to further the use of Irish music and art.

 **EASTER RISING 1916**

Based on the premise that England's difficulty is Ireland's opportunity a small more radical element of Irish nationalists took the opportunity of the war to stage a rising in 1916 in Dublin against British rule. The subsequent execution of the leaders of the Rising and the threat of conscription in Ireland in 1918 led to widespread support for Sinn Féin. The Great War was immediately followed by an Irish War of Independence and then the Irish Civil War. Ireland was partitioned into a new Northern Ireland and a new Irish Free State.

St Thomas' Church was built in 1758–62 in Marlborough Street, Dublin. The architect of this church was John Smith. The design is from one by Palladio. At the time it was considered to have the most beautiful façade of any church in the city. The Church was gutted by fire which destroyed most of Upper Sackville Street (now O'Connell Street) in the Civil War, July 1922. Although the main structure survived, the opportunity was taken to extend Gloucester Street (now Sean Mac Dermott Street) up to O'Connell Street. The new St Thomas' Church was erected in Cathal Brugha Street in 1930.
RCB ARCHIVE

Castle Bernard, Bandon, Co Cork
DAVID HICKS

This house, the home of the fourth Earl of Bandon, was burned by the IRA on 21 June 1921. Seventy year old Lord Bandon was kidnapped and held in a secret location until 13 July, after the Truce. He never recovered from this ordeal and died in 1924.

ÓuЬʒlas Óehíóe

an cRαοιЬιn αοιЬιηη 1860-1949

Céαó Uαċταράη
ηα h-ÉιReαηη
1938    1945

Memorial plaque to Douglas Hyde, founder of the
Gaelic League and President of Ireland, 1938–45,
in St Patrick's Cathedral, Dublin

**BURNING OF A BLASPHEMOUS PUBLICATION.**

A correspondent in the west of Ireland posted to the Editor of "Our Boys" four pages taken
from the Christmas number of a London publication.
   One of these pages contained a Christmas Carol, set to music, and ridiculing, in blasphemous
language, the Holy Family.
   On reading the horrible insult to God, the Editor immediately despatched messengers to the
principal Dublin newsagents, with instructions to buy up all unsold copies.
   The messengers returned with a large number of copies, which the Editor caused to be
burned in the public thoroughfare.
   It is worth noting that the copy which fell into the hands of our correspondent was given
him by a schoolboy.
   How long are the parents of Irish children going to tolerate such devilish literature coming
into this country?

Published in *Our Boys*, a C.B. publication, 5 February
1925 this extract is an example of the influence of
Catholic morality in the Free State in the early years of
the twentieth century.
LINEN HALL LIBRARY

The gradual shaping of social legislation to conform with papal teaching, for instance where divorce and family planning were concerned, and in the realm of state censorship of publications, was unwelcome to many, and not only in the Protestant community. It was not so much the case that members of the Church of Ireland wanted to avail themselves of such opportunities had they been available but rather the avowed acceptance by the state of Vatican teaching on such matters. The Mothers' Union precluded divorcees from its membership until 1974 and it was only in 1930 that the Lambeth Conference of Anglican bishops eased their congregations' consciences where the use of contraception within marriage was concerned. As late as 1948, at a time of high public controversy over proposals concerned with natal and post-natal care for mothers, John A Costello, Taoiseach (prime minister) told the Dáil (parliament's lower house) that he accepted 'without qualification in all respects the social teaching of the Church as interpreted by the Roman Catholic hierarchy of Ireland'. The contribution made by such statements (and their legislative implications) to Unionist perceptions of 'the South' as subject to 'Rome Rule' cannot be lightly set aside when we consider the policies of Unionist governments in 'the North'. Similarly, the statement by Lord Craigavon, Prime Minister of Northern Ireland in 1934 that 'we have a Protestant Parliament and a Protestant State' has to be seen in comparison with the statement made by Éamon deValera, head of the Irish government, broadcasting on St Patrick's Day in the following year, that spoke of Ireland as 'a Catholic nation'. Such quotations give a flavour of the sentiments of the time, but it should be added that, when deValera was framing his new constitution for the Irish state in 1937, he scrupulously consulted with the Church of Ireland archbishop of Dublin and refused to give his own Church the status that it would have liked.

While there were from time to time incidents that indicated a degree of religious discrimination in the Irish Free State, this was contrary to public policy. The political leaders of the time aspired to establish a parliamentary democracy with total freedom of religion, and many of them recognised that the coming into being of a sovereign Irish state owed much to the political and cultural endeavours of Protestant leaders over many generations.

### Unionism

The creation of what were originally intended to be two subordinate political jurisdictions, Northern Ireland and the Irish Free State, reflected the political realities of the time, and largely mirrored the religious demography of Ireland. The upsurge of nationalism had met an equally determined unionism, not confined to the north of the island, but with its greatest concentration there, to the extent that it was possible to devise a division of the country that catered for the great majority of northern Protestants. Witnessing social and cultural developments in the Free State, they found sufficient evidence to justify their claim that Home Rule would be Rome Rule. Unionist determination to have nothing to do with the Free State intensified under violent attacks by the agents of the Dublin government on military installations in the north, and, while the newly constituted Free State desisted from such activities (partly distracted by a civil war between a government that had accepted the dominion status offered by Britain and those who did not), a consistent 'anti-partitionist' propaganda campaign orchestrated from Dublin fanned the flames of northern resentment and deepened the sense of being

Gaelic-inspired art
from St Molua's,
Church, Stormont,
County Down
DERMOTT DUNBAR

William Albert Bell,
member of Rathboy
Parish, Co. Meath was one
of the first recruits in 192
to the new Irish police
force, later called the An
Garda Síochána.

besieged. To many northern unionists, the Roman Catholic people within Northern Ireland, substantial in number (about one third of the population and mostly identified, rightly or wrongly, with aspiring to a united Ireland under Dublin) were a threat to Northern Ireland's very existence. The parliament at Stormont, with a built-in Unionist majority, was in its turn perceived by the nationalist minority to preside over systematic discrimination, which greatly disadvantaged the Catholic population, especially in local government, public housing and educational provision. This in its turn motivated southern antipathy towards Northern Ireland.

None of what has been written above can be disregarded when we consider the experience of the Church of Ireland in the twentieth-century, and while this experience was shared with other Protestant Churches, two factors distinguished the situation of the Church of Ireland. First, while by far the majority of its people lived in Northen Ireland, its numbers in the Irish Free State were not inconsiderable, and, especially in Dublin, remained influential in the intellectual, professional and commercial life of the state. Second, because of the distribution of Church of Ireland members throughout the island, Dublin retained its position as the administrative centre of

Rev. Thomas Hamilton, first rector of St Mark's, Dundela, 1878–1900
Stained glass from the Lewis window in St Mark's

the Church. There was also, however, the stark reality that the Church of Ireland population in the south was in steep decline. This was a trend that long predated the partitioning of the island, especially in the south and west of the country. However, it accelerated considerably due to a number of causes, both political and ecclesiastical. The turbulence of the crisis years of 1912–22 led to a degree of migration by the Protestant population, most notably those living in what were now border counties, and for whom the more congenial atmosphere of Northern Ireland held out an appeal. There was also the great loss of life among the generation of young men who died in the service of the Crown, (and, as many of them perceived it, of Ireland) during World War I, the scale of which can readily be appreciated, not only by a study of the records displayed in the Garden of Remembrance designed by Sir Edwin Lutyens at Islandbridge in Dublin, but also by reading the lists of war dead commemorated in so many Church of Ireland places of worship throughout the land. To an already demographically threatened community was added the pressure exerted by the marriage regulations of the Roman Catholic Church, which required from both partners in an inter-Church marriage promises in writing that their children would be brought up in the Roman Catholic faith. The impact of these forces on the Church of Ireland in what is now the Republic of Ireland was very considerable, as was the emigration of younger members of the population, irrespective of religious denomination, looking for employment overseas, which contributed massively to a decline in the Church of Ireland population.

The Church addressed this huge fall in numbers in the Republic by a policy of drastic retrenchment. Parishes were united (sometimes as many as four being in the care of one incumbent (rector), and, likewise, there was some uniting of dioceses. The city of Dublin

The Irish National War Memorial Gardens, designed by Sir Edward Lutyens, is situated at Islandbridge, Dublin dedicated to the memory of 49,400 Irish soldiers who died in the 1914–18 war. The names of all the soldiers are contained in the beautifully illustrated Harry Clarke manuscripts in the granite bookrooms in the gardens. These gardens are not only a place of remembrance but are also of great architectural interest and beauty. This memorial was built in the 1930s but by the 1980s had fallen into disuse. In recent years a new appreciation of the bravery and sacrifice of these Irish soldiers has led to the restoration of the gardens by the Irish State.

## C.S. Lewis

Clive Staples Lewis, the author, was born in 1898 in Belfast, the son of a solicitor and a clergyman's daughter. He was also born a member of the Church of Ireland. Indeed, on his mother's side there were three generations of Church of Ireland clergy who went back to 1729. Both his parents were born in Cork. He was baptised in St Mark's Church, Dundela, in East Belfast, by his grandfather, Thomas Hamilton, who had been a curate in Holy Trinity Church, Rome, before coming to Belfast.

Most of Lewis's education and all of his academic career took place in England. Nonetheless, he retained very close connections with Ireland. He returned regularly to visit his family and friends. It is reckoned that his Belfast and Irish background strongly influenced his literary work. He was a noted medievalist and literary critic. His fictional work, in particular *The chronicles of Narnia*, has remained very popular.

As an author, however, his greatest impact has been in a number of influential Christian books, including *The screwtape letters* (1940) and *Mere Christianity* (1952). His writings have continued to attract a large audience of readers in the twenty-first century. Professor Alister McGrath has written that Lewis has become 'that rarest of phenomena-a modern Christian writer regarded with respect and affection by Christians of all traditions'.

As congregation numbers fell, parishes were united to form groups or unions. The parish of Arran, located on the islands off the coast of Co. Galway, was joined to the parish of Galway in 1923. St Thomas' Church on Inishmore, the largest of the Aran Islands, was still in use in the 1960s but is now a ruin.

PAUL JOHNSTON

posed a special case, due to the migration of the Church of Ireland population to suburbia, leaving centre-city churches bereft of congregations. Many of these were buildings of architectural or historic importance, and while some were closed and perhaps sold for secular purposes, others were grouped and, in some instances, placed in the care of one or other of the two cathedrals. There were also demographic changes in Northern Ireland caused by movement of population from city and town centres. New churches with ancillary buildings sprang up. In contrast with the amalgamation of bishoprics in the Republic, such as Cashel with Ossory and Limerick with Killaloe, Belfast and its environs were given an additional bishop in 1944 when the diocese of Connor was detached from Down and Dromore. However, the tensions associated with the political and communal turmoil of the last decades of the twentieth century impacted considerably on the distribution of Church of Ireland households in the north, and there has been a perceptible shift from area to area, and, where Belfast is concerned, further east.

The impact of 'the troubles' on people's lives in terms of suffering of one kind or another has made great demands on clergy, who have, throughout the North, and irrespective of denomination, shared in the dangers and other trauma of their people. However, a new factor that came into play in the 1960s, and full of promise where inter-Church relations were concerned, was a surge in ecumenical activity.

ABOVE: Belleek, Garrison, Slavin, Co. Fermanagh and Kiltyclogher, Co. Leitrim This group of parishes is the most westerly in the diocese of Clogher and throughout the later twentieth century there were constant problems due to the political situation. The Garrison group of parishes consists of approximately three hundred members. A minority community mostly involved in agriculture, situated on the border between Fermanagh on the northern side and Leitrim and Donegal on the southern side of the border between Northern Ireland and the Republic of Ireland. Two churches are used each Sunday, on a rotational basis, for Sunday services.

LEFT: Dublin Tourism purchased St Andrews in 1995 and the building has been restored and fully reconstructed to incorporate the Dublin Tourism Information & Booking Office, while retaining most of its original character and charm. It was opened as the Dublin Tourism Centre in 1996. This church was destroyed by fire in 1860 and replaced by the present church, designed for an architectural competition by WH Lynn, of Lanyon, Lynn and Lanyon, completed in 1862.

St Thomas', Clifton Street, Belfast, was lost in the Blitz, 1941
ST GEORGE'S BELFAST

## Inter-church relations

During the 1941 Blitz on Belfast a bomb destroyed the school to the rear of the St George's church, Belfast. In 1975, the church was damaged by a bomb which demolished the adjacent Winton's Hotel. Despite bomb damage on many occasions during the Troubles worship continued to a faithful congregation.
ST GEORGE'S, BELFAST

The modern ecumenical movement is generally dated to the Edinburgh International Missionary Conference of 1910, but it took on a new lease of life when it was espoused by Pope John XXIII and the Second Vatican Council. There had, of course, been relationships between the Irish Churches for many years prior to the holding of Vatican II, mainly through the agency of the Irish Council of Churches, founded in 1923, and of which the Church of Ireland was a founding member. The Council was in origin a body of Protestant Churches, the Russian and Romanian Orthodox having joined in 2003 and 2004, respectively. Vatican II, however, held out the prospect of more than simply cooperation between Churches, but of an aspiration to unity, and while there have, indeed, been 'conversations' between several Protestant Churches with a view to unity (the Church of Ireland and the

St Columba's Parish Church, Portadown
The Parish of St Columba came into being officially on 1 April, 1967. Large housing developments had been constructed on the west side of Portadown during the 1950s and 1960s and this new church was opened in 1970.

In the 1990s, serious controversy arose in another part of Portadown over an annual July Orange parade to Drumcreee parish church, whose traditional march went through a now nationalist area.

Methodist Church in Ireland are in a covenant relationship to that end) that is not the role of the Irish Council of Churches. The Church of Ireland has also been involved in the work of Anglican–Roman Catholic International Commissions, the first of which was co-chaired by the then Bishop of Ossory, later to be Archbishop of Dublin, HR McAdoo.

Ecumenism was only one of the concerns of Vatican II, which also made great changes in Roman Catholic forms of worship, introducing use of the vernacular, for instance. Such changes, together with a positive attitude on the part of the Vatican to shared worship among Christians, evoked a strong reaction from many Irish Christians, who welcomed the opportunity to join in worship together.

An early and far-reaching ecumenical development was the holding of regular meetings between representatives of the Roman Catholic Church and of the Irish

Church of the Transfiguration, Belvoir, Belfast, originally built in 1965, one of over 20 churches to be built in the Diocese of Connor and Down and Dromore in the period 1955–70. It was later rebuilt after total destruction by a bomb in 1992 at the Police Forensic Department on the other side of the road.
DERMOTT DUNBAR

A familiar sight during the Troubles. Clergy had more than their fair share of burials in tragic circumstances. Robert Crozier, a forty-six-year-old lance-corporal in the UDR was killed in an IRA explosion in May 1991.
MARTIN McCULLAGH

Cardinal O'Fiaich, Archbishop Eames, Bishop Poyntz and Bishop George Simms (former Archbishop of Armagh) in discussion at an Irish Inter-Church Meeting at Ballymascanlan in 1987
RCB LIBRARY

Council of Churches. First held at the Ballymascanlon Hotel, near Dundalk, half-way between Dublin and Belfast, these talks gave rise to a formal ecumenical instrument that addresses theological and social issues of common concern to all Churches. It can be said with confidence that the forming of relationships, both institutional and personal, that stemmed from closer ecumenical contacts greatly facilitated the opportunities for pastoral work that came with 'the troubles'. Not, of course, that ecumenical activity found favour with all Churches, or, indeed, with all members of some Churches. But the Church of Ireland and its leaders have never, sometimes at cost to themselves, diverged from their ecumenical commitment.

Acknowledging that from some points of view the Churches themselves have been part of Ireland's inter-community problems, the Church of Ireland took a series of steps to ascertain what its own responsibilities might be and what positive contribution might be made to making atonement where this was due. In 1997, as a starting point, the General Synod firmly declared its rejection of sectarianism, and set in train a process of self-examination to determine how '… to promote, at all levels of Church life, tolerance, dialogue and mutual respect between the Churches and society.' By now, however, it was becoming clear that the 'differences' that so often evoked sentiments of prejudice were not confined to those between Churches, but also, to quote an officially commissioned report, encompassed minority ethnic groups, people of other religions and issues of sexuality and gender. The educational process designed to combat sectarianism and also the prejudices directed against those who fall into these other categories, is an ongoing one.

Cardinal Cathal Daly with Archbishop Eames in the US, 19

## The place of women in the Church

It comes as a surprise to many people to learn that the Church of Ireland, so widely regarded as having an enlightened approach to lay participation in Church government, until comparatively recently restricted that participation to men! While it might be argued that this was in conformity with the role to which women were relegated in the sphere of national politics, it has to be admitted that it was several years after women had achieved the franchise in parliamentary elections that the first moves were made to admit them to the general and select vestries of parishes. Even then (in 1920) they might only hold six seats on a select vestry, a limitation that was only removed in 1960. It was not until 1949 that legislation was passed to allow for women to be elected to diocesan and general synods, in the face of some opposition from the male laity rather than the clergy.

A commonly rehearsed argument against the admission of women to synods was that this was the thin end of a wedge that would lead to women's ordination. If this was indeed the case, it was a very thin wedge indeed, for not until 1990, some forty years on, did the general synod vote to admit women to the offices of priest and bishop. That highly significant development proved not to be as contentious in the Church of Ireland as it was to prove elsewhere in the Anglican Communion. The issue had been carefully studied, and some years earlier the way had been cleared by the acceptance by a clear majority of the general synod that there were no theological barriers to ordaining women to the priesthood and the episcopate. In October 2013, an historic step was taken when the Church of Ireland elected Rev. Pat Storey as bishop of Meath and Kildare.

Chair of the Hard Gospel Committee at a Service to initiate the project. From left: Philip McKinley, Stephen Dallas, Archbishop Eames, Rev. Earl Storey and Archdeacon (now Bishop) Patrick Rooke

◆ **THE HARD GOSPEL PROJECT**

The Church of Ireland established the Hard Gospel Project in 2005 to tackle sectarianism and racism and to face the challenges of historic difference in the Ireland of the 21st century. Opportunity as well as challenge arises for the Church of Ireland, and all other Christian churches, in addressing two profound questions: How should we as a Christian church regard ourselves and our role in a rapidly changing, multi-faith and multicultural 21st century Ireland (north and south)?
How should we as individuals in the context of 21st century Ireland (north and south) regard ourselves and our responsibilities as:

- Individual Christians
- Members of the Church of Ireland
- Citizens of a wider community and society – living with our diverse 'neighbours'?

The Hard Gospel Project represents a commitment by the Church of Ireland to examine not only the challenges of faith which arise for Christians in the 'vertical' relationship in loving God but also the practical implications for the outworking of faith in 'horizontal' relationships as expressed in Christ's command to 'love your neighbour'.
The Hard Gospel Project is the Church of Ireland's response to the challenge to speak truth to, as well as to the world itself. Its core aim is clear – to strengthen the church for effective witness in a divided and changing society.

In 1990, the Church of Ireland legislated to ordain women to the priesthood. Following the General Synod's enactment on the matter on 17 May 1990, the first two women were ordained by Bishop Samuel Poyntz of Connor in St Anne's Cathedral, Belfast, 37 days later, on 24 June 1990. They were Kathleen Young and Irene Templeton. Canon Ginnie Kennerley was the first woman to be elected to a cathedral chapter, that of Christ Church Dublin in 1996.

Dean Katharine Poulton (Dean of St Canice Cathedral, Kilkenny, Diocese of Cashel and Ossory), was the first woman deacon to be ordained and the second woman Dean in the Church of Ireland. Dean Susan Patterson was the first. LEFT: Dean Poulton with Canon George Mitchell, the rector she served with when first ordained for St Comgall's, Bangor
CANON JOHN McKEGNEY

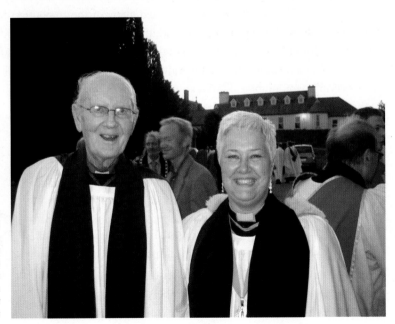

## Conclusion

This brief survey of the history of the Church of Ireland has traced its story from the origins of Christianity on the island through the best part of a millennium and a half to the present day. The foregoing pages have attempted to show how this part of the Irish Christian community, never from its earliest days a stranger to political influence, came to be the protégée of the Protestant state. The Established Church of Ireland remained so for some three-and-a-half centuries, until (against its wishes) it was cut adrift in 1871 – something that can now be regarded as having been, had its leaders but realised it, very much in its own interests. Rapidly on the heels of disestablishment and disendowment came the shock of virtual independence for twenty-six of Ireland's thirty-two counties, and devolved government within the United Kingdom for the other six. Shorn of the status and concomitant privileges that it had once enjoyed, the Church of Ireland now found itself part of a small Protestant minority in the Irish Free State, and, while a substantial part of a Protestant majority in Northern Ireland, having to come to terms with being but one of many Churches, including the strong and self-confident Presbyterian Church in Ireland.

In Northern Ireland, the Church is still coming to terms with the consequences of the political settlement of 1998 which created a devolved polity, based on a local assembly through whose Executive nationalists and unionists share power. In what became the Republic of Ireland in 1949, the Church of Ireland community long ago came to terms with Irish nationalism (to the growing strength of which, as has been shown, a small, but a highly significant number, of its members contributed vastly), and now finds itself in a Republic that has shed many of the attributes that once were uncomfortable for Protestants and in which it can surely be said that it is as comfortable as are most of its fellow citizens. Furthermore, after more than a century of numerical decline, it has found itself recovering demographically. To an extent, this is because some of the 'new Irish', the large number of immigrants who have in recent years come to our shores, are Anglican, though great numbers practise faiths other than Christianity, which has given a new imperative to our need to engage more fully in inter-faith dialogue. Irish Christians from other Churches who have made their spiritual home in the Church of Ireland have also contributed to a reversal of the demographic decline. So too has a very considerable relaxation of the Vatican's regulations with regard to inter-Church marriages. In a situation, at least in the Republic of Ireland, where an exceptionally high proportion of Church of Ireland members enter such marriages, the fact that there is a growing tendency for couples to decide for themselves the Church in which their children are reared is itself significant.

This volume is very largely devoted to a presentation of the Church of Ireland's 'built heritage', so to speak, and these initial

President Mary McAleese addressing the General Synod in Galway, 14 May, 2008

CHURCH OF IRELAND PRESS OFFICE

◆ THE PRESIDENT'S ADDRESS

This is, to my knowledge, the first time that a sitting President of Ireland has addressed the Synod like this, and it provides a welcome opportunity, I think, to reflect on the significant journeys that we have all made in Ireland, from a past which though steeped in the Christian tradition, has at times struggled to credibly showcase Christian values of love, forgiveness, mutual respect and good neighbourliness. Today, though, the story is an encouraging and reassuring one of transcendence, of remarkable progress, of a manifest shift from a culture of conflict to a culture of peace. For those who have always believed in and prayed for the triumph of the great discipline of love these are days to relish and to be grateful for. It is also a time to say thank you for the quiet, relentless and often courageous work of the Churches in nudging, cajoling, persuading and leading us in all our prickly differences to the increasingly secure common ground of mutual respect on which we build a shared future. We stand today at what I believe to be a pivotal moment in Irish history, one of those rare moments when all the accreted pain, planning and persuasion, do indeed lead to a sea change, to a sharp and manifest shift in direction.

EXERPT FROM PRESIDENT MCALEESE'S SPEECH TO THE SYNOD, 2008

The Church of Ireland began using its new and fifth edition of the Church Hymnal in September 2000. The first major new hymnal since 1960 introduces a far wider and more useful selection of texts and tunes.

JOHN HARRISON

One hundred and sixty four people, 82 men and 82 women, received the Maundy money from Elizabeth II at Armagh Cathedral on 5th March 2008 – the Thursday of Holy Week. The Maundy ceremony can be traced back to the twelfth century. Those receiving the purses of money were nominated by the leaders of the four main churches in Northern Ireland.

ST PATRICK'S CATHEDRAL, ARMAGH

pages aim to enhance the reader's appreciation of what must surely constitute a major part of Ireland's architectural and artistic patrimony. The buildings that feature in these pages exist for one primary purpose: the worship of Almighty God. But they are also there to be enjoyed by the visitor. Their impact may be an aesthetic one, but hopefully those who experience them will find sermons in stones.

# THE DOCK
## LIFE IN THE TITANIC QUARTER

ANNETTE MCGRATH

CHRIS BENNETT

The Bishop and the Lord Mayor of Cork are led to a reception at The Palace following the Festival and Civic Eucharist of St Patrick's Day at St Fin Barre's Cathedral.

In many churches and cathedrals throughout Ireland St Patrick's Day is widely celebrated.

The Dock is a fresh expression of church in the fast-emerging Titanic Quarter area of Belfast. On the historic land where the ill-fated liner was built, a new city district of apartments, offices, colleges, film studios and visitor attractions is being built - but a new urban development can be a lonely place without a heart and soul at its centre.

To respond to this need, Rev Chris Bennett was appointed in late 2009 as the first-ever Chaplain to the Titanic Quarter. As the area is a unique and precious opportunity for the churches to work in unity in a new part of the city, he has now been joined by co-Chaplains from five other denominations, who work together on the shared Dock project.

Initially intending to buy an old boat, the team were gifted a huge empty shop unit in early 2012 on a 'Meanwhile Lease'. This has become Dock Cafe – a unique 'Honesty Box Cafe' and shabby-chic community space open six days a week as an outreach to the growing numbers of residents, students, professionals and visitors in the area. Faith thrives informally in conversations, prayers and debates over lunch or a cup of tea – just as it did in the shipyards of *Titanic*'s day. And the old boat? After a fruitless search for a boat of their own, the Dock team were recently invited to hold Sunday services on board SS *Nomadic*, the beautifully-restored tender ship to *Titanic* moored right beside Dock Cafe.

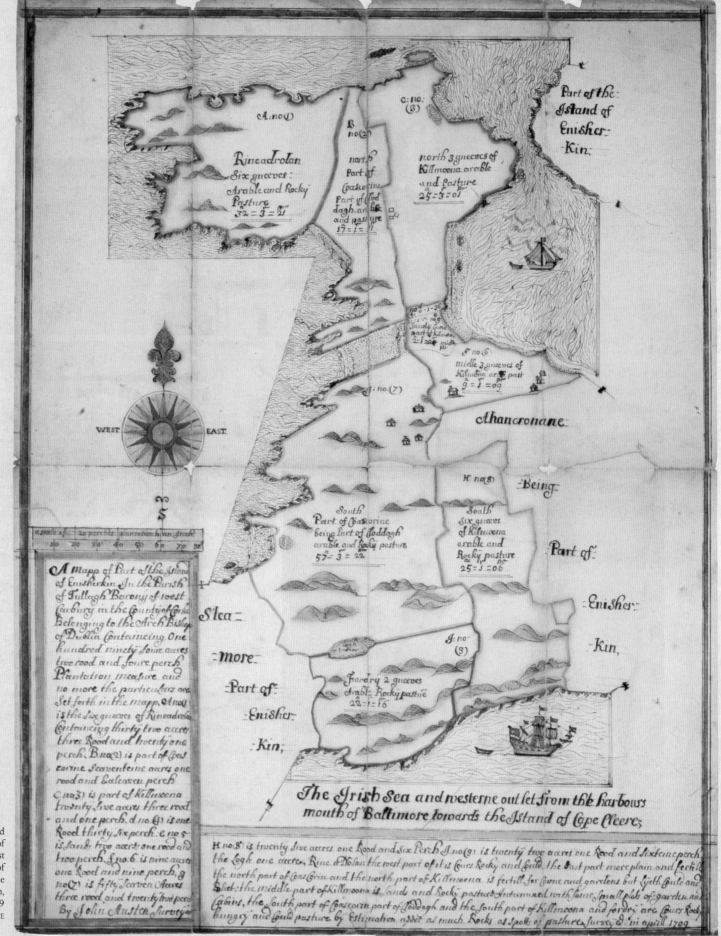

A Map of Part of the Island of Enisherkin in the Parish of Tullagh Barony of West Carbury in the County of Corke belonging to the Archbishop of Dublin, 1709

# Church of Ireland archives

RAYMOND REFAUSSÉ

Old Bawn House, Tallaght, from a
1654 map of the estates of the
Archbishop of Dublin
© RCB ARCHIVE

The archives of the Church of Ireland are, uniquely among those of the Irish Churches, not only the chronicles of a religious organisation, although they are that, but also are part of the records of state. For from the Reformation until disestablishment the Church of Ireland was the official Church of the state. Its parishes were units of local government, its courts were the centres for matrimonial and testamentary jurisdiction, its prelates and clergy were often important officers of state, and its parish churches were, for periods, the locations of the only acts of worship which were permitted under the law.

The Church of Ireland was always a minority Church but membership of the Established Church was critical not alone to ecclesiastical advancement but also to the attainment of office and the ownership of land. And so to the ranks of the Church of Ireland were attracted not only those who were convinced by its theology but many who out of political, social or economic expediency found it prudent to become, at least nominally, members of the Established Church. Thus the archives of the Church of Ireland reflect a much wider spectrum of Irish life than might otherwise be supposed.

Yet this apparently new dispensation was little more than a formalisation of what had gone before. The pre-Reformation Church was an integral part of the apparatus of state and performed many of the civil functions which were to be devolved on the post-Reformation Church of Ireland. The difference, of course, was that the headship of the reformed church was transferred from the papacy to the English monarchy and its representatives in Ireland, as were the archives which the pre-Reformation Church had created – or at least those of them which survived the Reformation.

And so the Church of Ireland, by this accident of history, has custody of the largest collection of medieval religious cartularies in Ireland. Among these, the seven registers of archbishops of Armagh from the fourteenth to the sixteenth century; the thirteenth-century *Credi Mihi* and the sixteenth-century *Liber Niger Alani*, which are registers of the archbishops of Dublin; and the thirteenth-century *Red Book of*

Calendar from the
sixteenth century *Liber
Niger* of Christ Church
Cathedral
© RCB ARCHIVE

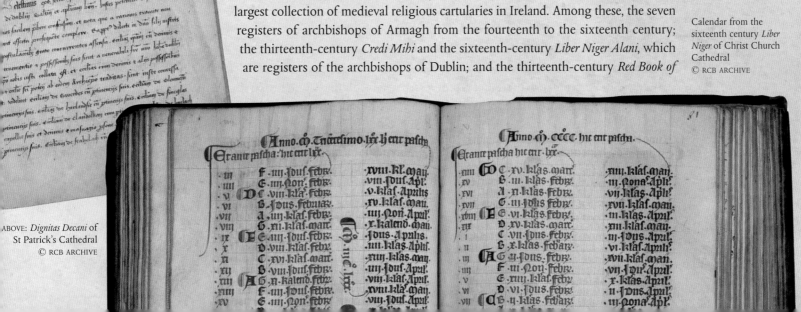

ABOVE: *Dignitas Decani* of
St Patrick's Cathedral
© RCB ARCHIVE

*Ossory*, the register of Bishop Richard Ledred are invaluable sources for the history of diocesan administration, and much else – the *Red Book of Ossory*, famously, contains a recipe for *acqua vita*. The *Liber Niger* and *Liber Albus* of the Augustinian priory of the Holy Trinity (which survived the Reformation as Christ Church Cathedral), and the *Dignitas Decani* of St Patrick's Cathedral give a sense of the administration of religious houses, both secular and monastic, and the interaction of the members of these communities with the Dublin Castle administration and with the city of Dublin. Alone among the parishes, that of St Werburgh, Dublin, has a sufficient body of documentation to give tantalizing glimpses of how parish life was led in Reformation Ireland.

For early modern Ireland the records of the parishes, and especially those in the cities, where there was a large enough population to require a range of services and enough people to pay for them, are rich sources for the history of Church life and the wider community. Registers of baptisms, marriages and burials, the earliest of which dates from 1619, record the population of the parish, while vestry minute books and churchwarden accounts, dating from the late sixteenth century, provide much detail on how the populace comported itself. Information on the church – buildings, furnishings, contents and, by extension, the organisation of worship – is complemented by details on the civil life of the parish – poor relief, fire fighting, policing, street cleaning and much more. By the eighteenth century, when the Church of Ireland, as the Established Church, was at its zenith, these records are bursting with a bewildering array of information on people, places, property (real and movable) and events.

As for the parishes, so too for the dioceses and cathedrals, the surviving records of which are often rich in unexpected detail. For example, the beautifully drawn maps of the estates of the archbishops of Dublin provide vivid detail of land holdings in Dublin, Wicklow, Westmeath and Cork, while the records of the diocese of Ossory include valuable material on the evolution of the borough of Irishtown in Kilkenny. The records of the cathedrals especially in Dublin, Kilkenny, Cork and Cloyne, and to a lesser extent in Kildare, Leighlin and Waterford are invaluable sources for their communities, and because the cathedral chapters were independent ecclesiastical corporations holding property in common, the scope of their collections often extends beyond their immediate localities.

Following Catholic emancipation the role of the Church of Ireland as an administrative support to the state gradually declined and as the nineteenth century progressed many of the Church's civil functions were transferred to central and local government. This process reached its acme with the complete separation of the Church of Ireland from the state under the terms of the Irish Church Act. However, although the church no longer generated records relating to civil matters the volume of archives which it produced from 1870 onwards did not diminish but significantly increased. A major consequence of disestablishment was the need to create a new administrative structure. Parish administration, and records which it

An engraving of St Werburgh, Dublin, with a page from records of St Werburgh's, opposite

Elizabethan coconut flagon presented by Queen Elizabeth I to Jonas Wheeler, bishop of Ossory 1613–40. Wheeler had been chaplain to Elizabeth and to James I.

St John the Evangelist Dublin Vestry Book
© RCB ARCHIVE

generated, continued much as before but to this was added the General Synod, which was replicated at local level by diocesan synods, and the Representative Church Body, all of which spawned a myriad of committees and commissions. In true Victorian fashion all generated minutes, accounts and reports – and still do.

Of course, the best known piece of information about Church of Ireland archives is that they were destroyed in the fire in the Public Record Office of Ireland in 1922. Many records were lost but many were never in PROI and so survived, while of those which were destroyed, rather more has survived in copy and extract form than was initially thought. The response of the Church of Ireland to the tragedy of 1922 was to set in train a process which led to the development of the Representative Church Body Library as the Church's archives. Today the Library manages the archives of 1038 parishes, chapels and chaplaincies, 20 dioceses, 20 cathedrals, and the non-current records of the General Synod and Representative Church Body, as well as over 950 collections of related ecclesiastical manuscript collections. In addition the Library maintains databases of episcopal portraits and church plate, and is developing a photographic collection.

It is certainly true that as a result of the events of 1922 there are aspects of the Church's life which cannot be articulated through its archives but there remains ample primary source material to satisfy the needs of the research community – local, national and international.

Portrait of William King, 1703–29
© RCB ARCHIVE

1834 Church Register
© NATIONAL ARCHIVES OF IRELAND

# The architecture of the Church of Ireland

MICHAEL O'NEILL

The architecture of the Church of Ireland is varied, of many periods, and is an integral part of the artistic, social, cultural and religious history of the island. Some of the buildings are nearly one thousand years old, and between fabric and furnishings, in some of the smaller cathedrals and large urban churches one can nearly trace a continuous history. However, more realistically, the visitor to these churches, by keeping perhaps a dozen buildings before the mind's eye, can construct a meta-narrative or social, artistic and architectural history of worship stretching back a millennium.

Plan of St Nicholas' Collegiate Church Galway

St. Nicholas' Collegiate Church, Galway. A late medieval aisled nave of four bays with long narrow transepts and a short chancel. The large urban medieval churches surviving in a number of towns often show continuity of worship over many centuries.
MICHAEL O'NEILL

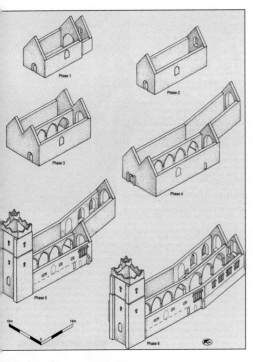

Major structural phases of St Audeon's Church, Dublin
Phase 1 – Late twelfth/early thirteenth century
Phase 2 – Early mid-thirteenth century
Phase 3 – Late thirteenth/early fourteenth century
Phase 4 – Early/mid-fourteenth century
Phase 5 – Early/mid-fifteenth century
Phase 6 – Late fifteenth/early sixteenth century

The medieval inheritance was the diocesan system – thirty-three dioceses in four archbishoprics, reflecting political divisions in the twelfth century. These in turn were divided into rural deaneries, sub-divided into more than 2,000 parishes; the parochial centres included the medieval parish churches, surrounding graveyards, glebe lands, priests' houses and sometimes chapels of ease. Secondly the Church inherited some thirty cathedral buildings, many no bigger than the larger urban parish church of the walled Anglo-Norman towns.

The larger rural medieval parish churches were generally nave and chancel churches (the chancels slightly narrower, with or without a chancel arch), un-aisled, with entrances to the nave in the side walls. In smaller buildings the internal division was created by a wooden rood screen. Tall buildings in themselves, a further vertical élan was achieved by the use of stepped battlements, residential western towers and occasionally belfries and, more often, bell-cotes. There was considerable building and rebuilding of medieval churches in the late medieval period. Two important subsets are the large urban churches of the thirteenth century in the major Anglo-Norman towns (New Ross, Galway, Youghal, Kilkenny, Fethard, Carrickfergus). These are cruciform in plan, with aisled naves. The other subset, often reflecting later medieval enlargements, are the twin-aisled parish churches of the Dublin region (St Audeon's, Lusk, Howth, Swords) with an outlier at Birr, often containing chantry chapels. Late Irish Gothic is a fascinatingly dynamic hybrid style, seen in the treatment of arcades, window tracery and tomb sculpture. Tudor reports in the reign of Elizabeth I, describing the parish churches being 'only like stables' doesn't seem to fit with what we know about the vibrant state of the late medieval Irish Church.

Medieval buildings often continued in use up to the late eighteenth century and indeed into the early decades of the nineteenth. The sense of this medieval inheritance is perhaps best captured now in the smaller cathedrals – Old Leighlin, Lismore, Cloyne, Clonfert and in the larger medieval parish churches – Galway, Kinsale, Youghal, St Audeon's, Carrickfergus. Without doubt there are many other parish churches with substantial medieval cores – St Doulagh's, Balgriffin; Freshford, Galtrim, Rahan to name but a few.

## The seventeenth century

There was some destruction of churches in the course of the long and bloody seventeenth century, but perhaps less than is sometimes portrayed. The Catholic majority entertained hopes of regaining the churches in the 1640s and again in the 1680s and were hardly likely to have deliberately destroyed them. The large number of medieval buildings maintained and repaired is one factor in understanding the phenomenon of Gothic survivalism. An early example was St Columb's Cathedral, Londonderry, rebuilt between 1628 and 1633 in a late Gothic style including Perpendicular style east window, substantial buttresses and stepped battlements. Again in Ballinderry Middle Church of 1664, late medieval window forms are used. The Irish Restoration bishops appear to have envisaged the traditional plan for a new church; the 1666 form of Consecration mentions going from the West Door to the Chancel Door, and from there 'ascend to the Communion Table', implying the medieval division of nave and chancel. However, given the need for new churches, particularly in the north, small aisleless buildings had to suffice: Hillsborough (1663) was a plain cruciform church (rebuilt 1772–4); Ballinderry is rectangular on plan; Waringstown (1681) has a hammerbeam roof; of the seven Dublin

St Doulagh's Church, Balgriffin, approximately ten kilometres from Dublin city is the oldest stone-roofed church still in use in Ireland. Its complex also comprises a stone pool-house and an octagonal baptistry – Ireland's only surviving standalone baptistry.
DIOCESE OF DUBLIN

The stepped battlements of St Columb's Cathedral, Londonderry
DERMOTT DUNBAR

churches built between 1610 and 1689 only St Michan's remains as it was – a plain cruciform church, which until 1818 has a wide but shallow eastern recess named in the plan of 1724 'Place of ye Altar'.

The end of the seventeenth century perhaps saw a second attempt at reformation before the tone changed to consolidation in terms of focussing pastoral care and the creation of manageable unions of parishes. As archbishop of Dublin (1703–19) William King 'procured 14 churches to be repaired, seven to be rebuilt, and nineteen to be erected in places where no Divine Service had been performed since the Reformation'. He also drew up 'Offices for the Consecration of a New Church …' (1719). The rubrics show that the plan of a new church had already been modified and the chancel was now a shallow recess; for the 'Chancel doors' of 1666 became the Doors of the Rails enclosing the Communion Table. King maintained 'that we ought to multiply the number of our churches than make them magnificent.'

## The auditory church

The auditory church was based on the Roman basilica (wide open hall space without crossing or transepts), the nave and aisles filled with box pews;

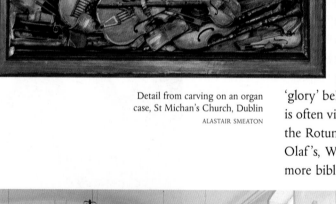

Detail from carving on an organ case, St Michan's Church, Dublin
ALASTAIR SMEATON

the large columnar arcade of the prototype was replaced with slender boxed-in shafts supporting a gallery which generally ran around three sides of the interior. In some cases the encased shafts continued up to support a compass (curved) ceiling (in lath and plaster). An elaborate organ often occupies the western gallery. Windows in two registers lit the 'aisles' under the gallery and larger ones above the gallery. The east end – often polygonal – generally had a wooden or stucco reredos, sometimes with a 'glory' behind the railed-in communion table. In both stuccowork and woodwork there is often virtuoso carving to be found. See for example St Michan's nave, St Werburgh's, the Rotunda Hospital Chapel and St Catherine's in Dublin, St Peter's in Drogheda, St Olaf's, Waterford (deconsecrated). The adaptation of extant medieval churches to the more bibliocentric form of worship, centred on the Book of Common Prayer and the Bible, often included enlarging the windows (Celbridge, Liscarton, Loughcrew), and the abandonment of either the nave or chancel, or the reduction of the nave aisles (Naas, Castledermot).

Detail from carvings in St Werburgh's Parish Church, Dublin
ALASTAIR SMEATON

A series of drawings for twelve churches by the architect Thomas Cooley dated 1773 outlines nine basic plan types that largely describe the stock of churches built in the last two decades of the eighteenth century and the first three of the nineteenth. In essence Cooley designed a rectangular hall space of three or four bays, with variations to east and west. At its simplest there is an east window where only the south elevation is fenestrated. Variations include

St Werburgh's Parish Church, Dublin. A more elaborate auditory church from the early eighteenth century, the interior furnishings date to 1750 following a devastating fire.
ALASTAIR SMEATON

a short chancel either square or apsed ended with either a three-light Gothic window form or a Serliana in the Classical version. West end variations include north-west and south-west entrances. Another is a central western pedimented entrance with vestry and robing room in the west bays under a gallery and vestibule into the church proper. A third is a belfry tower serving as entrance attached to the centre of the west gable. Variations of the tower front include incorporating the tower into the west bay with robing room and vestry to north and south.

## The Board of First Fruits

The Board of First Fruits (founded in 1717) became the most significant agent in Irish church architecture, particularly following the Act of Union. More than one million pounds passed through the hands of the Board between the Union and 1822 with over £322,000 expended on loans and gifts for Glebe Houses and over £54,000 on Glebe lands. The ready availability of gifts and loans also meant that the majority of the venerable medieval buildings which had continued in use were replaced by the hall-and-tower church type described above. Expenditure of over £400,000 resulted in a total of 697 churches being built, rebuilt or enlarged by the Board of First Fruits up to 1829. This phenomenon might be compared to the 600 'Waterloo' Churches built in England as a result of the Church Building Acts of 1818 and 1824.

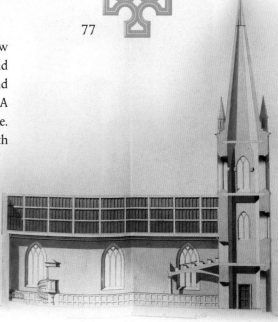

Thomas Cooley, architect: drawing from Album in Armagh Public Library. Cooley produced a series of hall and tower church designs in both Classical and Gothic idioms. Cooley enjoyed the patronage of many archbishops and bishops which might explain the proliferation of these church designs between *c.* 1780 and *c.* 1830.

Francis Johnston, the successor to Cooley at Armagh, and equally adept at Classicism and nascent Gothicism, made the wonderful harbinger of the Gothic Revival in Ireland – the Chapel Royal in Dublin Castle (1807–14) – an auditory church in Perpendicular Gothic style. The Spiky Gothic style was continued by George Semple, James Pain and William Farrell into the 1830s. Joseph Welland, initially architect of the Ecclesiastical Commissioners (successors to the Board of First Fruits) for Tuam diocese, became diocesan architect for the whole country in 1843.

Chapel Royal in Dublin Castle. Built between 1807 and 1814 by Francis Johnston. A Gothic Revival church having elaborate window and vault tracery while still retaining the essentially auditory church layout of galleries and west end organ. The original pulpit from this church is now located in nearby St Werburgh's church.

Welland's early tall double cube churches with west doorway and narrow tall lancets, are instantly recognisable. He was a good enough architect to re-imagine the parish church – doubtless influenced by Pugin and the Ecclesiologists to produce churches of far more incident – with separate spaces of nave, chancel, porches, belfries, medieval

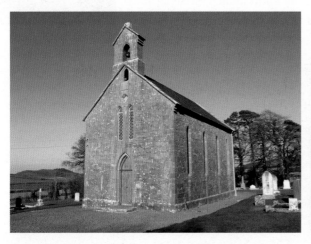

FAR LEFT: Dysert Enos, Co. Laois. Built in 1845 by the Ecclesiastical Commissioners. This simple Gothic Revival church typifies many of the small rural churches rebuilt in this period.

LEFT: Athlone Co. Westmeath. A large urban parish church. The polygonal chancel and Gothic chancel arch were added in 1869 to what was formerly a substantial hall and tower church. Many churches had chancel additions or internal refurbishments in the 1860s, in the decade leading up to disestablishment.

Ballinderry Middle Church Co. Antrim. Built by Jeremy Taylor, bishop of Down and Connor, soon after the Restoration, in 1664. A triple-decker pulpit is located in the nave, the modest holy table is enclosed by simple timber altar rails at the east end. The windows are examples of Gothic survivalism.
DERMOTT DUNBAR

Bannagher Church, Co. Offaly. This church has a shallow chancel; the stone communion rails follow the plan of the wooden predecessors. The Caen and coloured marble Gothic style stone pulpit and reader's desk replace a triple-decker pulpit which was located in the open space to the left of the brass lectern. Access to the communion rails was quite difficult as there were narrow passages between the pews and pulpit.

detailing to windows, asymmetrical planning and gables. In the final decade before disestablishment in 1869 the architectural partnership of Welland & Gillespie, in addition to building new churches, was generally responsible for the addition of chancels and transepts to the hall and tower churches of the early decades of the century. These churches include 'the dreary steeples of Fermanagh and Tyrone' as described by Churchill. In the interiors, triple-decker pulpits and box pews were replaced by carved wood Gothic detailing to pulpit and reading desk, located at the east end or arranged as part of a chancel addition. Gables, Gothic windows and internal rearrangements were major parts of their oeuvre.

After disestablishment the pace of building and re-building slowed, refurbishments became more common than new campaigns or further extensions to existing churches. In this period we have the wholesale introduction of Victorian Gothic elements – the polished brass rails, polished floor tiles, and carved stone reredos behind the holy table. The wooden pulpit and reader's desk were often replaced by ones executed in white Caen stone or coloured Irish marbles in the Early English style. The emphasis on the chancel is further enhanced by open bench seats facing eastwards for choirs and the insertion of commemorative stained glass. Victorian polychromy now dominated where previously clear light and oak or oak-stained furnishings (including wainscoting) ruled. The architects of the last decades of the nineteenth century included J.F. Fuller, Thomas Drew, and James Rawson Carroll, where there is an emphasis on apsed chancels, radiating roof timbers, polychromy and furnishings.

## Episcopal palaces and glebe houses

Two other building types for which the Church of Ireland was patron were the episcopal palaces and rectories or glebe houses. Their importance can only be hinted at here.

Gauntly impressive and curiously understudied, St Sepulchre's Archiepiscopal Palace in Dublin (St Kevin's Garda Station)

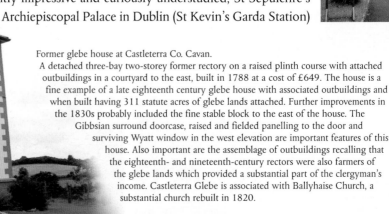

Former glebe house at Castleterra Co. Cavan.
A detached three-bay two-storey former rectory on a raised plinth course with attached outbuildings in a courtyard to the east, built in 1788 at a cost of £649. The house is a fine example of a late eighteenth century glebe house with associated outbuildings and when built having 311 statute acres of glebe lands attached. Further improvements in the 1830s probably included the fine stable block to the east of the house. The Gibbsian surround doorcase, raised and fielded panelling to the door and surviving Wyatt window in the west elevation are important features of this house. Also important are the assemblage of outbuildings recalling that the eighteenth- and nineteenth-century rectors were also farmers of the glebe lands which provided a substantial part of the clergyman's income. Castleterra Glebe is associated with Ballyhaise Church, a substantial church rebuilt in 1820.

Ballyhaise church
MIKE O'NEILL

hints at an important medieval legacy. Later examples include Sir Edward Lovett Pearce's Cashel Palace, Richard Castle at Ardbraccan, Co. Meath, replacing the medieval castle, Bishop Charles Este's (1735–40) improvements to the medieval Palace at Kilkenny and the magnificent Archbishop's Palace at Armagh, built for Archbishop Robinson by Thomas Cooley c.1770. Grandly impressive, it is unfortunate that so few now remain in the hands of the Church.

Glebe houses also have medieval roots, particularly in the residential towers placed at the west end of medieval churches – as at Leixlip, Lusk, Taghmon. In eighteenth-century visitations, 'miserable' 'Cabbins' on the glebe lands are noted, if rarely occupied by the incumbent or curate. In a highly stratified society, a clergyman manifestly poorer than his parishioners would have had little influence or standing. From 1711 the Board of First Fruits and Annates was involved in purchasing glebes and building glebe houses. In this context the 1757 book by Rev. John Payne *Twelve Designs for Country Houses*, published in Dublin, gives an important insight into the modest and more ambitious mid-century houses that might be suitable for a country parson. The majority, however, are nineteenth-century builds. Today when visiting rural parish churches, the visitor can scan the surrounding landscape and often identify the associated glebe house or rectory located within a convenient distance to the church.

Former Armagh episcopal palace. Built for Archbishop Richard Robinson by the architect Thomas Cooley around 1770. An additional storey and the porch to the entrance front were added by Archbishop John George Beresford in 1825, employing the architect Francis Johnston.

# Irish education,
# Church and State: an overview

SUSAN PARKES

The five Royal schools established in the counties of Ulster, such as Armagh Royal, above, all enjoy excellent grounds in which the schools are set.
ARMAGH ROYAL

## WILSON'S HOSPITAL SCHOOL

Founded in 1761 under provision of the will of Andrew Wilson. Wilson's Hospital School, situated in Multyfarnham in Co. Westmeath and now regarded as the diocesan secondary school for Meath and Kildare, was bequeathed to the Church of Ireland as a school for young Protestant boys and as a hospital for old men. Some of these pensioners earned their keep by teaching the pupils of the school their trades.
Over time the school ceased functioning as a hospital but naturally retained its original title although now entirely an educational establishment. It became co-educational in the late 1960s. Now a school for some 400 pupils (boarders and day pupils), it has grown and flourished considerably in recent years.

Ireland has had a long tradition of formal education. From the bardic and monastic schools of the Middle Ages through to the state-aided system of the twentieth century, education has played an important role in Irish society.

State intervention in Irish education began in the sixteenth century and schooling became a battleground in the religious conflict between Catholicism and Protestantism. As part of Tudor efforts to bring English 'order, habit and language' to Ireland, under an act of 1537 schools were established in every parish to teach English and the Protestant religion. In 1570, a further act established a grammar school in each diocese, and in 1592 Trinity College, University of Dublin was founded to educate the clergy and laity of the Anglican Church in Ireland. However, the overall failure of the Henrician reformation in Ireland meant that these measures did not create an effective education system. A further effort was made following the Ulster Plantation in 1608 whereby the Royal Schools were established in the

Kilkenny College ...ded 1684. Right, ...orts day *c.* 1920.
KILKENNY COLLEGE

## FRANCIS ROBERTSON
## 1737/8–91

Francis Robertson was born *c.* 1738, the son of Rev. John Robertson, rector of Aughanunshin. In 1764, he sailed for India, where he had a distinguished military career in the Bengal Army, eventually rising to the rank of colonel. Over the course of his career in India, Robertson became a very wealthy man.

In his will, Robertson made a bequest 'to the parishes of the Diocese of Raphoe, a sum of money, which by its interest at the rate of five percent shall be found sufficient to produce fifteen pounds sterling annually to each parish for or towards establishing a school therein …'. The sum bequeathed was £9,300. Thus each of the 31 parishes would receive £300, which, when invested, would produce enough interest to build and run the school and provide books and the master's salary.

Robertson died in 1791. The first schools were built at Raphoe and Killygarvan in 1810. Building continued throughout the 1810s, with schools at Donegal, Clondehorkey and Taughboyne being completed in 1824.

Eventually, the Irish state assumed control of education, and many of the Robertson schools closed. Nowadays, the governors of the Robertson endowments award grants to students at third-level institutions. Many thousands of young people over 200 years have good reason to be grateful to Colonel Francis Robertson.

DAVID CROOKS

counties of Ulster. Other Protestant endowed and charity schools were founded later including The King's Hospital (1670), Kilkenny College (1684), and Midleton College, Co. Cork (1696). The Erasmus Smith Trust (1669) was one of the largest educational endowments that established grammar schools and parochial 'English schools'. In 1733, the Incorporated Society for Promoting Protestant Schools in Ireland was founded with the purpose of converting pupils to Protestantism and providing a practical industrial education. These schools became known as 'charter schools' and later were much disliked for their proselytism and neglect of the children.

However, the majority of Irish people remained faithful to the Roman Catholic Church. As part of the Counter-Reformation Irish colleges were founded in Europe and men went abroad to study for the priesthood. In the eighteenth century the penal laws were introduced to prevent Roman Catholics from obtaining political or religious power. Roman Catholic education was prohibited and parents were forbidden to send their children abroad for education. However, these penal laws were circumvented by a clandestine education system of so-called 'hedge schools' where itinerant masters taught literacy and classical languages.

With abolition of the penal laws at the end of the eighteenth century, the prohibition on Roman Catholic education ceased and the Roman Catholic Church began to rebuild its educational provision of parish and diocesan schools, and by the founding of Irish religious orders such as the Irish Christian Brothers in 1803 and the Sisters of Mercy in 1820. The Anglican Church of Ireland as the Established Church still claimed the privilege of providing popular education and it began a further evangelical effort in the 1820s known as the 'Second Reformation' in which missionary education played a vital part. A number of Protestant education societies received government grants to support their work, the most important being the Society for Promoting the Education of the Poor of Ireland founded in 1811. It was a pioneer non-denominational society, but which required that the Bible be read daily in its schools 'without note or comment' – a rule that proved unacceptable to the Roman Catholic Church. The Kildare Place Society, as it became known from the location of its offices in Dublin, developed a countrywide network of schools, published textbooks and readers, established

The original building for Killaghtee School, Dunkineely, Co. Donegal, dates as far back as 1775. It became a National School in 1862 under the Rules for National Schools. In 1872, the school was rebuilt funded by local subscription raised by Mr Crooke (a late teacher). The school was housed in the stone building which is now Killaghtee Hall. It is under Church of Ireland patronage and is invested in the Robertson Board.

The Kildare Place Society Building, Dublin, founded in 1811 for the stated purpose of promoting non-denominational teaching for the poor. Ownership of the Kildare Place site was transferred to the Church of Ireland Training College in 1888. KPS gave grants towards the construction of schools. The illustration above is from the *Schoolmaster's Manual*.

CHURCH OF IRELAND COLLEGE OF EDUCATION

model schools for teacher training in Dublin, and set up an inspectorate. Its administrative structure was to have a marked influence on the subsequent national school system established in 1831.

The concept of a non-denominational education system began to gain favour and following the Act of Union in 1800, the government sought to gain control over the education of the poorer classes. In 1824, the government established a commission of inquiry, the Irish Education Inquiry, to survey the educational provision in every parish. Its report recommended that state grants to Protestant education societies should cease and instead a national system of non-denominational education should be established with the purpose of creating political and religious harmony. In 1831, the so-called 'Stanley Letter', written by the Irish chief secretary to the Duke of Leinster, president of the new Board of National Education, became the basis of the system. It was seen initially as an 'education experiment' and its rules were not enshrined in an act of parliament. The National Board provided grants for building and fitting up of schools, published suitable lesson books, provided gratuities for teachers and established a supervisory inspectorate. National schools offered combined secular and moral instruction with religious instruction taking place separately. Despite initial difficulties the national system grew and by 1900 there were over 8,000 national schools in the country. However, though remaining *de jure* a non-denominational system, *de facto* the churches used the system to sustain denominational schooling by applying separately for aid. The Irish language was not used in national schools as English was seen as the important imperial language, and this was one contributing factor to the decline of the Irish language.

The Church of Ireland objected in principle to the national school system because of the separation of religious from secular instruction and so its schools largely remained outside the national system until after disestablishment in 1870. The Church Education Society was founded in 1839 to support Anglican parochial schools and by 1850 there were 1,868 schools supported by the society. However, as the wealth of the Church declined, the schools gradually entered the national system but retained the rights of denominational management. The Church of Ireland Training College for Anglican national teachers was opened in 1884.

At secondary level the state did not intervene until the Intermediate Education Act of 1878 whereby state grants were paid to schools based on the pupils' performance in the intermediate public examinations. Both Protestant and Catholic voluntary secondary schools, including girls' schools, entered pupils for the

Queen's College Belfast
QUEEN'S UNIVERSITY BELFAST

examinations and the standard of secondary education was raised. Therefore the Protestant secondary schools remained autonomous institutions under their own management, aided by the state.

Technical education did not receive state support until the last decade of the nineteenth century and unlike primary and secondary education, its structure developed on a local authority basis. The 1930 Vocational Schools' Act later broadened the responsibilities of local authorities by introducing general continuation education in local vocational schools – clergy had the right to provide religious instruction for pupils attending.

However, in the higher education sector, religious issues were again to the forefront. At the beginning of the nineteenth century there was only one university in Ireland, namely Trinity College, Dublin, University of Dublin, founded in 1592. In the 1790s, the university was opened to Catholics and dissenters but it remained a privileged Anglican institution. In 1845, in an attempt to provide university education for the Catholic middle class, three secular Queen's Colleges in Belfast, Cork and Galway were established by the government. However, the Catholic Church refused to support these so-called 'godless colleges' and forbade Catholics to attend. As an alternative the Catholic hierarchy founded the Catholic University of Ireland in 1854 with Cardinal John Henry Newman as the first rector. However, the government refused to grant a charter to the Catholic University and so for the remainder of the century the 'university question' became a major issue in Irish politics. Various attempts were made to find a compromise, the Protestant churches upholding the historic religious identity of Trinity College and supporting the Queen's Colleges, particularly in Belfast, while the Catholic Church demanded a Catholic University as the only acceptable higher education institution for Catholics. In 1908, the National University of Ireland, consisting of three constituent colleges in Dublin, Cork and Galway was established as a non-denominational university, as was Queen's University, Belfast.

Thus in 1922, when the political partition of Ireland resulted in two jurisdictions, the Irish Free State and Northern Ireland, each inherited a denominational education system. In the Free State there was no radical structural reform of the existing church-state partnership, the new government concentrating on curriculum reform and the introduction of the Irish language, history and culture into schools. In Northern Ireland local education authorities became responsible for the three sectors, primary, secondary and technical, while the Catholic Church retained its own denominational system with part funding from the state. The education system in both parts of Ireland reflected the religious divisions of the respective societies with the Churches still having a major role in its provision.

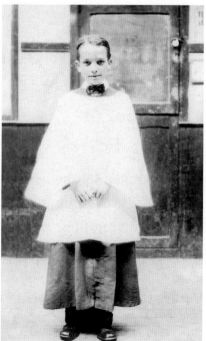

Edward Freeburn, a pupil at St George's Parish School, 1926. The school was situated behind the church on the site of the present hall. The school did not survive the 1941 Blitz.

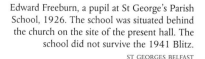
ST GEORGES BELFAST

ALEXANDRA COLLEGE

Alexandra College was founded in 1866 to give a new sense of purpose to the education of young middle-class ladies in Ireland. The prevailing system did not provide young ladies with any opportunities for real academic involvement; nor did it prepare them for any engagement in public, social or academic affairs.

Educating women for a domestic role was regarded at the time as the essential objective of a 'good' educational system. The system was largely in the hands of governesses who themselves lacked a grounding in mathematics, history, classics and philosophy.

Anne Jellicoe decided to address that inadequacy and put right the prevailing inequality against women. Her first idea was to open a college to educate governesses. This gave way to a wider plan to provide a liberal education for young ladies that would sharpen their academic consciousness, and encourage them to take up ideas and issues that exercised the minds of the thinking men of the time!

As Alexandra settled into its role, Anne Jellicoe was convinced that a major obstacle to the liberal education of women was their exclusion from the university campus. She passionately believed that until women were admitted to The Royal University (founded in 1880), the voice of women would not commonly be heard in politics, literature or in academic debate.

Some progress was made towards the end of the 1800s when lecturers from Trinity came regularly to Alexandra College to give university-type lectures to interested students.

When it was possible for women to prepare and sit for a degree by following these lectures, there was still no question of female students joining the student body on the Trinity campus. The doors of Trinity were finally opened to women in 1903 and Alexandra College students were the first to enrol. Alexandra College students were among the first to achieve successes at the Royal University from 1884 and at Trinity College from 1904.

*All the* CANONICAL BOOKES *of the* OLD TESTAMENT, *Translated, out of Hebrew, into the Irish Tongue, by the procurement of Doctor Bedell Bishop of Kilmore;*

A copy of the original translation by Bedell of the Old Testament from Hebrew into Irish
MARSH'S LIBRARY, DUBLIN

## The Church of Ireland and the Irish language

AONGHUS DWANE

Irish was the main language spoken by the Irish people for most of their recorded history. The language was brought by the Irish (the *Scotii*) to Scotland and the Isle of Man, evolving there into Scottish Gaelic and Manx respectively. Irish has the oldest vernacular literature in Western Europe. It is the first official language of the Republic of Ireland and is a recognised minority language in Northern Ireland. It is also an official language of the European Union.

From the middle of the sixteenth century onwards, the established Church of Ireland in the main followed the official policy of Anglicisation, which resulted in the Reformation principle of worship in the vernacular not being generally implemented in Ireland. Such Established Church interest as did exist focused principally on the possible use of the language in evangelising the Gaelic-speaking population, some of its clergy perceiving the shortcomings of preaching to them in English. John Carswell's *Foirm na nUrrnuidheadh*, a Gaelic translation of the (Presbyterian) Church of Scotland's *Book of Common Order* was published in Edinburgh in 1567. Intended primarily for Scottish worshippers, this publication was used in parts of Ireland also, in the absence of other worship materials at that stage.

The first book printed in Irish in Ireland was an Irish Alphabet and Catechism, *Aibidil Gaoidheilge 7 Caiticiosma*. This was printed by John Kearney with type presented by Queen Elizabeth I in 1571. William Bedell (1571–1642), a Provost of Trinity College Dublin, and later bishop of Kilmore, undertook the first translation of the Old Testament into Irish. This was printed in 1685, many years after Bedell's death along with a translation by William Daniel, archbishop of Tuam, of the New Testament – *Tiomna Nuadh*, the completed work was known as 'Bedell's Bible'. Daniel, who himself died in 1628, had also translated the *Book of Common Prayer* into Irish, and this was printed by John Francke in 1608. A number of later editions of the *Book of Common Prayer* were also translated into the Irish language.

When Bedell was Provost of Trinity College, those from a Gaelic background who were studying for the ministry were obliged to attend lectures in Irish in the College, again with a view to its utility in evangelisation.

*William Bedell, 1571–1642, undertook the first translation of the Old Testament into Irish.*

Wider European influences such as romanticism led to a greater interest in the study and conservation of the Irish language from the mid-eighteenth century onwards. Assisted by their access to universities and to research materials, many individuals including Church ministers, from an Irish Anglican background (as well as from other reformed traditions) were to the fore in such studies from this time onwards. These included such people as the antiquarian George Petrie (1790–1866), and the Rev. Maxwell Close (1822–1903), a key figure in the Society for the Preservation of the Irish Language. Charlotte Brooke (c.1740–93) published the first anthology of Gaelic poetry translated into English, her *Reliques of Irish Poetry* being published in 1789. Other prominent individuals from a Church of Ireland background were leaders in the Irish literary and cultural revival of the late nineteenth and early twentieth centuries, including the poet William Butler Yeats (1865–1939) the playwright Lady Gregory (1852–1932) and the writer John Millington Synge (1871–1909). The son of a rector from Frenchpark, Co. Roscommon, Douglas

Douglas Hyde was born in Castlerea, County Roscommon in 1860. His father became rector of Tibohine, and the family soon moved to neighbouring Frenchpark. Educated mainly at home due to childhood illness, the young Douglas became fascinated by the Irish language spoken by the local people. Rejecting family pressure to choose a career in the Church, he studied French, German, Greek, Latin and Hebrew at Trinity College Dublin. Between 1879 and 1884 he published more than a hundred pieces of Irish verse under the pen name *An Craoibhín Aoibhinn* (The Delightful Little Branch). Concerned at the continuing decline of the native language, he helped to found the Gaelic League (Conradh na Gaeilge) in 1893. He served as first President of Ireland, 1938–45.

A printed version of Bedell's translation of the Old Testament
MARSH'S LIBRARY, DUBLIN

St Finian's Church, Adelaide Road, Dublin, where services of the Irish Guild of the Church were held during the 1950s
ST FINNIAN'S LUTHERAN CHURCH, DUBLIN

Minutes of the Irish Guild of the Church from the inaugural meeting on 29 April 1914
RCB LIBRARY DUBLIN

Hyde (1860–1949), was a prominent Gaelic scholar and one of the founders of the Gaelic League (Conradh na Gaeilge) in 1893. The League soon established branches throughout the country attracting wide support across the denominational divide. Hyde was inaugurated as first President of Ireland in 1938, an acknowledgement by the nationalist political establishment of his immense cultural contribution.

Influenced strongly by the same cultural revival, *Cumann Gaelach na hEaglaise*, the Irish Guild of the Church (of Ireland) was founded in 1914 with the following aims:

1. to promote all that tends to preserve within the Church of Ireland the spirit of the ancient Celtic Church and to provide a bond of union for all members of the Church of Ireland inspired with Irish ideals;
2. to promote the use of the Irish language in the Church;
3. to collect from Irish sources suitable hymns and other devotional literature;
4. to encourage the use of Irish art and music in the Church.

The Guild flowered in the early years of the Irish state, and organised many social and cultural events for its members, while facilitating the publication and distribution of worship materials in Irish. It also had its own journal in the 1920s, *An tEaglaiseach Gaelach*, *The Gaelic Churchman*, featuring articles in both Irish and English of antiquarian, spiritual and literary interest with a celtic flavour. The Guild organised church services in the Irish language at various locations, including at St Finian's, Adelaide Road, Dublin in the 1950s. Since the 1960s, Christ Church Cathedral in Dublin has been home to Cumann Gaelach na hEaglaise.

In the early years of the independent southern Irish state, a preparatory college system was established by the Department of Education to improve the standard of Irish among primary school teachers. All but one of these was under Roman Catholic

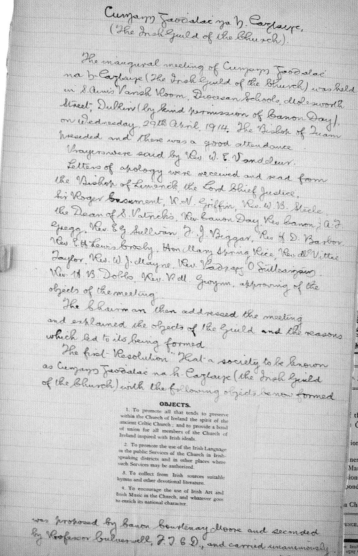

A large pseudo-Celtic Cross made of Caen stone stands in St Nicholas' Collegiate Church, Galway as a memorial to various parishioners who died during the First World War.

The cover of *An tEaglaiseach Gaelach, The Gaelic Churchman* – the journal of the Irish Guild of the Church, which appeared in the mid-20s to the mid/late-30s
RCB ARCHIVE

DUNBAR DESIGN

management. The singular exception was Coláiste Moibhí, founded in 1926 as a preparatory college to the Church of Ireland College of Education. Coláiste Móibhí offered secondary education through Irish, from Intermediate to Leaving Certificate level, until its closure in 1995. A detailed history has been written by Valerie Jones: *A Gaelic experiment – the Preparatory System 1926 to 1961 and Coláiste Moibhí* (the Woodfield Press, 2006).

A number of Archbishops of Dublin in recent times have been competent Irish speakers, including George Otto Simms (Abp 1956–69), Henry McAdoo (Abp 1977–85) and Donald Caird (Abp 1985–96).

Canon Coslett Quin (1907–95), Professor of Biblical Greek at Trinity College and priest in the Church of Ireland, produced a translation of the New Testament from Greek. *An Tiomna Nua*, was published in 1971. The *Alternative Prayer Book* 1984 was also translated into Irish. Noted Irish speaker and traditional musician Rev Gary Hastings undertook the translation of the Church's revised *Book of Common Prayer* in 2004, *Leabhar na hUrnaí Coitinne 2004* being launched at a festival in Down Cathedral, Downpatrick, in September of that year.

St Nicholas' Collegiate Church in Galway city regularly hosts performances of traditional Irish music. Traditional musician Rónán Browne is pictured here, along with the Rector, Rev. Gary Hastings.
ST NICHOLAS' COLLEGIATE CHURCH GALWAY

## DONALD CAIRD

Bishop Donald Caird (born 1925) has taken a keen interest in the Irish language throughout his life. He attended Dublin's Wesley College. He was fascinated to encounter Anglican worship in Irish in St Patrick's Cathedral, and first visited the Gaeltacht of Corca Dhuibhne and the Great Blasket in the early 1940s.

Donald studied at Trinity College and was ordained deacon in 1950. In 1960, he was appointed rector of Rathmichael, Co Dublin. He married Nancy Ballatyne-Sharpe and they have two daughters and one son. While bishop of Limerick (1970–76) he was appointed to Bord na Gaeilge. As archbishop of Dublin (1985–96), he was chairman of Coláiste Móibhí, the only Irish-medium Protestant school in the country.

Donald has spoken at numerous Irish language festivals, and assisted in translating hymns for the *Church Hymnal*. He retired in 1996, and in 2006 lectured on Douglas Hyde at the Celtic Revival Summer School on the Aran Islands.

In 2010, Donald celebrated 40 years in the episcopate. The Irish language Patrick Pearse Award (Gradam an Phiarsaigh) was awarded to him in recognition of his work for the language.

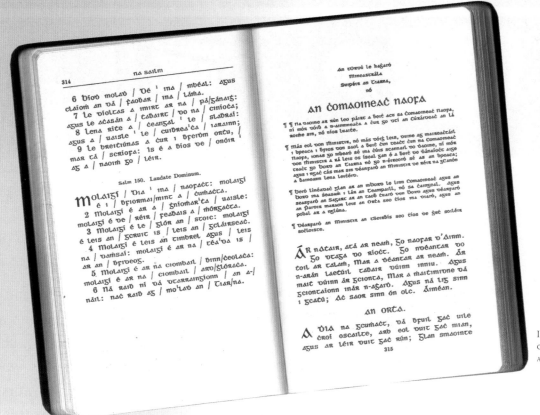

Irish translation of the Book of Common Prayer, 1926
AONGHUS DWANE

# Liturgy in the Church of Ireland

## BISHOP HAROLD MILLER

A Praise service at Willowfield
Parish Church, Belfast
DAVE BRADSHAW

There is good reason to describe the Church of Ireland as a 'liturgical Church'. It is liturgical in a variety of ways. The firm roots of the Church are in the *Book of Common Prayer,* and, of course, until relatively recently, that meant that pretty well every word used in worship was read directly from the book. The reason was that liturgical worship was a means of teaching and passing on the faith, and the words were therefore of vital importance.

The Church of Ireland, along with the Church of England, is both catholic and reformed. Many other reformed churches were more radical in their approach to liturgy, giving greater freedom to the minister to write prayers and design services of worship – though usually within a framework. But Anglicanism, as the communion of churches has become known, sought to retain all that was good in liturgy and to develop it in a way that cohered with and advanced the doctrines of the Reformation. This means, of course, that a Roman Catholic visiting a Church of Ireland service is likely to comment that the form of worship is very akin to their own, and a reformed person is likely to notice and resonate with the reformed doctrine. The Church of Ireland is a 'bridge' church.

One of the key aspects of worship which needed to be emphasised in the sixteenth century was the teaching of the Scriptures. The invention of printing was vital to this, and, as time went on, printed books were available to more and more people. So, Anglicanism was a creature of its day, and books, whether the King James Version of the Bible or *The Book of Common Prayer* grew in importance and more general use in that era. But the prayer book was also relatively simple and memorable. The model for reading the scriptures was, in essence, one chapter from the Old Testament and one from the New each morning and evening in sequence; the Psalms were read over in a monthly cycle, morning and evening; and memorable prayers and liturgical structures were regularly repeated so that those who could not read would know them 'off by heart'. So, in my childhood, everyone who worshipped regularly in the Church of Ireland knew the creeds, the canticles and the set prayers. They were stored common memory.

The Liturgical Movement of the twentieth century lay behind the revision of liturgies which began in Ireland with the setting up of the Liturgical Advisory Committee in 1962. New discoveries had influenced patterns for the word and sacrament which had, for example, been taken up in the new 'ecumenical' liturgy of the Church of South India. The Lambeth Conference of 1958 encouraged a review of

Bishop
Mant's crook
BELFAST
CATHEDRAL
ARCHIVE

PAUL HARRON

The Rev. Turner lights a candle in St George's, Belfast.
ST GEORGE'S, BELFAST

The Very Rev. Sandra Pragnell, Dean of Limerick, reading from the Old Testament
PAUL HARRON

liturgies in view of these discoveries and they began to emerge in the Church of Ireland with a new Liturgy for Holy Communion in 1967. This liturgy had a new shape, a new language (people were called 'you' but God was still 'thee') and new elements (for example the Peace, which had emerged from India but was rather like the emperor with no clothes at this stage because it was not actually shared). Over the next ten years, booklet after booklet was produced with new rites, and these were eventually revised and included in the *Alternative Prayer Book* in 1984.

Beneath the surface other important things were also happening:

Choristers singing at the *Sound of Singing Psalms*, St Nicholas' Church, Belfast, 2008    PAUL HAR

- Liturgy was becoming more participative.
- An ecumenical consensus was beginning to form, with different denominations realising that they could learn and benefit from the others.
- The concept of having every single word written down and fixed was changing. Prayers were to be more flexible and even 'open prayer' was allowed.
- The idea of the importance of the 'framework' or 'agenda' of worship into which the different parts fitted was strong.

- The horizontal dimension of worship was being increased, with a sense of the worship of the gifted community – an insight also helped by charismatic renewal.
- More variety was allowed, both in seasons and in ordinary worship. This was increased further with the later introduction of A Service of the Word, which was essentially a structure into which different elements could be fitted, and offered an alternative to Morning Prayer.

Children enjoying a praise party

ANNETTE MCGRATH

The end result of this over a few decades has been quite a transformation of the experience of worship in the Church of Ireland. The 2004 *Book of Common Prayer* allows a wide variety of styles of worship and these are used to the full. This means that, whereas fifty years ago you could go into any Church of Ireland church and experience essentially the same thing, the Church of Ireland has probably now become the denomination which offers the widest variety in worship styles. A visitor can experience, for example, a eucharist and music of exquisite beauty in the context of a cathedral, with Latin texts, candles, vestments and communion wafers, very close to traditional Roman Catholic worship; a quiet *Taize* service; Evening Prayer in Irish; the exuberance of charismatic worship; a preaching service with half an hour of biblical exposition; or straightforward Morning Prayer with three chanted canticles. And that is only the beginning of a list which could be much longer. Some of these services will be strictly within the bounds of what is allowed, but in others, creativity may have taken churches beyond those bounds.

In 2001, President Mary McAleese led a congregation of several hundred young people from all the Christian Churches in Ireland at a Taizé Service in Christ Church Cathedral, Dublin. During the service the President led prayers for Church Unity.
CHRIST CHURCH CATHEDRAL, DUBLIN

If the Bible and the *Book of Common Prayer* are the two key books of the Church of Ireland in worship, there is, nevertheless, an important third: the *Church Hymnal*. This was not always so. Some of the Churches of the Reformation wrote hymns, and indeed some of Luther's are still sung. But it was the Evangelical revivals of the eighteenth and nineteenth centuries, and the Tractarian movement of the nineteenth century which introduced many of our hymns into

## St Patrick's Day

On 17 March, The Rt Rev. Harold Miller, bishop of Down and Dromore, invites pilgrims to join him for the Annual St Patrick's Day Festival Service, followed by lunch in the grounds of Down Cathedral. The event is a joyful, cross-community occasion which attracts hundreds of visitors from Ireland and abroad. The celebrations centre around two historic sites – the cathedral and Saul Church, on the site of St Patrick's first church. The day begins with an early service of Holy Communion at Saul after which a group of pilgrims of all ages and nationalities makes a 45-minute prayer pilgrimage to Down Cathedral. The Festival Service is a lively event including traditional music and a guest speaker who addresses the congregation on the chosen theme. At 1pm special guests and local clergy take part in a wreath laying ceremony at St Patrick's grave before sharing an Irish stew lunch. The pilgrimage dates back to the 1950s and Bishop F.J. Mitchell. On one occasion the preacher at Down Cathedral was The Archbishop of Canterbury, Michael Ramsey. With the arrival of the Troubles more local celebrations, such as the pilgrimages, stopped for a time, although Bishop Gordon McMullan revived a large inter-denominational service in Down Cathedral in the 1980s.

Anglicanism. Indeed, for most Church of Ireland worshippers, although they can envisage worship without hymns in early and midweek communions, they cannot really imagine main services without them. Hymnody, especially for an older generation, is of vital devotional importance, usually accompanied by organ and choir. But for a new, younger generation, the preference is often to sing a group of songs led by a music group, with words and visuals projected onto a screen. These songs may be popular for a time and then be replaced by others. They do not have the same 'foursquare' style as hymns, and can at times be quite complex, at other times repetitive. But what is happening is that, just as Cranmer and his followers used the invention of printing to proclaim the Gospel, so today, the amazing developments in electronic communications media are being used for a new generation. To make the best use of these media could be considered a foundation principle of the Anglican way!

One final aspect of liturgy which pervades Anglicanism is the use of the Christian Year. For many visitors, indeed, it may be a service associated with a particular point in the year which is their means of access to the Church of Ireland. On the most obvious level, there is something very special about the Nine Lessons and Carols in the week before Christmas, or the Midnight Communion by candlelight on Christmas Eve. For some it may be a Good Friday Service or a Remembrance Service in early November. There is a sense in which liturgy takes us through the year, with both the re-telling of the story of salvation in Christ, and the reminder of aspects of our humanity and createdness in Harvest Thanksgiving and Lenten lamentation. Like the Jewish people, we keep telling the story over and over again, because worship engages, not just with the big story of God's work in the world, but 'our' story as the community of Christ's disciples today, and 'my' story as a sinner saved by grace.

GORDON GRAY

The use of technology, as here in Christ Church Cathedral Lisburn, is now commonplace in many churches.

The Very Rev. Katherine Poulton with the Discovery Gospel Choir at Mountjoy Gaol, Dublin

PAUL HARRON

Bishop Harold Miller lays a wreath on St Patrick's Grave, as part of a St Patrick's Day celebration at Down Cathedral, Downpatrick.

## Women in ministry in the Church of Ireland

The Church of Ireland General Synod approved the ordination of women as priests and bishops in 1990. The first women were ordained as priests in that year by Bishop Samuel Poyntz in St Anne's Cathedral, Belfast. The two candidates on that occasion were (the late) Irene Templeton and Kathleen Young (now Brown). The Church of Ireland General Synod also made it possible for women to be ordained to episcopal ministry. Across the 38 provinces of the Anglican Communion, 28 now ordain women as priests and 17 allow women to serve as bishops.

Katharine Poulton became the first woman ordained deacon in 1987. She is now serving as Dean of Ossory.

On 20 September 2013, Rev. Pat Storey, rector of St Augustine's Church, Londonderry, was elected as Bishop of Meath and Kildare

# Missionary work and the Church of Ireland

WILLIAM MARSHALL

The Verger Mr Gamble with Dr Darcy, bishop of Down, Dean Grierson and Canon Moore of Holywood, join in prayer with a Church Army mission outside St Anne's cathedral on Friday 7 July, 1911.
BELFAST CATHEDRAL ARCHIVE

The whole world nowadays is a mission field. Here in Ireland, churchgoing has greatly declined in recent years. Hence, for the missionary work of the Church of Ireland the obvious starting point is this island. In that sense this whole book describes such work. But the Church of Ireland is part of the worldwide Anglican Communion. Its mission entails giving to and receiving from other bodies in the universal mission. Moreover, mission work is not solely evangelism. The Church is an instrument of God and must promote the welfare of humanity. The following sections will give examples of the various aspects of mission associated with the Church of Ireland.

Rev. Adrian Empey, Dublin port chaplain, with seafarers

The Church of Ireland claims to be continuous with the church planted in this island by St Patrick and others. The example of these early missions has inspired the work of their modern successors. Archbishop Godfrey Day was Primate of all Ireland in 1939. In the sole address he gave to the General Synod he stated:

> May the Church of St Patrick, of St Columba … Robert and Louisa Stewart, George Pilkington, George Alfred Lefroy … and Marie Hayes … ever realise that her supreme purpose … was to preach [the] Gospel to all mankind.

Many of the names Day mentioned will appear in the following account. I shall deal largely with missionary expansion in the nineteenth- and early twentieth-centuries, noting developments since then.

## Mission societies

The Church of Ireland engages in mission work largely through voluntary societies. The 2013 *Church of Ireland Directory* lists 20 constituent members of the Association of Missionary Societies (AMS). All receive support from parishes. The oldest is the Society for Promoting Christian Knowledge (SPCK), founded in England in 1698. It is now chiefly a publishing firm, but in its earliest days sent missionaries abroad. Many AMS member societies work in specific places. Others, such as the Mission to Seafarers, have specific kinds of work. Some, like the Leprosy Mission, are interdenominational.

Missions usually emphasise their holistic role – both social work and proclaiming the gospel. Some societies are headquartered in England and have an Irish branch, often with considerable autonomy. The society that receives most support in Ireland is the Church Mission Society (CMS). The Irish branch, now called the Church Mission Society Ireland (CMSI), was formed in 1814. It now includes several former societies, such as the Church of England Zenana Mission.

Many missionaries of the past spent most of their lives on the mission field, with rare or no visits home. Today mission work is done mostly by Christian nationals of the countries concerned, with plenty of movement between churches. Ordinands of the Church of Ireland often have placements in Asia and Africa during their training.

## North America

Ireland provided many settlers in the American colonies in the eighteenth century and the Society for the Propagation of the Gospel (SPG, later United Society for the Propagation of the Gospel (USPG, now US)) ministered to them. It also worked among the indigenous peoples and African slaves there. SPG and CMS continued to send missionaries to North America in the nineteenth century as European

Father Pat, pioneer missionary in Canada, with Chinese employees of Bishop Sillitoe and his favourite dogs
RCB ARCHIVE

settlements expanded westwards. One of the most colourful Irish missionaries in Canada was Henry Irwin from Newtownmountkennedy. Known as 'Father Pat', he ministered to the miners, prospectors and builders of the Canadian Pacific Railway from 1885. He then moved to Vancouver, where his young wife died in childbirth and their child was stillborn. Father Pat returned to the mining camps, wearing himself out in reckless work. His bishop ordered him back to Ireland, but he got off the train a few miles from

## Charles Inglis (1734–1816)

Charles Inglis was the son of Rev. Archibald Inglis, rector of Glencolumbkille. He went to America in 1754. In 1758, he was ordained in London and took up duty as a missionary with the Society for the Propagation of the Gospel in the Dover Mission in Pennsylvania. He was appointed curate of the prestigious Holy Trinity Parish, New York in 1765 and rector of the same parish in 1777. The American War of Independence created problems for Inglis, who was staunchly loyal to King George III. With the loss of the American colonies, he departed for Canada. In 1787, he was consecrated first bishop of Nova Scotia, and was thus the first bishop of a diocese in a British colony. At that time, the diocese covered most of what is now Ontario.

Inglis travelled widely, building churches and establishing good standards of Anglican worship. He founded the University of King's College and the King's School at Windsor, Ontario. His son John became the third bishop of Nova Scotia in 1823. Inglis died in 1816, having worked hard to ensure the success of the early development of the church in Canada. His feast day is observed in the prayer book of the Anglican Church of Canada.

Helen Roseveare with Pastor Danga of Wamba on a return visit to the Congo in October 1989

## Helen Roseveare

Dr Helen Roseveare is renowned for her medical missionary work in the Belgian Congo and as a speaker and author. She is a parishioner of St Elizabeth's Dundonald on the outskirts of Belfast. Helen was born in England in 1925, becoming a committed Christian as a medical student at Cambridge University in 1945. She went to the Congo in 1953 through WEC International where she practiced medicine and trained others in medical work. Helen remained in the country throughout the infamous Simba Rebellion – a hostile and dangerous period of political instability in the early 1960s. In 1964, she was taken prisoner and for five months endured beatings and rape at the hands of the rebel forces. She left for England but, although humiliated by the rebels, Helen found that God gave her an even deeper love for the Congo people. In 1965, she returned to pick up her medical missionary work. Helen finally left Africa in 1973 and since then, she has spoken and written for an international audience and is well known throughout the world. A supportive member of her parish, Helen still loves to teach the Bible to young women in East Belfast through the Girl Crusaders Union.

Montreal and wandered around in the harsh Canadian winter. In spite of the care of the Notre Dame Hospital nuns in Montreal, he died and was buried beside his wife and child. The Canadian Pacific Railway carried the body of 'the best loved man in British Columbia' free of charge to his last resting place.

In the nineteenth century the Anglican Church in Canada became an autonomous province of the Anglican Communion. The interchange of personnel from there to Ireland continues to the present day.

## South America

Anglican missions in South America had no link with the colonial powers, but the South American Missionary Society (SAMS), along with other societies, worked in several countries there. South America's settlers were mainly Roman Catholic, so Anglican missions concentrated on the indigenous peoples.

Anglican mission societies in South America today work as part of the Anglican Communion. Movement between there and Ireland is two-way. A particularly inspiring SAMS meeting was held in Craigavon in October 2010. José Henriquez, one of those who had been trapped for 69 days in a Chilean mine, spoke about how the Christian faith had sustained him and his companions through their ordeal.

A survivor of the Chilean mine disaster José Henriquez shares his testimony at a SAMS meeting in Craigavon, 2011. Far right is Bishop Ken Clarke, director of SAMS.

## Africa

The nineteenth century was a time of great European expansion in Africa. CMS worked in many parts of Africa, with Irish participation in many cases. For example, George Pilkington (one of those mentioned by Day), who hailed from Westmeath, was an evangelist in Uganda and helped to translate the Bible into Luganda.

The Bible Churchman's Missionary Society (BCMS, now Crosslinks), founded in 1922, worked in Uganda, Tanzania and other African countries, with Irish people among its missionaries. The same is true of USPG, which was active in Tanzania, Zambia and Zimbabwe. By the end of the twentieth century all of Africa had self-governing Churches of the Anglican Communion.

## Asia

A new era of Protestant outreach began in Asia in the eighteenth century. India received special attention and the Church of Ireland contributed mission workers and money through SPG and CMS. Smaller, more regional societies also had Irish members. George Lefroy from County Down (mentioned by Day) was a foundation member of the Cambridge Mission to Delhi and later became metropolitan (equivalent of primate) of the Church of India.

The Church of Ireland had its own special mission in India the Dublin University Mission to Chota Nagpur (DUMCN) Assigned to the district of Hazaribagh, DUMCN founded a hospital, schools and a college. The Church of Ireland still supports DUMCN and frequent visits to and from India keep the link alive.

From left: Missionary in a topi and children, possibly in Hassardganj; Chitarpur hospital; Missionaries, with women and girls and their baggage, labelled 'lace school'

Though China (apart from Hong Kong) was never a European colony, Europeans had considerable influence there. The Dublin University Fukien Mission (DUFM) was founded in 1885 by a CMS missionary, Robert Stewart. DUFM opened many schools and a college in Fuzhou. Work in Fukien continued through times of great change, war and revolution, but by 1951 the communists had gained control and foreign missionaries had to leave. DUFM became the Dublin University Far Eastern Mission (DUFEM). Its missionaries went to work among the Chinese diaspora in Singapore, Malaysia and elsewhere. Today DUFEM has no missionaries working abroad but visits take place in both directions and DUFEM ministers among the large numbers of Chinese in Ireland. CMS and USPG have links with other countries of Asia such as Iran, Nepal, Pakistan, Sri Lanka, Korea and Japan.

Born in 1864, Rev. James Stratford Collins was the son of a Church of England rector, but ordained for the Church of Ireland in the diocese of Killaloe following his education at Trinity College, Dublin. He was the first missionary at the Dublin University Mission in Fukien, China in 1887. Unfortunately he drowned in 1897.
RCB LIBRARY, KILLALOE LANTERN SLIDE CHINA COLLECTION

## Australasia

Included in the mission of the Church of Ireland was ministry to the settlers in Australia, New Zealand and the surrounding islands. The British government appointed chaplains and SPG and CMS also supplied personnel. As dioceses were created in the nineteenth century, their bishops recruited clergy from England and Ireland until well into the twentieth century. Today there are autonomous Anglican churches in Australia, New Zealand and Melanesia.

## Mission in Ireland

The Church of Ireland is a minority Church in a predominantly Roman Catholic country, and its mission requires great sensitivity because of the malign legacy of history. There could hardly have been a worse form of mission than the penal laws. A long-lasting bitterness affected relations between the two communities in Ireland (mitigated by some notable exceptions of good relations). In the early years of the nineteenth century attempts were made to convert Roman Catholics. The Irish Church Missions (ICM) was founded in 1849 'to Protestantise Ireland'. Schools were established, churches built and people employed to distribute evangelical literature. At the height of the Great Famine the missions distributed food, clothing and medicine. Roman Catholics, however, resented the ICM's strong denunciation of their religion and the project had limited success. Today ICM ministers to students and young people and works among the homeless, those suffering from addiction and families affected by suicide.

The mission of the Church of Ireland at home is primarily the task of its parishes. Generally proselytism is avoided, but the growing numbers of unchurched Irish people mean there is plenty of scope for preaching the gospel. The Church Army served, and continues to serve, the church well in evangelism.

The mission of the Church throughout the world is one. This is especially true today but it was always true to varying degrees. Stories of heroic witness in far-off lands inspired more fervent Christianity in the 'home' church. Today the large numbers of African and Asian Christians living in Ireland can stimulate and challenge the Irish churches by their exuberance. The statement on the CMSI website is no doubt also true of the other missions: 'CMS Ireland is working to empower and equip the local church for local and global mission.'

Bishop Bill Love (Albany), Bishop Harold Miller (Down and Dromore) and Bishop Justin Badi Arama (Maridi).

## 'A threefold cord'

'A threefold cord is not quickly broken.' Ecclesiastes 4:12. This image perfectly describes Down and Dromore's link with Maridi Diocese which is a unique concept of mission across three continents: Albany Diocese (USA) and Down and Dromore sharing together in mission with the Church in South Sudan. The 3 dioceses have been linked since 2005, before South Sudan gained its independence on 9 July 2011. One of Africa's longest-running civil wars has ravaged the country and it has many needs in terms of basic infrastructure, education and health. With the help of CMS Ireland, the link has facilitated the building of schools and a clinic as well as the training of teachers and medical staff. The church also faces challenges as it seeks to care for and equip its clergy for ministry and to raise up a new generation of godly leaders, both for Church and country.

In October 2012, a ten-strong team from Down and Dromore and Albany visited Maridi Diocese – the first time in the history of the link that all three bishops were together in South Sudan.

# Protestant charitable endeavour in Ireland

MARIA LUDDY

Dr Kathleen Lynn with infants
The tradition of establishing
hospitals by members of the
Protestant community was still
evident in the twentieth century
when Dr Kathleen Lynn and
Madeline ffrench-Mullen
established St Ultan's Hospital for
Infants in 1919.
ROYAL COLLEGE OF PHYSICIANS
SU/8/3/1

An 1822, account of Dublin noted that many there lived 'in the most squalid and wretched conditions'. Eighty years later Rev. Gilbert Mahaffy observed that 'Dublin is relatively the poorest [city] in the kingdom'. It seems as if the circumstances of the poor had altered little in those 80 years; however, this ignores the extensive philanthropic provision that had developed throughout the eighteenth and nineteenth centuries.

Many philanthropic institutions of that time were supported by charitable individuals, particularly Protestants. Religion was an important motivating factor for charitable works. The scriptural basis for charitable involvement was much invoked in the reports of the various institutions formed in the period.

The Protestant charity network was developed in Ireland in the eighteenth century, especially in the area of health. By the 1840s Dublin city could boast 35 hospitals, dispensaries and asylums. There were few permanent institutions for the relief of the poor in the pre-Famine period, however. Such institutions as did exist operated only in cities and towns and were partly supported by the government. An extensive state dispensary system and a state-supported hospital system were in place by the 1840s. The major institution for the relief of the poor at this time was the workhouse. The Irish poor law, introduced in 1838, divided the country into 130 administrative divisions (later 162 designated unions), each of which constructed a workhouse. At their origin workhouses were managed by local Protestant elites. However, by the 1870s, control of poor-law boards began to pass to Catholic hands.

Many Protestant charities became the concern of individual families. The Female Orphan House in Dublin is typical of a successful charity; its leading supporters were the banking LaTouche family. Charitable initiatives were also sponsored by the rising middle classes, although institutional charities organised by Protestants did not receive substantial support from the Catholic community. There does appear to have been cooperation between Catholic and Protestant philanthropists, however, in rural areas.

One of the major areas of philanthropic intervention within the Protestant community was the care of children. Many 'poor' and 'charity' schools were established from the early nineteenth century. Alongside these were 'ragged schools', common in Dublin from around the 1850s. These were intended to entice street children away from a life of crime 'by training them in habits of industry'. Ragged schools in Ireland were controversial, being seen by Catholics as Protestant proselytising agencies. Mrs Ellen Smyly, associated with the Irish Church Missions, was an innovator in ragged schools. Her first Bible school opened near Grand Canal Street in 1850; by 1883, the number of children catered for in her various establishments amounted to 1,578.

A network of orphanages was also set up during this period. Among the most enduring of these is the Cottage Home for Little Children, established by Rosa M. Barrett in 1879 in Dún Laoghaire, and still working with children today. Rosa M. Barrett was a founding member of the Society for the Prevention of Cruelty to Children, formed in Ireland in 1889, in which many Protestants were active. Its work involved active intervention in the home, albeit with a strong belief that abusive parents could be reformed. The society helped to define how abuse and neglect were understood, thus challenging the popular understanding that 'such things' did not occur in Ireland. Unlike earlier, similar organisations, the society put pressure on legislators and achieved changes that improved the

Walter Blake Kirwan (1754–1805), Dean of Killala, a Catholic, converted to Protestantism and gained fame as a charismatic preacher. In November 1791, the governors of a newly founded home for destitute girls on the north side of Dublin invited Kirwan to preach. In 1800, the charity was incorporated by the Irish parliament as 'The Female Orphan House' and they paid £205 for the event to be immortalised in paint.

## LADY ARABELLA DENNY

Lady Arabella Denny was a supporter of The Foundling Hospital for the poor of Dublin. In 1760, she presented a clock to the Dublin Workhouse. It was put up in the nursery for foundling children, and used to regulate the feeding of infants.

She was instrumental in the reforming of the Foundling Hospital and in 1764 was thanked by the Irish House of Commons for her extraordinary bounty and charity. She worked with the Dublin Society, helping introduce lace-making into workhouses; in recognition of her work with the poor she was conferred with the Freedom of the City of Dublin in 1765. She was elected honorary member of the Dublin Society in 1766. In June 1767 she founded Magdalen Asylum for Protestant Girls in Leeson Street, which was a home for fallen women or penitent prostitutes, who were provided with accommodation, clothing, food and religious instruction.

In 1773, she founded the Magdalene Chapel frequented by many of high society in Dublin. The Governance of the Magadalene Asylum became the Leeson Street Trust, which was named in her honour the Lady Arabella Denny Trust, or Denny House, which is still a registered charity today. The Protestant Adoption Society which became PACT named its office Arabella House in her honour.

Arabella Denny retired in 1790, and died in Dublin on 18 March, 1792.

Osborne
February 11 1884

Dear Lady Meath
I am commanded by the Queen to let you know that Her Majesty will be happy to Patronize the Girls Friendly Society of Ireland. Her Majesty will also send a donation of Fifty Pounds to the Fund of the Society

Letter from Queen Victoria confirming patronage of the Girls' Friendy Society
RCB ARCHIVE

A hostel on non-denominational lines was set up by the Alexandra Guild in Castlewood Avenue, Rathmines, to provide safe accommodation for young girls seeking employment in Dublin. Although there were 'lodgings in Dublin at the GFS Lodge, the YWCA home and others, they were for the better paid business girls and others.'
ALEXANDRA COLLEGE

lives of many Irish children – for instance, the Prevention of Cruelty to Children Act of 1894 and the 1908 Children Act.

## Protestant Women and Philanthropy

Amongst the earliest forms of the organised charitable work of Protestant women were auxiliaries to Bible societies. Originally their function was to raise funds, but their members began also to visit the homes of the poor and distribute Bibles. By 1825, women were acknowledged as the 'life' of Bible associations. Also significant were foreign missionary societies. The two largest societies organised by women in Ireland were the Young Women's Christian Association, which opened its first branch in Ireland in 1866, and the Girls' Friendly Society, established in Ireland in 1877. The GFS offered training to young girls and sought permanent employment for them, while many members of the YWCA visited prisons and were strong temperance activists. Like most religiously inspired philanthropic groups of the time, both were socially conservative and did not urge legislation regarding the conditions of the poor.

Generally women in Protestant philanthropic organisations were more independent of clerical authority than their Catholic counterparts. Their minority position allowed a sense of community to develop and, in times of severe distress, local relief committees were organised. Many societies were national in scale, however. One of these was the British and Irish Ladies Society for Promoting the Welfare of the Female Peasantry in Ireland, established in 1822. Members of the aristocracy acted as local patrons, while the active work was carried on by the wives of the gentry and commercial classes. They visited the poor and distributed material aid to those deemed worthy. It was also assumed that the 'ladies' would influence the moral conduct of those they assisted.

## Twentieth-Century Developments

How, then, did this philanthropic endeavour evolve into what we understand as 'social work'? The emerging 'social worker' was shaped at the end of the nineteenth century, when debates were occurring around what this term meant.

Philanthropists sought to provide relief to the deserving poor only. And, in order to ascertain who were deserving, investigations were always carried out. In the late nineteenth century the belief emerged that workers should be trained to this end. The Charity Organisation Society, founded in 1869, was amongst the first to promote casework – the detailed investigation of the circumstances of each 'client' as a basis for judgement. At a lecture to the Irish Women's Reform League in March 1918 a Miss Cunningham pointed out the need for 'reasoned judgement' in social work: 'The feelings, she considered, should be the inspiration to action, but in action reason should be the guide.' The call, then, was for rational, educated people, almost always women, to be trained in social work.

Charity box

Students studying at
Alexandra College,
Dublin, c 1920s
ALEXANDRA COLLEGE

So, in Alexandra College, Dublin, the first training course in social work in Ireland was organised.

Another significant role was that of the hospital almoner. In Ireland the first almoner was appointed in the Adelaide Hospital in Dublin in 1921. From the early twentieth century, almoners, who were exclusively women, became involved in child welfare, social insurance and the prevention of disease. Most appear to have come from the middle classes – the poor, of course, could not investigate the poor. They were initially expected to be between 25 and 32 years old and to have some experience of social work. The first recognised form of training for almoners evolved from an apprenticeship into an integrated programme of practical and academic work. By 1920 basic training had become a two-year course with continuous-assessment certificates in addition to university awards. The Dublin branch of the Institute of Almoners was established in 1937.

After the establishment of the Irish state, initiatives in social work came from interested groups and individuals, not necessarily from government. A one-year diploma in social studies was introduced in Trinity College, Dublin in 1934. The course was at first considered suitable only for young women: one commentator described it as 'a pleasant interlude between school and matrimony'. In 1941, it was extended to two years, except for graduates, and a four-year honours degree course was established in 1962.

Echoes of the fears of proselytism expressed by Catholics in the nineteenth century were evident in the twentieth. In 1940, John Charles McQuaid, Roman Catholic archbishop of Dublin, formed the Catholic Social Service Conference. McQuaid helped create a social science diploma in University College, Dublin and offered his Catholic Social Welfare Bureau, established in 1943, as a practical training ground for students. McQuaid was anxious to control, as far as possible, the training of social workers, believing that the Churches working together on issues of welfare would only lead to confusion.

Eileen Younghusband, in a 1951 report, listed the social work courses available in Ireland. Amongst the subjects covered on the TCD diploma course were: social and political theory, industrial law, hygiene, dietetics, child and industrial psychology and penology. Practical work involved visits to a number of social welfare agencies. In 1950, there were 47 women and one man taking this course. Younghusband also noted that, as might be expected, the 'marriage mortality rate' was very high.

Degree courses in social science became available from 1954. By the end of the 1960s the profession had become well established and had expanded into a variety of areas including fostering and adoption, probation and housing services. The Dublin branch of the Institute of Almoners, formed in 1937, joined with the expanding Irish Association of Medical and Psychiatric Social Workers in 1964. This eventually led to the establishment, in 1971, of the current Irish Association of Social Workers.

Protestant philanthropic endeavour has a distinguished history in Ireland. There was no standing still in the philanthropic endeavours of the Protestant community – their work in charitable provision altered with the needs of the times and Protestant philanthropists sought legislative change to improve welfare provision. Their endeavours touched the lives of millions of Irish people over the centuries.

# The enrichment of Church of Ireland churches with stained glass and decoration

DAVID LAWRENCE

Farranthomas Church, Newcestown, Co. Cork, 1810, commissioned by the Board of First Fruits. Architect unknown

## Five eras of stained glass

The history of stained glass in Britain and Ireland can be divided into five periods and is closely related to matters of architecture, patronage and doctrine. The first period, which we shall term 'medieval', lasted from the thirteenth to the fifteenth century and, indeed, the art form reached its zenith in the thirteenth century. Stained glass then entered the doldrums for several hundred years, during which time the medieval techniques for producing windows were largely forgotten. The third period, which we shall call 'Gothic Revival' began in the mid-nineteenth century. Windows in this idiom continued to be made right through to, and beyond, the Great War, notably by the large established studios, such as Heaton, Butler & Bayne of London. But, by then, and in parallel to this, a fourth period of stained glass was already well underway. Starting in the 1890s in London, and in the 1900s in Dublin, windows in the Arts & Crafts style were made until at least the 1930s. During the remainder of the twentieth century, the art-form once again lost its way.

## Liberalisation of doctrine brings stained glass to the Church of Ireland

No intact medieval windows survive in Church of Ireland churches, but fragments have been found during excavations at St Canice's Cathedral, Kilkenny. Some small pieces of medieval glass and panels of sixteenth- and seventeenth-century Netherlandish glass have been salvaged from elsewhere and set into windows. There is just a handful of examples of, to our eyes, rather unsatisfactory attempts at producing coloured windows during the Georgian era, the oldest being that by Thomas Jervais at Agher, Co. Meath, made in 1770. In total, there are about two thousand five hundred stained-glass windows in Church of Ireland churches, only about fifty of which date from prior to 1860, whereas about three-quarters of them date from 1860 to 1920. Doctrine in the Established Church had been firmly opposed to the introduction of images into churches, especially images of Christ, until a gradual liberalisation unfolded during the first half of the nineteenth century. It began with a limited, but significant, 'High Church' movement, at the heart of which was John Jebb (1775–1833), bishop of Limerick. In England, this was to be followed by the Oxford Movement which aimed to reinstate pre-Reformation catholic traditions.

All Saints' Church, Kilmalooda, Co. Cork, 1858, by James Piers St Aubyn. This ecclesiological building by a well-known Gothic Revival architect is in striking contrast to the simplicity of Farranthomas.

Typical early nineteenth century 'Prayer-Book' interior

In Ireland, from the 1850s onwards, new churches were built which embodied ecclesiological principles and the emphasis shifted from the Word to the Sacraments. Such churches, many of them built by Joseph Welland (1798–1860) or by the partnership Welland & Gillespie, had substantial chancels, baptistries at the west end and decorative enrichment, including iconographic stained-glass windows. New churches were built in accordance with this new doctrine and many existing churches were converted by re-ordering and the addition of chancels. It has been estimated that half the cost of church-building in England in the second half of the nineteenth century was devoted to decorative elements and something of this mood gradually replaced former thinking in the Church of Ireland.

## The second golden age of stained glass

Further motivation for church-building and decoration was evident in the years immediately preceding and following disestablishment, the most illustrious example being the Cathedral of St Fin Barre at Cork with its highly elaborate furnishings and decorations in all media, including seventy-six windows. A vital consequence of the quest for the Church's medieval past was a determined and successful effort, by James Powell & Sons of London and others, spurred on by some of the great architects of the Gothic Revival, such as George Edmund Street (1824–81), to analyse and recreate the materials, techniques, colours, translucency and non-pictorial nature of thirteenth-century windows, notably those in the great French cathedrals. This led to an astonishing flowering of the art form and to what has been called the 'second golden age' of stained glass in the late 1850s and 1860s. There are some outstanding examples of windows from this period in Ireland, including Edward Burne-Jones's (1833–98) first design for stained glass, made by Powell's, at Trim Cathedral, Co. Meath; windows by Clayton Bell at Limerick Cathedral and at Street's Church at Ardamine, Co. Wexford, by William Wailes at St Patrick's Cathedral, Dublin; and by Lavers & Barraud at Clogher Cathedral, Co. Tyrone, Templebreedy Church, Crosshaven. Co. Cork and Ardcarne. Co. Rosscommon. In Ireland, by the time of disestablishment, there was not only the doctrinal freedom to sanction stained glass but also suitable patronage, often emanating from the families in the big houses.

*Pentecost*, designed by William Burges, 1869, cartooned by Horatio Lonsdale, executed by Saunders & Co., 1876. Cathedral Church of St Fin Barre, Cork

*Good Shepherd*, designed by Edward Burne-Jones, 1857, executed by James Powell & Sons, 1869, Cathedral Church of St Patrick, Trim, Co. Meath

*Baptism of Christ* by Clayton & Bell, *c.* 1860. Church of St John the Evangelist, Ardamine, Co. Wexford

## The later years of the nineteenth century

As the century progressed, styles evolved and changed and took on different influences, such as Classical and Aesthetic. Amongst the Irish studios, some of the best work came from the Earley studio of Dublin, but patrons mostly turned to English and German studios, from which came about 90% of the Gothic Revival windows made for the Church of Ireland during this period. Amongst all these, there are hundreds of examples of truly significant work of great beauty, demonstrating a thorough understanding of the medium and its role, as well as consummate drawing, painting and craft skills. Just a few can be mentioned in this short account, including those by Henry Holiday (1839–1927) at Abbeyleix, Co. Laois; by Powell's at Myshall, Co. Carlow and Rathmolyon, Co. Meath; by Clayton & Bell at Arklow, Co. Wicklow; by Wailes at Killarney, Co. Kerry; and by William Francis Dixon (1848–1928) for Mayer & Co. at Kilcluney, Co. Armagh.

*Ascension*, designed by John Milner Allen, executed by Lavers & Barraud, *c* 1862. Cathedral Church of St Macartan, Clogher, Co. Tyrone

*Nativity*, designed by William Dixon, executed by Mayer & Co., 1896. Church of St John, Kilcluney, Co. Armagh

## The Arts & Crafts movement and after

As the twentieth century began, the Arts & Crafts movement injected new life into stained glass in Ireland and this went hand in hand with a renewed nationalism in art and a revival of Celtic roots. The studio, Tower of Glass (An Túr Gloine), was established as a co-operative by Sarah Purser in 1903, enabling individual artists of considerable stature to design and paint windows in an idiom radically different from that of the nineteenth-century artists, but nevertheless founded on sound iconographic and figural precedents. There are about two hundred windows from these artists in Church of Ireland churches, superb examples being those by Michael Healey (1873–1941) at Castlecomer, Co. Kilkenny and by Beatrice Elvery (1883–1968) at Grange, Co. Armagh.

There are also about ten windows, for example those at Castlehaven Church, Castletownsend, Co. Cork, by the best-known of Irish stained glass artists, Harry Clarke (1889–1931). In the years following the heyday of the Arts & Crafts movement, two former Tower of Glass artists, Wilhelmina Geddes (1887–1955) and Evie Hone (1894–1955), pointed a possible way ahead with their powerful expressionism, but very few of their windows found their way into the Church of Ireland. For the remainder of the century, the nature of the developments in stained glass was, to a large extent, determined by the demise of the large studios and the loss both of the disciplines and apprenticeships which they provided and also of the exacting standards which they set. Instead, with the exception of the work of a few notable artists, there came ever-more diversity and dilution of styles, a search for self-expression and a tendency by some to ignore basic drawing and craft skills, architectural and liturgical considerations.

It is remarkable, there being, relatively speaking, so few windows in the Church of Ireland, that there are so many of outstanding quality, some of which are equal to any nineteenth-century stained glass anywhere in Europe. Furthermore, the work of Tower of Glass has an international reputation.

Above: *Parable of the Good Samaritan*, designed by Beatrice Elvery, executed by An Tur Gloine, 1910. Church of St Aidan, Grange, Co. Armagh

Right: *Adoration of the Magi*, by Harry Clarke, 1918, Castlehaven Church of St Barrahane, Castletownsend, Co. Cork

Choral Evensong at St Fin Barre's Cathedral, Cork
ST FIN BARRE'S CATHEDRAL, CORK

# Music in the Church of Ireland

JACQUELINE MULLEN

'Praise'. Stained glass in St Mary's Church, Carlow
KEN HEMMINGWAY

Music in the Church of Ireland has evolved from being almost non-existent following the Reformation to being an important part of Sunday worship (and other significant occasions within the Church year). While plainchant and some hymnody existed in the early and medieval Church (and Ireland is believed, by virtue of documentary evidence, to have had a rich musical heritage in its monasteries and large churches) it was to be the eighteenth century before music was included in worship in the Church of Ireland.

Instruments for a praise group accompanies the organ at St Cedma's Church, Larne. This organ was originally water powered by the River Inver that runs alongside the church.
DERMOTT DUNBAR

Metrical Psalms may have been sung in some larger churches, both at the beginning and end of services and before and after the sermon, being purely scriptural and therefore appropriate. These would have been 'lined out' by the minister or a lay clerk. Lining out involved the singing of one line or phrase by the leader; this was then echoed by the people. Obviously this process depended on the musicality of the leader and their ability to sing rhythmically. The advent of choirs and newly installed organs in the late eighteenth century must have been an improvement on what had gone before. It became customary for an organ voluntary to be played between the Psalm and the First Lesson (Scripture reading) at Morning and Evening Prayer.

During the nineteenth century many organs were installed in churches, usually paid for by benefactors or several subscribers. Organ builders found plenty of work in installing, renovating and tuning organs during this period. Organists were generally paid for their services, as were 'blowers': men employed to pump air into the bellows of the organ. Failure to keep up with the organist would cause the sound to die away and incur the wrath of the player. As time passed, electrification of organs meant that blowers were no longer needed although some organs retain the manual mechanism. In some rural churches it became the duty of the teacher in the parish school to play the organ in church each Sunday.

Bell ringing mats ready for practice
ST CANICE'S CATHEDRAL, KILKENNY

## Hymns, canticles and chants

The advent, in the eighteenth century, of hymns not taken directly from Scripture was at first led by Isaac Watts. This paved the way for hymn writers, including those of Irish descent, to reflect aspects of the faith in song. Translations of early Latin hymns were also added to the repertoire. The first hymnal to be compiled for the Church of Ireland was edited by the Rev. Hercules H. Dickinson, who commenced his ministry as curate of St Ann's Church in Dublin. He realised that a variety of books were being used in parish churches, and resolved to improve the resources available. In 1855, Archbishop Whately of Dublin gave permission for the work of collating hymns for the book to commence and it was subsequently printed under the title *Hymns for Public Worship*. It proved popular where approved by diocesan bishops. A reprint in 1859 included some extra hymns but the year 1864 saw a revised hymnal, with the addition of 100 hymns. This book was called *The Church Hymnal* and

The bells in St Columb's Cathedral, Londonderry
ST COLUMB'S CATHEDRAL, LONDONDERRY

was approved for the whole of the Church of Ireland. A chant book containing plainchant tones and Anglican chant alongside various other liturgical settings was also published. Chant permits lines of prose of unequal length to be sung, thus facilitating the singing of Psalms and Canticles. A Canticle, meaning small song, is a song from the Bible or Apocrypha. One such example is the *Magnificat* – the Virgin Mary's song of praise to God on hearing that she is to be the mother of Jesus. Canticles formed part of worship in monastic communities and some have been traced back to the fourth century. They were included in the *Book of Common Prayer* by Cranmer as he attempted to join together the various hours, which punctuated monastic life, to form Morning and Evening Prayer. Canticles to Anglican chant continue to be sung by some congregations, due to the unchanging words and familiar tunes, while Psalmody to Anglican chant is more likely to be sung in churches with a proficient choir.

Following disestablishment in 1871, a further revision of the hymnal occurred, with the approval of the General Synod of the Church of Ireland, for use in worship. This edition included 475 hymns. Subsequent revisions occurred in 1891, 1915 and 1935, words editions being followed by revised musical editions.

A complete revision of *The Church Hymnal,* including an amended musical version, was published in 1960, totalling 688 hymns and 31 Christmas Carols. Hymns for personal devotional use; several hymns for children; a section for use in schools and colleges and a number of hymns for choral singing were included. The repertoire of the Church was expanding. This book remained well loved within parish churches for the following 30 years. A supplement, entitled *Irish Church Praise* was published in 1990 to further resource the church. Subsequently, in 1994, a new committee was appointed and tasked with revising *The Church Hymnal*. This hymnal, totalling 719 items, includes a section comprising metrical canticles, and other sung liturgical resources. At the time of writing a further supplement is proposed to include contemporary material and additional liturgical items. The value of retaining a common hymnal, reflecting the broad sweep of Church of Ireland belief and worship, continues to be appreciated.

While hymn singing has been part of the Church of Ireland's heritage since the late eighteenth century there is also a strong choral history in many parish churches. The church choir led congregational singing and sang anthems during worship, and was also part of the social fabric of the parish community. Choral festivals became an annual event in many dioceses from the mid-nineteenth century onwards and from 1888 to 1947 a *Choral Festival Book* was published by the Kildare Choral Union. These festivals took the form of Evening Prayer and included hymns, the canticles *Magnificat* and *Nunc Dimittis*, an anthem, Bible readings and a sermon. A final rehearsal usually took place on the day itself, followed by refreshments. The choral festival service then took place in the evening. These occasions presented an opportunity for singers to attempt works requiring larger vocal resources than was available in one church; they also offered a social aspect which would have been important to small rural communities. In November 1947, the Church of Ireland Choral Union was formed, being an alliance of local choir festivals, to compile and publish the annual festival book. Subsequently a merger between the Royal School of Church Music and the Joint Committee for Church Music in Ireland took over the running of choral festivals until

St Gall Choristers celebrating the Royal School of Church Music Choir Sunday
ST GALL'S CHURCH, BANGOR

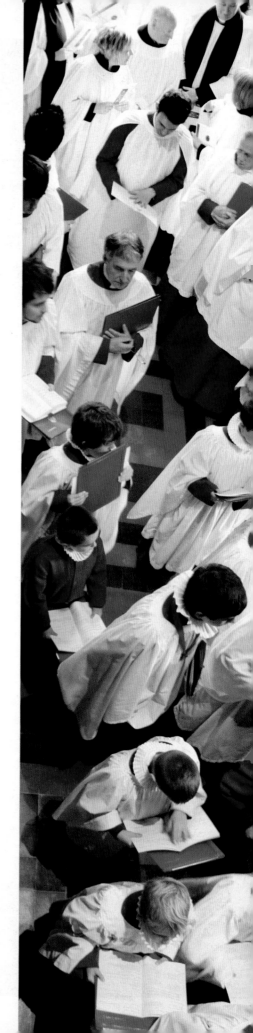

Charles Villiers Stanford

Edward Bunting, famous for his collection of Irish music, in 1784 began his apprenticeship to William Ware, the first organist in St Anne's Belfast. In 1813, Bunting organised a four-day sacred and secular music festival at which the first almost complete performance of Handel's *Messiah* was performed in Belfast. An Edward Bunting Harp Festival Concert is held annually in Armagh.

they ceased in the 1980s. Today, choirs exist in larger parish churches and continue to enhance worship to a high standard. To some extent the growth of community choirs offers singers the social aspect once solely provided by the church choir. Contemporary worship co-exists alongside the more traditional forms as band based worship or Gospel choirs. Training of parish church musicians remains a priority: courses being available in various dioceses.

## Music in Irish Cathedrals

At the time of the Reformation choirs existed in many Irish cathedrals made up of Vicars Choral, choristers and, in some cases, boys. Members of cathedral choirs were paid and boys were given a broad musical training. In some cathedrals they also received their general education; however, these schools closed gradually as time progressed. One such school exists today, at St Patrick's Cathedral, Dublin.

The upheavals of the seventeenth century must have affected music in cathedrals but during the eighteenth century the situation improved. Organs were restored or completely rebuilt while organists, choirmasters and singers from England took up duty in cathedrals, thus influencing the choral tradition. Some notable Irish composers such as Charles Villiers Stanford who was born in Dublin (1852) and Charles Wood (born 1866 in Armagh) contributed choral works and service music to the Church that are performed to this day.

Many of the Irish cathedrals have choirs of men and boys (although Christ Church Cathedral, Dublin has a mixed adult choir) and some now offer opportunities for females with the advent of girls' choirs. These choirs sing on a regular basis within their cathedrals and a musical education continues to be offered alongside this commitment.

## Recorded Music

Where no musical instrument exists, the work of the Recorded Music Committee has ensured that congregations may sing by the provision of recordings of church choirs, played during worship, enabling worshippers to sing along. Apart from this venture some dioceses within the Church of Ireland, believing that the musical heritage is of great value and wisely looking to the future, have set up training schemes for church musicians. These schemes offer valuable training in organ playing, choir training and liturgy.

Charles Wood, musician and composer, pursued his early musical career as a chorister in St Patrick's Cathedral, Armagh. In 1926, on his death, he left a legacy of over 250 sacred works plus a large number of hymn tunes. The Charles Wood Summer School is held annually in Armagh.

A mixed choir with choir master at St Fin Barre's Cathedral, Cork. As part of the training scheme choristers follow the Royal School of Church Music Voice for Life programme.

LEFT: Choir members preparing for service at St Columb's Cathedral, Londonderry
LUCY MCGONIGLE

Musicians prepare for the première of Philip Hammond's *Requiem for the lost souls of the Titanic* in St Anne's Cathedral, Belfast, 2012.
COI PRESS OFFICE

# The Dioceses

## The Province of Armagh

Downpatrick Cathedral from the River Quoile
SCENIC IRELAND

# The Diocese of Armagh

Even the name of Armagh itself suggests a long and colourful history. It derives from 'Ard Mhacha', the Hill or Height of Macha who was a formidable pagan goddess from pre-Christian celtic mythology. Today, the cathedral city of Armagh is the centre of a diocese that spreads in a long swathe from the town of Magherafelt at its northern end down into much of County Tyrone and onwards through the entire counties of Armagh and Louth to the River Boyne at Drogheda. Hence it is one of the four 'cross-border' dioceses of the present-day Church of Ireland. Since the twelfth century, the diocese of Armagh has claimed a pre-eminence over the other dioceses as the primatial see for the whole of Ireland, connected through its long history with Saint Patrick himself.

The Armagh Diocese of today is largely rural, although it contains a number of large towns, including Portadown, Dungannon, Magherafelt, Cookstown, Dundalk and Drogheda. It faces the challenges of life and Christian witness in the twenty-first century, as of course does every diocese throughout the Church of Ireland. During thirty years of horrific violence during the so-called 'Troubles' – from the 1970s through into the 1990s – many people in almost every parish in the diocese suffered dreadfully, and a legacy of trauma remains palpable today. A particular vocation for clergy and people alike in this part of Ireland is therefore to seek from God both healing of the past and hope for the future, and many set themselves to this essential task with a wonderful conviction, integrity and faith.

At present, Armagh Diocese comprises over forty parochial groupings, served by around fifty clergy. There is also a large corps of layreaders who provide invaluable assistance to the clergy in the provision of worship, Sunday by Sunday in almost ninety parish churches of the diocese. The styles of worship are extremely varied, and in many of the parishes there is strong emphasis on the needs of younger people in worship. At the centre of the diocese is the beautiful cathedral of St Patrick on the Hill of Armagh, continuing the glorious choral tradition of Anglicanism. Part of the heritage of the illustrious Richard Robinson, Archbishop of Armagh in the closing decades of the eighteenth century, is the splendid Library beside the Cathedral in Armagh and the world-famous Armagh Observatory on the outskirts of the city. Both of these great and historic institutions maintain fully their original links with the Archbishopric of Armagh.

But the Diocese of Armagh is not about a great inheritance or even a vibrant present. It sets its face to the future also. One of the great challenges we now must face with energy is the equipping of all the people of the Church to be evangelists for the faith. All Christian disciples must be enabled to account to others for the faith they claim for themselves. In the secularised culture of Ireland, north and south, east and west, the great commission of the Church is to equip all the people of God to speak persuasively with both confidence and clarity of the Gospel that is theirs to share with the world.

RICHARD ARMAGH

Navan
SCENIC IRELAND

## St Patrick's Cathedral, Armagh

Worship has taken place on the hill of Armagh since St Patrick founded the first church on the site in 444. In the ninth and tenth centuries the cathedral was repeatedly plundered and burned by the Danish invaders. Archbishop O'Scanlan rebuilt and extended it eastwards in 1268, and the crypt, now open to the public, dates from that time.

A restoration of the building took place under Archbishop Swayne in 1428. In the sixteenth century, however, it suffered during the conflict between the Uí Néill of Ulster and the Dublin authorities. Necessary repairs were effected after the restoration of the monarchy in 1660. When Archbishop Robinson came in 1765, he slated the nave for use as a parish church. He also decided to raise the tower to a height of 101 feet, but the foundations proved to be inadequate to support the extra weight and this scheme was abandoned.

A major restoration took place in 1834–9 under Archbishop Lord John George Beresford, who employed the English architect Lewis N. Cottingham. He strengthened the base of the tower and restored the side walls of the nave to the perpendicular.

KEITH DRURY

LEFT AND ABOVE ARMAGH CATHEDRAL

KEITH DRURY

ARMAGH CATHEDRAL

The Staff of Jesus, a crozier reputed to have been given to Patrick, illustrated in stained glass; the Bell and Shrine of St Patrick

He also covered the external walls with imported red sandstone cladding, concealing most of the ancient masonry. In recent years, extensive restoration work has been carried out.

In addition to fragments of an eleventh century high cross and a slab commemorating the burial of Brian Boru, the cathedral has a major collection of remarkable monuments and memorials. These include work by some of the leading sculptors of the eighteenth and nineteenth centuries.

The cathedral maintains an important musical tradition. A key feature of this is the annual summer music festival in honour of Charles Wood who was born in one of the houses on Vicar's Hill beside the cathedral.

The cathedral is a major focus for the entire diocese. Once a month a different parochial group is invited to worship in the cathedral. Important ecumenical occasions, concerts and civic events are held here. A number of ecumenical canons have been installed, including Dr Donald Watts, former Clerk of the Presbyterian General Assembly, and Dom Mark-Ephrem Nolan, Prior of Holy Cross Monastery, Rostrevor. On 20 March 2008, Queen Elizabeth II distributed Maundy Money to pensioners, the first time this ceremony has taken place outside England and Wales.

This gem of a building today stands serene on the hill of Armagh. It is a place not only of history and heritage but also of worship and praise.

LEFT: Monument to Dean Drelincourt, 1644–1722
RIGHT: Sir Thomas Molyneaux of Castle Dillon

Nor was his Charity delay'd till Death;
He chose to give what others but bequeath

ARMAGH CATHEDRAL

# The Diocese of Armagh

TED FLEMING AND PROF BRIAN WALKER

The diocese of Armagh extends from Magherafelt, Co. Londonderry, in the north to Drogheda, Co. Louth, in the south, a distance of some 72 miles, and thereby embraces both jurisdictions in Ireland. To the north-west it reaches into the hill country of Tyrone, and south Armagh is also mountainous. The area is primarily an agricultural region, at the heart of which is Co. Armagh, long described as 'the orchard of Ireland'. The Bramley apple is particularly suited to the soil: tradition says that St Patrick planted an apple tree east of Armagh city in the fifth century. The diocese includes a number of important urban areas, including Armagh, Portadown, Dungannon, Cookstown, Dundalk and Drogheda.

## St Patrick

St Patrick negotiates with Daire, the local chieftan

It is generally accepted that St Patrick, having preached the gospel in various parts of the country, came to Armagh around 444. He approached the local chieftain, Daire, who granted him a site for a church on low ground (now the site of St Patrick's Fold in Scotch Street). Patrick later obtained from Daire a more commanding site on the hill called the Sallow Ridge. There he built his great stone church, and ordained that it should have pre-eminence over all the churches of Ireland – a position Armagh still holds today.

Stained glass illustration of St Patrick laying the foundation stone of his church, AD 444

Both cathedrals dedicated to St Patrick stand out above the skyline in Armagh city.
SCENIC IRELAND

## The Early Church in Armagh

The Tandragee idol, a stone figure likely to belong to the Pagan Iron Age between 400 BC and 400 AD. It was found in the cathedral grounds and is now housed inside the cathedral.

The Irish church in the centuries after St Patrick developed a monastic system. Such a religious foundation grew up at Armagh. In the late seventh century it incorporated a school whose renown spread across Europe. At one time it is believed to have had 7,000 students. Armagh became a place of pilgrimage, and a poem written about the year 685 contains the lines:

> I found in Armagh, the splendid,
> Meekness, Wisdom, Circumspection,
> Fasting in obedience to the Son of God,
> Noble, prosperous sages.

From around the eighth century, the bishop-abbots of Armagh claimed ecclesiastical authority over all Ireland. This was openly acknowledged by the high king, Brian Boru, when he made a pilgrimage to Armagh in 1005 and presented 20 ounces of pure gold to the church. After his death at the Battle of Clontarf in 1014, Brian Boru was buried in the cathedral grounds.

The Culdees ('Servants of God') were members of a religious order, often married, who, from about the sixth century, lived a rigorous life of prayer accompanied by charitable deeds. In Armagh they maintained the choral services of the cathedral. For their support they held land in various places, from which they drew rents and in return employed clergy to minister to the local people. They continued to function until the time of the Reformation in the sixteenth century.

## The Coming of the Vikings

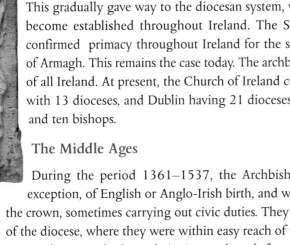

A 'cadaver stone' taken from the tomb of Sir Edmond Goldyng and his wife Elizabeth Fleming. It is built into the churchyard wall at St Peter's, Drogheda and shows two cadavers enclosed in shrouds which have been partially opened to show the remains of the occupants of the tomb. Estimated to be from the first quarter of the sixteenth century.

In the early ninth century, the Vikings plundered religious houses throughout Ireland. In 836, they landed at Newry and proceeded to Armagh, where they pillaged and burnt the city, drove out the students from the school and destroyed manuscripts and relics. Three years later, they plundered Armagh again.

Such ongoing attacks helped to bring about the decline of the monastic system. This gradually gave way to the diocesan system, which by the twelfth century had become established throughout Ireland. The Synod of Rath Breasail in 1111 confirmed primacy throughout Ireland for the successors of St Patrick in the see of Armagh. This remains the case today. The archbishop of Armagh is called primate of all Ireland. At present, the Church of Ireland comprises two Provinces, Armagh, with 13 dioceses, and Dublin having 21 dioceses. There are now two archbishops and ten bishops.

## The Middle Ages

During the period 1361–1537, the Archbishops of Armagh were, with one exception, of English or Anglo-Irish birth, and were generally on good terms with the crown, sometimes carrying out civic duties. They resided at Drogheda in the south of the diocese, where they were within easy reach of the seat of government in Dublin. We can learn much about their time and work from the medieval Armagh Episcopal Registers, the originals of which are housed in the Public Record Office of Northern Ireland. These volumes are a unique collection of material throwing light upon various aspects of current church and civil administration. For example, we find that in 1451, Archbishop Mey travelled north to Tullyhogue (parish of Desertcreat), Co. Tyrone, to crown Owen O'Neill as King of Ulster

Stained glass illustration of Ferdomnach scribe of the Book of Armagh

## The *Book of Armagh*

The parish of Ballymoyer was the home of the *Book of Armagh* for several centuries.

The book is a Latin copy of the New Testament made by the scribe Ferdomnach around AD 807, with fine initial capital letters and four drawings, one of each of the four evangelists. It is bound together with early writings about St Patrick. The small vellum volume was probably prepared for private study.

For several centuries, the MacMoyer family of Ballymoyer were the hereditary keepers of the book. Then, in 1679, Florence MacMoyer, a Franciscan friar, pawned it for the sum of £5 to pay his fare to London to give evidence against Archbishop Oliver Plunkett. Afterwards, the *Book of Armagh* was not redeemed.

By the year 1707 it had passed into the possession of the Brownlow family of Lurgan, County Armagh. In 1853, Dean (afterwards Bishop) William Reeves, the celebrated antiquarian and scholar, bought it from the Brownlows for £300. In 1858, the primate, Lord John George Beresford, defrayed the dean's outlay and presented it to the library of Trinity College, Dublin

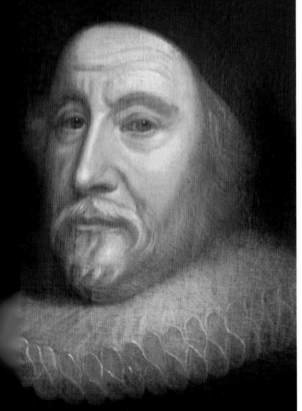

## Seventeenth and Eighteenth Centuries

Following the Flight of the Earls, the Plantation of Ulster brought important changes in land ownership in Co. Armagh. The arrival of protestant settlers, mainly from England, led to an increase in the number of the members of the Church of Ireland. After the Reformation (1530s), the Archbishops of Armagh continued to have their principal residence in the Drogheda area. The most famous of these was James Ussher (1625–56), a renowned scholar, writer and church historian, whose system of chronology placed the Creation at 4004 BC, a date adopted by some English editions of the bible. Hugh Boulter (1724–42) was involved in high government politics, but also built four houses for clergy widows on Vicars' Hill Armagh for clergy widows and did likewise in Drogheda, beside St Peter's church.

Undoubtedly, the archbishop who made most impact in the eighteenth century was Richard Robinson, Lord Rokeby (1765–74). He took up residence in Armagh. Apart from starting important restoration work on the cathedral, he revitalised the city by a series of building projects.

## Nineteenth Century

In the years preceding the Great Famine of 1845–9, Co. Armagh was one of the most densely populated rural areas in Ireland, the farms generally being small and often supported by weaving as a cottage industry. Many parishes were subdivided and new churches were built to accommodate the parishioners. In consequence of the population explosion, Armagh diocese in 1844 had 102 parochial units, each with a clergyman, augmented by 27 curates assistant, a total of 129 clergy.

Primate Robinson built *St Luke's Church, Tamlaght*, in the village of Coagh, in 1780.
COLIN BOYLE

These rural areas were badly affected by the famine and there was great loss of life. Many Church of Ireland clergy were involved in the diocese in efforts to provide relief, and often worked alongside clergy of other denominations. Death among clergy due to famine fever or exertions included the Rev. Henry Hobson, curate of the parish of Ballymascanlon, Co. Louth. His memorial in the church describes how 'Having freely devoted his energies to alleviate the sufferings of his poorer brethren, his mortal frame proved unequal to the task, and on the 2nd day August, 1847, he entered into his rest, aged 44 years.'

After the famine, population numbers continued to fall in the diocese, as elsewhere in rural Ireland, as many emigrated. To some extent, this population decline was ameliorated with the rise of important linen mills and factories in towns like Portadown and new mill villages as in Bessbrook. These developments necessitated the construction of new churches in a number of places.

## Archbishop James Ussher

James Ussher was born in Dublin in 1581 and was nephew of Henry Ussher (archbishop of Armagh 1593–1613). When Trinity College, Dublin was founded in 1592 he was one of the first students enrolled, and eventually became professor of divinity in 1607.

Ussher was ordained on the Sunday before Christmas 1601, and the following year was sent to England to buy books for Trinity College Library. He was a meticulous scholar in the fields of theology and early church history. He was rector of Trim in 1620, bishop of Meath in 1621 and archbishop of Armagh 1625–56, having his residence in Drogheda. When he was on a visit to England in 1640, the split between Charles I and parliament came to a head, and in the following year the Irish rebellion and unsettled state of the country prevented his return.

Ussher was a man of immense scholarship, whose works on theology and ecclesiastical history were published in 17 volumes. His system of chronology, placing the date of the creation at 4004 BC, was introduced into the second Oxford quarto edition of the bible in 1679.

Though a firm royalist, his tolerance of Puritans in Ireland earned the respect of Cromwell, who, when Ussher died on 21 March 1656, ordered that he be buried in Westminster Abbey. His library, consisting of 10,000 books and many early manuscripts, was placed in Trinity College, Dublin, after his death on the order of Charles II. He ranks as one of the most distinguished sons of the Church of Ireland.

MILLTOWN WEAVING FACTORY AND FINISHING WORKS.

GRANAGILL MILLS.

JOSEPH ORR & SONS,
Linen Manufacturers, Finishers,
&c.
Office—Granagill, Loughgall, ARMAGH.
Telegraphic Address: "ORRS, LOUGHGALL."

Bann Bridge,
Portadown 1861
PRIVATE COLLECTION

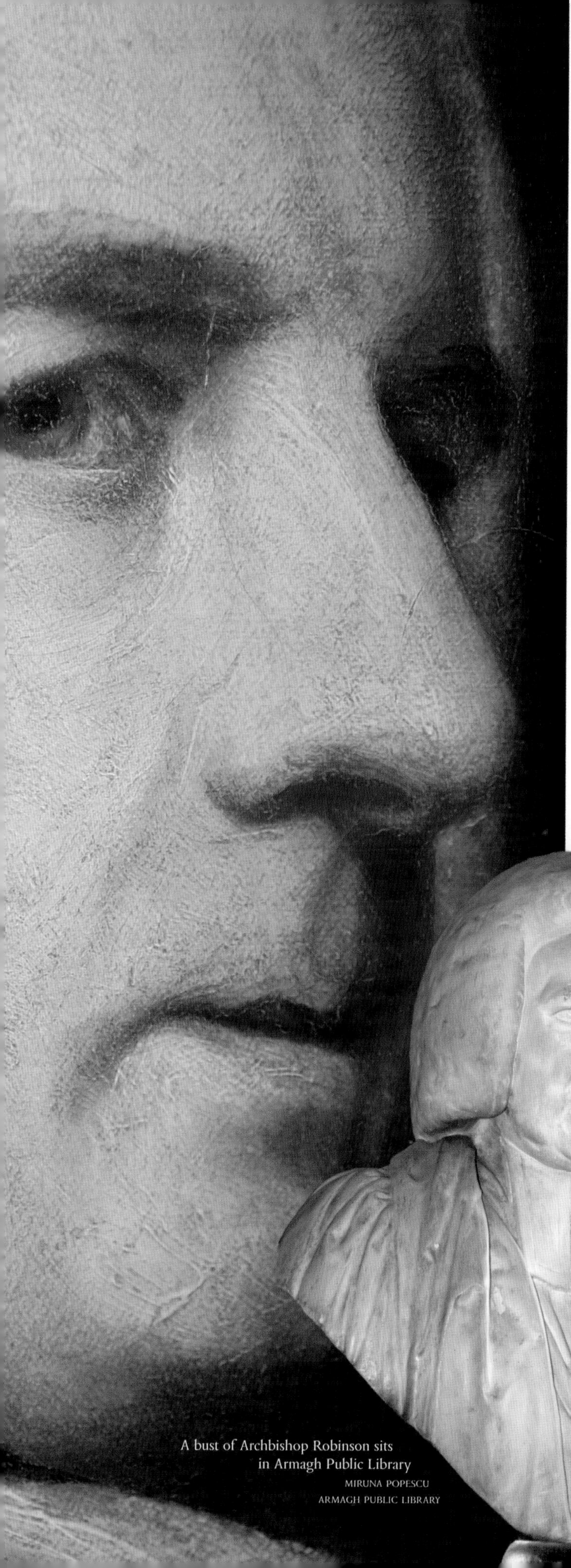

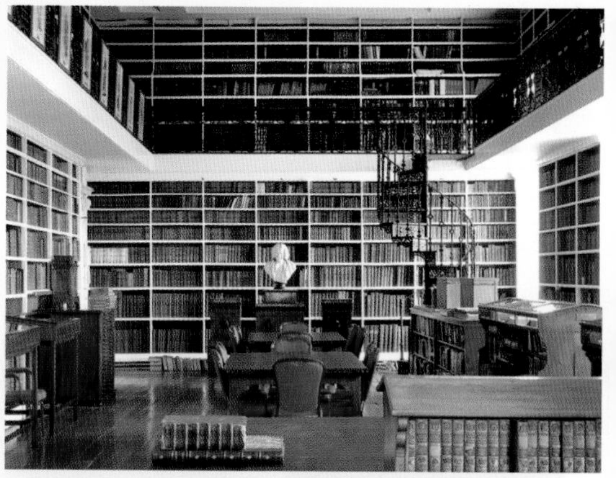

## Archbishop Richard Robinson

Richard Robinson, Lord Rokeby, was descended from the Robinson family of Rokeby in Yorkshire. He was educated at Christ Church College, Oxford and came to Ireland as chaplain to the lord lieutenant, becoming archbishop of Armagh in 1765.

The diocese of Armagh since the fifteenth century had been administered from two locations. The southern part, within the Pale, which was under the supervision of the archbishop living in Drogheda; the northern part, mostly under native Irish rule, was generally administered by the dean and chapter of Armagh Cathedral. Archbishop Robinson decided to have his official residence back in Armagh. Armagh, however, had lost much of

Armagh Observatory

its glory and was then little better than a huddle of mud cabins and a run-down cathedral. Robinson set about transforming the image of the primatial city, restoring the cathedral and building a primatial palace, a public library, premises for the Royal School and an observatory.

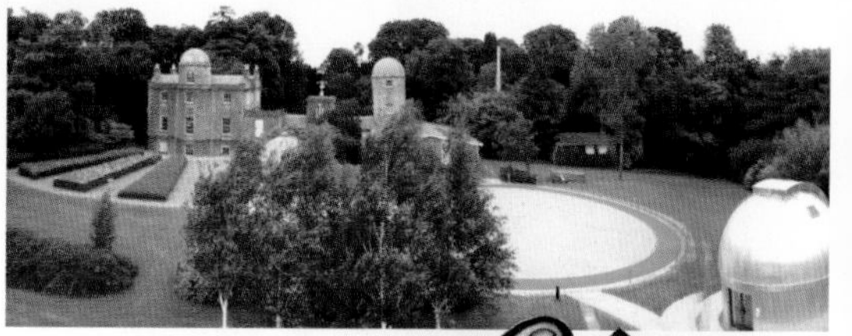

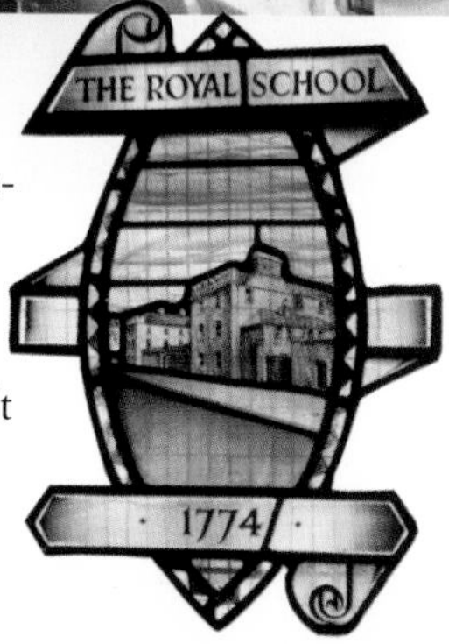

The Observatory, like several of the Archbishop's foundations, was built on a hill so that it could be seen against a natural woodland setting from his new palace. It was designed by Francis Johnston, the city architect, who was responsible for several fine buildings in Dublin; notably, the Chapel Royal and the GPO in O'Connell Street.

THE ROYAL SCHOOL

· 1774 ·

In 1771, Archbishop Robinson built and endowed a public library. The Robinson Library is one of the finest Georgian buildings in the city. It was designed by the architect Thomas Cooley and built in ashlar limestone. Archbishop Lord John George Beresford enlarged it around 1847, by the addition of a bay at each end and an entrance on the side next to the cathedral gates. The building also provides accommodation for the keeper.

Today the library, which continues to grow, houses a valuable collection of books, manuscripts and artefacts and provides an important resource for study and research.

He also devoted his energies to the needs of the diocese at large, encouraging the clergy to be resident. He died, unmarried, on 10 October 1794, aged 86, and is buried in the crypt of Armagh Cathedral.

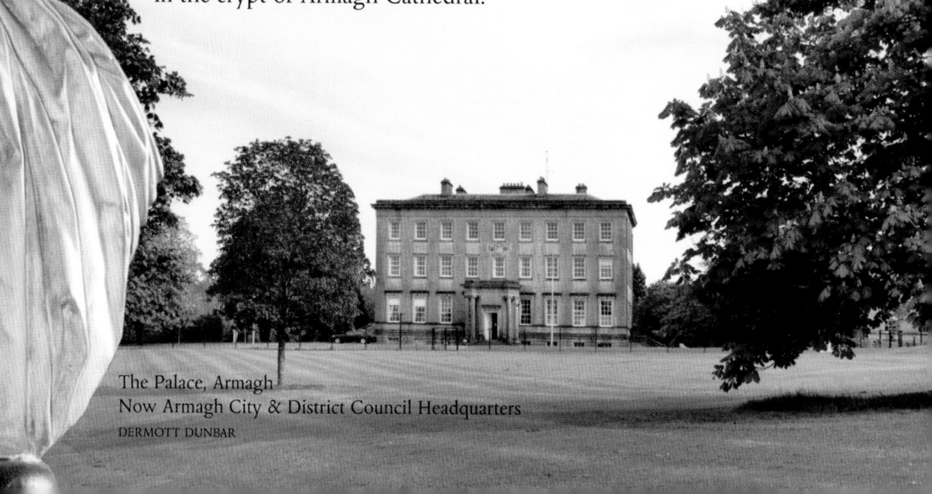

Laying the foundation stone of the Alexander Hall in memory of Archbishop Alexander, 27 July 1912. Archbishop William Alexander, bishop, theologian and husband of the famous hymnwriter Cecil Frances Alexander

Interior of Alexander Hall, Armagh
RICHARD WATSON

## The Twentieth and Twenty First Century

Disestablishment of the Church of Ireland in 1870 had been a shock to many in the church initially but it brought a number of advantages. Now the church relied entirely on its clergy and members. Local diocesan synods were elected to hold annual meetings to discuss church affairs. This led to the erection of a synod hall and church house near the cathedral in Armagh, opened in 1913 and called the Alexander Hall, in memory of Archbishop Alexander.

The two world wars had an immediate impact on churches and congregations throughout the diocese. War memorials record loss of life in every parish. Political changes in 1920–2 saw the diocese split into two jurisdictions but this did not affect its essential unity. Population decline continued during the twentieth century which has led to the grouping of parishes and a reduction in numbers of clergy. Today (2013) the Diocese of Armagh comprises 15 single parishes, 16 groupings of two parishes, 10 groupings of three parishes, and 2 groupings in excess of three parishes (in Co. Louth). The current parochial staffing is 51 clergy, inclusive of 7 serving in the non-stipendiary ministry.

The present Church of Christ the Redeemer, Camlough suffered substantial damage during a mortar-bomb attack on the nearby RUC station in Bessbrook in 1993.
COLIN BOYLE

Rev. Canon Robert Boyd with Bishop Isesomo the Bishop of North Kivu Diocese, Democratic Republic of Congo.
Rev. Gerald Macartney (Loughgall) and Canon Boyd (Killyman) visited the Democratic Republic of Congo, where the diocese plans to build a new orphanage for children displaced by violence, some of whom are the result of rape

DIOCESE OF ARMAGH

The last forty years have brought special challenges. A number of churches in Co. Louth and South Armagh have closed. New churches have been consecrated in Moygashel and Portadown. As a result of the 'Troubles' in Northern Ireland many families in the diocese have suffered bereavement and loss because of paramilitary activity. Community tension has been raised over confrontation relating to the annual Orange July parade to Drumcree.

These decades have witnessed much fine work by clergy and parishioners to maintain good community relations and to support efforts to encourage peace. In a number of places there are regular meetings of clergy of all denominations. St Patrick's Cathedral has been involved in founding the Centre for Celtic Spirituality, now based at Emain Macha/The Navan Centre, Armagh, which draws inspiration from the lives of the Celtic Saints.

Four archbishops have guided the diocese over this tumultuous period. Archbishop George Simms held the primacy from 1969 to 1980. Archbishop John Armstrong served for the period, 1980 to 1986. Archbishop Robin Eames held the position from 1986 to 2006. In 1995, he was awarded a life peerage for his contribution to building peace in Northern Ireland. Archbishop Alan Harper served the diocese from 2007 to 2012. On 15 December 2012, Bishop Richard Clarke was consecrated as Archbishop of Armagh and Primate of All Ireland.

Archbishop Robin Eames

Archbishop Richard Clarke with Rev. Grace Clunie outside the Centre for Spirituality, Armagh

## The Centre for Celtic Spirituality

The Centre for Celtic Spirituality was initiated in 2007. Subsequently Rev. Grace Clunie was appointed to the post of director and began the work of The Centre's development.

From the outset it was conceived as an inter-church project with the hope that Celtic Spirituality, representing the roots of all Christian traditions, would draw people from all denominations together in a spirit of respect, peace and reconciliation.

An interchurch management committee was created and the Centre – now also a registered charity – has Quakers, Catholics, Anglicans, Presbyterians and Methodists working together.

The Centre for Celtic Spirituality offers a local programme for groups and also works with international pilgrims offering sabbatical study and day programmes on Celtic Spirituality.

Since May 2013, the centre has been based at The Navan Centre, three miles from Armagh, where there is also a study library, shop and restaurant and many excellent facilities for visitors.

The Gala Concert held in St Patrick's Cathedral, Armagh with the students who attended the annual Charles Wood Summer School, 2013.
ST PATRICK'S CATHEDRAL, ARMAGH

# THE DIOCESE OF ARMAGH

St Mary's Church, Drumbanagher

Acton Church

## ACTON and DRUMBANAGHER

Acton Parish was formed out of Ballymore (Tandragee) in 1789. Drumbanagher was a district of Killeavy Parish until 1870.

*Acton Church* was built in 1789 at Poyntzpass, with the tower added in the 1820s.

*St Mary's Church, Drumbanagher* was erected in 1859–61. The font was taken from Killeavy Old Church, near Newry.

## ANNAGHMORE

Annaghmore Parish was formed in 1854 from the parishes of Loughgall, Killyman and Clonfeakle. The area's many small farmers produced fruit and vegetables, whose sale was greatly facilitated by the advent of the railway in 1858. *St Francis's Church, Annaghmore* was opened in 1856. The building is cruciform. The bell is rare in Ireland in that it is encircled by a bell wheel.

St Francis's Church, Annaghmore

Desertcreat Church

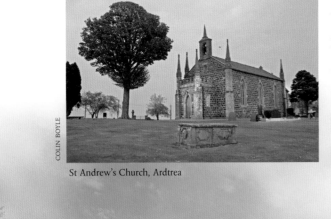

St Andrew's Church, Ardtrea

## ARDTREA and DESERTCREAT

Ardtrea means 'the height of Trea', a fifth-century virgin saint said to have been baptised by St Patrick. Desertcreat, East Tyrone, is an early Christian site. The parish contains the ancient mound of fort of Tullyhogue, where the kings of Ulster were inaugurated with the royal title and authority of the O'Nial.

*St Andrew's Church, Ardtrea* was constructed in 1822. It is built from whinstone with sandstone trim and has a pinnacled bell-cote.

*Desertcreat Church* dates from the early seventeenth century, with more recent renovations. The churchyard contains the grave of Phelim Brady, the 'Bard of Armagh'.

## ARMAGH, ST MARK'S

*St Mark's Church* was built in 1811 as a chapel of ease to Armagh Cathedral. It served as a garrison church to the local military barracks. The church was designed by Francis Johnston. Its fine three-storey tower has Primate Stuart's arms and the date 1811 over the entrance. The building was rebuilt in 1832 and a chancel and side aisles were added in 1866. In 1896, the present pulpit, believed to be the highest in Ireland, was erected. It became the parish church of Armagh in 1972.

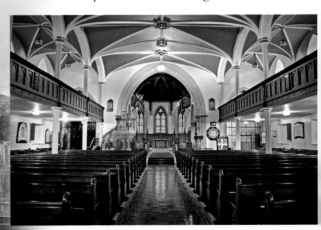

St Mark's, Armagh
COLIN BOYLE

St John's Church, Ballinderry

## BALLINDERRY, TAMLAGHT and ARBOE

Ballinderry was held by the Culdees of Armagh in 1367. Arboe is an early Christian site with an early tenth-century high cross.

*St John's Church, Ballinderry* was built in the 1840s, aided by a grant from the Salters' Company. It has a rood screen at the chancel entrance.

Primate Robinson built *St Luke's Church, Tamlaght*, in the village of Coagh, in 1780. A chancel was added in 1932.

The present *Arboe Church*, a small building, was consecrated in 1713. A small mural tablet commemorates Mary Ledlie, the first person buried in the churchyard.

Arboe Church

## BALLYMORE (TANDRAGEE)

The prosperous market town of Tandragee suffered when it was bypassed by the railway in 1852. Its nineteenth century castle occupies the site of an O'Hanlon stronghold. It is now a potato-crisp factory. *St Mark's Church, Ballymore* was built *c.* 1622 by Lord Grandison, with walls said to have been four feet thick. It was damaged during the 1641 Rebellion and later rebuilt. In 1812, this building was demolished and a new church with a tower was erected.

St Mark's Church, Ballymore

St Patrick's Church, Ballyclog

## BRACKAVILLE, DONAGHENDRY and BALLYCLOG

Coalisland village grew up in the nineteenth century around the industries of coal-mining, pottery, brickmaking and weaving. The parish of Brackaville was formed there in 1840 and a church was built the same year. Donaghendry is said to have been founded by St Patrick and contains the village of Stewartstown. Ballyclog, 'the town of the bell', is so called because the bell of St Patrick was found there. It is now kept in the National Museum, Dublin.

*Holy Trinity Church, Brackaville*, Coalisland was consecrated in 1861 to replace an earlier church which became too small for the rapidly growing population. The church bell, inscribed 'Eireann go brach' (Ireland for ever), was originally intended for the Roman Catholic church at Edendork, but was found to be too big for it.

Holy Trinity Church, Brackaville

*St Patrick's Church, Donaghendry*, in Stewartstown, was erected in 1875 to replace an earlier church building which had been destroyed during the rebellion of 1641 and rebuilt in 1694. This new church was burnt in 1877 but immediately rebuilt.

*St Patrick's Church, Ballyclog*, an attractive church of 1865, was designed by Welland and Gillespie, architects to the Church Commissioners. It has spiral bands of red stone on the apse and tower.

## CAMLOUGH and MULLAGLASS

A church was built in this parish in 1773, but the growing village of Bessbrook meant that a larger one was needed. The area owed its prosperity to the Richardson Quaker family, who built and ran the major linen mill in the village.

The present *Church of Christ the Redeemer, Camlough* was built in 1866 and enlarged in 1887. It suffered substantial damage during a mortar-bomb attack on the nearby RUC station in Bessbrook on 1 March 1993.

*St Luke's, Mullaglass*, positioned between Newry and Markethill, was consecrated in 1833. Originally in the parish of Killeavy it became a separate parish after disestablishment. It has pinnacles surmounting its buttresses. The entrance is under an iron archway.

St Luke's, Mullaglass

## CARNTEEL (AUGHNACLOY) and CRILLY

Aughnacloy was an important market town in the late eighteenth century. *St James's Church, Carnteel* was built in Aughnacloy in 1736. A tower and octagional spire were added in 1796 and a chancel in 1868.

St George's Church, Crilly* was originally erected in 1803 for the Independent Calvinistic Church, but in 1849 the Church of Ireland took it over as a chapel of ease, and trustees were appointed. The church was conveyed to the Representative Church Body only in 1966. The church bell was cast in 1851 by the Dublin firm of Thomas Hodges. On one side are a crown and shamrock with the inscription 'Venite Cum Voco' (Come when I call), and on the other side are a crown, harp and shamrock with 'Galea Spes Salutis'(A Helmet the Hope of Salvation).

St George's Church, Crilly

St James's Church, Carnteel

Holy Trinity Church, Drumnakilly

St Patrick's Church, Clogherny

## CLOGHERNY, SESKINORE and DRUMNAKILLY

Clogherny Parish includes the village of Beragh. Drumnakilly Parish, east of Omagh, was formed in 1843. *St Patrick's Church, Clogherny*, dating from 1746, incorporates part of an earlier church. The gallery and tower were added later and the chancel was built in 1885.

Seskinore Chapel of Ease* was erected in 1873 on the McClintock estate to the design of Robert A. Ferguson of Londonderry. It is a small Gothic-style hall with a bell-cote.

Holy Trinity Church, Drumnakilly*, a cruciform building, was consecrated in 1843. It was later enlarged by the extension of the nave.

## CLONFEACLE (BENBURB), DERRYGORTREAVY and EGLISH

An early Christian site at Clonfeacle was associated with St Patrick. Derrygortreavy was formed as a parish in 1819. In the seventeenth century, Eglish was connected to the deanery of Armagh. *St Patrick's Church, Clonfeacle*, in Benburb village, dates from 1618 and is one of the oldest churches in the diocese still in use. The tower was added in 1892, although the bell is dated 8 July 1688. The Rev. William Richardson, rector 1783–1820, who is believed to be buried within the church, was a prolific writer on various subjects including geology (the Giant's Causeway) and aspects of agriculture. On his large glebe of 532 acres he experimented with the growth of fiorin grasses for making winter hay. He was also instrumental in the formation of the yeomanry in September 1796 in conjunction with the Hon. Thomas Knox of Dungannon.

St Columba's Church, Derrygortreavy*, outside Dungannon, is a three-bay building with a tall, slender tower.

Holy Trinity Church, Eglish* was built at Drumsallan, four miles north-west of Armagh. The communion chalice was the gift of Dean Drelincourt in 1721 to an earlier church.

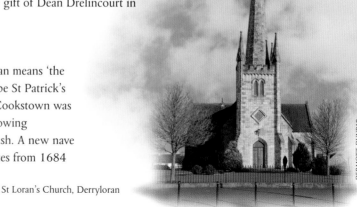

St Patrick's Church, Clonfeacle
COLIN BOYLE

Holy Trinity Church, Eglish

## DERRYLORAN (COOKSTOWN)

Cookstown is a plantation town founded by Allan Cook. Derryloran means 'the oak-wood of Luran'. St Luran, whose mother Darerca was said to be St Patrick's sister, was bishop in the fifth century. *St Luran's Church, Derryloran* Cookstown was built in 1822 because the existing church was too small for the growing population. The building is reputed to be to the design of John Nash. A new nave was built around 1860 and there were later additions. The font dates from 1684 and is inscribed: 'He that believeth and is baptised shall be saved'.

St Loran's Church, Derryloran

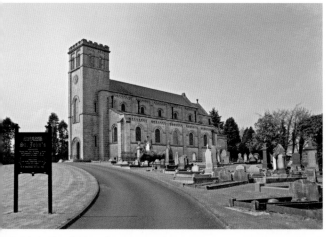

St John's Church, Desertlyn

## DESERTLYN (MONEYMORE) and BALLYEGLISH

In 1767, the site of the church for Desertlyn Parish was changed to Moneymore. Ballyeglish was formed as a parish in 1866.

*St John's Church, Desertlyn* was built in 1832 at a cost of £6,000, paid by the Drapers' Company. The building, using polished white sandstone, is in the Norman-revival style.

*St Matthias's Church, Ballyeglish* was consecrated in 1868. A hall with semicircular apse, it is built from white limestone from the Drapers' Company estate, relieved with bands of Moneymore sandstone. The Salters' and Drapers' Companies contributed to the cost of it.

St Matthias's Church, Ballyeglish

## Rev. Charles Wolfe

On 19 April 1817, a short poem was published anonymously in *The Newry Telegraph* and reproduced in other newspapers, causing excitement in London literary circles. Byron is said to have declared it the best ode in the English language. 'Burial of Sir John Moore' told the story of a general who was mortally wounded in battle at Corunna in January 1809. It began:

> Not a drum was heard, not a funeral note,
>     As his corpse to the rampart we hurried,
> Not a soldier discharged a farewell shot
>     O'er the grave where our hero we buried.

It was only after the death of Charles Wolfe in 1823 that the poem was established as his work. At the time he wrote the poem, Wolfe was a divinity student at Trinity College, Dublin. Ordained in 1817, his first clerical duty was in the rural parish of Ballyclog, where he arrived shortly before Christmas 1817. His devotion to his duties took a toll on his health, hastening the onset of tuberculosis.

In the following year Wolfe became curate of Donaghmore. This added to his health problems, and he was advised to travel to the south of France to recuperate. But it was already too late, and he died of tuberculosis *en route*, while awaiting ship at Cobh. He was buried in the nearby Clonmel Cemetery. His tombstone is inscribed:

> Here lie
> The Remains of
> The Rev. Charles Wolfe
> Late Curate of Donoughmore
> who died at Cove 21st Feb. 1823
> Aged 31 years.
> The record of his genius
> pity and virtue
> Lives in the hearts
> of all who knew him …

St Michael's Church, Donaghmore

## DONAGHMORE (CASTLECAULFIELD) and DONAGHMORE UPPER

St Patrick is said to have founded an abbey at Donaghmore. Castlecaulfield is a small plantation village founded by Sir Toby Caulfield, afterwards Lord Charlemont. Donaghmore Upper, which includes the village of Donaghmore, was created in 1843. There is a high cross, probably dating from the ninth century. It is 15 feet high, but has suffered weathering.

*St Michael's Church, Donaghmore*, in Castlecaulfield village, was built by Lord Charlemont in 1685. It has had numerous alterations.

*St Patrick's Church, Donaghmore Upper*, a four-bay churchwith a semi-circular apse, was built and dedicated in 1843.

St Patrick's Church, Donaghmore Upper

## DROGHEDA, KILSARAN, ARDEE, COLLON, TERMONFECKIN and DUNLEER

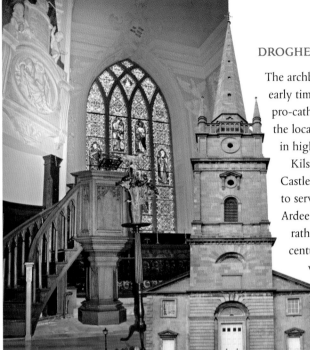

The archbishops who resided in Drogheda from early times regarded the church in Drogheda as a pro-cathedral and usually had a close bond with the local community. The primates were thus held in high esteem.

Kilsaran Parish includes the village of Castlebellingham, built in the seventeenth century to serve the Bellingham estate. The importance of Ardee in medieval times is evidenced by the large rath south of the town and the thirteenth-century castle in the main street. Collon Parish was part of the lordship of Mellifont. The old pre-Reformation church was repaired in 1763 and later enlarged.

Termonfeckin lies north-east of Drogheda and was the site of a twelfth-century monastery. Dunleer is a quiet village bypassed by the motorway. There seems to have been an abbey there in the sixth century.

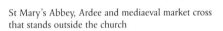

St Mary's Abbey, Ardee and mediaeval market cross that stands outside the church

St Peter's, Drogheda
DERMOTT DUNBAR\COLIN BOYLE

*St Peter's Church, Drogheda* was built 1749–52 on the site of the medieval church of St Peter. It has a handsome Palladian west front by Hugh Darley and a tower with a Gothic needle spire to the design of Francis Johnston. The interior has galleries around three sides. Eight primates were buried there between 1404 and 1613. The church contains many things of interest, including a medieval octagonal font, elaborate plasterwork in the chancel along with notable wall monuments and an eighteenth century organ presented by the corporation.

*St Mary's Church, Kilsaran* was erected originally in 1660; it was rebuilt in 1852, when a chancel was added. It is claimed that Napper Tandy, a United Irishman who died in 1803, is buried in the churchyard.

St Mary's Church, Kilsaran
COLIN BOYLE

St Feckin's Church, Termonfeckin
COLIN BOYLE

*St Mary's Abbey, Ardee* incorporates part of a medieval church with a Norman doorway. It is a five-bay hall with a short chancel and side aisles.

The foundation stone of the present *Collon Church* was laid in 1811. It was built to the design of the rector, Rev. D.A. Beaufort, and modelled on that of the Chapel at King's College Cambridge.

*St Feckin's Church, Termonfeckin* was erected in 1792, to the design of Francis Johnston, with the spire erected 1906. A high cross, probably from the ninth century, stands in the churchyard.

The present *Dunleer Church* is a four-bay hall built in 1830, but the adjoining tower possibly dates back to the thirteenth century.

Dunleer Church
COLIN BOYLE

Collon Church
COLIN BOYLE

## DRUMCREE

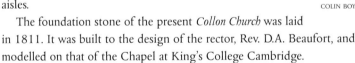

This ancient parish originally belonged to the Culdees of Armagh, whose duty it was to maintain the cathedral. Because of its rapid growth, Portadown was formed as a separate parish from Drumcree in 1824. The *Church of the Ascension, Drumcree* was built in 1856, on the site of a former church. 21 year old John Mitchel, later the Young Irelander, was married to 16 year old Jenny Verner in the earlier church, in 1837, after having eloped twice. The first time he was arrested and spent 18 days in Kilmainham Jail. The second time they were secretly married by the rector of Drumcree, Rev David Babington. In the 1990s Drumcree parish church received widespread media publicity because of controversy over an annual July Orange Order parade to the church via Garvaghy Road.

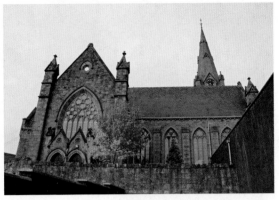

St Anne's Church, Drumglass
COLIN BOYLE

## DRUMGLASS (DUNGANNON) and MOYGASHEL

The town of Dungannon stands on the site of the ancient fortress of the Uí Néill and owes much of its prosperity to the linen industry in the nineteenth century. The village of Moygashel, south of Dungannon, expanded rapidly after World War II, chiefly owing to the famous Moygashel fabrics.

*St Anne's Church, Drumglass* Dungannon was consecrated in 1869 to replace another church which had become too small for the growing population. Erected in the Gothic Revival style to a design of W.J. Barre of Belfast, it is a large cruciform building with sizeable transepts.

*St Elizabeth's Church, Moygashel* was consecrated and dedicated to St Elizabeth in 2002. It had been built originally as a church hall in 1952 and was later converted into a chapel of ease to Drumglass.

St Elizabeth's Church, Moygashel
COLIN BOYLE

St Nicholas's Church, Dundalk

## DUNDALK, HEYNESTOWN, BALLYMASCANLAN, CREGGAN and RATHCOR (BUSH)

In the late eighteenth and early nineteenth centuries, Dundalk was a thriving commercial centre. Creggan belonged to the Culdees of Armagh.

*St Nicholas's Church, Dundalk* suffered in 1641 and 1689. It was restored in 1707 and has had more recent alterations. The spire was struck by lightning in 1932 and a new copper spire was dedicated on 1 January 1933. Due to the green appearance of the copper, the church is known locally as 'The Green Church'. There was a complete renovation of the church in 1991.

*St Paul's Church, Heynestown* dates from 1827 and has a three-bay nave and tower.

*St Mary's Church, Ballymascanlan* was built in 1821 and probably incorporates part of an earlier seventeenth century building. It is cruciform, with an elaborately painted sanctuary.

Creggan Church

St Mary's Church, Ballymascanlon

The present *Creggan Church* dates from 1758, and the tower from 1799. The graveyard is the burial place of the clan O'Neill and three eighteenth century Gaelic Irish poets. The Creggan Visitors' Centre, situated in the grounds of the church, is a vibrant cross-community project which received EU funding.

*Rathcor Chapel of Ease* (Bush Church) was built on the Carlingford Peninsula in 1844. It is a small hall with side buttresses and pinnacles. Originally known as 'Bush Church', the building was renovated in 1994 and dedicated to St Andrew. The Holy Table, which accommodates a seventeenth century altar stone, was transferred from Carlingford Church in 1968.

St Paul's Church, Heynestown
COLIN BOYLE

## ERRIGLE KEEROGUE, BALLYGAWLEY and KILLESHILL

Errigle Keerogue, west of Ballygawley, is probably a sixth-century foundation. Remnants of a round tower and ancient Celtic cross still survive there. Ballygawley was established as a perpetual curacy in 1829. Killeshill, between Dungannon and Ballygawley, is an ancient parish.

*Errigle Keerogue Church* was consecrated in 1832. The stone font is probably seventeenth century. Extensive repairs were carried out in 1994.

*Ballygawley Church*, with its double pinnacled bell-cote and battlemented porch, also dates from 1832.

*St Paul's Church, Killeshill* was built around 1732 and rebuilt in 1768, becoming cruciform by the addition of an apse and transepts and a low tower. It was enlarged in 1861 to the design of Welland and Gillespie.

Ballygawley Church
DERMOTT DUNBAR

St Paul's Church, Killes
COLIN BOYLE

Errigal Keeroge Church

Armabreague Church

St Matthew's Church, Keady

## KEADY, ARMAGHBREAGUE and DERRYNOOSE

Keady Parish was formed in 1773. Keady was a market town surrounded by linen mills and bleach greens, but it suffered with the decline of the linen industry. Armaghbreague became a parish in 1829, comprising parts of Keady and Lisnadill parishes.

Archbishop Robinson built *St Matthew's Church, Keady* in 1775. A tower was added in 1822.

*Armaghbreague Church*, with a bell-cote on the west gable, dates from 1831. It is the 'highest church', above sea level, in Armagh Diocese.

*St John's Church, Derrynoose* was consecrated in 1713. It was rebuilt in 1812 and the substantial tower was added in 1820.

## KILDRESS and ALTEDESERT

Altedesert Parish, which includes the town of Pomeroy, was formed in 1840.

*St Patrick's Church, Kildress* was built in 1818. It is a three-bay hall with tower.

*Altedesert Church*, in Pomeroy town square, dates from 1841. It has a side aisle and tower, with a spire added c. 1876.

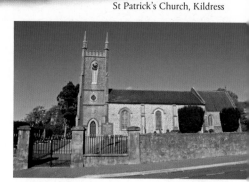

St Patrick's Church, Kildress

Altedesert Church

## KILLYLEA, CALEDON and BRANTRY

Killylea Parish was established in 1829. The village of Killylea was founded in the late eighteenth century by John Maxwell of Fellows Hall. Caledon Parish was formed in 1806; Brantry Parish was formed in 1843.

*St Mark's Church, Killylea* was built in 1832, with a chancel added in 1874. The pulpit and moulded stone in the sanctuary had been removed from Armagh Cathedral during renovations.

*St John's Church, Caledon*, a four-bay church, dates from 1768. The tower was built in 1785 and the third earl of Caledon added in 1808 the fine needle spire to the design of John Nash.

*Holy Trinity Church, Brantry* was built in 1844 at the expense of the countess of Caledon. It is a small hall with side porch and bell-cote. A replacement bell was obtained in 1976 from a disused church in the Clara group of parishes, Co. Laois.

St Mark's Church, Killylea

St John's Church, Caledon

Holy Trinity Church, Brantry

## KILLYMAN

This populous rural area was previously known as Derrybrochus. *St Andrew's Church, Killyman* was rebuilt in 1823 and enlarged in 1868. In 1967 a peal of eight bells was brought from Kilshane Church, Bansha, County Tipperary, and hung in the church tower.

## KILMORE and ST SAVIOUR'S

Kilmore, between Armagh and Portadown, is an ancient site of worship. The site was dedicated in honour of St Aidan, first bishop of Lindisfarne, who had Irish connections and died in AD 651. The ancient parish was very large, covering some 38 square miles. The parish of Mullavilly was formed out of it in 1755. In the nineteenth century, Richhill, St Saviour's and Diamond Parishes were also formed, thereby reducing Kilmore to about 4.5 square miles.

Thomas Preston, born in Kilmore, was a distinguished scientist, becoming professor of natural philosophy in University College, Dublin in 1891. St Saviour's Parish was carved out of Kilmore in 1857. The parish, which is locally known as 'the Dobbin', was reunited with Kilmore in 1979. *St Aidan's Church, Kilmore* was rebuilt in 1814. The church has an ancient tower with walls nine feet thick in places.

*St Saviour's Church*, along with a parsonage and school, was built in black whinstone at the expense of Mrs Louisa Baker of Richhill Castle in 1857.

St Saviour's Church

## LISNADILL and KILDARTON

Lisnadill, south of Armagh city, seems to have been held by the primates. Kildarton is an early Christian site. The parish was formed in 1840.

*St John's Church, Lisnadill* was built by Primate Robinson and consecrated on 2 November 1782. The plain east wall is inscribed with the Lord's Prayer, the Creed and the Ten Commandments. The organ, built in 1842, was purchased from Kilmore Church in the 1930s for £30.

*Kildarton Church*, a three-bay structure with a bell-cote on the west gable, was consecrated in 1841.

St John's Church, Lisnadill

Kildarton Church

## LISSAN

Lissan, near Cookstown, is an ancient Christian site. Lissan Rectory, a listed building, was designed by the architect John Nash and built in 1807. *Lissan Church* was described by Samuel Lewis in 1837 as 'a plain and very ancient structure'. A gallery on cast-iron Gothic columns was added to it in 1823 at a cost of £55.

## LOUGHGALL and GRANGE

In Loughgall, an attractive village in an apple-growing area, stand the ruins of an ancient church and graveyard. Loughgall is of plantation origin, built by the Cope family. Grange, a parish two miles north of Armagh, was created in 1776.

*St Luke's Church, Loughgall* was built in 1795 and later enlarged.

*St Aidan's Church, Grange* was built by Primate Robinson in 1773. There was a custom here that male members of the congregation sat on one side of the aisle and female members on the other.

St Aidan's Church, Grange

St Luke's Church, Loughgall

## LOUGHGILLY and CLARE

Loughgilly, between Armagh and Newry, is an ancient parish. An almshouse 'for the reception of four respectable old women of the parish' was built in 1811 and has recently been refurbished for parochial use. Clare Parish was formed in 1840. Rev. Frederick T. Hankin (perpetual curate 1858–77) is said to have sung for King George IV.

*St Patrick's Church, Loughgilly* was rebuilt in 1811 and a chancel was added in 1863. The stone font bears the name of Rev. George Synge (rector) and the date 1637.

*Clare Church*, a three-bay building with bell-cote, was built in 1840.

St Patrick's Church, Loughgilly          Clare Church

## MAGHERAFELT

St Swithin's Church, Magherafelt

This market town was founded by the Salters' Company in 1609. A church was built in 1622, but destroyed in the 1641 Rebellion; it was rebuilt in 1664 and in 1688 the Jacobites fortified it as a barracks. Magherafelt is the most northerly parish in Armagh Diocese. *St Swithin's Church, Magherafelt* was erected in 1856. The Salters' Company gave the site and about half of the cost. It is cruciform and in the Decorated Gothic Revival style. The spire was rebuilt in 1993 at a cost of £300,000. The church is dedicated to St Swithin, probably because the head office of the Salters' Company was in St Swithin's Lane, London.

St Swithin's Church, Magherafelt

## MILLTOWN

This parish was formed out of Tartaraghan Parish in 1840. Rev. Michael Angelo Holden (rector 1874–1907) claimed a family connection with the famous painter Michaelangelo Buonarroti. The district suffered greatly during the Great Famine. Today farmers in the area specialise in producing fruit and vegetables. *St Andrew's Church, Milltown* was erected in 1840. For about ten years prior to the building of the church, evening services were conducted by the Tartaraghan curate in Derrylee Methodist Church. The building was later enlarged, and part of the tower was rebuilt in 1949. The present font was obtained in 1969 from the select vestry of St Catherine and St James Parochial Group, Dublin.

## MOY

This attractive eighteenth-century village was built by the earl of Charlemont and is said to have been modelled on Marengo, Lombardy. It became renowned for its horse fairs. The parish was formed out of Clonfeacle. *St James's Church, Moy* was erected in 1819. It is a four-bay hall with tower, pinnacles and battlements. A south aisle was added in 1863 and a north transept was built in 1868.

## MULLABRACK, MARKETHILL and KILCLUNEY

Mullabrack seems to have belonged to the Culdees before the Reformation. Markethill in the parish is a vibrant business town.

*Mullabrack Church* was rebuilt in 1830. It contains the vaults of the Gosford family of Markethill.

*Markethill Chapel of Ease*, is in the old courthouse in the town. The building was purchased by the Mullahbrack rector and given as a gift to the parish on his retirement from the incumbency in 1859. It was consecrated in 1861.

*St John's Church, Kilcluney* was built on a new site in 1794, in place of an earlier church at Kilbracks. In the rectory grounds there stood a remarkable wooden building, with an arch, chancel and screen, and other furnishings, carved by Rev. Henry Hutchings (rector 1877–96), commonly called 'The Abbey', in which he held evening services. The building has now been re-erected near the parish church.

St John's Church, Kilcluney

Mullabrack Church

## MULLAVILLY

Mullavilly was formed out of Kilmore Parish in 1755. In the mid-nineteenth century the Sintons, a Quaker family, built a linen mill and the village of Laurelvale to house their employees, who in the 1880s numbered about 800. *Mullavilly Church* was built around 1750; the font is dated 1751. The church was later enlarged. In 1966 a bell was erected in the tower, being the gift of Delvin Parish, Co. Westmeath.

Mullavilly Church

## NEWTOWNHAMILTON, BALLYMOYER and BELLEEK

The parish of Newtownhamilton dates from 1773, the Hamilton family having built the town in 1770. Ballymoyer is so called because the MacMoyers, the hereditary keepers of the *Book of Armagh*, lived there. The area is associated with St Patrick. Belleek Parish was formed out of Loughgilly Parish in 1827.

*St John's Church, Newtownhamilton* was built in 1866 to replace an earlier church. It is a large building in black stone with a tower.

*St Luke's Church, Ballymoyer* was built in the Gothic Revival style in 1822. The elaborate font and cover (*c.* 1876) were designed by the renowned Victorian architect William Butterfield.

*St Luke's Church, Belleek* was described by Samuel Lewis in 1837 as 'a plain small edifice in the ancient style with a lofty square tower'.

St John's Church, Newtownhamilton

St Luke's Church, Ballymoyer

St Luke's Church, Belleek

## POMEROY

Pomeroy Parish was carved out of Donaghmore in 1775. *Pomeroy Church* was consecrated in 1782 at Crossdernott, three miles from Pomeroy village. It is a three-bay hall with a tower and diagonal buttresses. A north transept was added later.

Pomeroy Church

## PORTADOWN, ST COLUMBA'S

This is the youngest parish in Armagh Diocese, formed in 1967 out of St Mark's Parish. *St Columba's Church, Portadown*, built in 1970, is modern and symmetrical in the form of a Greek Cross. It is topped by a copper cross 65 feet above ground level. The foundation stone was brought from Gartan, Co. Donegal, the birthplace of St Columba. The baptismal font came from Trinity Church, Limerick.

St Columba's Church, Portadown

## PORTADOWN, ST MARK'S

Portadown owed its importance to a ford across the River Bann, which was eventually replaced by a wooden bridge. The Newry Canal opened the town to commerce and prosperity. St Mark's Parish, Portadown was formed out of Drumcree Parish in 1824. In the nineteenth and twentieth centuries, the town was renowned for the manufacture of fine linen and was an important railway junction. *St Mark's Church, Portadown* was built in the town centre in 1826. It was originally called St Martin's but was dedicated to St Mark in 1885, following extensive rebuilding. The tower was replaced by a taller one in 1928 as a memorial to the dead of the First World War. In 1993 the church building was badly damaged due to a bomb in Portadown town centre. The parish today has the largest number of parishioners in the diocese.

## RICHHILL

Richhill was named by the Richardson family, who built the castle there around 1665. In 1837 the parish was formed from the ancient parish of Kilmore. Archbishop Robinson lived at Richhill Castle while the palace in Armagh was being built. *St Matthew's Church, Richhill* was created when the old session house was converted into a church in 1837. The tower was added in 1912. A new clock and chimes for the tower were installed in 1959: the chimes were the composition of the rector Canon John Cockrill, and are a variation of the well known Westminster chimes.

## SIXMILECROSS and TERMONMAGUIRKE

The name of this perpetual curacy was changed from Cooley to Sixmilecross in 1837. The original church was erected in 1733 but closed in 1811. Before the new church was built, the local Presbyterian congregation allowed their church to be used for worship by the parishioners. Termonmaguirke is associated with St Patrick and St Columba.

    *St Michael's Church, Sixmilecross* was consecrated in 1836. It was later enlarged and the tower was added in 1885.

    *St Columbkille's Church, Termonmaguirke*, in Carrickmore village, was built in 1786. There are fine carvings on the gallery front, pulpit, prayer desk and reredos.

St Michael's Church, Sixmilecross

St Columbkille's Church, Termonmaguirke

## TARTARAGHAN and DIAMOND

In medieval times Tartaraghan was a grange of the abbey of St Peter and St Paul in Armagh. In the 1890s it was the most densely populated rural district in Ireland. Diamond Parish was formed in 1867, services being held in the Grange O'Neilland School until a church was built in 1926. The battle of the Diamond took place in the area in 1795.

    The present *St Paul's Church, Tartaraghan*, to the design of John Bowden, architect to the Board of First Works, replaced an older church in 1816.

    *St Paul's Church, Diamond*, in the Norman style, was built in 1926 to the design of R.C. Orpen.

St Paul's Church, Diamond

St Paul's Church, Tartaraghan

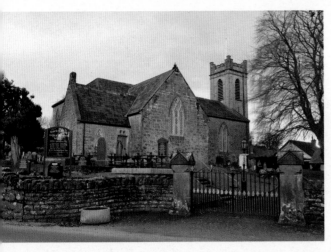

Holy Trinity Church, Tullanisken

## TULLANISKEN and CLONOE

The old parish church at Tullanisken was destroyed in the 1641 Rebellion, after which the parish was united with Drumglass (Dungannon). In 1789, it again became a separate parish. Clonoe Parish lies north-east of Coalisland.

*Holy Trinity Church, Tullanisken* was built in Newmills in 1793. Transepts were added in 1865, making the building cruciform.

*St Michael's Church, Clonoe* is an ancient, small, three-bay hall with bell-cote. Part of the building may date back to the 1430s. It was repaired in 1699, according to an inscription in the porch which ends with the words 'One Lord, One Faith, One Baptism'.

St Michael's Church, Clonoe

St John's Church, Middletown

## TYNAN, AGHAVILLY and MIDDLETOWN

Tynan village grew up around the church. It has four high crosses, the oldest of which is possibly ninth century.

Aghavilly Parish was established in 1841. Within it is the village of Milford, which grew up in the nineteenth century around a linen factory.

Middletown Parish was formed in 1792.

St Mary's Church, Aghavilly

Vindic's Church, Tynan

*St Vindic's Church, Tynan* was rebuilt in 1784 and transepts and a chancel were added in 1822; the tower has angled buttresses and tall pinnacles.

*St Mary's Church, Aghavilly* was consecrated in 1841. It is a three-bay hall with bell-cote and porch.

*St John's Church, Middletown* dates from 1793 but was not consecrated until 1822. It is a three-bay hall with tower.

Gracefield Church

## WOODSCHAPEL and GRACEFIELD

Woodschapel Parish, near Magherafelt, existed in pre-Reformation times and later became part of Ardtrea Parish, from which it was separated in 1823.

*St John's Church, Woodschapel* was consecrated in 1870, the site being a gift of the Salters' Company. It is a large cruciform building in basalt with sandstone trim and an unusual tower.

*Gracefield Church* is a late-eighteenth-century building which was originally a Moravian church. It was rented as a chapel of ease to the parish church in 1935 and purchased around 1946. It is a five-bay hall with two-storey tower surmounted by a wooden cupola. Nearby is a small Moravian graveyard.

St John's Church, Woodschapel

# The Diocese of Clogher

The countryside is rich in the diocese of Clogher. Even a newcomer like me can see that. It is rich in the range of its plants and animals, and richer still in the depth and variety of its people. As I look out over the hills beyond Mullaghfad towards county Monaghan, the view changes each day, and sometimes each hour of the day, with the changing light, and I realise in a fresh way, why Ireland is often thought of as an enchanted island.

Spend a week in the Diocese and you will soon recognise both the small truth and the enormous injustice in Winston Churchill's famous reference to '… the dreary steeples of Tyrone and Fermanagh …' No landscape, nor the people who have shaped it, will yield up their identity to a superficial or a cynical observer.

Since the time of St Patrick's strong helper, St McCartan, Christianity has been at work in shaping Clogher through the generations of believers. We know little enough about the lives and beliefs of many in those generations, and reconstruct what we can with the help of the surviving official records. I would not like my life to be judged only by what is kept in the official record.

In addition the discipline which we call 'history', where skilled researchers look dispassionately through old documents and artefacts, and assess them *in their own terms*, is very new to Ireland. Before the 1950s much history in this country was merely a form of ethnic propaganda. So today we are one of the few places in the world where it is the past that is unpredictable.

Nevertheless we do know that many expressions of the Christian faith and Christian commitment have flourished in the diocese. That particular way of being a Christian called 'Anglicanism' still flourishes and adapts itself to the changing circumstances of life in South Tyrone, Fermanagh and Monaghan.

In some parishes numbers are small, in others numbers are very large indeed, but all are held together in worship through the Offices of The Book of Common Prayer, and each has its part to play in the continuing drama that God has mapped out for us.

The Anglicanism which is 'bred in the bone' of the people of this part of the world is itself distinctive. The post-Reformation settlements of the Diocese (whether officially sponsored or private) were of English people who brought with them the religion of England; moderate and reserved. However, unlike much of the religion of England since, it has been largely unaffected by the legacy of the Oxford Movement or of modern academic scepticism. In many places it is what used to be described as 'Low', and values straightforward and unshowy devotion above all else. In other places there is a recognisably modern feel in the atmosphere and music of worship. Everywhere God is worshipped as Friend and Saviour, but also as a great King to whom stern obligations are owed. It is also a place of sincere welcome, and behind the natural diffidence of the countryman lurks shrewd observation and the hand of friendship.

JOHN CLOGHER

Devenish Island, 3 miles north west of Enniskillen contains the remains of an early medieval monastery founded by St Molaise. The site includes the small oratory known as St Molaise's house (twelfth century) a complete round tower (256 metres high) – one of the finest examples in Ireland and the ruins of a large church building. The Augustinian Abbey of St Mary is slightly detached from the former group. It has a datestone of 1449. The churchyard contains a fifteenth century cross with a crucifixion scene and some interlacing with vine leaves. The grave slabs of many of the leading Maguires of Fermanagh provide some notable grave art.
SCENIC IRELAND

# ST MACARTAN'S CATHEDRAL CLOGHER

Bishop John Stearne, 1717–45
CLOGHER CATHEDRAL

The present Clogher Cathedral dates from 1744, when it was built by Bishop John Stearne. James Martin appears to have been the architect he employed. Its early Christian and medieval predecessors have vanished, but the church is probably the fifth building on the site; the datestone of its predecessor (showing 1628) is preserved in the porch. It is a cruciform structure, with pedimented gables to the transepts and chancel. The broad west front, wider than the nave, also has a pedimented gable, but it is topped by a solid, square belfry tower with a balustrade and obelisk finials. All the windows are round headed except the east window, which is Venetian and of rare beauty.

The cathedral was remodelled by Dean Richard Bagwell in 1818 and reordered in the 1860s, when the galleries over the transepts were removed. The interior is homely and unadorned. There are several fine memorials, including the Gledstanes memorial, with its elegant urn, and the memorial to Bishop Porter, complete with mitre and crozier. Two mosaic-style memorials honour the Ellison Macartney family and there are fine brasses dedicated to the Taylors. There are nine stained-glass windows in all. The collection of bishops' portraits hung in the entrance lobby and the chapter room features work by Sir Thomas Lawrence, James Latham, Sarah Purser, James Sleator, Derek Hill, Peter Greenham and Andrew Festing. The seating dates from c. 1865.

Within the tower, the diocesan archive room houses visitation reports from 1666 as well as maps and chapter records. In the cemetery are two early Celtic crosses as well as 28 slab memorials from the seventeenth century. The former bishop's palace nearby, built between 1819 and 1823, is now St Macartan's Private Nursing Home. The former deanery (possibly designed by Thomas Cooley) was demolished in 1975.

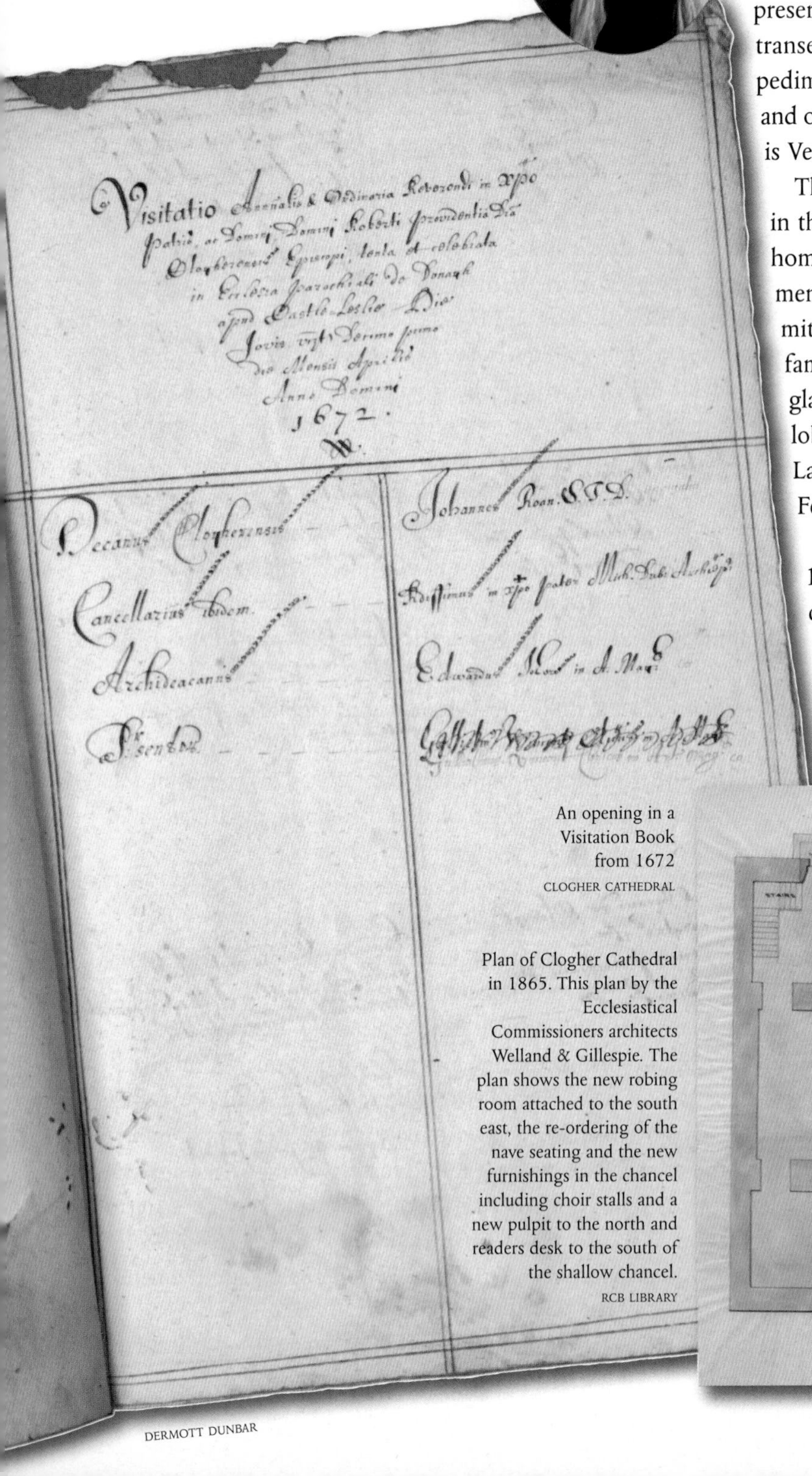

An opening in a
Visitation Book
from 1672
CLOGHER CATHEDRAL

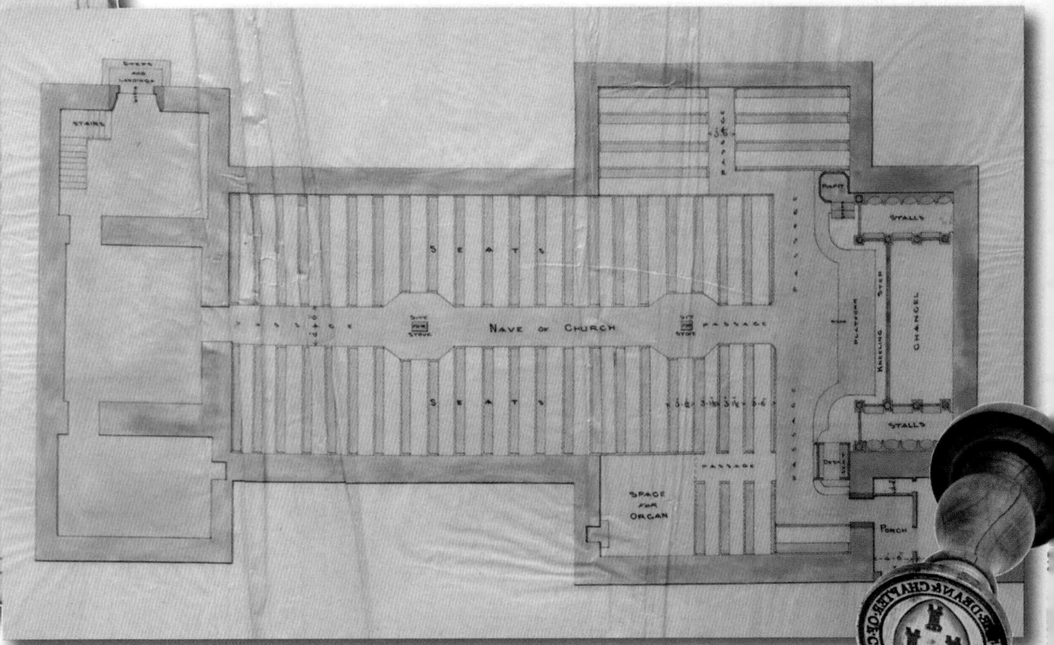

Plan of Clogher Cathedral in 1865. This plan by the Ecclesiastical Commissioners architects Welland & Gillespie. The plan shows the new robing room attached to the south east, the re-ordering of the nave seating and the new furnishings in the chancel including choir stalls and a new pulpit to the north and readers desk to the south of the shallow chancel.
RCB LIBRARY

DERMOTT DUNBAR

A seal from the archive in Clogher Cathedral
CLOGHER CATHEDRAL

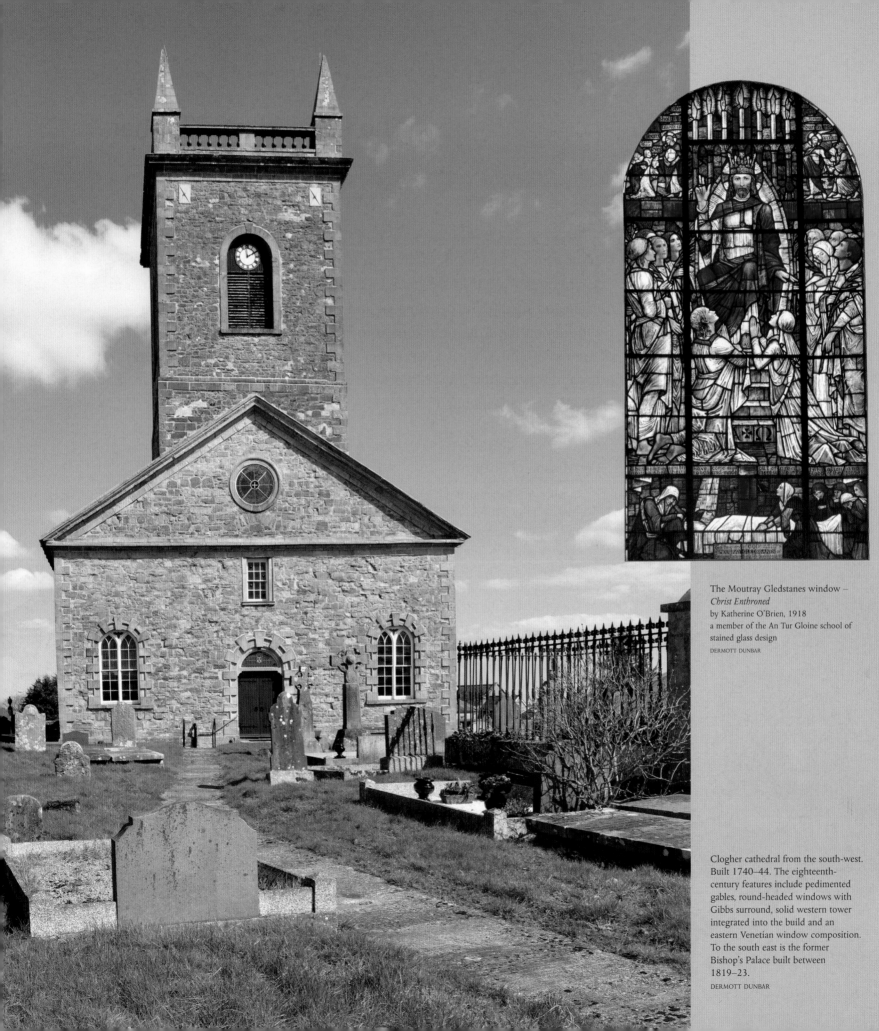

The Moutray Gledstanes window –
*Christ Enthroned*
by Katherine O'Brien, 1918
a member of the An Tur Gloine school of
stained glass design
DERMOTT DUNBAR

Clogher cathedral from the south-west.
Built 1740–44. The eighteenth-
century features include pedimented
gables, round-headed windows with
Gibbs surround, solid western tower
integrated into the build and an
eastern Venetian window composition.
To the south east is the former
Bishop's Palace built between
1819–23.
DERMOTT DUNBAR

# The Diocese of Clogher

JACK JOHNSTON

The diocese of Clogher today stretches through all or part of five counties – all of Monaghan, most of Fermanagh, a significant area in Tyrone and small parts of Donegal and Louth. It once extended from Bundoran on the Atlantic seaboard to Inniskeen near Dundalk – a distance of almost 80 miles, with a maximum width of about 30 miles. This territory is today fairly evenly divided between the political jurisdictions of Northern Ireland and the Republic.

## The Mission of St Patrick

St Patrick's Chair and Well sits in woodland at Altadavin in Co. Tyrone, supposedly this was an ancient druidic centre in the days before Christianity. St Patrick is said to have banished pagans from here, hence the name – Altadavin – The Demon Cliff.
DERMOTT DUNBAR

The church in Clogher dates from the mission of St Patrick in the fifth century. Tradition recalls how Patrick, travelling from the west, came through the Clogher Valley and forded the Blackwater. He appointed Macartan, his so-called 'strong man', as the first bishop and left him behind at Clogher as he moved on to Armagh. This tradition is reinforced by the presence of St Patrick's Chair and Well at Altadavin, between Augher and Clogher. Macartan died in AD 506 and was buried at Clogher, just a few yards south-west of the present cathedral, 'near a white-thorn bush'.

The High Cross standing
Clones town centre is be
to have come from two
century crosses. It was us
illustrate stories from the
to the congregation.

## The Medieval Period

The area of the diocese was originally coterminous with the kingdom of Oriel and did not have declared boundaries until the Synod of Ráth Breasail in 1111. Its extent was from the River Blackwater to Galloon and from Slieve Beagh to Slieve Largy, south of Omagh. This core area was later expanded to the south and west and also northwards as far as Ardstraw. Donnchadh O'Carroll, who became king of Oriel in 1125, pushed his kingdom into Louth and with it the emerging diocese. Indeed, the abbey of Louth served briefly as a cathedral church before the diocese was restored to Clogher in 1197.

By c. 1300 its present boundaries were more or less settled, with 25 medieval parishes recognised. Some of these very large parishes – Inishmacsaint, Devenish, Aghalurcher, Galloon and Clogher – could well have been seen as micro-dioceses in themselves, and in due course were split into smaller parishes. For example, Aghalurcher, traditionally one of the wealthiest parishes, at one stage included Aghavea within its borders, while Magheracross was originally a chapelry within the greater Derryvullen Parish. Seven of these 25 medieval parishes have records of clergy going back before 1400 – Clogher, Cleenish, Clones, Enniskillen, Derryvullen, Derrybrusk and Aghalurcher.

The Domhnach Airgid or Silver Shrine, now in the National Museum in Dublin, was kept in Clogher Cathedral from 1308 until 1525. It contained part of a copy of the

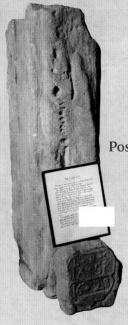

gospels that is said to have been given to Macartan by Patrick. The relic was venerated locally and belonged to the Maguire chiefs until the early 1800s.

## Post-Reformation Times

There was little change in parish structure over the next 200 years and by 1500 there were 30 parishes in the diocese.

Miler Magrath, who had been a Franciscan friar, was the first Protestant bishop of Clogher. He was a noted pluralist and held several benefices in addition to two and sometimes three sees, all concurrently. He was provided to Clogher in 1570, though there is some doubt as to whether he ever occupied his cathedral. Cornelius MacArdle was restored to the see the following year and it was not until the appointment of George Montgomery in 1605 that there was a Protestant successor. Montgomery, who was James I's chaplain, held the sees of Derry and Raphoe with Clogher before being translated to Meath in 1610. He held Clogher with Meath. Montgomery was more interested in the temporal life than the spiritual and amassed some 90,000 acres as a result of plantation grants.

Clogh-Oir or the Golden Stone from which Clogher may have derived its name and is reputed to be one of the three stones of Erin.
DIOCESE OF CLOGHER

The Domhnach Airgid book shrine – or Silver Church – is a splendid exercise in medieval retro. The earliest part, a yew-wood box covered by ornamental, tinned bronze plates, may be early 9th century in date. Some of the external embellishments date both to the mid-fourteenth and fifteenth century.
NATIONAL MUSEUM OF IRELAND

## The Seventeenth Century

Many of the medieval churches in the diocese were burnt or destroyed in the Nine Years' War and few were repaired after it. Things changed little with the arrival of the plantation settlers in 1610. The visitation of 1622 gives us a view of the diocese after a decade of plantation. Only nine Clogher churches were in repair, with twenty-eight in ruins. Bishop James Spottiswood, who was Montgomery's successor, wrote that his cathedral was 'altogether ruynous' and that the adjoining St Mary's Abbey had 'noe roofe'.

Little remains of the early churches at Clogher today except for some moulded pieces of doorways and window-mullions now incorporated into the graveyard walls. Two Celtic crosses stand opposite the west door of the cathedral and an early seventh-century cross, which some authorities consider to be a sundial, stands in the side porch. The main porch houses a large standing stone known as the Clogh-Oir. It is reputed to be one of the 'three stones of Erin', one of which is the Stone of Destiny in Edward the Confessor's chair in Westminster Abbey. There is a tradition that the Clogh-Oir, venerated as an oracle, was consulted by Concobar MacNessa, the high king of Ulster.

In the seventeenth century the diocese was ravaged by wars. In 1641, Bishop Spottiswood fled to London and his palace at Clogher was plundered in his absence. Henry Jones, his successor, abandoned the monarchists and threw in his lot with Cromwell and the Puritans, but returned to the Stuarts at the Restoration. Charles II promoted him to Meath, where he found his calling as a politician. John Leslie, the next bishop, was a decided royalist and was rewarded by Charles II with the grant of an estate in Monaghan, a property that is still in the hands of his descendants. The bishop, who lived to be 100, married an 18-year-old when he was 67. Roger Boyle, who held the see between 1672 and 1687, had a reputation for learning and piety, unlike his predecessors. The accession of James II meant that no appointment was made to Clogher after Boyle's death, with the result

Bishop John Leslie, Bishop of Clogher 1661–71, was granted an estate, Glaslough, Monaghan, Castle Leslie.
CLOGHER CATHEDRAL

The Castle Leslie Estate c. 1950s. Standing on the steps are Sir Shane Leslie, 3rd Baronet with his second wife Iris Carola Leslie. The estate remains in the family and is now a thriving hospitality business.
CASTLE LESLIE ESTATE

Bishop James Spottiswood, Bishop of Clogher 1621–45
CLOGHER CATHEDRAL

that for four years the revenues of the see were given to Patrick Tyrrel, the Catholic bishop.

Bishop Richard Tenison was translated to Clogher from Killala and Achonry in 1691. He spent just six years in the diocese, but during that time persuaded many Dissenters to conform to the Church of Ireland.

## The Eighteenth Century

Throughout the eighteenth century, the bishops of Clogher were mostly English, except for St George and Ashe and John Stearne. They all came on promotion and had each been in at least one Irish bishopric before being translated to Clogher. They were for the most part non-resident, with the exception of Stearne and John Garnett. It was said of Stearne, who was a scholar and a bibliophile, that he used to take his telescope up to the top floor of his palace to scan the countryside for a traveller that might bring him convivial company. John Garnett, his successor, was resident; he built the market house in Clogher and endowed a new schoolhouse. It is now the freemasons' hall, but the datestone reading '1780' may still be seen above the door. Garnett also actively encouraged his clergy to build new glebe houses: between 1771 and 1780 nine were constructed.

Bishop Roger Boyle, 1672–87
CLOGHER CATHEDRAL

There was a fairly casual attitude to religion in the more rural parishes, with attendances at the sacraments being sporadic. Philip Skelton, when he moved to live in Pettigo, complained that his parishioners 'scarce knew more of the gospel than the Indians of America'. He is reputed to have once locked the congregation in the church, where he catechised them vigorously and then examined them closely on what they had learnt.

Clogher was a wealthy bishopric – second to Derry in revenue – and as a result was much sought after. The Rt Rev. Sir John Hotham, from Yorkshire, who had been bishop of Ossory for three years, wrote to Sackville Hamilton, under-secretary to the lord lieutenant of Ireland, after he secured Clogher in 1782:

Pettigo, the present church built in 1838
DERMOTT DUNBAR

> When Mr Eden suggested it to me last Spring, I told him I would thank him heartily for Clogher, but not at all for Tuam … I was lately on an expedition … to Clogher … I took advantage of our present parliamentary recess to run down and see what sort of thing I had gotten … Since your Lordship was at Clogher things are greatly changed … My cathedral is no longer a miserable … but now a very neat and respectable church … It was rebuilt by Bishop Stearne and substantially repaired and beautified by the late bishop [Garnett] …
>
> Bishop Stearne also built the present palace … which though not so well contrived as it might have been, is far from a despicable place of residence, especially as my predecessor added two wings, the one an eating room of 30 feet by 20 and the other a library of 32 feet by 22, exclusive of the bow window in each …
>
> The demesne is sufficiently planted … and is in my opinion extremely beautiful … It measures 560 English acres and the whole surrounded by a stone wall, without a road or even a pathway through it … My beef, mutton, veal and lamb are all as good in their kind as can be, the decoy gives me teal and wild ducks … the warren supplies me with excellent rabbits … the pidgeon house with pidgeons, the water with carp, tench, trout, eels and perch … while the venison in the park is remarkably good …

Detail from 1745 Map of Bishop Clayton's demesne by James Leonard. Note the old and new cathedral shown on the plan.
DERMOTT DUNBAR

**THE REV PHILIP SKELTON, 1707–87** was a writer and philanthropist. He entered Trinity College Dublin as a sizar and had Dr Patrick Delaney as his tutor in college. He served curacies in Drummully and Monaghan before being appointed rector of Templecarne. He was Prebend of Devenish (1759–66) and of Donacavey (1766–87 ) during which time he published almost 100 items ranging from *An Account of Lough Derg* to *Some Reflections on Predestination*. He wrote several hymns and some poetry. He twice sold his library to raise money for his congregations in times of famine and hardship. He was a man of tremendous physique and administered justice with a cudgel when necessary. He was an eccentric in many ways and locked his congregation in church so that he could catechise them. His life was written by Samuel Burdy (1792).

Bishop John Garnett

The citie of Clogher stands on my ground and the citizens are all my tenants … The borough is at present secure and likely to remain so … and the roads are very good … the income of the See is not less that £4000 per annum … which in my judgement is no trifling emolument … Indeed [Clogher] … is the very great prize which I have had the good fortune to draw in the lottery of the world …

## Diocesan Reform

The first definitive list of parishes in the modern diocese comes from the visitations of the 1660s. By the mid-seventeenth century the diocesan visitations record 36 parishes within the diocese. There was no change in this figure until 1738, when Ematris was carved out of Galloon. A more rapid population growth after 1750 saw eight new parishes emerge in the next fifty years. Aghabog (1767), Drumkrin (1773) and Killeevan (1795) were also carved out of Galloon, while Ballybay (1798) was created out of Aghnamullen and Tullycorbet. In Fermanagh, Drumkeeran (1770), Trory (1778) and Belleek (1791) were created out of Magheraculmoney, Devenish and Templecarn respectively, while in Tyrone Fivemiletown (1791) secured perpetual-curacy status with territory drawn from Clogher and to a lesser extent from Aghalurcher.

By 1811 the diocese had 50 churches and chapels as well as one under construction. Two of the 44 parishes had no church, however – Derrybrusk and Galloon. The former, which was the smallest parish in the diocese, had never repaired its old pre-Reformation site in Fyagh townland. Instead, Derrybrusk parishioners worshipped once a month in Ballyreagh schoolhouse. Galloon's church, which had been on Galloon Island in earlier times, had been served by the church at Drumkrin before the reorganisation of Currin and Drummully as new parishes in 1804.

The last two decades of the eighteenth century and the first two of the nineteenth saw the construction of several new glebe houses, often supported by the Board of First Fruits. This building included substantial rectories at Magheraculmoney (1780), Kilmore (1792), Ballybay (c. 1805), Magheracloone (1816) and Devenish (1820). Dr Beaufort reported 26 glebe houses in the diocese in 1792 (half of that number in Monaghan), while 34 of the parishes had glebe houses by 1820, many of them constructed within the previous 50 years. The Board of First Fruits also supported church-building on a large scale and between 1825 and 1835 provided grants or gifts towards six of the twelve new churches or chapels erected in Clogher in that decade. In fact, the Board of First Fruits expended over £6,000 in gifts and over £16,000 in loans towards the building of Clogher churches during its lifetime.

There was also considerable support from landlords in the building of new churches. In the seventeenth century, Lord Balfour provided a new church at Lisnaskea (1622), though he was unable to have it declared the parish church for Aghalurcher, while Sir John Dunbar built a new church at Derrygonnelly in 1627. Over the following century, Richard Dawson built a church at Ematris to serve the Dartrey estate in 1727, Margetson Armar of Castle Coole built a chapel of ease at Fivemiletown in 1736 and Lord Rosse built a new church at Lisbellaw in 1764. In the next century the Victorian gentry

opy of Queen Elizabeth's
yer Book, 1590, from the
nive in Clogher Cathedral
CLOGHER CATHEDRAL

Belleek Church, built 1875
DERMOTT DUNBAR

### THE REV DR WILLIAM RICHEY BAILEY
### 1817–88

Dr Bailey was one of the most skilled and versatile clergymen in the diocese. He was an engineer, architect, musician, a wood carver and carpenter. He was also a profound classical scholar and took both his BD and DD from Trinity College. He served a curacy in Aghalurcher before being rector of Lisnaskea, Monaghan and Clogher in each of which he spent 12 years. He had expected to be made Dean in 1874 and when offered the Precentorship refused it. He spent his final three years in Kilmore diocese as Rector of Killesher. He restored with his own hands the stairway of Clogher cathedral and while in Clogher founded a philharmonic society. He was also an enthusiastic Orangeman and formed a flute band which he also taught himself. He was one of the founders of the Protestant Orphan Society. His father was a Methodist minister in Fermanagh.

Devenish parish, St Molaise at Monea, built 1890
DERMOTT DUNBAR

**CANON JOHN GREY PORTER**
**1789–1873**

was a generous benefactor to Kilskeery and
endowed other churches in the diocese at
Clabby, Lisbellaw, Derrybrusk and Barr. He
was a son of Bishop John Porter who
presided over the diocese from 1797 until
1819. The young Porter was a classmate at
both Harrow and Cambridge with Lord
Byron. John Grey Porter purchased Belle
Isle estate in 1830 and twenty years later
acquired the former bishop's palace which
he renamed Clogher Park. His munificence
came from a rental of almost 20,000 acres
which he acquired in Fermanagh, Tyrone
and Longford. He began the campaign for
the restoration of the See of Clogher, a
movement that was carried on by his son
John Grey Vesey Porter of Belle Isle
(1817–1903) There is a second window to
Canon Grey Porter's memory in Clogher
Cathedral.

saw church-building as an element of their families' prestige. In Clogher, the Irvines
built a church at Killadeas, the Archdales one at Castle Archdale, the Singletons one at
Errigal Shanco and Andrew Kerr another at Newbliss.

In 1860, the mother of the new proprietor of Augher Castle, Mrs Carmichael-Ferrall,
was so disappointed to find no church in the village that she immediately set about
providing one. She was not the only influential lady to promote worship in the diocese.
Another benefactress, Mary, countess of Enniskillen, generously refurbished and panelled
in oak the chapter room at Clogher Cathedral, while Mrs JE Taylor of Cheltenham
provided a new throne.

## Pluralism

In the eighteenth century, pluralism and non-residence were charges often placed at the
door of the clergy. Clogher was no different from any other diocese. In many cases, ill
health or the want of a glebe house were used as excuses for non-residence. Other clergy
had more plausible explanations: the rector of Carrickmacross, Dr Thomas Romney
Robinson, was the astronomer in Armagh, while the incumbent of Lisnaskea was
secretary to the Society for Promoting Christianity among the Jews, which meant he
had to live in Dublin. In the 1820s, Dr John Brinkley, rector of Clontibret (also
archdeacon of Clogher) was non-resident because he was a professor in Trinity College,
while Dr George Miller, rector of Derryvullen, was absent because he was the headmaster
of Armagh Royal School. A rector who was well connected seemed to get a licence for
non-residence with ease. The Rev. Sir Harcourt Lees, a political pamphleteer, who was
vicar of Killany, managed to spend his last 17 years out of the parish on the grounds of
his 'infirm and precarious health'.

Thomas Romney Robinson
1792–1882
ROYAL IRISH ACADEMY

Some of the bishops were not without blame either. Bishop Tottenham was a habitual
absentee and was attacked by William Trimble in his paper *The Impartial Reporter* in 1841,
when the new church at Rossorry was ready for dedication:

> Is there no possibility of our Diocesan … appearing within his diocese and performing this
> necessary ceremony? If the Bishop of Clogher cannot be induced after years of absence to
> return and consecrate the church, such inexcusable delinquencies must be exposed …

There was still a fair degree of pluralism at the beginning of the nineteenth century.
The rector of Muckno, Thomas Hackett, held another living in Elphin, while John Grey
Porter held Kilskeery and Donaghmoine simultaneously. The Rev. Sir Harcourt Lees
held prebendaries in both Clogher and Cashel in the 1830s. The practice was on the
wane by this time, however, and after 1829 it was illegal to hold more than one benefice
at any one time.

## The Nineteenth Century

The clergy of Clogher during the nineteenth century were
for the most part drawn from Irish families, many within
the diocese. The Leslies, Stacks, Storys, St Georges and

Belle Isle was bought by Canon John Grey Porter in 1829 and
occupied by the family until 1991 when the last Porter owner,
Miss Lavinia Baird sold it to the present Duke of Abercorn.
It is now a centre for hospitality and has a renowned cookery
school. The estate today runs to 470 acres and includes 8 islands
in Upper Lough Erne.
BELLE ISLE ESTATE

Aghavea Rectory
ROLAND EADIE

Tottenhams provided at least five clergy each. The twelve Leslies who served in the diocese were drawn from two branches of the same dynasty. In Aghavea, a Leslie father and son held the rectory for over 90 years, while in Clones a Roper father and son had almost the same longevity in office. In many cases, sons acted as curates to their fathers and in due course succeeded them. In Drumsnat, the Rev. John Edward Simpson pleaded increasing age and infirmity to permit him to be licensed for non-residence during his last 18 years in the parish on condition that his son, the Rev. Samuel Hoare Simpson, should occupy the glebe house and fulfil his duties as curate.

The rapid growth of population between 1800 and the Great Famine saw almost 20 new parochial units set up, either as perpetual curacies or as district curacies. By 1844, the diocese had 46 parishes and 14 perpetual curacies. There were 45 incumbents (32 being resident) and 44 curates, with a total of 66 places of worship. In 1834, the Church of Ireland population in the diocese of Clogher stood at just over 104,000, making it the second most populous Anglican diocese in Ireland.

## Union with Armagh

The Church Temporalities Act of 1833 reduced the number of dioceses from 22 to 12 and recommended that Clogher be united with Armagh once the see fell vacant. This happened in 1850 with the death of Bishop Tottenham. Consequently, Lord John George Beresford, who was the primate, became bishop of Clogher for the second time, as he had briefly filled the see in 1819–20. After Beresford's death in 1862, his cousin Marcus Gervais Beresford filled both the primatial see and that of Clogher.

The new arrangement meant that the bishop's palace was sold in 1853. It was bought by Canon John Grey Porter, the prebend of Kilskeery and a son of Bishop Porter. Porter settled his daughter Elisabeth and son-in-law John Ellison Macartney in the former palace and it remained their family home until 1921.

## Restoration of the See

The union with Armagh did not last long, however, and after Disestablishment there was a growing feeling in Clogher that the needs of the diocese would be best served by a separation. The Porter family, headed by Canon Grey Porter and his son, John Grey Vesey Porter of Bellisle, together with the earls of Erne, Belmore and Dartrey, pushed for the revival of Clogher diocese. They were charged by the General Synod with raising £25,000 for this purpose (the idea being that this sum invested at four per cent would yield a stipend of £1,000 a year). When the money had been raised except for the last £3,000, Porter stepped in and advanced the balance due. It was hoped to repay this in full, but with £1,000 still owing Porter wiped out the balance. Thus, in 1886, Clogher and Armagh were disannexed, with the archdeacon of Clogher, Charles Maurice Stack, being elected bishop.

Clogher had its own bishop once again, but no see house. The bishop lived at Knockballymore near Clones and then in the old Clones rectory now renamed Bishopscourt. After 1923 the See House moved north of the border to St Angelo near

Bishop Porter
1796–1819, father of
Canon Grey Porter
CLOGHER DIOCESE

## Famine Pit, St Mary's, Ardess, Kesh

Running right across and dividing the pre-plantation cemetery in two is a huge fourteen foot wide trench grave. Described locally as the Famine Pit the huge long narrow sunken grave of 120 feet had remained in an overgrown, unkempt state serving as a harsh visual reminder of the Great Famine period 1845–50. In 1997, the newly formed Ardess Community Association's immediate objective was to mark the 150th anniversary of 1847 (known as Black 47) by firstly restoring the unmarked famine pit and subsequently creating a sensitive memorial commemorating the many forgotten famine victims from North West Fermanagh.

The Famine Pit serviced the human tragedy that unfolded in the Lowtherstown (Irvinestown) Workhouse and it is estimated that the bodies of some two hundred victims of the famine period from throughout the Irvinestown Poor Law Union area were buried anonymously. Over time the trench emerged, after having been filled as a mound, when the large number of bodies it contained, decomposed. In death, as perhaps in life, the famine victims had nothing but the transient space their bodies occupied in an unmarked sunken trench grave. Using traditional stonemasonry methods and local grey limestone the tumbledown sides of the Famine Pit have been strengthened and preserved with the stonewalling tastefully blending in with the vaulted tomb marking the end of the Famine Pit.
ARDESS PARISH

The wives of several local rectors set up lacemaking as a cottage industry during the famine years. Lace from Clones, Carrickmacross and Inishmacsaint all flourished and provided a much needed income to many households.

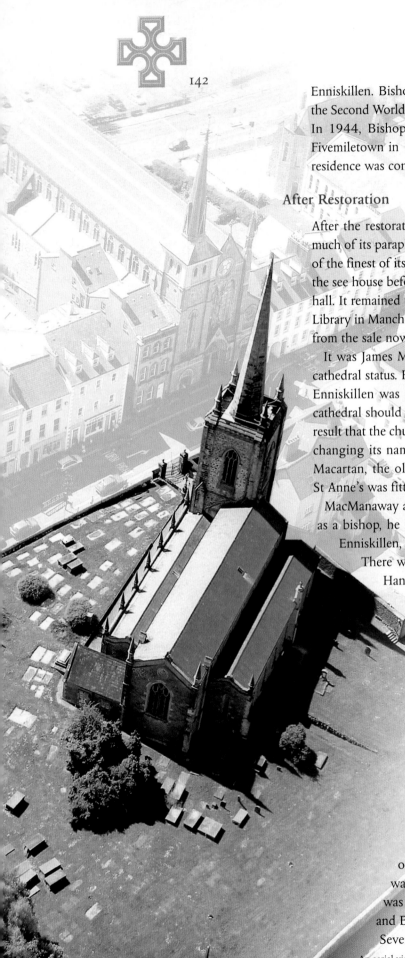

Enniskillen. Bishop MacManaway gave up St Angelo to the RAF on the outbreak of the Second World War. His last few years were spent in Aghavea House, Brookeborough. In 1944, Bishop Tyner reverted to Clones. A new see house was acquired at Fivemiletown in 1958 and since then the bishop has lived in Tyrone. A fine new residence was constructed there in the first years of the twenty-first century.

## After Restoration

After the restoration of the see in 1886, the diocese was centred on Clones and much of its paraphernalia was based there. The old diocesan library, which was one of the finest of its kind, dated from the mid-eighteenth century. It had been sited in the see house before 1850, but was now transferred to the boardroom of the synod hall. It remained there until it was dismantled and sold in 1954. The John Rylands Library in Manchester purchased the bulk of its early pamphlet collection. The proceeds from the sale now constitute the Moffett Prize Fund.

It was James MacManaway who raised St Anne's Parish Church in Enniskillen to cathedral status. He had been rector of Enniskillen from 1919 and believed that, since Enniskillen was the centre of the most densely populated part of the diocese, the cathedral should be moved there. His plan met with considerable opposition, with the result that the church in Enniskillen became a second cathedral for the diocese in 1923, changing its name to St Macartin's. Thus, Clogher has two cathedrals dedicated to Macartan, the older site retaining the original spelling of his name. In due course, St Anne's was fitted with stalls and a second throne.

MacManaway also moved the see house from Clones to Enniskillen. During his time as a bishop, he lived at three different Fermanagh addresses. The cathedral hall at Enniskillen, built in the 1960s, eventually replaced the old synod hall at Clones. There was also a diocesan office in Enniskillen. In 1972, Bishop Richard Hanson retrieved many of the older records of the diocese from Armagh and deposited them in a new diocesan archive room in Clogher Cathedral. The archive was named in memory of Bishop Samuel Heaslett, a native of Tydavnet Parish and the first Anglican bishop of Tokyo. The records stored here include diocesan visitations going back to 1666.

## After the Second World War

Most of the church-building in Clogher was completed during the nineteenth century. The only churches erected in the last 50 years have been Dromore and Colaghty. Dromore was built in 1958 at a cost of £23,000; part of the earlier church had collapsed during a service. In June 1963, work on repairing Colaghty began, but became so thorough that, in effect, a new church was erected. It was dedicated that October, having cost £9,500. Many other churches had major repairs carried out in these years. Over £500 was spent at Monaghan and Mullaghdun in 1939, while Errigal Shanco was overhauled in 1940. Aghavea was reroofed in 1959 and both Muckno and Boho were reroofed in 1960.

Several new halls were built after the Second World War. A new hall at

Bishop James MacManaway 1923–43

The first Anglican bishop of Tokyo, the Rt Rev. Samuel Heaslett 1875–1947

An aerial view of St Macartin's Cathedral, Enniskillen

War graves stand as a memorial to both World Wars at St Tigernach's Irvinestown
DERMOTT DUNBAR

Rev James Douglas, Rector of Aghalurcher 1938–42, killed in Normandy 5 August 1944
CLOGHER DIOCESE

Rossorry, erected in memory of Archdeacon Pratt, was opened in 1961. In the same year the Carmichael Hall at Augher was extended at a cost of £2,000. After that, commodious new halls were built at Fintona, Fivemiletown, Kilskeery, Garvary, Ardess, Aghavea, Clabby and Tubrid. The former cornmarket building in Lisnaskea was also converted into a fine parish facility. In many other parishes, more modest work has provided good accommodation for parish development. The legacy of William Dent and Richard Pierce as diocesan architects is to be found in all corners of the diocese.

## Women in the Ministry

Clogher Diocese was to the fore with women in the ministry. In 1971, two women from the diocese, Miss Susan Austin of Smithborough and Mrs Norah Stevenson of Clogher, were licensed as lay readers. Women were able to serve on select vestries from 1920 and be returned for the Diocesan and General Synod from 1949. In due course they were able to serve as churchwardens. Mrs Ethel Magill and Mrs Bertha Bailey were the first female wardens in the cathedral parish in 1982. Mrs Isabel Nixon was the first woman to be ordained for the ministry in Clogher Diocese in 1994, while in 2011 the Rev. Helene Steed was the first woman to be appointed to the chapter of Clogher. The diocese was also active in appointing non-stipendiary clergy and has currently five cures operating in this way.

Clogher has been served by 12 bishops since its separation from Armagh. They include Charles Fredrick D'Arcy, who became archbishop of Armagh in 1920, and two bishops who were subsequently translated to Dublin. the Rt Rev. Alan Buchanan served in Clogher from 1958 to 1969 and the Rt Rev. Michael Jackson

Helene Steed running the Belfast marathon in May 2013. The Rev. Canon Helene T. Steed is the Rector and Rural Dean of Clones, appointed incumbent of the Clones Group of Parishes (Clones, Killeevan, Currin and Newbliss) in February 2008. She was the first woman to be appointed incumbent in the Diocese of Clogher and in 2011 was appointed Prebendary of Devenish, again the first woman in this Diocese on the chapter.

As in other dioceses throughout the North of Ireland parishes were affected by the Troubles. This memorial hangs in Muckross parish.
CLOGHER DIOCESE

Bishop Michael Jackson, 2002–11 opening the Clogher Hostel at Jacaranda Farm, Kaduna Diocese, Nigeria, November 26, 2009.
CLOGHER DIOCESE

FROM LEFT: Bishop Alan Buchanan 1959–68,
portrait by Peter Greenham
Bishop Brian Hannon 1986–2001, portrait by Derek Hill
Bishop John McDowell, 2011
CLOGHER DIOCESE

served from 2002 until 2011. Bishop Brian Hannon and Bishop Gordon McMullan, are happily still with us. Another recent bishop, the Rt Rev. Robert Heavenor (who served from 1973–80), lived to celebrate his hundredth birthday.

## New Millennium

The 'Macartan 1500' project in 2006, sponsored by the diocese, marked 1,500 years since Macartan's death. It successfully organised several events that linked the two traditions and culminated in a visit to Clogher by the archbishop of York, the Most Rev. Dr John Sentamu.

Twenty-fifth Anniversary Remembrance
service at St Macartin's, Enniskillen
CLOGHER DIOCESE

On November 8 2012, the twenty-fifth anniversary of the Enniskillen Remembrance Day bombing was marked with a service of remembrance in St Macartin's Cathedral Enniskillen, and was attended by the Taoiseach, Enda Kenny TD. The Cathedral was also the venue in June 2013 of the visit by the Queen and Prince Philip to mark the Queen's Diamond Jubilee. The service was followed by a historic walk across Church Street to St Michael's Roman Catholic church. St Patrick's Day 2013, was celebrated in Clogher Cathedral and concluded with Choral evensong led jointly by the choirs of the Cathedral group of parishes joined by St Patrick's Roman Catholic Church, Clogher.

Queen Elizabeth's visit to
St Macartin's, Enniskillen, 26 June 2012
CLOGHER DIOCESE

# PARISHES IN THE DIOCESE OF CLOGHER

### AGHADRUMSEE, CLOGH and DRUMSNAT

These three parishes straddle the border between Fermanagh and Monaghan.
*St Mark's Church, Aghadrumsee* was completed in 1820, when it was a district curacy to Clones. It was extended between 1834 and 1865.

*Holy Trinity Church, Clogh* began as a chapel of ease to Clones. The church, built in 1828, has a very fine stained-glass window by Clayton & Bell of London, which was rescued from a church in County Meath.

*St Molua's Church, Drumsnat* was built in 1808–11, near a fourteenth-century monastery. The cemetery contains the graves of Oscar Wilde's two half-sisters, Mary and Emily, who lost their lives in a fire in nearby Drumaconnor House in 1871.

St Mark,
Aghadrumsee
CLOGHER DIOCESE

### AGHALURCHER with COONEEN and MULLAGHFAD

Garter banners
relating to the
Brooke family with
that of the Knights
of Malta in the
centre
CLOGHER DIOCESE

The medieval parish of Aghalurcher was most extensive. It stretched from Upper Lough Erne to Kiltermon in Tyrone and was bisected by Aghavea Parish, except for a strip of mountain at Carrickawick. The old church, about two miles south of Lisnaskea, was in ruins by 1622 and services were transferred to a new chapel of ease at Lisnaskea.

*Colebrooke Church*, the present parish church, was built in 1767. It has strong links with the Brooke family and the church has numerous votive tablets and memorials to them. Their garter banners also hang in the nave.

*Cooneen Church* was built between 1871 and 1873, largely at the expense of the Rev. Butler Brooke. The writer Kathleen Foyle was a daughter of the Rev. Walter Brown (rector 1899–1923).

*Mullaghfad Church* was built between 1836 and 1841 at a cost of £900. The cemetery contains the graves of two B-Specials who were shot in the Mullaghfad ambush in 1921. Both Cooneen and Mullaghfad were added to Colebrooke in 1965.

St Ronan's, Colebrooke
DERMOTT DUNBAR

### AGHAVEA

Aghavea Parish centres on the town of Brookeborough in east Fermanagh. The Leslie family has played a significant role in the life of the parish. The Rev. John Leslie and his son the Rev. William Leslie held the living for over 90 years between them.

*Aghavea Church* was built in 1806, close to the site of an earlier building. The north vestry, designed by Alexander Hardy, was added in 1855. A commodious new parish hall was completed in 2002. The cemetery contains the graves of Jeremiah Jordan, Protestant Home Rule MP, and John Macken, poet and newspaper editor.

*Tattykeeran Church*, which was consecrated on 29 October 1873, was closed in 1992. Tattykeeran was originally a district within Aghavea Parish.

Church and new hall,
Aghavea, Brookeborough
DERMOTT DUNBAR

## BALLYBAY, CLONTIBRET and MUCKNO

These three parishes cover most of east Monaghan and include the towns of Ballybay and Castleblayney. Ballybay Parish was created in 1798 from Aughnamullen and Tullycorbet.

*Christ Church, Ballybay* opened in 1801. It was built at the expense of Henry Leslie, the owner of Ballybay. A gallery was added in 1816 and a new chancel and sanctuary were provided in 1881. A brass plaque commemorates Surgeon-Major T.H. Parke, Henry Morton Stanley's medical officer in Africa. A fine new stained-glass window dedicated to the memory of Dean and Mrs Mollan, designed by Meg Lawrence, was erected in 2005.

*St Maeldoid's Church, Castleblayney*

For a time *St Peter's Church, Laragh* was attached to Ballybay. This little church, affectionately called 'the tin church', was built in 1891 and finally closed in 1962. It is now being restored.

*Crossduff Church* (built in 1827) was also briefly attached to Ballybay. It closed in 1979 but has since been handsomely renovated to accommodate occasional services and the burial of the dead.

Tullycorbet Church, now disused, was built in 1831 in the townland of Terrygeely on the site of a previous church. It was closed in 1974. Tullycorbet gives its name to one of the prebendal stalls in the cathedral chapter.

*Clontibret Church* was built in 1842 and a gallery added shortly afterwards. The First World War memorial to three parishioners has an attractive ivy-leaf motif along its sides. The east window was erected in memory of the Rev. Henry Swanzy (1803–87) of Avelreagh House. Clontibret was a separate cure until 1952.

*Christ Church, Ballybay*
DERMOTT DUNBAR

*St Maeldoid's Church, Castleblayney*, which dates from 1811, was the third parish church for Muckno. The St Cecilia window in the nave (1923) is from the Harry Clarke studio in Dublin.

## CARRICKMACROSS and MAGHERACLOONE with ARDRAGH

St Fin Barre's Church, Carrickmacross
CLOGHER DIOCESE

This grouping at the very tip of south Monaghan covers a large area with a small Church of Ireland population. Carrickmacross parish today is an amalgam of Inniskeen, Donaghmoyne and Killany, whose churches closed in the 1970s.

*St Fin Barre's Church, Carrickmacross*, built in 1779 at the end of Main Street, replaced the old church of Magheross, just outside the town, whose tower is still intact. St Fin Barre's has a window by Harry Clarke and two others by James Powell.

*St Molua's Church, Magheracloone* was built in 1824 at a cost of £800 and enlarged in 1891.

*Ardragh Church* was built in 1868 by William Slater of London for the Shirley family of Lough Fea, who raised the chancel end by four feet to accommodate their family vault in the undercroft. It has four fine windows by Clayton & Bell. Ardragh was completely restored by Colonel E.C. Shirley in the early 1950s.

St Molua's Church, Magheracloone
CLOGHER DIOCESE

## CLEENISH and MULLAGHDUN

This parish originally centred on a monastic site on Cleenish Island in Lough Erne. It stretched from Lisbellaw to Belcoo, but was much reduced at a later date when the perpetual curacies of Mullaghdun and Lisbellaw were carved out of it.

*Cleenish Church, Bellanaleck* dates from about 1760. It was altered and given a new seating plan in 1869.

*Mullaghdun Church* was created as a district curacy out of Cleenish around 1817, when the church was built. The church was reroofed in 1939 and a new vestry and Sunday-school room were added in 1983. The pulpit and prayer desk, dedicated at the rehallowing in 1983, came from St Luke's, Dolphin's Barn, Dublin. The original pre-Reformation chapel of ease was at Templenaffrin, near Belcoo.

Mullaghdun church
CLOGHER DIOCESE

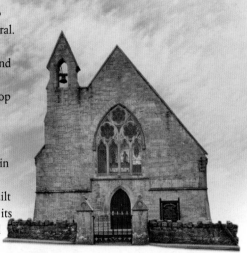

## CLOGHER CATHEDRAL GROUP of PARISHES

Clogher parish was staffed by the dean and two curates in earlier years. Today the group includes Augher and Newtownsavile, which were formerly chapels of ease to the cathedral. Portclare, part of Errigal Truagh Parish, was added to Clogher in 1965.

*St Macartan's Cathedral, Clogher* contains the bishop's throne and stalls for the chapter and prebends. The Clogh-Oir, from which the diocese takes its name, stands in the entrance foyer. Another stone there was dedicated in 2006 on the occasion of the visit of Archbishop John Sentamu.

*St Mark's Church, Augher.* Augher was originally a district curacy in Clogher Parish. Divine service was held in the market house before the present church was built in 1862–3. Tully House (built in 1867) was purchased for a rectory in 1891. It was sold in 1973 and a new rectory was built in 1981. The Carmichael Memorial Hall, which serves the church, was built in 1905.

Newtownsavile parish was carved out of Clogher as a perpetual curacy in 1816. The church was built then by John Bowden for the owner of the Cecil estate, the Rev. Francis Gervais. The parish obtained its first rector in 1872 and has been grouped with Augher since 1964, though not continuously. The old rectory was demolished in 2003 and a new house was built on its site.

*Errigal Portclare Church* was built in 1836 by John Corry Moutray for his tenantry at Favour Royal. There are several Moutray memorials in the church, including a lectern in memory of Stella Moutray, who died, heartbroken, when the family refused to countenance a romance she had with a local policeman. The original Telford organ is still in use.

*A view of the Cathedral grave yard from the oriel window*
DERMOTT DUNBAR

*St Mark's Church, Augher*
DERMOTT DUNBAR

## CLONES, CURRIN, KILLEVAN and NEWBLISS

This grouping nestles around the market town of Clones, in the north-western corner of County Monaghan. Clones is one of the oldest parishes in the diocese.

*St Tigernach's Church, Clones,* dedicated to the second bishop of Clogher, was built in 1823 and is possibly the fifth on the same site. It has a gallery on three sides and canonical stalls, reflecting its importance as a pro-cathedral during the union of Clogher Diocese with Armagh in the mid-nineteenth century. The pulpit, reading desk and font are fine items of sculpted marble, while the Walker organ dates from 1851. There is an ascension window by Miss Courtney (1910) as well as attractive box pews.

*St Andrew's Church, Currin* was built in 1810–12, although the parish dates from 1804. The church was restored and a chancel added in 1905–7. There is a memorial inside to Ernest Waldron King, assistant purser on the *Titanic*, who lost his life when that ship sank in 1912.

Killeevan Church, on a mound above the village, is a handsome building that dates from 1857. A history of Killeevan Parish was compiled by the Rev. V.H. Forster when he was rector in 1958.

*Newbliss Church,* built in 1841, was liberally endowed by Andrew Kerr of Newbliss House.

*Memorial to Ernest Waldron King purser on the* Titanic
CURRIN PARISH, SCOTSHOUSE

*St Tighernach's Church, Clones*
DERMOTT DUNBAR

## DERRYVULLEN SOUTH and GARVARY

These two parishes are on the eastern outskirts of Enniskillen and have been a joint cure since 1968. The 1622 visitation recorded that the church at Derryvullen was in poor repair. It was rebuilt in 1776 but abandoned in the mid-nineteenth century, when the site was moved to Mulrod.

The earl of Belmore laid the foundation stone for *St Tighernach's Church, Tamlaght* on 17 August 1852; it was consecrated two years later. The building has some notable stained-glass windows, mostly by Ward & Hughes of London. A new parochial hall was built in 1995. The parish was united with Garvary in 1968.

*Garvary Church* was built between 1865 and 1869 on a site given by Lord Belmore. The tower was added in 1871. Garvary Parish had been formed in 1865 from townlands taken from the parishes of Enniskillen, Derryvullen, Derrybrusk and Magheracross. The church's east window, depicting the ascension, was provided in 1910 by Mayer & Co. of Munich. Garvary Rectory, built at the expense of the earl of Belmore in 1867, was sold in 1973.

*Alms dish*
DERRYVULLEN SOUTH

*Garvary Church*
DERMOTT DUNBAR

## DERRYVULLEN NORTH and CASTLE ARCHDALE

The ancient parish of Derryvullen stretched from Irvinestown to Tamlaght. The old church at Irvinestown was rebuilt in 1734 and a square tower added by Dr Patrick Delaney. Only the tower now remains. Derryvullen Parish was divided into two halves by the Diocesan Synod in 1874.

*St Tighernach's Church, Irvinestown* was built at a cost of £2,300 in 1828. A vestry was added to it in 1895. The old glebe house at Tullyclea was sold to the Verschoyle family in 1896.

*St Patrick's Church, Castle Archdale* was built in 1905 to a plan by Sir Thomas Drew, replacing an earlier building. It was the gift of Edward Archdale. The interior has a finish inspired by the Arts and Crafts movement. The 'Te Deum' east window is the work of Alfred Child and Beatrice Elvery (Lady Glenavy) from the An Túr Gloine studio, while another (depicting St Patrick and St George) may also be attributed to Child. Some of the other windows are the work of Sarah Purser. The elaborate pulpit was carved principally by Henry Emery.

St Tigernach's Church, Irvinestown
DERMOTT DUNBAR

Arts and Crafts inspired pulpit at St Patrick's, Castle Archdale
CLOGHER DIOCESE

The window entitled 'Innocence walking in the fields of paradise' by the artist Wilhelmina Geddes, 1887–1955 in St Molaise's Church, Monea. Text on the window is 'Pure in Heart'.
DAVID LAWRENCE © RCB ARCHIVE

## DEVENISH and BOHO

Devenish Parish runs from the shore of Lough Erne across to Monea and Derrygonnelly, about eight miles from Enniskillen. The parish takes its name from the ancient monastic site on Devenish Island.

*St Molaise's Church, Monea* was built in 1890 to a plan by Sir Thomas Drew. It was financed by the Brien family of nearby Castletown Manor. The tower, which was part of the former church on the site, dates from 1803. The church contains an ancient stone window and a stone font taken from Devenish Abbey. There is a fine stained-glass window by Wilhemina Geddes in the north wall and two windows commemorating the late duke and duchess of Westminster. The window dedicated to Viola Westminster is by Alan Younger.

*Boho Church* was built in 1777 and restored in 1830. A medieval door case, which came from an earlier church nearby, is built into the west wall. The ninth-century high cross beside the Catholic church testifies to the antiquity of the parish.

## DONACAVEY and BARR

These two parishes in west Tyrone centre on the town of Fintona. The old church at Donacavey, about a mile north of the town, was destroyed in 1641. Its successor at Castletown was abandoned when the present church was built.

*Donacavey Church* was built in 1840 by William Farrell. Its impressive sanctuary window, in memory of Charles Eccles, is by Curtis, Ward & Hughes of London.

*Barr* was made a separate parish in 1843 and the church was built the same year. It was re-united with Fintona in 1924.

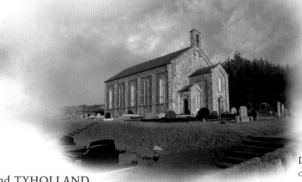

Donacavey Church
CLOGHER DIOCESE

## DONAGH, ERRIGAL TRUAGH and TYHOLLAND

These three country parishes in north Monaghan were once independent parishes in their own right, dating back to the fifteenth century. Tyholland Parish is of great antiquity and gives its name to one of the prebends in the chapter of Clogher.

*St Salvator's Church, Donagh*, on the Castle Leslie estate at Glaslough, was built in 1763.

*Errigal Truagh Church, Mullanacross* replaced an earlier building nearby, which stands in the centre of one of the oldest graveyards in the county.

The present *Errigal Church*, built in 1836, has an attractive east window, dedicated to the memory of Thomas Anketell of Dungillick. St Mellon's Well stands close to the church gate.

*Tyholland Church* was rebuilt in 1788.

St Salvator's Church, Donagh
CLOGHER DIOCESE

## DROMORE

This parish dates from the fourteenth century. The original church may have been at Kildrum, though by 1609 there was also a church in Dromore. It was replaced by a 1694 church, which was in turn replaced by a church built in 1846 by the Rev. Henry Lucas St George on the site of the present church. In 1954, one of the walls of this building collapsed during a service. Although no one was injured, the damage was so great that it was decided that a new building should be erected.

*Holy Trinity Church, Dromore* was consecrated by Archbishop Gregg in 1958 at a cost of £28,000. The stone used in the bell tower was brought from the recently demolished Aughentaine Castle, Fivemiletown.

Holy Trinity, Dromore
CLOGHER DIOCESE

## DRUMKEERAN, MUCKROSS and TEMPLECARNE

St John's Church, Muckross
CLOGHER DIOCESE

These three parishes between Kesh and Pettigo make up what was once, in area, the largest parish in the diocese. Drumkeeran was carved out of Templecarne, the original parish, in 1770. Muckross was then detached in 1865 as a perpetual curacy.

*Templecarne Church, Pettigo* was built in 1838 to a plan by William Farrell. A private chapel within Templecarne Parish was built at Castle Caldwell around 1716.

Drumkeeran Church was built in 1774. The former Vaughan Charter School at Tubrid is within the parish.

*St John's Church, Muckross*, on the shore of Lough Erne, dates from 1868.

## EMATRIS with ROCKCORRY, AGHABOG, AGHNAMULLEN and DRUM

This grouping, which contains three former distinct parish churches, is in west Monaghan, between Cootehill and Ballybay.

*St John the Evangelist's Church, Ematris* (Dartrey Church) was built in 1729 by the Dawson family. An 1887 stained-glass window by Clayton & Bell of London commemorates 'Augusta, Countess of Dartry'. There is an impressive First World War roll of honour in the church.

*St James's Church, Rockcorry*, which dates from *c.* 1855, has been united with Ematris since 1904.

Aghabog parish was formed in 1767 and was originally part of the greater Galloon parish. The old church was built in 1775 in the townland of Crover and replaced by the present Aghabog Church exactly a hundred years later.

*Christ Church, Aughnamullen* was built in the 1840s. It was enlarged and partly rebuilt by the Rev. Elias Tardy in 1864. Aughnamullen was once the largest parish in County Monaghan. Drum Church, just north of Cootehill, was built in 1828 and restored in 1902.

Christ Church, Aughnamullan
CLOGHER DIOCESE

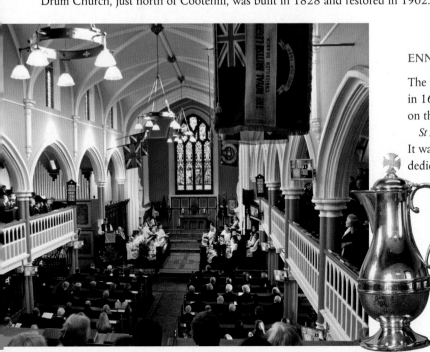

## ENNISKILLEN

The first church on the island of Enniskillen was built by Captain William Cole in 1627. It was replaced in 1841 by St Anne's Parish Church, which was built on the same site, although the original tower of Cole's church was retained.

*St Macartin's Cathedral, Enniskillen*, the new church, has galleries on three sides. It was constituted as a second cathedral for the diocese in 1923, when the dedication to St Macartin was invoked. Part of the nave was set aside as a chapel for the Royal Inniskilling Fusiliers in 1970. The cathedral has a fine Conacher organ (1936) and ten bells. A chalice made in 1638 and a flagon presented in 1707 form part of the communion plate in current use. The porch contains the interesting William Pockrich grave slab, while the stained glass includes a very early window by William Warrington. A new suite of offices with a cathedral hall was provided in 1964.

St Macartin's Cathedral, Enniskillen
CLOGHER DIOCESE

St John's Church, Fivemiletown
DERMOTT DUNBAR

## PORTORA ROYAL SCHOOL

*The School Chapel, Portora Royal School*, is in a converted loft above former stables. It contains a number of memorial plaques to teaching staff and several old Portorans. They include Paul Maxwell (pupil 1975–9), who was killed when Lord Mountbatten's boat was blown up at Mullaghmore, County Sligo, in August 1979.

## FIVEMILETOWN (with Kiltermon)

Fivemiletown was originally a perpetual curacy formed out of the parishes of Clogher and Aghalurcher. It obtained its own rector in 1870.

*St John's Church, Fivemiletown* was built by Margetson Armar in 1736, with a north aisle added in 1890. There are several votive tablets to the Montgomery and Burnside families. The 'Good Shepherd' east window (1927) in memory of Hugh De Fellenburg Montgomery is by A.K. Nicholson.

*Kiltermon Chapel of Ease* dates from 1841, while the parish burial ground dates from about 1740. A new parochial hall at Fivemiletown, costing £14,000 was opened in 1964.

## GALLOON, SALLAGHY and DRUMMULLY

The ancient parish of Galloon once stretched from the fringes of Lisnaskea to the outskirts of Cootehill. The old church on Galloon Island was in ruins in 1622. In the eighteenth century, a church at Drumswords served as the parish church.

*St Comgall's Church, Newtownbutler*, the present parish church, was built in 1821, replacing an earlier building on the same site.

Sallaghy Church was consecrated in 1843. It was served by district curates until 1958, when the first rector was appointed. A new hall costing £80,000 was opened in 1991.

*Drummully Church* was built in 1844. The original church, ruined by 1622, was replaced by one in Newtownbutler and then by another at Drumcrin. It served as the parish church from 1773 until the present church was built, a mile north of the original site.

St Comgall, Newtownbutler
DERMOTT DUNBAR

## GARRISON, SLAVIN, BELLEEK and KILTYCLOGHER

This union is situated in west Fermanagh and north Leitrim.

Garrison was originally part of Devenish and became a perpetual curacy in 1827.

*Garrison Church* was erected at that time with a grant of £738 from the Board of First Fruits.

*Slavin Church* was originally a district curacy in Inishmacsaint. Garrison and Slavin were united in 1891 and added to Belleek in 1951. Kiltyclogher, previously in the diocese of Kilmore, was added to the union in 2002.

*Belleek Church* was built in 1875 and extended in 2009, when a new chancel was provided. The three-light east window by David Esler was dedicated at the same time. Robert Williams Armstrong (1824–84), the architect and co-founder of Belleek Pottery (1857), is buried in the churchyard.

*Kiltyclogher Church*, built by Charles Henry Tottenham, dates from c. 1860.

The 2009 Esler window showing the potter's wheel
DERMOTT DUNBAR

This cross hanging in Belleek Church was a personal gift and a symbol of peace from Dr Finn, a member of the Roman Catholic Community, in 1972, at a time of great unrest in Northern Ireland.
DERMOTT DUNBAR

## INISHMACSAINT

This parish takes its name from the island in Lough Erne now joined to the shore by a causeway. The ruins of a church measuring 60 feet by 23 feet stand here, as does an impressive 14-foot high cross. The island church was replaced by a building at Drumenagh or Churchill in 1688; the present church was its successor.

St Ninnidh's Church, Derrygonnelly was built in 1831 and enlarged in 1871. It has stained-glass windows by Wilhemina Geddes and David Esler. The former rectory at Benmore was built in 1829. The Misses Maclean began lace-making classes here and developed the high-quality Inishmacsaint lace popular with the British royal family about a hundred years ago.

St Ninidh's, Derrygonnelly
DERMOTT DUNBAR

## KILSKEERY and TRILLICK

These two parishes lie along the Tyrone/Fermanagh border. The old church at Kilskeery was burnt in 1537. It was in the centre of the old graveyard in the village, where its successor also stood.

The present Kilskeery Church was built on a new site in 1790, at the expense of Archdeacon Hastings, then rector. The present tower dates from 1830. The sanctuary window by Beatrice Elvery (Lady Glenavy) is dedicated to the memory of the Rev. John Grey Porter.

Trillick Church was built in 1872, when Trillick was carved out of Kilskeery and became a separate parish. The church was provided by the Archdale family, heirs to the Mervyns of Castle Mervyn, the estate where the village is situated.

Kilskeery Church
DERMOTT DUNBAR

Trillick Church
DERMOTT DUNBAR

## LACK or COLAGHTY

This parish was created around 1835, from townlands taken from the three parishes of Magheraculmoney, Drumkeeran and Langfield.

Before Lack Church was built in 1844, services were held in the schoolhouse in Lack and at Edenaveigh Chapel of Ease. The chancel was restored in 1913. In 1963, the church was substantially restored and is now virtually a new building.

## LISBELLAW with COOLBUCK

Lisbellaw Church was built by Sir Ralph Gore (later Lord Ross) in 1764 as a chapel of ease to Cleenish. It was extended in 1793 and a bell tower added in 1894, the gift of John Grey Vesey Porter of Belle Isle. The main body of the church was enlarged and altered between 1841 and 1854.

Lisbellaw became a district curacy in 1838 and achieved parochial status in 1873. The impressive Venetian window in the chancel is by Jones & Willis of Liverpool. The church's pipe organ is a memorial to Dean Robert McTighe.

Coolbuck Mountain Church was originally a school where divine service was held. It became a church around 1870.

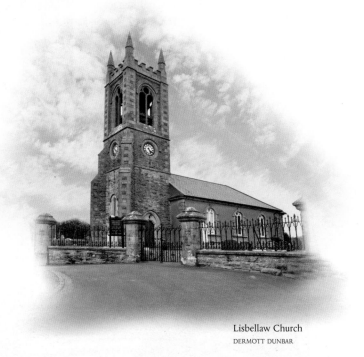

Lisbellaw Church
DERMOTT DUNBAR

## LISNASKEA

Lisnaskea was originally in the extensive parish of Aghalurcher.

*Holy Trinity Church, Lisnaskea* was built in 1852 to replace the old 1814 chapel of ease in the town. There is a chalice dated 1690 and a paten dated 1692. The latter had been used in the church's predecessor, Sir James Balfour's plantation church (1622), also at Lisnaskea. In 1971 an east window and other significant gifts were provided. A carved oak reredos in the right aisle was designed by Denis O'D. Hanna. The church is approached through elegant stone piers with lanterns surmounted on the capstones.

The medieval *Aghalurcher Church* lies just a mile south of the town.

Holy Trinity, Lisnaskea
DERMOTT DUNBAR

## MAGHERACROSS

Magheracross centres on the Fermanagh village of Ballinamallard. It is in area one of the smallest parishes, but in population one of the largest, in the diocese. The parish was originally part of Derryvullen and was for a time a joint cure with Kilskeery.

*Magheracross Church* dates from the mid-nineteenth century, except for the tower, which dates from 1785. There is a handsome stained-glass window depicting David and his sling, made by W.F. Clokey of Belfast, and a memorial tablet to Sir Alexander Armstrong, explorer and surgeon. The Archdale Memorial Hall, across the road from the church, dates from 1892. This building was given a major overhaul in 1982.

Magheross, Ballinamallard
DERMOTT DUNBAR

## MAGHERACULMONEY

The medieval parish of Magheraculmoney is situated around and north of Kesh in the north-east of County Fermanagh. It originally included Drumkeeran and Clogh, which were disannexed in 1793 and 1845 respectively.

White Island and Boa Island are both in the parish. The former has a ruined church with a Romanesque door and a carved head as well as six sculpted stone figures. The ancient churchyard of Caldragh is situated on Boa Island, where a causeway crosses to and from the island across Lough Erne. The double-headed Janus figure in the cemetery is a national monument.

At Kiltierney, in Castle Archdale deerpark, are the ruins of an early monastery and a passage grave.

*St Mary's Church, Magheraculmoney* was built in 1767. Its impressive glebe house was built 13 years later. The church's north aisle, the work of Welland and Gillespie, was added in 1867. There is a three-light window by Mayer & Co. of Munich in the sanctuary.

St Mary's, Ardess, Magheraculmoney
DERMOTT DUNBAR

Janus figure, Boa Island
DERMOTT DUNBAR

## MAGUIRESBRIDGE and DERRYBRUSK

These two parishes in mid-Fermanagh lie between Enniskillen and Lisnaskea. Maguiresbridge began as a chapel of ease in Aghalurcher Parish. Derrybrusk is one of the smallest parishes in the diocese, but also one of the oldest.

*Christ Church, Maguiresbridge* dates from 1841. The north transept and vestry were added in 1862. A votive tablet commemorates Lieutenant-Colonel John J.S. Irvine of nearby Drumgoon Manor.

*St Michael's Church, Derrybrusk*, originally a schoolhouse, was consecrated in 1886. There is a window in the nave by Beatrice Elvery and two brass plaques dedicated to the memory of the Porter family of nearby Belle Isle. The ruined ancient parish church in the townland of Fyagh has a well-preserved perpendicular east window.

Christ Church, Maguiresbridge
DERMOTT DUNBAR

## MONAGHAN, TYDAVNET and KILMORE

*St Patrick's Church, Monaghan* is the largest church in the diocese. It was built in 1835 to a plan by William Farrell, beside its predecessor, which was subsequently demolished. An earlier building at Rackwallace had served as a parish church before that. There are galleries on all three sides, with a recessed chancel containing a window dedicated to the memory of the third Lord Rossmore.

The church has several particularly fine tablets, including sculptures in relief by Thomas Kirk and his son Joseph R Kirk.

*St Davnet's Church, Tydavnet* is now sited at Bellanode, north of Monaghan. The old church and its graveyard stood at the centre of Tydavnet village. In 1754, the present church was built in a commanding setting at Bellanode from stones carted from the original site.

It was enlarged in 1830 at a cost of £471. The elegant clock in the tower was provided by the Wood-Wright family of Gola. The adjacent schoolhouse, now used as a hall, was built in 1826 but rebuilt and enlarged in 1903 in memory of Mrs Esther Moorehead.

Kilmore, to the west of Bellanode, is one of the oldest parishes in the diocese. *Kilmore Church* was built in 1788. The nearby former glebe house was built in 1792. Kilmore had a chapel of ease at Stranooden, which closed in 1978.

vnet's, Tydavnet
CLOGHER DIOCESE

St Patrick's Church, Monaghan
DERMOTT DUNBAR

eaders taking part in the Bible marathon at ossorry are from left, Rev. Sam McGuffin, Nick Hambly, John Houston, Neville Gamble, Dorothy lson and Rev. Arthur Barrett with Emma rwin with Alexandra and Jenna Wilson.
CLOGHER DIOCESE

## ROSSORRY

According to tradition, the original church at Old Rossorry was built in 1084 and dedicated to St Fanchea. The district was also served by the monastery at Lisgoole Abbey, which was destroyed by fire in 1360.

*Rossorry Church*, built on a new site in 1840, replaced the church at Old Rossorry, which was proving inadequate for the growing population. The new church was built to a design by William Hagerty and restored by an anonymous benefactor in 1911. The tower was added in 1915 in memory of Robert Johnston of Lisgoole. The 'Te Deum' window in memory of Alfred Johnston is by Sarah Purser. A commodious new parochial hall was built in 1961 in memory of Archdeacon Pratt, nicknamed 'Skip the Litany Pratt' as he invariably left out the litany if he was in a hurry. No trace now exists of the former church at Old Rossorry as the stones were drawn away to build a stable at the glebe house.

## TEMPO and CLABBY

These two rural parishes in east Fermanagh were once part of Enniskillen parish.

*Tempo Church* was built between 1780 and 1788 as a chapel of ease, becoming a separate parish upon disestablishment in 1870. The three-light east window commemorates Sir William Emerson Tennent of nearby Tempo Manor.

*St Margaret's Church, Clabby* was built between 1864 and 1870 by the Rev. J.G. Porter, with William Welland as the architect. The resurrection window by Ward & Hughes of London has five lights, while a window of similar date in the nave has three. Both were the gift of Archdeacon Francis James Hurst around 1885.

Tempo Church
DERMOTT DUNBAR

Detail from a window in St Michael's Church, Trory
CLOGHER DIOCESE

## TRORY AND KILLADEAS

This union north-east of Enniskillen comprises Trory, which was originally part of the medieval parish of Devenish, and Killadeas, which was carved out of Trory in 1866. The earliest reference to a church here comes from the Devenish vestry book of 1743, where mention is made of 'thatching the chapel at Trory'.

*St Michael's Church, Trory* was built between 1778 and 1788. Trory and Killadeas were taken from Devenish and constituted as a new parish in September 1778. Thornhill House served as the rectory between 1880 and 1921, when the parish was grouped with Enniskillen. Trory again became a separate parish in 1955 and the following year a new rectory was built at Rossfad. The parish was grouped with Killadeas in 1980.

*The Priory Church, Killadeas*, (left) endowed by the Irvine family of the Manor House, was built in 1881.

# The Dioceses of Derry and Raphoe

## TWO POLITICAL JURISDICTIONS, ONE KINGDOM OF GOD

Derry and Raphoe is one of four united dioceses in the Church of Ireland that have parishes in both Northern Ireland and the Republic of Ireland.

This means that we operate with two currencies, sterling and euro; we work with two education systems and with two child protection systems. While this complexity is an administrative challenge, it can also be a helpful reminder that the Kingdom of God transcends political boundaries and human institutions.

We are conscious of our missionary heritage and of the rich legacy of St Columba, who was born here. This legacy is a formative influence on our calling to be outwardly-focussed and actively engaged in our local community and in the wider world.

Our diocesan vision, which each parish works out in its own particular context, is *Transforming Community Radiating Christ.*

For us, *Transforming Community* means, firstly, that every parish must be a community in which those who belong to it are being transformed by our faith in Christ, learning, growing, developing our-God-given gifts, loving, serving and caring – and that the local church must be a means of providing us with ways to grow.

Secondly, each parish is looking out beyond its doors as we ask ourselves, 'What does God want us to do engage constructively in this neighbourhood, that is, *Transforming Community*? Parishes are actively involved in their local communities in many creative ways.

*Radiating Christ* means that what motivates us is the love of God. We are a people whose motivation is spiritual and whose desire is to honour Christ in serving others.

We have three additional values that further shape our diocesan focus and culture.

### We seek growth

We believe that church growth is possible. *Qualitative* growth usually comes first – that is, growth in welcome and compassion, in prayer and spirituality, in love and serving, in giving and caring. This kind of growth will often be followed by *quantitative* growth, as people are attracted by a faith community where they can see that lives are being changed, needs are being met and God is being encountered.

### We serve in teams

Clergy are a vital part of our churches' life. Their leadership is valued and their ministry is greatly appreciated and needed. However, we also take seriously the ministry of all of God's people, and we recognise the importance of serving in teams. We believe it is vital that all of us discover and use our God-given gifts, sharing and combining the various strengths God has provided us with.

### We encourage leaders

These are demanding and challenging times in which to lead, especially in churches. So we recognise the need to provide encouragement and support for those in positions of leadership, both lay-leaders and clergy. Rather than finding fault with our leaders, our aim is to strengthen and build them up in their God-given leadership role, so that the church and the community may benefit from more effective leadership and church life.

KEN DERRY AND RAPHOE

Doey Village, Horne Head,
Altantic Drive, Donegal
SCENIC IRELAND

# ST COLUMB'S CATHEDRAL DERRY

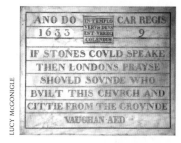

LUCY MCGONIGLE

In 1164, the Great Church was founded in Derry. This was destroyed in 1568, and replaced with the present cathedral in the parish of Templemore. In 1628 the foundations of this new cathedral were laid on a new site at the summit of the hill within the city walls. The builder was William Parrott, who had been commissioned by the Honourable the Irish Society. It was finished in 1633, having cost £4,000, and dedicated to St Columb. Its completion is marked by an inscription from the foundation stone, which can be seen in the porch. This reads:

If stones could speak then London's prayse should sound,
Who built this church and cittie from the ground.

LUCY MCGONIGLE

St Columb's was the first cathedral to be built in Ireland following the Reformation. It is in the planters' Gothic style. It is approached through the grand gates, which were erected in 1933 to mark the building's tercentenary. Composed of rubble schist walls with sandstone trim to the windows and doors, the cathedral has an aisled nave and a short chancel. The tower and spire date from 1822. The crenellated parapets of the aisles and clerestory are an interesting architectural feature.

The chapter house, built in 1910 by Thomas Drew, contains a museum with artefacts from the time of the siege of Derry. The cathedral possesses the oldest peal of bells in Ireland – one bell dates from 1614 – and the Promise Chalice from 1613, so called because it was sent from London on the basis of a promise that the cathedral would be built.

St Columb's Cathedral was at the centre of the siege of Derry in 1689. In the porch is a mortar shell fired at the besieged defenders, offering terms of surrender, which were not accepted. A spire of wood covered with lead originally surmounted the tower, but the lead was used for bullets during the siege.

The nave of seven bays has a fine hammer-beam ceiling dating from 1823. In the north-west corner of the north aisle is the baptistery, which commemorates the hymn writer Mrs Cecil Frances Alexander and her husband. The canopy over the bishop's throne dates from 1861 and contains a Chinese Chippendale chair from around 1765.

Over the last 50 years major restoration has been carried out. In 2011, during the incumbency of Very Rev. Dr William Morton, extensive renovations were completed. The Cathedral today plays a major role in the civic life of the whole community, hosting annual services for the Apprentice Boys of Derry as well as interdenominational events with St Eugene's Roman Catholic Cathedral.

One of the keys that locked the city gates now in St Columb's archive
LUCY MCGONIGLE

Carved pew end in St Columb's Cathedral
LUCY MCGONIGLE

SOUTH

Plate 82.

James Fittler Sculp.

PROSPECT OF THE CATHEDRAL CHURCH OF LONDON-DERRY. IRELAND.

# The United Dioceses of Derry & Raphoe

DAVID CROOKS

The united dioceses of Derry and Raphoe are situated in the north and west of Ulster, straddling the border between Northern Ireland and the republic. The north-west coast of Ireland in both Counties Donegal and Derry contains some of the finest scenery in Ireland. The main centre of population is the city of Londonderry, and there are several large towns including Coleraine, Omagh and Letterkenny. Until recent times, a major source of employment was the textile industry, which has almost disappeared.

## The Golden Age

The early Irish church, following St Patrick's mission, was organised in monasteries, which were established all over the country between roughly AD 450 and AD 800. Many of these were great seats of learning, such as Clonmacnoise, Glendalough and Movilla. The abbots were the heads of the monastic communities, and bishops, whose function was to ordain the clergy, were subordinate to them.

Stained-glass window in St Columb's Cathedral, Derry, celebrating the life of Columb.
LUCY McGONIGLE

In June 2013, a boat set sail from Iona for the Homecoming of Columcille (St Columb). The Return of Colmcille flooded the streets with contemporary tales of the city that has grown up since the Saint's departure in 547AD.

### St Columba and His Followers

SEAN GREEN TOURISM IRELAND

Outstanding amongst the great figures of the early Celtic church was St Columba. Columba founded a monastery in Derry (Doire Cholmcille, 'the oak grove of the dove of the church'), around AD 546. This institution is considered the origin of the diocese of Derry. The diocese of Raphoe originated in and was named after the huts inhabited by Columba's monks there – Ráth Bhoth, 'the fortress of the huts'. Columba's biographer, St Adamnan or Eunan (died 704), wrote his biography.

Attempts to form extra-monastic structures were made in the north-west in this period. St Eugene founded a 'diocese' at Ardstraw in County Tyrone around AD 540, but this was in no way similar to a modern diocese. Rather, it was an early example of the emergence of a bishop from the monastery, taking charge of territory. This 'diocese' lasted until around 1150, when Maurice O'Coffey moved the see to Maghera. The see was transferred to Derry around 1280. Meanwhile, for over a century before that, bishops had been based in the great abbey at Derry. The first of these was Flahertach O'Brolchain, around 1158.

## St Columba AD 521–97

*In the roll-call of God's sons, sounding sweet and solemn,*
*Name we mid his chosen ones, Ulster's own Saint Columb.*

These lines from a hymn by Mrs Cecil Frances Alexander call to mind one of the great figures of the early Celtic church. St Columba, the 'dove of the church', was born of royal patronage at Gartan in County Donegal in AD 521. He was educated at Temple Douglas, near Kilmacrennan, and at Clonard Monastery in County Meath. He was duly ordained a priest.

In the age of saints and scholars, Columba founded many monasteries. His greatest was at Derry, which he founded around AD 546. He also founded religious communities at Kells, Durrow and Swords. Many of these would have been small foundations. The monastic buildings on each site would have included a church, a dormitory, a refectory and a library, and there may have been a small farm.

Columba was very keen on copying books. He borrowed a Latin psalter from St Finnian of Moville and copied it. Finnian demanded both the original book and Columba's copy, claiming it on the grounds that, 'as to every cow belongs its calf, so to every book belongs its copy'. Columba refused to part with his copy. He sought the aid of Diarmit, king of Meath, who ruled against him. Being an impetuous man Columba gathered his clan and, with the help of the king of Connaught, attacked Diarmit. In the ensuing battle near Sligo, 3,000 men were slain. Columba felt so remorseful about the consequences of his impetuosity that he vowed to bring to Christ as many people as had lost their lives in the battle.

Columba resolved to leave Ireland forever. He and his 12 companions sailed in a curragh from Derry in AD 563 and continued their journey until Ireland was out of sight. They arrived in Iona, where they established a monastery. This became the base for the conversion of the Pictish people of Scotland.

Columba did return to Ireland a number of times, however. He attended the Convention of Drumceatt near Limavady in AD 575, held to sort out a dispute about whether the kingdom of Dalriada in Argyll should pay tax to the Irish king, and to determine the place and position of the bards.

Columba's long life ended on 9 June 597. That evening, he was copying Psalm 34, verse 10: 'They who seek the Lord shall want no manner of thing that is good.' He handed the work to his companion Baithin to finish. He died at the altar of his chapel that night.

In fulfilling his vow, Columba and his followers had begun the process that would lead to the eventual reconversion of Europe after the fall of the Roman Empire.

In June 1963, to mark the 1,400th anniversary of Columba's departure to Iona, a series of celebrations took place. The main events were a great service at Gartan, attended by about 10,000 people, and a voyage to Iona by curragh, rowed by 12 people. There was also a great service in the abbey at Iona, and a ship, the *Devonia*, was chartered to take pilgrims to the island. A large number of people in Derry and Raphoe and Iona planned the celebrations, under the leadership of the rector of Conwall and Gartan, Archdeacon Louis Crooks. The bishop was Rt Rev. Charles Tyndall. The fourteenth centenary of the death of Columba was also observed with celebrations in 1997.

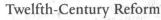

S. COLUMBA AT DRUMCEATT A.D.575
MEMORY OF WILLIAM PHILLIPS J.P.
THIS WINDOW WAS ERECTED BY HIS WIDOW

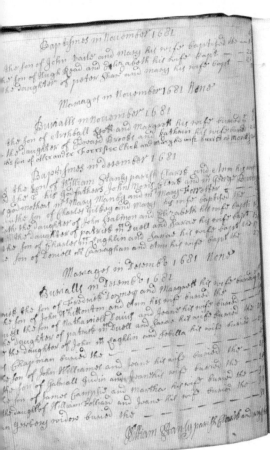

1681 Register of Births, Deaths and Marriages
ST COLUMB'S CATHEDRAL

## Twelfth-Century Reform

The dioceses of Derry and Raphoe, as we now know them, were formed at the Synod of Ráth Breasail in 1111. Derry Diocese was assigned most of what is now County Derry in the territory of Oriel as far east as the River Bann, along with the Inishowen Peninsula in Donegal, the western part of what is now County Tyrone and the parishes of Clonleigh and Donaghmore in east Donegal. Raphoe Diocese was assigned the territory of Cenél Conaill in Aileach in what is now County Donegal, except for the extreme south of the area, which went to Clogher Diocese.

## Post-Reformation Times and the Plantation

From the Synod of Ráth Breasail until the Reformation in the sixteenth century, the Irish church came under papal jurisdiction. At the Reformation, the church regained her independence, though for a century after that some bishops – including William McTaggart, bishop of Derry until 1609, and Donald McCongall, bishop of Raphoe in the 1560s – remained Roman Catholic. McCongall attended the Council of Trent in 1563, one of three Irish bishops to do so.

Though the Irish church originated in the mission of St Patrick some 1,200 years earlier, in the period following the plantation of Ulster from 1609, the church became much more anglicised. Pre-Reformation clergy were Irish; they spoke Irish and had Irish names. After the Reformation, and even more so after the plantation, the clergy were mostly Englishmen.

Detail of Reformation head
on Kilmacrennan pulpit

## The Plantation of Ulster

In the years following the 1607 Flight of the Earls, Scottish and English settlers planted Ulster. In 1600, Elizabeth I had sent Sir Henry Docwra to Ulster. Docwra chose Derry as a suitable location for a settlement because of the potential harbour. He befriended Cahir O'Doherty, son of the chieftain of Inishowen, who fought on his side against Henry Og MacShane O'Neill. For this he was made lord of Inishowen and awarded the forts at Buncrana and Burt. In 1606, Docwra left Derry, disappointed at his failure to establish a settlement. His successor George Paulet fell out with Cahir O'Doherty, who raised an army and sacked Culmore Fort. He went on to capture Derry, for which he was condemned as a traitor. In the end, O'Doherty was defeated and he was killed in 1608. It seemed to be the end of the attempt to establish a new city at Derry.

James I had since come to the throne and was determined to make another attempt to garrison Derry. He began the plantation of Ulster in earnest by sending so-called 'undertakers' to Ulster from Scotland and England. The planted counties were Donegal, Derry, Armagh, Tyrone, Fermanagh and Cavan. The land was to be divided into lots, varying in size from 1,000 to 3,000 acres, and allocated to undertakers who had taken the oath of supremacy. Most of the native Irish chieftains were expelled, but many Irish remained and worked for the planters on the land.

The plantation led to the creation of the new city of Londonderry and the county of Coleraine, which stretched along the north coast as far as Lough Foyle. In 1618, the walls were built. St Columb's Cathedral was erected between 1628 and 1633.

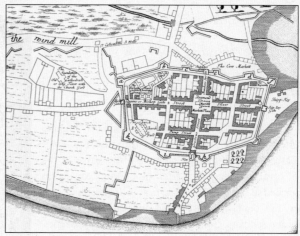

St Patrick's, Kilrea

In 1613, Londonderry was granted a charter by King James I, and the Honourable the Irish Society was formed to promote religion and trade. The medieval guilds came over and established themselves in the county. For example, the Worshipful Companies of Mercers, Masons, Cooks and Broderers (embroiderers) were based in Kilrea, and the Fishmongers' Company settled in Ballykelly.

Meanwhile, conditions for the native Irish deteriorated and became so bad that they rose up in a bloody rebellion in 1641. During and following this, many churches were damaged or destroyed. However, by that time the plantation had taken root, and to this day the planters' descendants continue to live in Ulster.

### John Bramhall (1594–1663)

Up until the time of the plantation of Ulster, conditions in the Irish church were in a sorry state. Churches were in bad condition or in ruins, and people were slack in matters of faith and discipline. The sudden surge in the population following the plantation brought about the building of whole new towns, especially in areas where the various London guilds established themselves. New churches were needed and fast. It was John Bramhall, bishop of Derry from 1634, who consecrated the new cathedral of his diocese. At the time, the population of about a thousand people had only the old Augustinian monastery church for a place of worship. The new cathedral, completed in 1633, fulfilled the people's need for a place of worship. Bramhall set about building new churches and rectories for the clergy all over his diocese. He also worked to ensure that the clergy had adequate stipends. In seven years, he built up capital for the diocese, which yielded the incredible sum of £40,000 per annum.

Bramhall was forced to flee Derry during the 1641 Rebellion. He was to spend the next years in the Netherlands. During this period he produced many great books in support of Anglican polity.

After the restoration of the monarchy in 1660, Bramhall returned to Ireland as primate, whereupon he set out to reorganise the Irish church. One of his first tasks was to consecrate 12 new bishops to fill the sees that had been vacated during the 1641 Rebellion and the Cromwellian period.

A painting by John Noah Gossett, of Derry and the River Foyle with St Columb's on the left and the old wooden bridge (demolished 1863) on the right.
HERITAGE AND MUSEUM SERVICE OF DERRY CITY COUNCIL

## The Siege of Derry 1689

There were three sieges of Derry during the seventeenth century. The first during the 1641 Rebellion, and the second during the civil war of the 1650s. The third and most significant was in 1689.

The Stuart King James II came to the English throne in 1685. Where Protestants had previously held all positions of power, James proceeded to replace them with Roman Catholics as quickly as possible. This caused alarm in England, as it was thought that he was undermining the Protestantism established there.

In Ireland, the people saw in James an opportunity to make a new attempt to gain independence. This raised fears among Protestants that the Irish were going to attack them in a rebellion similar to that of 1641. Things came to a head when, in December 1688, the regiment of the Roman Catholic earl of Antrim arrived in Derry to replace the largely Protestant garrison there. They were barred by 13 Apprentice Boys, who closed the Ferry Quay Gate in the city walls against them. The other three gates were closed soon afterwards.

Meanwhile, James was deposed and replaced by William III and Mary II. He fled to France but, with French troops in tow, landed at Kinsale in early 1689.

Lieutenant-Colonel Robert Lundy was appointed governor of Derry in March 1689, having taken an oath of allegiance to William and Mary. One of King James's army captains, Richard Hamilton, clashed with Lundy's forces in a skirmish just south of Derry. Lundy's forces were so easily defeated that Lundy was suspected of having Jacobite sympathies. He later defected and was replaced as governor by Rev. George Walker. Lundy later became governor of Gibraltar.

James arrived in Derry on 18 April. His calls for allegiance were met with shouts of 'No surrender!' Resistance hardened and the siege defences were strengthened. The Protestants held out in increasingly poor conditions for 105 days. There is a list of the items available to them for food in the chapter house of St Columb's Cathedral. The menu consisted of horses, dogs, cats, rats and mice. One pound of horse flesh cost 1s 8d, one quarter of a dog 5s 6d, a cat 4s 6d, a rat 1s and a mouse 2d. Provisions could not be brought into the city because a boom of timbers had been placed across the River Foyle. The citizens were rallied and encouraged by the sermons of Governor Walker in the cathedral.

When three ships laden with provisions, led by the *Mountjoy*, finally broke through the boom under heavy Jacobite gunfire James's army beat a retreat for Dublin. The Jacobite cause in Ireland came to an end with James's defeat at the battle of the Boyne on 1 July (12 July after adjustment to the Gregorian calendar) 1690. In Scotland, Bonnie Prince Charlie attempted to maintain the cause well into the eighteenth century, but it all ended at Culloden in 1746.

Today the siege of 1689 is commemorated by the Apprentice Boys of Derry in two annual events, the 'closing of the gates' and the burning of Lundy's effigy in December, and the 'relief of Derry' in August.

Londonderry depicted under siege

INSET ABOVE: Governor Walker
ABOVE: This siege cannon ball was fired from the city during the Siege of 1689. It has a stone centre covered in lead as lead was in short supply.
ST COLUMB'S CATHEDRAL

FAR LEFT: A coin celebrating the ascension of William and Mary to the throne
ORANGE ORDER

ORANGE ORDER

## The Seventeenth Century

Throughout the seventeenth century, the British Isles experienced much turbulence as Roman Catholicism and Protestantism vied with each other to gain or regain control and influence. The siege of Derry in 1689 was a pivotal turning point in these events.

This period can be characterised by a number of great figures associated with Derry and Raphoe.

### John Leslie (1571–1671)

John Leslie was born in Aberdeen in 1571. He spent much of his youth on the continent, where he was ordained. He was consecrated bishop of the Isles in 1628, and was translated to Raphoe in 1633. He built Raphoe Castle as much for defence against the rebels as for living in, and from there he managed to hold out successfully against the 1641 Rebellion. He was a staunch defender of the *Book of Common Prayer* during the Commonwealth, which made him subject to attack from that quarter too, but again his defences in Raphoe Castle proved impregnable. Leslie became bishop of Clogher at the age of 90 in 1661, and died in office five weeks before his one-hundredth birthday. Also a fine scholar, he was one of the most colourful characters of the period.

Raphoe Castle

### William King (1650–1729)

William King held incumbencies in the diocese of Tuam and in Dublin before becoming bishop of Derry in 1691. He was a staunch Williamite. In support of William's cause, he wrote *The State of the Protestants in Ireland under King James's Government*. After the battle of the Boyne in 1690, William promoted him to the see of Derry. He found the diocese in a miserable condition. During his 13 years in the see, King rebuilt and repaired churches and established the diocesan library, which today is housed at Magee College and possesses some fine seventeenth- and eighteenth-century tomes. He became archbishop of Dublin in 1702. The Archbishop King's Chair of Divinity in the University of Dublin was established in his memory.

## The Earl Bishop: Hon. Frederick Augustus Hervey
### 1730–1803

Hon. Frederick Augustus Hervey, fourth earl of Bristol, was the third son of John, Lord Hervey, whose father, also named John, had been created Baron Hervey of Ickworth in Suffolk in 1703 and earl of Bristol in 1714. Frederick inherited the title upon the death of his brother George in December 1779. He was educated at Westminster School and Corpus Christi College, Cambridge. In 1747, he enrolled at Lincoln's Inn to study law.

Hervey was ordained for Ely Diocese in 1754. In 1763, he was appointed chaplain to King George III. He was appointed bishop of Cloyne in 1767 by the favour of his brother, George, earl of Bristol. However, Hervey was anxious to become bishop of the wealthy see of Derry. He achieved his ambition upon the death of Bishop Barnard in 1768.

Frederick Hervey was an eccentric and colourful character. At first, he governed the diocese of Derry conscientiously. He was ahead of his time in that he favoured Roman Catholic emancipation. He gave £200 towards the building of the Long Tower Chapel in Derry. He sympathised with the Presbyterians, who also suffered religious discrimination.

Hervey had two great passions, building and travel, and he was a patron of art and literature. He built and enlarged several churches in Derry Diocese. He also built Downhill House with Mussenden Temple, overlooking Lough Foyle. Another of his great houses was Ballyscullion near Bellaghy, the classical facade of which is at St George's Church in Belfast. He erected a spire at Derry Cathedral, but this had to be demolished a few years later, as it was too heavy to be supported by the tower. As well as creating several fine buildings in Derry, he erected a bridge over the River Foyle. All this building activity earned him the title 'the Edifying Bishop'.

Hervey travelled more and more widely on the continent collecting art. The Bristol hotels in many European cities are named after him. His marriage to Elizabeth broke down, he quarrelled with her incessantly and did not see her for 20 years before her death. Bishop Hervey was absent from the diocese for the last 11 years of his episcopate. He died of gout at Albano in Italy on 8 July 1803.

Mussenden Temple overlooking Downhill, County Londonderry
DERMOTT DUNBAR

## The Eighteenth Century

The eighteenth century produced even more famous men, sons of Derry and Raphoe who contributed to worldwide Anglicanism as it spread beyond these shores.

### George Berkeley (1685–1753)

George Berkeley was one of the great thinkers of his day. Born at Thomastown, Co. Kilkenny, and educated at Trinity College Dublin, he was ordained. During an illustrious career, he served as Dean of Derry, 1724–34 (as seen in this painting). His philosophical writings earned him great fame during his lifetime and afterwards. While Dean he spent much time planning a missionary college in Bermuda, and to further that end he spent the years 1728–32 in the New World on Rhode Island. During his American sojourn he wrote, 'Verses on the prospect of planting arts and learning in the Americas'. Nearly one hundred and forty years later, on a hill side above San Francisco Bay, some developers and educationalists plotted a site for a new town and college. For a name, one of them, Frederick Billings, quoted from a poem by Berkeley, especially the lines 'Westward the course of empire takes its way', and suggested using the name Berkeley, after the famous Irish philosopher and poet.

Today, Berkeley University is one of the preeminent universities of the world, claiming 65 Nobel Laureates.

John F. Weir, *Westward the course of empire takes its way* (Bishop Berkeley), 1873
UNIVERSITY OF CALIFORNIA, BERKELEY ART MUSEUM AND PACIFIC FILM ARCHIVE; GIFT OF FREDERICK BILLINGS

## Nineteenth-Century Reform

Under the Church Temporalities Act of 1834, the dioceses of Derry and Raphoe were amalgamated. The last bishop of Raphoe as an independent diocese was William Bissett, who died that year. Thus Hon. Richard Ponsonby, bishop of Derry from 1831 became the first bishop of Derry and Raphoe. He held the united sees until his death in 1853.

Cloncha Church in Malin a Plantation villa built with Board of First Fruits funding.

Most of the churches in Derry and Raphoe date from the early part of the nineteenth century, and were in many cases partly provided for by the Board of First Fruits and later the Ecclesiastical Commissioners. Many of the churches built in the nineteenth century replaced at least one previous church that had fallen into disrepair, as we know from the royal visitation of 1622 and from surveys carried out in 1733 and 1768.

## The Twentieth Century

In 1978, the parishes of Inishowen, including Moville and Donagh and Fahan Upper and Lower, were transferred from the diocese of Derry to the diocese of Raphoe. This was done for administrative convenience, so that all the parishes in Donegal, in the republic, could be grouped together to administer matters such as education and finance.

A Free Gift for All is an initiative by churches from across the city community. Specially illustrated copies of Luke's Gospel will be hand-delivered to every home in the city. The four church leaders who made the presentation to the Mayor were Monsignor Eamon Martin (Diocese of Derry), Bishop Ken Good (Bishop of Derry & Raphoe), Rev Peter Murray (Superintendant of Methodist City Mission) and Rev Dr Robert Buick (Clerk of Presbytery).

Canon Leslie (1865–1952) has been described as a large-hearted man, generous to a fault who reeeked with the odour of tobacco smoke. He was usually clothed in a rough tweed jacket and cape.

The modern history of the dioceses of Derry and Raphoe has been greatly affected by the Troubles and civil unrest, which began in Derry in 1968 and continued until very recently. Many families on both sides of the political and religious divide suffered horrendously as their members were murdered and businesses and properties were damaged and destroyed. The churches in Derry Diocese produced many enlightened people, both lay and ordained, who gave courageous leadership throughout these difficult years, during the episcopate of Rt Revs Charles John Tyndall, Cuthbert Peacocke, Robin Eames, James Mehaffey and Kenneth Good, the present bishop. Local clergy of all denominations played their part too, as they ministered to bereaved families and made every effort to mediate.

In 1937, Canon James Blennerhassett Leslie, rector of Kilsaran near Castlebellingham in County Louth, produced a volume of succession lists of the clergy of Derry entitled *Derry Clergy and Parishes*. He published a similar volume, *Raphoe Clergy and Parishes*, in 1940. These were two of a series of such volumes for several of the dioceses published by Leslie. He also produced lists for most of the other dioceses, which were not published, and which are in manuscripts in the library of the Representative Church Body in Dublin.

There are some modern churches in Derry and Raphoe, built to modern designs in the middle of the twentieth century. The rest have had large sums spent on them, so they are now as well maintained and in as good a condition as they have been since they were first built.

His Royal Highness Prince Michael of Kent GCVO visited the Cathedral for the Service of Thanksgiving to mark the 70th Anniversary of 'the turning of the tide' in The Battle of the Atlantic 1939–45 on Sunday 12 May 2013.
FROM LEFT: Prince Michael, Dean William Morton and Sir Donal Keegan

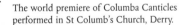

Bishop Ezekiel Hopkins
UNIVERSITY OF ULSTER

2009 saw completion of the magnificent Derry and Raphoe Library owned by the Church of Ireland and now housed in the purpose-built Rare Books Room at the Magee Campus of the University of Ulster. The library had its origins in the collections of two of the early bishops, George Downham and Ezekiel Hopkins. Bishop William King succeeded Hopkins in 1690 and he can be credited with founding the Derry Diocesan Library and bequeathing it for perpetual use.

The rich tapestry of what makes Derry/Londonderry special was celebrated by St Augustine's Church. Known affectionately as 'the wee church on the walls' the church marked UK City of Culture with The Big Weave Project, a worldwide community weaving project. As part of the newly opened Christian Heritage Trail, St Augustine's also launched its own app. Last year it welcomed well over 14,000 visitors through its doors, from all parts of the world.

The world premiere of Columba Canticles, an oratorio specially commissioned by The Culture Company and St Columb's Cathedral was performed as part of its contribution to the UK City of Culture 2013 celebrations.

The world premiere of Columba Canticles performed in St Columb's Church, Derry.

Participants busily involved in the Big Weave, a worldwide community weaving project, celebrated at St Augustine's Church, Derry.

163

St Patrick's Church, Kilrea
LUCY McGONIGLE

# PARISHES IN THE DIOCESE OF DERRY

### AGHADOWEY and KILREA

Aghadowey Parish lies along the River Bann south of Coleraine. St Guaire founded a church in the area in the seventh century, which was connected with his abbey at nearby Agivey. At the plantation, the Ironmongers' and Mercers' Companies received land nearby. In 1622, Aghadowey became one of the three prebends in Derry Cathedral.

*St Guaire's Church, Aghadowey* dates from 1797 and replaced an older church. The tower and a spire, later struck by lightning and never replaced, were provided by Hon. Frederick Augustus Hervey, the earl bishop. The church contains a bell that was provided by Queen Anne to her chaplain, Rev. Robert Gage, rector of Aghadowey, at the end of the seventeenth century.

*St Patrick's Church, Kilrea (Grey Church)* is situated in a small town in eastern County Derry. The ruins of the ancient church are adjacent to the present church, which was built in 1843. At the plantation, the Mercers' Company was established in the area. The organ in the gallery (not the one in present use) is said to have been played by Handel.

St Guaires, Aghadowey
LUCY McGONIGLE

### ARDSTRAW and BARONSCOURT, BADONEY LOWER and GREENAN, BADONEY UPPER

These five parishes, which were grouped in 1984, are situated in the hills between Strabane and Omagh. St Eugene founded the 'diocese of Ardstraw' around AD 540. This remained the seat of a bishop until around 1150, when Maurice O'Coffey transferred the see to Maghera. At the plantation, the chief planting family were the Stewarts, who gave their name to the village. The parish of Badoney, in the Sperrins in mid-Tyrone, is supposedly a Patrician foundation.

*St Eugene's Church, Newtownstewart* was built in 1724 and the spire was added in 1806. The organ in the gallery was presented in 1907 by Thomas Noble Mitter, a friend of the American philanthropist and patron of music, Andrew Carnegie. Several monuments in the church commemorate distinguished academic clergy from the eighteenth and nineteenth centuries, who held professorships and other senior positions in Dublin University along with the incumbency of Ardstraw.

*Baronscourt Church* in the woods and hills south-west of Newtownstewart is more English than Irish in style. It has the only lychgate in the Derry Diocese. The church was consecrated on 24 March 1858. Numerous monuments commemorate the Hamilton family, dukes of Abercorn. Baronscourt House, their ancestral home, surrounded by its estates and gardens, is amongst the grandest neoclassical houses in Ireland. The Hamiltons have lived at Baronscourt since 1566.

*St Patrick's Church, Badoney Lower*, in Gortin, was built in 1856 and replaced the original Badoney Lower Church, which was built in 1730.

*Greenan Church* was built in 1852.

*St Patrick's Church, Badoney Upper*, near Plumbridge, was built in 1784.

Baronscourt Church
LUCY McGONIGLE

St Eugene, Newtownstewart
in the parish of Ardstraw
LUCY McGONIGLE

A cross commemorating the
Duke of Abercorn at Baronscourt
LUCY McGONIGLE

### BALLYSCULLION

Ballyscullion Parish is situated around the village of Bellaghy. The ancient name was Inistoide, meaning 'Toit's island'. The Vintners' Company replaced the ruined church on Loch Beg in 1625. The Downing family, at one time resident in the parish, gave their name to Downing Street in London.

*St Tida's Church, Bellaghy* dates from 1794.

St Tida's Church, Bellaghy
GORDON GRAY

## BALTEAGH and CARRICK, TAMLAGHTARD and AGHANLOO

These four parishes to the south and north of Limavady were grouped in 2004. St Canice was the patron of Balteagh. Tamlaghtard Parish is supposedly a Patrician foundation. At the time of the plantation, Aghanloo was granted to the Haberdashers' Company.

*Balteagh Church* dates from 1815. The holy table and pulpit are finely carved.

Carrick Church
LUCY McGONIGLE

*Carrick Church* was consecrated on 25 May 1847.

*St Gedanus's Church, Tamlaghtard* was built some time between 1778 and 1787. Monuments in the church commemorate the Heygate, McCausland, Gage and Tyler families.

*St Lugha's Church, Aghanloo* was consecrated on 2 July 1826. The parish lies between Limavady and Castlerock.

## CAMUS-JUXTA-BANN

Camus-juxta-Bann is a parish at Macosquin near Coleraine. St Comgall is said to have founded a monastery here around AD 780, whilst St Colman was abbot of an earlier monastery. Around 1200, the O'Cahan family founded a Cistercian house, de Claro Fonte.

*St Mary's Church, Macosquin* dates from 1827, although at the royal visitation in 1622 it was reported that the Merchant Taylors' Company petitioned the primate for the building of a new church on the ruins of the monastery.

Stained glass, St Mary's Church, Macosquin
LUCY McGONIGLE

### CAMUS-JUXTA-MOURNE

Samuel Lewis's *Topographical Dictionary of Ireland* records that the earl of Abercorn built a chapel for the new town of Strabane in 1619.

*Christ Church, Strabane* was consecrated by Bishop Alexander in 1879. His wife, the celebrated hymn writer Mrs Cecil Frances Alexander, came from the parish. The east window, depicting the last supper, is a memorial to her parents. The church is a large and particularly fine building, cruciform, with a tower and spire.

## CAPPAGH and LISLIMNAGHAN

*Cappagh Church*, near Omagh, was built in 1768 in the classical style. It has some fine stained-glass windows and memorials to the Stack family.

*Lislimnaghan Church* was consecrated on 26 August 1862. The parish is near Omagh on the main Strabane Road.

Cappagh Church
LUCY McGONIGLE

## William and Cecil Frances Alexander

William Alexander and his wife, Mrs Cecil Frances Alexander, were two of the great figures of the dioceses of Derry and Raphoe in the nineteenth century. William was born in Derry on 13 April 1824, son of Rev. Robert Alexander, rector of Aghadowey and educated at Tonbridge School and Exeter College, Oxford. While at Oxford, Alexander came under the influence of John Henry Newman and the Tractarians, the party in the Church of England who wanted to bring the church back to a more catholic position in doctrine and liturgical practice. Alexander was ordained on 19 September 1847. He was curate of Templemore, then rector successively of Termonamongan, Fahan and Camus-juxta-Mourne, Strabane. He was consecrated bishop of Derry and Raphoe in 1867 and elected archbishop of Armagh and primate of all Ireland on 25 February 1896. He remained primate until his retirement in 1911 and died on 12 September 1911.

William Alexander was an outstanding bishop at a time of uncertainty for the Church of Ireland. He vigorously opposed disestablishment, speaking eloquently against it in the House of Lords, but to no avail. After disestablishment in 1870, Alexander set about guiding his dioceses of Derry and Raphoe as the church came to terms with its new position.

A fine scholar, Alexander won the Dover Prize for an essay on the divinity of our Lord. He was also awarded the University Prize for a poem. He graduated in 1867 with a doctorate in divinity. He was a prolific author and an eloquent preacher, becoming select preacher at Oxford, Cambridge and Dublin Universities, as well as Bampton lecturer in 1876. He published numerous books and sermons, including *Leading Ideas of the Gospels* (1872).

In October 1850, William married Cecil Frances, daughter of Major John Humphreys of Milltown House, Strabane. Her hymns and poems, which are world renowned, include such favourites as 'Once in Royal David's City' and 'All Things Bright and Beautiful'. Many, such as 'Do No Sinful Action', were written for the instruction of children. Mrs Alexander died in 1895, while her husband was still bishop of Derry and Raphoe. Portraits of Bishop and Mrs Alexander by C.N. Kennedy hang in the hallway of the deanery. The window in the east wall of the chapel in the cathedral, which depicts the ascended Christ, commemorates Bishop Alexander. The baptistery in the cathedral is Mrs Alexander's memorial.

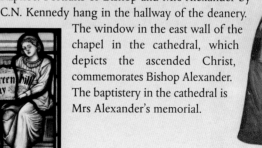

William Alexander from an 1895 illustration in *Vanity Fair*

GORDON GRAY

## CASTLEDAWSON

The parish of Castledawson in eastern County Londonderry was created in 1875 from parts of the neighbouring parishes of Magherafelt and Ballyscullion.

*Christ Church, Castledawson* was consecrated on 7 November 1876. It was an enlargement of the old church, built in 1760 by the Dawson family of Moyola Park, which in turn had replaced an earlier church of 1710. There are numerous monuments to the Dawson and Chichester-Clark families. Major James Chichester-Clark (1923–2002) was a one-time prime minister of Northern Ireland. An ancestor, Arthur, Lord Chichester of Belfast (1563–1625), was lord deputy of Ireland and may have commanded a ship during Drake's last voyage at the time of the Spanish Armada.

## CASTLEROCK, DUNBOE and FERMOYLE

Castlerock is a seaside town on the north coast of County Derry. The Hervey Bruce family of Downhill House in the parish, descendants of the earl bishop, were prominent in the area. Mussenden Temple, built by the earl bishop, is in the parish, on the edge of a cliff above Lough Foyle. Dunboe is a parish between Castlerock and Coleraine. St Patrick visited the area and found that Christianity was already established there. The village of Articlave in the parish was established by the Clothworkers' Company at the plantation.

*Christ Church, Castlerock* was built in 1867. The Clothworkers' Company contributed to the cost.

*St Paul's Church, Dunboe* was built in 1691, with later additions. A sundial on the south wall, dating from 1823, has the inscription, ''Tis greatly wise to talk with our past hours, and ask them what report they bore to Heaven.'

In 1843, *Fermoyle Church* was established in the foothills of the Sperrins.

## CLOONEY

Clooney is a large parish in the Waterside of Londonderry. A perpetual curacy was established in Glendermott Parish for Clooney district in 1863. A joint Methodist and Church of Ireland worship centre was opened at Strathfoyle in 1970, but is now closed.

*All Saints' Church, Clooney* was opened in 1867. It is both internally and externally an impressive building. The sanctuary has fine carved marble panelling around its three sides, surmounted by three sets of double stained-glass windows depicting the 12 apostles and various biblical scenes.

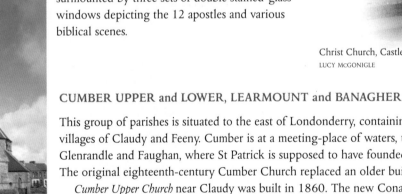

Christ Church, Castlerock
LUCY McGONIGLE

All Saints' Church, Clooney
GORDON GRAY

## CUMBER UPPER and LOWER, LEARMOUNT and BANAGHER

This group of parishes is situated to the east of Londonderry, containing the villages of Claudy and Feeny. Cumber is at a meeting-place of waters, the Rivers Glenrandle and Faughan, where St Patrick is supposed to have founded a church. The original eighteenth-century Cumber Church replaced an older building.

*Cumber Upper Church* near Claudy was built in 1860. The new Conacher organ was erected in 1999.

*Holy Trinity Church, Cumber Lower* is situated at Killaloo, on the main Derry to Belfast road. Built in 1796, it contains fine furnishings, including a beautiful marble eagle lectern, and some excellent windows depicting biblical texts.

*Learmount Church* in the village of Park was consecrated on 13 December 1831.

*Banagher Church,* at Feeny, was built by the earl bishop between 1780 and 1784. The ruins of a tenth-century church nearby contain the tomb of the patron, St Moresius. At the plantation, the Skinners' Company was established in the area.

Stained glass, Cumber Upper Church
LUCY McGONIGLE

St John's Church, Derg
LUCY McGONIGLE

St James's Church, Donagheady
LUCY McGONIGLE

## DERG and TERMONAMONGAN

Derg centres on the town of Castlederg.

*St John's Church, Derg* dates from 1731, though the tower is much older. It replaced a church in ruins since the 1641 Rebellion.

*St Bestius's Church, Termonamongan* at Killeter, near Castlederg, was built in 1822. It has a north aisle that is so large that it looks as if two churches, externally in different styles, have been joined together. In ancient times, it was known as O'Caireall's Church.

## DESERTMARTIN and TERMONEENY

Desertmartin Parish is in eastern County Londonderry. Its patron, St Martin, is supposed to have been an uncle of St Patrick.

*St Conghall's Church, Desertmartin* was built in 1820. Inside it is a large, spacious church, with a north transept containing a large four-light decorated window of 1869.

*Termoneeny Church* at Knockloughrim near Maghera dates from 1801.

## DONAGHEADY

Donagheady, named for St Caidinus, a companion of St Columbanus, is situated around the Tyrone village of Donemana.

*St James's Church, Donagheady* is a fine church built in 1879 to replace the previous church, which had fallen into bad repair.

167

St Conghall's Church, Desertmartin
LUCY McGONIGLE

## DRUMACHOSE

Limavady, County Londonderry is an important market town on the River Roe at the foot of the Sperrin Mountains. The town's name means 'the leap of the dog'. The parish name is Drumachose. The patron saint, Canice, was born in the area around AD 517. The Convention of Drumceatt in AD 575 was attended by St Columba. At the plantation, Sir Thomas Phillips allocated lands for the Haberdashers', Fishmongers' and Skinners' Companies. He established the town of Newtown Limavady, which received a charter in 1613.

*Christ Church, Limavady*, which dates from 1750, was extensively enlarged in 1881. The finest of the many monuments in the church is the memorial along the north aisle wall to those who fell in World War I.

Langfield Lower
LUCY McGONIGLE

Christ Church, Drumachose, Limavady
[T]his tailfin from an Avro Shackelton Mr Mk3 in Drumachose churchyard is dedicated to those who [se]rved at RAF Ballykelly, RAF Eglinton, RAF Limavady and RAF [M]aydown throughout [W]orld War II and the [s]ubsequent Cold War.
LUCY McGONIGLE

Drumragh wallhanging and interior
LUCY McGONIGLE

## DRUMCLAMPH, LANGFIELD LOWER, LANGFIELD UPPER and CLARE

Langfield Parish is situated around the village of Drumquin. Though medieval, the present-day village of Drumquin was founded during the plantation, around 1617, by Sir John Davies, who was attorney general for Ireland.

*Lower Langfield Church* was built in 1842, with later additions.

*Upper Langfield Church* dates from about 1803.

*Drumclamph Church*, near Castlederg, was built in 1846.

*St Andrew's Church, Clare* was consecrated on 21 February 1997.

## DRUMRAGH and MOUNTFIELD

Drumragh Parish is situated around Omagh. It contained a Franciscan friary dating from 1464 and a medieval castle.

*St Columba's, Drumragh* was consecrated by Bishop Alexander on 20 October 1871, and replaced an older church of 1777. The stained-glass windows are a notable feature of this church.

*Mountfield Church* near Omagh was built in 1862.

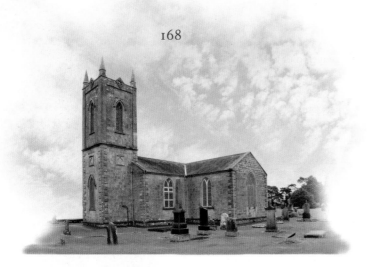

## DUNGIVEN and BOVEVAGH

Just outside Dungiven, County Derry, are the remains of St Mary's Priory, which became Augustinian around 1140. It is thought that St Neachtain founded a monastery here as early as the seventh century. At the time of the plantation, a church was built by the Skinners' Company on the site of the priory. Bovevagh is a parish to the north of Dungiven. Columba founded a monastery in the area in AD 557.

*Dungiven Church*, built in 1816, replaced an earlier one of 1718.

*Bovevagh Church*, which replaced older ones, was built in 1823.

Dungiven Church
LUCY McGONIGLE

## EDENDERRY and CLANABOGAN

*Edenderry Church* was consecrated on 23 June 1847. It contains monuments to the distinguished military family, the Auchinlecks, and the Sebastopol marbles, brought from the Crimea in 1856 after the Crimean War.

*Clanabogan Church*, just south of Omagh, is a splendid example of Welland & Gillespie architecture. It was consecrated on 22 December 1863. It is noted for its spectacular marble. The main furniture and fittings, including the altar, communion rails and pulpit, are made in a rich variety of marble in many colours from Ireland and abroad – from Connemara and Kilkenny, Siena and France.

Clanabogan Church
LUCY McGONIGLE

St Paul's Church, Errigal
LUCY McGONIGLE

## ERRIGAL and DESERTOGHILL

Errigal Parish at Garvagh in County Londonderry was anciently associated with St Eunan. Columba formed a monastic community here.

*St Paul's Church, Errigal* was built by the Canning family in 1670. A descendant, George Canning, was prime minister in 1827, and died that year in office.

*Desertoghill Church* was built in 1784.

## FAUGHANVALE, EGLINTON

The patron saint of the parish of Faughanvale at Eglinton, east of Londonderry, was St Canice (*c.* 517–*c.* 600), who also gave his name to Kilkenny. At the plantation, in 1615, the Grocers' Company of London was granted a manor of 15,900 acres along the southern shore of Lough Foyle.

*St Canice's Church, Eglinton*, alongside the ruin of the old one, was completed in 1826, with transepts and sanctuary being added later.

St Canice, Eglinton
LUCY McGONIGLE

## GLENDERMOTT

Glendermott is a large parish in the Altnagelvin area in the eastern suburbs of Londonderry. In ancient times, St Patrick, St Columba and St Canice founded churches in the area. In 1622, the Goldsmiths' Company built a church. The Church of Ireland Centre at New Buildings near Londonderry was built in 1988 to serve the needs of the people there, during the incumbency of Canon Noel Moore.

*Glendermott Church* dates from 1753. It is a fine building, both internally and externally, with some excellent windows and interesting monuments.

Glendermott Church
LUCY McGONIGLE

## KILCRONAGHAN, BALLYNASCREEN (DRAPERSTOWN) and SIX TOWNS

Kilcronaghan Parish is situated in the village of Tobermore in the foothills of the Sperrin Mountains. Its patron, St Cronaghan, is said to have baptised and taught St Columba. Ballynascreen is the ancient name of the plantation town of Draperstown in south County Derry. It was named after a shrine whose patron was St Columba. The earl bishop financially supported the building of a church in 1760.

*Kilcronaghan Church* was completed in 1858. A monument in the church commemorates Sir Hiram Shaw Wilkinson of the Consular Service in Japan, who was also crown advocate in Shanghai, chief justice of the Supreme Courts of China and Korea, high sheriff for County Londonderry and pro-chancellor of the Queen's University of Belfast.

*St Columba's Church, Draperstown* dates from 1887, retaining the tower and spire from the previous building.

The nearby *St Anne's Church, Six Towns* was consecrated in 1843.

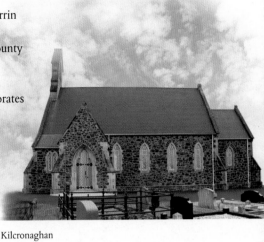

Kilcronaghan
GARY McMURRAY

Six Towns
GARY McMURRAY

## KILLOWEN

*St John's Church, Killowen* is situated on the west bank of the River Bann in Coleraine. In 1248, the English erected a castle and a bridge over the Bann. At the time of the plantation, the Clothworkers' Company was established in the area. They financed the building of the present church, which dates from 1830. This church was largely rebuilt in 1875.

## LECKPATRICK and DUNNALONG

Leckpatrick Parish, near Strabane, is a Patrician foundation. Further north towards Londonderry is the parish of Dunnalong.

*St Patrick's Church, Leckpatrick* was consecrated in 1821 and enlarged in 1824. There is an unusual two-decker pulpit with reading desk below. The windows are of clear glass, though some have figures etched into them, giving the whole building a large, airy feel.

*St John's Church, Dunnalong* was built in 1865. The steeply pitched roof and cream-coloured brick trim round the windows give the church a distinctive character.

St John's Church, Killowen

St Patrick's Church, Leckpatrick

## LONDONDERRY, CHRIST CHURCH, MUFF, CULMORE and ST PETER'S

*Christ Church, Londonderry* is a benefice in the parish of Templemore. It originated in 1830 when the Free Church was built on Northland Road to accommodate the poorer people in the area. The church was enlarged in 1882 and given the present dedication. A mission church was dedicated in 1903; it existed until 1967. The sanctuary has fine mosaic tiles commemorating Dean Potter, rector 1878–1903 and dean of Raphoe 1903–05. Christ Church was badly damaged by fire in 1996. The Conacher organ of 1886 and the east window were destroyed. The window has been replaced with an exact replica, and the firm of Wells Kennedy of Lisburn built a brand new three-manual organ completed in 2001.

The ancient *Muff Church*, north of Londonderry, originated in a Columban abbey. The present church was built in 1737 by the Hart family of Kilderry in the parish and, like Culmore, was one of the five chapels of ease in the parish of Templemore.

*Holy Trinity Church, Culmore* is situated to the north of Londonderry. In 1840, the Irish Society acquired land, and the church was built on it in 1867.

A new church, *St Peter's Church, Belmont*, was built because of the growth of Londonderry. It was consecrated on 8 October 1966. It is a fine modern building, containing some excellent windows.

Holy Trinity Church, Culmore
LUCY McGONIGLE

## LONDONDERRY, ST AUGUSTINE'S

*St Augustine's Church, Londonderry*, a benefice in the parish of Templemore, is situated on the historic walls of Derry, on the site of an ancient Augustinian abbey. The present church was consecrated on 11 June 1872. The Minton tiles in the sanctuary are a notable feature.

St Augustine's, Londonderry

GARY McMURRAY

St Lurachs Maghera

## MAGHERA and KILLELAGH

Maghera in County Derry was the seat of a bishop from around 1150 to around 1280, when the see was transferred to Derry. Lurach, the patron saint, lived in the sixth century. Killelagh is in the village of Swatragh near Maghera.

*St Lurach's Church, Maghera* dates from 1819 and stands adjacent to the ruins of an old church. There are many monuments and memorials in the church to the Clarks, a distinguished family in the area.

*Killelagh Church* was built by the Mercers' Company in 1855.

LUCY McGONIGLE

St Findluganus's Church, Tamlaghtfinlagan, Ballykelly

## TAMLAGHTFINLAGAN and MYROE

Tamlaghtfinlagan is a parish between Derry and Limavady. At the plantation the Fishmongers' Company erected a castle nearby at Walworth, named after Sir William Walworth, mayor of London at the time of Wat Tyler's revolt in 1381. In 1896, a parishioner, Thomas Nicholl, was ploughing a field close to Tamlaghtfinlagan Church when his plough struck an object in the ground. It turned out to be one of seven gold objects, including a model boat and a chain and some collars dating from the first century BC. These items, known as the Broighter Hoard, are now in the National Museum in Dublin.

*St Findluganus's Church, Tamlaghtfinlagan*, Ballykelly, was built by the earl bishop in 1795, with later additions.

*Myroe Chapel of Ease* was built in 1863.

## TAMLAGHT O'CRILLY UPPER and LOWER

The parish of Tamlaght O'Crilly is near Portglenone. The O'Crillys were erenachs (agents or stewards) of the church lands in the area in the later middle ages.

*Tamlaght O'Crilly Upper Church* was rebuilt in 1815, with the addition of the chancel in 1859.

*Tamlaght O'Crilly Lower Church* is in Innisrush. The present church, also rebuilt in 1815, replaces one built by the earl bishop in 1775.

Sion Mills

GARY McMURRAY

## TEMPLEMORE

Alongside his monastery founded in Derry in AD 546, St Columba founded the so-called Black Church. In 1164, the Great Church was founded. This was destroyed in 1568 and replaced with the present cathedral in the parish of Templemore.

## URNEY with SION MILLS

Urney is a parish on the banks of the River Finn to the south of Strabane.

The present *Christ Church, Urney*, built in 1865, replaces an earlier church of 1734. The rose window in the west wall is an interesting feature. The archway over the main entrance is in the Moorish style, and the east windows are also of good quality.

The *Church of the Good Shepherd, Sion Mills* is a chapel of ease in Urney Parish. Built in 1909 to replace the earlier church, too small for the congregation, it is a splendid building in the Italian Renaissance style, modelled on a church at Pistoia near Florence. Inside, seven steps lead to the chancel, with three more to the altar. There is a large marble pulpit and a reading desk on either side of the chancel. Sion Mills village was built in the early nineteenth century around Herdmans Mills in the village.

Church of the Good Shepherd, Urney

LUCY McGONIGLE

## ARDARA, GLENCOLUMBKILLE, INNISKEEL, GLENTIES and LETTERMACAWARD

This group of parishes is situated among the beautiful scenery of south-west Donegal.

*St Conal's Church, Ardara* was consecrated on 11 June 1820 as the parish church of the newly formed parish of Ardara. This building was replaced with the present church in 1833.

The present *St Columba's Church, Glencolumbkille* dates from 1828, and the tower from 1913. Columba is reputed to have founded a monastery here. Charles Inglis, (1734–1816), first bishop of Nova Scotia, was a son of the rector of the parish, Rev. Archibald Inglis.

*Inniskeel Church* was consecrated on 8 June 1828. Inniskeel contains the village of Portnoo.

*Glenties Church* was built around 1860.

*Lettermacaward Church* dates from around 1790. Lettermacaward is to the south of Dungloe.

t Conal's Church, Ardara

St Columba's Church, Glencolumbcille

GARY McMURRAY

## CLONDEHORKEY, CASHEL and MEVAGH, MILFORD

The ancient parish of Clondehorkey is located around Ballymore, to the east of Dunfanaghy, at the foot of Muckish Mountain on Donegal's scenic north coast.

*St John's Church, Clondehorkey* is a splendid example of Georgian architecture, dating from 1752. The altar and reredos and wood panelling in the interior are noteworthy.

Nearby *St Columba's Church, Cashel* is adjacent to the well-preserved ruins of Doe Castle on the shores of Sheephaven Bay.

St John's, Clondehorkey

*Holy Trinity Church, Mevagh*, in the village of Carrigart, was built around 1895. It is a fine building both outside and inside. The pulpit is of Caen stone and the font dates from 1681. The estates of the earls of Leitrim are in the parish.

*St Columba's Church, Milford* was consecrated on 7 August 1860. The church was severely damaged by lightning in 1982, and subsequently closed and demolished.

St Columba's Church, Cashel

## CLONDEVADDOCK

The parish of Clondevaddock occupies the northern part of the Fanad Peninsula.

The parish church, *Christ the Redeemer, Rosnakill* is very old, probably dating from before the seventeenth century. There are two chapels of ease.

*All Saints' Church, Portsalon* replaced an older church destroyed by a hurricane in 1961. It has excellent and striking modern glass depicting biblical and nautical themes. The bell came from RMS *Laurentic*, which was sunk by German submarines in Lough Swilly in 1917.

*Leatbeg Church* was built in 1843.

Christ the Redeemer, Rosnakill

All Saints', Portsalon, exterior and stained glass window

PHIL CROSS

## CONVOY, MONELLAN and DONAGHMORE

The perpetual curacy of Convoy, south of Raphoe, was created when a deed establishing a new chapel was issued on 24 July 1773.

*St Ninian's Church, Convoy* dates from 1824. There are three fine windows on each side of the nave.

*St Anne's Church, Monellan*, at Killygordon near Stranorlar, dates from 1833.

*St Patrick's Church, Donaghmore*, which is large and spacious, dates from the early part of the eighteenth century. However, St Patrick is said to have founded a church at Donaghmore near Castlefinn, between Lifford and Stranorlar.

St Ninian's Church, Convoy

St Patrick's Church, Donaghmore

ALASTAIR SMEATON

## CONWALL, LECK and AUGHANUNSHIN with GARTAN

Conwall is situated around the town of Letterkenny. Nearby are the ruins of the medieval abbey of Congbhail, of which St Fiachra was abbot. Leck and Aughanunshin, to the south and north of Letterkenny respectively, were small parishes and their churches are now closed.

The nave of *Conwall Church* dates from 1776, although the tower is from 1636 and the spire from 1832. The three-gable south aisle of 1865 has fine stained-glass windows. Within is a chapel dedicated to St Fiachra.

*St Columba's Church, Gartan*, in Churchhill, dates from 1819, with a tower dating from 1895. The fine east window with three lights depicts scenes from the life of St Columba. The Adairs of Glenveagh Castle were prominent parishioners in the nineteenth century.

St Columba's, Gartan
LUCY McGONIGLE

Conwall Chu

## DONEGAL, KILLYMARD, LOUGH ESKE and LAGHEY

Donegal is a medieval town. In the twelfth century, the O'Donnells built a castle there, and in 1474 a monastery was built for the Franciscans. The *Annals of the Four Masters* were compiled in Donegal in 1631. Killymard is a parish just to the west of Donegal, while Laghey lies to the south of Donegal.

*Donegal Church* dates from 1831, with later additions.

*Killymard Church* dates from 1830.

*Christ Church, Lough Eske* dates from 1846. The tower is capped by an unusual four-gabled structure, Scandinavian in style.

*Laghey Church*, which is in a distinctive architectural style, was built in 1834.

Lough Eske

## DUNFANAGHY, RAYMUNTERDONEY and TULLAGHOBEGLEY

The village of Dunfanaghy is situated on the beautiful north coast of Donegal. The parish was formed out of its neighbour, Clondehorkey, in 1872. The parish of Tullaghobegley lies on the other side of Falcarragh, towards Gortahork.

*Holy Trinity Church, Dunfanaghy* was consecrated on 2 May 1874 and is of an attractive, if somewhat unusual, design. Many of the memorials commemorate the Stewart family of Horn Head.

*St Paul's Church, Raymunterdoney*, near Falcarragh, dates from 1805.

*St Anne's Church, Tullaghobegley*, also called Killult, was built in 1820 and rebuilt in 1840. Tory Island is in the parish. The celebrated portrait and landscape painter Derek Hill (1916–2000) did much of his finest work on Tory.

St Anne's Church, Tullaghobegley
GARY McMURRAY

Stained glass in Holy Trinity, Dunfanaghy
LUCY McGONIGLE

## FAHAN UPPER and FAHAN LOWER

St Mura (died c. AD 645) founded a monastery and school at Fahan between Derry and Buncrana. A church was built there at the time of the plantation.

*St Mura's Church, Fahan Upper* was built in 1820, with the chancel added in 1897. In the south wall there is a window by the celebrated artist Evie Hone, depicting St Elizabeth of Hungary. The mosaic tiles on the sanctuary floor commemorate Mrs Cecil Frances Alexander, the celebrated hymn writer, whose husband was rector from 1855 to 1860.

*Christ Church, Fahan Lower*, on the Main Street of Buncrana, dates from 1804. The chancel was added in 1902. The fine east window depicts the ascension. The ceiling is also of note.

*Inch Church* on Inch Island in Lough Swilly and *Desertegney Church* to the north of Buncrana have been closed for many years. Their ruins can still be seen.

*Burt Church*, between Newtowncunningham and Derry, built around 1860, is a fine little building, now in private ownership.

GORDON GRAY

St Mura's Church, Fahan Upper

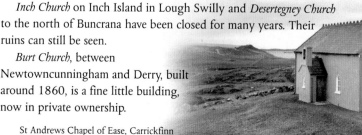

Christ Church, Fahan Lower
GORDON GRAY

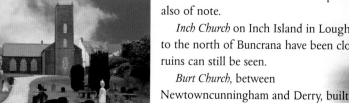

St Andrews Chapel of Ease, Carrickfinn

## GWEEDORE, CARRICKFINN and TEMPLECRONE

*St Patrick's Church, Gweedore* is located in Bunbeg in north-west Donegal. The church was built for use as a school as well as for worship in 1844, with the tower added in 1914.

*St Andrew's Chapel of Ease, Carrickfinn Island* was built in 1857. It was originally a watchtower and was later converted into a church.

*St Crone's Church, Templecrone* dates from 1844. The parish centres on the town of Dungloe on the west coast of Donegal. St Crone lived there in the seventh century.

St Crone's, Templecrone
JOHN CAMPBELL

## INVER, MOUNTCHARLES, KILLAGHTEE, KILLYBEGS and KILCAR

This group of parishes is situated along the south coast of Donegal.

*St John the Evangelist's Church, Inver* was built in 1807. The chancel was added in 1861.

*Christ Church, Mountcharles*, between Donegal and Inver, dates from 1860. Henry Conyngham, the first Marquis Conyngham (1766–1832), became Viscount Conyngham of Mountcharles in the Irish peerage. He had great influence in the court of King George IV, for which he was created Lord Minster of Minster Abbey in 1821.

John the Evangelist's Church, Inver

*St Peter's Church, Kilaghtee*, at Dunkineely, between Donegal and Killybegs, was erected in 1826. It replaced an older church whose ruins are nearby.

*St John's Church, Killybegs* was consecrated on 6 June 1828. The fine ceiling of the chancel is in the shape of the inverted prow of a ship, reflecting the fact that Killybegs is an important fishing port.

*Kilcar Church*, to the west of Killybegs, was built in 1828 and closed in 1960.

St John's Church, Killybegs
GARY McMURRAY

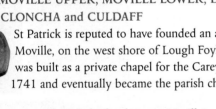

St Peter's, Kilaghtee

## MOVILLE UPPER, MOVILLE LOWER, DONAGH, CLONCHA and CULDAFF

St Patrick is reputed to have founded an abbey at Moville, on the west shore of Lough Foyle. A church was built as a private chapel for the Carey family in 1741 and eventually became the parish church.

St John's Church, Rossnowlagh

*St Finian's Church, Lower Moville* is at Greencastle, north of Moville. It was built in 1782.

As the town grew larger, it received a church of its own. *St Columb's, Moville* was built in 1858 as a chapel of ease in Lower Moville Parish. Memorials to the Montgomery family are in the church. Henry Hutchinson Montgomery was bishop of Tasmania in 1889–1901 and father of Field Marshal Bernard Law Montgomery, a key player in World War II.

*Upper Moville Church, Redcastle*, now closed, was consecrated on 18 August 1853.

*Donagh Church* at Carndonagh was built in 1769. Carndonagh was a very early Christian settlement, supposed to have been founded by St Patrick in AD 442. St Patrick's Cross, outside the church, possibly dates from the seventh century. The bell of the church is thought to have come from *La Trinidad Valencera*, a warship wrecked in the Spanish Armada in 1588.

*Cloncha Church* in Malin is the most northerly Church of Ireland church in Ireland. The first stone was laid by Mrs Harvey of Malin Hall in 1827.

*Culdaff Church*, built in 1747, has some fine monuments to the Young family.

*Clonmany Church*, built in 1772, was closed in 1927 and is now a ruin.

*Gleneely Church*, dating from 1856, was also closed in 1990.

St Patrick's Cross at Carndonough
GORDON GRAY

Cloncha Church, Malin

## KILBARRON, ROSSNOWLAGH and DRUMHOLM

*St Anne's Church, Kilbarron* is impressively situated, overlooking Ballyshannon. The abbey of Assaroe was nearby. The present church was built in 1795 and rebuilt in 1841. The massive four-storey tower contains a peal of eight bells. This huge church, which can accommodate 800 people, was once a garrison church for the nearby Finner army base.

*St John's Church, Rossnowlagh*, on the coast to the west of Ballyshannon, was consecrated on 21 September 1831.

*Drumholm Church* at Ballintra is another massive and spacious church. It was built in 1795 and remodelled in 1854. St Ernan (died *c.* AD 640) was the abbot of a monastery in the area.

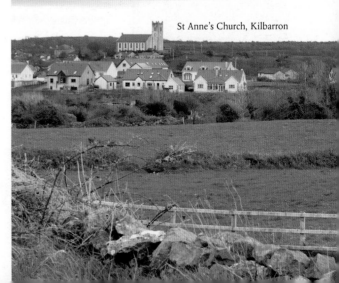

St Anne's Church, Kilbarron

## RAPHOE, RAYMOCHY and CLONLEIGH

Raphoe in east Donegal is the site of a monastery founded by
St Columba. This was later restored by St Eunan. The earliest record of a
bishop of Raphoe is Oengus O'Lappin in AD 959. The parish of
Raymochy is in the village of Manorcunningham, the seat of the
Cunningham family at the time of the plantation. In the parish are the
ruins of Balleighan Abbey, founded for the Franciscans in the fifteenth
century by the O'Donnell clan. Clonleigh is in the town of Lifford. The
patron saint, Lugadius, was one of the 12 companions who accompanied
St Columba to Iona in AD 563.

*St Eunan's Cathedral, Raphoe* has undergone much alteration over the
years, so that most of the present building dates from the seventeenth to
the nineteenth century. The earliest remains of any original building are
part of a ninth-century door lintel in the porch, with scenes carved on it
depicting the arrest of Jesus in the garden. There are also medieval
lancets in the south choir wall with unusual shamrock carvings
containing twelfth-century triple stone sedilia. Bishop Forster
built the tower and the Galilee porch in 1738 and provided
the Volt House in the town as a residence for the widows of clergy. He also founded the
diocesan library and provided fine new buildings for the Royal School, Raphoe in 1737.
Further substantial restoration work was carried out in 1893 by the Knox family of Prehen,
Londonderry. The two aisles were removed, as was the gallery at the west end.

The west door, with a series of representations of the four evangelists, were carved in
1907 by the wife of Canon J.W. McQuaide, rector of Raphoe. Inside, beyond the porch, is
the consistory court, which was where the bishop used to preside over such matters as the
granting of probate and the issuing of marriage licences. The font was presented by Bishop
Pooley in 1706. The intricately carved choir stalls date from 1908, and the
bishop's throne dates from 1665. The east window is particularly fine, and
depicts the ascension. There is a monument commemorating William
Bissett, the last bishop of Raphoe as an independent diocese, who died in
1834. Other monuments commemorate various former deans and prominent
families from the parish, and there are some fine windows, including a set in
the south wall depicting the four evangelists.

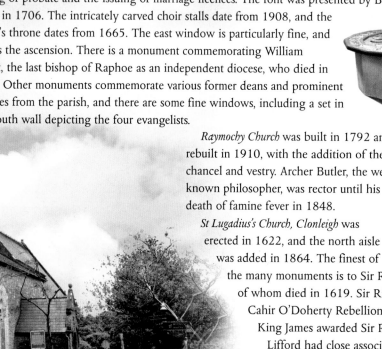

*Raymochy Church* was built in 1792 and
rebuilt in 1910, with the addition of the
chancel and vestry. Archer Butler, the well-
known philosopher, was rector until his
death of famine fever in 1848.

*St Lugadius's Church, Clonleigh* was
erected in 1622, and the north aisle
was added in 1864. The finest of
the many monuments is to Sir Richard Hansard and his wife, Dame Anne, both
of whom died in 1619. Sir Richard was governor of Lifford at the time of the
Cahir O'Doherty Rebellion, just before the plantation. For his part in it,
King James awarded Sir Richard the town of Lifford. The Prior School in
Lifford had close associations with the parish. It was provided for in
the will of Miss Eleanor Prior and opened in 1879. It was
amalgamated with the Royal School, Raphoe in 1971.

All photographs of St Eunan's Cathedral, Raphoe
ALASTAIR SMEATON

Church of the Ascension, Meenglass

## STRANORLAR, MEENGLASS and KILTEEVOGUE

Stranorlar is between Letterkenny and Donegal.

*Stranorlar Church*, built in 1729, was enlarged in 1733, with transepts being added in 1863. A bell in the porch is inscribed 'Henricus Paris me fecit 1677' ('Henry Paris made me 1677'). A peal of eight bells was added in 1999. The distinctive quatrefoils were installed in each window in the nave in 2001. Isaac Butt (1813–79), son of Rev. Robert Butt, perpetual curate of Stranorlar, was the founder of the Irish Home Rule movement.

The *Church of the Ascension, Meenglass*, to the south of Ballybofey, was consecrated on 27 May 1962. It replaced the previous church, which had been severely damaged by Hurricane Debbie on 16 September 1961.

*St John's Church, Kilteevogue*, to the west of Ballybofey, was consecrated on 16 July 1879.

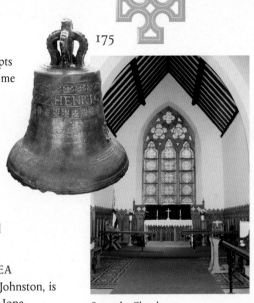

Stranorlar Church

LUCY McGONIGLE

## TAUGHBOYNE WITH CRAIGADOOISH, ALL SAINTS and KILLEA

The parish of Taughboyne in east Donegal, containing the village of St Johnston, is named after its patron, St Baithin, a cousin and successor of Columba at Iona.

*St Baithin's Church, Taughboyne* was found to be in ruins at the royal visitation in 1622, so a new church was begun in St Johnston. However, as this was too far from the centre of population, the old building dating from 1627 was restored. There are some curious fifteenth-century carved animal figures at the main entrance.

*St Columba's Church, Craigadooish* is a chapel of ease situated between St Johnston and Raphoe. The bell was obtained in 1966 from the light vessel HMS *Kittiwake*.

*All Saints' Church, Newtowncunningham*, halfway between Derry and Letterkenny, was also originally a chapel of ease in Taughboyne Parish. Like its neighbour Raymochy at Manorcunningham, it was a seat of the planting Cunningham family. The Forwards of Castle Forward, a landowning family of the eighteenth and nineteenth centuries, built All Saints' Church as their private chapel in 1722. The tower and chancel are later additions. All Saints became a parish in 1871. It possesses the only lychgate in Raphoe Diocese.

*St Fiach's Church, Killea* is on the main street of Carrigans. It dates from 1765. The east window, depicting the ascension, is of excellent quality, and the oak panelling in the sanctuary is finely carved.

St Baithin's Church, Taughboyne
RCB/DAVID CROOKS

All Saint's Church, Newtowncunningham
COLIN BOYLE

St Fiach's Church, Killea

GARY McMURRAY

Detail of Reformation head on Kilmacrennan pulpit

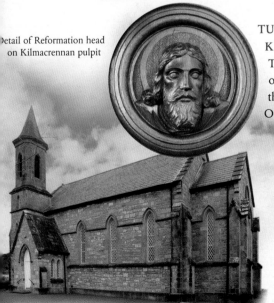

## TULLYAUGHNISH, KILMACRENNAN, KILLYGARVAN and GLENALLA

The parish of Tullyaughnish is situated on the west shore of Lough Swilly, with the town of Ramelton at its centre. The O'Donnell clan founded a Franciscan friary at nearby Killydonnell in the sixteenth century. At the plantation, Sir William Stewart moved the church from Aughinish Island to Ramelton. St Columba spent his childhood and received his education at Temple Douglas near Kilmacrennan, to the west of Ramelton. Killygarvan is a parish centred in the village on the scenic west coast of Lough Swilly, while Glenalla Parish lies between Milford and Ramelton.

St Finnian's and St Mark's, Kilmacrennan

JOHN CAMPBELL

St Paul's Church, Tullyaughnish

St Columb's Church, Killygarvan

*St Paul's Church, Tullyaughnish* dates from 1825. Its most distinguishing feature is the magnificent three-light, highly coloured, modern stained-glass east window dating from 1975, which depicts the creation.

*St Finnian and St Mark's, Kilmacrennan* was built in 1846. The pulpit, from a Congregational chapel in Galway, has finely carved heads of figures from the Reformation.

*St Columb's Church, Killygarvan* was built in 1814 and enlarged in 1887. The Batts, founders of the Belfast Banking Company, were a prominent family in the parish.

*Glenalla Church* was built around 1850 and dedicated to St Columba.

# The United Dioceses of Down and Dromore

The Diocese of Down and Dromore is one of only two Church of Ireland dioceses to be situated entirely in Northern Ireland. It is also one of the smallest geographically and one of the largest numerically. It is deeply rooted in the ministry and life of Patrick and the instinct of Patrick and his followers to make the mission of Christ their priority. That instinct took on a new dimension in the lives of the great missionary saints of the 6th Century, not least those from Bangor (including Comgall, Gall and Columbanus) who are still remembered for their evangelism and missionary endeavour in Europe.

Down and Dromore is a diocese of 76 parochial units covering the whole of Co Down (including a third of the city of Belfast), part of Co Armagh as far as the river Bann in Portadown, and a small portion of County Antrim. There are around 100 serving clergy and around 90,000 Church of Ireland people. The churches and sites range from the very ancient to the very new. Many churches were built during the 1960s and 1970s to serve new communities and housing estates. In recent years a new church has been built at Movilla Abbey (jointly with the Methodist Church) and another in Dollingstown.

There is also a developing desire in the diocese to make the Gospel relevant to the issues of the day. Reconciliation across the traditional divide in Northern Ireland is very important to us and was the lead strand in a diocesan programme called *Think again* in the first five years of the new millennium. We have also been developing youth work and, in recent years, seeking to respond to areas of poverty. Three *Christians Against Poverty* centres have been set up and *Via Wings*, a project which emerged in Dromore to help women going through difficult times in their lives, won the All-Ireland prize in its category in the *Pride of Place* awards. Several community centres have been set up by parishes including the multi-million pound *Jethro Centre* in Lurgan and the *Micah Centre* in East Belfast.

The diocese has also encouraged experimentation with new ways of doing church for a new generation. Some of these experiments have been within the life of ordinary parishes, such as parallel informal morning services for families, sometimes held in a parish centre rather than the church, evening events for young adults or *Messy Church* for children. Others have been even more 'out there', such as Wells and the Titanic Quarter. In the latter, the diocese took the decision to put a chaplain into the quarter to bring a spiritual dimension and he has been joined by five co-Chaplains from other denominations. The Dock Café is a hugely successful community space and the historic tender vessel, SS *Nomadic*, is now the venue for worship services.

Serving as bishop in the Diocese of Down and Dromore for the last decade and a half has been a great privilege. Life is never dull! One of my great joys is when the diocese comes together for events like the St Patrick's Day pilgrimage in Downpatrick, or the Bishop's Bible Week in the last week of August each year, or to share our missional life and experience at the Diocesan Synod. I always leave encouraged by the commitment and vision of the people. The future is good under God.

HAROLD DOWN AND DROMORE

County Down from the Mournes.
SCENIC IRELAND

# DOWN CATHEDRAL, DOWNPATRICK

In the period following St Patrick's death, the Hill of Down came to be regarded as his traditional burial place. There is a reference from AD 584 to a Fergus, who is named as bishop of 'Dun-lethglaise', when a timber church may have stood here.

As part of his reform of the church, St Malachy founded an Augustinian abbey on the site in 1138, naming it the Church of the Holy Trinity. In 1183, John de Courcy removed the Augustinian abbey and invited Benedictine monks from St Werburgh's in Chester to come and establish a monastery. The new foundation was named after St Patrick. Following the dissolution of the monasteries in the sixteenth century, the building gradually fell into ruin. In 1609, James I granted a charter to establish a dean and chapter, renaming the site the Cathedral of the Holy Trinity. Although the structure was still in ruins, bishops were consecrated within its walls.

Reputed burial place of St Patrick in the grounds of the cathedral
KEITH DRURY

Towards the end of the eighteenth century, Dean Annesley, along with Wills Hill (of Hillsborough) and many of the wealthy families of County Down, raised funds to restore the building. The work began in the 1780s and was completed in the early nineteenth century under the supervision of the architect Charles Lilly. Much of the interior of the cathedral dates from that period, in particular the box pews and the location of the organ above the canons' stalls. In the 1980s, and again in recent years, significant restoration work was carried out in the cathedral.

The capitals on the piers on both the north and south arcades are all thirteenth century work, but were heavily restored with plaster during the 1790 rebuild.

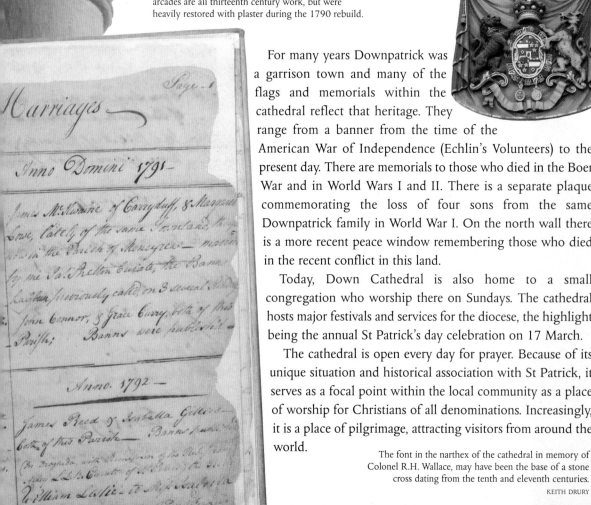

For many years Downpatrick was a garrison town and many of the flags and memorials within the cathedral reflect that heritage. They range from a banner from the time of the American War of Independence (Echlin's Volunteers) to the present day. There are memorials to those who died in the Boer War and in World Wars I and II. There is a separate plaque commemorating the loss of four sons from the same Downpatrick family in World War I. On the north wall there is a more recent peace window remembering those who died in the recent conflict in this land.

Today, Down Cathedral is also home to a small congregation who worship there on Sundays. The cathedral hosts major festivals and services for the diocese, the highlight being the annual St Patrick's day celebration on 17 March.

The cathedral is open every day for prayer. Because of its unique situation and historical association with St Patrick, it serves as a focal point within the local community as a place of worship for Christians of all denominations. Increasingly, it is a place of pilgrimage, attracting visitors from around the world.

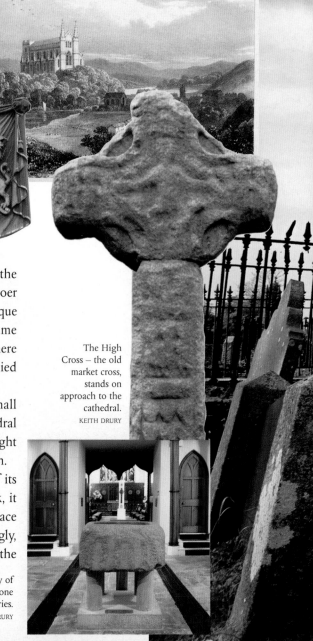

The High Cross – the old market cross, stands on approach to the cathedral.
KEITH DRURY

The font in the narthex of the cathedral in memory of Colonel R.H. Wallace, may have been the base of a stone cross dating from the tenth and eleventh centuries.
KEITH DRURY

# The United Dioceses of Down and Dromore

FRED RANKIN, ANNETTE McGRATH AND
BRIAN M WALKER

The dioceses of Down and Dromore cover a small area – County Down and portions of north County Armagh and south County Antrim. Nonetheless, they contain a large Church of Ireland population. These dioceses include a substantial part of Belfast (south and east of the River Lagan) as well as other major urban centres, such as Newtownards and Bangor in the east and Newry and Lurgan in the south and west. The mountains of Mourne and the Ards Peninsula are renowned for their special natural beauty. Many diocesan residents are employed in commerce and industry; the agricultural, fishing and tourist sectors are also important.

## The Early Church

This area has strong links with the early Patrician church. It contains the site of St Patrick's first church at Saul and also the reputed place of his burial, in the grounds of Down Cathedral in Downpatrick. Important early monastic sites include abbeys at Bangor, founded by St Comgall in AD 555, and at Movilla in Newtownards, founded by St Finnian in AD 540. The arrival of the Anglo-Normans led to the building of other impressive monasteries, such as at Inch and Greyabbey.

Holywood's rich ecclesiastical heritage is represented today by its most distinctive building, the Old Priory. The site is a monastery founded by St. Laiseran in the early seventh Century. The present ruins are twelfth century Anglo-Norman Augustinian Abbey built by Thomas Whyte and much of these ruins remain.
NORTH DOWN COUNCIL

## The Medieval Period

At a series of synods in the twelfth century, in particular Rathbrassil, convened to oversee the diocesan reorganisation of the whole country, the boundaries of the Down and Dromore dioceses were laid down. The boundaries of the modern dioceses relate quite closely to those drawn up at this time. The diocese of Down was united with Connor in the late fifteenth century. Dromore was joined to Down in 1842. Finally, in 1945, Connor became a separate diocese again, while Down and Dromore have remained united.

The twelfth century also saw the establishment of a parochial structure in both dioceses. These early parishes are documented in Pope Nicholas IV's taxation of the ecclesiastical benefices in Ireland. Until modern times and the growth of Belfast, this basic territorial structure of parishes remained in place, with comparatively minor modifications. Few church buildings have survived from this early period, but a number of today's churches do occupy the sites of earlier eccleciastical buildings.

This crucifixion scene, believed to be fifteenth century, was formerly above the doorway of the old church at Inch Abbey.
KEITH DRURY

The abbey at Grey
DERMOTT DUNBAR

## The Sixteenth, Seventeenth and Eighteenth Centuries

The sixteenth and seventeenth centuries witnessed important change, due not only to the Reformation but also to the arrival of Scots and English settlers. St Patrick's Church in Newry, erected in 1578, was probably the first Protestant church to be built in Ireland after the Reformation. Although not part of the official plantation of Ulster, County Down witnessed the arrival of many new Protestant settlers from England and Scotland in the early seventeenth century. The Scottish settlers tended to be Presbyterians, while the English ones were usually members of the Established Church, which took control of existing church buildings.

The first half of the seventeenth century saw great turmoil and many churches were destroyed. After the Restoration in 1660, church-building began in earnest in what might loosely be called the upper Lagan Valley. A cathedral was erected at Dromore and parish churches were built in places such as Seagoe, Donaghcloney and Magheralin. Until the Restoration, it was common for Presbyterian ministers to officiate at Church of Ireland churches in these dioceses, but this practice was ended in the 1660s by Bishop Jeremy Taylor, who, in the years 1661–7, served as bishop of Down and Connor and also administered Dromore.

In the eighteenth century, the building of new churches continued. On various occasions, local landlords contributed considerably to this process. St Mary's, Newry was erected largely through funding from the Kilmorey family. Other examples are the churches built by the Montgomery family in Greyabbey and the Waring family in Waringstown. Perhaps the finest example was Hillsborough Parish Church, which was erected by Wills Hill, later first marquis of Downshire, and which retained the name of St Malachi's, after the medieval church in the district.

Among the clergy of the two dioceses, some are of special interest. Bishop Jeremy Taylor earned a high reputation for his theological works, although Presbyterians resented his efforts to remove their ministers from parish churches in the 1660s. The literary writings of Bishop Thomas Percy, friend of Samuel Johnson and James Boswell, are regarded as influential. Both Taylor and Percy are buried at Dromore Cathedral.

## The Nineteenth Century

The 1800s saw continued construction of new churches and the improvement of earlier buildings. The Down and Connor Diocesan Church Accommodation Society was formed in 1838 by Rev. Thomas Drew, father of the architect Sir Thomas Drew. This led to the erection of a number of churches in places such as Groomsport, Tyrella, Hollymount and Kilwarlin. Elsewhere we see the replacement of churches by new, larger buildings to accommodate growing numbers in urban centres – for example, in Lurgan, where the Church of Christ the Redeemer, the largest parish church in Ireland, was consecrated in 1863. From the middle of the nineteenth century there was a significant rise in churchgoing, in some places due to the 1859 revival.

The greatest increase in church-building, however, occurred in the region of Belfast, which experienced enormous population growth in the nineteenth and early twentieth centuries, thanks in large part to the rise of the shipbuilding and linen industries. Until

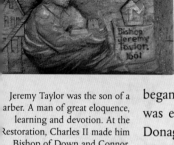

Jeremy Taylor was the son of a barber. A man of great eloquence, learning and devotion. At the Restoration, Charles II made him Bishop of Down and Connor, and then added Dromore. He rebuilt Dromore Cathedral, which he found in ruins, and which is represented by the model in his hands. He was buried under the chancel.

Clonallon Church, believed to have been built by Bishop Jeremy Taylor

Bishop Jeremy Taylor

### Dean Patrick and Mary Delany

Patrick Delany served as dean of Down in 1744–68. His wife, the renowned artist and writer Mary Delany, has left us in her published correspondence an intriguing picture of clerical life in Downpatrick and Lecale in the first half of the eighteenth century. She was also renowned for her fine flower collage work. The Delanys were friends of Dean Swift, Alexander Pope and Letitia Pilkington.

Bishop Thomas Percy, 1782–1811

Tyrella
GARY MCMURRAY

In the late nineteenth and early twentieth century the Church of Ireland ran a number of conferences to look at social and moral issues affecting Ireland. This photograph taken at the October 1910 Belfast Conference shows most of the bishops of Ireland in the front row.

1827, the area immediately south and east of the River Lagan at Belfast was served by the one parish church of Knockbreda, but by 1914 there were another seven churches. St Patrick's, in the heart of the shipbuilding area of Ballymacarrett, could accommodate 1,500 people.

William Reeves served as bishop of the united dioceses in 1886–92, but is best known for his extensive historical research, including the *Ecclesiastical Antiquities of Down, Connor and Dromore* (1847). Rev. William Butler Yeats was rector of Tullylish Parish in 1836–62 and grandfather of the poet W.B. Yeats. On 23 January 1847, at the height of the Great Famine, he wrote to the *Northern Whig* to plead for funds to alleviate the starving in his area:

> I ask, for our suffering fellowmen, in the name of common humanity and by the stern necessities of justice, that you will do your duty, and give liberally.

The success of this appeal enabled a relief committee to purchase large quantities of meal for famine relief.

## The Early Twentieth Century

The impact of World War I on the lives of so many parishioners is clearly revealed in the war memorials erected in most churches in the dioceses. The roll of honour in St Gobhan's church, Seagoe Parish, records a total of 264 names, including 49 killed and 57 wounded. After the war the population continued to grow, especially in the Belfast region. On 21 April 1922, the *Church of Ireland Gazette* noted:

> In Belfast the Church of Ireland, we are proud to say, is the church of the poor, the very poor. Everyday five souls are added to our church population in Belfast. In less than a week more souls are added to the church in Belfast than are to be found in some parishes in Ireland.

All Saints, Tullylish
KEITH DRURY

By the mid 1930s, members of the Church of Ireland in these three dioceses numbered nearly 250,000 and there were 230 clergymen. Eventually, in 1945, Connor was separated from Down and Dromore. New buildings from the interwar period included the churches of St Finnian, St Christopher, St Clement and Cregagh in east Belfast, St Columbanus in Ballyholme and St Patrick in Saul, Downpatrick.

One of the last bishops of the three united dioceses was Frederick MacNeice (bishop 1934–44), father of the poet Louis MacNeice. During the riots in Belfast in 1935, he took a leading role in seeking to promote reconciliation in the city.

John Leishman, a parishioner at St Mary's Ballybeen, who served in World War II at El Alamein and Normandy, seen at a Jubilee Celebration in June 2012.

## The Second Half of the Twentieth Century

From the 1950s onward, there was a resurgence in church-building. Development of housing away from Belfast city centre to the suburbs and parts of north Down created a need for extra venues for worship. The 1950s and 60s, under Bishop F.J. Mitchell, saw the building of 13 new churches in areas in Belfast such as Belvoir, Stormont and Knocknagoney, as well as in Bangor, Dundonald and Lurgan. The 1970s saw the construction of four churches, including St Mary's, Ballybeen and Movilla Abbey, Newtownards.

Under the leadership of Bishop George Quin (bishop 1970–80), the two dioceses witnessed a significant campaign of renewal, which led to a rise in ordinations and a reinvigorated lay involvement in church life. Important new relations with the Methodist Church resulted in the development of a number of joint churches and parish initiatives.

The Troubles, of course, had a direct bearing on both dioceses. Considerable numbers of members of the church lost their lives or were seriously injured through political violence. Some areas witnessed major displacement of population owing to important economic and social changes, such as the decline of the Belfast shipyards and the redevelopment of parts of east Belfast.

Attempts to improve community relations meant that clergy and laity became involved in various ecumenical and reconciliation efforts. In 1974, Cecil and Myrtle Kerr founded the Christian Renewal Centre at Rostrevor to encourage inter-church relations and reconciliation. Bishop Gordon McMullan (bishop 1986–97) organised a series of annual lectures in Irish history for schoolchildren, known as the Rockwell Lectures, at Queen's University, Belfast in the 1990s, to promote better understanding of our past.

## The twenty-first century

Two new church buildings have been erected at Dollingstown and Movilla (the latter jointly with the Methodists) and two large community centres governed by Parish Caring Associations: The Jethro Centre in Lurgan and the Micah Centre in Willowfield. Bishop Harold Miller (1997–present) is the longest-serving bishop of Down and Dromore since the mid-nineteenth Century. He led the 5-year 'Think Again' strategy at the start of the new millennium with its threefold goal of Reconciliation, Outreach and Young People, and will lead a Year of Mission in 2015. Moving forward, the diocese has set as its priorities: developing young leaders, planting new churches and reaching the next generation for Christ.

Cecil and Myrtle Kerr

### BORING WELLS

Boring Wells was born in 2003 out of a desire to bore down into the bedrock of our communities to see if there is fresh water to be found, especially among those who find themselves culturally distanced from the church in its inherited structures. We have tried to create communities of faith among different sorts of people and in some very different sorts of places – pubs, schools, community centres, and coffee shops. We are working in three areas – teenagers with severe and profound learning difficulties, inner city east Belfast and an interface community. We have been granted one of the first Diocesan Mission Orders to develop a new Christian community in the St Christopher's area of east Belfast.

### MESSY CHURCH

Craft, worship, food: Messy Church is a simple formula with a huge appeal. Mount Merrion Parish in Cregagh is running a very popular 'Messy Church' on the third Friday of every month, straight after school. Refreshments are served and then the adults and children can play games or make crafts together. After an hour, everyone moves into church for some lively worship, puppets, a Bible talk and prayer. The afternoon finishes at 5.30pm with a meal together. More parishes in the diocese are exploring Messy Church as a possible method of creating community and family moments as they seek to forge links and build relationships within the communities they are a part of. Kilkeel, Mount Merrion, St Dorothea's, Knockbreda, Bangor Parish and Boring Wells in Mersey Street are just some of the churches seeing discipleship opportunities increase by using the Messy Church idea.

Detail from a stained-glass window in Drumgooland church that replaced one of three blown out by a bomb in 1975.
DERMOTT DUNBAR

Dromore Cathedral's 'Snyf' group at Summer Madness
ANNETTE McGRATH

# THE PARISHES IN THE DIOCESE OF DOWN

## BALLYBEEN

*St Mary's Church* was planted as a daughter congregation of St Elizabeth's, Dundonald, establishing a Church of Ireland witness in the new Ballybeen estate. The site was conveyed by the Northern Ireland Housing Executive in 1966 and the hall/church was dedicated in 1973. Ballybeen received parochial status in 1983, at which time the present church was built. Rev. Ken Clarke, later bishop of Kilmore, was the first curate-in-charge. The current church building, designed by S.V.W. McCready, opened in September 1984. It houses the first baptismal pool in the diocese.

St Mary's,
Ballybeen
DERMOTT DUNBAR

## BALLYHALBERT AND ARDKEEN

St Andrew's Church, Ballyhalbert
DERMOTT DUNBAR

Ballyhalbert was grouped with Ardkeen in 1967. Situated on the Ards Peninsula, *St Andrew's Church*, Ballyhalbert was built in 1850. The church has fine stained glass and a notable organ. The pulpit is unusual in that it is entered directly from the vestry, a reminder of the period when the preacher removed his surplice before preaching the sermon.

*Christ Church, Ardkeen* replaces a much earlier building on the shore of Strangford Lough and was consecrated in 1847.

## BALLYHOLME

Stained glass at St Columbanus's Church, Bangor
NORTH DOWN COUNCIL

The first building to house the congregation at Ballyholme, Bangor, was a wooden hall on the Groomsport Road. It was constructed in 1927 on a site bought earlier by Bangor Parish. Services were held there until the new church was built. Ballyholme remained a daughter church of Bangor Parish Church until 1955. *St Columbanus's Church* was consecrated on 22 June 1940. The stone used came from Roxborough Castle in Moy and the bell came from St Patrick's Cathedral in Dublin. A new purpose-built parish centre was completed in 2006, allowing the parish to further its ministry to the community.

## BALLYWALTER AND INISHARGIE

There has been a parish church in Ballywalter since the thirteenth century or earlier. It was originally known as Whitechurch and the ruins may still be seen. The present *Holy Trinity Church* was consecrated in 1849.

*St Andrew's Church*, Balligan was consecrated in 1704. It was restored in 1844, 1966 and 2004, but retains its eighteenth-century character. Unusually, it is lit entirely by candles and evensong takes place regularly in this atmospheric light.

Holy Trinity
Church,
Ballywalter
DERMOTT DUNBAR

St Andrew's Church, Balligan
DERMOTT DUNBAR

## BANGOR

By the late nineteenth century, Bangor Abbey was in need of considerable repair and plans were laid to build a new church in the centre of the town. By 1877, funds had been raised and R.E. Ward of Bangor Castle donated the site. The new church, *St Comgall's*, was consecrated in 1882. In the twentieth century, the organ was installed as a memorial to those who fell in World War I and refurbished in memory of those who served in World War II. Among the former clergy of this parish are at least seven bishops and archbishops.

After fire damage in June 2012, the church has undergone significant repair and remodelling.

St Comgall's, Bangor

## BANGOR ABBEY AND KILCOOLEY

*Bangor Abbey* is built on the site of the early Christian monastery founded by St Comgall in AD 558. Sacked by the Vikings, then revived by St Malachy around 1140, the ruined abbey was rebuilt in 1617 by Sir James Hamilton. The church was demolished in 1830 and replaced by the present building in 1833. When St Comgall's was built in 1882 in the centre of Bangor, the abbey church was abandoned. It remained unused until 1917, when it was restored and reopened. In 1935, it became a separate parish.

*St Columba Church, Kilcooley* was opened in October 1973 as a daughter church of Bangor Abbey, to cater for the growing population in the Kilcooley area. It is a dual-purpose building, serving as both church and hall.

Bangor bell
NORTH DOWN MUSEUM

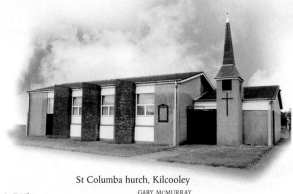

St Columba hurch, Kilcooley
GARY McMURRAY

## BANGOR (THE PRIMACY)

*Christ Church* was built in the Primacy area of Bangor to cater for the large number of new residents who moved there in the 1970s. It was opened in 1983 as a daughter church to St Comgall's, but became an independent parish in 1998. Christ Church is located on the Balloo Road. It is a modern multi-purpose facility for the whole community. It is shared with the local Methodist congregation. Primacy is one of the parishes in the diocese that have partnered with Christians Against Poverty to open a much-needed debt-counselling centre.

## BELFAST

### BALLYMACARRETT

Ballymacarrett Parish was created in 1828, the first new parish to be carved out of Knockbreda Parish to cater for the spread of the population of Belfast to the east of the Lagan caused by industries such as shipbuilding and ropemaking. The original church was rebuilt several times to cater for the rapid rise in numbers. *St Patrick's Church* was built in 1893. The building was badly damaged during World War II, with the loss of most of the stained glass. It was almost totally rebuilt after the war and rededicated in 1952. In recent decades, the loss of heavy industry, the redevelopment of the area and the movement of much of the population to other areas, such as Newtownards and Dundonald, has led to a much-depleted congregation. Former clergy of the parish include four bishops, namely Cyril Elliott of Connor, George Quin and Gordon McMullan of Down and Dromore and James Mehaffey of Derry and Raphoe.

*St Christopher's Church* and *St Martin's Church*, Ballymacarrett, built in the 1930s within the parish, closed in 2011. The latter was founded by the Southern Church Mission. Its rector was originally appointed by the bishop of Meath.

St Patrick's Church, Ballymacarrett

## BALLYNAFEIGH

*St Jude's Church*, on the Ormeau Road, was the first church to be erected in Ireland after disestablishment in 1870. The architect was Sir Thomas Drew, who was also responsible for the addition of the south aisle 30 years later. In 1990, a two-storey suite of rooms was built inside the church to give added space for other meetings. The stained glass beside the north-east entrance, portraying Ruth and St Jude, was designed by the well-known Ulster artist Olive Henry.

DERMOTT DUNBAR

DERMOTT DUNBAR

## BELVOIR

The *Church of the Transfiguration* is one of the generation of churches built on the housing estates that arose with the post-World War II shift to the suburbs. Its foundation stone was laid on 11 April 1964 and the church was consecrated almost a year later. The design was by A.F. Lucy. A terrorist bomb exploded across the dual carriageway in November 1992, wrecking the building and forcing its demolition. It was rebuilt to the original design and reconsecrated in December 1993.

## CREGAGH

The parish of Cregagh was formed to cater for an area not far from Knockbreda Parish Church which, after World War I, saw much new housing, including 150 homes for ex-servicemen and their families. Streets had names such as Picardy and Thiepval. The foundation stone for *St Finnian's Church*, Cregagh (left) was laid in September 1931 and the building was consecrated on St Finnian's Day, 10 September 1932. It was awarded parochial status in 1946. A former rector, James Mehaffey, became bishop of Derry and Raphoe in 1980.

DERMOTT DUNBAR

## DUNDELA

Dundela in east Belfast achieved parochial status with the increase in population of the area around Strandtown in the nineteenth century. *St Mark's Church* was designed by William Butterfield, an internationally known architect of the 'high' school. The foundation stone was laid in 1876 and the church was consecrated in 1878. The church has strong links with C.S. Lewis, whose childhood home was nearby and whose name is entered in the baptismal register.

## C.S. LEWIS AND ST MARK'S DUNDELA

The parish of St Mark's, Dundela, has rich associations with the Lewis family. Its first Rector was Revd Thomas Hamilton, CS Lewis' grandfather. On 29th January 1899, the Revd Hamilton baptised his grandson, Clive Staples Lewis, at the font in the west end of the church. Albert Lewis, father of CS, was a successful solicitor in Belfast and a loyal member of the parish. He served as Churchwarden and as the first Sunday School Superintendent. Jointly with his brothers and sisters, Albert gave the church the silver vessels still used for Holy Communion. Albert died in 1929 and in 1932, CS and Warren presented a stained glass window to St Mark's in memory of their parents. The Lewis Window may be seen in the south aisle. Michael Healy, a noted Dublin artist in stained glass, portrayed three Saints – Luke, James and Mark. CS Lewis also presented St Mark's with a portrait of his grandfather.

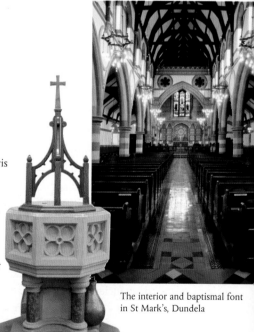

The interior and baptismal font in St Mark's, Dundela

## GILNAHIRK

On the edge of east Belfast, *St Dorothea's Church* was built and consecrated in 1956, but it did not become a separate parish until July 1959. The church was designed by Desmond Hodges, a son of the then-bishop of Limerick, and much of the funding came from a bequest from the brother of a former rector of Holywood. His legacy to the dioceses of Down, Dromore and Connor for the erection of churches was conditional upon his being allowed to specify their dedications. The dedication to St Dorothea is a rare one. The baptismal font came from Kilmore, County Tipperary.

## KNOCK

The foundation stone of *St Columba's Church* which replaced an iron church, was laid in 1895 and the chancel and transepts were consecrated a year later. A newspaper report of the consecration noted that the district had become 'immensely popular as a residential place on account of its splendid scenery and close situation to the city'. Additions continued and the building was not completed until 1932. The original architect was R.M. Close and the final work was the responsibility of his son, also called R.M. Close.

## KNOCKBREDA

Originally, the parish of Knockbreda covered a large area in County Down to the east and south of the town (later the city) of Belfast. This ran from Drumbo to Holywood. As the population grew, many new parishes with their own churches were created within its original boundaries. *Knockbreda Church* was built in 1737 by Lady Middleton, a grandmother of the duke of Wellington. It was designed by the eminent German architect Richard Cassell, whose other buildings included Leinster House in Dublin. The chancel, the work of Sir Thomas Drew, was added in 1883. In the graveyard are several mausolea of considerable architectural and historic importance. Knockbreda is the oldest Church of Ireland church in the Belfast area, although at present it is outside the city boundaries.

DERMOTT DUNBAR

## KNOCKNAGONEY

DERMOTT DUNBAR

The *Church of the Annunciation* was designed by Desmond Hodges and built in the early 1960s to serve new housing in Dundela and Holywood Parishes. Initially a bishop's curacy, in 2011 the parish became a full incumbency. The foundation stone was laid in March 1963 and the church was consecrated a year later. Lady Dunleath opened the building, the organ having been presented by Lord Dunleath. The pulpit was made by prisoners in Crumlin Road Gaol and came from the old church of St Elizabeth at Dundonald, where it was no longer in use. In the Mothers' Union chapel is a stone taken from Rachel's tomb in Jerusalem and presented to the church by Mrs Kathleen Mitchell, wife of Bishop Mitchell.

## MOUNT MERRION

The *Church of the Pentecost* was built as a daughter church to St Finnian's Church, Cregagh, to cater for the increasing population in the adjacent housing estate. Initially, only a hall was built, but the church followed. It was designed by Denis O'D. Hanna and consecrated on 16 March 1963. It sits in front of Ravenhill Stadium, home to the Ulster rugby team. Mount Merrion became a parish in its own right in 1962 and remains so, although for a few years it was a curacy to Willowfield Parish.

DERMOTT DUNBAR

Decorative wall art, Church of the Pentecost, Mount Merrion

## ORANGEFIELD

The history of *St John the Evangelist's Church* on the Castlereagh Road in east Belfast, goes back to St John's Church, Laganbank, which was built in 1853 but closed owing to population movement and finally demolished in 1943. The endowments and furnishing of the original St John's were transferred to this new church in east Belfast. The new church, designed by R.H. Gibson and E.D. Taylor, was consecrated on 2 November 1957. The building, whilst being of modern construction, has a very traditional interior.

A daughter church, *St Brigid's Church*, Braniel, designed by J.P. Jury, was licensed for worship on 18 June 1964 to serve the Braniel district. It has been agreed that new models of mission be developed in the area covered by St Brigid's.

## ST BRENDAN'S, SYDENHAM

*St Brendan's Parish* was carved out of nearby Dundela in 1923. At first it had only a wooden hut, and this eventually became the parochial hall. The parish became independent after the war. The Larkfield Road site of *St Brendan's Church* was purchased in 1943. The church, dedicated to the patron saint of sailors, was built in 1962 to designs by Denis O'D. Hanna and the foundation stone came from Ardfert Cathedral. The church was completely demolished in a storm in January 1965 but, luckily, much inside was saved. A new church, designed by Gordon McKnight, was consecrated on 21 October 1967.

## ST CLEMENT'S, TEMPLEMORE AVENUE

This east-Belfast parish was originally served by an iron church, which was moved from a site on the Beersbridge Road to a new site on the Castlereagh Road. The present *St Clement's Church* built of stone, was consecrated on 20 April 1929. The architects were Blackwood and Jury.

## ST DONARD'S, BLOOMFIELD

The site of *St Donard's Church* at the junction of the Beersbridge and Bloomfield Roads in east Belfast, was acquired in 1900. Initially an iron church was erected to cater for the needs of the increasing population of Ballymacarrett. Plans were soon afoot to build, and a stone church was dedicated in the name of St Donard on 1 June 1912. The vestry room was added in 1922. Shortly afterwards, the lease of the site was bought out and transferred to the Representative Church Body. This enabled the church to be consecrated on 15 June 1929.

## STORMONT

*St Molua's Church* was designed by Denis O'D. Hanna. It was built in 1961–2 and financed largely by diocesan funds, supported by substantial contributions from Knock Parish. The parish was drawn from the parishes of Knock, Gilnahirk, Dundonald and Dundela. A large mural, *The Son of Man* by Desmond Kinney, fills the east wall behind the sanctuary; there are also bronze sculptures by James McKendry. The organ came from St Matthias's Church in Dublin. The church has a very strong musical tradition and frequently mounts choral concerts.

DERMOTT DUNBAR

## WILLOWFIELD

*Willowfield Church* was consecrated in 1872 and was the seventh and last church built by the Belfast Church Extension and Endowment Society. The building has undergone major alterations throughout its history. It has twice had a spire, which has twice been dismantled for reasons of safety. In September 2007 there was a massive reordering and restoration of the church, including the replacement of the pews with movable chairs. The construction of the adjoining Micah Centre was also completed as part of this project. Willowfield has a burgeoning inner-city congregation of all ages and is very active in the community.

## BRIGHT, BALLEE, KILLOUGH AND RATHMULLAN

Ecclesiastical records of the late twelfth century list churches in the parishes of Bright and Ballee. Bright and Ballee were grouped in 1922, with Killough added in 1968 and Rathmullan in 2008.

*Bright Church* was built in 1745. The first Sunday school in Ireland was begun here in 1782, when up to 363 pupils attended.

*Ballee Church* was erected in 1749. A tower was added as late as 1913.

*St Anne's Church*, Killough was originally a chapel of ease for Rathmullan, dating from 1716 but rebuilt in 1802. The wooden spire, a notable landmark for sailors, was blown down in 1839.

*Rathmullan Church* was built in 1701 on the site of an earlier building. The tower and spire were constructed in 1886.

Bright Church

St Anne's Church, Killough

## CARNALEA

This parish in west Bangor was constituted in 1960 with a temporary building from St Molua's Church, Stormont. The parochial district was formed in 1962, comprising portions of the parishes of Bangor Abbey and Glencraig. *St Gall's Church* designed by Edward Leighton, was consecrated in March 1966. The stained-glass windows depict, in addition to Christ and the way of the cross, St Gall and a bear (his companion, according to legend) and St Comgall. A stone from St Gallen in Switzerland is exposed in the wall of the vestibule. The church was, for some time, shared for worship with the local Methodist congregation.

St Patrick's Church, Millisle

## CARROWDORE AND MILLISLE

Carrowdore is the last resting place of the poet Louis MacNeice, of international fame, whose father was a former bishop of the diocese.

In 1837, the primate of all Ireland, Lord John George Beresford, decided to build a new church, *Christ Church*, at Carrowdore at his own expense, because of his links to the Dunbar family in the parish. The church was consecrated in August 1843. Designed originally by William Farrell, the firm of Lanyon and Lynne was responsible for additions to the church in 1860.

The nearby *St Patrick's Church*, Millisle was built in 1953. Initially, Millisle was a daughter church of Donaghadee Parish, but it was transferred to Carrowdore in 1965.

Christ Church, Carrowdore

DERMOTT DUNBAR

Statue of General 'Rollo' Gillespie on Comber Square in front of St Mary's Church

## COMBER

*St Mary's Church* is situated in the centre of Comber on what was almost certainly the site of an ancient Cistercian Abbey. Although there is evidence of a church here as early as the seventeenth century, the present church, designed by William Farrell, was consecrated in 1840. In 2008 a south transept was built and the Cistercian and Quarry windows added. Among famous parishioners was General Hugh Robert 'Rollo' Gillespie, a British army officer who died at the battle of Nalapani in 1814; his last words were 'One shot more for the honour of Down!' His statue stands in the town square in front of St Mary's Church.

## DONAGHADEE

This parish can be dated back as far as the 1306 taxation. The present *Donaghadee Parish Church* appears to have been built by Viscount Hugh Montgomery in 1626. It took the form of a cross. The tower, asymmetrically placed at the north end of the cross, would seem to have been the stump of an earlier tower house. Many examples of tower houses can still be found around the County Down coast. The tower was completed in 1833 and the church was enlarged in 1878, thanks to the generosity of the local landed Delacherois family, who were of Huguenot origin. The church was extensively restored in 2011.

BRIAN M WALKER

Saul, Downpatrick, where St Patrick had his first church. This was taken about 1960, and shows the rector, Canon H.C. Marshall, the Archbishop of Canterbury and Lady Fisher, with Mrs Walker, wife of former rector Leslie Walker, in the background.

## DOWN CATHEDRAL and THE LECALE GROUP (SAUL, BALLYCULTER, KILCLIEF, DUNSFORD, ARDGLASS)

This group consists of these five parishes along with Down Cathedral.

*St Patrick's Church*, Saul, is close to where St Patrick landed and made his first convert Dichu, the local chieftain. The present building which replaced an earlier one on the site, was consecrated on 1 November 1933 as part of the celebrations to mark the 1,500th anniversary of the arrival of Patrick in Ireland. The architect was Henry Seaver, who modelled the building on an early Celtic pattern.

*Christ Church*, Ballyculter was built in 1723, with the tower and spire added in 1770. The church was virtually rebuilt, complete with lychgate, in 1881–2 by the Ward family of Castleward as a memorial to Viscountess Bangor.

The site of *St Caelan's Church*, Kilclief has links to the early Christian period. The present structure was completed between 1834 and 1843. It is simple in style, with a fireplace at the south-west corner.

*St Mary's Church*, Dunsford dates from the eighteenth century. Dunsford was grouped with Ardglass in 1928.

*St Nicholas' Church*, Ardglass is dedicated in the name of the patron saint of mariners and dates from 1813. It is built on the site of St Mary's Abbey; the tiles at the foot of the pulpit were part of the original abbey floor.

St Nicholas' Church, Ardglass

Christ Church, Ballyculter

St Caelin's, Kilclief

# DOWN GROUP (DOWN, HOLLYMOUNT, TYRELLA, LOUGHINISLAND)

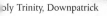

Seaforde Church

NOEL THOMPSON

The present *Holy Trinity Church*, Downpatrick is thought to have been built in 1735, although there are earlier records of the steeple and belfry. Despite its dedication, it is known locally as St Margaret's.

*Hollymount Church* was designed by Sir Charles Lanyon and consecrated as a chapel of ease for Down Parish in 1841. It was remodelled in 1885 by Sir Thomas Drew and restored in 2004.

As with other parishes in Lecale, *Tyrella* has a history that goes back to the Anglo-Norman period. The present church was built by the Montgomery family of Tyrella House in 1839–40. Although there is no record of formal dedication, the church is known as St John's.

*Seaforde Church* was built for the parish of Loughinisland around 1723. Rev. Dr Thomas Drew, father of the architect of the same name, was incumbent in 1859–70, and it is likely that his son was responsible for important additions to the church in 1861.

oly Trinity, Downpatrick

## DRUMBEG

Drumbeg Parish originally included Dunmurry and Finaghy parochial districts. To accommodate the growing population, these districts were transferred to the diocese of Connor. A church was built in 1798, but its wooden spire was blown down in 1831 and replaced by a stone tower and spire in 1833. *St Patrick's Church* designed by Sir Thomas Drew, was built in 1870 on the same site as the original church, and retained the 1833 tower and spire. It is known to all who pass it as 'the church with the lychgate'. The lychgate was built in 1878 as a memorial to John Ferguson Montgomery.

DERMOTT DUNBAR

## DRUMBO

*Holy Trinity Church*, built in 1791, is in the village of Ballylesson. The architect was Charles Lilly, who was also responsible for the restoration of Down Cathedral. Drumbo has a peal of eight bells, six of which were installed when the church was built; the other two were added in 1977. The lighting was designed by Stephen Dykes Bower, who was then surveyor emeritus to Westminster Abbey, and made by Harland and Wolff. Buried at Drumbo is Michael Sadler, MP for Newark, who died in 1835 after a career campaigning for social justice in the industrial revolution.

## DUNDONALD

There are two parish churches adjacent to each other at Dundonald. The older building, dedicated in the name of St Elizabeth of Hungary, dates back to the eighteenth century, with additions from the nineteenth century. *St Elizabeth's,* a new church with the same dedication, was consecrated on 17 September 1966, having been built to accommodate the large numbers of people who moved to the area in the 1960s. The older church was deconsecrated in 1967. The organ in the new church came from St Barnabas's in Dublin, which had closed in 1965. St Mary's, Ballybeen was a daughter church of Dundonald until it achieved independent parochial status in 1983.

## GLENCRAIG

*Holy Trinity Church* was consecrated in 1858. The parochial district was taken from Holywood, Bangor and Newtownards. By 1886 it had become necessary to provide additional accommodation and the nave was lengthened. The chancel was enlarged in 1921 and a side chapel was added in 1975. The church was built at the request of Miss Anne Symes, who lived at Glencraig House, now the Camphill Community, who always wanted it to be known as Glencraig Church.

Ballyphilip Church

## GREYABBEY AND KIRCUBBIN
## WITH BALLYPHILIP AND ARDQUIN

Greyabbey is dominated by the ruins of the nearby Cistercian abbey, founded by the wife of John de Courcy in 1193 and dissolved in 1541. The first Viscount Montgomery enclosed part of the abbey's nave for use as a parish church until 1778, when a new church was built.

*St Saviour's Church, Greyabbey*, consecrated in 1869, is the third church to serve the parish. The interior is richly furnished with ornamental brickwork and carvings. Greyabbey has been united with Kircubbin since 1975. In 2008, Ballyphilip and Ardquin joined the union.

*Holy Trinity Church, Kircubbin* was designed by Sir Charles Lanyon in the Greek-revival style and built in 1843 by the Ward family of Bangor. Lord Dunleath donated the organ.

*Ballyphilip Church* is in the town of Portaferry, near the southern tip of the Ards Peninsula. The present church was built in 1787.

*Ardquin Church* was consecrated in 1827 and known as the Abbacy Church, after the seventeenth-century manor house of that name.

St Saviour's Church, Greyabbey

## GROOMSPORT

*Groomsport Church* was built in 1842 as a chapel of ease to Bangor, on a site donated by the Maxwell family of Groomsport and Finnebrogue. The architec was Sir Charles Lanyon. The church was not consecrated until 1850, when Groomsport became a parish independent of Bangor. A condition of the Maxwell gift was that it be called Groomsport Church (thus there is no dedication) and that there be no graveyard. Over the years there have been additions – the chancel was added in 1909 and the transepts in 1932.

## HELEN'S BAY

Initially, *St John the Baptist's Church*, was a chapel of ease to Glencraig but, by the early years of the twentieth century, the parishioners of the district wanted their own church. A site was donated by the dowager duchess of Dufferin and Ava, from nearby Clandeboye, and she laid the foundation stone of a new church on 3 August 1909. In November of the same year it was consecrated. Extensions were added in 1924 and 1964, almost doubling the size of the original building.

GARY MCMURRY

## HILLSBOROUGH

*St Malachi's Church* the only church with this dedication in the Church of Ireland, is one of the best examples of eighteenth-century church architecture in Ireland. There was an earlier church on the site, erected by Arthur Hill, but it was reconstructed and enlarged by Wills Hill, the first marquis of Downshire. Since it reopened in 1773, it has been little altered, retaining the original high box pews and pulpit, complete with sounding board. The east window is the only one in Ireland designed by Sir Joshua Reynolds, first president of the Royal Academy. Hillsborough Church was traditionally the church where successive governors of Northern Ireland worshipped. For many years its organist was William Harty, whose son, Sir Hamilton Harty, became conductor of the Halle Orchestra and was one of the foremost musicians of his day.

## HOLYWOOD

The ruins of the priory church, with its medieval origins, can be seen in High Street, Holywood. It was burned by Brian Phelim O'Neill in 1572 and largely restored by Sir James Hamilton in 1615. Thereafter, it served as the parish church for over 200 years. *St Philip's and St James's Church* on Church Road, was designed by Charles Lanyon and consecrated in 1844. It was later enlarged with the addition of nave, chancel and north aisle and reconsecrated with the present dedication. The church has a peal of eight bells and much notable stained glass. The organ, rebuilt in 1914, has been played by some famous musicians, including Sir Edward Elgar, Sir Henry Wood and Sir Hamilton Harty.

St Ignatius Church, Carryduff

## KILLANEY AND CARRYDUFF

Originally, an iron church from London was erected at Killaney, but this was replaced by a stone building, consecrated on 18 April 1867. Curiously, the church was dedicated in the name of St John the Evangelist, but is now known as *St Andrew's*.

To cater for the post-World War II movement of population from Belfast, a dual-purpose hall/church was built at Carryduff in 1954. A new church, designed by Donald Shanks, was consecrated on 2 October 1965. It was dedicated in the name of *St Ignatius*, the third bishop of Antioch, which is rare in Anglicanism. Appropriately, the preacher at the consecration was Very Rev. Anthony Bloom, archbishop of Sourozh, of the Russian Orthodox Church.

St Andrew's Church, Killaney

## KILLINCHY AND KILMOOD

GARY MCMURRY

St Mary's Church, Kilmood

In 1928, Kilmood joined with Killinchy and Tullynakill (whose church was demolished in 1971) to form the Killinchy Union of Parishes.

*Killinchy Church*, situated in Killinchy village, with views of Strangford Lough, was built in 1830 in succession to a number of earlier churches in the parish.

*St Mary's Church*, Kilmood was opened for worship in 1822. The building retains its original box pews. The church has three fine chandeliers including one of Dutch origin.

## KILLYLEAGH

*St John the Evangelist's Church* was built in 1812 by Lord Dufferin of Clandeboye. The first church on the present site had been built in 1612 by his ancestor, Viscount Clannaboy. The church has undergone considerable alteration. New pews were installed in 1859 and, in recent years, major refurbishment took place. Killyleagh was the home of Hans Sloane, founder of the British Museum, in whose memory the church's font cover was installed in 1961. A former rector was Dr Edward Hincks (rector 1825–66), a noted Egyptologist and scholar of oriental manuscripts.

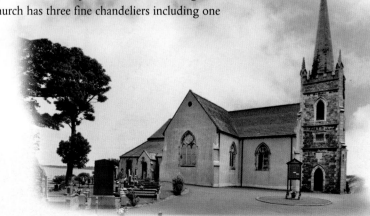

## KILMORE AND INCH

Inch Parish was originally grouped with Saul. It was grouped with Kilmore in 1982.

The first church at Kilmore was erected in 1792. By the 1860s the congregation had outgrown it and the new building, *Christ Church*, was consecrated in 1870. Extensive renovations and repairs were carried out in 2003. In 1978 the original church was taken down and reconstructed at the Ulster Folk and Transport Museum.

Originally, *Inch Church* stood close to the ruins of the Cistercian Abbey in the area. The present church, dedicated in the name of St Patrick, was erected in 1742. Various additions were made in the eighteenth and nineteenth centuries.

Inch Chur[...]
KEITH DRUR[...]

## KILWARLIN UPPER AND LOWER

GARY MCMURRY

Both these churches were built in 1840 as necessary outreach to the more distant parts of Hillsborough Parish. Upper and Lower Kilwarlin were grouped in 1969.

*St James's Church*, Lower Kilwarlin is situated on the Hillsborough–Moira Road. It was designed by Charles Lanyon.

*St John's Church*, Upper Kilwarlin is a stone-built church on the Ballygowan Road in the townland of Corcreeny. Its parish district includes parts of Moira and Dromore, as well as Hillsborough.

## MOVILLA

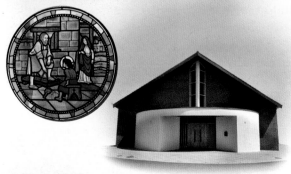

*Movilla Abbey Church* was built to cater for a growing population in the Newtownards area, due in large part to the movement of people from east Belfast. The remains of the original abbey of Movilla, founded by St Finnian in AD 540, are close to the present church. A church was opened here in 1980, but such was the increase in members and organisational needs that a new, larger, modern building had to be erected in 2002. Originally a daughter church of the parish of Newtownards, Movilla Abbey became independent in 1990. Worship and the building are shared with the Methodist Church.

## NEWTOWNARDS

The ruins of the old Dominican abbey in Court Street, Newtownards still survive. The abbey was in use as the parish church until the new church was built. *St Mark's Church* was consecrated in 1817. The baptistery, created in 1965 in the south transept, contains some medieval glass from the old church and there is a stone in the south wall believed to originate from Movilla Abbey. More recently, a side chapel with a glass screen was created in the north aisle and the church underwent extensive restoration, including the cleaning of the exterior stonework.

## SAINTFIELD

The first church here appears to date from around 1633 and is possibly the one whose remains can be seen in the graveyard of the present church. *Saintfield Church* was built in 1766 and the gallery was added a century later. The fine east window was installed in 1929 in memory of Major and Mrs Blackwood Price, whose family presented a silver chalice and paten to the parish in 1724. They are still used. The double line of yew trees at the entrance to the church was a gift from Hugh Armitage Moore of Rowallane in 1881.

Christ Church, Kilmore

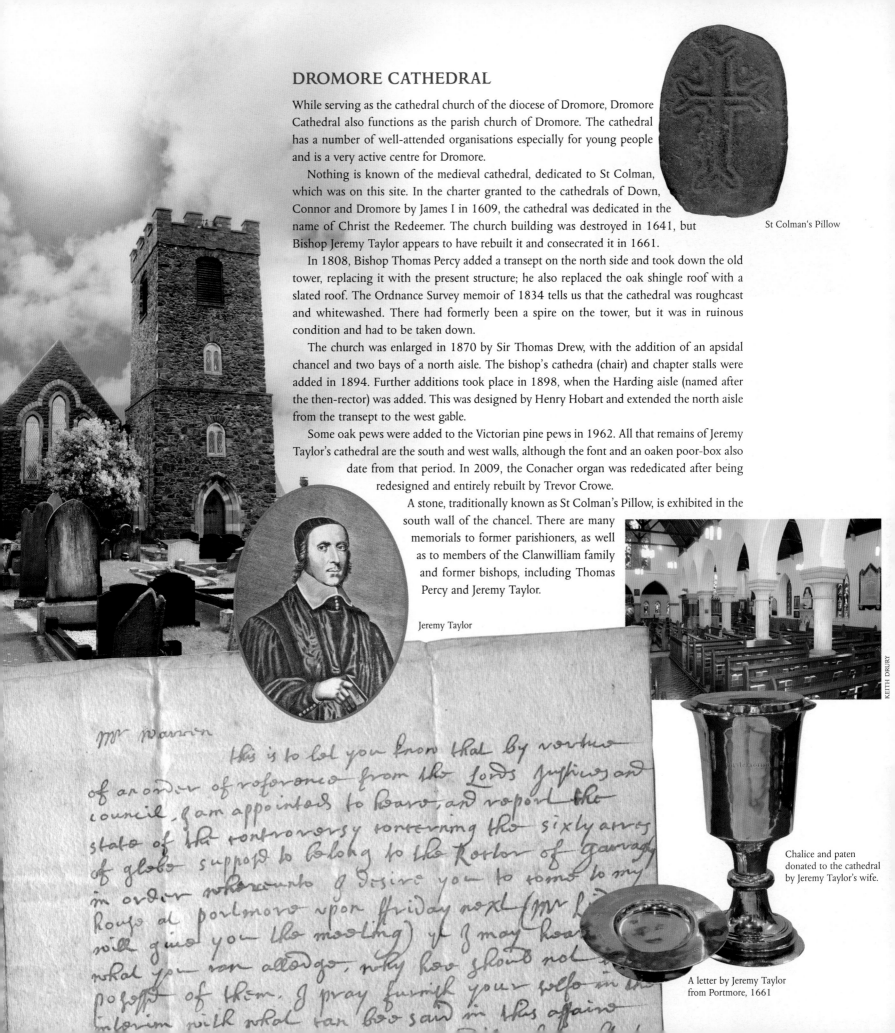

# DROMORE CATHEDRAL

While serving as the cathedral church of the diocese of Dromore, Dromore Cathedral also functions as the parish church of Dromore. The cathedral has a number of well-attended organisations especially for young people and is a very active centre for Dromore.

Nothing is known of the medieval cathedral, dedicated to St Colman, which was on this site. In the charter granted to the cathedrals of Down, Connor and Dromore by James I in 1609, the cathedral was dedicated in the name of Christ the Redeemer. The church building was destroyed in 1641, but Bishop Jeremy Taylor appears to have rebuilt it and consecrated it in 1661.

In 1808, Bishop Thomas Percy added a transept on the north side and took down the old tower, replacing it with the present structure; he also replaced the oak shingle roof with a slated roof. The Ordnance Survey memoir of 1834 tells us that the cathedral was roughcast and whitewashed. There had formerly been a spire on the tower, but it was in ruinous condition and had to be taken down.

The church was enlarged in 1870 by Sir Thomas Drew, with the addition of an apsidal chancel and two bays of a north aisle. The bishop's cathedra (chair) and chapter stalls were added in 1894. Further additions took place in 1898, when the Harding aisle (named after the then-rector) was added. This was designed by Henry Hobart and extended the north aisle from the transept to the west gable.

Some oak pews were added to the Victorian pine pews in 1962. All that remains of Jeremy Taylor's cathedral are the south and west walls, although the font and an oaken poor-box also date from that period. In 2009, the Conacher organ was rededicated after being redesigned and entirely rebuilt by Trevor Crowe.

A stone, traditionally known as St Colman's Pillow, is exhibited in the south wall of the chancel. There are many memorials to former parishioners, as well as to members of the Clanwilliam family and former bishops, including Thomas Percy and Jeremy Taylor.

St Colman's Pillow

Jeremy Taylor

KEITH DRURY

Chalice and paten donated to the cathedral by Jeremy Taylor's wife.

A letter by Jeremy Taylor from Portmore, 1661

St Mellan's, Loughbrickland

St Matthew's Church, Scarva

## AGHADERG, DONAGHMORE and SCARVA

*St Mellan's Church*, Loughbrickland was originally built for the parish of Aghaderg around 1688, but was considerably altered in the nineteenth century. It is said that the small bell in the church tower was given by King William III.

*St Bartholomew's Church*, Donaghmore was built in 1741. There is a Celtic high cross, possibly from the tenth century, standing in the churchyard, reflecting earlier ecclesiastical buildings on the site.

*St Matthew's Church*, Scarva was consecrated on 15 September 1850. The church is dramatically situated on a height overlooking the village, at the top of a flight of 84 steps.

## AGHALEE and MAGHABERRY

This parish, known locally as Soldierstown, is situated in south County Antrim.

*Holy Trinity Church*, Aghalee was built during the reign of Charles II and dedicated on 1 May 1667. Major renovations were carried out in the nineteenth century and the church was reconsecrated in 1899. Richard Owen, the engineer of the Lagan Navigation, is buried in the churchyard.

The *Church on the Hill*, Maghaberry was formed when the Church of Ireland and Methodist congregations in Maghaberry joined for worship in 2006. The congregation meets every Sunday morning in the building close to the primary school, and the church offers a range of youth and children's activities throughout the week.

## ANNAHILT and MAGHERAHAMLET

Church of the Ascension, Annahilt

The *Church of the Ascension*, Annahilt was consecrated on 29 July 1856 on the site of earlier churches. The pulpit, dated 1571, was removed from Turvey Parish Church in Bedfordshire in 1852 and purchased for Annahilt in 1905.

*Magherahamlet Church*, near Ballynahinch, was built on the shore of Lake Macawley or Ballymacarn Lake. It was consecrated on 12 May 1815 and extended in 1870. A major refurbishment took place between 1977 and 1979.

Annalong Church

## ANNALONG (KILHORNE)

Originally part of the parish of Kilkeel, Kilhorne became a parish in its own right in 1884. The foundation stone for *Annalong Church* had been laid in 1840 by Viscount Newry and Mourne, who gave the site and was largely responsible for building the church. The chancel was added in 1883 and the tower was erected in 1889. The stained glass, by Gibbs of London, is in memory of Viscount Newry and Mourne.

Holy Trinity Church, Aghalee

## ARDMORE (MOYNTAGH)

The parish of Ardmore, or Moyntagh, was carved out of the parish of Seagoe in 1766. *Ardmore Church* was built in 1785 in the townland of Derryadd, an earlier building having been destroyed in a storm in 1783. The original spire was blown down in 1883 and the present one erected in 1886. On the same occasion, the pulpit was presented by St Mark's, Portadown. The parish centre at Esky was built as Esky Mission Hall in 1885 and the font from Rahan Church (diocese of Cork) was donated in 1962.

Ardmore Church, Moyntagh

## CASTLEWELLAN and KILCOO

*St Paul's Church, Castlewellan* was built in 1853 as a proprietary chapel of ease within the parochial district of Kilmegan by the fourth Earl Annesley, and contains many memorials to his family. Prior to disestablishment, Castlewellan was served by a chaplain to the Annesleys but, after 1871, was served by an incumbent. On the surrender of patronage by the Annesley family in 1977, St Paul's became a parish church and Castlewellan was grouped with Kilcoo Parish.

*Bryansford Church*, for the parish of Kilcoo, is thought to have been built in 1712. The tower was added in 1812, as were the four panels of early sixteenth-century Flemish glass above the nave window, presented by Lord Roden.

St Paul's Church, Castlewellan
DERMOTT DUNBAR

## CLONALLON and WARRENPOINT with KILBRONEY

There was a church at Clonallon as early as the sixth century, founded by Dallan, a blind poet contemporary with St Columba. Kilbroney was grouped with Clonallon and Warrenpoint in 2011. The present *Clonallon Church* is believed to have been built in the 1660s by Bishop Jeremy Taylor.

*Warrenpoint Church* was built in 1825 in the parish of Clonallon. Established as a perpetual curacy, it was separated from its mother church in 1871, but rejoined it in 1922.

The foundation stone for *St Bronach's Church, Rostrevor* was laid in 1818. It has a memorial to Major-General Robert Ross, who commanded the British forces against America in 1814.

Warrenpoint Church

St Bronach's Church, Rostrevor

## CRAIGAVON

From 1969, services were held in Moylinn Community Hall in the new city of Craigavon, served by curates from Shankill Parish. By 1971 the services had moved to Tullygally Community Hall and a curate-in-charge had been appointed. *St Saviour's Church, Tullygally* was consecrated in 1972 in and in 1977 the parish was grouped with Ardmore (Moyntagh). The new *St Saviour's Church* designed by G.P. and P.H. Bell, was built at Drumgor West Road in the early 1980s, the move having been forced by population movement and vandalism. Sadly, there have since been three arson attacks and more vandalism. The church has been restored each time and continues its faithful witness to the community.

COLIN BOYLE

## DONAGHCLONEY and WARINGSTOWN

*Holy Trinity Church, Waringstown* was built in the seventeenth century and maintains much of the original design and architecture. Destroyed in 1641 and rebuilt in 1681, it is perhaps the best example in Ulster of a Jacobean church.

*St Patrick's Church, Donaghcloney* came into being when a school built in 1903 was taken over by the parish and transformed into a church to serve the people of the village.

Holy Trinity Church, Waringstown

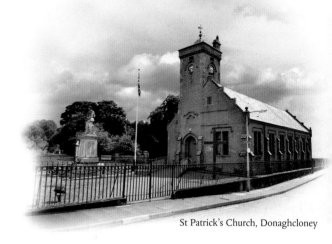

St Patrick's Church, Donaghcloney

St John the Evangelist's, Dromara

DERMOTT DUNBAR

Moses the Musical at Garvaghy

ALMA FERGUSON

## DROMARA and GARVAGHY

Garvaghy was grouped with Dromara in 1885.

The site of *St John the Evangelist's Church, Dromara* is believed to have been used for Christian worship from at least the fourteenth century. Ruined by fire in 1641, the church was restored in 1744. Many changes were made during the nineteenth century and in 1896 it was reconsecrated.

The present *Garvaghy Church*, near the village of Waringsford, is thought to have been built in 1699 and reconstructed in 1885. It is a singing community, the parish having written and performed two original musicals to date.

## DRUMGATH, DRUMGOOLAND, CLONDUFF and DRUMBALLYRONEY

Drumgath was united with Drumballyroney in 1902 and with Clonduff in 1936. It was grouped with Drumgooland in 1976.

The original *St John's Church, Drumgath* (Rathfriland) dates from 1733, but was rebuilt in 1818 and added to in 1892.

The foundation stone of *Drumgooland Church* was laid in 1821 by the rector, Rev. Thomas Tighe. He appointed Patrick Brontë (father of writers Emily and Charlotte) schoolmaster in Drumballyroney and prepared him for Cambridge, where he studied for ordination. When the church was restored following a bomb blast in 1975, two stained-glass windows were installed in honour of Patrick Brontë.

St John's Church, Drumgath

DERMOTT DUNBAR

Drumgooland Church

DERMOTT DUNBAR

*St John's Church, Clonduff* (Hilltown), probably designed by Charles Lilly, was consecrated in 1771, but regular worship ceased there in 1983.

*St John's Church, Drumballyroney* was built around 1800. It closed for worship in 1970 and eventually became the Brontë Heritage Centre.

## GILFORD

Gilford Parish was carved out of Tullylish Parish in 1867. It was given full parochial status in 1995. *St Paul's Church, Gilford* was consecrated in 1869. The church, designed by the architectural firm of Lanyon, Lynn and Lanyon, was largely endowed by linen-mill owner J.W. McMaster of Dumbarton House. The east window is by Caldwell of Canterbury and represents, in medallions, the resurrection, the ascension, the four evangelists, the good Samaritan, the feeding of the five thousand, the acts of mercy and the conversion of Saul. The west window, by Mayer of Munich. Unusually, the church has no centre aisle.

## KILKEEL

Originally this parish was known as Morne [*sic*] and was under the control of the Kilmorey family, who were lay abbots of Newry.

*Christ Church, Kilkeel* was part-funded by the earl of Kilmorey and designed by Patrick O'Farrell. It was consecrated on 14 August 1818. After disestablishment, Kilmorey control was ended. Additions were made to the building later in the nineteenth century.

The *Pratt Memorial Church, Carginagh*, a small daughter church, was built in 1889 in memory of a former rector, Rev. E.O'B. Pratt. One incumbent, Rev. James Mehaffey, became bishop of Derry and Raphoe in 1980.

Christ Church, Kilkeel

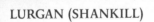

## KILMEGAN (DUNDRUM) and MAGHERA

*Kilmegan Church*, built in the late eighteenth century, was originally attached to the church in Kilkeel. Kilmegan Parish did not become a parish in its own right until 1884. It was then united with Maghera and transferred to the diocese of Dromore. The church is two miles from Dundrum.

*Maghera Church* was built in 1825 and consecrated in 1827.

*St Donard's Church, Dundrum* was built by the fifth marchioness of Downshire as a chapel of ease within the parish in 1887. Three of the tower's pinnacles have had to be removed for safety reasons. Dundrum Church is still a chapel of ease in Kilmegan Parish.

St Donard's Church, Dundrum

Kilmegan Church

## THE JIMS PROJECT

In the Spring of 1998 a 12-week pilot youth project was set up in Kilkeel. The temporary premises were laid out in the theme of Star Trek (hence the name JIMS) and the project offered a soft drinks bar, snack food, music and games. JIMS attracted up to 40 young people each weekend and a permanent JIMS Youth Centre eventually opened in the middle of the town under the auspices of the Kilkeel Parish Bridge Association. The project has gone from strength to strength, adding many more programmes to the original Saturday night drop-in. JIMS provides an alternative and safe place for kids from the town to hang out and have fun. Young people are encouraged in multiple aspects of their lives - mental, social, emotional, and spiritual – and as a neutral venue, JIMS is well placed to carry out its cross-community work.

## KNOCKNAMUCKLEY

The parish of Knocknamuckley was constituted in 1837 out of the existing parishes of Seagoe and Tullylish. *St Matthias's Church* was consecrated on St Matthias's feast day, 23 February 1853. Initially only the nave was built, the chancel and organ chamber being added in 1912. The pulpit is in memory of those who fell in the First World War. Whilst there are wall memorials, Knocknamuckley has no stained glass. A new porch was erected in 1987 to mark the 150th anniversary of the parish.

### JETHRO CENTRE

The Jethro Centre first opened its doors in September 2006 and is managed by the Shankill Parish Caring Association (SPCA). The vision of the Shankill Parish Caring Association is to seek to promote the well being of the inhabitants of Lurgan and its environs and to promote the Christian faith among them. Many varied and interesting courses take place within the Centre, which meets the needs of the Local Community and enables The Shankill Parish Caring Association fulfil its mission.

## LURGAN (SHANKILL)

Lurgan town is situated in the parish of Shankill. The church in the centre of the town, *Christ the Redeemer*, replaced an earlier building. It was designed by architects Welland and Gillespie to cater for the rapidly expanding population of Lurgan and was consecrated in 1863. Today it seats 2,000 people and is the largest parish church in Ireland.

*St Andrew's Church, Lurgan* (the Brownlow Hall) opened in 1963. Expansion of the town at that time necessitated the building of another hall/church.

## LURGAN (ST JOHN'S)

*St John the Evangelist's Church* opened in May 1888. The building was originally intended as a mission hall within Shankill Parish, but in fact became a national school and Sunday school, the needs for which were more pressing. The building was transferred back to Shankill Parish in 1935 and became known as the Mission Hall. Population growth in the area led to the parish of St John the Evangelist being formally constituted on 1 March 1968. The puppet ministry in St. John's commenced in September 2007. The aim of the ministry is to present the gospel primarily to children but also adults in a simple and fun way. The team work with a variety of puppet characters allowing them to tell bible stories, do sketches, sing choruses and mimes to popular Christian music. Many of their performances are themed e.g Easter, Christmas, Mother's day.

Magheradroll Church,
Ballynahinch
DERMOTT DUNBAR

## MAGHERADROLL

The ruins of a previous church with a datestone reading 1607 are in the old graveyard at Magheradroll. *Magheradroll Church, Ballynahinch* was built by the earl of Moira as a private chapel. This church, in turn, was rebuilt in 1829, incorporating the original tower. It was enlarged, with a second aisle and porch and spire added, in 1870. The Conacher organ was installed in 1899. Fine stained-glass windows were added in the 1950s and the sanctuary was reordered in the 1970s.

St John the Evangelist's Church,
Magherally

## MAGHERALLY and ANNACLONE

Magherally and Annaclone were amalgamated in 1902. Until 1977, the parochial group was a bishop's curacy, but in that year full parochial status was granted.

*St John the Evangelist's Church, Magherally* was consecrated in 1887. In the graveyard at the old church lies Helen Waddell, the world-renowned medieval scholar and classicist, who was born at nearby Kilmacrew House; her sister was married to a former rector.

*Christ Church, Annaclone* was built in 1860 and added to in 1896.

## MAGHERALIN and DOLLINGSTOWN

The *Church of the Holy and Undivided Trinity, Magheralin* is Gothic in style. Rebuilt a number of times, it was consecrated in 1845. It has some fine stained glass by the An Túr Gloine studio of Dublin and also by Sarah Purser. The site has associations that go back to the Celtic church of the sixth century.

*St Saviour's Church, Dollingstown*, a daughter church to Magheralin, was licensed for worship in 1914. It was demolished in 2004 to make way for a fine modern church, which was consecrated in 2005.

St Saviour's, Dollingstown

## VIA WINGS

Award winning charity, Via Wings, is based in Dromore and cares for those in greatest need from all sections of the local community. Founded in 2009 by Dromore Cathedral parishioner, Gail Redmond, the project employs a Centre Manager and can call upon an invaluable pool of volunteers. Projects include the 'House of Hope', a place of friendship and learning and 'Dare2Care', a Dromore project that provides essential provisions such as food and heating oil to local families in need. In June 2012, Via Wings opened a community venture called 'Hope & Soul'. It's a second-hand store selling key pieces of barely worn, stylish clothing and vintage and locally made jewellery, along with some upcycled furniture and fittings. Upstairs is a coffee bar called the Olive Branch and a soft play area. Hope & Soul and the Olive Branch are staffed entirely by volunteers. All profits are ploughed back into the mother charity to continue the work of showing God's love in a caring, practical and non-judgmental way. In 2011, Via Wings won top prize in the Community Health Initiative category of the All-Ireland 'Pride of Place' Awards.

## MOIRA

Originally part of Magheralin, Moira Parish was established in 1722. The clergy of the parish have included Rev. John Dubourdieu, author of the statistical surveys of Down (1802) and Antrim (1812). *St John's Church, Moira* was built in 1725, largely financed by the Rawdon family. The tall copper-clad spire, replacing the original slate steeple (which was blown down in a storm in 1884), is visible for miles. Otherwise, the church is little altered. Of interest within is the ancient reredos with the Creed inscribed in gold letters on Irish linen. The inner west door and communion rails are said to have come from Moira Castle.

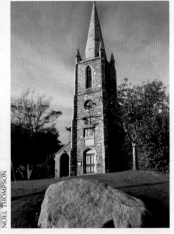

St John's Church, Newcastle

NOEL THOMPSON

## NEWCASTLE

Newcastle was dedicated a parochial district within the parish of Kilcoo in 1868. *St John's Church* built by the third Earl Annesley and designed by the architect John Lynn, was opened for worship in 1832, but for legal and financial reasons was not consecrated until 1 December 1853. The church remains under the private patronage of the Annesley family. Mayer of Munich and An Túr Gloine studio of Dublin were responsible for some of the stained glass in St John's.

*St Colman's Church, Tullybrannigan* was built in 1927 and used as a cemetery chapel, although regular services are held by the clergy of the parent parish.

St Mary's Church, Newry

St Patrick's Church, Newry

DERMOTT DUNBAR

## NEWRY

*St Patrick's Church* built by Sir Nicholas Bagenal in 1578, was one of the first post-Reformation Protestant church built in Ireland. It became a chapel of ease in 1819. St Patrick's regained its parochial status in 1870. Renovated and restored, it opened for a new era of ministry in 2004.

*St Mary's Church* was opened in the town centre in 1819. St Mary's was generous in scale and built to a very high standard. Architects Patrick O'Farrell and Thomas Duff were involved in its construction. St Mary's was grouped with Donaghmore from 1922 until 1950 but has been grouped with St Patrick's since 1993.

## SEAGOE

Former clergy of Seagoe Parish include Jack Shearer, dean of Belfast, and Most Rev. David Chillingworth, primus of the Episcopal Church of Scotland. Seagoe Primary is the only Church of Ireland maintained school in the diocese. *St Gobhan's Church, Seagoe,* close to Portadown, reflects in its dedication connections of the site to an early Christian saint. The current church was built in 1814 and enlarged by Sir Thomas Drew in 1891. The font dates from 1660. A fine new church hall has recently been constructed adjacent to the church.

St Gobhan's Church, Seagoe

COLIN BOYLE

## SEAPATRICK

The present Seapatrick Parish comprises the large parish church of the Holy Trinity and the smaller St Patrick's. Joseph Scriven, author of the hymn 'What a Friend We Have in Jesus', was a famous Seapatrick parishioner, as was Captain F.R.M. Crozier, the nineteenth-century polar explorer..

*Holy Trinity Church, Banbridge,* consecrated in 1837, replaced a much older church elsewhere in the parish of Seapatrick. A peal of ten bells was presented in 1920 by a Mrs White of Chicago, on the condition that 'Home Sweet Home' should be played each Hallowe'en as a reminder of emigrants who have left the parish. This tradition is continued to the present day.

*St Patrick's Church, Seapatrick,* consecrated in 1882, lies adjacent to the historic site of the original parish church. It was formerly an old school.

Holy Trinity, Banbridge

## TULLYLISH

The foundation stone for *All Saints' Church* was laid in 1861. It replaced a church which was abandoned as it was too small to contain the influx of people from the 1859 revival. Unusually, it has no centre aisle. The parish once included Gilford and two townlands given to Knocknamuckley in 1839. See page 182.

'It is a living place where day by day the cycle of worship is maintained and which welcomes visitors as tourists, pilgrims, regular worshippers, or merely those who seek a quiet place to ponder alone.' DEAN JOHN MANN

# Belfast Cathedral

St Anne's Cathedral, Belfast was built on the site of an older church, also dedicated to St Anne. In a statement proposing its construction written in 1896, it was observed that the city required a building 'capable of accommodating large congregations for important services or festivals'. The foundation stone was laid in 1899 and the nave was opened for public worship on 2 June 1904. Gradually, the cathedral was extended and beautified. The building was effectively completed with the consecration of the north transept in 1981. A striking metal spire was added in 2007.

The cathedral is a Romanesque building and possesses elements that reflect that style: five large pillars on each side of the central nave with half pillars in the walls at either end; huge single-light windows; mosaics in two ceilings; the four archangels carved high in the corners of the nave; an apse and ambulatory at the east end; and massive round arches throughout the whole building.

Laying the Foundation Stone of the new cathedral

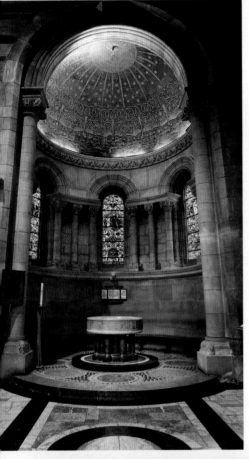

There is a great deal of artistic merit in the finer detail of the building. The chapel of the Holy Spirit, added in 1932 to celebrate the 1,500th anniversary of St Patrick's arrival in Ireland, is immediately to the left on entering the cathedral. All its stained-glass windows relate to the Holy Spirit. On the opposite side of the cathedral is the baptistery, one of the most photographed features of the building. The carvings are by Rosamund Praeger, who also designed the bronze plaque above Lord Carson's tomb. Carson is the only person buried in the cathedral.

The detailed nave pillar capitals were carved, each with a different theme, over a period of 12 years, chiefly by Morris Harding, whilst the fine carving on the west facade of the cathedral is the work of Esmond Burton. Completed in 1927, it is a memorial to those who lost their lives in World War I. The cathedral's mosaics of Italian glass are the work of two sisters, Gertrude and Margaret Martin, who spent seven years in this work. The mosaic over the font is said to hold more than 150,000 pieces.

SCENIC IRELAND

This siver baptismal bowl was presented by the Government of Northern Ireland. It contained earth from the six counties which was strewn on the coffin of Lord Carson at his interment in the Cathedral.
DERMOTT DUNBAR

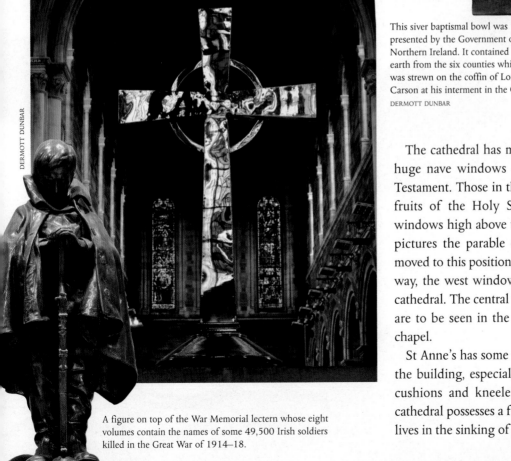

DERMOTT DUNBAR

A figure on top of the War Memorial lectern whose eight volumes contain the names of some 49,500 Irish soldiers killed in the Great War of 1914–18.

The cathedral has many stained-glass windows. The huge nave windows depict characters from the Old Testament. Those in the ambulatory show some of the fruits of the Holy Spirit. There are three abstract windows high above the altar, whilst the east window pictures the parable of the Good Samaritan. It was moved to this position from the old St Anne's Church. Looking the other way, the west windows are perhaps the most impressive of the whole cathedral. The central window depicts Christ in glory. Modern windows are to be seen in the chapel of unity and the Royal Irish Regimental chapel.

St Anne's has some very fine needlework on display in many areas of the building, especially the individually designed hand-sewn tapestry cushions and kneelers, all of which are different. In addition, the cathedral possesses a funeral pall recently made to commemorate the lost lives in the sinking of the *Titanic*. It hangs on the south wall of the nave.

The *Titanic* memorial pall
DERMOTT DUNBAR

# The Diocese of Connor

Connor is one of the most populous dioceses in the Church of Ireland. Covering 1,700 square miles, it encompasses the urban sprawl of north and west Belfast and the stunning rural landscape of the Antrim coast. It has more than 70 parishes in very diverse locations.

The diocese is divided into three archdeaconries, each covering nine rural deaneries. Diocesan administration is carried out in Church of Ireland House, Belfast. The dean and chapter of St Saviour, Connor have their seats in Christ Church Cathedral, Lisburn. Connor shares St Anne's Cathedral, Belfast with the diocese of Down and Dromore.

Since my enthronement in September 2006 I have been wrestling with the impact of change in the culture in which we minister. Connor is embracing this change, and in recent months we launched our vision strategy for the future of ministry here – *Connections: Engaging Culture, Empowering Ministry, Effecting Change.* This followed a lengthy period of listening – to responses to an extensive survey, to clergy, to those who consider themselves very much a part of our church and to those who do not. This research allowed us to acknowledge the many ways in which churches and individuals are seeking to serve God. It also highlighted, with striking uniformity across our parishes, key areas of concern.

At the Diocesan Synod in 2011, the survey team presented their findings. Although some of it was difficult to hear, we had to listen. We discerned a lack of engagement with – and even awareness of – the culture in which we live, and a critical need to grow and develop leadership at every level, lay and ordained. We learned that even where there is an awareness of the need to change, we often do not know how to go about it.

We are now at a critical, yet exciting, juncture. As bishop, I have appointed a team to explore how we will progress our vision. A key member of this team is our new Parish Development Officer Trevor Douglas.

In January 2013, I visited our partner diocese of Yei, South Sudan for the first time, witnessing how this link, established in 2007, is thriving. It was a privilege to meet the people of South Sudan, who have experienced indescribable pain through decades of war. I visited the rural school built with funds raised in Connor Diocese, and was delighted to co-sign a second five-year partnership agreement with Bishop Hilary of Yei.

In Connor, we have a strong Mothers' Union, whose members run initiatives including a very successful parenting progamme. In March 2011, we organised our first diocesan pilgrimage to the Holy Land. This was a joy-filled time in a God-filled place for all 85 pilgrims from all parts of the diocese.

ALAN CONNOR

A memorial dedicated by the mother of Brigadier General John Nicholson, to keep his memory alive.

Part of the morning service at the cathedral

Centre detail from the East window

The bishop's throne dedicated in 1893

# Christ Church Cathedral
# Lisburn

Detail from one of the windows which form a memorial to Sir Richard Wallace, 1818–70. He was a great benefactor in Lisburn and his art collection is famous as the Wallace Collection in London.

The first church, called St Thomas', was built here in 1623 by Sir Fulke Conway, who had been granted the territory around Lisnagarvey by the crown c.1609. Damaged during the 1640s, it was later repaired and a western tower and gallery was added in 1674.

The parish church of Lisburn was constituted the cathedral church for the diocese of Connor by royal charter of Charles II, on 27 October 1662, and now known as Christ Church. The bishop at the time was Jeremy Taylor, Bishop of Down and Connor and administrator of Dromore 1661–67. The cathedral in Lisburn replaced St Saviour's, Connor, as the diocesan cathedral but the cathedral chapter is still known as the chapter of St Saviour.

The cathedral, town and castle were destroyed in a disastrous fire on 20 April 1707. The foundation stone for the new cathedral was laid on 20 August 1708, the work of construction took several years.

The plan of the rebuilt church was an aisleless nave of four bays retaining the tower at the west end. The clock and bells were a gift from the Second Marquis of Hertford in 1796. The slender octagonal spire was added between 1804 and 1807.

The cathedral has fine memorial tablets, including one of 1780 to William Dobbs, with sea battle, by Edward Smith. A window commemorates Sir Richard Wallace, local landlord and founder of the Wallace Collection in London.

The building has seen several major exterior changes over the centuries; it has been reconstructed, reinforced, enlarged and made more visible by the addition of its lofty spire. The interior has changed also by the addition of the gallery and a chancel area. This area has changed in recent years by moving the choir seating into the main body of the building. With increased space in the chancel, it is possible to have many differing arrangements of musicians and singers for some of the newer forms of service like praise services and family services.

Lisburn Cathedral is home to a vibrant church community. Services are well-attended and offer a mix of traditional and contemporary worship. The cathedral is open during the week allowing people to come and use the church for quiet prayer. It also now contains an attractive coffee shop, which has been added recently. The vision of the cathedral is to 'be a blessing to the community', 'praying for the peace and prosperity of the city, where we are situated'.

# The Diocese of Connor

JOHN F.A. BOND

Situated in the north-eastern corner of Ireland, this diocese covers County Antrim and part of County Londonderry. At its southern end are the cities of Belfast and Lisburn. The west of the diocese borders the River Bann, while the east and north of the county overlook the North Channel, with Scotland just 21 miles distant. The north coast is dramatic, with its cliffs and volcanic rock features. Among these rocks, the Giant's Causeway, a mass of symmetrical basalt columns, stretches out into the sea. The seaports of Belfast and Larne are within the diocese, as is Belfast International Airport and major educational institutions and hospitals. Belfast is Northern Ireland's commercial hub. Many people in the diocese make their living from commerce, tourism, farming, the arts and education.

## The Beginnings of Christianity in Ireland

It is likely that, with sea-trading links, Christianity already had a footing in the north of Ireland when St Patrick arrived in AD 432. Patrick's first ministering efforts took place in this district. He founded many churches and ordained a bishop for every area. Tradition has it that as a slave Patrick looked after animals on Slemish in County Antrim, close to the heart of the present diocese of Connor.

## The Early Church and the Monastic System

Outside the Roman Empire, the primitive Church of Ireland was essentially monastic, episcopal in character and influenced by tribal custom. Irish rule differed in many ways from the customs of the Roman church and a strong spirit of independence animated the early Irish church. Round towers were erected near some ecclesiastical foundations in Connor Diocese, such as at Armoy and Antrim and on Ram's Island in Lough Neagh, and provided places of safety and defence in times of danger. In time, Connor came to be recognised as the principal church of Dalriada. However, monasteries and churches became special objects of destruction as the Vikings raided the north coast.

Slemish mountain
SCENIC IRELAND

## The Diocese of Connor

The diocese of Connor (meaning 'oak wood of the hounds') takes its name from Connor village in County Antrim, five miles south-east of Ballymena. A monastery was founded there in the sixth century; Aengus Mac Nissi was the first recorded abbot and bishop of Connor. He was baptised by St Patrick, educated by Patrick and Olcan and is said to have founded the church and monastery of Connor following a visit to Jerusalem. He died *c.* 513 and is buried in Connor.

The bishop of Connor had the church of Connor as his cathedral and enjoyed the rents of lands attached to small sees incorporated in the see of Connor. The abbot of Kells had advowson and rectorial tithes of the churches. For centuries these offices were held by one cleric, but they were separated in the twelfth century. Connor was burned in AD 612.

A drawing of the ruined first cathedral of St Saviour in the Diocese of Connor

## The Medieval Period

Connor seems to have been an important place until the middle of the fourteenth century. Rebellion in Scotland during the reign of Edward II gave the Irish some hope of casting off the English. They chose Edward Bruce as their king and crowned him in Dundalk. When the Scots invaded in 1315, Connor was the scene of a military engagement in which Edward Bruce defeated the Anglo-Norman forces under the command of Richard de Burgh, earl of Ulster. The town was plundered by Scottish soldiers and never recovered.

The diocese of Connor was established by the Synod of Ráth Breasail in 1111; Ireland was divided into 24 dioceses at this time. In 1152, the Synod of Kells confirmed diocesan boundaries and jurisdictions. The parochial system dates from Malachy's episcopate. In 1439, it was proposed that the diocese of Connor should be united with the diocese of Down, but this proposal was not implemented until 1453.

The seal and insignia of the Dean and Chapter of St Saviour. The Chapter of Connor dedicated to St Saviour (i.e. our Lord) was brought into being by the Charter of James 1 in 1609.
DIOCESE OF CONNOR

Stone cross dated 1164, discovered in St Nicholas' Church, Carrickfergus, during renovation work to the chancel floor, 1760.
DERMOTT DUNBAR

## The Sixteenth Century

When Henry VIII determined to abolish papal supremacy in England and Ireland, Conn O'Neill of Ulster repudiated the authority of the pope. He sent a submisssion to Henry VIII regarding corruption in the church in Ireland under Roman supremacy, which resulted in several reforms being put into action. However, there was little appetite in Ireland for church reform. Most of the population spoke Irish and papal supremacy was useful to higher clergy in furthering their own plans. Thus, little progress was made. Wars and infighting were widespread. Churches in Connor lay in ruins, neglected and disused. Shane O'Neill, a fractious man, claimed sovereignty of Ulster, but his death in 1567 brought relative peace. His successor, Hugh O'Neill, submitted to the crown, but later rebelled.

## The Seventeenth Century

Although not part of the official part of plantation of Ulster, ownership of land in County Antrim was taken under the control of English and Scottish settlers who brought with them tenants and labourers. Territory in what became County Londonderry was granted to various London companies.

James I established a chapter for the cathedral of Connor by charter in 1609. The

Dean Swift and below, the rectory
at Kilroot, 1685

ancient church at Connor was restored and became the cathedral of the
diocese of Connor, with a dean and chapter. The chapter of Connor was
dedicated to St Saviour, and each member at that time was allotted a corps
or group of benefices for his sustentation. There appear to have been no
deans in the diocese of Connor before this – the archdeacon was the
principal official. Today, unlike other cathedral foundations, the
archdeacon ranks next to the dean in Connor.

Connor Cathedral was badly damaged during the Rebellion of
1641. There were few members of the Church of Ireland resident
in the village, so there was little incentive or money to rebuild the
cathedral. It continued to be used, though in ruins. In April 1695
Jonathan Swift read divine service in Connor.

### Bishop Jeremy Taylor

At the restoration of Charles II, the fortunes of the Church
of Ireland were improved. Jeremy Taylor was made
bishop of Down and Connor and administrator of
Dromore. He entered fully into the trials of the Irish
Church, however, his conduct was severely
criticised at the time. Today, however, we view
his role in a more favourable light. His work on
liturgical reform and episcopacy shows that he was a
champion of the Established Church against its
Presbyterian and Roman Catholic opponents. In his short life, Bishop
Taylor completed an enormous amount of work, writing eight octavo
volumes. His two most popular works were 'Holy Living' and 'Holy
Dying'. Strictly Anglican in his theology, he emphasised devotional
writing, church-building, baptism and holy communion. Bishop Taylor
died of a fever aged 54. In 1662, a Royal Charter of Charles II
established the parish church of Lisburn as the Cathedral of Christ
Church for the Diocese of Connor.

The Chichester monument in St Nicholas', Carrickfergus is probably the
finest Jacobean monument in Ireland. It depicts Sir Arthur Chichester,
Lady Chichester and the casket of their baby son. It is believed to have
been made in 1625 by craftsmen from the Continent.

### Cromwell (1649–60)

Great social changes took place in the middle
of the seventeenth century. The new Scottish
settlers brought with them their own
ministers who had little reverence for
episcopal order. It was a time of religious
conflict and intolerance. Rebellion broke out
in 1641. The arrival of the Scottish army
under Munro quelled the rebellion. They
established a presbytery at Carrickfergus and
sent commissioners all over the area to
administer the Scottish Covenant.

The Church of Ireland suffered severely
both during and following the 1641
Rebellion and under Oliver Cromwell's
Commonwealth. In the 1650s the
Commonweath authorities forbade
exercise of the church's rites, such as
use of the prayer book. In the
meantime, the full cathedral
organisation existed at Connor, but there were
few people to enjoy it. The prebendary and
rector of Connor, James Watson (1637–61),
seems to have retained his position through the
Commonwealth period. Elsewhere, clergy
remained with their flocks and often held
services within the walls of ruined churches.

1723 detail from
Ballintoy Church
GORDON GRAY

## The Glorious Revolution and the Eighteenth Century

The succession of James II brought new dangers for the Church of Ireland. However,
the Glorious Revolution, with the victory of William III brought new stability.

Bishop Francis Hutchinson was appointed bishop of Down and Connor,1720,
and is best remembered for building St Thomas's Church on Rathlin Island in
1723. Because the inhabitants of Rathlin understood only the Gaelic
tongue, he arranged for a catechism to be printed in parallel columns
of English and Irish.

The church suffered from economic problems at this time because of
impropriate use of rectorial tithes by laymen. The average income of
the clergy varied considerably and was very unequally distributed.

In the 1760s, the area was in a disturbed state, with many secret
societies in existence and widespread opposition to the collection of
tithes. Another problem beset the diocese – pluralism. Most clergy

St Thomas' Church, Rathlin Island
COLIN BOYLE

Siege ball found in St Nicholas'
Church, Carrickfergus
DERMOTT DUNBAR

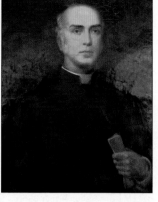

served several parishes at the same time, and many were perceived as lax in parish matters.

As republican principles were spreading in France, Ireland became unruly. The Orange Order was founded in 1795 as a result of political division between Protestants and Roman Catholics. Many Church of Ireland clergy were chaplains in the lodges, and even today pictures of churches and former clergy are sometimes seen on Orange banners.

Rev Dr Richard Kane, 1841–98 was appointed rector of Christ Church, serving the Sandy Row area of Belfast. At the end of 1884 he was elected Grand Master of Belfast County Grand Orange Lodge, a position he occupied until his death.
ORANGE ORDER ARCHIVE

## The Nineteenth Century

The union of English and Irish parliaments occurred in 1800 and took effect in 1801. The English and Irish churches also united. The Irish church was reorganised into two provinces, with Connor Diocese in the northern province of Armagh. The number of churches and clergy increased. At disestablishment in 1871, the Church of Ireland became independent once again.

Ramoan Parish introduced the Mothers' Union to Connor in 1892.
GARY MCMURRAY

### The Growth of the Church of Ireland in Belfast

As Belfast grew to become the epicentre of the industrial revolution in Ireland, the population expanded greatly. St Anne's, built in 1774, and St George's, built in 1815, did not provide seating for the poor of Belfast. Rev. Arthur Macartney, vicar of Belfast, took the initiative to build a free church, the new Christ Church, College Square North, Belfast. The Rev. Thomas Drew was appointed perpetual curate of the church, opened in 1833. Drew devised a programme to reclaim the poor and unchurched of the Belfast area. He introduced a clothing society, libraries for adults and children, a day school and Sunday school and a singing class. In 1838 his congregation reached 1,000 on Sundays. The Down and Connor Diocesan Church Accommodation Society was formed by Drew in 1838 and was responsible for building sixteen churches in the dioceses.

The Belfast Church Extension and Endowment Society was formed in 1863 and was responsible for building another seven churches in Belfast including six in Connor. Women contributed much to the life of the church; as the value of their work was appreciated in the parishes, they gained the right to vote and the right to serve on parish vestries. In time, they became members of the Diocesan Synod and General Synod (1920). The Mothers' Union was introduced to Connor in Ramoan Parish in 1892 and in 1894 it reached St Luke's Parish, Belfast. Missionary societies developed and support for their work spread throughout the diocese.

Christ Church, College Square North, Belfast, restored in 2003 by the Building Preservation Trust for Inst.
DERMOTT DUNBAR

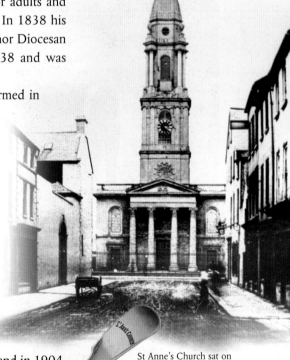

### Belfast Cathedral

The growth of Belfast led to demands for a cathedral. The chosen site was the existing parish church of St Anne (built in 1776) and the walls of the new cathedral were constructed around it. The first part of the new St Anne's Cathedral was consecrated by Bishop Welland in 1904. The building was finally completed in 1981. The Spire of Hope was added in 2007. St Anne's has a cross-community, civic and religious role and is very much part of the life of Belfast. Both the bishop of Connor and the bishop of Down have

A surreal view of the Spire of Hope in St Anne's Cathedral, Belfast, 2013

St Anne's Church sat on the site of the current St Anne's Cathedral, Belfast

Silver plate of 1697 and strainer spoon from St Anne's Church, Belfast

ST CATHERINE'S, KILLEAD

Lord Molyneaux was baptised in St Catherine's, Killead, where he has worshipped all his life except during World War II when he served with the RAF in Europe and was one of the first British Servicemen to enter Belsen Concentration Camp towards the end of the conflict. 'I witnessed terrible scenes in Belsen which I have never forgotten and I was relieved to come home to my church to pray for the Jewish inmates,' he said.

a seat in St Anne's Cathedral, Belfast. Lord Carson, the Unionist leader, is buried in St Anne's.

## Home Rule and the Early Twentieth Century

Special sessions of the General Synod took place when the Home Rule Bills were introduced in 1886, 1893 and 1912. It was feared that the Protestant faith would be jeopardised under Home Rule. Numbers in the Orange Order swelled. In 1912 Bishop D'Arcy preached to a packed St Anne's Cathedral before the signing of Ulster's Solemn League and Covenant in the city hall.

World War I was to bring sorrow and sadness to many families, as fathers and sons left for the battlefields of Europe. Today, many memorials record the names of those who served and gave their lives in the trenches.

Many clergy served as chaplains with their parishioners in World War II. Air raids in 1941 brought death and devastation to parishes in the north and west of Belfast. St James's Church was left only with its spire among the ruins, while areas around St Anne's Cathedral were flattened. In north and west Belfast four churches were completely destroyed and another four badly damaged. Families were forced to seek a home in the housing areas of outer Belfast.

Bishop Arthur Butler (bishop of Connor, 1969-81) served six years as army chaplain to the forces.

The Commonwealth Air Force men from Australia, Canada, New Zealand and the UK who were killed during World War II are commemorated in stained glass in Eglantine Church's Battle of Britain Memorial West Window.
GORDON GRAY

## The Twentieth Century and Today

After the war reconstruction of war damaged churches was a priority. This was followed by a major programme of building of new churches to cater for new housing estates and developments in the 1950s and1960s, under the direction of Bishop Cyril Elliott.

The Troubles began in 1969 and raged for around 30 years. Significant changes, exacerbated by sectarian tensions, brought about a shift in population from Belfast to other places within the diocese, such as Lisburn and Carrickfergus. Over the past 40 years it is estimated that over 30,000 members of Connor Diocese have moved out of greater Belfast. Belfast saw some of the worst of the Troubles, particularly in the 1970s, with rival paramilitary groups active on both sides.

Throughout this period of change, the diocese built new churches in areas of growth, while restructuring parochial boundaries and groupings. Today, many parishes suffer from severe social and environmental problems, family fragmentation, high levels of unemployment and poor housing. In the current economic climate, the parishes with the greatest pastoral needs are hard pressed both financially and for lack of human resources.

Canon Edgar Turner a significant figure in Connor diocese for over forty years serving as Diocesan Registrar and a renowned constitutional expert. He examines some of the bomb damage at St George's, Belfast, during the Troubles.
ST GEORGE'S BELFAST

### BLACK SANTA

The 'Black Santa' tradition at Belfast Cathedral was started by Dean Sammy Crooks in 1976. Concerned at the emphasis being placed on necessary and costly building programmes at the Cathedral, Dean Crooks decided to stand on Donegall Street in front of the Cathedral and beg for the poor and charitable causes. With a small barrel in which donations could be placed, and dressed in the familiar black, Anglican clerical cloak, Dean Crooks 'sat out' each day of the week before Christmas. Thus began the tradition of Belfast's Deans sitting out for charities. The local press described Dean Crooks as, Belfast's Black Santa, and the description struck a lasting chord with the public.

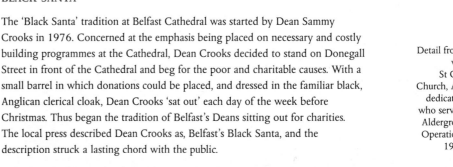

Detail from a Peace window in St Catherine's Church, Aldergrove dedicated to men who served at RAF Aldergrove during Operation Banner, 1969–2007.

Kathleen Young and Irene McCutcheon on ordination to the priesthood – 24 June 1990

Today, hope for lasting peace is encouraged by communities working together, accommodating different viewpoints, aspirations and culture. The Church of Ireland has an open-table policy and Christians of other denominations are welcome to receive the Sacrament.

The diocese of Connor has endeavoured to respond to the challenges experienced by parishes to meet the demands of ministry and mission in modern times. The Alternative Service Book was introduced in Connor in 1984. Bishop Samuel Poyntz ordained Kathleen Young and Irene McCutcheon to the diaconate in 1988 and to the priesthood in 1990, the first in Ireland. In 2000, the Building for Generations strategy was put forward, with six themes emphasising the family, communications, family support, youth, training and the elderly. The diocese engaged in partnership with other, quite different, dioceses – Edinburgh, Linköping (Sweden) and Yei (South Sudan), taking the opportunity to exchange experiences with Christians from different parts of the world. Building for Generations has been superseded by the Connor Diocesan Vision Strategy, which focuses on empowering ministry, engaging culture and effecting change.

A new church building – St Columba's – was dedicated in 2011 in Whiterock, along with a new 64-bed nursing home. A similar project is planned for St Hilda's, Seymour Hill. The diocese has a vibrant Mothers' Union, which is actively emgaging with families in the diocese and overseas. The Church of Ireland has chaplains serving in hospitals, prisons and universities in the diocese of Connor. Connor is a diocesan family working together in the mission of bringing the gospel to God's people. We are confident that as a diocese the tasks ahead of us are not as great as the Power behind us.

Signing of the Methodist Covenant September 2012. Back, from left: Rev John Alderdice, Methodist Chaplain at Queen's; Prof Alan Hibbert, Chair, Church of Ireland Executive Committee; Rev Donald Ker, Methodist chair of the Chaplaincy Committee; Rev Barry Forde, Church of Ireland Chaplain at Queen's. Front, L–R The Rt Rev Alan Abernethy, Bishop of Connor and Rev Heather Morris, now President of the Methodist Church in Ireland.

Young people enjoy the spirit of Summer Madness
CHRIS NELSON PHOTOGRAPHY

Connor diocese is blessed with vibrant youth organisations. Summer Madness is the largest Christian youth event in Ireland and has been held at Glenarm Castle in the parish of Tickmacrevan in recent years.

### Connor Holy Land Pilgrimage

The Bishop of Connor, the Rt Rev. Alan Abernethy, leads a Service of Holy Communion held on the shores of the Sea of Galilee during the first ever Connor Diocesan Pilgrimage to the Holy Land in March 2011. More than 80 people from parishes across Connor Diocese took part in the pilgrimage which was led by the Dean of Belfast, the Very Rev John Mann.

## Ecumenical Relationships

The Church of Ireland is a member of many ecumenical bodies. Until recently, the diocese of Connor shared a partnership with the diocese of Linköping in the Lutheran Church in Sweden, whereby parishioners had an opportunity to enjoy exchange visits to Linköping parishes.

In Connor, valued opportunities for lay and clerical training have been shared with the Methodist Church. The Moravian congregations at Gracehill and Belfast have enjoyed and continue to enjoy fellowship with their Church of Ireland neighbours.

Ecumenical services and events are held in the diocese during the Week of Prayer for Christian Unity and there has been a growing understanding between the different Christian churches over the years. The well-established link between St Anne's Cathedral, Belfast and St Peter's Roman Catholic Cathedral has made a positive impact on Belfast. In recent years, Belfast has become a place of diversity, where religions, cultures and people meet.

In some of the deaneries in Connor, clergy and people from different denominations meet regularly for prayer and support. Women's church organisations meet, pray together, worship together and share in the Women's World Day of Prayer and fellowship days to encourage one another.

# THE PARISHES IN THE DIOCESE OF CONNOR

## AGHERTON

Agherton Old Church is now a ruin. It was replaced in 1826 by a new church across the road. Soon afterwards, the church was dismantled and reerected. *St John the Baptist's Church, Agherton*, Portstewart, was rebuilt in the Diamond and opened for worship in 1839. A Mr O'Hara, however, who owned cottages opposite the church, let them for free to tenants as long as they 'burnt tar during the hours of divine service on a Sunday'. The church survived this opposition and in 1879, a new chancel and sanctuary were built. The bells in the tower were installed as a memorial to parishioners who died in World War I.

DERMOTT DUNBAR

## AHOGHILL AND PORTGLENONE

Ahoghill was originally the largest parish in County Antrim. It was divided into three parts in 1840. After the religious revival of 1859, the original church was unable to accommodate the congregations. Portglenone was originally a perpetual cure within the parish of Ahoghill. In 1840, it became a rectory in the patronage of the crown. Ahoghill and Portglenone were grouped in 1976.

*St Colmanell's Church, Ahoghill* was consecrated on 24 August 1865. The church is cruciform, with a tower and spire over the porch. Atop the spire is a wrought-iron cross by Skidmore of Coventry.

*Portglenone Church* was consecrated in 1735. A porch was added and dedicated on 13 February 1912. The church was reroofed in 1929.

Portglenone Church
COLIN BOYLE

St Colmanell's Church, Ahoghill
GORDON GRAY

## ANTRIM

*All Saints' Church, Antrim* was first erected in 1596, and rebuilt several times. The original door was hit several times during the battle of Antrim in 1798. The parochial records date from 1700. In 1816, the lofty tower and octagonal spire were erected. In 1869, a new transept for the choir and a vestry were added and in 1870 the magnificent east window, depicting ten scenes from the life of Christ, was put in place.

GORDON GRAY

## ARDCLINIS, TICKMACREVAN AND LAYDE

The sixteenth-century ruins of the original church stand in Ardclinis townland. In 1953, the parish was grouped with Tickmacrevan (Glenarm). Tickmacrevan means 'the house of MacCrevan', one of St Patrick's disciples, who reputedly ministered to the people here.

The foundation stone of *St Mary's Church, Ardclinis*, Carnlough, was laid in 1835. The church was consecrated on 19 July 1841. The tower was added ten years later and the bell, a gift from the marchioness of Londonderry, dates from 1866. The organ and organ loft were added in 1885. Repeated restorations have been carried out, most recently in 2005.

Building work on *St Patrick's Church, Tickmacrevan*, Glenarm, began in 1763, using stone from the old friary. It was the first church in Ireland built in the Strawberry Hill Gothic style. It was consecrated in 1769. The south transept and a vestry room were added in 1823, while the baptistery was added in 1878. The chancel was extended in 1892. The organ was presented by Lady Jane McCann, dowager countess of Antrim, in 1871. There are fine examples of Victorian encaustic tiling in the baptistery and chancel. Major work was carried out in 2005–6.

*St Ciarain's Church, Layde* was built and consecrated in 1831. In 1855, a new chancel and organ chamber were added. The church is built from red sandstone and is distinguished by the pinnacles on its facade and on the porch. There are some fine stained-glass windows. Much restorative work has been done to the church.

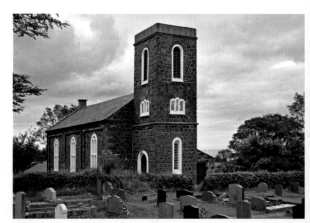

St Mary's Church, Ardclinis, Carnlough
COLIN BOYLE

## ARMOY, LOUGHGUILE and DRUMTULLAGH

It is believed that St Patrick founded a monastery at Armoy around AD 461. A recent archaeological dig just outside the graveyard revealed 1,000-year-old pottery and metal fragments, evidence of lignite jewellery and the remains of medieval walls.

*St Patrick's Church, Armoy* was built in 1820 and enlarged some 20 years later. The east windows came from Balla Church in County Mayo in the 1960s. In the graveyard are a well-preserved round tower and the grave of Rev. Ralph Wilde, grandfather of Oscar.

*All Saints' Church, Loughguile.* In the eighteenth century, the parish church of Loughguile was a tiny building deep in the grounds of Lissanoure Castle. In 1846 this much larger church was built on the edge of the estate. The church has three graveyards.

*Drumtullagh Church* started life in 1841 as a chapel of ease for Derrykeighan and became a parish church in 1875. The architect Sir Charles Lanyon designed it. The church was extended in 1910. It has an unusual complete set of art-nouveau windows.

St Patrick's Church, Armoy
COLIN BOYLE

## BALLINDERRY

Bishop Jeremy Taylor paid to have *Middle Church, Ballinderry* built in 1664, locating it halfway between Upper and Lower Ballinderry. Consecrated in 1668, it is simple and unadorned, a fine example of a seventeenth century plantation church in Ireland. It is used in the summer months.

A new *Ballinderry Church* with its handsome lofty spire was built near the village of Ballinderry Upper and was consecrated in 1824 leaving Middle Church to be preserved in its original condition.

Middle Church, Ballinderry
DERMOTT DUNBAR

## BALLINTOY, DUNSEVERICK and RATHLIN

Originally, Rathlin was a vicarage attached to Ballintoy, but later it became a separate parish. It was united with Ballintoy in 1963. The parishes were grouped with Dunseverick in 1978.

During the rebellion of 1641 Ballintoy church was a place of refuge from the insurgent army. Father McGlaime, a local priest, at great risk to himself, secretly supplied the people with food until relief came. In 1813, *Ballintoy Church* was completed on the site of the earlier church. It is two bays in length, with a single north transept. The tower comes from the earlier building. Originally the church had a spire but was blown down during a storm and never replaced. Unusually the church is white painted. Ballintoy has a sundial, which was apparently used to record tidal movements and is dated 1817.

*Dunseverick Church*, on the edge of Lisnagunogue village, was constructed in 1831. Three bays in length, the main structure is supported by a castellated three-storey tower to the west. A new north aisle and robing room were added in 1864. Further renovations were carried out in 1890.

*St Thomas' Church, Rathlin* was erected around 1812. It occupies the site of an earlier church. Of single-bay design with adjoining tower, the church is finished in basalt and limestone. There are some fine carved memorials and a heavy stone font. St Thomas's Church was renovated and rehallowed in July 2004.

St Mark's, Ballymacash

## BALLYMACASH

The Ballymacash area was part of the parish of Derriaghy until 1967. The original church was a chapel of ease, erected in 1892. The present *St Mark's Church, Ballymacash* was erected in 1975, the population having grown rapidly with the development of Lisburn. The church and hall are built on a hill site and incorporated into one building.

Interior of Ballintoy Church
GORDON GRAY

St Thomas' Church, Rathlin
COLIN BOYLE

COLIN BOYLE

Ballintoy Church
DON GRAY

## BALLYMENA (KILCONRIOLA), DUNCLUG and BALLYCLUG

The original parish church of Kilconriola was situated two miles north of Ballymena. It was in a ruinous state in the seventeenth century. A parish church in Church Street was consecrated in 1721; only the tower and graveyard now remain. As the population grew, this church proved too small and was replaced by the present church.

The foundation stone of *St Patrick's Church, Ballymena* was laid in 1853 and the building was consecrated in 1855. The Adair family of Ballymena Castle gave the ground for the present site and contributed to the cost of £5,000. Rebuilt in 1879 after a fire, the building has remained much the same since, although there have been renovations. St Patrick's is the only parish church in Northern Ireland with a ring of twelve bells and unusually boasts two splendid Art Nouveau stained windows.

*St Columba's Church, Dunclug* is a multi-purpose building. It was built in 1975 because of new housing developments. The church offers a range of youth activities and has mission links with India and Nepal.

*St Patrick's Church, Ballyclug* is situated in the townland of Ballymarlagh, about a mile from Ballymena. The present church was built in 1844, but today it has a finer appearance owing to the addition of a chancel, vestry porch and more windows. The whole building was refurbished in 1994 to mark its 150th anniversary.

St Patrick's, Ballymena
GORDON GRAY

St Patrick's, Ballyclug

## BALLYMONEY, FINVOY and RASHARKIN

*St Patrick's Church, Ballymoney* was constructed in 1782. on the site of earlier ecclesiastical buidings. Of this original church the tower and nave remain. Extensive renovations by Welland and Gillespie were carried out in 1868. An organ was installed in 1912 and further renovations took place in 1962.

*Finvoy Church.* In the early eighteenth century, Benjamin Galland donated land to build a church at Finvoy, but many people were unwilling to pay for the building. Galland therefore accompanied the collector on his rounds. One gentleman, a Mr McShee, refused them entry to his home and put his back to the door. Enraged, Galland thrust his sword through a crack and right through the man's body. Tradition has it that McShee's daughter smeared her father's shirt, wet with blood, on the church walls. The building became known as the 'Bloody Church'. The church, erected in 1721, was replaced by a new church in 1826.

*St Andrew's Church, Rasharkin* was built in the 1860s, replacing an older building. It has a high roof and low walls.

St Patrick's, Ballymoney

GORDON GRAY

St John's Church, Ballyclare

GORDON GRAY

Christ Church, Ballynure

## BALLYNURE and BALLYEASTON (BALLYCLARE)

The original church in Ballynure was built in 1602. It was very small and situated in the graveyard. Part of the tower still remains. Ballynure and Ballyclare became the united parish of Ballynure and Ballyeaston (Ballyclare) in 1888.

*Christ Church, Ballynure* was designed by Joseph Welland of Dublin. The foundation stone was laid in 1854 and the church was consecrated on 19 August 1856. The organ was a gift from the Orange Order.

*St John's Church, Ballyclare* was built in 1903 and consecrated on 12 December 1903. It is in early Gothic style. In 1986 an extension was added.

## BALLYRASHANE and KILDOLLAGH

Loughan village is situated adjacent to an excavated Mesolithic site, which produced the earliest human settlement found in Ireland. Historians believe that there has been a religious community in Kildollagh since earliest times.

*St John the Baptist's Church, Ballyrashane* was consecrated in April 1827. During the protectorate of Cromwell, the incumbent of Ballyrashane was dispossessed and an Englishman installed. After the restoration, a troop of dragoons demanded possession of the church in the king's name. As it was a Sunday and a service was in progress, the incumbent requested permission to finish the service. This was granted.

*St Paul's Church, Kildollagh.* Advent 2005 marked the 150th anniversary of the laying of the foundation stone of the present building. The original diamond-paned windows are arranged in five bays with paired lancets. The black oak sanctuary chair bears the date 1685.

GARY MCMURRAY

St Paul's Church, Ballyrashane

## BALLYWILLAN (PORTRUSH)

The ruins of the old Ballywillan church are in Crossreagh, about 1.5 miles from Portrush. *Holy Trinity Church, Ballywillan* was licensed for public worship on 24 September 1842 and consecrated on 19 July 1843. The building consisted of a nave and square tower, built in irregular Gothic style. A south transept was added in 1863 and two aisles were added in 1887. The chancel was built in 1890 and a new organ installed in 1889. In 2001, extensive renovations of the church were carried out restoring original Victorian features.

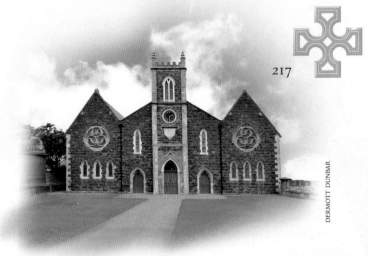

217

DERMOTT DUNBAR

# BELFAST

### ALL SAINTS', UNIVERSITY STREET

The original church in this parish was erected in the 1880s. It was the largest iron structure of its kind in Ireland. The foundation stone of the present *All Saints' Church, Belfast* was laid in 1897. The church was designed by W.J. Fennell in the early English Gothic style, with seating for 1,000. The nave was completed in 1898 and the chancel in 1906. An organ was largely funded by American millionaire Dr Andrew Carnegie. Recently a parochial hall has been built adjacent to the church.

GORDON GRAY

### FINAGHY AND UPPER MALONE

This parish grew out of a Sunday school started in the mid-1920s. As the population increased, it was decided that Finaghy should become a separate parish.

The foundation stone of *St Polycarp's Church, Finaghy* was laid on 27 December 1930 and the building was consecrated on 2 April 1932. A late Gothic-style church, it is dedicated to the bishop of Smyrna (who died *c.* AD 155).

The *Church of the Epiphany, Upper Malone* was dedicated on 23 September 1962. Finaghy select vestry had purchased the site in Sicily Park for a dual-purpose church and hall in response to the postwar building boom. The two churches have since been grouped.

GORDON GRAY

St Polycarp's Church, Finaghy

### CHURCH OF THE RESURRECTION QUEEN'S UNIVERSITY/THE HUB

There has been a Church of Ireland Dean of Residence since the opening of Queen's College in 1849. The current church, with accommodation for students, was consecrated in October 1996, for the care of Church of Ireland students at Queen's. In recent years there has been major refurbishment of the centre with the addition of a café.

### HOLY TRINITY AND ST SILAS WITH IMMANUEL

The original Holy Trinity Church was consecrated on 17 January 1843 and situated on what is now Clifton Street. It was destroyed in the Belfast Blitz in April 1941. In the 1930s, the Joanmount area was developed with new housing and St Bride's Church Hall was built as part of St Mark's Parish, Ballysillan. In 1943, it was decided to transfer the old Holy Trinity Parish to St Bride's district. Immanuel Church Hall originally served the community of Ardoyne and Deerpark. However, over half of the parishioners left the area at the outbreak of the Troubles in 1969. In the early 1990s Immanuel was grouped with Holy Trinity Parish.

The foundation stone of the present *Holy Trinity Church, Ballysillan* was laid on Saturday, 1 May 1954 on the corner of the Oldpark and Ballysillan Roads. Mr E.P. Lamont was appointed architect.

*St Silas's Church, Joanmount*, opened in 1958, was deconsecrated in the early 1990s, owing to profound demographic shifts. Holy Trinity Parish then became Holy Trinity and St Silas's.

*Immanuel Church, Ardoyne* was consecrated on 24 March 1963. The pulpit, baptismal font, lectern, pews and much of the stained glass for the church came from the redundant St Aidan's in Dublin. The church continues to serve the Ardoyne area.

Holy Trinity Church, Ballysillan

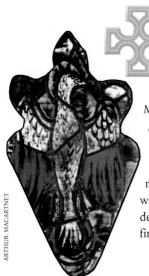

ARTHUR MACARTNEY

218

## MALONE

The *Church of St John the Evangelist, Malone* was built in 1893. It replaced an older St John's Church a short distance away. The north and south transepts were added in 1906, and in 1908 a new choir vestry and meeting room were erected. The choir vestry was extended in 1921 to form a minor hall. A new baptistery was dedicated on 19 June 1980. The church building is noted for its fine stained glass and organ.

GORDON GRAY

ARTHUR MACARTNEY

## ST AIDAN'S, SANDY ROW and ST MARY MAGDALENE'S

In the late nineteenth century, the growth of the linen industry led to an increased population in the Sandy Row area. In July 1893, the Diocesan Council decided to form St Aidan's Parish. St Mary Magdelene Parish on Donegall Pass was part of the parish anciently called Shankill. In neighbouring Donegall Pass St Mary Magdalene Church and Asylum was established in the mid-nineteenth century for 'penitent females' but eventually came to serve a large local congregation. In 2007, in response to the dwindling number of parishioners, it was decided to ask these two parishes to amalgamate.

St Aidan's Church

DERMOTT DUNBAR

St Mary Magdalene Church

*St Aidan's Church, Sandy Row* had its foundation stone laid on 27 October 1894. At that time there were 10,000 Church of Ireland members in the parish. In the mid-1960s the area was redeveloped and the parish lost many members. The church was closed for renovation to mark the eightieth anniversary of its consecration, and was rehallowed in October 1970.

*St Mary Magdalene Church*, Donegall Pass, stands on the site of *Ulster Magdalene Asylum and Episcopal Chapel* opened on 1 December 1839. A fire broke out in December 1898, after which the church was rebuilt using Scrabo stone. St Mary Magdalene was home to the first Irish Boys' Brigade company, which began in 1888.

## ST ANDREW'S, GLENCAIRN

In the twentieth century, many people from the Sandy Row and Ardoyne areas were rehoused in the new Glencairn estate, north Belfast. Glencairn was given independent parish status in 1982. *St Andrew's Church, Glencairn* was consecrated on 30 November 1971 by the bishop of Connor and the president of the Methodist Church in Ireland. It is owned jointly by the Church of Ireland and the Methodist Church. The church building is stark and plain on the outside, with a bright and welcoming interior. Decorations include some stained glass from the old St John's Church, Laganbank (1853–1942).

Harvest Thanksgiving, St Andrew's Church, Glencairn

## Mission to Seafarers

The Missions to Seamen was founded by a Church of Ireland rector, Rev. Dr John Ashley in the mid-nineteenth century. The current Flying Angel Seafarers' Centre is based at Prince's Dock Street and provides companionship and home comforts to the many sailors who visit Belfast.

DERMOTT DUNBAR

## ST BARTHOLOMEW'S, STRANMILLIS

Until late in the nineteenth century, Stranmillis Road was within St Thomas' Parish. In 1918, St Bartholomew's Parish was created, incorporating areas from St Thomas' and Malone Parishes. The lease of a two-acre site at Mount Pleasant was purchased for a church in 1925. *St Bartholomew's Church* was consecrated on 13 September 1930 in response to substantial residential development. The church bell was a gift from St Patrick's Cathedral, Dublin. The exterior of the church is in Ballycullen stone, quarried near Newtownards.

## ST GEORGE'S, HIGH STREET

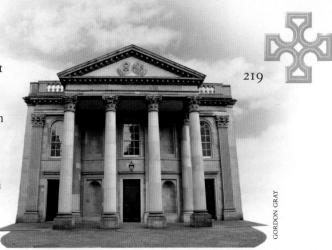

St George's is the oldest church building belonging to the Church of Ireland within the city boundaries of Belfast. It has been a site of worship from at least the fourteenth century. It became the parish church of Belfast in 1616 but was demolished in 1774 when St Anne's, Donegall Street, became the parish church of Belfast. A new church, the present St George's, opened on this site in June 1816. The portico of the church came from Ballyscullion House, former home of Frederick Hervey, the Earl of Bristol and Bishop of Derry. During the Troubles the church was damaged on seventeen occasions by IRA bombs. Nonetheless, St George's maintained its unique traditions and distinctive 'High Church' ethos which have attracted parishioners from across the Greater Belfast area and beyond. It is believed that St George's was the first Anglican church in Ireland to introduce Harvest Thanksgiving.

GORDON GRAY

## ST KATHARINE'S, DUNLAMBERT PARK

St Katharine's was originally part of St Peter's Parish and was set up in 1944. *St Katharine's Church, Dunlambert Park* was consecrated on St Katharine's day, 24 November 1956. At this time, St Matthias's Church in Dublin was scheduled to close and its furniture was transferred to St Katharine's. The pulpit came from St Patrick's Cathedral, Dublin and tradition says that Jonathan Swift preached from it.

## ST MARK'S, BALLYSILLAN

GORDON GRAY

*St Mark's Church, Ballysillan* was consecrated in 1856. The architect was Sir Charles Lanyon. The building was intended as a chapel of ease to the parish church of Belfast. It cost £1,000 to build and could accommodate 180 people. St Mark's is the loftiest church in Belfast, standing some 500 feet above sea level. It boasts some fine stained glass. In 1865, a new nave was added, increasing capacity to 320. Extensive repairs and renovations were carried out in 1960.

## ST MARY'S with HOLY REDEEMER, CRUMLIN ROAD

The first housing in this area sprang up in the 1860s, mainly to accommodate the linen workers on the Crumlin Road. The closure of the mills in the 1960s hastened the physical decline and social decay of the area.

*St Mary's Church, Crumlin Road*, a Gothic-style high-Victorian church with an enormous central tower, is built of Mourne granite and sandstone. In the Easter Tuesday blitz of 1941 the church was badly damaged and was finally restored in 1946. Refurbishment work on the church organ was completed in August 2006 at a cost of £22,000.

The *Church of the Holy Redeemer, Riga Street* was consecrated in 1961. Fifty years earlier students of Trinity College Dublin established a mission in part of St Mary's Parish. They ran several Sunday Schools and church halls before the church was built. It closed for worship in 1995 and parishioners and organisations transferred to St Mary's.

St Mary's Church,
Crumlin Road
GORDON GRAY

## ST MATTHEW'S, SHANKILL

This parish has its origin in a church founded by Rev. Thomas Drew in the late 1830s. The first church, on the site of the present parish hall, was opened in 1839, with seats for 150. The present *St Matthew's Church, Shankill*, originally with seating for 700, was consecrated in 1872. It was built in the shape of a shamrock, with a round tower. The exterior is in white brick, with red-brick ornamentation. The interior is a simple dome-shaped space, created for preaching. A comprehensive renovation of the church was completed in 2003. The sanctuary was remodelled to create a dais in front of the communion rail. The area at the back of the church was enclosed with a glass screen to create the St Patrick room. A window of St Patrick was added in 2006.

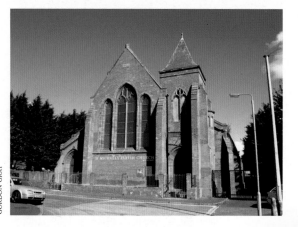

## ST MICHAEL'S, CRAVEN STREET

The parish of St Michael was carved partly from Holy Trinity Parish in 1894. Holy Trinity School was used for Sunday services and weekday activities until a site was purchased for a new church. Foundation stones were laid on 4 May 1899. *St Michael's Church, Craven Street*, in Gothic style, has seating for 900. The external finish is of red brick with dressings of Dumfries stone.

## ST NICHOLAS'S, LISBURN ROAD

Towards the end of the nineteenth century, the population of the Lisburn Road grew steadily. In March 1898 a building fund was launched for a new church. *St Nicholas's Church, Lisburn Road* was consecrated on 9 February 1901 by the bishop of Down, Connor and Dromore. In 1910, the nave was extended. The church boasts some beautiful stained-glass windows, a pulpit of Caen stone, an oak reredos and a two-manual organ.

## ST PAUL'S, YORK STREET and ST BARNABAS'S

St Paul's Parish was created to meet the needs of the migrants who flocked to Belfast in the middle of the nineteenth century. St Barnabas's Parish was created in 1891 to accommodate mill and factory workers in the area. A church was erected in Duncairn Gardens in 1892, but it was destroyed during the Blitz of Easter 1941.

*St Paul's Church, York Street* was built in the mid-nineteenth century. The German air raid of May 1941 resulted in a fire bomb through the roof but was extinguised by the sexton. The fin of the bomb is mounted in a glass case on a wall in the church. A major renovation plan was put in place in St Paul's during the mid-1990s.

The foundation stone for *St Barnabas's Church, Duncairn Gardens* was laid in 1955. In 1967, Captain Terence O'Neill opened a new suite of halls. The Troubles and redevelopment in the Duncairn area had a devastating effect on the parish. Following its amalgamation with St Paul's in 1992, St Barnabas's Church and halls were demolished in 1995 to make way for new offices and factories.

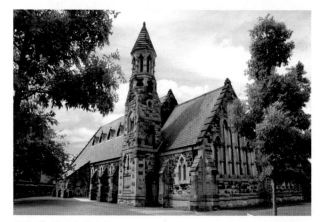

St Paul's Church, York Street
GARY McMURRAY

## ST PETER'S and ST JAMES'S, ANTRIM ROAD

In 1996, the parish of St James was grouped with the parish of St Peter. On 1 October 2005 they became one united parish.

*St Peter's Church, Antrim Road* was consecrated for worship on 29 June 1900. The building was extended and completed in 1933. In 1944, St Katharine's was set up as a daughter church. The church is built of Scrabo sandstone in Gothic style with Giffnock dressings and all of the wood is oak. In July 1987, a car bomb exploded in a neighbouring hotel car park, causing extensive damage to the church and halls. It was subsequently restored.

*St James's Church, Antrim Road* was consecrated on 2 March 1871. The style of the church is decorated Gothic and it is built in sandstone from St Bee's, Cumberland. The tower is surmounted by a metal cross. The church was enlarged in 1881. It was mostly destroyed in the Blitz of April 1941, but the tower, steeple and belfry remained intact. The church was rebuilt and consecrated on 11 September 1954. St James's closed for worship by the Church of Ireland on 29 June 2008 but is currently used by the Antiochion Orthodox church.

## ST SIMON'S and ST PHILIP'S (DREW MEMORIAL), DONEGALL ROAD

A site for a church for St Simon's Parish was purchased in 1900 for £829. An iron church, formerly used in St Donard's Parish, was erected on the site and opened for worship in August 1911. Despite high unemployment in the area in the 1920s, it was decided to build a new church, which was then joined to the iron church. *St Simon's Church, Donegall Road* was consecrated in June 1924. St Simon's was the first to benefit from 1928 Belfast Additional Church Act, with grants totalling £10,481. The old iron church was reconstructed on a nearby site to serve as parish hall. The renovated church could accommodate 500. Organists have included the young Barry Douglas, concert pianist.

## ST STEPHEN'S, MILLFIELD and ST LUKE'S, LOWER FALLS

Situated close to the city centre, *St Stephen's Church, Millfield* was consecrated on 28 October 1869 as the first free church in Belfast (that is, no rental was charged for any pews or seats). Seating was provided for 1,000 souls. Redevelopment in the area has resulted in a major dispersal of parishioners. In the 1970s the halls were requisitioned by the British Army. The church building contains many irreplaceable stained-glass windows. During major road construction in the 1970s, the original facade of the church was taken away, and replaced with the current facade incorporating the tower and the cross that is lit up every night. The rest of the original building remains.

*St Luke's Church, Lower Falls* was closed in 2006 and St Stephen's and St Luke's became a united parish.

St Stephen's Church, Millfield

## ST THOMAS', EGLANTINE AVENUE

The architect of *St Thomas' Church, Eglantine Avenue* was John Lanyon of Lanyon, Lynn and Lanyon. It was consecrated on 22 December 1870. *St Thomas'* is one of the best examples of high-Victorian Gothic ecclesiastical architecture in Ulster. The Hill organ of 1874 was enlarged by its builder in 1906. There is a peal of eight bells and the building has many fine stained-glass windows. Major renovations and restoration work were carried out in 2008 and the church was officially reopened on 19 September of that year.

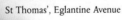

St Thomas', Eglantine Avenue

## UPPER FALLS

*St John the Baptist's Church* was consecrated to be the parish church of Upper Falls in 1861. The Troubles had a major impact on the parish. The church was damaged in June 1982 by a rocket attack on the nearby Woodburn Police Station and restored and re-dedicated in 1983. A faithful witness is maintained by a small number of families and clergy. *St John the Baptist* celebrated its 150th anniversary in 2011.

St John the Baptist's Church, Upper Falls

## WHITEROCK

The foundation stone of Belfast's smallest church, the chapel of ease at Whiterock, was laid on Queen Victoria's coronation day in 1838. It was known as the Luther Church. In 1948 St Columba's, incorporating the Luther Church, was established. The new parish of Whiterock came into being in July 1953, when it was decided to build a new dual-purpose church/hall. The new building was consecrated in November 1962. The Whiterock area suffered badly during the Troubles. The Luther Church was repeatedly vandalised and had to be closed and deconsecrated after serving the community for 130 years. A brand-new *St Columba's Church, Whiterock* was dedicated on 17 January 2011. Adjacent to the church is a new 64-bed nursing home. The church has a modern café, named the Luther Café. Some items from old St Columba's have been incorporated into the new building.

St Columba's Church, Whiterock
COLIN BOYLE

## BILLY and DERRYKEIGHAN

This scattered parish includes Northern Ireland's only UNESCO World Heritage Site, the Giant's Causeway.

The monastery of Derrykeighan was founded in AD 460. The ruins of the old church can still be seen at the Derrykeighan crossroads. A very ancient Celtic stone from the walls of the old church is now in the Ulster Museum. On 1 July 1976, the rector of Billy assumed charge of the parish of Derrykeighan.

*Billy Church* was consecrated in 1815. The chancel, erected and consecrated in 1890, contains some fine twentieth-century stained-glass windows by Michael Healy. In 1834, Billy Parish expended the sum of £9 for the purchase of a parish hearse. Half a crown was to be paid by any person using the hearse and a second half crown lodged as security for its safe return. It was last used in 1900 and can now be found in the Transport Museum at Cultra. In 2005, the church underwent major restoration work.

The foundation stone for *St Colman's Church, Derrykeighan* was laid in 1829 on a site offered by George Macartney of Lissanoure. The church was consecrated on 9 September 1831. It is in the later English style of Gothic architecture. An extensive restoration of the church began in 2012.

## BROOMHEDGE

*St Matthew's Church, Broomhedge* was erected as a chapel of ease for Lisburn Cathedral and was consecrated in September 1848. It was served by curates from Lisburn Cathedral until 1867. The parish of Broomhedge was established in 1880 with Rev. John Leslie as the first rector. He served for forty seven years until his death in 1927.

## CARNMONEY

Carnmoney Parish was originally part of the parish of Shankill and seven medieval parishes in east Antrim. The present church *Church of the Holy Evangelists, Carnmoney* was consecrated on 23 December 1856 and was named after the east window, probably a gift of the Smythe family. In subsequent years, the church has undergone various restoration works and improvements.

## CARRICKFERGUS

*St Nicholas's Church, Carrickfergus* was also certainly built by John de Courcy who founded Carrickfergus in 1182. It is the oldest parish church in continuous use in Northern Ireland. A reconstruction was carried out for Sir Arthur Chichester in 1614. The Norman pillars were encased in the present walls and did not come to light until 1907 when they were uncovered. Two unique features of the church are its crooked aisle and the fact that the chancel is longer than the nave.

## CLOUGHFERN

In 1950, it was decided to create a new parish of Cloughfern out of the parish of St John Whitehouse to cater for new housing developments. Originally services were held in a hall while the church was being built. The *Church of the Ascension, Cloughfern* was consecrated on Ascension Day, 1954. In 1959, full parochial status was granted, again on Ascension day. The church buildings were refurbished and officially reopened in 2002, on the fiftieth anniversary of the building of the first hall.

222

GORDON GRAY

Billy Church

Canon John Leslie

GORDON GRAY

The baptistery, St Nicholas's Church, Carrickfergus

Background Norman arch St Nicholas's Church

DERMOTT DUNBAR

## COLERAINE

Coleraine is the largest parish in the Church of Ireland, with over 1,500 families. *St Patrick's Church, Coleraine* was already practically in ruins when rebuilt in 1613–14 by the Honourable the Irish Society. During the 1641 Rebellion, St Patrick's was a shelter for refugees from surrounding areas; hundreds, including the rector, died of disease and starvation. Despite various renovations, by the 1880s the church was in bad repair and it was decided to rebuild it. The new building was dedicated on 28 April 1885. In the 1890s the church received new glass – east and west windows, a peal of eight bells and an organ. Following damage from a terrorist bomb in the town centre in 1992 extensive refurbishment gave an opportunity to reconsider the layout of the interior.

*St Andrew's Church, Ballysally* is a daughter church of St Patrick's consecrated in 1981.

Patrick's Church, Coleraine
RDON GRAY

## CONNOR and ANTRIM

*St Saviour's Church, Connor* was consecrated in the early nineteenth century. It stands on the site of the former cathedral which had links to the fifth-century monastery founded by Aengus Mac Nissi. It gives its name to the largest diocese in Ireland.

*St Patrick's Church, Antrim* was consecrated in May 1976. It is situated in the Steeple housing estate, Parkhall, to the north of Antrim town.

St Patrick's Church, Antrim
COLIN BOYLE

St Saviour's Church, Antrim
COLIN BOYLE

## RAIGS, DUNAGHY and KILLAGAN

hese parishes were grouped together in 1960. The parish of Craigs, a mile or so outside ullybackey, came into existence in 1839–41, taking over 22 townlands from the overlarge parish f Ahoghill. There are burial grounds related to a medieval foundation in the parish. The previous uined) parish church at Dunaghy may be seen in Clough Cemetery. This church was rebuilt in e 1630s and 1740s, on the site of previous structures probably dating back to the post-Patrician a. Killagan was grouped with Dunaghy and Newtowncrommelin from 1894 to 1960.

*Craigs Church*, designed by Sir Charles Lanyon, was consecrated on 14 July 1841. Transepts ere added in 1870 and the chancel was rebuilt in 1888. There are two 'wagon-wheel' handeliers, two 150-year-old yew trees at the gate and an imposing graveyard, one feature of hich is a plot dedicated to victims of the Great Famine. In 1961, Craigs was the venue for the rst broadcast of a communion service from a church in Northern Ireland.

*St James's Church, Dunaghy* is in the centre of Clough village. The present church was designed by Sir Charles Lanyon and consecrated on 21 December 1842. The Rev. Monsell (1846), author of the hymn 'Fight the Good Fight', was a former rector. The pinnacles on the tower of the present church were removed in the 1960s for reasons of safety and replaced with facsimiles in the early 2000s. Between 1998 and the present day, much work has been done to restore the fabric of the church.

*Killagan Church* is situated on the outskirts of the village of Cloughmills. Also designed by Sir Charles Lanyon, it was consecrated on 25 November 1840. The grounds are pleasantly laid out and there is a scenic graveyard. The finely designed wrought-iron gates on both entrances to the church property are particularly remarkable.

## DERRIAGHY

Situated between Lisburn and Dunmurry, Derriaghy is the mother church of several parishes. Parish records survive from 1696, but the earliest documentary evidence of a church here is dated 1204.

*Christ Church, Derriaghy* was built in 1872, one of the strikingly original churches by William Gillespie, architect to the Ecclesiastical Commissioners, of Welland and Gillespie. The church has a simple but impressive interior and the spire has been described 'like a rocket ready to be launched'.

*St Andrew's Church, Colin* was built in 1957 to serve the Colin and Castlerobin areas of the parish but was closed in 1974 due to the almost complete exodus of protestant families from the area.

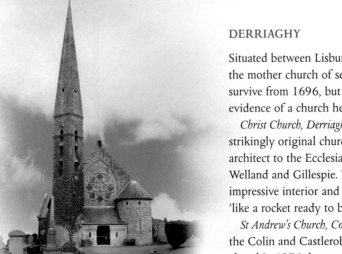

GORDON GRAY

Christ Church, Derriaghy

Killagan Church
GARY MCMURRAY

GORDON GRAY

## DERRYVOLGIE

Derryvolgie Parish was founded in 1963 because of increased population in the area. It was formed from the adjoining parishes of Lisburn, Lambeg and Derriaghy. Services were originally held in shop premises on Moss Road; later, parishioners worshipped in a hut on the present site. *St Columba's Church, Derryvolgie* was built in 1966. Its focal point is a cross above the holy table, made from reclaimed wood from pews and the hut that was originally used for services.

## DRUMMAUL, DUNEANE and BALLYSCULLION

The ancient parish church of Drummaul was situated on the western bank of the River Maine and dedicated to St Brigid. In the 1700s, a new church was built in a more convenient location, probably because of the increasing importance of the town of Maine Water (Randalstown).

The present *St Brigid's Church, Drummaul* was built in 1831 in the churchyard of the former church, in the early English style of architecture. The oak pulpit was dedicated in 1960 in memory of the third Baron O'Neill, killed in action in Italy in 1944 and his brother Arthur O'Neill killed in action in Norway in 1940.

The east wall and two side walls of *Duneane Church* formed part of a much larger ancient church. The present church was downsized by local landlord Major Dobbin in a rebuilding of 1729. The porch and vestry were added in 1788.

*Ballyscullion Church*, Grange, was consecrated in 1848. Before the church was built, services were held in a licensed cabin that could hold about 60 people.

COLIN BOYLE

Duneane Church

## DUNLUCE

Dunluce Parish consists of the village of Portballintrae, the town of Bushmills and Benvarden estate. The ruin of St Cuthbert's is next to Dunluce Castle. Built in the seventeenth century as a chapel to the castle, St Cuthbert's was used as the parish church until the new church was built in Bushmills. *St John the Baptist's Church, Dunluce*, Bushmills, beside the River Bush, was erected in 1822 on the ancient church ruin of Portcamon.

## DUNMURRY

The people of Dunmurry first worshipped in a building known as the assembly rooms, constructed in 1874 and in use today as the parochial hall. *St Colman's Church, Dunmurry* was consecrated on 25 April 1908. It was built in the late perpendicular Gothic style; the architects were Messrs Blackwood and Jury. The parish was linked with Drumbeg until 1932. A Garden of Remembrance for the ashes after cremation was consecrated in 1963.

GORDON GRAY

St John the Baptist's Church, Dunluce

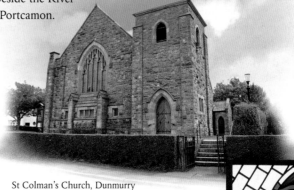

COLIN BOYLE

St Colman's Church, Dunmurry

GORDON GRAY

## EGLANTINE

*All Saints' Church, Eglantine* is closely linked with the Mulholland family, who lived in nearby Eglantine House. The church was built in memory of two members of that family. A parochial district was formed from parts of Christ Church and Broomhedge Parishes. Before and during WW2 All Saints' was surrounded by temporary buildings which were part of the former Long Kesh Air Base which stretched to Sprucefield. In Eglantine Graveyard lie the graves of 21 Commonwealth Air Force men from Australia, Canada, New Zealand and the UK who were killed during that war. They are also commemorated in stained glass in the church's Battle of Britain Memorial West Window.

## GLENAVY

Full historical lists for this parish date from 1622. In 1690, a detachment of the duke of Schomberg's army was billeted in the parish. The parish holds an engraved silver chalice presented to the church by officers of the duke's army. During the second world war a search light battery of the Royal artillery, stationed at Glenavy presented another chalice to the church.

St Aidan's Church, Glenavy dates from 1812. A transept was added in 1863 and the church was enlarged in 1894. A fire completely destroyed it in 1938, but it was repaired and consecrated in 1939.

St Andrew's Church, Tunny, a chapel of ease dating from 1854, was enlarged in the twentieth century, with a church room added.

St John's Church, Crumlin dates from 1903.

Church of the Holy Name, Greenisland

COLIN BOYLE

St Aidan's Church, Glenavy

## JORDANSTOWN

Jordanstown Parish was carved out of the ancient parish of Coole or Carnmoney. Tradition has it that King Fergus of Scottish Dalriada was buried in the old graveyard at Monkstown around AD 531. St Patrick's Church, Jordanstown was built in 1866–68 to the designs of W.H. Lynn, one of the finest examples of the Celtic Revival. In the porch is a very beautiful Rosamund Praeger carving of St Patrick as a shepherd boy on Slemish mountain.

## GREENISLAND

Greenisland is between Jordanstown and Carrickfergus. In the early 1950s, members of St Patrick's, Jordanstown decided to establish a daughter church in this large residential area. The Church of the Holy Name, Greenisland was consecrated on 4 September 1954. Greenisland became a separate parish ten years later.

GARY McMURRAY

DERMOTT DUNBAR

St Patrick's Church, Jordanstown

## KILBRIDE

There has been a church in the Kilbride area for some 1,400 years. In 1609, the charter of James I saw Kilbride and Donegore Parishes united. Rev. George H. Johnston was appointed rector in 1814 and built a church at Kilbride at his own expense. It was used as a chapel of ease, but the bishop refused to consecrate it because he had not been consulted. The present St Bride's Church, Kilbride, early English in style, was consecrated on 9 June 1868.

GARY McMURRAY

## KILMAKEE

In the 1950s, the Connor Diocesan Council obtained a central site for a church in this rapidly expanding area with new housing estates at Seymour Hill and Conway. On 20 May 1956, services began in Kilmakee Orange Hall. St Hilda's Church, Kilmakee, a dual purpose church/hall was dedicated on May 17 1958. As Dunmurry Parish is known as St Colman's, it was fitting that its daughter church should be dedicated to St Hilda, who supported St Colman at the Synod of Whitby in AD 664. On 1 August 1964, the Diocesan Council constituted the Parish of Kilmakee. A new church building, pictured, was consecrated on 19 December 1970. This has since been deconsecrated (April 4 2011) and demolished. In 2013, a new church building is under construction.

St Colman's Church, Kilroot
GARY McMURRAY

## KILROOT and TEMPLECORRAN

In the late seventeenth century Jonathan Swift served as prebend of the parishes of Kilroot, Templecorran and Ballynure. However, he had very few parishioners and his church buildings were in a ruinous state. Eventually Kilroot became attached to Carrickfergus Parish. It remained so until the industrial expansion of Carrickfergus in the second half of the twentieth century. Land was purchased close to Downshire Gardens for a temporary church hall, which was dedicated in December 1971. The hall was named St Colman's. Templecorran was grouped with Kilroot in 1990.

St Colman's Church, Kilroot was dedicated in 1981.

St John's Church, Templecorran, situated in Ballycarry, was consecrated in 1847.

## KILWAUGHTER (CAIRNCASTLE) with ALL SAINTS', CRAIGYHILL

The earliest evidence of a church in Cairncastle Parish is in the taxation of 1291. The present *St Patrick's Church, Cairncastle* was built in 1815. The chancel and the stained-glass east window, by Mayer of Munich, were added in 1891. In 1993, a Sunday school/vestry room was built on and in 2006, a major conservation programme was undertaken. In 1992, the parish was united with All Saints', Craigyhill.

*All Saints' Church, Craigyhill* was built in 1962 to serve the newly built Craigyhill estate in Larne. It was originally a daughter church of St Cedma's. In 2002, the church was reroofed and extended. Its fortieth anniversary was celebrated with a visit by Archbishop Robin Eames.

St Patrick's Church, Cairncastle

## LAMBEG

There is some evidence that a place of worship existed in Lambeg as far back as 1306, but the first definite mention of a church is from 1598. The original small church was in ruins before 1649. *Lambeg Church* was consecrated on 25 September 1737. The church was rebuilt in 1849 and, just before disestablishment, was enlarged to a seating capacity of 480 by the addition of a south aisle. The churchyard was extended in 1921 and the parochial hall opened in 1937. Major refurbishment was carried out in 1967 and again in 2000.

Lambeg Church

St John's Church, Glynn

## LARNE AND INVER with GLYNN and RALOO

In medieval times there were three churches in Larne – Drumalis, Inverbeg and Invermore. The parish church of Larne, dedicated to St Cedma, occupies the site of the ancient church of Invermore. In 1838, the parish of Glynn was separated from Larne and Inver. Services were regularly held in a temporary building in the village of Glynn until the present church was built.

*St Cedma's Church, Larne* stands on the site of earlier churches dating back to Norman times. The building was extensively remodelled in the nineteenth century, but retains some of its older character. Its grounds are entered through a lych gate made of Burma teak. In the churchyard, the oldest headstone is dated 1677. Two of the windows in the church were made by Wilhelmina Geddes in the 1920s. The dramatic dado on the east chancel wall and the chancel floor are made of encaustic tiles.

*St John's Church, Glynn* is a picturesque building designed by Sir Charles Lanyon and built in 1840. It has a small bell tower at one end. The church was completely refurbished in 2001. Within the well-kept graveyard are the ruins of the medieval church.

*St Columba's Church, Gleno* was built in 1842 to serve the parish of Raloo. This church was also designed by Charles Lanyon. It is built of rough-hewn basalt, with a decorative campanile over the west gable and a small porch attached to the centre of the south wall. On Easter Sunday 2006, following a major restoration, the church was rededicated by the bishop of Connor.

## LISBURN (HILLSBOROUGH ROAD)

*Christ Church, Lisburn* was designed by Sir Charles Lanyon and opened for worship on 20 November 1842, providing free sittings for linen workers. After the religious revival of 1859, the north and south transepts and the gallery were constructed. The church was consecrated on 24 September 1863.

During the incumbency of Rev. Canon Arthur Noble (1961–82), a massive reconstruction programme was carried out. In 1982, the porch of the church was rebuilt and enlarged, the church halls were renovated and new pews and flooring were installed. In 2011, the east window was completely replaced, with major repairs done to the sandstone around the three main windows.

St Cedma's Church and piscina, Larne

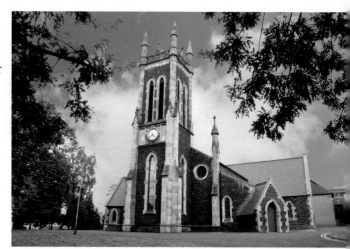

## LISBURN (LONGSTONE STREET)

*St Paul's Church, Lisburn* was originally a daughter church of Christ Church and was intended to serve new housing estates planned for south of Lisburn. The site was purchased by Christ Church in October 1959. Two army huts were acquired and dedicated on 8 September 1962. The foundation stone of the present church was laid on 10 November 1962 and the church was consecrated on 25 January 1964. St Paul's became a separate parish in 1966.

## MAGHERAGALL

The parish of Magheragall first appears in a document of 1210 under the name of Drumchale. The present *Magheragall Church* was consecrated on 2 June 1831. One of the hymn boards was made from the oak beams from the previous church. The organ was brought from St Patrick's, Coleraine in 1875. The church was reroofed and a new vestry room was built in 1988–9. From 1990 to 1999 the parish spent over £400,000 on restoring the church, rectory and parochial hall.

## MALLUSK

Mallusk was linked with Carnmoney until 1974. *St Brigid's Church, Mallusk*, Glengormley, was originally built in 1958. The 130-year-old bell was a gift from the parish of Killoscully, County Tipperary. A new, larger church was built and consecrated in 1964 beside the existing church; the existing church then became the parish hall. The current circular church has a redwood ceiling that slopes to a high central point, while windows in the roof direct sunlight onto the holy table. The modern church was consecrated on 3 June 1989.

St Brigid's Church, Mallusk

## MONKSTOWN

Monkstown was part of the parish of Jordanstown. The foundation stones for a church and hall to be used by Methodist and Church of Ireland worshippers were laid in 1969. Both church organisations have joint membership and carry out joint services on Sunday evenings. The *Church of the Good Shepherd, Monkstown* was consecrated in 1970. It is modern in architectural design. On 1 April 1991, Monkstown became an independent parish.

## MOSSLEY

The village of Mossley was built around a spinning mill. The area was originally part of Carnmoney Parish, but on 30 May 1971 the parish of Mossley was born to cater for new housing estates. The main features of the *Church of the Holy Spirit, Mossley* are an imposing cross-shaped window in the east wall with flame-coloured glass, and all-white sanctuary furnishings in a modern style. The church was dedicated on 5 December 1969.

St Catherine's Church, Killead
COLIN BOYLE

## MUCKAMORE, KILLEAD and GARTREE

*St Jude's Church, Muckamore* was built in 1841 on land belonging to the Thompson family of Muckamore Abbey. The architect was Charles Lanyon and the church could accommodate 300 people.

*St Catherine's Church, Killead* was dedicated by the bishop on St Catherine's day, 25 November 1712. The church has a bell-cote and lychgate. Restoration work was carried out in 2003. The church building is sited in the middle of an RAF Station. Lord Molyneaux, former leader of the Ulster Unionist Party, was a member of the choir for an incredible 80 years retiring on his 91st birthday in 2012.

*Gartree Church* was built by architect Edward Sands in 1830–1 and cost £1,200. Situated on the site of the ancient church of Kilmacheret, it has a square tower 30 feet high and an ornate gateway.

Lord Jim Molyneaux and the choir of St Cartherine's

## RAMOAN and CULFEIGHTRIN (BALLYCASTLE)

The parish of Ramoan is believed to have connections with St Patrick, through his disciple Ereclacius.

*St James's Church, Ramoan* is about a mile outside Ballycastle and lies a short distance from the original site. It was built in 1849.

*Holy Trinity Church, Ballycastle,* is in the Diamond. It was built in Greco-Italian style by Colonel Hugh Boyd in 1756 and is regarded as of outstanding architectural merit. It was a chapel of ease for the Boyd family for many years and was given to the Church of Ireland in the 1950s.

*Culfeightrin Church* dates from 1829 and is located close to the Corrymeela Centre.

GORDON GRAY

Holy Trinity Church, Ballycastle

GARY McMURRAY

## RATHCOOLE

St Comgall's Church, Rathcoole

Rathcoole Parish is north of Belfast, in the extensive Rathcoole housing estate. In March 1962, formal ties with Carnmoney Parish were severed and Rathcoole became independent. *St Comgall's Church, Rathcoole* was consecrated on 1 December 1956 by Bishop Cyril Elliott. According to tradition St Comgall's birthplace was in the parish. Thanks to its unusual architectural design, this modern church is a listed building with the church hall being on the ground floor and the church on the first floor.

## REV CANON JOHN GRAINGER

Former rector at Broughshane Rev. Canon John Grainger, 1869–91, was a renowned antiquarian and scholar. He toured extensively collecting fossils, minerals, fine art, books and curios, which he lodged with Belfast Central Library in 1891, shortly before his death. This vast collection of artefacts encouraged the City Fathers to build a municipal museum which became the Belfast Museum and Art Gallery, now the Ulster Museum. A replica of a 10th century Monasterboice cross marks his grave.

St Patrick's Church, Broughshane
COLIN BOYLE

## STONEYFORD

Stoneyford was originally part of Derryaghy parish and became an independent parish in 1867. *St John's Church, Stoneyford* was licensed for public worship on 6 October 1841. The marquis of Hertford had given the ground for the new church the previous year. The cost of the new building, designed by Sir Charles Lanyon, was £554. The church and churchyard were consecrated on 28 October 1874.

## SKERRY, RATHCAVAN and NEWTOWNCROMMELIN

The ruin of Skerry Church was formerly a place of pilgrimage. Tradition ascribes its foundation to St Patrick.

*St Patrick's Church, Broughshane,* erected by Charles O'Neill of Shane's Castle in 1765, was enlarged in 1829. In 1859, a chancel transept was added. The stone pulpit, designed by Sir Thomas Drew, is a memorial to his father, Rev. Thomas Drew (curate 1827–9). There are lych gates at the front and rear of the church. St Patrick's was refurbished in 2007. It was one of the first churches in Connor Diocese to broadcast services to the housebound on shortwave radio.

*Rathcavan Church* was separated from Skerry by the River Braid.

GARY McMURRAY

229

## TEMPLEPATRICK AND DONEGORE

A church of Patrick may have existed at Templepatrick from the fifth century. It is thought that the Knights Templar took over an existing church in the twelfth century and built their priory nearby. The earliest record of a church at Donegore occurs in the taxation of Nicholas IV in 1306. After the battle of Antrim in 1798, the rebels retreated to Donegore. In 1864, Donegore Parish separated from Kilbride. The united parishes of Templepatrick and Donegore gained parochial status in 1868.

*St Patrick's Church, Templepatrick* was consecrated in 1827. In 1889 the church was added to by the Templetown family. St Patrick's contains a brass font that originally belonged to a church in Sebastopol. Restoration work was completed in 1993 after dry rot was discovered.

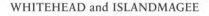

*St John's Church, Donegore* bears the date 1659 over its doorway. In 1871 the tower and belfry were added; the east window was added in 1875. In the south-west corner of the churchyard is the witch-house, or corpse-house, built in 1832 to foil the attempts of bodysnatchers. The churchyard contains the grave of Sir Samuel Ferguson, Irish scholar and poet, who died in 1886. Repair works to Donegore Church were carried out in 1962 and 1980, but major restoration work is now required.

St John's Church,
Donegore
COLIN BOYLE

## WHITEHEAD and ISLANDMAGEE

In 1961, the united parish of Whitehead and Islandmagee was formed. The Templecorran part of the parish was split between Raloo and Kilroot.

Before work began on *St Patrick's Church, Whitehead* in 1907, the congregation had been meeting in a lifeboat shed. The church is built of basalt and sandstone. St Patrick's is unusual in that the floor slopes towards the front, so that those at the back can see more easily.

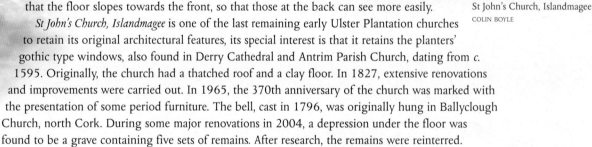

St John's Church, Islandmagee
COLIN BOYLE

*St John's Church, Islandmagee* is one of the last remaining early Ulster Plantation churches to retain its original architectural features, its special interest is that it retains the planters' gothic type windows, also found in Derry Cathedral and Antrim Parish Church, dating from *c.* 1595. Originally, the church had a thatched roof and a clay floor. In 1827, extensive renovations and improvements were carried out. In 1965, the 370th anniversary of the church was marked with the presentation of some period furniture. The bell, cast in 1796, was originally hung in Ballyclough Church, north Cork. During some major renovations in 2004, a depression under the floor was found to be a grave containing five sets of remains. After research, the remains were reinterred.

GORDON GRAY

St Patrick's Church, Whitehead

## WHITEHOUSE and ST NINIAN

Whitehouse was originally part of Carnmoney Parish. The population boomed with the growth of the textile industry and a small church was built.

*St John's Church, Whitehouse* opened in 1840 and was consecrated in 1843, Sir Charles Lanyon having given his services for free. The church was enlarged in 1873 and the organ installed in 1877. Rev. R.H.B. Cooper (rector 1890–1912) was a co-founder of the Boys' Brigade in Ireland and St John's was one of the first companies. The first Irish company of Girl Guides was formed in the parish in 1909.

The foundation stone for *St Ninian's Church, Whitehouse* was laid in 1962. An unusual feature of the new building is a columbarium for depositing ashes in single niches.

## WOODBURN (CARRICKFERGUS)

Woodburn gained parochial status on 23 April 2000. *Holy Trinity Church, Woodburn* first opened its doors on 6 December 1992. It was built on land bequeathed by the late Miss Henly of Prospect House. In 2004 Holy Trinity was extended to accommodate the growing congregation.

Holy Trinity Church, Woodburn

St John's, Whitehouse

COLIN BOYLE

# The United Dioceses of Kilmore, Elphin and Ardagh

The dioceses of Kilmore, Elphin and Ardagh, trace their history back to the Synod of Rathbreasil in 1111. They have been united together for over 170 years since 1841. Geographically, the united diocese is spread over three provinces: Connacht, Leinster and Ulster. The landscape in the northern midlands is characterised by drumlins, laid down by ice and interspersed by a labyrinth of lakes. To the west, the landscape becomes progressively more rugged with large limestone hills and ridges.

The diocese has a rich cultural heritage. In the early seventeenth century Kilmore produced the eminent Bishop William Bedell, who translated the Old Testament into Irish. Many icons of Irish culture, had their roots in Kilmore, Elphin and Ardagh: Maria Edgeworth, Oliver Goldsmith, Percy French, Douglas Hyde, Thomas Sheridan, and Jack and William Butler Yeats.

Apart from the urban centres of Cavan, Longford and Sligo, the dioceses are largely rural and agricultural. Around 10,000 people identified themselves with the Church of Ireland in the area, according to the most recent census. Like many parts of Ireland, there has been an influx of people into the region through immigration in the last decade or so.

Administratively, the united diocese is made up of around 100 church communities, clustered together into 24 groups, serviced by teams of clerical and lay leaders. The diocese is overseen by the bishop, two archdeacons, two deans and two lay secretaries. There are two cathedrals, in Kilmore and Sligo. Educational provision is maintained by 21 primary and two secondary schools: Royal School Cavan, and Sligo Grammar School, under Protestant management.

The Mothers' Union is very active in the diocese with some 400 members in 19 branches. Likewise, there is an energetic youth ministry at work in the diocese in the shape of YKEA! (Youth in Kilmore, Elphin and Ardagh). In recent times, the diocese has partnered with overseas links in the Anglican Communion, in Kenya, Paraguay and with the Diocese of South Carolina, in the United States.

At the turn of the century, the diocese, building on the achievements of the past, came together and agreed the Forward programme, seeking to be Christ Centred, Character Building and Community Transforming. The diocese is still going forward in good heart, as these lofty aims are worked out on the ground.

FERRAN KILMORE, ELPHIN AND ARDAGH

Benbulben
SCENIC IRELAND

## Kilmore Cathedral

The trowel used by Lady Farnham in laying the foundation stone of Kilmore Cathedral
CAVAN COUNTY MUSEUM
COURTESY OF DIANA,
LADY FARNHAM

William Bedell
Bishop of Kilmore

Occupying an attractive hillside site about five kilometers to the west of Cavan town sits St Fethlimidh's Cathedral, Kilmore. In geographical terms it is the most centrally located cathedral of the Church of Ireland. The old cathedral at Kilmore, now the parochial hall was constructed around 1400 and was given cathedral church status in 1454. When William Bedell arrived as bishop in 1629, he noted 'the church here built, but without Bell, Steeple, Font or Chalice'. By early 1858, the old cathedral was in poor condition and too small to accommodate the large body of parishoners. Under the guidance of Bishop Marcus Gervais Beresford, and with his financial support and the Ecclessiastical Commissioners and local landed families, especially the Farnham family, the present cathedral was constructed. Lady Anna Farnham, wife of Henry 7th Baron Farnham, laid the foundation stone in summer 1858.

The architect of the cathedral was William Slater of London who designed the cathedral in the Gothic Revival style on a cruciform plan with a central tower.

Bishop Beresford envisaged that the cathedral would be a memorial to his first wife, Mary who had died in 1845, and the famed Bishop Bedell. Sculptures representing the head of Mary Beresford and William Bedell are found on either side of the base of the chancel arch.

Bishop Beresford's second wife provided the new cathedral with its bell and it is inscribed 'To worship the Lord in the beauty of holiness in the year of our Lord 1860 Elizabeth Beresford gave me to this church.'

Illustration of architectural drawings for the Cathedral
RIGHT: Mary Beresford

The church was consecrated in June 1860, and during that service it was referred to as the 'Bedell Memorial Church' a name by which it is often referred to by today. The inscription that Bedell had composed for his own gravemarker was altered to 'Gulielmi Bedelli Quondam Kilmorensis Episcopi in memoriam' and included in the tympanum over the west door of the cathedral.

One of the most important architectural features of the cathedral building is the twelfth century Romanesque doorway incorporated into the north side of the building. It has been recognised as being one of the finer examples of such a doorway in Ireland. Tradition states that the doorway was brought from the Premonstratensian Canons priory church on Trinity Island in Lough Oughter sometime during the early to mid-seventeenth century and that it was incorporated within the old cathedral and then in the 1860s into the present cathedral.

The interior of the cathedral is well endowed with a good range of stained-glass windows dating from the later 1860s to the early 1970s. The most dominant window is that presented by Bishop Hamilton Verschoyle in 1868 depicting the parables of the Ten Virgins, the Good Samaratin and the Prodigal Son. It came from the studio of William Wailes, Newcastle-upon-Tyne.

Slater's design brief for the cathedral included the reredos depicting the Last Supper and the bishop's throne and choir stalls which were made by the firm of Forysthe of London. The organ constructed in 1860 by the Sheffield based organ builder Charles Brindley is one of the very earliest examples of his work.

This beautiful cathedral has recently undergone an extensive refurbishment programme at the cost of €1 million, raised with the help of diocesan members, the local community, county council, and statutory bodies. The building work was completed in 2010, on the 150th anniversary of the consecration of the cathedral. It continues to play an imprtant part in diocesan life.

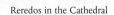

Reredos in the Cathedral

GARY MCMURRAY

# The United Dioceses of Kilmore, Elphin and Ardagh

JONATHAN CHERRY

The united dioceses of Kilmore, Elphin and Ardagh include parts of three Irish provinces: Ulster, Connacht and Leinster. The diocese of Kilmore covers most of County Cavan, north County Leitrim and small areas of the neighbouring counties of Fermanagh, Longford and Donegal. Elphin covers most of County Roscommon, north County Sligo and a small part of east Galway. Ardagh encompasses most of County Longford, the southern part of County Leitrim and a small area of County Westmeath.

## The Early Church

A number of prominent saints and monastic settlements are associated with the united dioceses. St Fethlimidh, born around 500AD, is traditionally accepted as having been the first bishop of Kilmore diocese. St Patrick is reputed to have founded the See of Ardagh around 435AD and appointed his nephew St Mel as its first bishop. Another of St Patrick's monastic settlements at Elphin was placed in the charge of Assicus, a renowned craftsman around 450AD. In the sixth century, St Mogue of Templeport was strongly linked with the monastic settlement at Drumlane that had been established by St Columba. Around these and other religious centres the early church grew and established itself.

The boundaries and extent of the dioceses of Elphin and Ardagh were established and settled at the synods of Rathbreasil (1111) and Kells (1152). Co-existing within this new diocesan framework were a number of religious orders who were already established or arrived in the dioceses during the thirteenth and fourteenth centuries. These included the Augustinians at Drumlane and Mohill and the Franciscans in Cavan town. The fourteenth century seal of the diocese of Kilmore, depicts the Virgin and Child seated and to their right a bishop kneeling in adoration.

## Post-Reformation and the Seventeenth Century

Throughout the early decades of the seventeenth century, the structures and institutions of the existing church were vested in the newly appointed Protestant bishops and clergy. This facilitated the 'newcomers' who came as part of the various plantation schemes at this time. The first bishop appointed in 1603 to Kilmore and Ardagh was Robert Draper. It is, however, one of his successors, William Bedell, appointed in 1629, who became one of the outstanding personalities at both diocesan and national level during the seventeenth century. Although many of the improvements and

Drumlane Abbey
©NATIONAL MONUMENTS SERVICE
DEPT OF ARTS, HERITAGE AND THE GAELTACHT

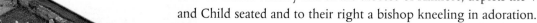

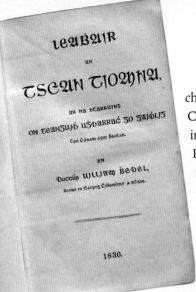

The title page of Bedell's translation
RCB ARCHIVE

changes brought about by William Bedell in terms of the organisation of the Church in the diocese and the provision of a resident clergy proficient in the Irish language were thrown into turmoil as a result of the 1641 Rebellion, his personal legacy as a tolerant yet reforming bishop remained. Bedell was responsible for the first translation of the Old Testament into Irish.

After a vacancy of two years following his death in 1642, Robert Maxwell was appointed as his successor. In 1664, Bishop Maxwell purchased the Waldron estate of over 7,000 acres which bounded the church lands at Kilmore and so laid the foundations from which his descendants – the Lords Farnham – would build up what was to become by the mid-nineteenth century the largest landed estate in county Cavan, extending to over 30,000 acres. The legacy of Bedell was felt again towards the end of the century, when William Sheridan, was appointed bishop in 1682. A son of Denis Sheridan, one of the native Irish who had become a clergyman during Bedell's period and in whose home Bedell had died, Bishop Sheridan was to gain prominence as a *non-juror* in 1692, when he was removed from office for failing to take the oath of allegiance to William and Mary.

Killeshandra Church built 1688
Although now in ruins, the Jacobean church is of national importance in terms of its architecture.
MICHAEL O'NEILL

## The Eighteenth Century

One clergyman of special note in the eighteenth century, Rev. John Richardson, was rector of Annagh between 1709 and 1747. He published a number of religious works, including several of his sermons in Irish. Bishop Wetenhall lent him support in 1711 when he presented a petition in London to the lord lieutenant, the second duke of Ormonde, calling for the publication of bibles and catechisms in Irish. During the same period, Bishop Edward Synge, was transferred to Elphin from Ferns and Leighlin and remained as bishop until his death in 1762. An advocate of religious tolerance, he was critical of the penal laws. In 1749, he undertook a census of his diocese, using a specially designed form and his churchwardens as his enumerators. The original manuscripts comprising the census are held today by the National Archives of Ireland. In the absence of other source material containing such social and demographic detail, the 1749 Census of Elphin provides a unique insight into a rural region of Ireland in the mid-eighteenth century.

Marcus Gervais Beresford, Bishop of Kilmore, 1854–62, Archbishop of Armagh, 1862–85
RCB ARCHIVE

## The Nineteenth Century

Rev. Charles Leslie, later Bishop of Kilmore
IAN S ELLIOTT

Throughout the seventeenth and eighteenth centuries the dioceses of Kilmore and Ardagh were occasionally held together. Following the death of Power Le Poer Trench, Archbishop of Tuam and Bishop of Ardagh in 1839, the dioceses were again united under Bishop George de la Poer Beresford. The dominant ecclesiastical dynasty in the dioceses during the latter half of the eighteenth century and throughout most of the nineteenth century were the Beresfords. Bishop George Beresford built the See House at Kilmore in the Grecian Revival style between 1835

Corravahan House is a substantial early nineteenth-century classical house, built *c.* 1840 as a rectory by the Beresford family in the Georgian style. It replaced the eighteenth-century parsonage at Drung and was bought by Reverend Charles (later Bishop) Leslie, a cousin of the Leslies of Glaslough, in 1855. The Leslies lived at Corravahan until 1972. The house now belongs to the Elliott family.
IAN S ELLIOTT

**Rev. Joseph Robert Garven Digges: the father of modern bee-keeping in Ireland**

Rev. J.R.G. Digges was private chaplain to the Clements family at Lough Rynn Castle, county Leitrim, from 1885 until his death in 1933. At Clooncahir Rectory on the western shores of Lough Rynn, he had his first lesson in bee-keeping in 1885. From this grew what was to become a life long passion and Digges became a well-known and much respected apiarist and expert on bee-keeping.

County Leitrim alongside other counties along the Western seaboard were designated 'Congested Districts' in 1891. Characterised by high population densities on poor quality land, over-reliant on traditional agricultural employment and subject to much emigration, the government sought to bring about greater diversity in employment. In particular they attempted to develop fishing, cottage industries and other small scale enterprises such as bee-keeping.

Digges promoted, lectured and demonstrated the art of bee-keeping throughout the country and developed the Congested Districts Hive. He published *The Irish Bee Guide* in 1904. It was renamed *The Practical Bee Guide: A Manual of Modern Bee-Keeping* and was reprinted on at least sixteen occasions throughout the twentieth century, illustrating its popularity as the handbook of bee-keeping. He was Chairman of the Irish Bee-Keepers' Association, 1910–21. Following his death, a stained-glass window by Ethel Rhind was installed in Farnaught Church. Appropriately, it depicted St Modomnoc bringing the bees from Wales to Ireland. Digges' name is commemorated by several bee-keeping clubs in county Leitrim today.

and 1837 to a design attributed to the Dublin based architect William Farrell. His son Bishop Marcus Gervais Beresford oversaw the construction of Kilmore Cathedral and later as Archbishop of Armagh and Primate of All Ireland, lead and guided the Church of Ireland during disestablishment.

The ecclessiastical landscape of the united dioceses was dramatically altered in the nineteenth century as new churches and rectories were constructed and older churches rebuilt and renovated through funding provided by the Board of First Fruits. The elegant churches of eighteenth century origin that survive in the united dioceses to the present day are primarily located in urban settings, such as at Ballyconnell and Longford. Some of the rural eighteenth century churches include Ardcarne and Tashinny.

This church building boom produced a portfolio of churches in the dioceses that ranged from simply designed and constructed hall and tower churches, to those where the generosity of local benefactors resulted in superior quality buildings, displaying high quality stone craftsmanship and additional ornamentation on both the exterior and interior. In addition, the landowning class of Ireland, the landlords, also provided sites and paid for the construction of churches on their own lands, which would serve their own family needs and those of their estate workers. Examples of these nineteenth century 'estate churches' include Castle Saunderson, County Cavan and Clongish, County Longford, which date from the 1820s, while those at Aghanagh, County Sligo and Quivvy, County Cavan, date from 1840 to 1860.

Across the united dioceses a number of clergy played important roles in attempting to alleviate the widespread suffering caused by the mid-nineteenth century Great Famine. Many sat on Local Relief Committees, and attempted to use their influence and position through report and letter writing to government authorities, to highlight the plight and suffering of those in their parishes. In the parish of Mullagh, the Rev. Charles Atkinson Caffrey and his son Fitzherbert have gone down in local folklore as 'the kind-hearted Caffrey' due to their influential role in securing funding from local landlords, provision of famine works and the establishment of a soup kitchen. Rev. James Godley, rector of Ashfield during the famine, is recalled in local folklore as having sold his horse to buy food for the hungry, while Rev. Charles Beresford, rector of Bailieborough, a tireless

Carrigallen Church was constructed between 1812 and 1814 with funds provided by the Board of First Fruits.
COLIN BOYLE

worker for the relief of the poor, died from famine fever in August 1848. At Tomregan (Ballyconnell) Church several famine burial plots within low walled enclosures in the graveyard serve as poignant reminders of this period in Ireland's history.

## The Twentieth Century

Challenges and opportunities have faced the united dioceses during the course of the 20th century. In County Cavan, opposition to Home Rule in the form of the Ulster Covenant in September 1912 drew great support from the Church of Ireland population and clergy. Eleven clergy were amongst the 56 organisers of the signing of the document in county Cavan, reflective of the strong Unionist views of many in the area at this time. Later in the 1920s, as the border was drawn, the Fermanagh portion of the united dioceses now fell within Northern Ireland. At this time, a significant number of Church of Ireland people from the border region moved to Northern Ireland for a variety of socio-political reasons and more practical ones such as gaining employment in the industrial regions.

Since the mid-twentieth century, rural de-population and dwindling Church of Ireland populations have brought about the closure of a number of churches in the dioceses. In Elphin diocese at least twelve churches have closed over the last sixty years, while in the same period ten churches have closed in Ardagh and six in Kilmore. Some of these churches such as Bumlin (Strokestown) have found new functions as heritage centres, while others such as Kilbryan have become family homes. Others remain as spectacular ruins on the landscape such as Mount Talbot, county Roscommon, with Quivvy Church, Belturbet closed, in 1986, finding new use as a music recording studio.

A number of people from the dioceses have helped shape the Irish education system during the latter decades of the twentieth century. Florence (Florrie) Armstrong of Drumaloor Church was principal of the Dalkey School Project in Dublin from 1978 and, from this, the Educate Together schools of today have evolved. She has been hailed as 'one of the key pioneers in Irish education' whose child centred approach to education was to become 'The New Curriculum' of 1971. More recently, Dr Harold Hislop of Kilmore diocese, since 2010, has been Chief Inspector in the Department of Education and Skills in Dublin.

Nine bishops have served the dioceses over the course of the twentieth century. From Kilmore several have gone on to hold other high offices in the Church of Ireland including Arthur William Barton who was elected Archbishop of Dublin in 1939; Frederick Julian Mitchell who was elected Bishop of Down and Dromore in 1955; Charles John Tyndall who was elected to Derry and Raphoe in 1958 and Michael Hugh Gunton Mayes, elected Bishop of Limerick and Killaloe in 2000.

Lt Hugh Gore-Booth from Lissadell, Co. Sligo, lies buried in a commonwealth graveyard on the island of Leros in the Aegean Sea. A member of the 2nd Battalion of the Royal Irish Fusiliers, he died in action during the battle for the island in November 1943. Surrounding him are the graves of soldiers from Co. Tyrone, Co. Tipperary and Co. Donegal, including that of his commanding officer, Lt Col. Maurice French, from Wellington Bridge, Co. Wexford. Hugh's brother, Brian, was drowned when his ship was sunk during convoy duty in the Atlantic in 1940. They were sons of Sir Josselyn and Lady Gore-Booth and nephews of Countess Markievicz.

Famine grave, Ballyconnell
JONATHAN CHERRY

Kilmore clergy, 1956, at Carrick-on-Shannon
RCB ARCHIVE

At the turn of the millenium, Ken Clarke was appointed Bishop of Kilmore, Elphin and Ardagh. In 2005, he initiated a programme entitled *Forward Growing Healthy Parishes* and led the dioceses until 2012 when he became the Mission Director of the South American Mission Society (SAMS) UK & Ireland. In 2013, Bishop Ferran Glenfield, a former rector of Hillsborough, county Down and Kill of the Grange, Dublin was elected bishop of the united dioceses. He and his wife, Jean and family are the first residents of the new See House at Kilmore completed in summer 2013. The diocesan archive is housed in the library of the RCB.

One of the most striking features of the make up of the diocesan clergy in 2013, when compared to the mid-twentieth century are the number of female clergy. Of the 23 clergy currently serving in the united dioceses, eight are female. The clergy are assisted by a team of over 20 diocesan readers and numerous parish readers in leading services.

A range of organisations operate within the parishes of the dioceses. One of the most popular is the Mothers' Union established in the diocese in 1897 by Mrs Gertrude Clements of Lough Rynn. Today, nineteen branches of the Mothers Union with 415 members meet across the dioceses. Since 2011, Dean Raymond Ferguson of Kilmore has been All Ireland Chaplain to the Mothers Union. In many parishes children and youth groups such as the scouts and guides and the Girls Friendly Society also exist, while Youth of Kilmore, Elphin and Ardagh (YKEA) provides a meeting place for teenagers from across the dioceses.

The church buildings detailed in the following pages are maintained by in some instances relatively small yet dedicated groups of parishioners. Those who clean these structures, arrange flowers for Sunday services, provide music, teach Sunday School and maintain these historic structures and graveyards remain the unsung heroes of the Church of Ireland. It is hoped that what follows provides some sense of their 'home' churches.

Rev. George Davison and Bishop Ken Clarke present the New Forward Banner, 2009.

Parishioners from Kinawley and Holy Trinity Parish Church enjoy the Queen's Diamond Jubilee Event at Crom Castle, Co. Fermanagh, 4 June 2012

Diocesan Mothers' Union Service, May 2012

# DIOCESE OF KILMORE

PHOTOGRAPHS BY COLIN BOYLE

## ANNAGH (BELTURBET), DRUMALOOR, CLOVERHILL and DRUMLANE

This group of parishes, centred on the town of Belturbet in north Cavan, contains four churches. *Annagh Church* is the oldest in the group. The original parish church, located close to Butlersbridge, was unroofed at the Ulster plantation. By the 1620s, a new parish church in the recently established town of Belturbet had been constructed. Built on an elevated site overlooking the town, the church was noted in 1733 as being in 'very good order'. It was rebuilt in 1828 in a cruciform plan with three galleries. The tower dates from 1814 and was attached to the earlier, seventeenth-century church. The graveyard surrounding the church contains the imposing Knipe and Maudsley family mausolea. Bishop Samuel Poyntz spent some of his early years in this parish, when his father James Poyntz was rector, between 1932 and 1944.

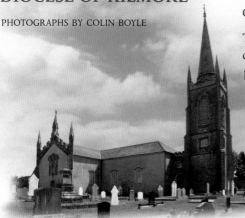

Annagh Church

St Andrew's Church, Drumaloor

St John's Church, Cloverhill

St Columba's Church, Drumlane

COLIN BOYLE

*St Andrew's Church, Drumaloor*, nestling beneath one of Cavan's many drumlins, was designed in Gothic-revival style by James Rawson Carroll. The building was opened for worship in early 1871 and consecrated in June 1875.

*St John's Church, Cloverhill*, one of several estate churches in the diocese of Kilmore, was consecrated in 1860 as a chapel of ease for the parish of Annagh. Designed by Joseph and William J. Welland in the Gothic-revival style, the cost of constructing the church, amounting to over £4,400, was provided by the local landlord, Mary Anne Sanderson, who also provided the site for the building.

The original parish church lay in close proximity to Drumlane Abbey, once an important Augustinian friary, located just outside the village of Milltown. *St Columba's Church, Drumlane* was completed in 1821 to a design by John Bowden. Its construction was funded by the Board of First Fruits. In the 1860s, a transept and robing room were added to the church and in 1964 a stained-glass window from Monivea Church, County Galway was installed. More recently, in 2004, over €60,000 was invested in an extensive programme of repairs to the church, a huge achievement for this small rural parish.

## ARVAGH (ARVA), CARRIGALLEN, GOWNA and COLUMBKILLE

These four parishes straddle the border between Counties Cavan, Leitrim and Longford. It is here that the boundaries of Ulster, Connacht and Leinster also meet.

*Arva Church* was constructed in 1821. The funding for both the construction of the church and the addition of the north transept in 1827 was provided by the Board of First Fruits. The contrast between the rubble stone tower and the rendered walls of the church is a notable architectural feature.

*Carrigallen Church*, situated in extensive grounds to the west of the town of Carrigallen, was constructed between 1812 and 1814 at a cost of £1,384, provided by the Board of First Fruits. The castellated finish to the tower and the ornate entrance porch add architectural interest. The remains of a fifteenth-century church lie in close proximity to the present church, illustrating the importance of the site as an ecclesiastical settlement. James Agar, a son of Archbishop Charles Agar, is to date the longest-serving rector, having served from 1809 to 1866.

Overlooking Lough Gowna, *Gowna Church*, built around 1840, is located on the site of an ancient church of *c.* 1100, sited within a ringfort. The addition of an ornate entrance porch in 1908 greatly enhances the aesthetic appeal of the building in its picturesque setting.

*St Thomas' Church, Columbkille*, County Longford was consecrated in 1829. Although funded by the Board of First Fruits, its design is quite different from the more traditional hall-and-tower churches. The use of stone pinnacles at the corner of the roof, above the porch and bell-cote, coupled with the painted window stones and contrasting wall paint, adds great interest to this most picturesque of buildings.

Carrigallen Church

COLIN BOYLE

St Thomas' Church, Columbkille

COLIN BOYLE

Arva Church

Gowna Church

## BAILIEBOROUGH, KNOCKBRIDE, SHERCOCK and MULLAGH (AUGHNACLIFFE)

This group of parishes, located in east Cavan, stretches towards the border with County Meath.

*Bailieborough Church* is situated in a commanding position at the lower end of the town's main street. The church, dating from 1835, with a vestry, transept and porch added in the 1860s, replaced an earlier one sited to the north-west, constructed around 1780, the ruins of which remain. The burial vault of Sir John Young, the first governor general of Canada, is located in the graveyard.

*Bailieborough Church*

*Knockbride Church*, built on an ancient ecclesiastical site, occupies an elevated, picturesque position atop one of Cavan's many drumlins. It was constructed in 1825 and enlarged in 1858 and again in 1870, when transepts and a vestry were added.

*Knockbride Church*

*Shercock Church*, like so many Church of Ireland churches in urban settings, occupies a central position on the town's main axis. A distinguishing architectural feature of the church, which was constructed around 1780, is its apsed (rounded) chancel. A tower was added to the building in 1830.

*Mullagh Church*

*Shercock Church*

*Mullagh Church*, lying close to the county border with County Meath, is in an idyllic lakeside location. It was constructed in 1819 with a loan of £1,107 from the Board of First Fruits. The ruins of the ancient Templekelly Church are located a short distance to the south-west of the church and a memorial stone to 'the three hundred and twenty sons and daughters of Mullagh' who died during the Great Famine is found in the graveyard. St Killian, martyred in Würzburg, Germany around AD 689, was born in Mullagh around AD 640.

## CLOONCLARE (MANORHAMILTON), KILLASNETT (GLENCAR), LURGANBOY, DRUMLEASE (DROMAHAIRE), ROSSINVER (KINLOUGH), FINNER (BUNDORAN) and INNISMAGRATH (DRUMKEERAN)

With the exception of Christ Church, Finner in Co. Donegal, all the parishes in this grouping are located in north County Leitrim.

The town of Manorhamilton was established by Sir Frederick Hamilton during the early 1600s as part of the plantation of Leitrim. By 1637, evidence suggests that a church had been constructed there. The present *Cloonclare Church, Manorhamilton*, built in 1783, is located on the site of the former barracks, within a star fort.

*Cloonclare Church*

*Kilasnett Church*

*Killasnett Church*, Glencar was constructed around 1821.

*Lurganboy Chapel of Ease*, located a mile to the north-west of Manorhamilton, was built in 1862. It is a rare example of a corrugated-iron church or 'tin church'. Its architectural significance was recognised by the Heritage Council, who granted financial assistance for its conservation in 2002. It stands on the site of a late-medieval earthen star fort.

*Drumlease Church*, located off the main street of Dromahaire, was constructed in 1806 and rebuilt in 1816 at a cost of £1,044. The east window by Mayer & Co. of Munich dates from 1913.

*Drumlease Church*

*Rossinver Church*

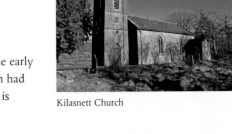

*Innishmagrath Church*

*Rossinver Church*, built by 1820, is located on a wooded site in the village of Kinlough.

*Christ Church, Finner* has the distinction of being the only church in the diocese located in County Donegal. It was transferred to the diocese of Kilmore from Clogher in 1974. Occupying a very pleasing seafront site in the town of Bundoran, the church was constructed in 1839 at a cost of £2,150, to a design by William Hagerty. The substantial nature and size of the church for a small Irish country town reflects Bundoran's importance as a nineteenth-century seaside resort.

*Innismagrath Church*, Drumkeeran was constructed in 1828 at a cost of £1,115. The east window dates from *c.* 1910.

*Christ Church, Finner*

*Lurganboy Chapel of Ease*

## DRUMGOON (COOTEHILL), ASHFIELD, KILLESHERDONEY and DERNAKESH

This group of parishes, centred on the town of Cootehill, close to the border with County Monaghan, covers an extensive area of north-east Cavan.

*All Saints' Church, Drumgoon* is the dominant architectural feature of Cootehill's main street. The church, constructed in 1818 on a site within Bellamont Forest Demesne, may have been designed by the renowned architect Francis Johnston. Its elegant cut-stone spire is notable. The site of the earlier parish church from the eighteenth century, located on Church Street, remains, with its associated graveyard. Later additions to the church in the 1860s and again in the 1960s complete the existing building.

*Ashfield Church*, occupying a rural, picturesque site, was constructed in 1796 on lands owned by the Clements family of nearby Ashfield Lodge. A tower and spire were added in 1820 and, in the 1860s, the transepts and chancel were added. The involvement of the Clements family in the life of the parish is reflected in their patronage of the church's several stained-glass windows – from the studios of Clayton and Bell, London and Mayer & Co., Munich – dating from the late nineteenth and early twentieth centuries.

Ashfield Church

All Saints' Church, Drumgoon

*Dernakesh Chapel of Ease* was built in 1834 to a design by William Farrell. His use of castellations and pinnacles on the porch and bell-cote add charm to the building. A pot-bellied stove in the nave of the church reveals the heating system once used.

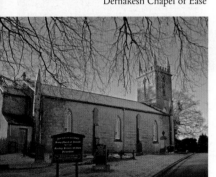

Dernakesh Chapel of Ease

*St Mark's Church, Killesherdoney*, built in 1855 to a design by Joseph Welland, replaced a late-eighteenth-century church, the site of which lay to the south-east of the present church. The east window, by Solaglas Caldermac, Lisburn, was installed in 1993.

St Mark's Church, Killesherdoney

## DRUNG, CASTLETERRA (BALLYHAISE), LARAH AND LAVEY and KILLOUGHTER (REDHILLS)

This group of parishes extends across an extensive area of Cavan, running in a southerly direction from Redhills in the north of the county to Lavey, which lies to the south-east of Cavan town. *Drung Church* was constructed in 1834 to a design by William Farrell, replacing an earlier church of 1728. Marcus Gervais Beresford, later archbishop of Armagh, was vicar of the parish at this time. His interest in the building of the church and that of the Clements family of nearby Rathkenny House is reflected in the quality craftsmanship exhibited in the building. The parlour pew of the Clements family, which opens into the nave from the first floor of the tower, is an interesting architectural feature of the church.

Drung Church

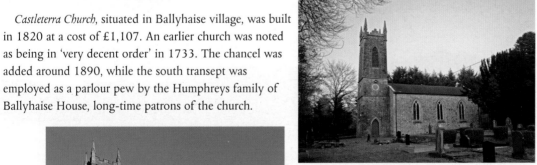

*Castleterra Church*, situated in Ballyhaise village, was built in 1820 at a cost of £1,107. An earlier church was noted as being in 'very decent order' in 1733. The chancel was added around 1890, while the south transept was employed as a parlour pew by the Humphreys family of Ballyhaise House, long-time patrons of the church.

Castleterra Church

Larah Church

*Larah Church*, built in 1832, replaced an earlier church to the north. The Ordnance Survey memoirs of Ireland from the 1830s stated that it was a 'neat oblong building, capable of accommodating about 250 parishioners'. It was the family church of the Burrowes family of Stradone House, who funded the installation of the east window from the studio of Heaton, Butler and Bayne of London in 1893.

Killoughter Church

*Lavey Church* was built in 1822, replacing an earlier, eighteenth-century church through a gift of £830 from the Board of First Fruits.

*Killoughter Church (Redhills)* was constructed between 1812 and 1814. A chancel was added in 1860. The east window, from the studio of Catherine O'Brien, Dublin, depicting the parable of the sower, was installed by the Whyte-Venables family in 1954. An impressive wall monument erected by Eliza Whyte in memory of her sons John Boyle (died aged 22 in 1827) and James (died aged 24 in 1830) dates from 1831.

## KILDALLON, NEWTOWNGORE AND CORRAWALLEN, SWANLINBAR, KINAWLEY, TEMPLEPORT and TOMREGAN (BALLYCONNELL)

Christ Church, Kildallon

Extending across the border into County Fermanagh, this group of parishes covers a large area of west Cavan and south Leitrim. It is one of the largest groupings of parishes in the dioceses.

*Christ Church, Kildallon* was built around 1750, with a tower designed by John Bowden added in 1815 and a transept added in 1827. The original church there was founded by St Dallan, a nephew of St Mogue, in the sixth century. An ancient cemetery, known as 'the Relic', located to the south-west of the existing church, is the likely location of Dallan's church. The 1733 visitation of the diocese of Kilmore records 50 families in the parish.

RCB/DAVID CROOKS

*Newtowngore Church*, County Leitrim, constructed around 1850, replaced an earlier church in the vicinity. *Corrawallen Church*, adopting a similiar architectural style to Newtowngore Church, was built in 1854.

Newtowngore Church

Corrawallen Church

*St Augustine's Church, Swanlinbar* was built in 1849, replacing an older chapel of ease dating from the 1760s, at which time the village was one of Ireland's well-established spa sites. A memorial to William Grattan, curate of the church for 37 years, alongside memorials to the Johnston and Hutton families, adorn the interior walls. Stained-glass windows were installed in 1898, 1900 and 1920, in memory of members of the Brooks and Hutton families.

*St Paul's Chapel of Ease, Kinawley* is located on an elevated site in the village of Kinawley, County Fermanagh. It is the youngest church in the diocese, consecrated in February 1932. The east window, depicting the resurrection, was installed in 1948.

St Augustine's Church, Swanlinbar

Kinawley Chapel of Ease

*St Peter's Church, Templeport* was built in 1819 at a cost of £1,382, replacing an earlier church. It occupies a beautiful position on the shores of Templeport Lake. St Mogue, born in the parish, established a church on an island in the lake in the sixth century and the ruins of this remain to the present day. A chancel was added to the present building in 1860. The east window, from the studio of Heaton, Butler and Bayne, London, was presented in 1929 by Robert Henry Johnstone in memory of his wife Mary Elizabeth Johnstone. Mary Elizabeth, whose portrait is contained within the window, was one of the leading lights in the revival of the Association of Loyal Orangewomen of Ireland at the turn of the twentieth century, and rose to the rank of grand mistress before her retirement in 1923.

St Peter's Church, Templeport

A church has occupied the site where *Tomregan Church, Ballyconnell* now stands since at least the sixteenth century. The present building was constructed around 1756 by the patronage of Col. George Leslie Montgomery, and enlarged around 1820. Pigot noted in 1824 that 'the church, with its spire, built of stone, in the Gothic order, is a handsome building and was finished about three years ago'. The interior of the church is rich in interesting memorials and furnishings. The ten commandments are recorded on decorative panels on either side of the sancturay window. The twelfth-century Tomregan Stone was moved to the church in the early 1960s. It has been suggested that it is a rare example of a male exhibitionist sheela-na-gig.

Tomregan Church

## KILDRUMFERTON (KILNALECK), BALLYMACHUGH and BALLYJAMESDUFF

This group of parishes is located in south Cavan, to the west of the town of Virginia.

*St Patrick's Church, Kildrumferton*, a short distance to the north-east of Kilnaleck, County Cavan, was built in 1812 at a cost of £1,200 and consecrated in 1816.

St Paul's Church, Ballymachugh

*Ballyjamesduff Church* was built on an elevated site in 1834 at a cost of £1,125. It follows the traditional hall-and-tower plan typical of the Board of First Fruits, who provided a loan of £900 towards the cost. The town of Ballyjamesduff has grown dramatically in size over the last decade.

*St Paul's Church, Ballymachugh*, overlooking Lough Sheelin, was constructed around 1800 with a gift of £500 from the Board of First Fruits and transferred from the diocese of Ardagh to Kilmore in 1910. The east window, depicting the ascension, dates from 1903 and was presented by the Maxwell family, a minor branch of the Farnham family, who held property at Arley and Fortland in the area. They funded the construction of the north transept around 1837.

St Patrick's Church, Kildrumferton

Ballyjamesduff Church

Killegar Church

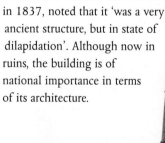

Derrylane Church

## KILLESHANDRA, KILLEGAR and DERRYLANE

The existing *Killeshandra Church* was constructed by 1842, following a design by William Farrell, with a pinnacled roofline. The impressive east window by Alexander Gibbs & Co. of London is dated 1882 and depicts the parables of the prodigal son and the lost sheep. The 1842 church building replaced the older Jacobean church, built in 1688 by Viscount Southwell of Castle Hamilton on a site where a church was recorded in 1436. Samuel Lewis, writing in 1837, noted that it 'was a very ancient structure, but in state of dilapidation'. Although now in ruins, the building is of national importance in terms of its architecture.

*Killegar Church* and its associated parsonage, in County Leitrim, was built by 1825. The cost of £1,100 was covered by the local landowner, John Godley (ancestor of the Lords Kilbracken). The church was consecrated in 1837 and the first rector, Hon. Henry O'Brien, son of Sir Edward O'Brien of Inchiquin, who was married to Godley's daughter Henrietta, served between 1827 and 1860. Many memorials to members of the Godley family adorn the interior of the church.

*Derrylane Church*, designed by William Farrell, was built in 1833 with a loan of £800 from the Board of First Fruits and a donation of £100 from Lord Farnham, the major landowner in the area. It was constructed as a chapel of ease for the parish of Killeshandra. The cast-iron roof trusses are an interesting feature of the church's design. The east window depicting the ascension is dated 1968 and came from the Irish Stained Glass studio in Dublin.

Killeshandra Church

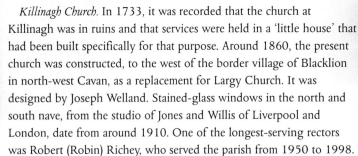

## KILLESHER (FLORENCECOURT), DRUMINISKILL
## and KILLINAGH (BLACKLION)

These parishes lie in the stunning landscape of south-west Fermanagh and north-west Cavan.

*St John's Church, Killesher* lies to the north of Florencecourt House and Demesne, the former home of the Cole family, earls of Enniskillen. The original church dated from around 1791. The Board of First Fruits granted a loan of £553 in 1819 to assist with the construction of a pair of transepts, a chancel and an elegant tower and spire. In September 1979, the main body of the church was destroyed through accidental burning and a new church was built and reconsecrated in 1982. The church is particularly well endowed. It has seven stained-glass windows, all of which date from between 1982 and 1985 and come from the Caldermac studio in Belfast and the Solaglas Caldermac studio in Lisburn. Several of the earls of Enniskillen are buried in the adjoining graveyard. In terms of number of parishioners, Killesher is one of the largest parishes in the dioceses.

St John's Church, Killesher

*Druminiskill Chapel of Ease*, County Fermanagh is an interesting red-brick church with grey stone trim. It was designed in the mid-1850s by John Macduff Derick and is the only example of his work in Ulster. Its completion was delayed until 1860, after Derick emigrated to America in 1858 and died there the following year. The completion of the church's construction was overseen by Carmichael and Jones of Dublin.

*Killinagh Church.* In 1733, it was recorded that the church at Killinagh was in ruins and that services were held in a 'little house' that had been built specifically for that purpose. Around 1860, the present church was constructed, to the west of the border village of Blacklion in north-west Cavan, as a replacement for Largy Church. It was designed by Joseph Welland. Stained-glass windows in the north and south nave, from the studio of Jones and Willis of Liverpool and London, date from around 1910. One of the longest-serving rectors Killinagh Church was Robert (Robin) Richey, who served the parish from 1950 to 1998.

Druminiskill Chapel of Ease

## KILMORE and BALLINTEMPLE

Ballintemple Parish was grouped with Kilmore Cathedral in 1950.

The present *Ballintemple Church*, located to the south of Ballinagh town, was completed by 1821 through funding provided by the Board of First Fruits. It most likely replaced an earlier church sited in ancient graveyard on the opposite side of the road. A cut-stone plaque above the entrance door reads, 'This Church was Built by the Parish of Ballintemple for the Service of God. Anno Domini 1821 W. Magenis A.M. Dean of Kilmore and Vicar of Ballintemple Rev. James Pollock A.M. curate.' Pollock, ordained in 1774, was to remain curate at Ballintemple until around 1827, at which stage he had served in that capacity for 39 years. Altogether, he served as curate in the diocese for 54 years. The chancel of the church was added in 1931 and the east window was added in the mid-1950s. The font in the church was a gift from Oldcastle Church, County Meath and was installed in 1962.

Ballintemple Church

## KINAWLEY (DERRYLIN), DRUMANY and CROM

This group of parishes lies in south Fermanagh, between the villages of Derrylin and Newtownbutler. The network of lakes that comprise Upper Lough Erne add great variety to the landscape of the area. *Kinawley Church* is located at the southern end of the border village of Derrylin. The original parish church was in the nearby village of Kinawley. The church was constructed by 1825, and the north aisle was added by Welland and Gillespie between 1860 and 1861. The stained-glass window depicting Christ as the good shepherd dates from the 1970s.

Kinawley Church

Christ Church, Drumany Chapel of Ease

*Christ Church, Drumany Chapel of Ease* was opened in December 1883. *Holy Trinity Church, Crom* was completed by 1842, construction having begun two years earlier. Tradition has it that John Crichton, third earl of Erne, had quarrelled with the bishop of Clogher and deliberately sited the church on Derryvore Peninsula, 200 yards across Lough Erne from Crom Castle, within the confines of the diocese of Kilmore. It is one of the most idyllically sited churches in the diocese. Various architects have been said to have designed the church, including Edward Blore, George Sudden and John Shipton Mulvany. It cost £7,200 to construct. The chancel was added around 1867 and the tower, designed by William Fullerton, was added in 1885 in memory of Selina, countess of Erne, wife of the third earl. The east window in stained glass depicting Christ blessing the children was provided by the Crichton family (earls of Erne). It was made by the famed stained-glass painter Jean-Baptiste Capronnier in Brussels and dates to 1869. In fine weather, visitors to the estate, which is now run by the National Trust, can sail across to the church for services from Crom Castle.

Holy Trinity Church, Crom

## LURGAN (VIRGINIA), BILLIS, KILLINKERE and MUNTERCONNAUGHT

This group of parishes is centred on the town of Virginia in south Cavan. *Lurgan Church (Virginia)* was mentioned in the 1733 diocesan visitation for Kilmore as the only church in the diocese that was slated. This church was located about four kilometres from Virginia, just off the Ballyjamesduff Road. It is one of the key landmarks as one travels onwards to Cavan town. Mature yew, lime and chestnut trees delimit the site. The church was designed by the Cavan-born architect Arthur McClean. Construction began on it in 1818 and was completed by 1821, at a cost of £2,492. A fire on Christmas night 1830 destroyed a good deal of the roof, which was repaired with donations of £900 'contributed chiefly by the diocese and the parishioners'. The east window, from the studio of Clayton and Bell, London, dates from around 1870 and was installed by the Taylour family (marquises of Headfort), who kept a hunting lodge on the shores of Lough Ramor, just a short stroll from the church. The ornate reredos, also donated by the Taylour family, depicts Christ in majesty with saints and dates from 1890. It came from the studio of James Powell & Sons, London.

Killinkere Church

*St Bartholomew's Church, Billis* was completed by 1844. The tower was added around the 1860s, at which time the north transept was also constructed. The east window in memory of William Jennings dates from 1907 and depicts the resurrection. It came from the studio of Campbell Brothers, Franklin Street, Belfast. The pulpit is in memory of Walter Cunningham Peyton, rector of the church from 1848 until his demise in 1896.

*Killinkere Church.* The present building was constructed in 1817. A transept and other additions were made in 1866 by Welland and Gillespie. The organ, by the renowned organ builders Telford and Telford of Dublin, was dedicated in 1911.

*Munterconnaught Church* was built in 1832 to a design by William Farrell, as a chapel of ease for the parish of Lurgan. It was funded by a gift of £900 from the Board of First Fruits. The original box pews are a unique feature of the furnishings of the church.

St Bartholomew's Church, Billis

RCB/ DAVID CROOKS

Lurgan Church

Munterconnaught Church

## URNEY (CAVAN), DENN AND DERRYHEEN

This group of parishes is centred on the town of Cavan, which is located roughly in the centre of County Cavan.

*Urney Church.* The former Franciscan abbey of St Mary in Cavan town had been appropriated for use as the parish church of Urney at the time of the plantation. The present church, on a slight incline to the northern end of Farnham Street in Cavan town, was constructed in 1815 at a cost of £4,963, to a design attributed to Joseph Bowden, on a site given by John James Maxwell, earl of Farnham. Mid-nineteenth-century additions by Joseph Welland include the chancel, transepts and galleries. The size of the church building illustrates the garrison status of Cavan town. The collection of stained-glass windows that adorns the church was donated by several prominent local families, including the Farnhams, Halpins and Roes. The east window, dating from around 1850, was donated by the de la Poer Beresford family and came from the studio of Ward and Nixon, London. An impressive memorial by the sculptor Sir Francis Leggatt Chantrey of London for John James, earl of Farnham, who died in 1823, dominates the south chancel wall.

RCB/ DAVID CROOKS

Urney Church

Derryheen Church

*Denn Church* is located on the road between Cavan town and Ballyjamesduff. It was constructed by 1817 at a cost of £1,218, of which over half had been raised through parochial assessment (cess). Because of this level of financial commitment to the construction of the church, it has been suggested that the parishioners may have had a greater say than usual in the design of the building, hence the inclusion of late-Georgian architectural ideas. Unlike the traditional Board of First Fruits churches, the main hall of the church has a cubic character.

Denn Church

*Derryheen Church* was constructed at a cost of £900 in 1834. It was funded by a gift from the Board of First Fruits.

# THE DIOCESE OF ELPHIN

## BOYLE, TAUNAGH (RIVERSTOWN), AGHANAGH (BALLINAFAD), CROGHAN, ARDCARNE, TYBOHINE (FRENCHPARK), BALLYSUMAGHAN and KILMACTRANNY

This is the largest grouping of parishes in the diocese of Elphin. It is served by eight churches, stretching from north Roscommon into south-east Sligo.

*Boyle Church*, built in cruciform plan in 1770, sits on an elevated site overlooking the town of Boyle, County Roscommon. The pedimented entrance front and the castellated tower reflect the eighteenth-century origins of the building. It was enlarged and improved around 1818 at an expense of £1,846. Stained-glass windows by Watson & Co. of Youghal, dating from the second decade of the twentieth century, add character to the interior of the church.

Boyle Church

*Taunagh Church, Riverstown*, County Sligo was begun in 1816 on a site donated by the local landowning family, the Coopers of Coopershill. The church was consecrated in 1818 and follows a typical hall-and-tower design. However, the detail and craftsmanship reflect the influence of the Cooper family. Originally in Toomna Church, the east window by A.E. Child depicting the Resurrection dates from 1928. It was installed in 2000.

*Aghanagh Church, Ballinafad*, County Sligo was designed by James Welland in 1850 and consecrated in September 1855. It replaced an older church on the shores of Lough Arrow. The Ffolliot family of nearby Hollybrook were the main patrons of the church.

Taunagh Church, Riverstown

Aghanagh Church, Ballinafad

*Tybohine Church*, Portahard, County Roscommon is located a short distance to the north-east of the village of Frenchpark. Built in 1740, the church was extensively renovated in 1988 by Roscommon County Council. Today it also functions as interpretative centre known as the Dr Douglas Hyde Centre, in memory of the parish's most famous son. Hyde's father, Rev. Arthur Hyde, was rector of the parish between 1866 and 1905.

Ardcarne Church

*Holy Trinity Church, Croghan*, County Roscommon was designed by Joseph Welland. Construction was completed by 1862. A stepped tower that leads to an octagonal tower is a defining feature of the church. The site was donated by local landowner Guy Lloyd of Croghan House.

A church has existed on the site of *Ardcarne Church*, County Roscommon since the early sixth century. The present building was constructed around 1750, enlarged in 1828 and repaired in 1859, following a fire the previous year. An extensive collection of stained-glass windows enhances the interior of the church. The earliest, dated 1860, came from the studio of Lavers and Barraud, London. There are also works by Burlison and Grylls, London (1888), A.E. Child from An Túr Gloine (1911, 1920 and 1921) and Evie Hone from the same studio (1935).

Tybohine Church

Holy Trinity Church, Croghan

Ballysumaghan Church

*Ballysumaghan Church*, County Sligo was built in 1829 at a cost of £1,233. The site, along with a substantial gift towards the construction of the church, was provided by the local landowner, Col. Neynoe of Castle Neynoe. The projecting transepts give the building a much more elaborate appearance when compared with most Board of First Fruits churches.

*Kilmactranny Church*, constructed in 1816 at a cost of £738, is located in a rural setting in south-east Sligo, close to the county border with Roscommon.

Kilmactranny Church

RCB/DAVID CROOKS

Calry Church

## CALRY

*Calry Church*, located on the Mall in Sligo town, on an elevated site overlooking the Garavogue River, was consecrated in 1824. The church was built in a plain Gothic style, with stone quarried from the site as a chapel of ease to the parish church of St John (now the cathedral), at a cost of £5,246. It was consecrated in response to the growing Protestant population of the town at the time. Samuel Lewis commented on the tower and spire, added at a later date, in his *Topographical Dictionary of Ireland*, published in 1837. The catacombs of the church have recently adopted a new use, as both a parish meeting place and a childcare facility known as Cosy Cats, which caters for the entire community. The church has a long-established link with the adjacent Sligo Grammar School and boarders from the school frequently attend services there. This is the only single-incumbency church in the diocese of Elphin.

St Columba's Church, Drumcliffe

## DRUMCLIFFE, LISSADELL and

*St Columba's Church, Drumcliffe* in Sligo has Benbulbin Mountain as a stunning backdrop. The church was built in Gothic style in 1809 at a cost of £738, given by the Board of First Fruits. The tenth-century high cross and associated remains of a round tower reflect the longevity of Christian worship on the site – Columba established a monastery at Drumcliffe in AD 574. Today the church is known internationally as the burial place of the poet William Butler Yeats, whose great-grandfather, John Yeats, was rector of the parish between 1811 and 1846. Extensive internal renovations to the church were carried out around 1999. The Yeats connection causes it to be one of the most visited rural church buildings in Ireland.

Lissadell Church

St Kevin's Chapel of Ease, Munninane

*Lissadell Church* was built and endowed by Sir Robert Gore-Booth of Lissadell House during the early 1840s. The chancel, nave, tower and porch designed by Joseph Welland were added in the mid-1850s and the church was finally consecrated in 1858. The Gore-Booth family burial ground lies to the east of the church and the stained-glass windows were all provided by the Gore-Booth family. The east window, dated 1857, is by William Warrington of London. Another, dated 1906, is by Ethel Rhind and another, dated 1950, is by Catherine O'Brien.

*St Kevin's Chapel of Ease, Munninane* was built in 1896 by the Gore-Booth family. This tiny church in the Tudor-revival style is the youngest Church of Ireland church in Connacht.

## ROSCOMMON, KILTULLAGH (BALLINLOUGH), RATHCLINE (LANESBOROUGH) and DONAMON

St Coman established an ecclesiastical settlement, which was later to become an Augustinian abbey, in the area of present-day Roscommon in the early sixth century. The place-name 'Ros Comáin' may be translated as 'the wood of Coman'. The present *Roscommon Church* is dedicated to St Coman. Constructed in 1775, the building has an eighth- and fourteenth-century doorway, as well as seventeenth-century memorials, incorporated within it. A report in *The Irish Builder* in February 1888 outlined several improvements that had been made to the church, including the removal of several galleries. At this time a pulpit of Caen stone, with columns of red and green marble designed by C.W. Harrison of Dublin, was presented to the church by Hon. Mrs Dillon of Clonbrock, County Galway. A large range of engraved headstones from the eighteenth century is to be found in the attached graveyard. One of the most unusual and detailed depicts a ploughman with his horse and plough. It is memory of Dall Cullane of Roscommon, who died in 1736.

*Kiltullagh Church*, sited on a hill overlooking the village of Ballinlough, County Roscommon, was commissioned in 1824 and completed by the end of that year by the architect and builder Thomas Cosgrove. An earlier church on the site had been destroyed by fire in 1821.

Roscommman Church

*Rathcline Church*, Lanesborough, completed to a design by Joseph Welland and consecrated in April 1862, occupies a site where a number of previous churches have stood, as attested to by the late-seventeenth-century gravestones in the attached graveyard. The church bell, cast in Eagle Foundry, Church Street, Dublin, was presented by Col. Henry White, the local MP (later the first baron Annaly of Annaly and Rathcline) in 1859. It is emblazoned with a bunch of shamrocks and the inscription 'Erin go Brath'.

In 1836, *Donamon Church* was 'capable of accommodating 150 persons, but although in good repair is very old and was originally a chapel to the castle at Dunamon'. This older church was replaced by the existing church in 1854, to a design by Joseph Welland, on the demesne lands of the Caulfeild family of Donamon Castle. An interesting architectural feature of the church is the lean-to bell-ringing room that projects from the rear gable of the building.

Rathcline Church

Donamon Church

## SLIGO CATHEDRAL GROUP

*St Mary's and St John the Baptist's Cathedral, Sligo*. Following the destruction of Elphin Cathedral by a storm in February 1957, a bill was passed at the General Synod in 1958 which removed the seat of the dioceses of Elphin and Ardagh to St John's Church, Sligo. Afterwards, St John's was known as the Cathedral Church of St Mary the Virgin and St John the Baptist. St John's was constituted as the cathedral for Elphin and Ardagh in October 1961. Located on John Street, in the heart of Sligo town, it has been suggested that the site of the cathedral was occupied by a hospital and parish church in the medieval period. Richard Castle designed the church around 1732 in the style of a Roman basilica. In the early nineteenth century the church was remodelled in the Gothic style at a cost of £4,259 and, in 1883, it was further enlarged. The bishop's throne and chapter stalls made from Belize mahogany are by Hearne of Waterford.

The reredos, depicting angels and people praising God, was painted by Percy Francis Gethin and dates from 1912. It was installed in memory of Gethin's brother Reginald Owen Gethin of the British South African police, who had died while serving the army in South Africa in 1899. Percy Gethin, born at Holywell, Sligo in 1874, was an accomplished artist, draughtsman and etcher, who settled in London around 1905 and taught life drawing at the Central School. He was killed at the Somme in 1916. Most of the stained-glass windows in the church came from the studio of Mayer & Co. of Munich and date from between 1883 and 1901. Another, from An Túr Gloine, designed by A.E. Child, dates from 1927. One of the Mayer windows depicting Christ blessing children was installed in 1892 by the Pollexfen family in memory of William and Elizabeth Pollexfen, who were important merchants and traders in Sligo. Their daughter Susan Mary Pollexfen had married John Butler Yeats in the church in 1863. Their children included the poet William Butler Yeats and the artist Jack Butler Yeats.

St Mary's and St John the Baptist's Cathedral, Sligo

*St Anne's Church, Knocknarea* is located to the north-east of the seaside village of Strandhill in County Sligo. Knocknarea Mountain provides a scenic backdrop to this small Gothic-revival-style church, constructed in 1843 to a design by Sligo native, Sir John Benson. An ornately carved font is an interesting component of the interior.

St Anne's Church, Knocknarea

*Rosses Point Church*, overlooking the sea to the south, was constructed in the mid-1850s. Designed in Gothic-revival style by the Dublin-based architect William Deane Butler, the church was constructed for Edward Joshua Cooper of Markree Castle.

Rosses Point Church

St Mary's and St John the Baptist's Cathedral, Sligo

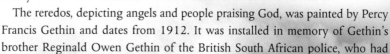

# THE DIOCESE OF ARDAGH

### ARDAGH, MOYDOW, TASHINNY, SHRULE (BALLYMAHON) and KILCOMMICK (KENAGH)

These five parishes lie to the south and south-east of Longford town.

*St Patrick's Church, Ardagh*, constructed by 1810, is located at the eastern end of the village. The remains of an eighth-century church known as St Mel's Cathedral lie to the south-east of the church. In the 1860s, James Rawson Carroll designed the village of Ardagh for the local landlord Sir Thomas Fetherston, who wished to improve the village as a memorial to his uncle, Sir George Fetherston. The lychgate found at the entrance to the church dates from the improvements carried out in the 1860s.

St Patrick's Church, Ardagh

Moydow Church

*Moydow Church*, constructed around 1765 and altered several times during the nineteenth century, has been disused since 1987.

*Holy Trinity Church, Tashinny* most likely occupies the site of a medieval church mentioned in the *Annals of Loch Cé*. The church was built or rebuilt in 1720, rebuilt again in 1785 and rebuilt again around 1825. A fine marble memorial monument dated 1753 by the renowned sculptor John Van Nost the Younger is an important feature of the church's interior. It is dedicated to the memory of Judge George Gore, attorney general of Ireland during the early eighteenth century, and his wife Bridget, of Tennalick House.

Holy Trinity Church, Tashinny

St George's Church, Kilcommick

*St Catherine's Church, Shrule* in Ballymahon was constructed on a cruciform plan around 1800, replacing an earlier church in the vicinity. It was rebuilt in 1824. Following the standard tower-and-hall layout with some later nineteenth-century additions, its graceful needle spire is a dominant skyline feature of Ballymahon.

*St George's Church, Kilcommick*, built to a Gothic-revival design by William Farrell, was constructed by 1832 in the village of Keenagh under the patronage of Jane, dowager countess of Ross, at a cost of £2,500.

St Catherine's Church, Shrule

Covering an extensive area of south Leitrim, this group of parishes is served by nine churches, the largest grouping in the diocese of Ardagh. It includes Carrick-on-Shannon, the county town of Leitrim. With a population of 3,980 in 2011, Carrick-on-Shannon is the smallest county town in the Republic of Ireland.

St Mary's Church, Mohill

*St Mary's Church, Mohill*, built on the site of a former Augustinian monastery, was described in 1836 as 'so old that the date and cost of its erection are unknown'. It was enlarged in 1815 with a loan of £348 from the Board of First Fruits. Welland and Gillespie, architects to the Ecclesiastical Commissioners, carried out some internal works in the church in the mid-1860s, including the pulpit, reading desk and chancel railing. Several stained-glass windows adorn the interior of the church, including one depicting Christ as the good shepherd.

St Mary's Church, Farnaught

*St Mary's Church, Farnaught* was completed by 1853 by Joseph Welland as an estate church for Lough Rynn, home of the Clements family (earls of Leitrim). A later tower, designed by Sir Thomas Drew and constructed in 1883, has four gargoyles based on the symbols of the evangelists contained within it. The architecture and setting in Lough Rynn Demesne add much to the character and beauty of this church. Three stained-glass windows by Ethel Rhind from An Túr Gloine in Dublin also add greatly to the interior of this church.

*Aughavas Church*, a former schoolhouse, was built in the 1840s.

*Oughteragh Church (Ballinamore)* was built around 1785. In 1910, it was transferred from the diocese of Kilmore to Ardagh. The east window, depicting women at the tomb of Jesus, dating from 1909, came from the studio of A.L. Moore & Co. of London.

Oughteragh Church

*Drumreilly Church*, overlooking Garadice Lake, was constructed in 1737, replacing an earlier building on the site. A range of late-medieval carved stone masks is incorporated within the church structure.

*St Brigid's Church, Kiltubride* is another eighteenth-century church in the grouping. It was built in the 1780s on an elevated site overlooking Lough Scur.

*St John's Church, Drumshambo* was built in 1828 through a loan of £1,200 provided by the Board of First Fruits.

St Brigid's Church, Kiltubrid

St George's Church, Kiltoghart

*St George's Church (Kiltoghart)* occupies a prominent site on Carrick-on-Shannon's main street. It was built in 1827 at a cost of £2,500 and replaced a late-seventeenth-century church. Following an extensive renovation, completed in 2006, the church now also acts as a heritage centre. A rare example of an early Telford organ from 1847 is housed in the church. Canon William Slator, rector between 1966 and 1981, was a prolific poet and accomplished musician. He was named Leitrim person of the year in 1975.

*St Ann's Church, Annaduff*, located along the banks of the River Shannon, was built in 1820. A memorial in the church commemorates Admiral Sir Josias Rowley, also known as the 'Sweeper of the Seas', who, during the Napoleonic Wars, captured the islands of Réunion and Mauritius. He was owner of the Mountcampbell estate at Drumsna, which lay close to Annaduff. He died in 1842 and is buried in the attached graveyard.

St Ann's Church, Annaduff

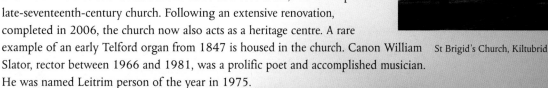

Drumreilly Church

St John's Church, Mostrim

## MOSTRIM (EDGEWORTHSTOWN), GRANARD, CLONBRONEY (BALLINALEA), KILLOE, RATHASPECK (RATHOWEN) and STREETE

This group of parishes, served by six churches, extends from north-east Longford, where the churches of Mostrim, Granard, Clonbroney and Killoe are located, across the border into County Westmeath, where the parish churches of Rathaspeck and Streete can be found.

*St John's Church, Mostrim* sits on an extensive site to the north-east of Edgeworthstown. This church was rebuilt, enlarged and altered on numerous occasions during the eighteenth and nineteenth centuries. The local landlord Richard Lovell Edgeworth designed and funded the construction of an unusual steel and copper spire for the church in 1811. The steel and copper were replaced around 1935 with slate. The remains of his daughter, the noted writer Maria Edgeworth, lie in the family vault in the attached graveyard. A stained-glass window in the church depicting Christ blessing children was removed from Elphin Cathedral around 1959.

*St Patrick's Church, Granard* occupies a prominent site in close proximity to the impressive Anglo-Norman motte there. The present church, completed by around 1760 following a standard Board of First Fruits style, most likely occupies the site of an earlier building. In 1930, the church was remodelled in a Classical style by the Dublin-based architect Ralph Henry Byrne.

St John's Church, Clonbroney

*St John's Church, Clonbroney (Ballinalea)*, built in 1825 in a Gothic-revival style to a design by John Hargrave, was funded (according to Lewis (1837)) by a gift of £1,110 from the Board of First Fruits. Grave markers from the eighteenth century in the adjoining cemetery suggest that the present church occupies the site of an earlier church building.

Built in 1824, *St Catherine's Church, Killoe* was also designed by John Hargrave and has many architectural similarities to St John's Church, Ballinalee. The *Down Survey* maps of 1654 record a church at Killoe, indicating the longevity of an ecclesiastical settlement on this site.

St Thomas' Church, Rathaspeck

St Catherine's Church, Killoe

*St Thomas' Church, Rathaspeck (Rathowen)* was built in 1814 and enlarged in 1821, with the addition of two single-storey vestibules either side of the tower. Their construction was financed by loans provided by the Board of First Fruits.

*Streete Church*, rebuilt around 1810, most likely retains some fabric of an earlier church, as indicated by the irregular spacing of round-headed windows along the nave of the church, coupled with the presence of a memorial to Miss Thomazin Crofton, dated 1767.

St Patrick's Church, Granard

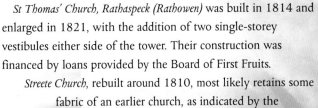

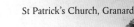

Streete Church

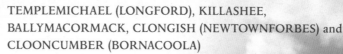

## TEMPLEMICHAEL (LONGFORD), KILLASHEE, BALLYMACORMACK, CLONGISH (NEWTOWNFORBES) and CLOONCUMBER (BORNACOOLA)

253

*St John's Church, Templemichael* is located on an extensive site in Longford town. It was built in 1710, replacing an earlier church that stood on the site of a medieval Dominican priory established around 1400. The present church was altered in the 1780s. Rev. Daniel Beaufort, visiting in 1787, wrote of the 'very handsome new church'. It was enlarged between 1810 and 1812 to a design by M. McCleland, a local architect, at a cost of £3,221, to provide accommodation for the town's garrison.

St Paul's Church, Killashee

St John's Church, Templemichael

St Paul's Church, Clongish
RCB/DAVID CROOKS

*St Paul's Church, Clongish (Newtownforbes)* was built during the 1820s to a cruciform plan on the site of an earlier church, components of which may have been incorporated into the new building. Designed by John Hargrave, who was working at Castle Forbes at the time, the church was built under the patronage of the major local landowners, the Forbes and Achmuty-Munster families. The parapets to the gables of the church, in Scottish baronial style, are an interesting feature of the building and may have been employed by the Forbes family to reflect their origins in Aberdeenshire. The box pews with their fielded (raised) panelling, which are mid-eighteenth-century in style, are reputedly the only surviving example of such features in Ireland.

*Clooncumber Church (Bornacoola)* in County Leitrim, on the border with County Longford, was built as chapel of ease in 1832. In terms of its scale and architecture, it provides great contrast with the grandeur of many of the other churches detailed and illustrated throughout this book.

*St Paul's Church, Killashee* was constructed between 1837 and 1840 with a grant of £1,211 from the Ecclesiastical Commissioners. It replaced an earlier church that had existed on this site. Gothic- and Tudor-revival styles are evident in the church, particularly in the chimney stacks, elegant tower and decorative buttresses that adorn the exterior of the church.

*Ballymacormack Church*, set in a rural landscape to the east of Killashee, was built in 1827 with a gift of £900 from the Board of First Fruits. Henry Maxwell, who succeeded to the title Lord Farnham in September 1838 and held it until his death a month later, was rector of the church between 1813 and 1838.

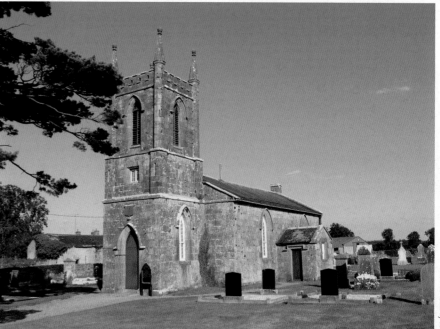

Clooncumber Church

Ballymacormack Church

RCB/DAVID CROOKS

# The United Dioceses of Tuam, Killala and Achonry

The Dioceses of Tuam and Killala were formed at the Synod of Rathbreasil in 1111, and the Diocese of Achonry at the Synod of Kills in 1152. The Diocese of Tuam was one of the four Archbishoprics in the Irish Church until it was reduced to a Bishopric in the Ecclesiastical Province of Armagh following the death of the last Archbishop in 1839. The three dioceses have been united since 1834 and, although geographically they form one of the largest dioceses, numerically they make up the smallest in the Church of Ireland with less than two thousand parishioners spread across nine parochial groups. Twenty-nine churches remain open and each is well maintained and lovingly cared for by loyal and devout parishioners.

In the Southern end of the United Dioceses is the large and vibrant city of Galway. Its rich culture, commerce and industry, its university life and tourist appeal have drawn many to the capital of the West. *Gaillimh*, the town of the foreigners, was said to be the fastest growing city in Europe during the era of the 'Celtic Tiger'. Its cosmopolitan population ensures a healthy mix of faith communities. Indeed, there are now many more Muslims in Galway than Church of Ireland members. These faith communities work closely together, with the ancient Collegiate Church of St Nicholas acting as a focus for much of this inter-faith activity.

By contrast, most of the rest of the United Dioceses is rural and, in some parts, rugged and spectacular. Dry fly fishing on the numerous lakes and rivers is a particular attraction for locals and visitors alike. Connemara in West County Galway, Westport, the seaside town further up the coast, and the picturesque island of Achill, are popular holiday destinations and in the summer months congregations are greatly enhanced by the tourist population. Many of the resident population, however, live in the north between Killala to the west and eastwards along the coast to the diocesan border near Sligo. Rural life in the West is tough and often isolated as distances are great and amenities can be limited. Hence, small parish communities play an important role in providing opportunities for spiritual and social interaction. Six Church of Ireland National Schools are located around the United Dioceses and these offer the mandatory early education entitlement, within the framework of a Church of Ireland ethos.

Ministry in the West is often a ministry of presence, although Church of Ireland clergy and people do play a significant and dis-proportionate role in the local communities of which they are part. Ecumenical relations are strong and in many places, churches are maintained thanks to the support of the local Roman Catholic congregation. Thus we have much of which to be proud and much to encourage our people of faith in 'the West'.

PATRICK TUAM

Derryclare Lake, County Galway
SCENIC IRELAND

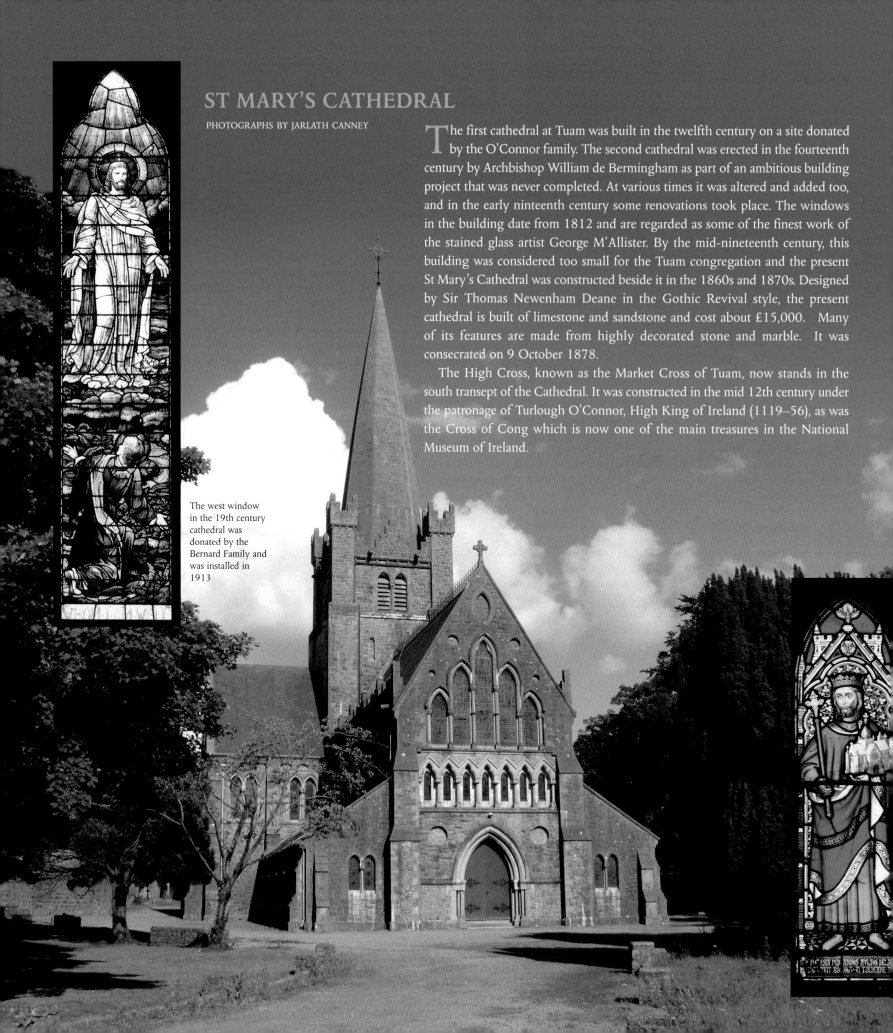

# ST MARY'S CATHEDRAL

PHOTOGRAPHS BY JARLATH CANNEY

The first cathedral at Tuam was built in the twelfth century on a site donated by the O'Connor family. The second cathedral was erected in the fourteenth century by Archbishop William de Bermingham as part of an ambitious building project that was never completed. At various times it was altered and added too, and in the early ninteenth century some renovations took place. The windows in the building date from 1812 and are regarded as some of the finest work of the stained glass artist George M'Allister. By the mid-nineteenth century, this building was considered too small for the Tuam congregation and the present St Mary's Cathedral was constructed beside it in the 1860s and 1870s. Designed by Sir Thomas Newenham Deane in the Gothic Revival style, the present cathedral is built of limestone and sandstone and cost about £15,000. Many of its features are made from highly decorated stone and marble. It was consecrated on 9 October 1878.

The High Cross, known as the Market Cross of Tuam, now stands in the south transept of the Cathedral. It was constructed in the mid 12th century under the patronage of Turlough O'Connor, High King of Ireland (1119–56), as was the Cross of Cong which is now one of the main treasures in the National Museum of Ireland.

The west window in the 19th century cathedral was donated by the Bernard Family and was installed in 1913

A well preserved face on one of the column capitals of the twelfth century arch
JARLATH CANNEY

In the 1880s, the old cathedral became known as the Synod Hall. For many years it contained eighteenth century Italian choir stalls, the Diocesan Registry and the Henry Library, the gift of the Reverend Joseph Henry, a member of a local family resident close to Tuam for many years. This library contains over 4,500 volumes and is now accessible in the James Hardiman Library, National University of Ireland, Galway. Henry's grand nephew Bobby Burke, a Christian Socialist, was a well known citizen of Tuam in the mid-twentieth century, giving up much of his estate for the relief of rural congestion and setting up a farming co-operative with his workers on a profit and management sharing basis.

The Synod Hall now functions as a fine venue for concerts, lectures, conferences and other public events as well as the annual diocesan synod. The cathedral is open to visitors on specific days of the week during the summer months and continues to be the centre for diocesan services and the weekly place of worship for the parish of Tuam.

JARLATH CANNEY

is window depicts rist the King and rected to the mory of Sir omas Deane who s the architect of nineteenth tury Cathedral.

The John Vesey Chalice

The Market Cross

The interior with the twelfth century Chancel Arch

# The Dioceses of Tuam, Killala and Achonry

BRIGID CLESHAM

The Cross of Cong
Constructed for the High King Turlough O'Connor, it
was to be used as a processional cross at the new
cathedral in Tuam but was soon afterwards moved to the
Abbey at Cong where it remained in the care of the
Augustinians throughout the centuries.
NATIONAL MUSEUM OF IRELAND

Time worn figures of the High King Turlough
O'Connor and the first Archbishop Aodh
O'Hessian, (Hugh O'Hession) carved on the base
of the High Cross in St Mary's Cathedral, Tuam
JARLATH CANNEY

The Church of Ireland dioceses of Tuam, Killala and Achonry contain much, but not all, of the province of Connacht, encompassing the whole of County Mayo and parts of Counties Galway, Sligo and Roscommon. The Atlantic Ocean sweeps the western seaboard of the dioceses and the peak of Croagh Patrick towering over Clew Bay indicates the presence of Ireland's patron saint in the locality during the fifth century. Today, this area is primarily dependent on agriculture, tourism, manufacturing and the service industries. The main centres of population are Galway city and the towns of Ballina, Castlebar, Tuam and Westport. The Church of Ireland community forms a small minority of the total population and most of its members reside in the north of the dioceses, from Killala to Ballisodare, and in the south around Galway.

## The Diocese of Tuam

The see of Tuam was originally founded by St Jarlath in the sixth century and at the Synod of Kells, in 1152, it became one of the four archbishoprics of Ireland. By the nineteenth century, the Anglican ecclesiastical province of Tuam included the dioceses of Tuam, Elphin, Clonfert, Kilmacduagh, Killala and Achonry. From 1742, the archbishop of Tuam also held the bishopric of Ardagh. The diocese of Achonry was

Pilgrims ascending Croagh Patrick
overlooking Clew Bay
SCENIC IRELAND

united with the diocese of Killala in 1622, and the united dioceses of Killala and Achonry were joined to Tuam in 1834 under the terms of the Church Temporalities Act. In 1839, following the death of Archbishop Trench (archbishop 1819–39), the province of Tuam was incorporated into the province of Armagh and the see ceased to be an archbishopric.

In the mid-1830s, the diocese of Tuam was described as being the most extensive in Ireland, measuring 77 miles in length and 63 miles in breadth and amounting to approximately 1,135,650 acres. The archbishop at this time derived an income of over £8,000 from lands belonging to the diocese. The chapter consisted of a dean, a provost, an archdeacon and eight prebendaries, and there were 34 single parishes or unions of parishes with 31 churches in the Diocese. Tuam Diocese is now made up of four parish groups with thirteen churches.

## The Diocese of Killala

The diocese of Killala is located for the most part in north County Mayo, but includes a small area of County Sligo. The establishment of the diocese possibly dates back to the time of St Patrick and the cathedral site is a very ancient one, as indicated by the souterrain on the east of the building and the nearby round tower. A cathedral certainly existed here prior to the fourteenth century. The royal visitation of 1615 records the cathedral as a ruin.

St Patrick's Cathedral, Killala
COLIN BOYLE

The present cathedral, St Patrick's, dates from the 1670s and was erected by Bishop Otway (bishop 1671–9). In the early nineteenth century, the diocese of Killala had 13 parishes or unions of parishes. The dean, precentor, archdeacon and five prebendaries made up the cathedral chapter.

## The Diocese of Achonry

From the early seventeenth century, the diocese of Achonry, located mainly in County Sligo, but also partly in Counties Mayo and Roscommon, was held with the see of Killala. The cathedral, known as St Crumnathy's, was opened in 1822 but closed for regular worship in 1997. During the Great Famine, the Dean of Achonry, Edward N. Hoare, worked alongside local Roman Catholic clergy to provide soup kitchens and famine relief. At a meeting in Tubbercurry, 23 September 1847, a resolution, put forward by

St Crumnathy's Cathedral, Achonry
COLIN BOYLE

Rev. James Gallagher, P.P., recorded thanks to Dean Hoare, 'for his unwearied and very efficient exertions as chairman of the Tubbercurry Relief Committee'. In the early nineteenth century, the diocese contained 13 parishes or unions of parishes. At present the dioceses of Killala and Achonry contain three parish groups and two parish unions with 16 churches, compared to 24 churches 180 years ago.

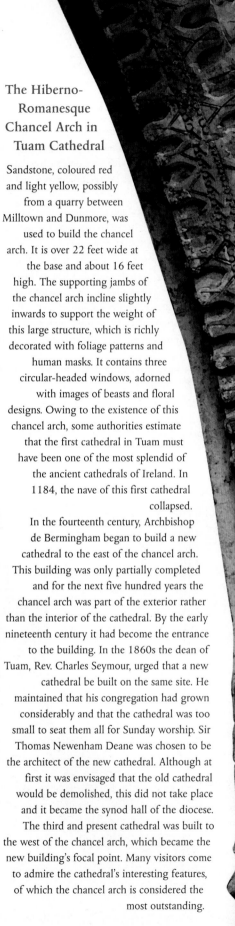

### The Hiberno-Romanesque Chancel Arch in Tuam Cathedral

Sandstone, coloured red and light yellow, possibly from a quarry between Milltown and Dunmore, was used to build the chancel arch. It is over 22 feet wide at the base and about 16 feet high. The supporting jambs of the chancel arch incline slightly inwards to support the weight of this large structure, which is richly decorated with foliage patterns and human masks. It contains three circular-headed windows, adorned with images of beasts and floral designs. Owing to the existence of this chancel arch, some authorities estimate that the first cathedral in Tuam must have been one of the most splendid of the ancient cathedrals of Ireland. In 1184, the nave of this first cathedral collapsed.

In the fourteenth century, Archbishop de Bermingham began to build a new cathedral to the east of the chancel arch. This building was only partially completed and for the next five hundred years the chancel arch was part of the exterior rather than the interior of the cathedral. By the early nineteenth century it had become the entrance to the building. In the 1860s the dean of Tuam, Rev. Charles Seymour, urged that a new cathedral be built on the same site. He maintained that his congregation had grown considerably and that the cathedral was too small to seat them all for Sunday worship. Sir Thomas Newenham Deane was chosen to be the architect of the new cathedral. Although at first it was envisaged that the old cathedral would be demolished, this did not take place and it became the synod hall of the diocese. The third and present cathedral was built to the west of the chancel arch, which became the new building's focal point. Many visitors come to admire the cathedral's interesting features, of which the chancel arch is considered the most outstanding.

## Kilcommon Church, Hollymount

Many disused churches dot the landscape of the west of Ireland, reminders of a time when the Church of Ireland population on this island was much greater than it is now. One such building is the church in Hollymount, a small village between Ballinrobe and Claremorris and once a halt for mail cars.

The original church was built as a chapel of ease by John Vesey, archbishop of Tuam in 1679–1716, who had erected a country seat for himself close by. It became the parish church in 1714, when the archbishop granted the 'parcel of ground on which the new church of Hollymount alias Moyla stands, circa 243 feet in circumference, in the town of Hollymount' to Rev. George Vesey, rector and vicar of Kilcommon, and his successors at the cost of one shilling. At the time of its consecration in September 1714, the church measured 60 feet east to west and 26 feet north to south. It was dedicated to St Charles the Martyr.

An inscribed stone above the doorway records the rebuilding of the church in 1816 with the support of a loan of £1,000 from the Board of First Fruits. The west doorway of Ballintubber Abbey was inserted into this nineteenth-century church and the building had oak panelling, box pews and a cast-iron spire. This unusual spire still dominates the skyline in the vicinity of the church. It is believed to have been made in

Birmingham and was transported in one piece by sea, canal and road to Hollymount. Openings in the spire, which appear decorative, were in fact designed to lighten its weight.

The church continued to be a place of worship until it was deconsecrated in 1959. In 1964, the stonework at the south-west door was returned to Ballintubber Abbey for the abbey's 750th anniversary. The church bell went to Immanuel Church, Ardoyne, Belfast and the lectern, dedicated to the memory of members of the Fair family, is now in St Mary's Church, Cong. The fine stained-glass window, depicting Christ in the days before his passion and during his ascension, was transferred to Sloan Street Mission Hall in Lurgan, County Armagh, which became the place of worship for the newly constituted parish of St John the Evangelist, Lurgan in 1968.

The graveyard at Hollymount contains some fine mausolea, particularly those dedicated to the memory of members of the Bingham family, Barons Clanmorris and the Ruttledge family. Robin Ruttledge, the well-known Irish ornithologist, who lived to celebrate his 102nd birthday, was buried here in January 2002. Rev. Charles Porter, curate of the parish, died of famine fever during the year 1847.

The window above is the odd one out in St Mary's Cathedral. This window depicting St Patrick and St Bridget was originally made for the Church of Ireland church in Crossboyne which closed in the 1960s. The window was removed from the Church for safekeeping with the idea that it might be used somewhere, sometime. The size of the window was remodeled to fit in its present position. It was installed by Aria Stained Glass in July 1997 and was blessed by Bishop John Neill.

RIGHT: Crossboyne Church

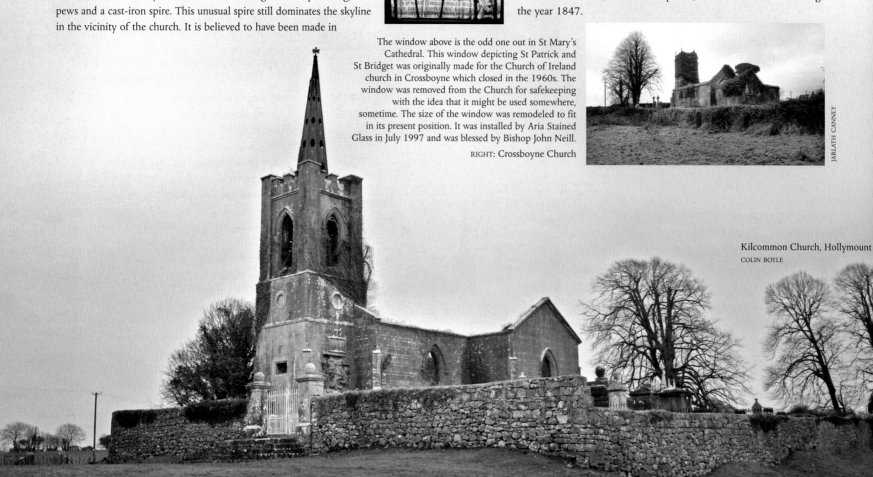

Kilcommon Church, Hollymount
COLIN BOYLE

## Parish Records

The main constituents of parochial records are the registers of baptisms, marriages and burials. Within the dioceses of Tuam, Killala and Achonry, entries from eighteenth-century registers survive for six parishes – Cong, Crossmolina, Emlaghfad, Killala, Kilmaine and Kilmoremoy. By the mid-nineteenth century, many clergy were keeping registers and 1844 legislation ensured that marriage registers and duplicates were kept from 1845 in every parish. These records reveal much about the families resident in a parish and the nature of their employment, and provide demographic statistics on subjects such as birth and death rates. Unfortunately, further legislation in 1875 meant that many of the pre-1870 baptism and burial registers were in the Public Record Office when it was destroyed in 1922. Parish records also include vestry minutes, lists of registered vestrymen, parochial account books and preachers' books. These records are important sources for the history of a particular parish and its parishioners. Most of the surviving parochial records of these dioceses not in current use are held in the Representative Church Body Library.

Sometimes parochial records can reveal details of local incidents. An entry in the Kilmaine combined register of baptisms, marriages and burials for 1744–78 records the death of a Robert Miller of Milford, County Mayo, in a duel in January 1748. This duel was fought at Musicfield, just outside the village of Kilmaine in south Mayo. Miller was fatally shot by his opponent, John Browne of the Neale, ancestor of the Barons Kilmaine. Miller managed to ride home, but died a few days later and was buried under the altar in Kilmaine Church. Before he died, Miller ordered that his horse, Hobnob, should be shot and buried with him.

When alterations were made to the church in Kilmaine in the 1850s, the jawbone of a horse was found.

The entry dated '21 Jan 1747/8' in the register reads as follows:

> On Jan 21st being Thursday Robert Miller Esq. late of Millford was fatally wounded by John Brown the Elder of Neal, of which wound he died on Tuesday the 26th following about ten in the morning. On Wednesday the 27th the Coroner's Inquest brought in their verdict that he was willfully murdered on the Lands of Musick Field, by sd. John Brown & on the 28th he was interred under the Communion Table in the Church of Kilmain greatly lamented by all good men especially those that knew, how much virtue adorned so good and so young a man. He was aged 35 Nov. 14. 1746.

The preacher's book for the same parish records how a tenant-right meeting in the village was dampened by 'torrents of rain' in November 1879. Other comments in this volume reveal the prevalence of illnesses such as influenza, scarletina, whooping cough and measles in the late-nineteenth century.

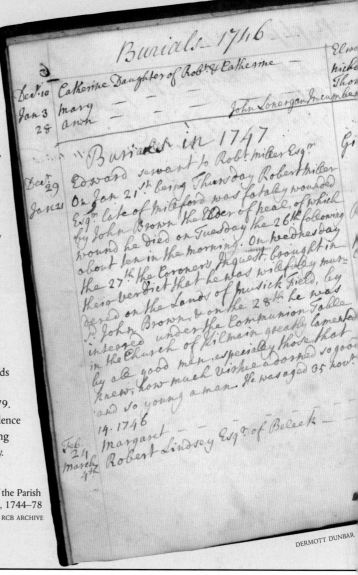

From the Register of the Parish of Kilmaine, 1744–78
RCB ARCHIVE

DERMOTT DUNBAR

Pictorial map of Galway 1651–52, a well developed town and busy port
Original copies in NUI, Galway and Trinity College, Dublin

## Seventeenth and Eighteenth Centuries

At the beginning of the seventeenth century, the Protestant population of Connacht was very small. Many of the clergy were non-resident and there were only a few churches. Small enclaves of Protestants lived in towns such as Galway, Castlebar and Tuam and some Elizabethan soldiers and settlers had acquired land in Connacht. Numbers grew slowly with the extension of English rule to the more remote areas of the province. The 1641 Rebellion caused many Protestants to leave their homes, including the archbishop of Tuam and the bishop of Killala and Achonry. Ensuing Cromwellian and Williamite land settlements brought into the region new landed families, often Protestant and English in origin, some of whom married into existing Gaelic and Norman landed families. By the eighteenth century, most land ownership had become vested in the hands of members of the Established Church, due to the penal laws. Nonetheless, especially in Co. Galway, a number of Catholic landowning families survived, due to leases from sympathetic and often related Protestant owners.

Many landowners employed Protestants, often from outside the locality, on their estates and in the big houses that became a feature of the Irish countryside. Wealthy landowners were often patrons of the Established Church, giving sites for the building of churches and paying for their erection. Agricultural

# The Episcopate of Tuam, Killala and Achonry

## Archbishops Nehemiah Donnellan and William Daniel

In the post-Reformation period, the archbishops of Tuam were appointed by the crown to establish and maintain the interests of the church and the state in the dioceses under their control. Many of them were not of Irish birth; some were scholars and theologians; others had important political connections. Archbishop Nehemiah Donnellan (archbishop 1595–1609) is among the better known of the Tuam archbishops. He was born in Galway, a graduate of Cambridge University and a fluent Irish speaker. In association with others, he began to translate the New Testament from Greek into Irish. In 1603, this task was completed by William Daniel or O'Donnell, who became Donnellan's successor in 1609. Archbishop Daniel (archbishop 1609–21) was a doctor of theology and one of the first elected fellows of Trinity College, Dublin. In 1608, his Irish translation of the *Book of Common Prayer* was published.

## Archbishops Richard Boyle, John Maxwell and Samuel Pullein

On the outbreak of the 1641 Rebellion, Archbishop Richard Boyle (archbishop 1638–45) fled to Galway, where he was joined by John Maxwell, bishop of Killala and Achonry, who became archbishop in 1645. No one was appointed to succeed Archbishop Maxwell (archbishop 1645–9) during the Commonwealth regime. The son of the rector of Ripley, Yorkshire, Samuel Pullein, first came to Ireland as private chaplain to the duke of Ormonde. During the 1641 Rebellion he was living in Cashel and was sheltered by a Jesuit priest, James Saul. Following the restoration of Charles II, he was one of twelve bishops consecrated by his brother-in-law, John Bramhall, archbishop of Armagh, in St Patrick's Cathedral, Dublin, on 27 January 1661. Among the treasures of Tuam Cathedral are the seventeenth-century paten and chalice inscribed with Archbishop Pullein's name.

## Archbishops John Vesey and Edward Synge

Archbishop John Vesey's prelature (1679–1716) saw the archdiocese of Tuam into the eighteenth century. Much of the archbishop's time was spent in providing for his family (he had 14 children). He was vice-chancellor of Trinity College, Dublin; he served on the Privy Council and was appointed three times as a lord justice of Ireland. His retention of the *quarta pars Episcopalia*, a quarter of the tithes, for his own use was out of step with most of the other bishops, who had given up this entitlement so that it could be used for the benefit of their clergy. He was often absent from Tuam and in 1686 was in danger of forfeiting his position due to his absenteeism. He had an estate at Hollymount, about ten miles from Tuam, where he built a large mansion and a chapel of ease. His successor was Edward Synge (archbishop 1716–41), who built a new bishop's palace in Tuam in the late 1710s. Both Archbishop Synge's sons became bishops in the Church of Ireland and he was a direct ancestor of the playwright John Millington Synge.

RCB ARCHIVE/DERMOTT DUNBAR

Archbishop John Vesey
1679–1716

Archbishop Edward Synge 1716–41
JARLATH CANNEY

The 'Parable' window in St Mary's Cathedral, Tuam was donated by Bishop Plunkett.

Bishop Thomas Plunkett, 1839–66

JARLATH CANNEY

## Archbishop Power Le Poer Trench

Hon. Power Le Poer Trench, son of the earl of Clancarty of Garbally, Ballinasloe, County Galway, was appointed archbishop in 1819. An evangelical, he was the last archbishop of Tuam and served for 20 years. Trench's work during the Connacht Famine of 1821–22 has been described as of 'inestimable importance'. He raised funds and involved local Roman Catholic clergy in providing food for the whole population, 'without distinction of creed'.

Archbishop Power Le Poer Trench, 1819–39, the last archbishop of Tuam
JARLATH CANNEY

## Bishops Thomas Plunket and Charles Brodrick Bernard

Thomas Plunket became bishop of Tuam, Killala and Achonry in 1839. He was the eldest son of William Conyngham Plunket, lord chancellor of Ireland and first Baron Plunket. Bishop Plunket became a keen supporter and promoter of the Irish Church Missions and many churches and schools were built in the western part of the dioceses. He died in 1866 and his successor was Charles Brodrick Bernard. Dr Bernard was one of the three Irish representative bishops in the House of Lords in 1869. He was very strongly opposed to the Irish Church Act of 1869, which disestablished the Church of Ireland. During his episcopacy the new cathedral at Tuam was built and consecrated.

Bishop Charles Bernard
The Bernard family donated the West Window to St Mary's Cathedral, Tuam.

JARLATH CANNEY

## Bishop Owen O'Connor and His Successors

By letters patent of Queen Elizabeth I, Owen O'Connor, dean of Achonry, was promoted to the see of Killala in December 1591. In 1607, he was succeeded by Miler Magrath, the notorious archbishop of Cashel and noted pluralist, who held the see with that of Achonry *in commendam* from 1613 until his death at Cashel in 1622. Bishop John Maxwell, when escaping from Killala in the winter of 1641, was the main figure in the party of persons who were attacked at the bridge of Shruel on the Mayo–Galway border in February 1642, while being escorted to the protection of Galway city. The bishop survived the incident. Thomas Otway, bishop of Killala from 1670 to 1679, is recorded by Sir James Ware as 'a hospitable, charitable and good prelate' who rebuilt the cathedral with his own funds and made it into a parish church.

## Archbishop Richard Robinson and His Successors

Archbishop Robinson of Armagh, primate of all Ireland (1765–94), still widely known for his library in Armagh and as the builder of the Armagh Observatory and the Archbishop's Palace there, began his episcopal career as bishop of Killala and Achonry in 1752. Another bishop, William Cecil Pery (bishop 1781–4), was formerly chaplain to the Irish House of Commons. William Preston, John Law and John Porter undoubtedly owed their advancement to the episcopacy to the influence of different lord lieutenants of Ireland, whom they served as chaplains. Joseph Stock (bishop 1798–1810) is one of the best known bishops of Killala and Achonry, as he played a prominent role in the town during the rising of 1798, when the French landed in Killala Bay. James Verschoyle, the last bishop of Killala and Achonry (1810–34), served for 24 years and was responsible for repairing the cathedral and bishop's residence and building schools and glebe houses in the dioceses.

The Rishworth window in St Mary's cathedral, Tuam. The Rishworth family came to the Tuam area *c.* 1846 and established a vibrant woollen trade, exporting Galway wool to the mills in Northern England. They also established the first factory in Tuam in 1885, known as the Curragh Match factory which unfortunately burned down in 1895.
JARLATH CANNEY

A monument to Bishop Joseph Stock in Waterford Cathedral
KEN HEMMINGWAY

improvements and industries – weaving, for example – were promoted, and people with such skills were encouraged to settle in towns such as Castlebar, Westport, Turlough and Ballymote. Thus, a Protestant middle class evolved.

One archbishop of Tuam in the mid-eighteenth century, Josiah Hort (archbishop 1742–51), was concerned for the spiritual well-being of his flock. At his primary visitation, held on 8 July 1742, he issued instructions to the clergy of the diocese of Tuam under two general headings: their conduct in the actual performance of the divine offices in church, and their behaviour at large towards their parishioners. He encouraged the clergy to reside in their parishes, to promote Bible study, to visit their parishioners regularly and to set a good example.

As the penal laws began to wane in the second half of the eighteenth century, religious tolerance grew. However, this was shattered by the events of 1798, when the arrival of a French fleet in Killala Bay sparked off another rebellion. Joseph Stock was bishop of Killala and Achonry at this time and his presence in Killala helped to maintain some degree of order.

## Bishop Stock of Killala

Joseph Stock, bishop of Killala and Achonry from 1798 to 1810, Classical scholar and author, is best remembered for the vivid account he wrote of the events in Killala in 1798. Newly arrived in the locality, he was conducting his first visitation, when the French under General Humbert arrived in Killala Bay in August 1798. He and his family remained in Killala with some of his clergy during the rebellion as prisoners of the French. During this time the bishop was respected by both the French and the Irish as interpreter, advisor and mediator. He spoke fluent French so was able to communicate well with the French officers, and his home, Killala Castle, became their headquarters. The gate of the castle for a time bore a flag inscribed 'Erin go brách'. His calm handling of the situation in Killala may well have prevented the massacre of the prisoners at Killala, including himself and his family, as retribution for the executions of the Irish prisoners following the defeat of the combined French and Irish force at Ballinamuck.

Bishop Stock continued as bishop of Killala and Achonry until 1810, when he moved to the more lucrative dioceses of Waterford and Lismore. He died there in 1813. Before becoming a bishop, he had been headmaster of Portora Royal School in Enniskillen. He was married twice. His first wife was Catherine Palmer, a widow. She was the mother of his ten children. His eldest son, Rev. Edwin Stock, was rector of Crossmolina in the early nineteenth century and first occupied the new glebe house there in 1814. Edwin's grandson, St George William Joseph Stock, was a Classical scholar at Oxford. It was he who, in 1898, the centenary of the 1798 Rebellion, presented Bishop Stock's journal to the library at Trinity College, Dublin. The journal gave an eyewitness account of the events at Killala a hundred years previously. Edited by Grattan Freyer, it was reprinted in 1982.

RIGHT: Clifden Workhouse, 1850. These workhouses were meant to provide relief for the starving but they were often overcrowded and underresourced. In Clifden, workhouse conditions were particularly harsh.
LEFT: A Famine Pot found in the garden of the rectory at Cong.

*THE ILLUSTRATED LONDON NEWS*

## The Nineteenth Century

Records of visitations give some insight into the state of the church in the dioceses of Tuam, Killala and Achonry in the nineteenth century. Clerical residency slowly improved, evidenced by the building of glebe houses, and education spread, with many parishes recording a resident schoolmaster. Churches were built or rebuilt with aid from the Board of First Fruits. The press recorded how, during the Great Famine, many Church of Ireland clergy and clergy families strove to alleviate hunger, sickness and general suffering. It was reported in April 1847 that the Rev. Patrick Pounden, rector of Westport, 'died of fever, rendered fatal by the exhaustion of mind and body in the course of his unremitting labours for the poor and needy – the famishing and dying'. In March 1848, Jane Little, wife of the rector of Dunfeeny, died of famine fever 'caught in the discharge of a charitable duty, which she was always foremost in performing.'

August 2013, an ambitious re-enactment of the French invasion of Mayo in 1798 with Humbert's landing at Killala was carried out. The English troops fire on the French.
GORDON GRAY

The glebe house in Cong painted by Heather Marshall. This rectory was built in 1817 with aid from the Board of First Fruits. It was also the home of Kathleen Lynn during her teenage years. Her father became rector of Cong parish in 1886.

## Dr Kathleen Lynn (1874–1955)

Dr Kathleen Lynn, the republican daughter of a Church of Ireland clergyman, spent her childhood in the dioceses of Tuam, Killala and Achonry. It is thought that the poverty she encountered as a child in County Mayo influenced her thinking in adult life. She was born in the parish of Ballysakeery in the diocese of Killala in 1874, the second daughter of Rev. Robert Young Lynn and his wife Catherine Wynne. She attended Alexandra College, Dublin, and eventually graduated as a doctor in 1899.

Kathleen Lynn was a devout member of the Church of Ireland throughout her life, attending daily service whenever possible. Interested in public health, she became politically active in the early years of the twentieth century. Initially influenced by the suffragette movement, she came to embrace nationalism and on Easter Monday 1916, she played an important role as the medical doctor assigned to City Hall. As a result of her republican activities, she was imprisoned.

On her release in 1917, she joined the Sinn Féin executive. Elected to the Dáil in 1923, she did not take her seat. She continued to work for improvements in the areas of public health and inner-city housing for the rest of her life. In 1919, she founded St Ultan's Hospital for Sick Children with Madeleine ffrench Mullen. The hospital was instrumental in combating tuberculosis among Dublin children in the first half of the twentieth century.

## The 'Second Reformation'

The growth of the population and the poverty of the Connacht region in the mid-nineteenth century were perceived by the supporters of the 'second Reformation' as fertile ground for the promotion of their doctrines. One result of their proselytising activities was another raft of church-building, which commenced in the 1850s under the auspices of the Irish Church Missions. Many of these churches were in remote areas along the west coast of the dioceses and their upkeep became unsustainable, especially after the establishment of the Irish Free State in 1922. Missions on Achill Island and in Clifden and Tourmakeady in particular caused a hostility between the two main Christian churches, which has taken a long time to dissipate.

St Thomas' Church, Dugort, Achill Island
St Thomas' was the principal church of the Achill Mission, which was founded by Rev. Edward Nangle in 1831. A significant act of worship took place here in 2011 when the Roman Catholic and Anglican communities came together for a Service of Reconciliation.
COLIN BOYLE

## Disestablishment

Disestablishment in 1871 brought many changes to the Church of Ireland, with the laity taking a more active role in church affairs and the Diocesan Synod becoming an important event in the annual church calendar. The first to be held in the new synod hall at Tuam took place on 15 November 1882. The dean, Very Rev. W.C. Townsend, was praised for his work in fitting up the synod hall as the venue.

A replica of the Bell of Armagh was presented to President Mary McAleese when she attended the General Synod of the Church of Ireland in May 2008 in Galway.
JANET MAXWELL

Ballinrobe Church, now the local library
COLIN BOYLE

## Twentieth Century

Congregation numbers in the west of Ireland declined in the early 20th century due to emigration, the establishment of the Irish Free State and casualties from World War I. Following amalgamation of parishes, there has been closure of churches and some have found alternative uses, such as those at Ballinrobe and Claremorris, which have become branches of the county library service, while the tiny church at Clonbur is the proposed centre for the Joyce Country Geopark. Nonetheless, the remaining parishes continue to have the support of loyal and dedicated congregations. The last decades have seen a great improvement in inter-church relations and a number of ordained women minister in the dioceses. Parish congregations continue to support and maintain their local church, often travelling long distances to do so, and play an important role in ecumenical activities in their locality.

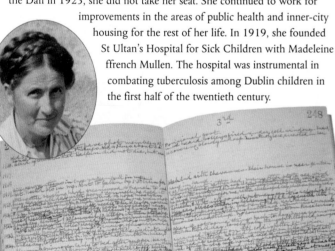

Kathleen Lynn and a spread of her tightly written diary from 3 May 1916–37
ROYAL COLLEGE OF PHYSICIANS IRELAND

## The Twenty-First Century – Parish Groups and Unions

At present there are seven parish groups and two parish unions within the united dioceses – Aughaval, Ballisodare, Galway, Killala, Kilmoremoy, Omey, Skreen, Tuam and Tubbercurry. The clergy provide services in 29 churches throughout the dioceses.

## Tuam, Killala and Achonry today

BISHOP PATRICK ROOKE

Archdeacon Gary Hastings presents medals to students at the Schola Cantorum.

MICHAEL BURKE

Towards the end of 2010, Bishop Richard Henderson announced his intention to resign the Bishopric of Tuam, Killala and Achonry. When the vacancy occurred early in 2011, it was recommended that there might be a moratorium for a minimum period of one year before an electoral college would be called to elect a new Bishop. This would give the Church 'a little time to think about how episcopal ministry can best be done in the West of Ireland'. Hence a special meeting of the General Synod was called to debate and decide on a Bill, proposed by two bishops, that would give effect to this. The result was an overwhelming defeat of the Bill and thus an electoral college was summonsed to meet a few weeks later.

Bishop Patrick Rooke on his way to hold a service at Holy Trinity Church on Innishbiggle Island

This debate, and the emotions aroused, highlighted two important issues. First, the need to examine episcopal needs and structures, not just in Tuam, Killala and Achonry, but throughout the country. Secondly, the deep desire there is in rural dioceses to retain a local episcopal presence. The difficulty, however, is the cost involved in supporting the episcopate in a diocese with only nine cures.

What is true at the diocesan level is true too when it comes to the parochial ministry. Parishes in the West of Ireland, as elsewhere, can no longer sustain the number of clergy currently employed. There are neither sufficient numbers of people nor the necessary finance. Yet each parish strives to hold onto its rector. Amalgamations, multi-church groups, church closures, services on alternative Sundays, part-time priests; all are practical but unpopular solutions.

With a Bishop and full compliment of clergy in place, Tuam, Killala and Achonry is in good heart. Under the leadership of its Diocesan Council, it is gently working at building up links between parishes and, despite the vast distances involved, small numbers and economic constraints, there is a determination to maximise potential in terms of 'Growth, Unity and Service'. Clergy and laity are realistic enough to know that change is inevitable and are beginning to consider new structures and patterns of ministry that are suitable and sustainable for the twenty-first century. In all likelihood, the present diocesan area will have to be expanded and parishes will need to prepare themselves for new forms of lay and ordained local ministry offered in a voluntary capacity. That in itself will bring its own challenges but encouraged by the support of the wider church, Tuam, Killala and Achonry has its part to play in ensuring that the Church of Ireland is alive and active in the West of Ireland.

## SCHOLA CANTORUM

St Nicholas' *Schola Cantorum*, in less than a year, has established three new ensembles and drawn close to one hundred people into the life of the St Nicholas Collegiate Church community. The youngest of the new groups is the *Choristers*, consisting of 12 boys and 12 girls aged 8–14. In their first year they have sung at seven services and two concerts. The next ensemble to be established was the *Choral Scholars*: students at NUI Galway awarded scholarships funded by the university. In their first year they sang four services of Compline and took part in various concerts and events in both St Nicholas' and the university. The third ensemble, *St Nicholas' Singers*, are a large allcomersgroup of between fifty and sixty singers, which gave two concerts of major choral works appropriate to the season.

The Parish Choir, the workhorse of the Schola Cantorum, these dedicated folk provide music for the parish Eucharist most Sundays. With the establishment of the Schola Cantorum a new chapter has begun in the history of this ancient church in Galway.

## AUGHAVAL (WESTPORT), DUGORT, CASTLEBAR and TURLOUGH

Aughaval group covers the area around Clew Bay on the western Atlantic coast, stretching north to include Achill Island and inland to Castlebar the county town of Mayo and its hinterland. The town of Westport is a thriving cultural centre and attracts visitors from all over the world while Castlebar contains all the elements of a busy town in which the headquarters of local government is situated. Congregation members are therefore from many diverse backgrounds and occupations but share a great involvement in the life of their towns and parishes.

*Turlough Church* is situated a few miles outside Castlebar and was built on a site donated by the Fitzgerald family in 1816. Worship is now held there on Saturday evenings.

Turlough Church
JESSICA PRIDDY

*Christ Church, Castlebar* is located in the centre of the county town of Mayo, on the edge of the Mall, the former cricket green of the Earls of Lucan. The church was built in 1739. A carved datestone set into the wall of the church grounds records Richard Castles as its architect. The church was damaged during the Rising of 1798 and a major reconstruction was completed in the late 1820s. It was the place of worship for the soldiers from the military barracks in the town for many years and a memorial remembers privates of the Fraser Fencibles killed in 1798.

*Holy Trinity Church, Westport* was consecrated on 26 September 1872. It was built in a central location in the expanding port town and replaced a late eighteenth-century church in the immediate vicinity of Westport House, which had become too small for the number of local parishioners and the influx of summer visitors. Holy Trinity is reputed to be the last church built before the disestablishment of the Church of Ireland. The church, designed by Sir Thomas Newenham Deane in the neo-Gothic style, has a very highly decorated interior, including mosaics, murals depicting scenes from the gospels and stained-glass windows. Many of the interior features were donated by parishioners as memorials to deceased family members. An extensive restoration of the church took place in the mid-1980s, with the help of a cross-community committee. Rev. James Owen Hannay, who wrote many novels under the *nom de plume* George A. Birmingham, was rector of this parish from 1892 to 1913.

Christ Church Castlebar

JESSICA PRIDDY

*St Thomas' Church, Dugort* is associated with the Achill Mission of the Rev. Edward Nangle in the 1830s and 1840s. Much of the hurt caused by the Mission has now been healed by inter church fellowship. An example of this was a special ecumenical service, held on 24 September 2011, at which the bishops of both denominations began to mark with crosses unknown graves from Famine times in the graveyards on Achill and Innisbiggle islands.

# GALWAY and KILCUMMIN (OUGHTERARD)

The most southerly group of parishes in the dioceses is centred on the city of Galway and along the shores of Galway Bay encompassing the Aran Islands and stretching up the west shore of Lough Corrib to the town of Oughterard. St Nicholas' Church in Galway is the oldest Irish medieval church still in parish use and is the focus of this vibrant, multi-cultural and very inclusive group. The rector is supported in his ministry by a curate and assistant priest who help to care for the congregations of the two churches in this group.

LEFT: Interfaith service for Japan
ABOVE: The Chapel of Christ; the Crusader's Tomb lies in the centre of the floor.

*The Collegiate Church of St Nicholas, Galway* is located in the centre of Galway city. It is said that Columbus worshipped here on his trip to Ireland in 1477, and Robert O'Hara Burke, the famous Australian explorer, was baptised in the church in July 1822. In the past, many of its parishioners were involved in military or maritime occupations or were employed by the civil administration. Until the mid nineteenth century the parish was part of the Wardenship of Galway, an unusual institution set up in 1484, whereby a college, (hence collegiate), comprised of a warden and eight vicars was appointed by the Mayor and Corporation of the town to administer the parish independent of episcopal control. The church, now a cruciform structure, was founded in 1320 on the site of a previous church and was enlarged in the sixteenth century by the building of north and south aisles under the patronage of the ffrench and Lynch families. It has many interesting carvings and tombs relating to the merchant 'tribes' of Galway and other memorials to more recent residents. A former institution associated with the church in Galway was the Grammar School, whose pupils included Peter Freyer from the parish of Sellerna in Connemara who was to become a pioneering doctor with a practice in Harley Street, London. An annual medical symposium is held in his honour at the university in Galway.

The population of Galway today is very cosmopolitan and to some extent transient, and many find a peaceful haven in the confines of St Nicholas'. The interior of the church contains a wonderful space for worship and prayer and is also used as a venue for musical concerts and cultural events. Interfaith services have been held with different communities and the church provides a place of worship for other denominations such as the Russian Orthodox and the Syriac Orthodox. The parish has a National School and besides its regular parish choir has recently formed a Schola Cantorum, a choir school for children and students attending the university.

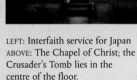

The flags of the fourteen 'Tribes' of Galway displayed on Eyre Square, Galway

*Kilcummin Church*, built in 1810, is situated in the town of Oughterard, a few miles to the west of Galway city. An interesting feature of this church is an enclosed area in the north transept in which prisoners sat during church services when a garrison was stationed in the town. The Martin family of Ross were prominent parishioners in the nineteenth century. Violet Martin and her cousin Edith Somerville were the famous literary duo known as Somerville and Ross.

Plan of St Nicholas' Church

Kilcummin Church
RCB/DAVID CROOKS

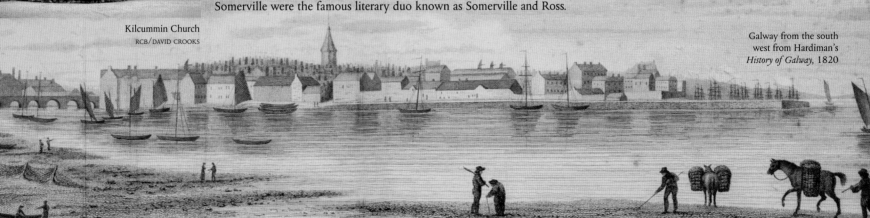

Galway from the south west from Hardiman's *History of Galway*, 1820

## OMEY (CLIFDEN), BALLINAKILL, ERRISLANNON and MOYRUS (ROUNDSTONE)

The Omey group covers an extensive part of west Co. Galway including much of the Connemara region. Clifden is a busy coastal town and a lively centre for art and cultural events and draws many visitors in the summer months. Roundstone, a small fishing village, located on the spectacular Atlantic coastal drive, was founded by the Scottish engineer Alexander Nimmo in 1820, and is now a popular holiday destination. This group of parishes has a small number of permanently resident parishioners but it is well supported by regular visitors to the area. There are extremely good community relations in Clifden and plans are currently being put together to transform the church into a venue for musical and other community events.

*Christ Church, Clifden* is situated in the town of Clifden, founded by John D'Arcy. It was built in 1812 but later demolished. A new one was built on the same site in 1853. This church was badly damaged by Hurricane Debbie in September 1961 and in the rebuilding it was shortened and a baptistery included. The silver cross (modelled on the Cross of Cong) and candlesticks were a gift from the family of Sir William Murphy in 1966. His father, Canon R.W. Murphy, was rector of the parish in 1905–16, and his son is the poet Richard Murphy.

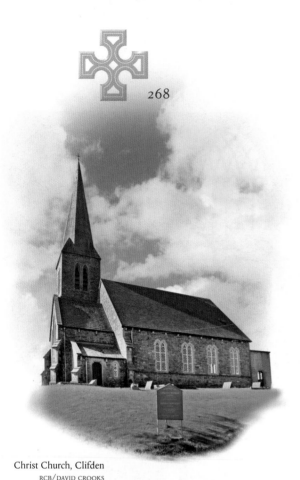

Christ Church, Clifden
RCB/DAVID CROOKS

Holy Trinity Church, Errislannan
RCB/DAVID CROOKS

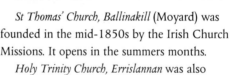

St Thomas'
Church, Ballinakill
RCB/DAVID CROOKS

*St Thomas' Church, Ballinakill* (Moyard) was founded in the mid-1850s by the Irish Church Missions. It opens in the summers months.

*Holy Trinity Church, Errislannan* was also founded by the Irish Church Missions in the mid-1850s. It closed in 1955 but was reopened thirty years later for services in July and August and is cared for by the Friends of St Flannans.

*St Mary's Church, Moyrus* (Roundstone) was designed by architect, Joseph Welland, and built by H. Carroll. The church was consecrated on 14 September 1843. The registers for this parish, currently located in the Representative Church Body Library, begin in the 1840s and cover the Famine years.

St Mary's Church, Moyrus
RCB/DAVID CROOKS

## TUAM, CONG and AASLEAGH (LEENANE)

The three parishes in the Tuam group, including that of St Mary's Cathedral, Tuam, transverse the full breadth of the Diocese of Tuam stretching from the Killary fjord in the west to the boundary of the dioceses in the east beyond Tuam. This group of parishes reflects the great diversity in the buildings of worship in these dioceses ranging from St Mary's Cathedral in an urban setting at Tuam to a small rural church located on the extreme western perimeter of the dioceses. Parishioners travel long distances to attend Sunday services which are held on a weekly basis at Tuam and Cong and summer visitors are always welcomed in all three churches. An annual fête is run by a cross community committee.

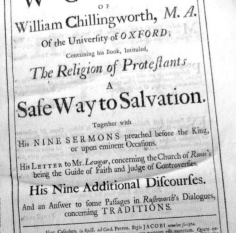

THE

# WORKS
OF

## William Chillingworth, M. A.
Of the University of OXFORD;

Containing his Book, Intituled,

*The Religion of Protestants*
A

## Safe Way to Salvation.

Together with

His NINE SERMONS preached before the King,
or upon eminent Occasions.

His LETTER to Mr. *Lewgar*, concerning the Church of *Rome's*
being the Guide of Faith and Judge of Controversies.

His Nine Additional Discourses.

And an Answer to some Passages in *Rushworth's* Dialogues,
concerning TRADITIONS.

*The Works of William Chillingworth* from the Henry Library
NATIONAL UNIVERSITY OF IRELAND, GALWAY

St Mary's Church, Cong
RCB/DAVID CROOKS

Abbey of Cong
RCB/DAVID CROOKS

St Mary's Church, Cong
ALISTAIR GRIMASON

*St Mary's Church, Cong* is situated in the village of Cong which is best known as the location for Ashford Castle Hotel and for the making of *The Quiet Man* film in 1951. Two church buildings in the village of Cong have served the Church of Ireland congregation for over two and a half centuries. The first church, now a ruin, dates from the early eighteenth century and is located immediately opposite the Abbey of Cong. The present church stands on the avenue from Ashford Castle and was consecrated on 28 July 1855. The 1850s heralded the arrival of the Guinness family in the Cong area. Benjamin Lee Guinness took a great interest in the church and paid for the stained glass windows designed by John Casey of Dublin and the erection of a tower and spire in 1861. In the following decades many members of the congregation worked for the Guinness family. Sir Benjamin's only daughter Ann married William Conyngham Plunket, Fourth Baron and Archbishop of Dublin (1884–97), and it was their descendants who in more recent times gave a beautifully carved wooden replica of the Cross of Cong to the church.

*St John the Baptist's Church, Aasleagh* was founded by the Irish Church Missions in the early 1850s. Located at the head of the Killary fjord and close to the Aasleagh Falls, the church is open only in the months of July and August and occasionally for a special service. Its picturesque setting has seen it host a video to promote the Irish American singing group 'The Kelly Family' and feature in the making of the film *The Field* based on the play by John B. Keane and starring Richard Harris among other well known actors.

A replica of the Cross of Cong

St John the Baptist's Church, Aasleagh and the Aasleagh Falls
JESSICA PRIDDY

# THE DIOCESES OF KILLALA AND ACHONRY

## KILLALA, DUNFEENY and CROSSMOLINA

The Killala union of parishes is located to the west of Killala Bay, an area very much linked to the tradition of St Patrick and the seventeenth century cathedral is named after him. The Céide Fields, one of the most extensive Stone Age archaeological sites, is located near the village of Ballycastle on the coast road. The regular congregations of this union of parishes are increased by visitors to the area. Killala supports its own primary school at Newtownwhite which is attended by children from all denominations. Parishioners participate in community based celebrations such as the annual festival which marks the rich history and culture of this locality.

Killala Cathedral and Round Tower
EAMONN O'BOYLE

Killala Cathedral
GORDON GRAY

*St Patrick's Cathedral, Killala* was certainly in existence here prior to the fourteenth century. A monastic settlement grew up around this first cathedral and had developed into a small town by the medieval period. The royal visitation of 1615 records the cathedral as a ruin. The present cathedral dates from the 1670s. It was built by Thomas Otway, Bishop of Killala and Achonry, (1671–80) with his own funds. It incorporates a small doorway from the original building. The spire is an early nineteenth century addition. The building is in the Gothic style of architecture and contains box pews and a Telford organ. This fine building with its interior stone walls has stood the test of time and continues to be a place of worship in the twenty-first century.

St John the Evangelist's Church, Dunfeeny
COLIN BOYLE

St Mary's Church, Crossmolina
COLIN BOYLE

*St John the Evangelist's Church, Dunfeeny* is situated in the village of Ballycastle on the north coast of County Mayo, close to the Céide Fields, an extensive Stone Age settlement. The church was built in 1810.

*St Mary's Church, Crossmolina* was also built in 1810. Samuel Lewis described it in the 1830s as a 'neat plain edifice, with a square tower and spire'. A register of births, marriages and burials survives for Crossmolina from 1802, with earlier eighteenth-century extracts, the previous register having been lost in the 1798 Rebellion.

The town of Ballina, situated at the mouth of the famous fishing river the Moy, is the main centre of the Kilmoremoy union. The area stretches along the coast east from Ballina towards the town of Sligo where the parishes of Castleconnor, Kilglass and Easkey are situated and south to the village of Foxford.

*St Michael's Church, Ballina*, the largest church in the Union, is currently exploring what it might mean to become a developing parish with a focus on community, both within and outside the church doors. There are two parish primary schools in the union and active branches of the Girls' Friendly Society and Mothers' Union. People travel long distances to attend services, especially at the Foxford end of the union with a large area to the east with no Church of Ireland presence. To meet that need an outreach service is held on the first Sunday of the month in the McWilliam Park Hotel, Claremorris and this is proving very successful.

Sited at Ardnaree, a part of the town of Ballina on the Sligo side of the River Moy, St Michael's was founded in 1763 when a nave, chancel and tower were built. In 1815, it was enlarged by the addition of a north east transept by Thomas Ham and, in 1892, by a new chancel. A special feature of the church is the rare stained-glass window of Charity and Wisdom designed by the cartoonist George Parlby in 1899.

*St Michael's Church, Kilmoremoy*
ALAN SYNNOTT

Kilglass Church
ALAN SYNNOTT

*Killanley Church, Castleconnor* is reputed to be named after an earlier church dedicated to St Patrick's sister Kill-Anley. This church is located in the parish of Castleconnor on the coast road from Ballina to Enniscrone. The site was given by Edward Wingfield, a large landowner in the locality and the church was consecrated on 3 October 1818. Previously, parishioners would have attended an earlier church at Enniscrone, known as Valentine's Church. Rev. Thomas Valentine, vicar of Kilglass and Castleconnor, 1712–65, left money in his will for the maintenance of clergy widows and Protestant schools.

*Kilglass Church* was built in 1829 with aid from the Board of First Fruits. Services are now held there twice a month, alternating with St Anne's Church, Easkey.

*St Anne's Church, Easkey*. In 1768, Rev. James Hutchinson gave the churchwardens of Easkey Parish a part of the glebe lands for the site of a new church. This building was destroyed in 1798. A new church, financed by a loan from the Board of First Fruits, was built in 1820 on the same site and incorporated the tower of the old church. One of its main features is a stained-glass window depicting Jesus Christ

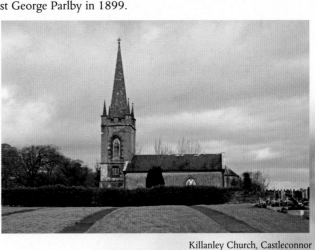

Killanley Church, Castleconnor
COLIN BOYLE

as the light of the world, which was commissioned from Kitty O'Brien of An Túr Gloine. The church building has undergone major renovations on a number of occasions, the most recent in 2002, made possible by generous support from the local community and others from further afield.

*Straid Church*, located to the south of Ballina, in the centre of the small town of Foxford, was built in 1801. A tower and gallery were added in 1826. The Faith, Hope and Charity stained-glass window by Mayer & Co. of Munich is the main feature of this church. Because of the church's elevated position, its tower was used as a lookout point by members of the Irish Free State army in the early 1920s. Killedan House in the vicinity was once the home of the family of Emily MacManus, the renowned and reforming matron of Guy's Hospital in London (1927–46).

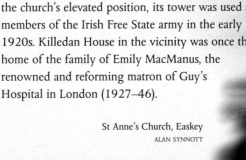

Straid Church, Foxford
ALAN SYNNOTT

St Anne's Church, Easkey
ALAN SYNNOTT

St Mary's Church, Kilmacshalgan
ALAN SYNNOTT

# SKREEN, KILMACSHALGAN and DROMARD

Skreen group of parishes is situated along the coast road from Ballina to Sligo and contains three churches. *Christ Church, Dromard* is the mostly easterly of these and is situated in the woods at Beltra while *St Mary's Church, Kilmacshalgan* is located just outside the small village of Dromore West with Skreen in the centre.

Sunday school, baptisms and marriages testify to youthful congregations in this group not adverse to bible study and socialising at parish dances and annual lunches. Weekly services are held in all three churches and a family service and a healing service on a monthly basis.

The present *Skreen Church* was built in 1819, although St Colmcille founded an early Christian monastery at Skreen and the remains of a medieval church still exist in the graveyard. When George Coulter died in 1902, aged 95, he had been the parish clerk of Skreen for over 70 years. The most notable features of this church are the many box tombs in the graveyard, with very fine carvings by members of the Diamond family, local stonemasons. Sir George Gabriel Stokes, a prominent nineteenth-century mathematician and physicist, was born in Skreen rectory in 1819. Rev. Edward Nangle was rector of Skreen from 1851 to 1873.

*St Mary's Church, Kilmacshalgan*, located on the main road into Dromore West, was built in 1820.

*Christ Church, Dromard* was originally built close to the sea around 1764 but now, thanks to drainage works, lies further inland. It is located along a narrow lane in a beautiful woodland setting. The interior is unique, with the altar and pulpit at opposite ends of the building, east and west. Oil lamps are still in use, as there is no electricity, and the church still retains its box pews.

Christ Church, Dromard
RCB/DAVID CROOKS

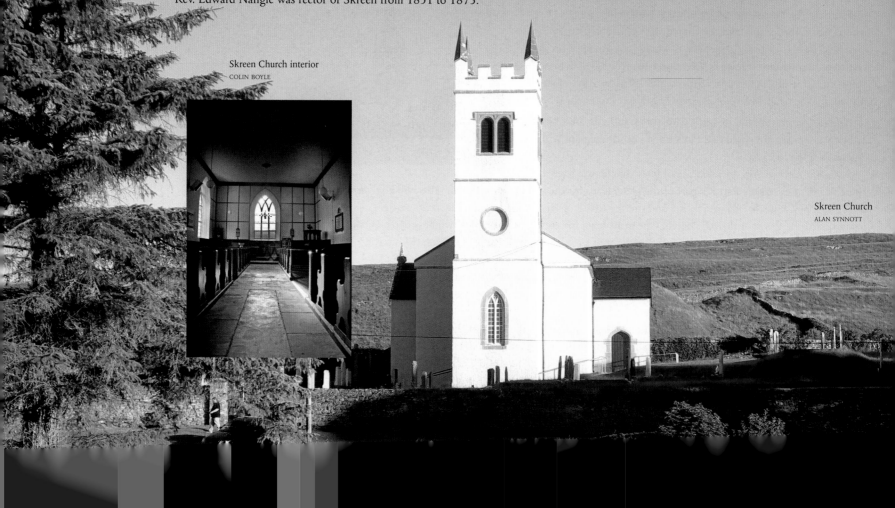

Skreen Church interior
COLIN BOYLE

Skreen Church
ALAN SYNNOTT

## BALLISODARE, COLLOONEY and EMLAGHFAD (BALLYMOTE)

Holy Trinity Church, Ballysodare
COLIN BOYLE

Ballisodare group situated in the north east of the dioceses stretches in a north to south direction from the coastal commuter town of Ballisodare, Co. Sligo, to a more rural southern end on the border with Co. Roscommon. This group of parishes is blessed with congregations of all ages. Weekly services are held in all three churches and worship is varied with appropriate liturgies for all. The three teacher primary school at St Paul's, Collooney, serves the needs of the children at national school level.

*Holy Trinity Church, Ballisodare* was built in 1839 as a chapel of ease to nearby St Paul's, Collooney, by Edward Joshua Cooper of Markree. The building contains a stained-glass window by Thomas Willement, dated 1862.

In the north transept of *St Paul's Church, Collooney*, a large marble monument made in Florence commemorates Edward Joshua Cooper's first wife Sophie, who died in 1822.

The present *Emlaghfad Church*, in the village of Ballymote, stands on what is locally known as the Rock and was originally built in 1818. Ballymote gave its name to the Book of Ballymote compiled in the late fourteenth century and is now held in the Royal Irish Academy. The building was substantially refurbished and rededicated for worship in 2002. An earlier church in the townland was roofless by the 1830s. The graveyard of this church contains an unusual profile portrait on the headstone of Robert Moore, who died in 1781.

St Paul's Church, Collooney
ALAN SYNNOTT

Emlaghtfad Church
RCB/DAVID CROOKS

## TUBBERCURRY and KILLORAN (RATHBARRON)

Located in Co. Sligo, Achonry group of parishes mainly cares for a prosperous farming community. The town of Tubbercurry is situated on the southern side of the Ox Mountains and has a growing population of more than seventeen hundred people. It hosts annual Irish traditional music and theatre festivals.

*St Crumnathy's Cathedral, Achonry.* St Finan founded a monastery at Achonry around the year AD 530. His pupil Nathy, commonly called Crumthir, soon took charge, and the nineteenth-century cathedral was dedicated to him by the name St Crumnathy's. The cathedral, the smallest of the Church of Ireland cathedrals, closed in 1997.

St George's Church, Tubbercurry
COLIN BOYLE

Rathbarron Church, Killoran

*St George's Church, Tubbercurry* This rectangular building with a small sanctuary addition was erected in 1830 in the Gothic style as a chapel of ease with an octagonal tower. Major renovations were initiated at St George's in 1997 and internal furnishings were bought from churches at Castlerea and Newport. The church was rededicated on 14 May 1999. The former church school located within the church grounds, which provided education for the children of the parish for 150 years, is now the parish centre.

*Rathbarron Church, Killoran.* In 1767, Charles O'Hara of Annaghmore gave an Irish acre of ground for the building of a church at Rathbarron. The church that was built on this site was recently described by David Lawrence as a 'classical cruciform church' with a 'tall tower and broad apsidal sanctuary … in a magnificent hilltop setting'. It contains a fine stained-glass window depicting the resurrection by the German studio of Mayer & Co.

# The Dioceses

## The Province of Dublin

St Patrick's Cathedral
ALASTAIR SMEATON

# St Patrick's Cathedral, Dublin

ANDREW SMITH & GAVAN WOODS
PHOTOGRAPHS ST PATRICK'S CATHEDRAL

The story of this site may go back to the time of Saint Patrick himself. According to legend he used a well somewhere onsite to baptise converts to the Christian faith. Celtic grave slabs discovered in 1901 beside the Cathedral prove that the site has been in use for at least a thousand years. The first mention of a church on the site occurred in 890AD. It is referred to as 'Saint Patrick's in-insula' because in those days the area was surrounded by water from the river Poddle.

The site changed dramatically in the twelfth Century with the arrival of the Normans to Ireland. The first Anglo-Norman Archbishop of Dublin, John Comyn, raised the status of Saint Patrick's from a parish church to that of a collegiate church in 1191. The status was raised again sometime between 1212–23 to that of a Cathedral. The building itself was constructed between 1220–60 and the Lady Chapel completed in 1270.

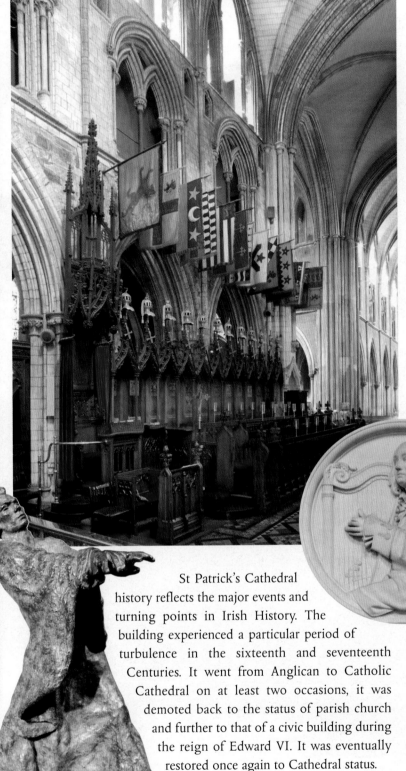

Lee Guinness, of the brewing family. However, he insisted that he be allowed to undertake the restoration without any interference. The changes he made caused quite a lot of controversy. Guinness took the decision to remove the partitions which separated the cathedral into different parts. He felt that an 'open plan' lay out was more attractive and in keeping with Anglican worship. He also decided to extend a ceiling around the entire building. Despite some opposition to these changes the Cathedral reopened in 1865 to enormous celebrations.

The Cathedral is the final resting place for up to 700 people. Arguably the most famous man buried in the building is Jonathan Swift who is most commonly known as the author of *Gullivers Travels*. Swift was Dean of the Cathedral from 1713–45 and he used this influential position to speak out against social injustice and inequality.

Bust of Jonathan Swift
DERMOTT DUNBAR

Music has played a central role in the life of the Cathedral. The Choir School, which is located directly opposite the Cathedral, was founded in 1432 and is the oldest school in Ireland. The boys and girls from the Choir school continue to sing in the Cathedral twice a day during term time. Matins in the morning and Evensong in the evening. One of the most famous choral performances in the life of the Cathedral took place when the combined choirs of Christ Church and Saint Patrick's Cathedrals sang the first performance of Handel's Messiah on 13 April 1742.

In 1869, the issue of Dublin having two Cathedrals was finally resolved when St Patrick's became the National Cathedral for the Church of Ireland and Christ Church was made the Cathedral for the Dublin and Glendalough diocese.

Today, the Cathedral welcomes around 400,000 visitors a year and the money raised from tourist visits helps pay for the enormous cost of maintaining the building and ensures that worship continues onsite.

St Patrick's Cathedral history reflects the major events and turning points in Irish History. The building experienced a particular period of turbulence in the sixteenth and seventeenth Centuries. It went from Anglican to Catholic Cathedral on at least two occasions, it was demoted back to the status of parish church and further to that of a civic building during the reign of Edward VI. It was eventually restored once again to Cathedral status.

By the mid-nineteenth Century the Cathedral had fallen into a poor state of repair, and in the 1860s, it was restored thanks to the generosity of Sir Benjamin

LEFT: St Patrick by Marion Le Broquy
ABOVE CENTRE: Monument to Carolan, the blind harpist
DERMOTT DUNBAR

ALASTAIR SMEATON

# The United Dioceses of Dublin and Glendalough

The United Dioceses of Dublin and Glendalough cover terrain which in itself is akin to the broad sweep of the witness of the Church of Ireland country-wide. By this I mean that our parishes are located in the rural, the sub-urban and the inner city parts of the Greater Dublin area. This gives scope for a broad range of ecclesiastical and community life in the parishes, together with the opportunities for fresh experiences and fresh expressions of an enriched and enriching life with people who belong to the places where we are and who make a vital contribution to the total shape of society. We also are involved in a number of educational and healthcare establishments and seek, through them, to serve the whole community from the perspective of the Church of Ireland ethos.

A number of shifts in emphasis must be carefully noted. The range of people who live in the Greater Dublin area has changed beyond imagining in the last twenty years. Some have come by choice; some have been forced to flee their own countries and make a home in Ireland. In the Dioceses we are the beneficiaries of such movement of people. It has expanded our understanding of the Anglican and Christian traditions. It has sent us out beyond our comfort zones to experience diversity as something human, tangible and challenging of our own particular brands of settled Christian identity. The second major shift is the engagement with people of Faiths other than Christianity. This is, of course, a feature of life right across Ireland, but in these Dioceses we are blessed by opportunities for encounter and engagement with people who want to contribute to a renewed Irish society through the expression of their Faith as part of their identity. Inter Faith encounter worldwide teaches us that presence among and engagement with people who are other than us stretches and elasticates our understanding of our own identity, as well as enabling those who are the others to be our neighbours and our friends. Thirdly, the urban dilemma is strong, vibrant and will not go away. Within a decade, more than half of the world's population will live in cities. There is no underestimating the pressures this will bring to bear on human lives and on lived environment in ways which we cannot either envisage or predict. These three challenges consume much of our thinking and our energy as we face the future with hope and with a sense of excitement.

Settled communities are one part of who we are. Transient communities are another part. The number of training colleges at second and third level, to give but one example, means that hundreds of thousands of people pass through the doors of educational establishments, year on year. Chaplaincy is an urgent priority in responding to the need for human welcome and belonging in the name of Jesus Christ. There is no doubt that Dublin will continue to change and develop in the years ahead. It is, and always will be, a fast-moving place and people. The United Dioceses are committed in every way to playing our part in this development of the future and to making our contribution to it with vigour and confidence.

MICHAEL DUBLIN AND GLENDALOUGH

St Kevin's Church and the
Round Tower, Glendalough
SCENIC IRELAND

## Christ Church Cathedral, Dublin

STUART KINSELLA

CAPTIONS BY LESLEY-ANNE CAREY
PHOTOGRAPHS CHRIST CHURCH CATHEDRAL

In 1028, the Hiberno-Norse king of Dublin, Sitriuc 'Silkbeard' with Flannacán Ua Cellaig of Brega made a pilgrimage to Rome. That this was to establish a new Dublin cathedral is suggested by a set of relics and a surviving martyrology acquired contemporaneously in Cologne. Holy Trinity or Christ Church, as it was later known, was staffed by Benedictine monks until the twelfth century, while the diocese itself deferred to Canterbury. After the synod of Kells-Mellifont in 1152, Dublin was integrated into the Irish church as an archbishopric and, shortly afterwards, its second archbishop, later patron saint, of Dublin, Lorcán Ua Tuathail, reformed the chapter to the use of St Augustine's rule, which remained until the Reformation.

A large salver reputedly presented to the cathedral by William of Orange, part of a larger collection of cathedral and parish silver and manuscripts on display in the cathedral crypt.

The Anglo-Normans rebuilt the cathedral in a grander style, first in a transitional Romanesque still evident in the transepts (c.1186–c.1200), and later in the Gothic visible in the nave (1230s–50s). The elevation of the collegiate church of St Patrick's to cathedral status in the early thirteenth-century, fired not only architectural but capitular rivalry, the latter only resolved in 1300 when the two chapters agreed a *pacis compositio* for peace. While the Augustinian community was supported by relic-visiting pilgrims, their main income derived from extensive estates accumulated since its foundation. An extension to the choir in the late 1350s–60s was the only significant architectural innovation of the later middle ages, while a choir of four choristers, established in 1480, would lay the more enduring foundations for the cathedral's musical tradition.

Dublin's oldest structure, Christ Church crypt dates from at least the 12th century. It is unique in these islands in running the entire length of the cathedral.

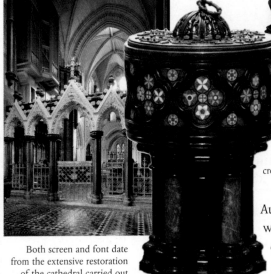

Both screen and font date from the extensive restoration of the cathedral carried out between 1871 and 1878.

Strongbow, leader of the Cambro-Normans who captured Dublin in 1170. He was buried within sight of the cross in the cathedral nave.

The cathedral's north wall dates from the thirteenth century and leans almost one foot out of plumb. It is considered one of the finest examples of the Early English Gothic style in Ireland.

The Reformation saw the dissolution of the Augustinian cathedral priory and its re-establishment, with the same personnel, as a secular cathedral. The collapse of the nave south wall in 1562 destroyed the architectural elegance of the nave along with the Strongbow monument, bequeathing dubious Tudor repairs, while the old monastic buildings were reused in 1608 for the four courts of the judicary. The crypt beneath harboured public alehouses spilling out onto John's Lane. Crown involvement, with two lord deputies restoring the choir: Henry Sidney (1560s) and Thomas Wentworth (1630s) saw the cathedral act increasingly as a chapel royal, a title acknowledged by Charles II after his Restoration and two further choir refurbishments took place before the 1688 rebellion. The long eighteenth century saw Dublin shift from its medieval core and by 1796, the courts had abandoned the cathedral cloister for the quays.

The cathedral's famous mummified cat and rat, immortalised by James Joyce in *Finnegans Wake*, who wrote 'as stuck as that cat to that mouse in that tube of that Christchurch organ'.

The Lady chapel was designed to accommodate meetings of the cathedral chapter.

Attempts were made to refurbish Christ Church, by then a mixture of styles, but by the 1814 opening of Johnston's chapel royal at Dublin castle, cathedral claims to royal status were futile. Matthew Price's gentrifying neo-Gothic restoration (1831–3, 1842–6) was so unimpressive, that the restoration by G.E. Street (1871–8), funded by the Dublin whisky distiller, Henry Roe, swept it aside, entirely removing the old long choir. Roe also generously donated a synod hall to the newly disestablished Church of Ireland which Street cleverly built around the tower of the old St Michael's church. The twin towers of cathedral and synod hall (now an exhibition of medieval Dublin called Dublinia) linked by an elegant bridge is a fusion of medieval Gothic and Victorian idealism that today remains an iconic silhouette on the Dublin skyline.

Christ Church today is a major tourist attraction where people come to admire the beautiful building, with its Norman and Victorian features, and to visit the crypt with its important historical displays. Above all, of course, the cathedral remains a vibrant centre for worship and for important diocesan and civic events.

The bridge connecting the cathedral to the former synod hall, now the Viking and medieval Dublin exhibition, Dublinia.

# The United Dioceses of Dublin and Glendalough

ORLA RYAN & LYNN GLANVILLE

The united dioceses of Dublin and Glendalough are one of five diocesan units in the Church of Ireland province of Dublin. The archbishop of Dublin is bishop of Glendalough and primate of Ireland and metropolitan. The united dioceses are located in Leinster and take in County Dublin, County Wicklow and part of County Kildare. Although geographically relatively small, Church of Ireland members in the south are numerically most high in the capital and its surrounds – an area that integrates urban, sprawling suburban and rural components

## The Early Church

The early Irish church was primarily monastic and parish based. There were several monasteries in the Dublin and Wicklow area, but Glendalough ('the valley of the two lakes'), founded by St Kevin in the sixth century, was one of the most significant. The city of Dublin was founded by Vikings around AD 841. The Hiberno-Norse king of Dublin, Sitriuc (the first Christian king of the city), when visiting Rome in 1028, formally established the diocese of Dublin and its cathedral, Christ Church, under its first bishop, Dúnán or Donat.

Coin featuring Sitriuc

## The Medieval Period

A decision was made at a synod held in 1111 to divide Ireland into 24 dioceses in addition to the primatial see of Armagh. The diocese of Dublin was ignored in this regard as it was subject to Canterbury and not Armagh. However, in 1152, the pope sent a legate to Ireland to bestow pallia on the archbishop of Dublin as well as his counterparts in Armagh, Cashel and Tuam. The dioceses of Dublin and Glendalough were unified following the death of William Piro, the last bishop of Glendalough as a separate diocese, in 1214. The unification of the two dioceses was confirmed by Pope Honorius III in 1216.

The parish church of St Patrick was granted collegiate status by Archbishop John Comyn in 1191. His successor, Henry of London, raised the church's status to that of a cathedral, leaving Dublin in the unusual position of having two medieval cathedrals. The situation became convoluted and litigious, as an archbishop could not be appointed without the sanction of both cathedral chapters – each of whom proposed their own candidate. The year 1300 saw the drawing up

Remains of Medieval Abbey, Swo

Helmets displayed in St Patrick's Cathedral, Dublin
ALASTAIR SMEATON

of a *composicio pacis*, or peace agreement, which officially recognised both as diocesan cathedrals. This status remained until the 1870s.

Throughout the Middle Ages, England continued its attempts to anglicise the Irish people. In 1367, a law was introduced that made it illegal for Irishmen to hold office in the church in areas under English jurisdiction. As a result, all pre-Reformation archbishops were English, with the sole exception of the Anglo-Irishman Walter Fitzsimons (archbishop 1484–1511).

## Post-Reformation Times

In 1536, Henry VIII was declared the 'supreme head of the Church of Ireland' and all clergy had to take the Oath of Supremacy. Henry was a theologically traditional man but his reign also heralded the traumatic dissolution of monasteries throughout the land in 1539. The only exception in this regard was granted to Christ Church Cathedral, which retained its property. The prior (Robert Castle) and monks became dean and canons. During the sixteenth and seventeenth centuries, the cathedral's crypt was used as a market and, at one stage, a public house. A new cathedral constitution was drawn up in 1660.

'The Printing Office of Trinity College is situated on the north side of College Park. The University press was erected in 1734 under the munificence of Dr John Stearne, Bishop of Clogher, and Vice-Chancellor of the College. The College shared with the King's printer in Ireland the exclusive privilege of printing testaments and Bibles …'
DUBLIN PENNY JOURNAL 1835

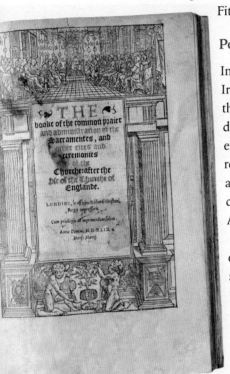

The 1549 Book of Common Prayer
RCB ARCHIVE

The Reformation in the sixteenth century split the Irish church. The established Church of Ireland was Protestant, state approved and supported. Nevertheless, the Roman Catholic Church was supported by the majority of the people, particularly outside of the Pale (an area which took in Dublin and part of its neighbouring counties), where the crown's authority was weakest.

The *Book of Common Prayer* (1549) was not widely available in Ireland until Henry Powell chose it to be the first publication he printed at the printing press he established on Dublin's Winetavern Street in 1551, the country's first. The book was used for the first time in Christ Church Cathedral on Easter Sunday of that year, making Dublin's archbishop, George Browne, one of the five members of the Irish episcopate to adopt the book (alongside the bishops of Meath, Kildare, Leighlin and Limerick).

Trinity College, Dublin was founded in 1592, during the tenure of Elizabeth I and had close connections with the established Church of Ireland. For most of the next two hundred years, Roman Catholics and dissenting Protestants were not able to attend the college. Women were not admitted until 1904.

Christ Church Cathedral, Dublin
ALASTAIR SMEATON

Score book Christ Church Cathedral, Dublin, 1795
RCB ARCHIVE

Monument to Sir Richard Boyle, Lord High Treasurer of the King's privy Coucil, and his wife Lady Katherine, Countess of Cork, in St Patrick's Cathedral, Dublin, 1629
ALASTAIR SMEATON

## The Seventeenth and Eighteenth Centuries

The expansion of Dublin in the reign of Charles II (1660–85) and into the early eighteenth century saw the subdivision of a number of parishes and the consequent building of new churches, particularly under Archbishop William King (archbishop 1703–29). The King's Hospital (the Bluecoat School) was founded in 1669. A number of church organisations were founded in the eighteenth and nineteenth centuries, including: an Irish branch of the Society for the Propagation of the Gospel in Foreign Parts in 1714; the Association for Promoting Christian Knowledge in 1792; the Sunday School Society for Ireland in 1809.

The penal laws implemented following the Williamite conquest (1689–91) banned Roman Catholics and dissenting Protestants from owning land, serving in any public office or the army, receiving education or intermarrying. The most austere of these laws had been repealed by the end of the eighteenth century. The passing of the Catholic Emancipation Act in 1829 allowed Roman Catholics to sit at Westminster.

## The Nineteenth Century

In 1833, the Church Temporalities Act was passed. This amalgamated several dioceses to leave two archbishops and ten bishops (reducing two archbishoprics, Cashel and Tuam, to bishoprics in the process). The act also united the diocese of Kildare, on the death of Bishop Charles Lindsay in 1846, with that of Dublin and Glendalough. Bishop Lindsay was also the dean of Christ Church, a position which had been jointly held since 1681. The act led to the amalgamation of the deaneries of the two cathedrals. This rationalisation freed up a considerable amount of money, which was earmarked to aid the restoration and building of churches and increase the income of clergy in poor parishes under the auspices of the newly founded Board of Ecclesiastical Commissioners (which supplanted the Board of First Fruits).

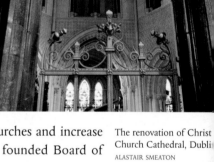

The renovation of Christ Church Cathedral, Dublin
ALASTAIR SMEATON

In 1869, William Ewart Gladstone put forward a bill for disestablishing the Anglican Church in Ireland. It was passed in both houses of parliament in July of that year and resulted in the disestablishment of the Church of Ireland on 1 January 1871.

In Dublin the act saw St Patrick's Cathedral deemed the national cathedral, while Christ Church became the cathedral of Dublin Diocese. The archbishop of Dublin, Richard Chenevix Trench, took the position of dean of Christ Church (later relinquished again to an independent dean in 1887).

The two cathedrals had major restorations carried out during the nineteenth century. Benjamin Guinness paid for reconstruction in St Patrick's from 1860 to 1865. The renovation at Christ Church (1871–8) was funded by Dublin whiskey distiller Henry Roe at a cost of £230,000.

Archbishop Richard Chenevix Trench
BELFAST CATHEDRAL

A statue of Benjamin Lee Guinness stands outside St Patrick's Cathedral, Dublin
ALASTAIR SMEATON

## Jonathan Swift, 1667–1745

BELFAST CATHEDRAL

Jonathan Swift, man of letters, political pamphleteer and Dean of St Patrick's Dublin, was born in Dublin and educated at Kilkenny College and Trinity College Dublin. In 1694, he took holy orders in the Church of Ireland, and was appointed to Kilroot parish in Co. Antrim. In 1699, he moved to Dublin before his appointment the following year as rector of Laracor, Co. Meath. In 1714, he became Dean of St Patrick's Cathedral, Dublin, where he remained until his death.

Swift was the author of a number of brilliant satirical works, including *Gulliver's travels*, *A tale of a tub*, and *The Battle of the books*. Much of his writing, often on pamphlet form, served to address social and economic problems of Ireland. In *A modest proposal* he attacked poverty in the country, while in *A proposal for the universal manufacture of Irish manufacture* and in *The drapier's letters* he supported strongly Irish interests against English misrule. This work gained him the title of 'Hibernian Patriot' and the freedom of the city.

At the same time, Swift supported the constitutional and material interests of the established church, and links between church and state which he saw as an essential part of the constitutional arrangements of the 'Glorious Revolution'. He attacked poverty and other social and political injustices but did not challenge legal disabilities against both dissenters and Roman Catholics.

ROBERT WELCH, ED., *The Oxford companion to Irish literature* (Oxford, 1996)

The work was carried out by the architect George Edmund Street, who also converted the old St Michael's Church into a hall for meetings of the General Synod, the Church of Ireland's new governing body. The growth of the Dublin suburbs in the nineteenth century led to the construction of many parish churches.

## The Twentieth Century

The twentieth century brought significant changes and challenges. During the First World War, many parishioners joined the ranks of the 200,000 Irishmen who volunteered to fight. Memorials in churches throughout the united dioceses attest to their bravery and loss. The 1916 Easter Rising, the War of Independence and the Civil War led to a new state and a new political environment. Although many were forced to leave and many others left because they did not like the changed conditions, the majority of Church of Ireland members in these dioceses stayed and were determined and happy to support the new government.

The next 50 years brought significant developments. Wise leadership from successive archbishops of Dublin ensured that the church faced the new challenges effectively. John Allen Fitzgerald Gregg was archbishop from 1920 to 1939. Arthur William Barton followed him, holding the office from 1939 to 1956, and George Otto Simms was archbishop from 1956 to 1969.

John Allen Fitzgerald Gregg, Archbishop of Dublin, 1920–39

In Dublin city during this time, the church faced various problems. A fall in overall numbers of the Church of Ireland population, especially among the Dublin working class, and also a movement of church members from inner Dublin to the suburbs, resulted in amalgamation and closure of city-centre churches and schools, while many suburban parishes flourished.

The social problems of Dublin brought an important response from church members such as Dr Kathleen Lynn, daughter of a Church of Ireland rector and a 1916 veteran, who founded and ran St Ultan's Hospital for Children. In June 1938, Douglas Hyde, son of a Church of Ireland rector and founder of the Gaelic League, was inaugurated as first president of Ireland. In July 1949, his funeral was held in St Patrick's Cathedral. Members of the Irish cabinet came to the cathedral but declined to enter, because of Catholic Church rules.

This window was erected in St Ann's, Dublin in memory of Ray Lancaster Bell, Lt 2nd Dublin Fusiliers, aged 19 years, killed at Ypres, 1915

Students and staff at the back of the Church of Ireland Divinity Hostel, Mountjoy Square, 1938

Changes in Irish society during and after the 1960s affected the fortunes of church members in these dioceses, as elsewhere in Ireland. The rise in ecumenism brought significant improvement in inter-church relations. On St Patrick's day 1972, Fr Michael Hurley S.J. became the first Roman Catholic priest since the Reformation to preach in St Patrick's Cathedral. In the early 1970s, all public commemorations on Remembrance Sunday were ended because of the threat of violence against the participants. St Patrick's

Church and State honour the Governor General, c. 1928: LEFT TO RIGHT, Professor John O'Sullivan, minister of education, Rev. James McCaughey, moderator of Dublin presbytery, W.T. Cosgrave, president of executive council, T.M. Healy, governor general, Archbishop Edward Byrne, Lord Glenavy, chairman of senate, Chief Justice Hugh Kennedy, and Archbishop John Gregg.

Archbishop Michael Jackson and Archbishop Diarmuid Martin carry a Taizé Cross on the Walk of Witness from Christ Church Cathedral to St Mary's Pro-Cathedral on Good Friday, 2013.

While some congregations are branching out and expressing the life and worship of the church in new and imaginative ways, others, particularly in the inner city, are experiencing a resurgence as they reach out to their communities and welcome the New Irish among them.

Cathedral, under the leadership of Dean Victor Griffin, became the focus for the principal commemoration of this event in the state, attended by members of the public from all denominations and ambassadors from many countries. Since 1993, this event has been attended by the Irish president.

## New Millennium

In 1977, Kildare Diocese was removed from Dublin and Glendalough and united with Meath. Dublin Diocese currently incorporates 41 parishes, unions or grouped parishes, while Glendalough comprises 15.

The twenty-first century has seen a reinvigoration within the church as it reaps the benefits of multiculturalism and warm ecumenical relations with other denominations and traditions. While some congregations are branching out and expressing the life and worship of the church in new and imaginative ways, others, particularly in the inner city, are experiencing a resurgence as they reach out to their communities and welcome the New Irish among them.

Peata Christmas Carol Service at Christ Church Cathedral, Dublin

An example of the strong ecumenical relations is the Walk of Witness, which now takes place through the streets of Dublin city centre on Good Friday, led by the Church of Ireland and Roman Catholic archbishops of Dublin. The procession took place for the first time at Easter 2012 and saw Archbishop Michael Jackson and his Roman Catholic counterpart, Archbishop Diarmuid Martin, carry a Taizé cross from Christ Church Cathedral to St Mary's Pro-Cathedral. The ecumenical event was a resounding success, with hundreds of people turning out to witness faith on the streets. The walk is now an annual fixture.

Mission and social action are now at the heart of the Church of Ireland community in Dublin and Glendalough. The dioceses have been finding new ways to reach people who are experiencing disadvantage or isolation. In 2012, the Dublin and Glendalough Diocesan Committee for Social Action split into two strands – one urban and one rural. The urban strand channels its energies primarily into the Solas Project, which works with inner city children and young people, while the rural strand tackles social exclusion and isolation.

RIGHT: Urban Soul
FAR RIGHT: The Solas Project

# PARISHES IN THE DIOCESE OF DUBLIN

PHOTOGRAPHS BY ALASTAIR SMEATON

### BOOTERSTOWN and MOUNT MERRION

*St Philip and St James' Church, Booterstown* was consecrated on 16 May 1824. It stood on land given by the eleventh earl of Pembroke. It was constructed to designs of John Bowden and finished after his death by Joseph Welland. At the time it was described as 'handsome, in the later English style, with a square embattled tower with crocketed pinnacles at the angles, and surmounted by a lofty spire'. Additions were made to the church later in the nineteenth century. The current school building was opened by Taoiseach Éamon de Valera. In the grounds of the church stand the Barrett Cheshire Home, the parish centre and the rectory.

    *St Thomas' Church, Mountmerrion* was opened for worship on 3 December 1874.

St Philip and St James', Booterstown

### BRAY

*Christ Church, Bray* was erected in 1863 to accommodate the bourgeoning population of the town, thanks to the the extension of the Dublin to Kingstown railway in 1854. It was built with local granite. The large spire came later in 1870, but it was not until 1880 that the peal of eight bells was hung. Legend has it that the impetus for the hanging of the bells came with a visit to Bray by William Ewart Gladstone in 1877. Gladstone is said to have remarked that 'so noble a church tower as this should not be silent'. In the grounds of the church is a memorial to Rev. James Scott and his son Rev. George Scott, who were rectors of the parish for an extraordinary 80 years, from 1863 to 1943.

Christ Church, Bray

### CASTLEKNOCK, MULHUDDART and CLONSILLA

The three parishes of Castleknock, Mulhuddart and Clonsilla have their origins in medieval times.

The present *St Brigid's Church, Castleknock* was completed in 1810 with the aid of a grant from the Board of First Fruits. The tower houses two bells, one cast in Dublin in 1855 and the other in Gloucester in 1747. The church is home to a stained-glass window designed by Harry Clarke in 1927 that depicts St George, St Hubert and St Luke. A president's pew is also present, as Áras an Uachtaráin lies just inside the parish boundary.

Mary's Church, Clonsilla
MARCASOCALLANAIN

    *St Thomas' Church, Mulhuddart.* By the nineteenth century, Mulhuddart Church had been in ruins for many years. A new church, to designs by Welland and Gillespie and dedicated to St Thomas the Apostle, was opened on 19 December 1871.

    *St Mary's Church, Clonsilla* stands on land believed to have an ecclesiastical history dating back to AD 500. The present church was built in 1845, while its tower was added in 1850. Acting on advice he had received from a medium, in 1907 Sir Arthur Vickers, the Ulster king at arms, came to Clonsilla to search for the stolen insignia of St Patrick (the Irish crown jewels). Despite this visit ending in failure, rumours still persist that the jewels are hidden somewhere in the grounds. St Fiacre is depicted in a stained-glass window designed by Evie Hone of An Túr Gloine, which was erected in the church in 1935. In 2005, an extension to *St Mary's* was completed, providing a parish centre.

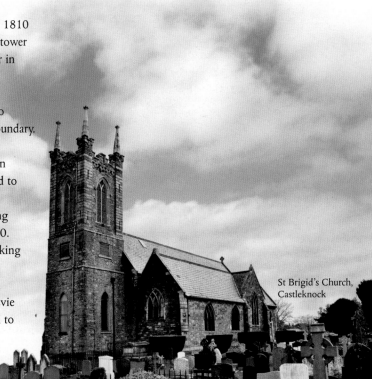

St Brigid's Church, Castleknock

## CHRIST CHURCH CATHEDRAL GROUP

*St Michan's Church, Church Street*, the oldest church within the Christ Church grouping, was dedicated in 1095 to serve the post-Clontarf Hiberno-Norse settlement of Oxmanstown. The church's medieval nave was rebuilt in 1685, while the Greek-revivalist interior largely dates from a restoration of 1828. Among the church plate is a gold chalice dating from 1516. St Michan's has strong links with music – its fine frieze of 17 musical instruments featured on the old £50 note, and the west gallery organ of 1725 (by Jean-Baptiste Cuvillé) is alleged to have been played by Handel. The church's vaults are famous for the mummified corpses that have been conserved owing to the fact that the magnesium salts in the limestone walls absorb moisture from the air. Notable figures associated with the church include Edmund Burke and Robert Emmet. The funeral service of Charles Stewart Parnell took place here in 1891.

St Michan's Church

*St Werburgh's Church, Werburgh Street* was built in 1716, but largely destroyed by fire in 1754. The interior dates from 1756. The church's tower was demolished in 1837 – it was considered a security risk as it provided a vantage point overlooking Dublin Castle. While serving as chapel royal of the viceregal court, it was one of the most fashionable Dublin churches. The viceregal pew, with its fine blazon of arms, can be seen in front of the organ (1766). The impressive pulpit by Francis Johnson, incorporating the arms of the bishoprics of Ireland, came from a later chapel at Dublin Castle. Famous parishioners included the composer John Field, and Lord Edward Fitzgerald, who died of wounds inflicted by Major Sirr on the eve of the 1798 Rebellion. By strange coincidence, Fitzgerald and Sirr lie buried within feet of each other.

St Weburgh's Church

*All Saints' Church, Grangegorman* began as a simple ailseless rectangle in the 'chess-piece' perpendicular-Gothic style of 1828. The Tractarian movement was an early influence on the parish through the long tenure of a leading high-church cleric, Dr William Maturin, perpetual curate from 1843 to 1887. Tractarianism inspired various additions, including the chancel in 1856 and the baptistery in 1889. The interior, richly decorated with wall paintings, stained glass and stencilling, was badly damaged by fire in 1966, but later restored. A succession of rectors, in particular Raymond Jenkins (1939–74), have sought to maintain the sacramental and devotional ethos of the church. Today, a choir of 20 local people advance the work of devoted predecessors such as Victor Leeson, organist from 1943 until 1987.

All Saints Grangegorman

## CLONDALKIN

*St John's Church, Clondalkin* stands in an area of south Dublin with strong connections to the early Christian church, as seen in its fine eighth-century high-tower with its original conical cap. The present St John's was built in 1789 and substantially extended in 1854 by Joseph Welland. There are some remains of a medieval monastery in the church grounds.

*Rathcoole Church* was consecrated on 1 April 1738. The church had strong connections to the Kennedy family of the neighbouring Beech Park estate.

St John's Church, Clondalkin

Rathcoole Church

## CLONTARF

Clontarf is reputed to have had close links in the early Christian period to St Comgall of Bangor. *St John the Baptist's Church, Clontarf* was consecrated in 1866 to replace an earlier church, built in the early seventeenth century. This new and larger church was required for the growing suburban population. The period from the 1930s to the 1940s saw another building boom in this area, which created a large Church of Ireland population. In 2007 a new parish centre was built in the grounds of the church.

## CORE ST CATHERINE'S

The year 2013 marks the twentieth anniversary of CORE, an evangelical and charismatic expression within the Church of Ireland, located at St Catherine's Church in inner-city Dublin. CORE stands for City Outreach through Renewal and Evangelism, and was started in 1993. In 1998, the group moved into their new home on Thomas Street. *St Catherine's Church, Thomas Street*, built in the 1760s and now beautifully refurbished, was the first Church of Ireland church to be reconsecrated in the modern era, following its closure in 1966. There has been significant growth over the past few years. The Sunday morning congregation has risen to around 200, with a large number of children and young adults attending. Over 20 nationalities are represented in the diverse congregation, with more people attending from within the local community. Part of the vision for St Catherine's in the coming years is to be a hub for the local community, a place for people from all walks of life to gather for music, arts, education, friendship and spiritual renewal.

## CRINKEN

*St James's Church, Crinken* near Shankill in South Dublin was consecrated on 16 October 1840. The architect was William Farrell. This church was one of a number erected in the south Dublin/north Wicklow area at this time by some prominent evangelicals, including Lady Powerscourt. The church has maintained a strong evangelical tradition. In 2011 and 2012, children from the parish raised significant sums of money for the faith-based charity Fields of Life, which seeks to provide drinking water in deprived areas of the developing world. The rector at this time was Rev. Trevor Stevenson, founder of Fields of Life.

## CRUMLIN and CHAPELIZOD

The parish of Crumlin had medieval links to St Patrick's Cathedral. The present *St Mary's Church, Crumlin* was built in the mid-twentieth century, to replace a building dating from 1817. The landmark yellow-brick building at Dolphin's Barn was consecrated by Archbishop Arthur Barton on 15 July 1942 and has been described as 'remarkably innovative' in its style. The architects and designers, Messrs McDonnell, Dixon and Crosby, combined modern and art-deco features.

St Laurence's Church, Chapelizod acquired its name from the third-century martyr whose moniker also once labelled the townland of Palmerstown Parish and a local twelfth-century infirmary. The early Victorian church as it now stands was consecrated on 6 June 1840. It possesses a distinguishing feature in the shape of a much older rectangular bell tower enveloping a round tower, reputedly built in the fourteenth century.

St Laurence's Church, Chapelizod

St Mary's Church, Crumlin

## DALKEY

*St Patrick's Church, Dalkey.* In 1836, a committee was formed to build a church to serve the growing population of Dalkey and Sandycove. A site was procured from the Ballast Office (now Dublin Port Company), adjoining their quarry, which supplied stone for Dublin's quay walls. The ashlar granite for the church was quarried and cut on the site. Architect Jacob Owen's design featured tall Gothic lancet windows and tower openings. The church was

consecrated in August 1868. The present floor plan was designed by Edward Carson (father of Sir Edward Carson) in 1879. The stone arcading around the east end was placed there as a memorial to those who fell in World War I.

A major redevelopment in 1999, designed by David Jordan, added a new four-teacher school and additional meeting rooms linked to the church. The Northover Hall was named to honour the chief parish benefactor for this project.

St Patrick's Church, Dalkey

## DONNYBROOK and IRISHTOWN

Donnybrook (meaning 'the church of St Broc') originated in the eighth century.

The present *St Mary's Church, Donnybrook* was rebuilt in 1726 in the centre of the village of Donnybrook. Population growth meant that the church had to be rebuilt once more in 1830 on the present site in Simmonscourt. The architect was John Semple of the Board of First Fruits. The church's spire was removed in 1839, while a chancel, transepts and vestry were added in 1859–60. The communion silver dates from 1693 and the font is dated 1729. The parish records are almost complete from 1712. As the population rose, daughter parishes were separated from Donnybrook.

*St Matthew's Royal Chapel, Irishtown* became the church of Irishtown Parish in 1872. *St Matthew's* had been built in 1704 for the seafarers and fishermen of this port area. It was enlarged in 1879.

St Matthew's Chapel, Irishtown

St Mary's Church, Donnybrook

St John the Baptist's Church, Drumcondra

St Barnabas's Church, North Strand

291

## DRUMCONDRA and NORTH STRAND

The present *St John the Baptist's Church, Drumcrondra* was rebuilt in 1743 at the expense of Miss Mary Coghill of Drumcondra House. The churchyard is the final resting place of a number of luminaries, including: the renowned architect James Gandon, designer of Dublin's Custom House and the Four Courts; Patrick Heeney, composer of the music for 'The Soldier's Song', now the Irish national anthem; and members of the Jameson whiskey-distilling family. The present-day church was built in 1838.

The origins of *North Strand Church* can be traced back to a Sunday and day school that was established in 1786. Services commenced in the present church in 1840. *St Barnabas's Church, North Strand* was consecrated in 1870 and eventually closed in 1965. The playwright Sean O'Casey was among its parishioners.

## DÚN LAOGHAIRE

The completion of Dún Laoghaire (formerly Kingstown) Harbour in the 1820s and the opening of the Dublin to Kingstown railway in 1834 gave rise to a large increase in population, turning a sleepy fishing village into a large residential area. Within the next 20 years, a number of Anglican churches were built, where previously there had been only one, namely Monkstown Parish Church.

*Christ Church, Dún Laoghaire* was built in 1836. It was originally called Bethel Episcopal Free Chapel. When it was extended in 1870 by the addition of two transepts and a chancel, it was renamed *Christ Church*.

The Mariners' Church, Dún Laoghaire

Recently, the rise in homelessness and other problems in the current recession has led to an initiative by church members to provide assistance. In September 2012, three parishioners started work on the No Buck's Café, a mobile café operated by Tiglin, an organisation that helps people overcome and find life beyond addiction. The bus travels to four different locations each week, stopping at Eblana Avenue in Dún Laoghaire on one night. The volunteers feed and talk to homeless people, with some people bringing food and some serving it. Clothes and sleeping bags are also distributed when available.

The *Mariners' Church, Dún Laoghaire* was erected in the town in 1843 to meet the spiritual needs of the seafarers of the area. In the 1950s, the Mariners' Church was grouped with Christ Church and the church was finally closed in 1972. It now houses the National Maritime Museum of Ireland.

## GLENAGEARY

*St Paul's Church, Glenageary*, situated on the corner of Silchester and Adelaide Roads, is one of a number of churches that were built in the old parish of Monkstown. St Paul's was consecrated in July 1868. The building was funded by Jane Shannon, originally of Belfast, who is commemorated in the church with by a window in the west wall of the transept, now the Memorial Chapel. St Paul's is built in the Gothic style. The tower in the south-west corner is 120 feet tall. The architect was A. Jones. The church's organ was built by Messrs Andrews and Foster of Hull in 1869, and then rebuilt in 1993 under the direction of parish organist Derek Verso. In May 2007, the new parish centre, situated in the grounds of the church, was opened by the then-president of Ireland, Mary McAleese..

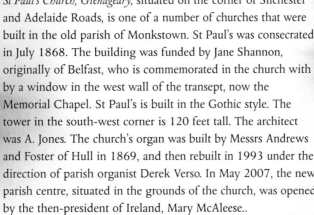

St Paul's Church, Glenageary

Christ Church, Dún Laoghaire

## HOLMPATRICK, BALBRIGGAN and KENURE

*Holmpatrick Church, Skerries* was consecrated on 2 September 1868. It was built from limestone from Milverton Quarries. In the graveyard are the ruins of an earlier church. Some of the memorials from this earlier church are in the new building.

*St George's Church, Balbriggan* was consecrated on 20 October 1816, but suffered a serious fire in 1835. The church was then restored and enlarged, in a more Gothic style. Again, in 1862, Welland and Gillespie carried out improvements to the church. The main window behind the altar was created in memory of Thomas Edward Taylor of Ardgillan Castle, MP for County Dublin for an amazing 42 years (1841–83).

Kenure Church, Rush

*Kenure Church, Rush,* designed by J.E. Rogers, was built in 1866 by Sir William Palmer.

St George's Church, Balbriggan

Holmpatrick Church, Skerries

## KILL O' THE GRANGE

*Kill O' the Grange Church,* was consecrated in 1864. It was one of a number of churches built in south County Dublin to cater for increased numbers of members of the Church of Ireland living in the area, due to the building of the railways. Then, in the 1960s, economic expansion under Sean Lemass, a new influx of parishioners came into the district. Recent years have seen restoration work on the church and a new building for Kill national school.

Kill O' the Grange Church

St Mary's Church, Howth

## HOWTH

The impressive ruins of St Mary's Abbey, built in the fourteenth century, overlook the harbour in Howth. The present *St Mary's Church* was consecrated on 3 July 1866 to replace an earlier church, consecrated on 27 October 1816.

## KILLINEY (BALLYBRACK)

In the nineteenth century, Dún Laoghaire pier was built and the railway line was extended from Dublin to Bray. This encouraged wealthy people to move to the district of Killiney. *Killiney Church,* on Church Road, was designed by the architect Frederick Darley. In April 1835, it was consecrated and described as being 'in the later English style ... built of the white granite that is found in great abundance locally; at the east end is an embattled tower with pinnacles'. The chancel and transepts were added in the 1870s under the supervision of Welland and Gillespie Architects. In 1887, a parish hall, which would later become a designated first-aid post during the 'Emergency' in 1941, was built. Three adjacent parishes, St Matthias's, Holy Trinity and Glenageary, established a jointly managed primary school in 1973 at Wyvern.

Killiney Church

## KILLINEY (HOLY TRINITY)

*Holy Trinity Church* answered the need for a second Killiney church. Churchgoers proved ready to participate in the building process, particularly Robert Warren, the owner of what is today the Fitzpatrick Castle Hotel, who gave the site and contributed largely towards the church's funding. Designed by Sandham Symes, it opened on 15 May 1859. Among the church's notable internal features are its stained-glass windows, among them *The Angel of Peace and Hope* (1918), designed by Harry Clarke, and the west window, which depict the annunciation and crucifixion. In 1958, the Carry Hall, built on land given by the Kirwan family, was opened. This facility enabled the development of local youth organisations such as the Guides and the Sunday Club. The parish's Garden of Remembrance was opened in 1995.

Holy Trinity Church

## CLONDALKIN

*St John's Church, Clondalkin* stands in an area of south Dublin with strong connections to the early Christian church, as seen in its fine eighth-century high-tower with its original conical cap. The present St John's was built in 1789 and substantially extended in 1854 by Joseph Welland. There are some remains of a medieval monastery in the church grounds.

*Rathcoole Church* was consecrated on 1 April 1738. The church had strong connections to the Kennedy family of the neighbouring Beech Park estate.

St John's Church, Clondalkin

Rathcoole Church

## CLONTARF

Clontarf is reputed to have had close links in the early Christian period to St Comgall of Bangor. *St John the Baptist's Church, Clontarf* was consecrated in 1866 to replace an earlier church, built in the early seventeenth century. This new and larger church was required for the growing suburban population. The period from the 1930s to the 1940s saw another building boom in this area, which created a large Church of Ireland population. In 2007 a new parish centre was built in the grounds of the church.

## CORE ST CATHERINE'S

The year 2013 marks the twentieth anniversary of CORE, an evangelical and charismatic expression within the Church of Ireland, located at St Catherine's Church in inner-city Dublin. CORE stands for City Outreach through Renewal and Evangelism, and was started in 1993. In 1998, the group moved into their new home on Thomas Street. *St Catherine's Church, Thomas Street*, built in the 1760s and now beautifully refurbished, was the first Church of Ireland church to be reconsecrated in the modern era, following its closure in 1966. There has been significant growth over the past few years. The

Sunday morning congregation has risen to around 200, with a large number of children and young adults attending. Over 20 nationalities are represented in the diverse congregation, with more people attending from within the local community. Part of the vision for St Catherine's in the coming years is to be a hub for the local community, a place for people from all walks of life to gather for music, arts, education, friendship and spiritual renewal.

## CRINKEN

*St James's Church, Crinken* near Shankill in South Dublin was consecrated on 16 October 1840. The architect was William Farrell. This church was one of a number erected in the south Dublin/north Wicklow area at this time by some prominent evangelicals, including Lady Powerscourt. The church has maintained a strong evangelical tradition. In 2011 and 2012, children from the parish raised significant sums of money for the faith-based charity Fields of Life, which seeks to provide drinking water in deprived areas of the developing world. The rector at this time was Rev. Trevor Stevenson, founder of Fields of Life.

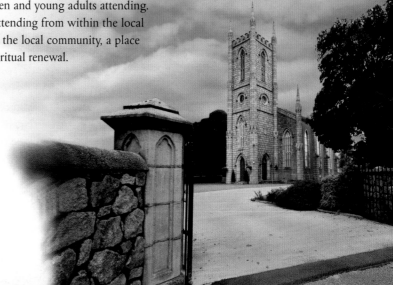

## CRUMLIN and CHAPELIZOD

The parish of Crumlin had medieval links to St Patrick's Cathedral. The present *St Mary's Church, Crumlin* was built in the mid-twentieth century, to replace a building dating from 1817. The landmark yellow-brick building at Dolphin's Barn was consecrated by Archbishop Arthur Barton on 15 July 1942 and has been described as 'remarkably innovative' in its style. The architects and designers, Messrs McDonnell, Dixon and Crosby, combined modern and art-deco features.

St Laurence's Church, Chapelizod acquired its name from the third-century martyr whose moniker also once labelled the townland of Palmerstown Parish and a local twelfth-century infirmary. The early Victorian church as it now stands was consecrated on 6 June 1840. It possesses a distinguishing feature in the shape of a much older rectangular bell tower enveloping a round tower, reputedly built in the fourteenth century.

St Mary's Church, Crumlin

St Laurence's Church, Chapelizod

## DALKEY

*St Patrick's Church, Dalkey.* In 1836, a committee was formed to build a church to serve the growing population of Dalkey and Sandycove. A site was procured from the Ballast Office (now Dublin Port Company), adjoining their quarry, which supplied stone for Dublin's quay walls. The ashlar granite for the church was quarried and cut on the site. Architect Jacob Owen's design featured tall Gothic lancet windows and tower openings. The church was

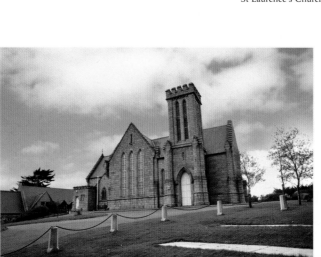

consecrated in August 1868. The present floor plan was designed by Edward Carson (father of Sir Edward Carson) in 1879. The stone arcading around the east end was placed there as a memorial to those who fell in World War I.

A major redevelopment in 1999, designed by David Jordan, added a new four-teacher school and additional meeting rooms linked to the church. The Northover Hall was named to honour the chief parish benefactor for this project.

St Patrick's Church, Dalkey

## DONNYBROOK and IRISHTOWN

Donnybrook (meaning 'the church of St Broc') originated in the eighth century.

The present *St Mary's Church, Donnybrook* was rebuilt in 1726 in the centre of the village of Donnybrook. Population growth meant that the church had to be rebuilt once more in 1830 on the present site in Simmonscourt. The architect was John Semple of the Board of First Fruits. The church's spire was removed in 1839, while a chancel, transepts and vestry were added in 1859–60. The communion silver dates from 1693 and the font is dated 1729. The parish records are almost complete from 1712. As the population rose, daughter parishes were separated from Donnybrook.

*St Matthew's Royal Chapel, Irishtown* became the church of Irishtown Parish in 1872. *St Matthew's* had been built in 1704 for the seafarers and fishermen of this port area. It was enlarged in 1879.

St Matthew's Chapel, Irishtown

St Mary's Church, Donnybrook

## KILTERNAN

*Kilternan Parish Church* in south county Dublin lies under the shadow of Three Rock Mountain, at the north-eastern margin of the Wicklow Mountain range. There has been a Christian presence in the area since at least 1185, when the lands of Kilternan were in the possession of St Mary's Abbey in Dublin. The present church of Kilternan was designed by John Semple in his characteristic slender, Gothic style. The church was consecrated on 10 December 1826. The parish also possesses a fine collection of silver, dating from 1760 to 1970. A Department of Education proposal in 1970 advising the amalgamation of Kilternan National School (1922) with the national school in Dundrum was vigorously opposed and eventually defeated. The school has flourished in recent times; a new building was erected in 1985 and extended in 2007. In 2000, the parish ceded a 3.2-acre field to Cowper Care Ltd for a nursing home and sheltered housing. The Kilternan Care Centre was opened in 2007, providing high-quality nursing for 48 residents. It is surrounded by a crescent of 22 houses offering sheltered independent living.

Kilternan Parish Church

## MALAHIDE, BALGRIFFIN

*St Andrew's Church, Malahide* was built in 1822, funded by a grant from the Board of First Fruits and a donation from the Talbot family, and enlarged in 1870. The church was further expanded in 2004, with the addition of St Marnock's Chapel, as well as a new entrance. The year 2004 saw the opening of a new parish centre, which is home to some 25 parish and community organisations.

*St Doulagh's Church, Balgriffin* dates in part to around 1140 and can claim to be the oldest church in Ireland in regular weekly use. Christian usage of the site by the anchorite (hermit) and teacher after which it is named, Doulagh, can be traced back to the sixth century. At the entrance to the church stands a granite cross (suggesting a pre-1300 date). The church was restored and reconsecrated in 1865. The anchorite's cell is directly under the prior's chamber, and they are connected by a spiral staircase. St Doulagh's Well and St Catherine's Pond are located adjacent to the church. The well is unique in that it is the only extant detached baptistery in the country.

St Andrew's Church, Malahide

St Doulagh's Church, Balgriffin

## MONKSTOWN

The building of Dún Laoghaire Harbour (begun in 1817) and the opening of the railway in 1834 led to a mushrooming population and the need for larger church than the existing one, built in the 1780s.

The present *Monkstown Church*, designed by diocesan architects John Semple & Son and seating 1,200, opened in 1831. It was a spectacular modification of the 1789 church. The Semples knocked down the east end and added two huge transepts to the west end, creating a T-shaped building. In the 1860s, the layout in Monkstown was altered and Victorian interiors were added. In 1883, Thomas Drew installed a reredos and stone arcading. The church contains more than 50 wall monuments. Monkstown has a long history of charitable work and social outreach. The Pim sisters founded the Mission to Lepers in 1874, while Canon Billy Wynne, then rector, founded the Samaritans in the Irish Republic in 1970. Following its setup in 1984, the Diocesan Employment Bureau operated from the Knox Hall for almost 20 years, finding jobs for up to 1,000 people.

Monkstown Church

St John the Evangelist's Church, Coolock

## RAHENY and COOLOCK

*All Saints' Church, Raheny* was dedicated on 16 December 1889. The building, which replaced an earlier church, was paid for by Lord Ardilaun, who lived in the nearby St Anne's Estate. The architect was George Ashlin. Recent years have seeen extensive restoration work to the church.

*St John the Evangelist's Church, Coolock* was consecrated on 21 September 1760. Originally located in a rural setting, major urban development in the area in recent decades has resulted in a large growth in the congregation.

All Saints' Church, Raheny

## RATHMICHAEL

Rathmichael is believed to have links with the Patrician church. Constituted a parish in the thirteenth century, with links to St Patrick's Cathedral, there was no church in the area from the restoration until the mid-nineteenth century. To cater for a growing population, local landlord Sir Charles Domville provided land for a church building. Rathmichael Parish National School, established in 1825, is a 12-teacher school. The newly built *Rathmichael Church* was consecrated by Archbishop Richard Trench on 12 December 1864.

Rathmichael Church

## RATHFARNHAM

Records show that a church has existed here since the early thirteenth century. This was confirmed by the discovery some years ago of a decorated granite slab dating to pre-Norman times, now in the parish centre. A parish school was built adjacent to the church in the early nineteenth century. The school has since been relocated to Washington Lane and the new parish centre incorporates the original building. The parochial hall, Rathfarnham War Memorial Hall, is situated in Terenure and was built in memory of those of all denominations in the district who fought in the First World War. Like the church, the memorial hall has been extended and renovated, most recently in 2009. Whilst many of the stained-glass windows date from the nineteenth century, three modern windows have been installed. They were designed and made by parishioner Dr Joan Forsdyke. The present *St Peter's and St Paul's Church, Rathfarnham*, is a plain rectangular building. It was consecrated on 7 June 1795, though it has since been enlarged with many additions.

St Peter's and Paul's Church, Rathfarnham

## RATHMINES

*Holy Trinity Church, Rathmines*, designed by John Semple, dates from 1828. In the mid-1880s the building was extended to accommodate a growing congregation. On its centenary in 1928, following the First World War and Irish independence, the parish noted a decline in its congregation. This decline continued throughout the twentieth century as newer suburbs developed. In 1990, the building was adapted to meet the needs of a smaller congregation and became a multipurpose parish centre with a worship area to accommodate about 250 people. It contains a lauded stained-glass window in the north transept by Michael Healy of An Túr Gloine. Among its notable parishioners was Dr Kathleen Lynn, daughter of a rector in County Mayo and medical officer for the Irish Citizen Army in 1916, who surrendered City Hall in Dublin to the British authorities. Her interest was in the medical care of the poor in Dublin and she went on to found St Ultan's Children's Hospital. *Harold's Cross Church*, at the gate of Mount Jerome Cemetery, was opened in 1837. It closed in June 2001 and reopened as a Russian Orthodox church.

Holy Trinity Church, Rathmines

Bram Stoker, St Ann's Church

## ST ANN'S

St Ann's Parish was created in 1707 at a time when the eighteenth-century Dublin suburbs were beginning to envelop the site provided for the church by Sir Joshua Dawson, from whom the name of the street is derived.

The building of *St Ann's Church, Dawson Street* did not commence immediately, but was described as being 'well advanced' in 1721. The present imposing neo-Romanesque front of 1868 was designed by Sir Thomas Deane. The Georgian interior was designed by the architect Isaac Wills. There is believed to be more stained glass per square metre in St Ann's than in any other church in Dublin; some of it was created by members of An Túr Gloine. Another notable feature of the church is the bread shelf located by the choir. Since 1723, the shelves have contained loaves of bread for the poor of the city by bequest of Lord Newtown of Newtownbutler. The bread can be removed without risk of question and, although this seldom happens today, the charity still exists and is continued in the Black Santa Appeal, which raises funds each Christmas for charities working with those in need. The church also incorporates a number of memorials, including a reredos commemorating 32 men who died in World War I. Many famous people have been associated with the church, among them Theobald Wolfe Tone, co-founder of the United Irishmen, who was married here in 1785, as was Bram Stoker, author of *Dracula*. Thomas Barnardo, the founder of the Barnardo's children's organisation, went to Sunday school in the parish, while the Irish writer and poet Oscar Wilde was baptised on 26 April 1885 in St Mark's Parish, now united with St Ann's.

*St Stephen's Church, Upper Mount Street* was consecrated on 5 December 1824. Designed by John Bowden, the building is famed for its iconic copper domed cupola and has been known to generations of Dubliners as the 'Pepper-Canister Church' because of its distinctive shape. Sir Charles Villiers Stanford (1852–1924), the eminent composer and conductor, received his early musical education as a member of the choir. The poet William Butler Yeats was also associated with the parish; the funeral of his artist brother Jack Yeats took place in the church on 30 March 1957.

St Stephen's Church

## ST BARTHOLOMEW'S with CHRIST CHURCH

*St Bartholomew's Church, Clyde Road*, the vision of the architect Thomas Wyatt, was consecrated in 1867. The building was conceived as a jewel of Gothic-revivalist architecture with sumptuous features both inside and out. Many of the interior original features are still intact, such as the elaborate mosaics, the fresco scheme and the iron choir screen. Later important additions include a set of fine stained-glass windows by Catherine O'Brien of An Túr Gloine. The church is celebrated for its fine music: the choirs of men and boys or men and girls continue to sing at services throughout the year and the repertoire is fully representative of the major styles of choral music from the sixteenth century up to the present day. The church maintains a liturgical tradition that is broadly related to that of the Anglo-Catholic tradition which stems from the Tractarian movement of the 1830s.

*Christ Church, Leeson Park* is the second church in the parish.

St Bartholomew's Church

## ST CATHERINE and ST JAMES
## WITH ST AUDEON

In 2012, the inner-city St Catherine's and St James's Parish with St Audoen's came into being. Formerly the St Patrick's Cathedral Group of Parishes, in 2010 it was deemed that the parish was able to exist on its own. A resolution at General Synod that year allowed the group to become a union under one incumbent. In the 1950s and 1960s, the parish experienced serious depopulation as people moved to the suburbs, and declining numbers saw a number of churches being grouped around the two Dublin cathedrals. On gaining independence, Canon Mark Gardener, who had been vicar of the St Patrick's Cathedral Group, became rector of the new parish. Much else stayed the same, but the parishioners were now able to manage their own affairs. *St Catherine's and St James's Church, Donore Avenue*, opened in 1897, now hosts a flourishing congregation in an increasingly vibrant area of Dublin's south inner city.

In the medieval *St Audoen's Church, Cornmarket*, Sunday services are maintained.

St Catherine's and
St James's Church

St Audoen's Church

## ST GEORGE and ST THOMAS'

St George's and St Thomas' Parish covers a large geographical area from O'Connell Street East to Commons Road and north to Phibsborough, taking in significant landmarks such as Croke Park and part of the Dublin docklands. It is an amalgamation of a number of city-centre parishes, namely St George's, St Aidan's and the Free Church, which were closed due to declining numbers. St George's was designed by Francis Johnston and consecrated in 1814. It closed in 1990.

The original St Thomas' Church was consecrated in 1762. The design was from one by Andrea Palladio and, at the time, the building was considered to have the most beautiful façade of any church in the city. On 6 July 1922, during the Irish Civil War, the church was completely destroyed.

*St Thomas' Church, Cathal Brugha Street.* The architect of the present church, consecrated in 1931, which was built in the Lombardic style, was Fredrick G. Hicks. His work on the church led him to receive the gold medal of the Royal Institute of Architects. The excellence of design shown in the original building was sustained when a wooden insertion at the back of the church won a special prize in the Royal Institute of the Architects of Ireland Awards in 2009. The current community includes people from many diverse backgrounds and nationalities, and the parish's current rector, Rev. Obinna Ulogwara, is the diocesan chaplain to the international community.

St Thomas' Church

St George's Church, Hardwicke Place

## SANDFORD and MILLTOWN

At present, Sandford and Milltown Parishes each have a vibrant Sunday school and both are served by active and enthusiastic Guide and Scout troops, a youth group (linked with Methodist Centenary Church) and a well-supported parish social group aptly named the Sandmillers.

*Sandford Church* was built in 1826, thanks to the initiative of local banker and evangelist Robert Newenham. Its architects, Lanyon, Lynn and Lanyon of Belfast, were inspired by Romanesque churches in northern Italy. Some 40 years later, the church was enlarged to accommodate the growing population and the new front incorporated the fine rose window we see today. The Harry Clarke stained-glass window with its striking depictions of St Peter and St Paul was added in the 1920s and is complemented by the 2011 addition of the St Francis window, designed by George Walsh.

*St Philip's Church, Milltown* was aptly consecrated on St Philip's and St James's day in 1867. The church was designed by Sir Thomas Drew on a site given by Lord Palmerston. It was originally intended to seat 200 but was extended by the addition of a side aisle in 1878. The building has various stained-glass windows, one of the most notable being the war memorial *Sacrifice, Peace, Victory* by Alfred Child, added in 1920.

Sandford Church

## SANDYMOUNT

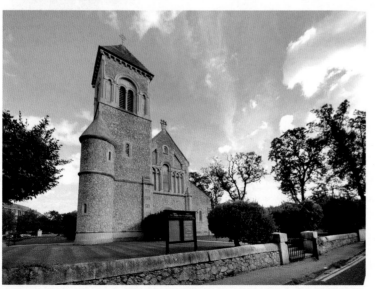

*St John the Evangelist Church's, Sandymount* was built in 1850. It was funded by Sidney Herbert, brother of the earl of Pembroke. The architect was Benjamin Ferrey, pupil and biographer of A.W.N. Pugin. Unusually for the time, Ferrey chose a neo-Romanesque style. The church contains windows by Joshua Clarke (father of the renowned window designer Harry Clarke). St John's has always been associated with the Anglo-Catholic tradition. Ferrey's original exterior included sculpted beasts, but the then-archbishop, Richard Whately, ordered their removal before the church might be consecrated. The course of the Anglo-Catholic tradition has not run smoothly at St John's. In 1937, the then-vicar, Rev. S.R.S. Colquhoun, was brought before a consistory court, consisting of three bishops and four judges (three from the north and one from the south) over certain high-church practices, including stations of the cross. The court suspended Rev. S.R.S. Colquhoun for six months and the stations of the cross were removed. Fortunately, the stations were rediscovered some 60 years later and returned to St John's, where they now hang.

## SANTRY, GLASNEVIN and FINGLAS

The small rural parish of Santry was transformed as the city spread northwards and the airport developed. Santry also incorporates the former parish of Cloghran.

*St Pappan's Church, Santry* is dedicated to the sixth-century hermit St Pappan, whose holy well is located near the parish hall. The present church was

St Pappan's Church, Santry

built in 1709. It boasts a fine carved altarpiece of that period and memorials to the lords of Santry. St Pappan's contains a small number of stained-glass windows. One is of patterned glass (from the mid-nineteenth century, commemorating Lady Helena Domville, who redesigned Santry as a Swiss village) and three creations from An Túr Gloine (from the 1920s and 1930s, in memory of the Poë family and Charles Vernon, who died in the First World War).

In 1994, the Blessed Margaret Ball Chapel was opened as a chapel-of-ease to Whitehall Roman Catholic Church, and the two congregations worship together from time to time.

St Mobhi's Church, Glasnevin

Among the many prominent names associated with Glasnevin Parish are Dr Patrick Delaney, sometime rector and friend of Jonathan Swift, whose home, Delville, is now the Bons Secours Hospital. *St Mobhi's Church, Glasnevin* commemorates a famous early saint of that name. A medieval tower was renovated in the seventeenth century and amalgamated with the present-day church when it was built in the eighteenth century, housing the baptistery. The church was enlarged and altered at the end of the nineteenth century.

*St Canice's Church, Finglas* is a small country church of the 1840s with later alterations, which contains some beautiful monuments from the earlier building, including commandment boards.

St Canice's Church, Finglas

St David's Church, Kilsallaghan
COLIN BOYLE

## SWORDS and DONABATE

St Columba's Church, Swords

Swords in north County Dublin was an important monastic site with links to St Columba. There are remains of a fourteenth-century medieval Norman square tower on the site of the parish church – the only surviving portion of the medieval abbey that once stood there.

The present *St Columba's Church, Swords* was built between 1811 and 1817, under the architect William Farrell.

*St. Patrick's Church, Donabate* was built around 1775. It came under the benefaction of the Cobbe family of Newbridge House around 1754. The ornate plasterwork of the ceiling in the balcony dates is copied from ceiling plasterwork in Newbridge House.

Worship has been offered on the site of *St David's Church, Kilsallaghan* since the late twelfth century. The present building was built in 1811 and dedicated to St David, patron saint of Wales. The structure conforms to the Gothic-revival style, with a castellated entrance tower at its western end.

St Patrick's Church, Donabate
COLIN BOYLE

## TALLAGHT

Until the latter half of the twentieth century, Tallaght parish was a rural one. Since then, the population of Tallaght has grown to over 70,000. The parish has benefitted from this growth, welcoming, among others, members of African and Indian communities to its worship. Until 1980, it was joined with Clondalkin and Rathcoole, but then became an independent parish. *St Maelruain's Church, Tallaght* stands on the site of a monastic settlement founded in the late eighth century by the saint of the same name. The present church, probably the third on the site, was designed by John Semple. It was consecrated on 1 November 1829. It is in Gothic style, decorated with buttresses, pinnacles and narrow lancet windows.

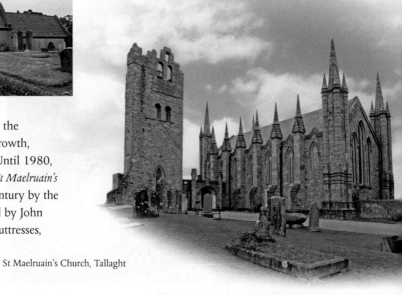

St Maelruain's Church, Tallaght

## TANEY

Tradition has it that St Nathi established a monastery on a hill in this parish in the eighth century. *Christ Church, Taney* (built in 1818), with its striking four-pinnacled tower, stands on one of the highest points in south Dublin, overlooking the village of Dundrum. From the Gothic-style tower, the famous peal of eight bells (originally held in St George's Church, Dublin and reinstalled in Taney in time for the new millennium) rings out every Sunday. The church's striking appearance represents a relatively recent phase of Taney's history linked to the expansion of suburban Dublin and its growing population.

Christ Church, Taney

The present *St Nahi's Church* was consecrated on 8 June 1760. Restored in the twentieth century in Celtic-revival style, its interior features needlework pictures by Misses Yeats, sisters of poet W.B. Yeats, of the Dun Emer craft studio. The font, which was moved from *St Kevin's Church*, is the one in which Arthur Wellesley, later to become the duke of Wellington, was baptised on 30 April 1769. The window, whose central panel portrays the Annunciation, is by An Túr Gloine's Evie Hone.

St Nahi's Church with the Luas Bridge

## TULLOW

There are twelfth-century monastic ruins in the area covered by this parish. *Tullow Church, Carrickmines* was consecrated on 14 April 1864. The erection of this new church was necessitated by a sudden rise in population after 1854, when a railway station was built at Foxrock. The church was extended in 1904. A war memorial on the exterior front wall of the church lists the names of 13 male parishioners, plus one female, Sophia Violet Barrett, who gave their lives in 'the cause of freedom and justice'.

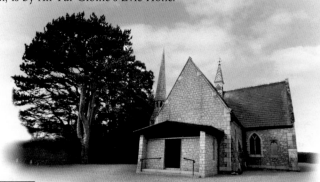

Tullow Church, Carrickmines

## WHITECHURCH

The twelfth-century ruins of the 'Old Whitechurch' church on Whitechurch Road contain two decorated slab stones of Viking Christian origin. The early 1820s saw the procurement of a new site for a church, school and teacher's residence on Whitechurch Road. From the 1980s onwards, what had originally been a largely rural parish experienced major urban development. In response, a new national school was built and opened in 1990 on a freshly-purchased site. An extension was added in 2008. In 1997–8, the old national school was restored and extended, to serve as a community facility.

In 1827, *Whitechurch Church*, known as 'New Whitechurch Church', was consecrated. Major internal and external church restoration projects were undertaken between 2002 and 2006. One of the stained-glass windows, the work of Joshua Clarke, depicts a resurrection scene.

Whitechurch Church

## ZION (RATHGAR)

*Zion Church* was erected in 1861 to serve the expanding population of Rathgar. Its founder, Dublin stockbroker John Gould, had been deeply influenced by the Christian revival and left his entire estate to endow 'a place in which the worship of God should be conducted in simplicity and the Gospel of Jesus Christ faithfully preached'. Evangelical in inspiration, Zion nonetheless bears witness to the influence of the Ecclesiologists and Tractarians – as is clear in the church's architectural design. Everything in the church was of the best quality, but in extremely restrained manner – perfectly appointed for the celebration of the measured liturgies of the Irish Church. *Zion Church* was consecrated on All Saints' day in 1861, and the Patronal Festival in 2011 saw the celebration of 150 years of service.

# PARISHES IN THE DIOCESE OF GLENDALOUGH

## ARKLOW, INCH and KILBRIDE

Inch Church

Kilbride Parish was formed from the parish of Arklow in 1833.

*St Saviour's Church (the Church of the Holy Saviour), Arklow* is an iconic landmark. Its spire, which for many years was used as a compass by sailors, dominates the town's skyline. The church was built by the third earl of Carysfort, William Proby, as a gift to the people of Arklow. It was consecrated on 12 August 1899. All of the church's windows were designed by George Daniels, a leading designer of the late Gothic-revival period. Another notable feature is the fine ring of bells, which was cast in 1898 by the Loughborough firm of John Taylor. The history of St Saviour's Church is closely linked with Carysfort National School, the local junior Church of Ireland school. The first school was opened in the area in May 1823. Later schools were erected and eventually, following the amalgamation of several smaller schools, the new Carysfort School opened its gates in September 1974 on the Wexford Road in Arklow, where it still stands today.

St Brigid's Church, Kilbride

The present *Inch Church* was built in 1831. The stained-glass window in the sanctuary commemorates Lieutenant George Brooke, First Battalion Irish Guards, who died on 7 October 1914.

*St Brigid's Church Kilbride* was consecrated in September 1834. A clock in its tower pays homage to Robert Valentine Kearon, who lost his life in a submarine attack on 12 September 1917. The most outstanding feature of St Brigid's is the stained-glass Resurrection window by Harry Clarke.

St John the Evangelist's Church, Fontstown    Kilkea Church    Kilberry Church

## ATHY, KILBERRY, KILKEA, and FONTSTOWN

*St Michael's Church, Athy* was consecrated on 22 September 1841, and replaced an earlier church in Pery Square in the town. Rev. Frederick Trench was rector from 1848 to 1860, and on his death left money to fund a yearly donation of food to the poor of Athy. Nowadays, money is distributed from the fund to the poor of the town.

*Kilberry Church* was consecrated on 9 September 1834.

*Kilkea Church* was built by the duke of Leinster and licensed for divine service on 28 April 1865.

*St John the Evangelist's Church, Fontstown* was consecrated on 24 June 1827.

St Michael's Church, Athy

St Mary's Church, Blessington

St Mary's Church, Blessington

## BLESSINGTON, MANOR KILBRIDE, BALLYMORE EUSTACE and HOLLYWOOD

The pupils of Blessington school have recently played their part in helping those less well off by giving the gift of education to children in Kolkata. Working with the aid agency GOAL, the pupils – all aged under 12 years – raised €10,000 to refurbish a school building on a dump in Kolkata. Archbishop Michael Jackson dedicated Khanaberia Primary School in Dhappa Dump at a special gathering in Blessington in the spring of 2013.

*St Mary's Church, Blessington*, the largest church in the union, is in the centre of Blessington. It was built for Archbishop Michael Boyle and dedicated in 1683. The church's tower houses what is believed to be the oldest working turret clock in Ireland, alongside a peal of six bells, cast in 1682 and bearing the coat of arms of Archbishop Boyle.

*St John the Baptist's Church, Manor Kibride*, at Clougleagh, was built in 1833.

*St John's Church, Ballymore-Eustace*, built in 1820, is the third church to have been built on the site. An ancient font and an early sixteenth-century FitzEustace effigy are preserved within its walls, while its graveyard is distinguished by the presence of two unusual high crosses.

*St Kevin's Church, Hollywood* was built on the site of one of the pilgrim churches on the way to Glendalough. The present building dates to the early 1700s.

COLIN BOYLE

St John's Church, Ballymore-Eustace

St Kevin's Church, Hollywood

## CASTLEMACADAM, BALLINATONE and AUGHRIM

The area around Castlemacadam has a long history of Christian worship. It is reported that Palladius had connections to these parts in the fifth century.

St John the Evangelist's Church, Aughrim

Ballinatone Church, Ballinaclash

*Holy Trinity Church, Castlemacadam* was built in 1870, replacing an 1817 building, and stands on a two-acre site in the scenic valley of Avoca, County Wicklow. It was executed in the French provincial and old English style following a grant from the Ecclesiastical Commissioners and with the assistance of the local business, farming and mining community. The Hartin Hall was built adjacent to the church in 1995.

*Ballinatone Church, Ballinaclash*, was erected in 1834. The stained-glass window depicting Faith, Hope and Charity was commissioned by the Kemmis Family of Ballinacor in 1900 and made by Mayer & Co. of Munich.

*St John the Evangelist's Church, Aughrim* is located in the so-called Granite Village. Built as a chapel of ease on land donated by the earl and countess of Meath, it was consecrated on 31 May 1913.

Holy Trinity Church, Castlemacadam

## CELBRIDGE, STRAFFAN and NEWCASTLE LYONS

*Christ Church, Celbridge* was consecrated in August 1884 on a site originally granted by Sir Thomas Conolly of Castletown for an earlier church. Designed by Sir Thomas Drew, the interior arches are mainly of Bath stone, while the exterior work is of red Whitehaven stone. In 1998, sadly, a fire gutted the vestry. Many of the contents, including records, were destroyed.

*St Finian's Church, Newcastle-Lyons* dates from the fifteenth century, although its adjoining tower is thought to be older still. The chancel is now in ruins, but the remainder of the nave and church are intact. The beautiful Gothic east window was moved to its present position in 1724 and the carved woodwork dates from the same time. The granite stone cross in the graveyard is from the seventh to ninth century. The tower is a fascinating building with a spiral staircase of 76 steps, and two rooms, where the priest would have lived in medieval times.

Christ Church, Celbridge

Straffan Church was built by Hugh Barton as a private chapel for the use of his family and the estate workers of Straffan House (now the K Club). It was consecrated in 1837. The organ, built by Peter Conagher, was installed in 1897; the font, unusually situated at the top of the nave, dates from 1875. The church remained a private chapel with its own chaplain until it was handed over to the Representative Church Body in 1933 and the chaplain, Canon Lionel Fletcher, became rector of the amalgamated parishes of Celbridge and Straffan.

Straffan Church

Christ Church, Delgany

COLIN BOYLE

## DELGANY

COLIN BOYLE

It is believed that St Mogorog, a friend of St Kevin of Glendalough, arrived in Ireland from Britain in the late sixth or early seventh century and built his cell at or near the area of the old churchyard in the centre of Delgany village. By the late eighteenth century, the church on that site was small and in poor repair. Delgany National School, situated in the church grounds, has been rebuilt and extended a number of times to cater for the rise in pupil numbers – from 115 in 1978 to over 200 at present.

Christ Church, Delgany. In 1787, Peter La Touche, a member of the Huguenot and banking family, built at his expense a new parish church. According to an inscription on the west door, the building was erected in 1789. In 1870, a fire destroyed the building. Following reconstruction, the church was reopened on 7 November 1871.

lavin Church

COLIN BOYLE

## DONOUGHMORE, DONARD and DUNLAVIN

Donoughmore Church was built in 1711 and a tower was added in 1821.

Donard Church was consecrated on 30 December 1835.

Dunlavin Church, in west Wicklow, was consecrated on 24 October 1817. It replaced an earlier church in Dunlavin village, where there had been bitter fighting and destruction during the 1798 Rebellion. To seek to heal divisions, the local landlord family, the Tyntes, gave land for the building of both the Church of Ireland and the Roman Catholic churches. Both were dedicated to St Nicholas of Myra. In the early eighteenth century, Jonathan Swift had been prebendary of Dunlavin before he became dean of St Patrick's Cathedral.

Donoughmore Church

Donard Church

## DUNGANSTOWN, REDCROSS, CONARY

St Kevin's Church, Dunganstown, in County Wicklow, was built in 1702. It was enlarged in 1821 thanks to a loan from the Board of First Fruits.

Holy Trinity Church, Redcross, situated in the heart of rural Wicklow, introduced a new style of worship in the last decade, transforming a traditional service into a contemporary format to appeal to all age

St Bartholomew's Church, Conary

St Kevin's Church, Dunganstown

groups. This led to the weekly congregation growing from 25 to over 150. They outgrew their small church and now worship in Trinity Hall, a temporary building in the grounds of the church that can accommodate up to 200. Children and youth make up a significant part of the congregation. Outside Sunday mornings, a range of activities has been developed to provide care and fellowship for members of the church and the local community.

St Bartholomew's Church, Conary was built in 1859 for the men who worked in the local mines. It was restored in 1892.

Holy Trinity Church, Redcross

St Patrick's Church, Greystones

## GREYSTONES

*St Patrick's Church, Greystones* was built in 1857 to the design of Welland and Gillespie. The town's rapid growth as a popular summer residence soon led to a number of additions to the building. Among the stained-glass windows in the church is a memorial window to a member of the La Touche family, who gave the land for the church. In 2005, major building work developed the church into a much larger integrated worship and recreation centre.

## LEIXLIP, LUCAN

*St Mary's Church, Leixlip* has links to a medieval church of the same name and on the same site, built by the Anglo-Normans. The tower is believed to be from the fifteenth century. The church was rebuilt and restyled in the seventeenth and eighteenth centuries. Recently, important conservation work has been carried out.

    *St Andrew's Church, Lucan* was consecrated on 7 December 1823. The design of the church was influenced by the architect James Gandon, who gave the land for the church and who died at his home in Lucan in 1823.

St Mary's Church, Lucan

## NARRAGHMORE, TIMOLIN, CASTLEDERMOT and KINNEIGH

*The Holy Saviour's Church, Narraghmore*, in south Kildare, was consecrated 17 July 1863.

    *St Mullin's Church, Timolin* was consecrated for worship on 28 July 1738. The church has a well-preserved thirteenth-century effigy of Robert FitzRichard.

    *St James's Church, Castledermot* stands on the site of an important ninth-century monastery. In the grounds are the remains of a very fine Romanesque doorway, a round tower and two high crosses.

*Kinneigh Church* was built in 1832.

## NEWCASTLE, NEWTOWNKENNEDY and CALARY

Dating back to the Norman invasion, the parishes of Newcastle, Newtownmountkennedy and Calary are situated in east County Wicklow.

    In Newcastle, St Francis's Parish School was opened in 1982. St Catherine's Assocation, which provides education, training, healthcare and residential and respite care for children with intellectual and other disabilities, started in 1972. It was the brainchild of Canon Robert Jennings, a former rector, who managed the school for 23 years. There are now approximately two hundred children benefitting from its services.

Newcastle Church

St James's Church, Castledermot

    Rev. Henry Irwin was once rector of the Newtownmountkennedy. His son Henry, known as Father Pat, went to British Columbia, where he ministered to the miners and railway workers. He built the first Anglican church in the Rockies and is honoured by having his own special day in the Canadian church calendar.

Calary's most famous curate was Rev. John Nelson Darby, who came to the area in 1826, before the parish was formally constituted. He became disenchanted with the Established Church and founded the Darbyites, now known as the Plymouth Brethren. He was widely known as a theological and biblical commentator. Over the years, Calary has blossomed into a centre for music and the arts, becoming a favourite performance venue for instrumentalists and vocalists alike.

    *Newcastle Church* was erected in 1788.

    *St Matthew's Church, Newtownkennedy* was built in 1836. The communion table is said to have been used by the bishop of London, Nicholas Ridley, one of the Oxford Martyrs. As such, it is often referred to as 'Ridley's altar'. Memorials in the church commemorate members of the Irwin family. .

    *Calary Church* was consecrated in 1834.

Calary Church

## POWERSCOURT, KILBRIDE

In Powerscourt Parish, the earliest church, dedicated to St Beccan, was built at Stagonil in the twelfth century; the second, next to Powerscourt House itself, was built in the early 1600s. Henry Grattan was churchwarden there in 1793.

A rector of note in the parish was Robert Daly, a noted Gaelic scholar who began his ministry at Powerscourt in 1814, remaining there for almost 30 years until he was appointed bishop of Cashel. He was responsible for the building of the school in 1818 (still in use), a glebe house and a parochial hall. His strong evangelical leadership had wide influence in north Wicklow, especially among local landowners. Known as a powerful preacher, his followers would travel long distances to hear him.

At Kilbride, new developments took place in 2012. A new school and rectory (the fifth since Rev. Robert Daly first built his), both with the most up-to-date technology, were completed, adding a new dimension to the life of the parish.

Kilbride Church

St Patrick's Church, Powerscourt

Kilbride Church

In 1863, *St Patrick's Church, Powerscourt* was consecrated in the village of Enniskerry. It was paid for by Elizabeth, Viscountess Powerscourt, as a gift to the parish when her son, Mervyn Edward, came of age.

*Kilbride Church* was consecrated in 1859. Two of the memorial windows were designed by famed artist and architect Sir Ninian Comper. The headstones in the graveyard bear witness to the lives of warriors engaged in numerous wars, as well as artists (including Paul Henry), engineers, musicians, academics, clergy, farmers and estate workers, with names still familiar in the valley of Glencree. The church building remains Victorian inside and out, in keeping with the design of the village.

### RATHDRUM

Glenealy Church

*St Saviour's Church, Rathdrum* was erected in the centre of the village of Rathdrum in 1793.

*Glenealy Church* was consecrated in 1792.

*St John's Laragh* is in the ancient parish of Derralossary, which contained the famous Glendalough monastic settlement. The church was erected by local subscriptions and opened in 1867. Former president Erskine Childers is buried in the old Derralossary graveyard.

St John's Church, Laragh

St Saviour's Church, Rathdrum

COLIN BOYLE

### WICKLOW and KILLISKEY

*Wicklow Parish Church.* There has been a place of worship at this site on Church Hill since at least the time of the Danes. The present building was constructed in 1700; a tower was added in 1777 and a chancel was added in 1912. There is much evidence to suggest that an old church stood in what is now the centre of the graveyard, a place that dates back to at least 1600. The church's original doorway is located to the right as you enter the existing building. On the outside of this door is a Hiberno-Romanesque arch that probably came from a medieval church elsewhere in the parish. This type of doorway appeared in Ireland between 1000 and 1160, meaning that it predates the Norman settlement in Wicklow. In the south-east corner of the nave is a font of similar age and construction as the doorway.

*Killiskey Church* was consecrated on 20 October 1817 to replace an earlier church, which had fallen into ruin.

Wicklow Parish Church

Killiskey Church

COLIN BOYLE

# The United Dioceses of Meath and Kildare

The historic dioceses of Meath and Kildare have been united only since 1976. Until then, Meath was a separate diocese. Kildare was also separate for much of its history, although for a period of 130 years before joining with Meath, it had been united with Dublin and Glendalough.

Geographically, the dioceses of Meath and Kildare are placed in the eastern midlands of Ireland, mainly in the province of Leinster, running from the River Shannon in the west to the Irish Sea north of Dublin in the east, and extending from eastern Cavan nearly a hundred miles south to County Laois in the central midlands.

In all, there are around 9,000 people who claim some affiliation with the Church of Ireland in this region. The dioceses today incorporate 57 parish-church communities, all but one of them grouped together with others in clusters of parishes known as 'unions' or 'groups'. (In a union there is a single administrative structure for all the parishes included, whereas in a group there is more than one such structure.) Most of the clusters of parishes in these dioceses are unions.

Primary pastoral care is in the hands of a group of ordained clergy under the leadership of the bishop – usually just under 20 stipendiary priests with half a dozen auxiliary (non-stipendiary) priests. They are assisted by a corps of diocesan readers and pastoral assistants.

The dioceses also have the supervision of church primary schools in almost all of the parish unions. There is, in addition, a thriving diocesan boarding and day secondary school, Wilson's Hospital School, to the west of the dioceses. There are large numbers of young people living in Meath and Kildare Dioceses. In recent years the decision was taken to employ a youth officer with particular responsibility for ministry to young people. This has proved a highly successful initiative.

There is a considerable range in the local social context, from small, settled rural communities (which have changed little over the passing of time), to large country towns (some of which have grown beyond recognition in recent years), to conurbations closer to Dublin (which are essentially outer suburbs of that city).

Early in the twenty-first century, the people of Meath and Kildare Dioceses set themselves the goal of 'becoming a series of interconnected Christian communities, each so vibrant in its worship, so open-hearted in its fellowship and so effective in its service to those around, that others would be unable to resist becoming part of such a community'. This, of course, resonates clearly with the vision statement set out by the archbishops and bishops of the Church of Ireland some years later – that *growth, unity* and *service* should be the essential bywords of the Church of Ireland as it moves into the future. Our hope is that the Christian aspirations that we in the dioceses of Meath and Kildare have envisioned will sustain and challenge us into the future.

RICHARD ARMAGH

Dusk at Clonmacnoise
SCENIC IRELAND

## St Brigid's Cathedral Kildare

Working backwards in time, it should probably be pointed out that what is visible today is largely a nineteenth-century reconstruction by the great Victorian architect George Edmund Street. Street (who died in 1881) did not live to see the completion of the project, which was rededicated in September 1896 in a splendid ceremony at which the archbishop of Canterbury, Edward White Benson, was the preacher. (The archbishop died in the course of his return journey to Canterbury, while staying in Hawarden in north Wales as a guest of William Gladstone.) Before the nineteenth-century restoration, for over two hundred years the cathedral had been a poorly constructed building site among the ruins of the fine thirteenth-century Norman cathedral of Ralph of Bristol. There is little of that building to be seen today, although there are remnants of the older cathedrals, including an altar tomb of Bishop Walter Wellesley, a sixteenth-century member of the family that would later produce the duke of Wellington. In recent years the cathedral has again undergone further restoration.

This ecclesiastical site has important links to the early church. The cathedral, of course, is dedicated to St Brigid who is believed to have ministered in the Meath and Kildare area in the late fifth and early sixth centures. It is likely that her early church was built of wood. Close to the cathedral is a round tower, the base of which dates from the sixth century. There is a stone baptismal font which is not original to the cathedral but which dates from the medieval period. The west window is in honour of St Brigid, St Columba and St Patrick. The cathedral continues today as an important centre of worship for parishioners and diocesan occasions.

# The Diocese of Meath

ARCHBISHOP RICHARD CLARKE

Meath Diocese today covers the counties of Meath and Westmeath in their entirety and parts of the counties of Offaly, Longford, Cavan and Louth (with the addition of parishes within the counties of Roscommon and Kildare in recent times). Its history is firmly rooted in the ancient kingdom of Meath, meaning simply 'middle', reflecting its geographical location within the island of Ireland.

## THE DIOCESE OF MEATH

### The Early Church

Although the early Christian centuries in this part of Ireland inevitably remain shrouded in mist, there are a number of specifics that may be regarded as historical certainties. Whatever the mission we associate with the name of St Patrick may have been, it had major associations with the great kingdom of Meath. In a period when the Irish church was primarily monastic and based on the local tribe or *tuath* rather than on parochial or diocesan structures as we know them, Meath could boast significant centres of Christian spirituality and learning, which have retained their reputation to the present day.

Mosaic in St Michael's and All Angel's Church, Clane
ALASTAIR SMEATON
An aerial view of Clonmacnoise and the river Shannon

The stained-glass windows in Coolcarrigan Church depict images from the Book of Kells.

One of the greatest of all the Celtic illuminated manuscripts of the gospels bears the name of Kells. It is one of the glories of western Christendom. The origins and precise provenance of the *Book of Kells* are uncertain (and subject to a number of competing theories), but it is now generally accepted that it dates from the very early ninth century. It is beyond question, however, that the abbey at Kells protected this wonderful manuscript through countless Viking raids (the *Book of Kells* was briefly stolen from the abbey in the early eleventh century, but thankfully recovered after a few months). It was kept safely in the town of Kells until the Cromwellian period, when it was transferred to Dublin for safe keeping. It has remained there (in the library of Trinity College Dublin from 1661) ever since, although not without some degree of controversy.

Anthony Martin, Bishop of Meath, 1624–50
ST ANNE'S CATHEDRAL, BELFAST

Close by the graveyard of St Columba's church, Kells, stands a small stone roofed Oratory (St Columcille's House). This probably dates from the eleventh century. Access to the monks' sleeping accommodation aloft is by ladder. This small rectangular building is positioned at one of the highest points in the town.
ALASTAIR SMEATON

Illustrious names associated with Meath's history in the early Christian period include St Finnian, founder of the monastery of Clonard in the early sixth century and regarded as one of the fathers of Irish monasticism, and his pupil St Kieran (numbered among the so-called 'Apostles of Erin'), who founded Clonmacnoise monastery in the mid-sixth century. Clonmacnoise, with its position at the real crossroads of Ireland, where the major land route running east–west across the country in those days met the great River Shannon flowing southwards from Cuilcagh Mountain in Cavan down to the sea near Limerick, became (with Clonard) a monastic settlement of European reputation. Between the ninth and twelfth centuries it was a major centre not only for learning and spirituality but also for trade and culture. Several of the high kings are buried in its precincts.

## The Medieval Period

As Norman influences became ever stronger, Meath (with the rest of Ireland) adapted to the diocesan and parochial structures that operated in wider Europe. Through the church synods of the twelfth century, the number of dioceses within Meath was reduced from eight to three (Clonard, Kells and Duleek) and, by the beginning of the thirteenth century, Meath Diocese had taken the shape we would recognise today. The first of the Norman bishops, Simon de Rochfort, moved the centre of the diocese to Trim, where the substantial remains of the largest Norman castle in western Europe may still be seen, along with ruins of a large medieval cathedral, and where the centre of Meath Diocese remained until the reign of Henry VIII.

The Clonmacnoise Cross of the Scriptures from the east
ALASTAIR SMEATON

The Norman Castle at Trim
SCENIC IRELAND

## Reformation to Disestablishment

The immediate post-Reformation period was to see the incorporation of Clonmacnoise into the diocese of Meath. With a few minor adjustments in the diocesan boundaries, this structure has remained. Two bishops in particular, Bishop Anthony Dopping and Bishop Lewis O'Beirne, between the Reformation and the disestablishment of the Church of Ireland in 1869 have provided us with useful information regarding the diocese, owing largely to their intense zeal for higher standards.

Bishop Anthony Dopping

### Bishop Lewis O'Beirne (1749–1823)

A century later, a more colourful (and, it has to be said, more effective) bishop also changed the face of the diocese. He was Thomas Lewis O'Beirne, who was bishop from 1798 until 1823. A convert from Roman Catholicism, O'Beirne had studied in France before his conversion to Anglicanism and had been a naval chaplain, a poet, a playwright and chaplain to the viceroy in Dublin. He became bishop of Ossory before his move to Meath. More than any of his individual predecessors, he succeeded in eradicating much of the absenteeism and pluralism that was rife among the clergy. He also built churches, 57 in all. In addition, he was able to ensure that clergy could not claim legitimate reasons for non-residence, by procuring the building of 72 new glebe houses for clergy in different parishes. The principal historian of the Church of Ireland diocese of Meath, John Healy, has written that 'Bishop O'Beirne's episcopate, extending over a period of about twenty-five years, is the story of continuous improvement and reform.'

### Bishop Anthony Dopping (1643–97)

Anthony Dopping was bishop of Meath (having previously been bishop of Kildare) in that period at the end of the seventeenth century when it seemed entirely possible that the monarchy might become Roman Catholic, with all that this would have entailed for church life in both England and Ireland. Very much a supporter of the Protestant cause and hence of William of Orange, Dopping walked a hazardous path in dangerous times. He was, however, an unusually conscientious bishop for his time – he had refused to leave his diocese during the Jacobite period, unlike many of his colleagues. In the early 1690s he undertook a thorough visitation report on Meath Diocese, which yielded interesting if alarming information. Although the diocese had almost 200 parishes, all but a handful of the churches were in ruins (some since the 1641 Rebellion) and there were a mere 60 clergy to serve the diocese, most of whom Dopping regarded as entirely useless. Although many of his ideas for reform did not come to fruition, he worked for a greater education for the clergy and also propounded theories for the social and economic improvement of the region. He also advocated training mission preachers to preach in Irish to the general population.

## After Disestablishment

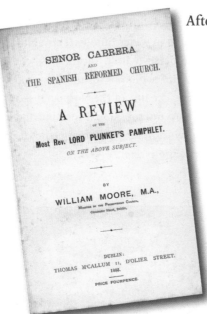

The disestablishment of the Church of Ireland in 1869 dealt a huge blow not only to the confidence of the Church but also to its material prosperity. Until then, the Church had been able to rely on the state for the upkeep and maintenance of its buildings, and even to build some new churches. The determination of both clergy and laity to make proper provision for the secure future of the Church of Ireland was remarkable, and it is probably fair to say that Meath Diocese showed a particularly courageous realism in coming to terms with its new situation. But Meath did not concentrate only on itself. William Conyngham Plunkett, bishop of Meath from 1876 until 1884, was hugely involved in bringing the reformed churches on the Iberian Peninsula into the Anglican fold, and remains a household name in the Spanish Reformed Episcopal Church.

Meath Diocese clearly possessed far too many parishes (and churches) for its needs in the late nineteenth century and had the courage to amalgamate parishes and close churches in some numbers before the end of that century. It has repeated that exercise with regularity since then, albeit not without pain. As a result of its courage, the Church of Ireland in the diocese of Meath (and in its sister diocese of Kildare) is for the most part not over-encumbered with buildings that are no longer required. Far from being damaging to morale, this has (in retrospect, at least) allowed the dioceses to concentrate on the mission and ministry of the church into the future, rather than on perpetuating the past.

William Conyngham Plunkett and pamphlet
RCB ARCHIVE

# THE DIOCESE OF KILDARE

The diocese of Kildare covers the northern part of County Kildare, eastern County Offaly and a small segment of County Laois.

## The Early Church and St Brigid

The story of Kildare Diocese is inextricably linked, historically, with the figure of St Brigid. It is difficult to know where history topples over into legend when writing about the fifth century, but there are several certainties that are of massive significance for some of the developments of Celtic Christianity.

Based in or near the modern town of Kildare, Brigid was abbess of a monastery that provided for both male and female religious. In these early centuries of the Christian mission in Ireland, bishops and dioceses were of relatively little account and Brigid undoubtedly dominated the ecclesiastical scene in this part of the island. Kildare does feature prominently in church annals from the seventh and eighth centuries, and Brigid did make claims to a preeminence within the church, particularly in her relationship with the kings of Leinster. There are interesting references in the twelfth-century annals to Cormac Ua Cathasaig as 'archbishop of Leinster' but also as a 'successor of Brigit', which is fascinating in view of the fact that Brigid was not a bishop (although there is one legend that suggests that she was accidentally ordained one).

A sculpture of St Brigid stands at St Brigid's Well, St Brigid''s Cathedral, Kildare.
ALASTAIR SMEATON

## The Medieval Period

It was, however, with the arrival of the Norman bishops that the history of Kildare became more consequential. These centuries were not an easy time for the diocese and it suffered heavily from war, neglect and mismanagement. In the thirteenth century, for example, the diocese split apart in a struggle as to who should be bishop, the dean of Kildare or the treasurer of Kildare. After a lengthy struggle, the pope (Nicholas III) finally annulled both elections and declared a third individual, Nicholas Cusack, bishop of the diocese.

But there were, of course, good times also. Ralph of Bristol, as his name implies, was an Englishman. He became a canon and treasurer of St Patrick's Cathedral, Dublin. In 1223, he was consecrated bishop of Kildare. He repaired and rebuilt the cathedral in the town. He introduced religious orders into the life of the church, generally reorganised the dioceses and also wrote a life of St Laurence O'Toole.

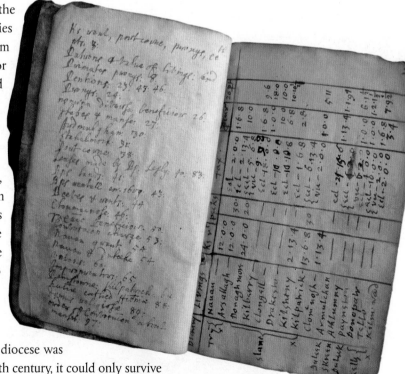

## The Seventeenth and Eighteenth Centuries

It has to be said, however, that Ralph was the exception. The diocese was in a sufficiently impoverished state that, from the late seventeenth century, it could only survive financially by the expedient of linking the bishopric with the deanery of Christ Church Cathedral in Dublin.

It should not be assumed, however, that there was no mobility, vitality or commercial enterprise within the diocese at this time. In the seventeenth century, for example, the area around Portarlington was (somewhat unsuccessfully) populated with English settlers, but at the end of the

Bishop Jones Account Book, 1661–81
RCB ARCHIVE

century there was an influx of French Huguenots whose influence remained strong until the nineteenth century. Indeed, services were held in the French language in the specifically designated French Church (now the parish church) until the 1820s. Mountmellick in the late eighteenth century was known as the 'Manchester of Ireland', such was the level of industrial enterprise.

## The Nineteenth and Twentieth Centuries

In 1846, the diocese of Kildare was united with the dioceses of Dublin and Glendalough, where it remained until 1976, when it was linked to the diocese of Meath. Kildare was probably fortunate in that its final bishop before it was united with Dublin was a particularly energetic individual, Charles Dalrymple Lindsay, who shook the diocese to the core. He was bishop of Kildare for over 40 years until his death in 1846. Lindsay's visitation book shows that he did not hesitate to make damning criticisms of inadequate care of churches or of any more general lethargy he encountered. He restored chapter meetings, held confirmations at regular intervals and revived the spirit of the diocese to a considerable degree.

The superb restoration of St Brigid's Cathedral took place at the end of the nineteenth century, when the diocese had been united with Dublin and Glendalough. For much of the twentieth century, Kildare Diocese remained with Dublin and Glendalough, until its amalgamation with Meath in 1976.

## New Millennium

The population growth of the city of Dublin and its subsequent expansion into the surrounding counties has meant that the part of Kildare Diocese closest to Dublin has, over the past generation, meant definable growth in a number of the parishes close to the capital city. This development has undoubtedly brought encouragement to a number of the parishes of the united dioceses, albeit with all the challenges that inevitably accompany such an increase in church population.

The House of Bishops of the Church of Ireland meeting in September, 2013, in Dublin appointed the Rev. Pat (Patricia) Storey as the new Bishop of Meath and Kildare, to succeed The Most Rev. Dr Richard Clarke, who became Archbishop of Armagh in late 2012. (The appointment of the new bishop had passed to the House of Bishops as the Episcopal Electoral College which met on 28 May 2013 failed to appoint a Bishop of Meath and Kildare dioceses.) The Rev. Pat Storey, who until her appointment as bishop was Rector of St Augustine's Parish Church, Londonderry, became the first woman to be appointed a bishop in the Church of Ireland and the first woman bishop in these islands.

Bishop Charles Dalrymple Lindsay's
Visitation Book, 1808
RCB ARCHIVE

Rev. Pat Storey, the
first woman to be
appointed a bishop in
the Church of Ireland
CHURCH OF IRELAND
PRESS OFFICE

Stained glass in St Brigid's Cathedral, Kildare
ALASTAIR SMEATON

# THE DIOCESE OF MEATH

PHOTOGRAPHS BY ALASTAIR SMEATON

Centred on the town of Athlone, which stands on the borders of Westmeath and Roscommon, and hence of the provinces of Leinster and Connacht, the Athlone parishes cover a large geographical area, extending into County Longford and County Roscommon and including the ancient site of Clonmacnoise, where services are held in the summer months. The town of Athlone was of major strategic importance in Ireland's history and in consequence was at the centre of violence and destruction during the many periods of warfare in Ireland.

*St Mary's Church, Athlone* dates from within the last two hundred years, scarcely surprisingly given the area's history of conflict. It is a fine building with an older tower and, as with so many churches in the diocese, a repository of some fascinating monuments.

St Mary's Church, Athlone

*St Mary's Church, Moate* is also an imposing church, dating from the late eighteenth century and situated at the centre of Moate, not far from Athlone. One of the most distinguished incumbents of this parish was Dr William Maxwell, who was rector at the end of the eighteenth century. Maxwell was a noted scholar in his own right, but was also a friend of Dr Samuel Johnson (and assisted James Boswell in his famous biography. He was the father-in-law of Rev. Henry Francis Lyte, who wrote the famous hymn 'Abide with Me'.

*Benown Church* near Lough Rea still boasts its original box pews.

*St Munis's Church, Forgney*, in County Longford, noted for some very fine glass, has the further distinction of being the parish in which Oliver Goldsmith was born, his father being incumbent of the parish, although the church in which Goldsmith's father ministered was replaced by the present early nineteenth-century building. The present church has a stained-glass window with the inscription:

To the glory of God and in Memory of Oliver Goldsmith, Poet, Novelist, Playwright, born in this parish, of which his father was for twelve years Curate. This window is erected by lovers of the man and his genius.

*Templeconnor Church, Clonmacnoise* lies on the monastic site itself. During the summer months, worship is held there every Sunday. On one Sunday every July there is a large open-air service to which people travel from many parts of the country. Since its inception over 50 years ago, this has become an established tradition of the diocese of Meath.

St Mary's Church, Moate

Benown Church

St Munis's Church, Forgney

Templeconnor Church,
Clonmacnoise

## CASTLEPOLLARD, OLDCASTLE and MOUNT NUGENT

The three churches of this union are situated in three different counties –
Westmeath, Meath and Cavan respectively. The parishes cover an area of enormous

historical interest and also of natural beauty. Near Castlepollard there is a seventh-
century monastic site at Fore, and close to Fore are the ruins of a medieval
Benedictine abbey, founded by the powerful Norman de Lacy family. The abbey
controlled most of the present-day parishes in this grouping, a large geographical
area, until the Reformation.

St Bride's Church, Mount Nugent

The Oldcastle area was the birthplace of St Oliver Plunkett, the famous Roman
Catholic martyr, an archbishop of Armagh, who was executed in 1681. He was the most famous
member of the Plunkett family, who had owned the estate land in this area prior to the Cromwellian
plantations. There is also an unusual ecumenical dimension to Oldcastle: the Gilson School in
the town involved both Roman Catholic and Church of Ireland authorities in its governance
from the outset. As it was founded in the early nineteenth century, this was indeed a
prophetic stance.

Mount Nugent is the smallest of the parishes. The name of the village derives from the
local Nugent family. Major-General Sir Oliver Stewart Wood Nugent was the officer of the
British Army in command of the Ulster Division during World War I.

The present *St Michael's and All Angels'*
*Church, Castlepollard*, a
nineteenth-century church
of considerable elegance, is set

Oldcastle Church and the
sculpture at the Gilson School

beautifully at one end of the village green.

*Oldcastle Church*, also dating from the nineteenth century, is
placed in a dominant setting at the centre of the town. There is
evidence that it stands on the site of a pre-Norman church, as
remains of early crosses have been found in its vicinity.

*St Bride's Church, Mount Nugent* has St Brigid as its patron
because of the parish's long association with holy
wells.

St Michael's and All Angels' Church,
Castlepollard

## DUNBOYNE AND RATHMOLYON WITH DUNSHAUGHLIN, MAYNOOTH, AGHER and RATHCORE

Today, the most populous of the parishes in the diocese, six parishes are combined within this cluster of
churches. Dunboyne, designated as the primary parish, has a history reaching back to medieval times.
It was said in the visitation of 1622 that Dunboyne 'is a great parish and the church and chancel are both
ruined'. It was reported in the early nineteenth century that 'the town was burnt down in the
disturbances of 1798; the present village contains 82 houses'. It has grown considerably since then,
and such has been the general increase in population in this area over recent years that a new
Church of Ireland primary school was built in the opening years of the twenty-first century.

Maynooth is a busy university town today. The history of the town, with its impressive castle, is
linked with the Geraldine family, later to become the earls of Kildare and dukes of Leinster. St
Patrick's Roman Catholic Seminary (St Patrick's College) now shares a campus with a constituent
college of the National University of Ireland, NUI Maynooth. The parish has built up a good
friendship with the colleges and the ecumenical spirit is fostered through this relationship.

The village of Dunshaughlin stands on the 'old' Navan Road – now superseded as the main road
by a motorway – some 30 kilometres north of Dublin. The first Christian site is believed to date
back to the fifth century and to St Seachnall, from whom the town derives its name. Early tradition
claims that Seachnall was born in Italy, became a disciple of St Patrick and was one of the first
bishops of Armagh. Although it may well be that the direct connection with Patrick was a later
invention, it seems certain from topological evidence that the Christian settlement of Dunshaughlin
appears very early in the history of Celtic Christianity. The Church of Ireland church in the
village is associated with the site of an early church. Between the census years of 1996 and
2006, Dunshaughlin's population grew by some 50 per cent. This has been reflected in an
increase in church population that has added to the vitality of the local parish.

St Mary's Church, Maynooth

St Seachnall's Church, Dunshaughlin; St Peter's and St Paul's Church, Dunboyne; St Ultan's Church, Rathcore

The three country parishes to the west of Maynooth – Rathmolyon, Agher and Rathcore – have worked together for many years. Their three churches are still in regular use for worship. Agher Parish has the distinction of having had Jonathan Swift as incumbent in 1699–1745 – although, as was customary in that period, they did not have him to themselves.

*St Peter's and St Paul's Church, Dunboyne*, although of fairly standard design, has a very attractive open timber roof and was designed by an English architect, somewhat unusual for Irish churches during that period (the 1860s). It is believed to be the third church built on the site.

*St Mary's Church, Maynooth* was once the private chapel to the Fitzgeralds, the earls of Kildare. It has a long and interesting history. The church (then a chapel) was part of a gift from Strongbow to Maurice Fitzgerald in 1176. The tower was originally part of the College of the Blessed Virgin Mary, which was established in the early sixteenth-century but closed shortly afterwards with the arrival of the Reformation in Ireland.

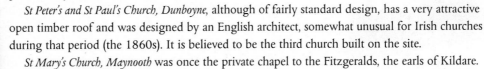

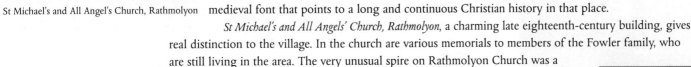

Although the present *St Seachnall's Church, Dunshaughlin* is an early nineteenth-century building, there is a lintel that may date from the first Christian millennium on the site, and an unusual medieval font that points to a long and continuous Christian history in that place.

St Michael's and All Angel's Church, Rathmolyon

*St Michael's and All Angels' Church, Rathmolyon*, a charming late eighteenth-century building, gives real distinction to the village. In the church are various memorials to members of the Fowler family, who are still living in the area. The very unusual spire on Rathmolyon Church was a memorial to one member of the family, Robert Fowler, who was bishop of Ossory Diocese in the eighteenth century.

*Agher Church* was provided by the local Winter family in 1804. It was described by Bishop O'Beirne a few years after it was built as 'finished in the handsomest manner'.

*St Ultan's Church, Rathcore* is small, simple and neat in style and certainly of earlier date than Rathmolyon and Agher, with which it has close associations. O'Beirne had this to say about Rathcore: 'The Church, also, is but in indifferent repair, owing to the unwillingness of the Parishioners to consent to any additional cess.' (A cess was a tax.) Happily, the church is now is good repair.

Agher Church

## JULIANSTOWN

Julianstown is the only single-church incumbency in the united dioceses at present. The parish church is in a fairly rural setting, but the parish extends into the nearby busy town of Drogheda. Until the late 1990s, the parish maintained a church there also.

Julianstown today is largely a commuter district for Dublin, which lies a little over 40 kilometres to the south. This is naturally reflected in the composition of the Church of Ireland parish. Part of the Irish possession of the Welsh abbey of Llanthony, the parish later came into the hands of the earls of Drogheda, who had the right of appointment of the clergy until the disestablishment of the Church of Ireland. Its original ecclesiastical title was Nanny, derived from the river that runs through the parish to the sea at the nearby small town of Laytown. Julianstown achieved some fame as the site of a battle in 1641, in what was intended by the rebel leader, Sir Phelim O'Neill, as a prelude to a siege of Drogheda. Although the rebels were successful in routing the English and Scottish soldiers at Julianstown, the siege

St Mary's Church, Julianstown

of Drogheda itself was not as successful. However, it has been argued that the reputation achieved in Julianstown by the rebels led to the spread of the rebellion to other parts of Ireland.

The church in Drogheda (also dedicated to St Mary) was destroyed by Oliver Cromwell in 1649 and replaced twice after that date. The best-preserved section of the old town wall of Drogheda is the southern boundary of the graveyard beside the church. The boundary between the dioceses of Meath and Armagh is marked in Drogheda by the River Boyne. This now marks a provincial boundary also, as Meath was transferred to the southern province of the Church of Ireland in 1976, when the dioceses of Meath and Kildare were united.

The army camp at Gormanstown (once a famous internment camp during the Irish Civil War) lies within the parish of Julianstown, and over many years important pastoral relationships with the Church of Ireland parish have developed. For many years, Butlin's holiday camp operated close by, at Mosney, again within the parish. Part of the role of successive rectors of the parish was to provide Sunday worship for holidaymakers.

*St Mary's Church, Julianstown*, dating from the late eighteenth century, has been modified and enlarged several times, fortunately in architectural harmony with the original design.

St Mary's Church, Julianstown

St Patrick's Church, Donaghmore

## KELLS and DONAGHPATRICK

In the early years of Christianity in Ireland, Kells was of major importance as a monastic centre, associated in particular with St Columba. The site of the present Church of Ireland church in Kells has been in continuous use for worship since the early ninth century. The small oratory close by – known as Colmcille's House – may well date from the ninth century.

Although the *Book of Kells* is no longer kept in the town, the great Celtic tradition is evident in many other ways. Near the church are a number of high crosses (one in particular is in excellent condition) and also a round tower. In 1152, the Synod of Kells played a major role in continuing the transition of the Irish church from a largely monastic structure to the diocesan organisation that has remained to the present day. (This synod was based at Mellifont Abbey and is probably more properly named the Synod of Kells-Mellifont.)

Nearer to our own time, the historian and Irish nationalist Alice Stopford Green (1847–1929) was a daughter of a rector of Kells, Archdeacon Edward Stopford. Although a strong supporter of Home Rule (and not opposed to the use of force if necessary), she did not give support to the Easter Rising of 1916. In the early years of the Irish Free State, she was a friend and strong ally of W.B. Yeats in his desire to see the place of the Church of Ireland maintained in public life. She, like Yeats, was a member of the Irish Senate. Defying normal convention seems to have been a family trait: her father was one of the few Church of Ireland clergy who were fully in support of the disestablishment of the Church of Ireland, and in the late 1860s even gave advice to the British prime minister, William Gladstone, on how this might best be achieved.

The other parish within this grouping, Donaghpatrick, may have an even older heritage. Souterrains (which may well be pre-Christian) and some standing stones have been found close to St Patrick's Church. The name of the area suggests a connection with Patrick, although no direct evidence has been found.

*St Columba's Church, Kells* dates from 1778. The tower beside the building, which can be seen from a great distance on the approach to the town from the south, is Anglo-Norman. It is now surmounted by a spire, built shortly after the church.

*St Patrick's Church, Donaghpatrick* is a beautiful and compact late-Victorian building.

St Columba's Church, Kells

Kingscourt Parish is the most northerly in the united dioceses and, other than Mount Nugent, the only parish with a base in the province of Ulster. Although the present market town of Kingscourt dates from the eighteenth century, the Christian origins of this area probably go back far earlier, as the St Ernan who is believed to have worked near here died in the seventh century. One of the interesting episodes in Kingscourt's history relates to a local Presbyterian minister who was nominated by the British crown to be rector of Kingscourt in the 1840s. Robert Winning was an Irish scholar and was also involved in founding the Irish Church Missions, intended to convert Roman Catholics to Protestantism. He is buried in the graveyard of Kingscourt, with a large headstone marking his grave.

St Ernan's Church, Kingscourt

The present *St Ernan's Church, Kingscourt* stands overlooking the town and has been modified many times since it was built.

*St David's Church, Syddan*, the other church in the Kingscourt Union, is in County Meath. A fine and impressive-looking church (built in 1880) in a country setting, it too has pre-Reformation roots. It was at one time part of the abbey of St Thomas in Dublin.

St David's Church, Syddan

## MULLINGAR, KILLUCAN, KILBIXY and ALMORITIA

Now a populous grouping of parishes, Mullingar has grown considerably in recent years, primarily because of a major increase in population as the area became part of the outer commuter belt for Dublin, although some 80 kilometres away. The population of the town of Mullingar and its surrounding area is approaching 20,000.

One of the more colourful rectors of Mullingar in the period immediately after the disestablishment of the Church of Ireland was Charles Parsons Reichel, who was later to become bishop of Meath Diocese. A controversialist, bitterly anti-Roman Catholic in his views, such was his unpopularity in the town of Mullingar that he provoked riots and at one stage required police protection. Fortunately, times have changed greatly in the ecumenical atmosphere of modern Mullingar.

One of the other parishes in the union, Killucan, is also based around an ancient site, in this case a monastery founded by St Etchen, a bishop of Clonard in the sixth century. St Etchen is believed to have baptised St Columba.

The third of the parishes has a remarkable history. Kilbixy was a particularly important town in western Meath in Norman times, but the church derives its dedication from an earlier era. St Bigseach founded a community, perhaps even before St Brigid's in Kildare, for men and women. Kilbixy came into its own in the Norman period. Near the church can be seen the remains of the bailey of a late twelfth-century castle and also what are believed to be the ruins of a lepers' hospital. The Norman town was destroyed twice in the fifteenth century and Kilbixy is now very much a rural area.

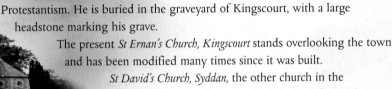

All Saint's Church, Mullingar

*All Saints' Church, Mullingar* celebrated 800 years of existence in 2002, and the list of rectors and vicars dates back to the early fourteenth century. There were alterations to the church over the centuries and the present church is a very fine nineteenth-century building. It contains some particularly beautiful stained glass.

*St Etchen's Church, Killucan* dates from the early nineteenth century, although it has a thirteenth-century font.

*St Bigseach's Church, Kilbixy* was built by a bequest of Lord Sunderlin at the end of the eighteenth century. It has had its own dramatic history. In 1960, much of the roof collapsed. Part of the church at the (east) chancel end was reroofed and retained for worship, while the nave section became a fine courtyard. Set in scenic and very well-maintained surroundings, it is an unusual and fascinating part of the diocese.

*St Nicholas's Church, Almoritia* is now used only on festive occasions.

St Bigseach's Church, Kilbixy

St Etchen's Church, Killucan

## NAVAN, SLANE and KENTSTOWN

Navan is the core of the three parishes within this grouping. The town of Navan itself has grown hugely in recent years. Already a large town, its population increased by more than 25 per cent between 2002 and 2006 alone.

One of the other parishes, centred on the village of Slane, has traditional connections with St Patrick. An ancient tradition has it that St Patrick lit a paschal beacon on the hill of Slane, but that the pagan king Laoghaire saw this fire (lit before the fire of spring that he, as king, was to light) from

St Mary's Church, Navan

the nearby hill of Tara, became outraged and travelled instantly to Slane with the purpose of killing Patrick. However, the exchange concluded not with Patrick's death, but with the king being persuaded that Christianity was to be protected rather than destroyed.

The great site of Tara itself – the seat of the Irish high kings – also has a church, no longer in the hands of the Church of Ireland, although provision is made for some services to be held there, including a traditional outdoor service at the end of June each year.

St Patrick's Church, Slane

*St Mary's Church, Navan*, as is often the case in these dioceses, is connected to an earlier monastic site and to a later abbey. The church building has direct antecedents going back to late-medieval times, when it was a chapel for the abbey. Although major reconstruction was carried out in 1683, the building of today is largely an early nineteenth-century restoration. Much of the design was the work of the incumbent of the time, who was greatly interested in architecture. He was Daniel Augustus Beaufort, son of the previous incumbent, a Huguenot refugee. Daniel Beaufort was man of varied talents and was one of the founders of the Royal Irish Academy. His son was the renowned Sir Francis Beaufort, who created the Beaufort scale for the measurement of wind force. A professional sailor who had fought in a number of naval battles in the Napoleonic Wars, Beaufort rose to the rank of rear-admiral, his scientific exploits being recognised by a knighthood and fellowship of the Royal Society.

*St Patrick's Church, Slane* is in the village of Slane, but ruins on the site of its predecessors are still to be found on the hill above the village.

*St Mary's Church, Kentstown* was built at the very end of the eighteenth century. It has an excellent pipe organ for a building of its size. There is a long and close connection between Kentstown Church and the Somerville family. Inside the door of St Mary's is a plaque that tells us that 'Sir James Quayle Somerville Baronet built this steeple Anno Domini 1797'.

St Mary's Church, Kentstown
Stained glass, Trim

## TRIM and ATHBOY

The parishes of Trim and Athboy are today united as a compact group of parishes. The historic town of Trim is home to the cathedral of the diocese of Meath, although the dean of the cathedral (in an important allusion to the ancient diocese of Clonmacnoise, which became part of Meath Diocese in 1569) is styled dean of Clonmacnoise. Although an important ecclesiastical centre through the Middle Ages, the church at Trim became a cathedral for the diocese as recently as 1955.

A parish's history, however, is about more than just buildings. Jonathan Swift was at one time vicar of the nearby parish of Laracor (now incorporated into Trim Parish). The duke of Wellington's family came from near Trim and he received his early education in the diocesan school in the town. Trim remains of great importance in the context both of the diocese and of the county.

Athboy, a few miles from Trim, is, from its Gaelic derivation, the 'town of the Yellow Ford'. The Yellow Ford is a river close to the border between the counties of Meath and Westmeath. Athboy was a walled town guarding the Pale and part of the old wall can still be seen behind the Church of Ireland parish church.

St Patrick's Cathedral, Trim

St Patrick's Cathedral, Trim

The Carmelite religious order came to Ireland in the mid-thirteenth century, and one of their four chief monastic houses was in Athboy, founded early in the 1300s. The parish has a further unusual distinction in that from the sixteenth century, for a considerable period, the archbishops of Armagh were also rectors of Athboy. Needless to say, they did not trouble themselves a great deal with the parish and left any pastoral work that might have been done to underpaid vicars.

St Patrick's Church, now *St Patrick's Cathedral, Trim*, has its origins as early as the fourteenth century, and the beautiful tower that still dominates this end of the town dates from the fifteenth century. The church itself was largely rebuilt at the beginning of the nineteenth century. There are many interesting features within the cathedral, not least the ornate piscine, now used as a font, with carvings of animals and devils in disguise. Close by is the first ever stained glass designed by Sir Edward Burne-Jones, part of the cathedral's west window.

*St James's Church, Athboy* stands on the site of the Carmelite friary of the fourteenth century. It was reported in 1622 that the church was 'ruinous'. Today, this fine church represents different periods of church architecture (eighteenth and nineteenth centuries), standing in the shadow of the impressive medieval tower.

St James's Cathedral, Athboy

## TULLAMORE, RAHAN, TYRELLSPASS and CLARA

St Carthach's Church, Rahan

Tullamore, the principal town and parish in this cluster of parishes, is unusual in the context of the dioceses of Meath and Kildare in that, although there appears to have been a church and a parish here in the sixteenth century, there followed a period of 150 years when there was no permanent Church of Ireland church in the town (although the family of the first Lord Tullamore built a small chapel in the eighteenth century for the use of townspeople). In 1785, the town suffered an unusual tragedy when a hot-air balloon crashed on the town and burst into flames, burning down more than a hundred houses (which, as has been often pointed out, gives Tullamore the grim distinction of being the place of the first known aviation disaster). The town was slowly rebuilt. In 1806, the select vestry petitioned the lord lieutenant to build a new church on a better site, as the parish church of Kilbride (the ecclesiastical name for Tullamore to this day) was in ruins and had not been used for worship 'within the memory of man'.

The first royal astronomer of Ireland, Charles Jasper Joly, was born at St Catherine's Rectory, Trim in 1864, the eldest child of the rector, Rev. John Swift Joly. Charles Joly was elected to fellowship of Trinity College, Dublin in 1894, and became professor of astronomy at the university. In 1897, he was appointed royal astronomer, before dying at a young age in 1906.

Close to Tullamore is a church that reaches back into antiquity. Rahan has two small churches on an ancient Christian monastic site. One of these is in ruins, but the other, St Carthach's, is in near-perfect condition.

: Brigid's Church, Clara

Tyrellspass (scene of a famous battle against the English in 1597) is the centre of another parish in this union. It lies closer to Dublin. Clara, the fourth of the parishes, has long connections with the textile and milling industries, as well as with the Quakers. For many years, large numbers of parishioners were employed by the Goodbody factory in the town. Among distinguished townspeople of Clara were Anne Jellicoe, the founder of Alexandra College in Dublin, and Vivian Mercer, the literary critic and academic.

The present (and very impressive) *St Catherine's Church, Tullamore* was built in 1816 on the hill overlooking the town.

St Catherine's Church, Tullamore

320

St Carthach's Church, Rahan has been fully and carefully restored in recent years. Although the main part of this building belongs to the eighteenth century, the settlement itself may be as early as the sixth century, and remnants of this small church date from the twelfth century. Still visible are some striking Romanesque features at the east end of the building, including a chancel arch decorated with beautiful ornamental sculptures. Rahan Church is used in the summer months for worship.

St Sinian's Church, Tyrellspass has a particularly picturesque setting overlooking a village green.

St Brigid's Church, Clara is in a very prominent position at the top of the village green. It was built late in the eighteenth century.

St Sinian's Church, Tyrellspass

# THE DIOCESE OF KILDARE

St Michael's and All Angel's Church, Clane

## CLANE, COOLCARRIGAN and DONADEA

The town and parish of Clane has likely origins in the sixth century, when an abbey was founded in Clane with St Senchel as its first abbot. One of the most interesting local saints was St Ultan Tua, who would place a stone into his mouth to prevent him from speaking for the duration of Lent. The old abbey in Clane was for centuries the parish church, until local landowner Thomas Cooke Trench donated a site a couple of kilometres out of the town for a new church. The son of a former rector of this church, Archdeacon Brian Handy, is the Irish management writer and broadcaster Charles Handy.

The wider parish of Clane is known as the place where the 1798 Rebellion began. In the nearby village of Prosperous, the barracks occupied by members of the North Cork Militia and a Welsh cavalry unit was attacked by the rebels. Near the town of Prosperous is a small private chapel on the Coolcarrigan estate, owned by the Wilson-Wright family but used regularly for parish worship.

Coolcarrigan Church

St Peter's Church, Donadea

St Michael's and All Angels' Church, Clane (known generally as 'Millicent') was consecrated in 1883. It is a stunning building, generally regarded as one of the most beautiful churches in Ireland. It contains some wonderful artwork, including rare examples of sgraffito (a technique for fresco which applies layers of tinted plaster in contrasting colours), and the entire church is richly decorated in mosaic, alabaster and onyx. The roof timbers are very ornate, built in Riga oak. The windows, too, are notably beautiful.

Coolcarrigan Church, modelled on one of the churches of Clonmacnoise, is in a beautiful setting and is one of the only churches in Ireland to have a lychgate at its entrance. There are texts on the walls of the church in Gaelic script (although in English), which were designed by Dr Douglas Hyde, the first president of Ireland and a noted champion of the Irish language in the earlier part of the twentieth century. The windows depict images from the Book of Kells.

St Peter's Church, Donadea, situated deep in the Donadea woods, dates from the early nineteenth century, although the ruins of an earlier church are visible around the present building. A relatively small church, it contains a flamboyant Renaissance-style funeral monument to Sir Gerald Aylmer (who died in 1634). The monument was moved from the older church and contains, on its plinth, images of Saints Jerome, Gregory, Ambrose and Augustine in addition to depictions of the Aylmer family at prayer.

Coolcarrigan Churc

## CLONSAST, RATHANGAN, MONASTERORIS (EDENDERRY) and CARBURY

This union of parishes, large both in area and in population, is centred on the village of Clonbullogue in County Offaly, close to that county's border with Kildare and Laois. The name of Clonbullogue suggests pre-Christian roots, pointing to the place of worship for Bolg, a Celtic sun-god. Although a small village, Clonbullogue has an interesting history. From Cromwellian times, it bore all the marks of a plantation town, with a significant proportion of its population belonging to reformed traditions. In less ecumenical times, in 1731, a local clergyman wrote about his parish: 'I bless God for the comforting assurance I have that there is no reputed friary, nunnery, friars, nuns or Popish schools.' More recently, a member of the local parish (and a son of the rector), John Joly (1857–1933), became a noted and brilliant scientist, whose experiments with radiotherapy have been integral to the treatment of cancer over many generations. He also made breakthroughs in geological dating and he may be credited with the creation of one of the first processes for colour photography. Among many other honours, Joly was made a member of the Royal Society at a young age, and a crater on the planet Mars has been named in his memory. An older cousin of Joly's, Dr Jasper Robert Joly, was an eminent book collector who, when he died, left his collection of over 23,000 volumes to the Royal Dublin Society. In 1877, his library became the basis for the collection housed in the National Library of Ireland.

St Kevin's Church, Clonbullogue

The nearby parish of Rathangan also has a colourful history. Bishop Thomas Lindsay's visitation book of 1804 tells us:

> the place suffered much in the rebellion of 1798. Since that time the church has been made a kind of citadel though fortunately it has not been resorted to in any way other than that of worship.

Lindsay writes of the windows being built up, with holes for firing out upon any attackers. The bishop's advice was that, although he could understand the fears of parishioners, they should nevertheless conceal their defences 'from the sight and knowledge of strangers and the female part of the congregation'. In more recent times, although still on a warlike note, the local Colley family provided southern Africa briefly with a high commissioner, Sir George Pomeroy Colley, who had served as a British Army major-general and who was killed at the battle of Majuba Hill in 1881.

Rathangan Church

The principal town in this grouping of parishes is Edenderry. Between the census years of 1996 and 2006, the population of Edenderry increased by over 50 per cent to almost 6,000. The church is known as 'Castropetre', although the ecclesiastical name for the parish is Monasteroris. Castropetre is a reference to the castle of Peter de Bermingham, a descendant of Sir John de Bermingham, who founded an abbey for the Franciscans in the early fourteenth century. Monasteroris means 'the monastery of Mac Feoris', an Irish name for the founder.

Carbury, close to Edenderry, is the remaining parish of the Clonsast Union. On the hill where the church stands is an old motte, which was for a time part of the de Bermingham land. At the bottom of Carbury Hill is the Trinity Well, the source of the River Boyne.

*St Kevin's Church, Clonbullogue* is believed to date from the late eighteenth century, although on an older foundation. Parish records are unfortunately only extant from a relatively recent date, the beginning of the nineteenth century.

*Rathangan Church* dates from 1770.

*Monasteroris Church* (Castropetre) stands on a hill overlooking the town. The site was given by the Downshire family and the present church was consecrated in 1778. The roofing of the church on the site of the old monastery was a constant anxiety in the mid-eighteenth century and the parishioners, with their clergy, demanded a new church. The vestry records give us some interesting indications of the process. In August 1774, the vestry demanded that the 'site of said Parish Church be changed and a new Church erected in the town of Edenderry', and petitioned for funds. Castropetre was completed by 1778 at a cost of £685 14s 11¾d, of which £400 was given by the Board of First Fruits.

*Carbury Church* is built on Carbury Hill (known also as Fairy Hill), overlooking the village, close to the ruins of the Tudor castle at the top of the hill, built by the Colley family. This eighteenth-century church has an unusual feature – the altar is placed at the west rather than the east end of the church.

LEFT: Monasteroris Church
RIGHT: Carbury Church

Killeagh Church

## GEASHILL AND KILLEAGH

St Mary's Church, Geashill

Until the close of the twentieth century, Geashill Parish was unique within the law of the Church of Ireland in that its rector was, by virtue of his office, automatically a canon of Kildare Cathedral, the prebendary of Geashill. The parish was also unusual in the post-disestablishment Church of Ireland, although not unique, in that a local family held the patronage of the parish. With the departure of the Digby family from the country, however, this situation changed. Appointments to the parish are now made in accordance with the normal procedures of the Church of Ireland. The prebendal stall of Geashill in St Brigid's Cathedral has therefore lapsed.

The other parish in this grouping is centred on the nearby village of Killeigh. An older Christian site than Geashill, Killeigh dates from the sixth century and in medieval times had a surprisingly large number of monastic houses for a relatively small community – Augustinian canons, Augustinian nuns and Greyfriars were all present. Following the Reformation, Killeigh's ecclesiastical buildings were almost certainly destroyed and the lands sequestered by the British crown. In 1578, Killeigh was rented to Gerald, earl of Kildare and his heirs; afterwards, through marriage, it came for a period into the possession of the Digbys.

*St Mary's Church, Geashill* is a Board of First Fruits church. It dates from the early nineteenth century, with some later enlargements and alterations.

*Killeagh Church*, which has seventeenth-century origins (although reconstructed in the nineteenth century), is physically attached to the striking ruins of the ancient Killeigh Abbey, once the third-largest abbey in the country.

St Patrick's Church, Newbridge

St Patrick's Church, Carnalway

St John's Church, Kilcullen

St Paul's Church, Curragh

## KILDARE, CURRAGH AND KILMEAGUE AND NEWBRIDGE, KILCULLEN and CARNALWAY

The cathedral parish of Kildare, although one of the smallest in the diocese in terms of Church of Ireland population, is nevertheless the custodian of the beautiful cathedral of St Brigid.

Part of this parish union is the Curragh military camp. There is a Church of Ireland chaplaincy involvement with the camp. The Curragh camp has a long military history, as its location made it an ideal mustering point for an army, and it served for this purpose under the command of the earl of Tyrconnell in support of King James II. Formerly a British Army camp, it is now a main command centre for the Irish Army. It was the setting of the Curragh 'mutiny', in which a number of the British officers at the camp in 1914 planned to resign rather than enforce Home Rule militarily against the will of the unionists.

With a population of almost 20,000 according to the 2006 census, Newbridge has seen large population growth in recent times and a large expansion of the parish school in consequence. Nearby are two other parishes, Kilcullen and Carnalway.

*St Paul's Church, Curragh* is a garrison church attached to the military camp.

*Kilmeague Church* is unusual because of its tower, the pinnacles of which resemble claws.

*St Patrick's Church, Newbridge* is in the Moorefield part of the town. It is an early nineteenth-century building in the early English style.

*St John's Church, Kilcullen* is known as the 'Yellow Bog Church'. It has particularly unusual circular stained-glass windows.

Kilmeague Church

St Patrick's Church, Carnalway

*St Patrick's Church, Carnalway* is also somewhat unusual. Built in the late nineteenth century in Hiberno-Gothic style, it includes a small stained-glass window by the famous Harry Clarke. The novelist George A. Birmingham (Rev. J.O. Hannay) was rector here for a few years at the end of World War I and wrote that his church was 'tiny but very attractive'.

## MOUNTMELLICK, ROSENALLIS and COOLBANAGHER

At the southern tip of the united dioceses, the Mountmellick Group consists of three parishes – Mountmellick, Coolbanagher and Rosenallis. The history of the town of Mountmellick is inextricably bound up with the Quakers, the Religious Society of Friends. The arrival of the Quakers in this area in 1657, led by William Edmundson (hailed as the first Quaker to settle in Ireland), led to the rapid expansion of Mountmellick to an eventual population of some 8,000. By the late eighteenth century, the town was home to many industries, including tanneries, breweries and glassworks. It was to become associated particularly with linens, Mountmellick embroidery becoming world famous in the nineteenth century. Joanna Carter, who is credited with the introduction of these particular lace processes, was a member of the Church of Ireland. She also ran a small school, which catered for both Church of Ireland and Roman Catholic pupils in the town. Although Mountmellick diminished in size and importance through the period of the Great Famine, it remained a centre for light industry.

St John's Church, Coolbanagher

Rosenallis was also important in the history of the Quakers in Ireland, and William Edmundson is buried in a Quaker graveyard near the village. The Church of Ireland church is dedicated to St Brigid, who, tradition suggests, may have founded a monastic settlement in the area.

The other parish in the grouping is Coolbanagher, near the Emo estate. St John's Church replaced an older church, which may have been destroyed by arson while worship was in progress. The rector of the time, Anthony Fleury, had the unenviable reputation of being 'the crossest man in Europe'.

*St Paul's Church, Mountmellick* was once a chapel of ease – in effect, a daughter church – for Rosenallis, now a village some ten kilometres distant. Given that Mountmellick is now a large town, this seems difficult to comprehend. St Paul's was built in 1828 at a cost of £1,828. It is a bright and spacious building sited just off the town square.

*St Brigid's Church, Rosenallis* is an attractive church on a small hill at the entrance to the village (from the direction of Mountmellick). In the graveyard is buried Roger Byrne, who died at the age of 53 in 1808, weighing 52 stone. It is assumed that he holds the record as Ireland's all-time heaviest man.

*St John's Church, Coolbanagher* is one of the architectural glories of the diocese. It was consecrated in 1785, having been built to a design by James Gandon, architect for the Custom House and the Four Courts in Dublin. Lord Carlow paid for the church, although it seems that his wife may not have been enamoured with events at the time of the consecration. She wrote to her sister in March 1785:

We are going to have great doings here next week. The new church is to be consecrated on Tuesday; the Bishop and all the clergy in the neighbourhood are to attend, besides all the country, I suppose, and Lord Carlow will ask them all to dinner both on that day and the next, as there are races within three miles of us. I own I am sorry to begin all this sort of work so soon, but there is no help for it.

Although a few alterations were made in later times to the original plan, the church has remained very true to its design. St John's also contains a medieval font, which is believed to have been rescued from an old and now disappeared church in Ardrea.

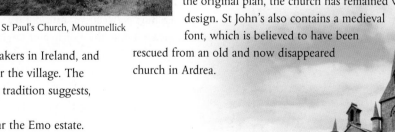

St Paul's Church, Mountmellick

St Brigid's Church, Rosenalis

## NAAS, RATHMORE and KILL

Although today there are few historical remains of its past, Naas hosted meetings of the kings of Leinster before the time of the Normans. In 1176, the barony of Naas was given to William Fitzmaurice, 'together with the adjacent territory and various important privileges, with a market and a very extensive jurisdiction'. It became a walled town, and before the Reformation there were four great churches in Naas. The present Church of Ireland church is the sole survivor of these. Its dedication to St David suggests that there may have been Welsh settlers among the Normans who came to Naas, although it was also said that the saint's mother was Irish. The sense of connection with St David lived on for centuries – until the close of the eighteenth century, it was a custom for the people of Naas to wear a leek on St David's day. The town's population has now grown to more than 20,000. Naas is the county town of Kildare and the centre for local government. It has a number of modern industrial enterprises in addition to being a commuter town for Dublin. The parish has been stimulated considerably by the influx of new families in recent decades.

There are two other, smaller parishes in this grouping. Rathmore is a country parish which, earlier in its history, was part of the diocese of Dublin. Samuel Lewis's *Topographical Dictionary of Ireland* (1837) gives us some indication of the parish at that time. Lewis describes it as follows:

> [Rathmore is a living] in the diocese of Dublin, united by act of council, in 1833, to the vicarage of Kilteel, and in the patronage of the Archbishop. The tithes amount to £336. 9. 5 ½., of which £97. 13. 6 ½. is payable to the impropriator, and £238. 15. 10. to the vicar. The glebe-house was built by aid of a loan of £200 from the late Board of First Fruits, in 1821; the glebe comprises 12 acres.

Kill Parish, originally on the main road from Dublin to the south (although now bypassed by a dual carriageway, the first to be opened in the republic of Ireland), was based around on old staging post on the road to Kilcullen.

In *St David's Church, Naas* there is a splendid font dating from the thirteenth century, which is testimony to the ancient Christian traditions of Naas. Only a few other aspects of the church, such as details on some of the columns, evidence the early origins of the church, which has been altered considerably over the centuries.

*St Columbkill's Church, Rathmore* was described by Samuel Lewis as follows:

> The church is a small plain structure, with a square tower, erected by aid of a grant of £450, in 1766, from the same Board.

*St John's Church, Kill* was built in the nineteenth century. It possesses an excellent chamber organ, a gift of the Bourke family, the earls of Mayo.

St David's Church, Naas

St John's Church, Kill

St Columbkill's Church, Rathmore

## PORTARLINGTON, LEA, CLONEYHURKE, MONASTEREVIN, NURNEY and RATHDAIRE

Portarlington, although possessing a strong Huguenot history, is perhaps unusual in that those Huguenots who settled here were not for the most part exiles from persecution. Instead, they were given grants of land in reward for services to the monarch of England, in this case William III. William granted Henri Massue, marquis de Rouvigny and later earl of Galway, the right to settle the area of Portarlington with his soldiers. Lord Galway built two churches in Portarlington, one French and one English. Although initially Calvinist, the French Church very quickly came under the sway of the bishop of Kildare and became part of the Established Church, although liturgies remained in French. Lord Galway referred to the French Church in a letter as the 'Église conformiste' (conformist church). The English Church now serves as a hall for the Portarlington parishes.

St Paul's Church, Portarlington

Stained glass in
St John the Evangelist's Church,
Monasterevin

The Church of the Ascension, Rathdaire

Peter Burrowes, friend of Wolfe Tone and the barrister who defended Robert Emmet at his trial, was a native of Portarlington. Burrowes was a strong supporter of Catholic emancipation and the reform of the Irish political system (although he did not support the more extreme elements of the United Irishmen movement).

St John the Evangelist's Church, Monasterevin

Portarlington is another town close to Dublin within the dioceses of Meath and Kildare which has seen a massive population growth in recent years, expanding by more than 50 per cent between 2002 and 2006. Near the town of Portarlington is the townland of Lea and the remains of a large Norman castle built in the mid-thirteenth century by William de Vesey. Also close to Portarlington is the parish of Cloneyhurke.

Closer to Dublin is a cluster of parishes around Monasterevin. The town of Monasterevin derives its name from a monastery that was built as a place of refuge in the seventh century and peopled by monks from Munster, led by St Eimhin. Although a place of sanctuary, there is a reliable tradition that the seizure of this monastery by King Cearbhall was the cause of a war in AD 908 between Cearbhall and Cormac Mac Culinan, king of Munster. The Cistercian monastic estates later moved into lay hands and became Moore Abbey. The great tenor Count John McCormack lived there from 1925 to 1939. In 1945, the Sisters of Charity of Jesus and Mary bought the house and made it a home for people with learning disabilities. This community is very much part of the life of Monasterevin. In the early nineteenth century there were more than six hundred children attending schools of different types in the town, mainly under Protestant auspices. In recent years, an increase in the population of the town has seen a proportionate increase in the size of the Church of Ireland parish.

Close to Monasterevin is the country parish of Nurney, at one time part of the corps of Kildare Cathedral and, indeed, almost within sight of that building. For more than a quarter of a century – from 1912 until 1938 – as curate and later as rector, nearby Rathdaire Parish was served by Rev. James O'Connor, an enthusiastic and fluent Irish speaker. His ministry is honoured by a memorial lectern in the church.

*St Paul's Church, Portarlington* (French Church), originally built by Lord Galway, was reordered in the nineteenth century.

*Lea Church*, dating from the early nineteenth century, is used for worship during summer months.

*Cloneyhurke Church* was built in the nineteenth century on a site given by the Warburton family of Garryhinch.

*St John the Evangelist's Church, Monasterevin* is a late eighteenth-century church built by the Drogheda family of Moore Abbey. The church was altered in the nineteenth century and today has the appearance of that period. In recent years the church has been renovated again.

*Nurney Church*, a simple and unpretentious building, was built in the 1830s.

*The Church of the Ascension, Rathdaire* stands on the old main road from Monasterevin to Port Laoise, near the village of Ballybrittas. Built in 1887 (originally as a chapel of ease for Lea Parish) in memory of members of the local Adair family, it is unquestionably one of the architectural beauties of the diocese. Constructed from cut stone in Hiberno-Gothic style, it has superb carvings over the west door. Although the cruciform church is not large, it gives a sense of spaciousness internally and is crowned by a wide semicircular apse.

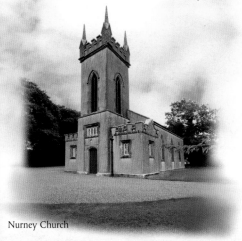

Nurney Church

Cloneyhurke Church

Lea Church

# The United Dioceses of Cashel, Ferns and Ossory

Each of the Irish dioceses has its own distinctive characteristics, but what makes Cashel and Ossory special is the sheer variety within it. I do not simply think of the landscape, although this diocese includes mountain ranges, glorious coastline and stunning valleys. What is even more important, however, is the rich historical variety that is our heritage, and the great pastoral diversity which is the legacy of that heritage today.

So it is that this diocese includes extensive parts of both Munster and Leinster. Our clergy serve in Kilkenny which was once the seat of medieval government, in the port city of Waterford famed world wide for its glass production, in Wexford with its quaint narrow streets and international opera festival, in places like Baltinglass or Lismore where the atmosphere of ancient monastic sites and their worship textures the air. Remarkably we have no less than six ancient cathedrals in this bishopric, each a symbol of continuity and faithful witness, of places where for centuries in the poet's phrase 'prayer has been valid'.

Amid all this variety and beauty we acknowledge the reality of to-day's challenges. The Church of Ireland is a small, if now slightly growing, church. It is charged with the responsibility of making fruitful ecumenical use of a huge built heritage without being overwhelmed by the demands of that heritage. It is a challenge as a bishop to create a sense of diocesan family and shared purpose across a huge geographical area that extends from parts of Dublin commuter-land to the edge of county Cork, and from the passenger port at Rosslare to the site near Birr where St Ciaran reputedly established the diocese of Ossory. It is all too easy to be so captivated by scenery and history that the great questions of today, of the preservation of the rumour of God in an Ireland hugely different from that of even a generation ago, can sometimes be for a moment temptingly sidestepped. However, we live among a people hungering for spirituality, for meaning and for hope … and the muse of history, important as it is, does not always speak instantly to their souls.

At the end of the day the church exists only to preserve, in the very best sense, the haunting, disturbing and loving memory of Jesus in the world. We do this as the apostles did, in their case without any of the accretions that surround us, through gathering the people, breaking the bread and telling the story. And we seek to be equipped to serve the society of which we are part – comforting its afflicted and disturbing its comfortable, making it known that the prophetic voice is not yet silent in this land. In due course only history can judge the faithfulness of our witness in our time.

The most famous (in my view) of all bishops of Ossory, Richard Ledrede, lies buried in a fourteenth century tomb in the sanctuary of St Canice's Cathedral. The bishop's effigy is of a man gloriously attired, but on his feet he wears the sandals of a simple Franciscan – the order in which his ministry had begun. His tomb is a parable about never forgetting roots, about relishing simple things, about knowing what is foundational for our values and beliefs. Such fruitful and faithful contemplation of roots is the real goal of the pages that follow.

Hook Head, County Wexford
SCENIC IRELAND

MICHAEL CASHEL, FERNS AND OSSORY

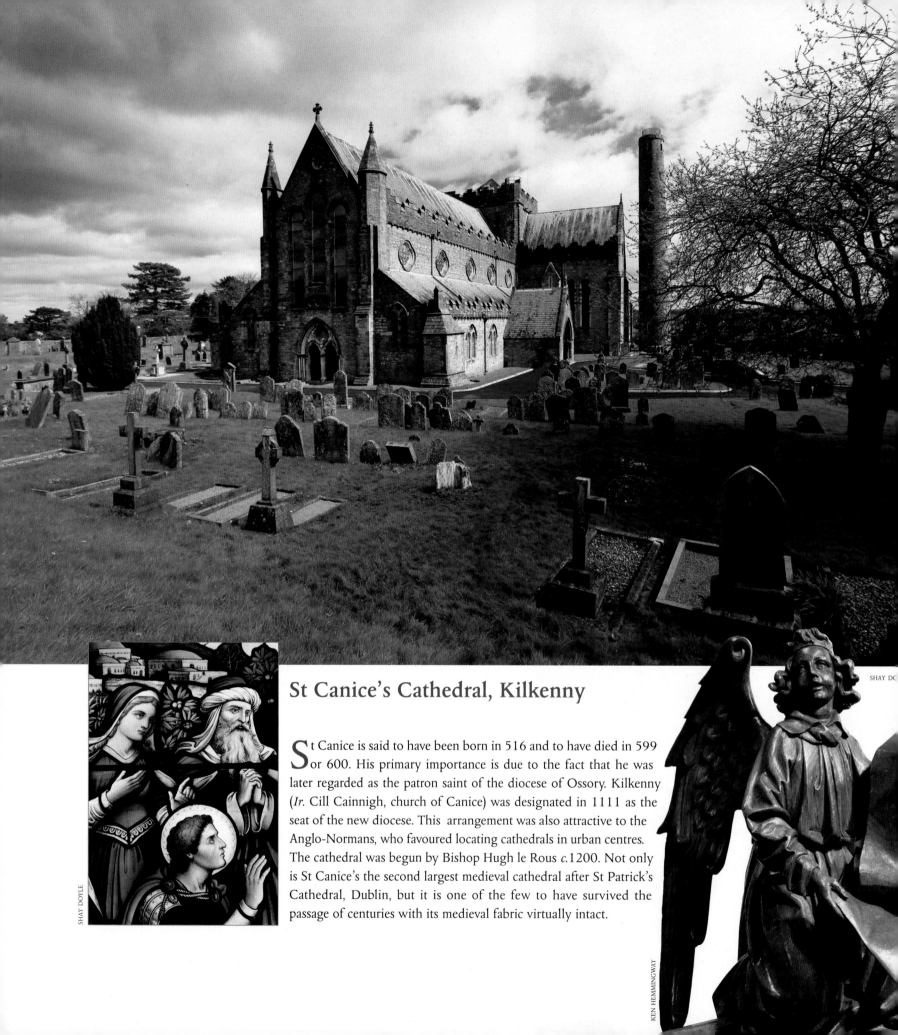

SHAY DOYLE

SHAY DO

KEN HEMMINGWAY

## St Canice's Cathedral, Kilkenny

St Canice is said to have been born in 516 and to have died in 599 or 600. His primary importance is due to the fact that he was later regarded as the patron saint of the diocese of Ossory. Kilkenny (*Ir.* Cill Cainnigh, church of Canice) was designated in 1111 as the seat of the new diocese. This arrangement was also attractive to the Anglo-Normans, who favoured locating cathedrals in urban centres. The cathedral was begun by Bishop Hugh le Rous *c.*1200. Not only is St Canice's the second largest medieval cathedral after St Patrick's Cathedral, Dublin, but it is one of the few to have survived the passage of centuries with its medieval fabric virtually intact.

The nave looking east

The construction of the cathedral was carried out in phases. Its Gothic style marks a sharp break with the Romanesque that had prevailed in Ireland before the conquest. The eastern section – the choir and transepts – were probably commenced under the first Anglo-Norman bishop, Hugh de Rous (*c.* 1202–18), while the stylistic changes in the nave suggest a second phase around the middle of the thirteenth century. The tower, which collapsed on 22 May 1332, is the latest part of the medieval fabric. The round tower, the only architectural survival of the earlier monastery that occupied the site of the cathedral, dates from around the eleventh century. The cathedral was fortunate in that the restoration carried out by Thomas Deane (1863–70) was conservative. He added the castellation over the aisle walls and the magnificent hammer-beam roof.

Apart from its beauty and well preserved architectural integrity, St Canice's possesses by far the largest collection of medieval monuments in Ireland. More than half of the surviving eighty-one monuments belong to the sixteenth century. Adjacent to the eastern end of the cathedral is the bishop's palace, now the National Headquarters of Heritage Council of Ireland. Concealed within its Georgian facade are significant elements of a fourteenth-century episcopal dwelling attributed to Bishop Ledrede and also a three-storey early sixteenth-century tower built by Bishop Milo Baron (1527–55). This makes the palace Ireland's earliest surviving medieval domestic residence. The present episcopal residence is located in its grounds. At the western end of the cathedral stands St Canice's library, the original site of Kilkenny College (founded *c.* 1530), and the *alma mater* of Jonathan Swift. The cathedral is an essential focus of the cultural life of the city, attracting many tourists and hosting arts and music events. Above all, St Canice's Cathedral remains an important place of worship, prayer and pilgrimage.

The tomb of Piers Butler, earl of Ormond and Essory

KEN HEMMINGWAY

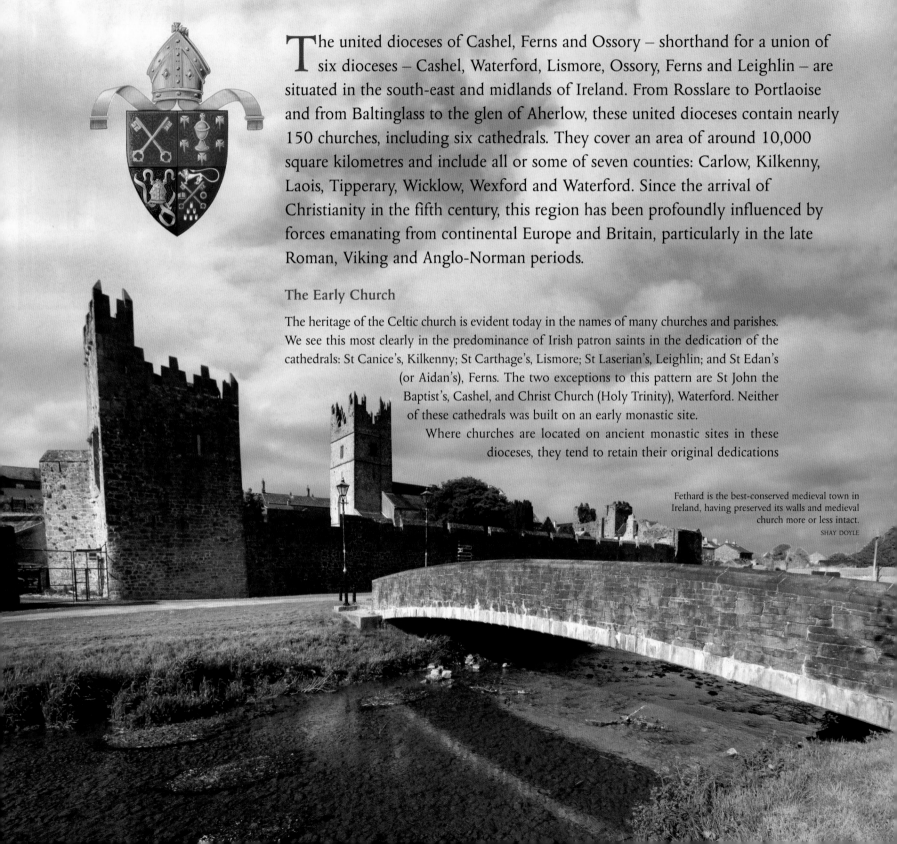

# The United Dioceses of Cashel, Ferns and Ossory

ADRIAN EMPEY

The united dioceses of Cashel, Ferns and Ossory – shorthand for a union of six dioceses – Cashel, Waterford, Lismore, Ossory, Ferns and Leighlin – are situated in the south-east and midlands of Ireland. From Rosslare to Portlaoise and from Baltinglass to the glen of Aherlow, these united dioceses contain nearly 150 churches, including six cathedrals. They cover an area of around 10,000 square kilometres and include all or some of seven counties: Carlow, Kilkenny, Laois, Tipperary, Wicklow, Wexford and Waterford. Since the arrival of Christianity in the fifth century, this region has been profoundly influenced by forces emanating from continental Europe and Britain, particularly in the late Roman, Viking and Anglo-Norman periods.

## The Early Church

The heritage of the Celtic church is evident today in the names of many churches and parishes. We see this most clearly in the predominance of Irish patron saints in the dedication of the cathedrals: St Canice's, Kilkenny; St Carthage's, Lismore; St Laserian's, Leighlin; and St Edan's (or Aidan's), Ferns. The two exceptions to this pattern are St John the Baptist's, Cashel, and Christ Church (Holy Trinity), Waterford. Neither of these cathedrals was built on an early monastic site.

Where churches are located on ancient monastic sites in these dioceses, they tend to retain their original dedications

Fethard is the best-conserved medieval town in Ireland, having preserved its walls and medieval church more or less intact.
SHAY DOYLE

– for example, St Fintan's (Durrow) and St Munna's (Taghmon). Traces of Irish saints are also preserved in names like Sierkieran (St Ciaran) and St Cormac (Kilcormac). Very often the names of parish churches, even when they lack a formal dedication, betray memories of earlier churches when they contain elements such as 'Kill' or 'Temple'. Irish dedications, of course, may be accompanied by the highly distinctive and very visible Irish round tower – for example, in Cashel, Kilkenny and Ferns.

## The Medieval Period

The Viking age in the south-east began in earnest with raids on Lismore (AD 833) and Ferns (AD 839). While severely disrupting the Irish church, they led to the construction of the region's first major trading towns, most notably at Waterford and Wexford. The arrival of the Anglo-Normans in 1169 brought further sweeping changes to church life. The Anglo-Normans favoured new dedications, reflecting the ecclesiastical tastes of the late twelfth or early thirteenth centuries, with a notable emphasis on St Mary. Above all, they created the great network of parish churches around this time, with the result that a significant proportion of them are dedicated to her.

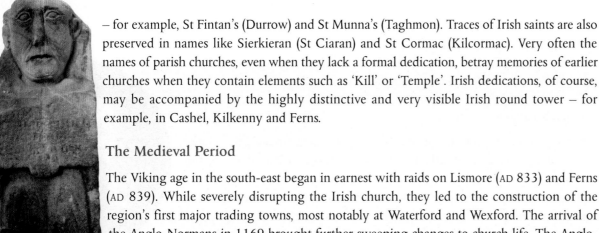

Stone figure from St Carthage's Cathedral, Lismore
SHAY DOYLE

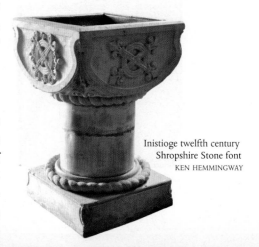

Inistioge twelfth century Shropshire Stone font
KEN HEMMINGWAY

While the Anglo-Normans brought the Irish church into close institutional conformity with the continental church, significant changes had also taken place in the half century before their arrival. A series of reforming synods, beginning with Ráth Breasail in 1111, resulted in the creation of four provinces, reflecting the territories of the provincial kings. These, in turn, were divided into their constituent dioceses, framed on the basis of their respective subkingdoms. Thus, the present diocesan map of Ireland, with few exceptions, reveals the political divisions of Ireland on the eve of the Anglo-Norman invasion. Cashel, the ancient royal seat of the Eóghanacht kings of Munster, became the seat of the archbishop of Cashel.

If territorial dioceses were late arrivals in medieval Ireland, exactly the same may be said of the parochial system, which was essentially created by the Anglo-Normans. Just as the dioceses reflected the political realities of pre-conquest Ireland, so too the parishes, in most cases, reflect the territorial unit of the Anglo-Norman manor. A significant number of Anglo-Norman lords founded towns on their manors – for example, Kilkenny and Carlow – each of which supported an important parish church. Many Church of Ireland churches in the united dioceses are located on the site of thirteenth-century manors, and always close to castles, wherever they have survived.

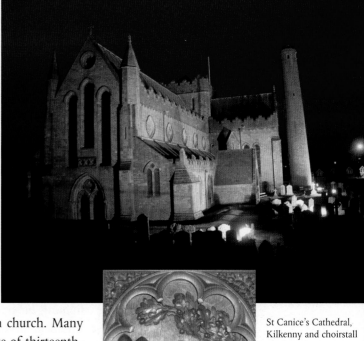

The Anglo-Norman architectural inheritance is omnipresent. The landscape of large areas of the united dioceses is dominated by Anglo-Norman castles, monastic foundations and churches. At the same time, the passage of centuries, the disruption of the Protestant Reformation and devastating wars, particularly in the seventeenth century, have all taken a heavy toll on medieval church buildings. By far the best-preserved Gothic cathedral is St Canice's, Kilkenny. Many parish churches were abandoned over the course of two centuries

St Canice's Cathedral, Kilkenny and choirstall carving
ST CANICE'S CATHEDRAL, KILKENNY

The ruins of the Cistercian monastery beside St Mary's Church, Baltinglass, founded by Dermot MacMurrough, king of Leinster, in 1148

John Bale, Bishop of Ossory,
1553–63
BELFAST CATHEDRAL ARCHIVE

ST. MARY'S CHURCH AND ABBEY, NEW ROSS.

A print of St Mary's Church New Ross, 1835

Richard Chevenix, Bishop of
Waterford and Lismore, 1746–79
BELFAST CATHEDRAL ARCHIVE

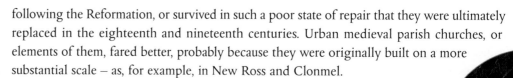

Bishop Miler Magrath
CLOGHER CATHEDRAL

following the Reformation, or survived in such a poor state of repair that they were ultimately replaced in the eighteenth and nineteenth centuries. Urban medieval parish churches, or elements of them, fared better, probably because they were originally built on a more substantial scale – as, for example, in New Ross and Clonmel.

## Post-Reformation Times

Whereas in most of Europe the majority of the population espoused the religion professed by the ruler, exactly the opposite process occurred in Ireland. Attempts by the state to promote religious reforms in a context where regional loyalties were deeply divided and where power could only be exercised through constantly shifting alliances met with limited success at best. Such a highly volatile and unpredictable religious situation produced some remarkable individuals, whose survival skills were more in evidence that their piety.

Chief among them was Miler Magrath (archbishop of Cashel 1571–1622), who survived the political turmoil of the Desmond Rebellion, the Nine Years' War and innumerable political intrigues, all the while retaining a papal appointment to the sees of Down and Connor, in spite of his marriage. To Miler's live-saving (or life-enhancing) ambivalence one may add his ecumenical ambivalence: his wife, five sons and four daughters were Roman Catholic. Miler, who reputedly lived to the age of 100, died in the bosom of the Church of Ireland. He was buried in the old cathedral, where his tomb is still situated.

## The Seventeenth Century

The conclusion of the Elizabethan conquest of Ireland in 1603 brought with it the prospect of political and religious stability. The first four decades allowed some rebuilding of churches and church life. But whatever progress was gained in the first four decades of the century was quickly annulled by the destruction and instability of the next two. First, there was the Eleven Years' War (1641–52 in Ireland), which was an overspill both from the civil wars in Britain and the Thirty Years' War in continental Europe.

The Irish campaigns were particularly bitter, inflicting death and confiscation on the south-eastern counties in the course of the Cromwellian campaign. Numerous towns – such as Wexford and Waterford – were subjected to sieges. Some of these surrendered without much fighting, but others, particularly Wexford, Kilkenny and Clonmel, experienced heavy fighting. Churches inevitably suffered in the course of these conflicts, including the beautiful cathedral of St Canice in Kilkenny. The Cromwellian victory resulted in the suppression of bishops of the Church of Ireland and the abolition of the *Book of Common Prayer*.

When Charles II was finally restored to the throne in 1660, the process of rebuilding the Church of Ireland began once again. The church was to suffer more dislocation during the Williamite Wars (1689–91), although this time the south-eastern counties were spared most of the ravages. It is scarcely surprising that no church building survives from this highly troubled century.

## The Eighteenth Century

In the eighteenth century the church was beset by a range of systemic problems deriving from the Tudor age. Among them were absenteeism, politicised patronage and a degraded infrastructure. At the same time, these dioceses benefitted greatly from the activities of some improving bishops, who devoted their episcopates to raising the standard of the parish clergy, provided libraries for their edification (for example in Cashel, Waterford and Kilkenny), repaired or replaced ruinous churches, established schools and promoted social-improvement schemes. The building or remodelling of splendid episcopal residences (Waterford, Cashel, Kilkenny) signalled their resolve to reside in their dioceses. Included in the ranks of these improvers were Nathaniel Foy (bishop of Waterford and Lismore 1691–1707), who improved his palace and founded Bishop Foy's School; and Theophilus Bolton (archbishop of Cashel 1730–44) – known as 'River Bolton' as a consequence of his water scheme in Cashel – who founded the famous library, built a splendid palace and endeavoured to maintain the crumbling medieval cathedral, much of it at his personal expense.

The episcopal residence Kilkenny
KEN HEMMINGWAY

Bishop Bolton's Library, Cashel Cathedral
RCB/DAVID CROOKS

Richard Pococke, the famed traveller (bishop of Ossory 1756–65), may also be classed as an improver, since he carried out works on both the bishop's palace and the cathedral of his diocese, founded a school and established a linen-weaving factory at Linstown, near Kilkenny. Perhaps the best example of a dedicated prelate, however, was Charles Agar (archbishop of Cashel 1779–1801), who not only completed the building of the new cathedral, but also actively supervised his clergy by encouraging the repair and restoration of parish churches, as well as the construction of glebe houses.

Important as the achievements of the church in this period undoubtedly were, the fact that they rested on insecure foundations should not be forgotten. In the first place, the penal laws against the Roman Catholic majority were difficult to defend once the passions of the previous century's religious conflicts had subsided. While many Anglicans questioned the propriety of the penal laws, they saw no prospect of surviving without the protection of the state – a state that they perceived to be defending personal liberties and freedoms in a European order dominated by autocratic, illiberal Catholic powers. They considered the Church settlement to be an essential pillar of a free social order. From such a perspective, they were known to defend the penal laws while at the same time promoting harmonious relations with Catholic clergy. Archbishop Agar was uncompromising in his support for the laws, but at the same time was on excellent and personally friendly terms with the Catholic parish priest in Cashel and the Catholic archbishop. In much the same spirit, Bishop Pococke, on his visit to Rome in 1734, paid courtesy calls to the Irish Dominicans at San Clemente and to the Irish Franciscans at San Isodore, where he was warmly entertained.

Bishop of Ossory, Richard Pococke, 1756–65
BELFAST CATHEDRAL ARCHIVE

Bust of Bishop Charles Agar, Leighlin Cathedral
KEN HEMMINGWAY

Defeat of the rebels at Vinegar Hill, 1798

This comfortable political and religious status quo was profoundly shaken by the outbreak of the French Revolution in 1789. In 1791, the Society of United Irishmen was formed. It was deeply imbued with the spirit of French Republican ideology, and demanded radical political reform and a union of Irishmen of every religious creed. In spite of their privileged position, a significant number of the leaders were Anglican. This was especially true of the leaders of the Wexford Rebellion in 1798, who included Beauchamp Bagenal Harvey, president of the Wexford Council of United Irishmen, his brother James, his cousin John Boxwell and several others, many of whom were closely connected to the Church of Ireland. The diocese of Ferns witnessed some of the heaviest fighting of the uprising at New Ross and Vinegar Hill.

## The Nineteenth Century

The union of Great Britain and Ireland, which came into legal effect in 1801, also involved the union of the Church of Ireland with the Church of England. Such a union offered the prospect of greater security and stability for Irish Anglicans, but in reality nothing could have been farther from the truth. To begin with, a long series of parliamentary reforms, beginning with the Irish Church Temporalities Act of 1833, led inexorably to disestablishment in 1869, resulting in the church being stripped of its inherited privileges and property and left to sink or swim. One of the early casualties of reform was the reduction of the archdiocese of Cashel to a bishopric, consisting of a united Cashel, Emly, Waterford and Lismore, in 1833. Two years later, Ossory, Ferns and Leighlin were united. Eventually, in 1977, these two surviving unions were joined to form the current diocesan union (Emly was assigned to the united dioceses of Limerick and Killaloe at this time).

The future of the church looked bleak. Outside observers suspected that it would implode once the prop of the state was removed, while many insiders feared that the forces released by the Evangelical revival might take the church out of the Anglican fold. In the event, the church emerged from all of these challenges renewed and invigorated. How could this be?

The Church of Ireland was transformed by pressures as much from within as from without in the first half of the nineteenth century. Relieved of their political role in the Irish parliament after the Act of Union, bishops concentrated their efforts increasingly on improving both the quality of the parish clergy and the diocesan infrastructure. The church was fortunate to have a body of increasingly dedicated bishops, clergy and laity to provide leadership at points of crisis.

*Kilcooley Church* in eastern County Tipperary was built in 1829 with a grant from the Board of First Fruits.
RCB/DAVID CROOKS

Another sign of this nineteenth-century renewal was the astonishing scale of church-building and restoration, which not only transformed the architectural landscape but also enriched the worshipping environment. Between 1808 and 1829 hundreds of churches were built in Ireland, often to replace ruinous or ruined medieval buildings, funded by private donations or by grants from the Board of First Fruits. These latter churches were generally rather basic structures, consisting of a square tower and rectangular hall, a form of design known as 'First-Fruits Gothic' in Ireland. Plain and unpretentious, they are nevertheless a distinctive feature of the Irish rural landscape. Churches of this style are well represented in these dioceses.

Other readily identifiable churches from this period are the products of the Gothic revival. St Paul's Church, Cahir (1820), designed by the great architect John Nash, who laid out much of London's West End, is a particularly interesting example of the early revival. Most revival churches, however, were built some decades later. Examples of neo-Gothic churches include Christ Church, Gorey (rebuilt 1858–61), and Holy Trinity, Portlaw (1852), designed by William Tinsley. The last in the series of Gothic-revival churches is the charming church of Christ the Redeemer, Myshall (1913), modelled on Salisbury Cathedral. Other nineteenth-century rebuilding activity consisted of restoration work, chiefly in connection with the cathedrals.

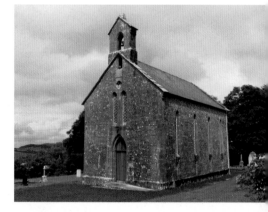

*Holy Trinity Church, Dysert Enos* was built in 1845 but, because of the Great Famine, was not opened until 1849.
RCB/DAVID CROOKS

Thus, by the time the Church of Ireland was disestablished in 1870, it was well stocked with churches and glebes, but also spiritually very much alive and equipped to meet the enormous challenges that would face it in the next five decades. Disestablishment proved a boon in many ways. The Church of Ireland, now having no connection with the state, became the sole responsibility of its members, who responded faithfully and enthusiastically. From this time, diocesan synods were held annually to deal with local church affairs, with delegates drawn from parishes.

## The Twentieth Century

During the twentieth century, the united dioceses of Cashel, Ferns and Ossory hosted a number of distinguished bishops. John Henry Bernard (bishop 1911–15), was a scholar and gifted teacher, archbishop of Dublin (1915–19) and provost of Trinity College (1919–27). He played an important role in the tumultuous politics of Home Rule and the eventual partition of Ireland. Conservative by inclination, he was also pragmatic. His conservatism did not prevent him from campaigning successfully for higher education for women.

John Allen Gregg (1915–20), who succeeded him, became archbishop of Dublin (1920–39) and then archbishop of Armagh (1939–59). His leadership in the early decades of Irish independence was crucial in reconciling southern Anglicans to the new regime. Henry Robert McAdoo (1962–77) was subsequently archbishop of Dublin (1977–85). As a recognised authority on the Caroline divines, McAdoo played an important role in the Anglican Communion, particularly as chairman of the Anglican–Roman Catholic International Committee.

St Mary's Inistioge, has a very fine triple-lancet memorial stained-glass east window from An Túr Gloine (1919), dedicated to the memory of Major Peter Connellan, who was killed in the First World War. The figures portrayed represent valour, resurrection and charity.
KEN HEMMINGWAY

Scholarship was not confined by any means to the rank of bishop. St John Seymour (1880–1950), archdeacon of Cashel and Emly and vice-president of the North Munster Historical Society. Like James Graves, MRIA, rector of Ennisnag and founder of the Kilkenny Archaeological Society (d.1886) before him, his publications drew extensively on archival sources since destroyed. He was a well regarded historian and a member of the Royal Irish Academy. His wide-ranging publications included history, Anglo-Irish literature, the Puritans in Ireland, and ghost stories. Others, like Robert Wyse-Jackson, dean of Kilkenny, and F.R. Bolton, dean of Leighlin, were notable scholars in the second half of the twentieth century.

Parishioners celebrate 150 years of the Church of St John the Evangelist at Ardamine in Co. Wexford in bright sunshine on 27th May 2012.
HERBIE SHARMAN

## New Millennium

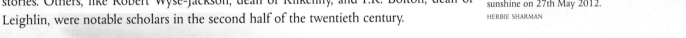

At present, the diocesan community consists of around 14,000 people, served by approximately 45 full-time and non-stipendiary clergy. The 33 parish unions within the united dioceses support nearly 150 churches. There is also a guild of around 30 diocesan lay readers. There are a considerable number of schools under church patronage and many parish organisations. The Diocesan Synod assembles once a year to oversee diocesan business. In recognition of recent rationalising changes, the title of the diocesan union most commonly used is Cashel, Ferns and Ossory.

FROM LEFT: Bishop Michael Burrows opening the new national school at Abbeyleix South on Monday 30 April 2012.

The future of the church? Good Friday at St Laserian's Cathedral 2013

Youth Group from the Dunleckney Union of parishes.
ALF HARVEY

HERBIE SHARMAN

## DIOCESE OF CASHEL

PHOTOGRAPHS BY SHAY DOYLE

### CASHEL, MOGORBAN, TIPPERARY, CLONBEG and BALLINTEMPLE

*St John the Baptist's Cathedral and St Patrick's Rock, Cashel.* Unlike most Irish cathedral sites, the Rock of Cashel – the seat of the kings of Munster since the fourth century – had no ecclesiastical associations until the twelfth century, when King Muirchearteach O'Brien granted the site 'to Patrick and the Lord'. In 1111, Cashel was chosen as one two Irish archiepiscopal sees. After the Reformation, the thirteenth-century Gothic building continued to serve as the Anglican cathedral until it was abandoned in 1749.

Founded on the site of the demolished medieval parish church of St John, the new cathedral was opened on Christmas day 1783. It was largely the achievement of Archbishop Agar (archbishop 1779–1801). Its Classical elegance makes no concessions to the medieval past. While we know that Richard Morrison's name appears on the design of the steeple, which was a slightly later addition, we are not sure who was responsible for the main building. Built from grey stone, it has arched windows and a cushion frieze supported by Ionic pilasters which, however, are omitted on the opposite, less conspicuous, side.

The original interior was remodelled in 1867, so that little of it remains except the western gallery (with its stalls) and the organ. In the eighteenth century, the Anglican archbishops bequeathed to posterity not only a fine Classical cathedral, but also Archbishop Bolton's gracious Palladian palace (1732), designed by the brilliant Edward Lovett Pearce. Bolton also created a splendid library, which still bears his name and which is fittingly located in the grounds of the cathedral.

St Mary's Church, Tipperary

*The church of the Holy Spirit, Mogorban* was built in 1816.

A new *St Mary's Church, Tipperary*, replacing an earlier building, was completed in 1830 with a loan from the Board of First Fruits. The church was extensively rebuilt in 1857–64 by Joseph Welland, with the addition of a north transept. The memorials provide ample evidence of the ravages of the First World War: the fine east window (1918), designed by John Archibald Davies and representing the adoration of the Magi, is a memorial to three members of one family, who perished in 1916. Another memorial records the names of 39 former pupils of the Abbey School who were killed. Between them they were awarded five Military Crosses and a Croix de Guerre. Among those buried in the churchyard is Christopher Emmet, grandfather of Robert Emmet.

*St Sedna's Church, Clonbeg*, in the glen of Aherlow, is an attractive estate church built in 1840 and designed by John Pain. It has a collegiate chancel complete with flying canopies for the clergy stalls. The interior is lit by 11 finely executed stained-glass windows from the studio of Watson & Co., Youghal, dating from between 1902 and 1908.

*St Mary's, Ballintemple*, at Dundrum, was rebuilt in 1861, replacing an earlier church.

SHAY DOYLE

St Sedna's Church, Clonbeg

RCB/DAVID CROOKS

Crohane Church

RCB/DAVID CROOKS

## KILCOOLEY, LITTLETON (BORRIS) and CROHANE

The Kilcooley Union in County Tipperary has many historical associations. The imposing remains of the Cistercian abbey of Kilcooley, founded *c.* 1182 by Donal O'Brien, king of Munster, are situated close to the parish church. In the eighteenth century, a considerable number of immigrants from the German Palatinate settled in the area.

*Kilcooley Church* in eastern County Tipperary was built in 1829 with a grant from the Board of First Fruits.

KEN HEMMINGWAY

*St Mary's Church, Littleton* is situated in a small village that originated in the eighteenth century as a stagepost on the old Dublin to Cork road. Built in 1786 with the assistance of the Board of First Fruits, it incorporates alterations made in 1822 and 1826. The church has a very fine east window dedicated to the ascension, executed by the studio of Watson & Co., Youghal, in 1908.

*Crohane Church* was designed by Joseph Welland in 1852. The east window, dating from 1900, is the work of Mayer & Co. of Munich.

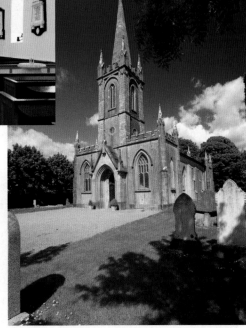

St Mary's Church, Littleton
KEN HEMMINGWAY

## TEMPLEMORE, THURLES and KILFITHMONE

Thurles was one of the major manorial towns of the vast Butler lordship, founded by Theobald Walter, brother of Hubert Walter, archbishop of Canterbury, in 1185. The large manor of Templemore was granted by Theobald to one of his most trusted vassals, Hugh Purcell, probably shortly after 1185. Hugh granted the tithes of the parish church, St Mary's, to the abbey of St Thomas, Dublin, dedicated to the memory of Thomas Becket, the martyred archbishop of Canterbury.

The present *St Mary's Church, Templemore* was built in 1789 and consecrated in 1794 by Charles Agar, archbishop of Cashel. The clock church tower was restored and floodlit as part of a millennium project.

The present *St Mary's Church, Thurles* replaced an earlier building in 1780, presumably on the site of the medieval parish church. More work seems to have been carried out on it in 1812, thanks to a loan from the Board of First Fruits.

The parish church of *Kilfithmone* was rebuilt in 1821.

Kilfithmone Church
RCB/DAVID CROOKS

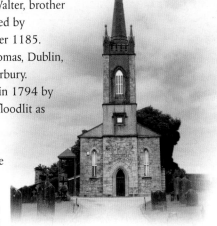

St Mary's Church, Thurles
RCB/DAVID CROOKS

# DIOCESE OF WATERFORD

## WATERFORD, KILLEA, DRUMCANNON and DUNHILL

*Blessed Trinity (Christ Church) Cathedral, Waterford.* The previous building to occupy the site of the present cathedral was a substantial Anglo-Norman Gothic building constructed primarily in the thirteenth century, which may have incorporated elements of an even earlier Hiberno-Norse cathedral. The Gothic building was demolished in the late eighteenth century, to be replaced by a new building, designed by a Waterford architect, John Roberts (1712–96), who was also responsible for completing the bishop's palace, Waterford town hall and the Roman Catholic cathedral. The resulting Classical building is one of the finest Georgian churches in Ireland, with its Doric portico, slender Corinthian columns, rococo stucco-work and magnificent reredos.

The cathedral contains a number of monuments rescued from its Gothic predecessor. One remarkable medieval survival is the beautiful collection of fifteenth-century vestments – the only complete set to have survived the Reformation in Britain and Ireland – discovered during the demolition of the old cathedral. They are now on display in the Waterford Museum. A brass plaque records that Col. E. Roberts lost five grandsons during the Great War, four in France and one in Gallipoli. There is a fine stained-glass window attributed to A.E. Childs from An Túr Gloine.

A full programme of concerts, exhibitions and events now takes place in the cathedral. For over a thousand years this site has continued to be an important place for Christian worship and prayer.

Interior of Blessed Trinity Cathedral, Waterford
KEN HEMMINGWAY

*St Andrew's Church, Killea,* at Dunmore East, was consecrated in 1821. It is not known who designed the chancel and nave, but the fine tower and large south transept are the work of Joseph Welland. The stained-glass windows are of high quality, the majority of them coming from An Túr Gloine.

Christ Church, Drumcannon, Tramore
SHAY DOYLE

*Christ Church, Drumcannon,* at Tramore in south-eastern County Waterford, is a fine six-bay neo-Gothic church overlooking one of Ireland's most popular seaside towns. Its cruciform design is attributed to Abraham Denny (1820–92). It was built in 1851 with high-quality local masonry. The interior is enhanced by delicate stained-glass panels, carved stone wall monuments and an exposed timber roof construction. Of particular interest is the memorial obelisk in the churchyard, commemorating the tragic loss of the crew of the Seahorse, a Royal Navy ship carrying 16 officers, 287 soldiers, 38 women and 38 children, which foundered in a storm in Tramore Bay on 30 January 1816. Only 30 of those on board survived.

*St John the Baptist's Church, Dunhill,* at Annestown, was completed in 1856.

Blessed Trinity
Cathedral, Waterford
KEN HEMMINGWAY

# DIOCESE OF LISMORE

### FIDDOWN, CLONEGAM, PORTLAW and KILMEADEN

*St Paul's Church, Fiddown*, in Piltown, south-western County Kilkenny, was designed by George Edmund Street (1824–81), one of the leading church restorers in these islands in the nineteenth century. The site, donated by the earl of Bessborough, is located on the Bessborough Demesne. The new church was completed in 1863 and consists of a three-bay nave and two-bay chancel. It has a good number of fine stained-glass windows, mainly executed in various London studios. Not surprisingly, many of the windows are associated with the Bessborough family.

*Clonegam Church* is situated on a hill on the Curraghmore estate of the marquises of Waterford. It was built in 1741 for Sir Marcus Beresford, earl of Tyrone, and Countess Catherine de la Poer. Their marriage brought about the union of the Beresford and de la Poer families. The church contains some remarkable funerary monuments.

*Holy Trinity Church, Portlaw*, a neat neo-Gothic church, is closely associated with the Beresfords (marquises of Waterford), whose family seat is at Curraghmore. The village of Portlaw owes its existence to the remarkable industrial enterprise of a Quaker named David Malcolmson, who established a highly successful cotton mill employing more than 700 people in 1824. Holy Trinity was completed in 1852. The east windows, reredos, oak pews and black and white tiles in the nave are all gifts of the Beresfords.

*St Mary's Church, Kilmeaden* may incorporate elements of the earlier medieval church that stood on the site. It contains a number of interesting memorials. The eighteenth-century pulpit originally came from Lismore Cathedral. The interior of this beautiful church was restored in Classical style in recent times through the generosity of the late Ambrose Congreve of Mount Congreve.

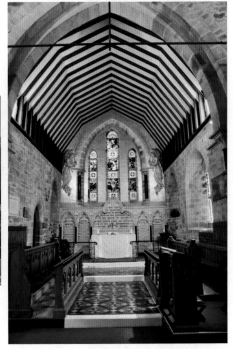

St Paul's Church, Fiddown, Piltown
KEN HEMMINGWAY

### ST MARY'S (CLONMEL), INISLONAGH, FETHARD, CAHIR and TULLAMEELAN

*St Mary's Church, Clonmel*, in south-eastern County Tipperary, incorporates much of the fabric of the medieval parish church that owes its origin to the first Anglo-Norman lord, William de Burgo, who died in 1205. Although it is unlikely that elements of the existing fabric extend as far back as William's time, the east and west windows are of fifteenth-century provenance. The six bays in the nave, largely rebuilt in the nineteenth century, together with the side aisles, reflect the importance of Clonmel, the largest town in Tipperary and the administrative centre of the palatinate of Tipperary until its demise in 1715. St Mary's was considerably restored in the nineteenth century, probably by John Welland.

Remnants of the town wall form the northern and western boundaries of the churchyard. In the chapel of St Michael there is a memorial to the Gough family: three brothers became generals, and two of them earned the Victoria Cross.

*St Patrick's Church, Inislonagh* stands on the site of a Cistercian abbey. Although the present church dates from 1818, it incorporates elements of the old abbey, most notably the well-preserved Romanesque doorway and the east window. Notable also is the fine stained-glass memorial window in the south nave, portraying St George and commemorating Brigadier General John Edmund Gough, VC, KCB and *aide-de-camp* to King George V.

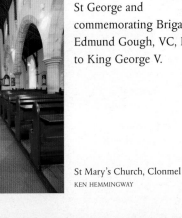

St Mary's Church, Clonmel
KEN HEMMINGWAY

## LISMORE, CAPPOQUIN, KILWATERMOY, DUNGARVAN, KILROSSANTY, STRADBALLY and KILMACTHOMAS (ROSSMIRE)

Dungarvan in southern County Waterford was the centre of an enormous royal manor created by King John that once extended over much of that county. The parish church is accordingly located close to King John's Castle in the oldest part of the town.

*St Carthage's Cathedral, Lismore.* The cathedral probably occupies the site of the famous monastery of Lismore, founded by St Carthach (*alias* Carthage) shortly before his death around AD 638. In the course of its long existence, the monastery was renowned for its learning, rivalling the great monasteries of Clonmacnoise and Glendalough. The original Anglo-Norman cathedral was destroyed in the course of the Munster Wars in the 1590s. Over the course of the next three centuries, the cathedral was subjected to successive restorations and rebuilding. However, most of what we see today was the result to two major nineteenth-century restorations. The tower, elegant spire, nave windows and nave vault were constructed in 1826–7 by James and George Richard Pain. More radical changes were carried out in the 1870s. An important nineteenth-century addition to the cathedral was the Cotton Library (1851) in the north transept, which was restored, refurnished and catalogued in the 1990s.

There is a very fine stained-glass window by the pre-Raphaelite Edward Burne-Jones, the only one of its kind in Ireland. The altar-tomb of John and Catherine Magrath, in the north-western corner of the nave, was erected in 1548. The relief shows St Gregory the Great wearing the papal triple crown.

PHOTOGRAPHS OF ST CARTHAGE'S CATHEDRAL BY SHAY DOYLE

*Holy Trinity Church, Fethard* was the parish church of the archiepiscopal borough of Fethard, the best-conserved medieval town in Ireland, having preserved its walls and medieval church more or less intact. Much of the fabric of Holy Trinity is medieval, including the vault over the nave (the roof is more recent), although it was once longer than it is today. Besides retaining its fine fifteenth-century tower, the church contains tracery windows and tombs commemorating the leading medieval borough families such as the Everards and the Hacketts. The coat of arms of King Edward VI (the only son of Henry VIII), who died in 1553, are visible in the south aisle near the vestry.

*St Paul's Church, Cahir* is a particularly interesting early neo-Gothic church designed by John Nash (1752–1835). Cahir was his only commissioned church in Ireland.

*Tullameelan Church*, at Knocklofty, was originally the estate church of the earls of Knocklofty. It was built between 1799 and 1813.

y Trinity Church, Fethard
HEMMINGWAY

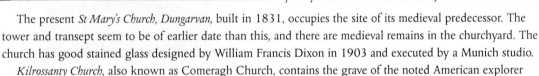

Holy Trinity Church, Fethard
SHAY DOYLE

St Mary's Church, Dungarvan
KEN HEMMINGWAY

*St Anne's Church, Cappoquin* was consecrated in 1820. The chancel, with its imposing east window (depicting the four evangelists), and the vestry date from 1869. The church was closely connected to the Keane family of Belmont.

*St Mary the Virgin's Church, Kilwatermoy* was built in 1831 as a chapel of ease in the parish of Tallow. It has some interesting stained-glass windows by Mayer & Co. of Munich and James Powell & Sons of London.

The present *St Mary's Church, Dungarvan*, built in 1831, occupies the site of its medieval predecessor. The tower and transept seem to be of earlier date than this, and there are medieval remains in the churchyard. The church has good stained glass designed by William Francis Dixon in 1903 and executed by a Munich studio.

*Kilrossanty Church*, also known as Comeragh Church, contains the grave of the noted American explorer Colonel John Palliser, who died in 1887. Palliser's Pass in the Rockies is named after him.

*St James's Church, Stradbally* was built in 1802 and enlarged in 1830. The ruins of the earlier Anglo-Norman parish church stand in the churchyard.

*Rossmire Church*, built in 1829, is situated in the village of Kilmacthomas.

St James's Church, Stradbally

## DIOCESE OF OSSORY

### CASTLECOMER, THE COLLIERY CHURCH, MOTHEL and BILBOA

*St Mary's Church, Castlecomer*, in north County Kilkenny, stands on the site of the medieval parish church. The town of Castlecomer was destroyed in the 1798 Rebellion. The church was restored by Lady Anne Ormonde. It possesses a fine triple-lancet east window from the An Túr Gloine studio by Michael Healy. The window was erected in 1920 in memory of Lt Christopher Prior-Wandesforde, who was killed on the western front in 1917. It portrays St Christopher (perhaps a reference to the lieutenant's heroic efforts to rescue his men after a gas attack, which cost him his life), St Martin of Tours (the Roman soldier-saint who gave his cloak to a beggar at Amiens, close to the western front), and the angel of Resurrection.

Holy Trinity Church, Bilboa

*The Colliery Church* was built on the Wandesforde estate to serve the spiritual needs of the local mining community. The coal-mining industry in the Castlecomer region was already well established by the beginning of the eighteenth century. Mining continued until the 1960s, when the mine was closed. The church was built by Rev. Henry Richard Dawson, rector of Castlecomer, a well-known antiquary, who died aged 48 in 1840, from fever contracted while visiting his parishioners. Another interesting absentee rector was Jacques Abbadie (d. 1727), a distinguished Huguenot scholar and theologian, who accompanied Marshal Schomberg on his Irish campaigns.

Also in this union are *Mothel Church* and *Holy Trinity Church, Bilboa*.

The Colliery Church
KEN HEMMINGWAY

## CLONENAGH (MOUNTRATH), OFFERLANE, BORRIS-IN-OSSORY, SEIRKIERAN, ROSKELTON and LACCA

Lacca Church

342  Seirkieran ('Kieran's fountain') in County Offaly is quite literally a place apart, since it is an Ossory parish in two parts, several kilometres east of Birr, inside the diocese of Killaloe. According to various medieval biographies, Kieran was not only Ossory's first saint, but also the first ordained bishop in Ireland consecrated by the pope before the coming of Patrick. The accuracy of these sources is doubtful. What is not in doubt, however, is that a monastery was established here possibly as early as the sixth century.

*St Peter's Church, Clonenagh (Mountrath),* just inside the diocese of Leighlin, is the principal church in this parish group. The town developed on the estate of the Cootes, earls of Mountrath, and has its origins in the seventeenth century. The church was consecrated in 1801 and subsequently enlarged in 1832.

St Peter's Church, Clonenagh

The present *St Kieran's Church, Seirkieran,* erected in 1844, is probably built on the site of the monastic church. It is located in the centre of an extensive network of earthworks, which are still quite visible. Other survivals of its early history include fragments of two ninth-century high crosses and the base of a round tower. The present church has a fifteenth-century east window, which was doubtless salvaged from the late medieval Augustinian priory on the site. Further interest is provided by St Kieran's Well and St Kieran's Bush (often draped in pieces of cloth). A curious medieval survival is a Sheela-na-gig, a naked female figurine, now on display in the National Museum. This intriguing object would have been located near the door of the late medieval church. Such figurines are the subject of extensive historical debate. They were possibly intended to ward off evil spirits, although others interpret them as fertility symbols.

*Offerlane Church, St Mark's Church, Borris-in-Ossory, Roskelton Church, Lacca Church* are also in this union.

Offerlane Church
RCB/DAVID CROOKS

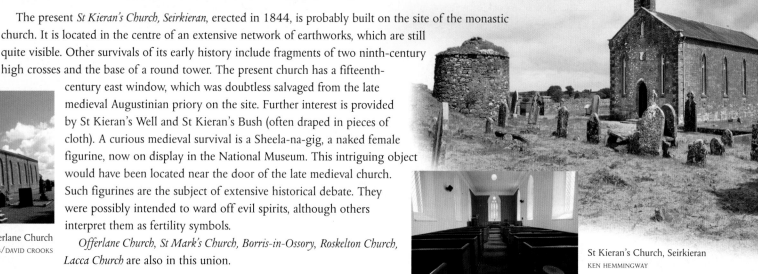

St Kieran's Church, Seirkieran
KEN HEMMINGWAY

## KELLS, KILMOGANNY, ENNISNAG, INISTIOGE and KILFANE

*St Peter's Church, Ennisnag,* on the Kilkenny side of Stoneyford village on the Kilkenny to Waterford road, is a charming church in this parochial group. The church was built in 1816 to serve the spiritual needs of workers in the nearby Merino Woollen Factory. It is likely that it was constructed on the site of a medieval parish church that served the episcopal manor of Ennisnag. It has an unusual window (An Túr Gloine, 1940) in the south wall of the nave, showing Ossory saints Ciaran and Moling in the company a fox and a hound respectively. Above them is a hunting scene, reflecting the patron's passion for hunting. Just to the west of the tower, a sharp-eyed visitor will note the epitaph to Hubert Butler (1900–91), a noted Anglo-Irish essayist and writer, and his no-less-remarkable wife, Susan Margaret (1905–96): 'Ossa damus medicis animam mandamus amicis' ('We bequeath our bodies to medicine and our spirits to our friends'). The head of the tombstone is inscribed 'Timor domini fons vitae' ('The fear of the lord is the fountain of wisdom'), a quotation from Proverbs 14:27. The Butlers lived nearby in Maiden Hall, Bennettsbridge.

*St Mary's Church, Inistioge,* located in the wooded valley of the Nore in south-eastern County Kilkenny, is in one of the most charming villages in Ireland. The village green of Inistioge is dominated on the north side by the medieval tower of the church, which originally belonged to the Augustinian priory. The fine square tower was completed around 1525. The present rather handsome eight-bay nave was built in 1824 on the site of the medieval chancel. Two other elements of the medieval priory are located on the north side of the church and so are not visible from the square. One is a tower, which probably served as the prior's residence in the later medieval period. The other seems to have been a medieval lady chapel running parallel to the present nave. St Mary's has a very fine triple-lancet memorial stained-glass east window from An Túr Gloine (1919), dedicated to the memory of Major Peter Connellan, who was killed in the First World War. The figures portrayed represent valour, resurrection and charity.

Also in the parochial group are *St Mary's Church, Kells, St Matthew's Church, Kilmoganny, Kilfane Church.*

St Mary's Church, Inistioge
KEN HEMMINGWAY

St Mary's Church, Inistioge
KEN HEMMINGWAY

## FERTAGH (JOHNSTOWN)

*St Mary's Church, Fertagh* (Johnstown), constructed in 1799, is associated with an ancient site at Fertagh. According to one tradition, a monastery was founded there by St Ciaran of Seirkieran, a shadowy figure supposed to have lived in the fifth century and said to have been the first saint of the diocese of Ossory. The pre-Norman round tower dominates the skyline for many miles around. *St Mary's* has a late-medieval window opening taken from the old priory.

### KILKENNY, ST JOHN'S, AGHOUR and KILMANAGH

*St Canice's Cathedral, Kilkenny.* The cathedral is an essential focus of the cultural life of the city, attracting many tourists and hosting arts and music events. Above all, St Canice's Cathedral remains an important place of worship, prayer and pilgrimage.

*St John's Church, Kilkenny* is a former chapel of an Augustinian priory, most of which had been demolished by the late eighteenth century. The chapel was restored and reroofed in 1817 as a parish church.

St Lachtan's Church, Aghour
SHAY DOYLE

*St Lachtan's Church, Aghour* is in Freshford in north-eastern County Kilkenny. Although altered, it retains much of its medieval fabric. The church, located in the centre of the town of Freshford, is dedicated to St Lachtan, abbot and bishop, who died in AD 620, according to Irish sources. An archaeological assessment of the church carried out in 2001 concluded that the western half of the church incorporates masonry from the ninth and tenth centuries. Early architectural features include the original antae projecting at either end of the north and south walls, and, most obviously, the fine twelfth-century Romanesque porch and doorway. In the thirteenth century, the original east wall was demolished to enable the construction of narrower chancel, which was renovated in the fourteenth and fifteenth centuries. It seems clear, therefore, that with the arrival of the Anglo-Normans the existing monastic church was converted into a parish church. The church was reroofed and renovated in the 1730s and again in the mid-nineteenth century. It remains, nonetheless, the most completely preserved medieval parish church in use in the diocese of Ossory. St Lachtan's has several stained-glass windows: the east window, depicting angels with scrolls, and the south nave window, depicting the transfiguration and ascension, were made in the O'Connor Studio around 1860. A more recent window (1956) in the south chancel by an unknown artist depicts St Cecilia, patron of music.

The remaining church in this union is *Kilmanagh Church*.

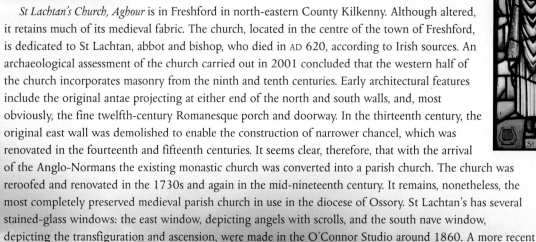

SHAY DOYLE

## RATHDOWNEY, CASTLEFLEMING, DONAGHMORE, RATHSARAN and AGHAVOE

*St Andrew's Church, Rathdowney*, in south-eastern County Laois, is built on the site of the medieval parish church. The present church was built in 1815 with a grant from the Board of First Fruits. Additions and improvements were made later in the century. Edward Ledwich (curate 1770–2 and vicar of Aghavoe 1772–97) was a noted if somewhat disputatious antiquary. He was the author of the widely read *Antiquities of Ireland* (1790).

*St Canice's Church, Aghavoe* was the seat of the bishop of Ossory in the second half of the twelfth century, until the see was removed to Kilkenny around 1200. The present parish church dates from 1818 and is built on the site of the monastery founded by St Canice before his death around AD 599. The remains of the fourteenth-century Dominican friary are quite well preserved, while there is an Anglo-Norman motte in the vicinity of the church.

*Castlefleming Church, St Patrick's Church, Donaghmore* and *St Columba's Church, Rathsaran* are also in the union.

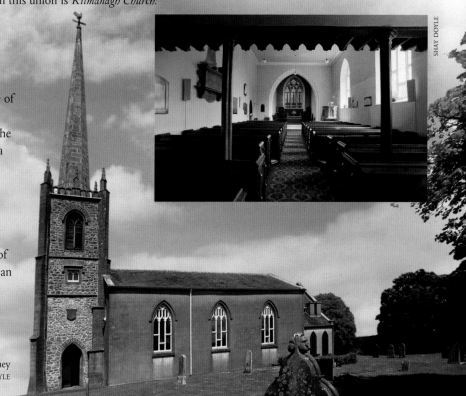

St Andrew's Church, Rathdowney
SHAY DOYLE

# DIOCESE OF FERNS

## ARDAMINE, KILTENNEL, GLASCARRIG (CLONEVAN), KILMANAGH, KILMUCKRIDGE and MONAMOLIN

St John the Evangelist's Church, Ardamine

*St John the Evangelist's Church, Ardamine* is the latest of a succession of buildings that almost certainly reaches back to the late twelfth century. The present church, however, was rebuilt in 1861–2 close to the ancient site. It was designed by George Edmund Street (1824–81), a leading light in shaping the high-Victorian architectural style. The church was built in the early English Gothic style with an apsidal chancel, partly as a memorial to Mr and Mrs Richards of Ardamine. Polychromatic brickwork is a notable feature of the church, especially in the chancel arch and window surrounds in the chancel and nave. There is a timber roof both in the nave and in the apse, each of a distinctive design. The handsome pulpit and font are of Caen stone. The fine stained-glass windows (1860) are from the studio of Clayton & Bell, London.

The date of *Kiltennel Church*, at Courtown, is uncertain. The nave seems to have been built in 1770, but the south aisle and memorial chapel were added in 1880. It is well furnished with stained glass, including a fine representation of St Brigid by Hubert McGoldrick from An Túr Gloine (1937). There was a manor and rural borough of Courtown in the thirteenth century, so the original parish church must derive from around 1200. The church benefitted from the patronage of the earls of Courtown.

*St Patrick's Church, Glascarrig (Clonevan)* is likewise situated on an ancient Norman manor, granted by Strongbow to his brother-in-law, Raymond le Gros, who married Strongbow's sister Basilia in 1175. The present church was built in 1844 and a new chancel was later added.

*St John's Church, Kilnamanagh* was built in 1813.
*Kilmuckridge Church* dates from 1815.
*St Moling's Church, Monamolin* was built in 1828.

Kiltennel Church

St John the Evangelist's Church, Ardamine
KEN HEMMINGWAY

St John's Church, Kilnamanagh
COLIN BOYLE

St Moling's Church, Monamolin
COLIN BOYLE

St Fiace's Church, Clonegal
COLIN BOYLE

St Mary's Church, Bunclody
KEN HEMMINGWAY

St Paul's Church, Kildavin
COLIN BOYLE

## BUNCLODY, KILDAVIN, CLONEGAL and KILRUSH

Both the town and the parish of Bunclody are comparatively modern creations. The town had taken its original name, Newtownbarry, from James Barry, sheriff of Dublin in 1577.

*St Mary's Church, Bunclody.* The nave and tower of the present cruciform church date from 1776. In 1869, the transverse chancel and nave were constructed, followed in 1877–8 by the memorial west front with its striking rose window and an additional bay designed by William Burges (1827–81). His stained glass matched the finest work of Morris & Co. The west rose window in St Mary's, depicting the Good Samaritan, was designed by Burges and executed by Saunders & Co. of London in 1877. The east chancel window (1927), also of high quality, is by Catherine O'Brien from An Túr Gloine studio and depicts Faith, Hope and Charity.

*St Fiace's Church, Clonegal*, which dates from 1819, was restored in 1904–5. The pulpit and candelabrum were presented by members of the Robertson family of Huntingdon Castle. Unfortunately, a consignment of choice woods for panelling the chancel never arrived from Vancouver because the Russians seized and confiscated the cargo during the Russo-Japanese War. The north nave window portraying the angel and women at the tomb (1900) is from the studio of Joshua Clarke & Sons, Dublin. Joshua was the father of Harry Clarke.

The remaining churches in this union are *St Paul's Church, Kildavin* and *St Brigit's Church, Kilrush*.

St Brigit's Church, Kilrush
COLIN BOYLE

All Saint's Church, Carnew
KEN HEMMINGWAY

## CROSSPATRICK UNION: KILCOMMON, KILPIPE, PREBAN and CARNEW

*Kilcommon Church*, Tinahely, south County Wicklow, was built in 1828 on a site given by Earl Fitzwilliam, together with a new churchyard. Among the interesting characters associated with this parish is Rev. James Bartley (curate of Crosspatrick 1901–2). Born in Ireland, he spent several colourful years wandering in the United States, but eventually returned to Ireland to study divinity in Trinity College. He became a fluent Irish speaker and played a part in the Gaelic-revival movement.

*Kilpipe Church*, which was built in 1765, has some fine stained-glass windows.

*St John's Church, Preban* was built in 1827.

*All Saints' Church, Carnew* was rebuilt in 1846–7 and contains an interesting memorial from an earlier church to Captain J. Chamney of the Coolatin Yeomanry, who was killed in 1798 in battle against the insurgents.

Kilcommon Church, Tinahely
COLIN BOYLE

## ENNISCORTHY, CLONE, CLONMORE, MONART and TEMPLESCOBIN

*St Mary's Church, Enniscorthy* was extensively damaged when much of the town was burned during the 1798 Rebellion. The present church, designed by Joseph Welland in 1843–6, occupies the site of its medieval precursor. The spire was added in 1850. The organ formerly belonged to the Royal Chapel in Dublin Castle and was first used at the thanksgiving service for the victory at Waterloo in 1815. In the mid-1990s, when St Aidan's Roman Catholic Cathedral was being renovated, cathedral services were held for a year in St Mary's.

St Paul's Church, Clone dates from 1833.

St John's Church, Clonmore was built in 1828.

St Peter's Church, Monart was built in 1805–8. There are a number of famine graves in the churchyard.

St Paul's Church, Templescobin dates from 1818.

Holy Trinity Church, Kilbride
KEN HEMMINGWAY

SHAY DOYLE

St Mary's Church, Enniscorthy
KEN HEMMINGWAY

## FERNS CATHEDRAL, KILBRIDE, TOOMBE, KILCORMACK and BALLYCARNEY

*Holy Trinity Church, Kilbride* is situated in the picturesque Ballymore Demesne in north County Wexford, close to a late twelfth-century Norman motte, which was probably attached to the great seigneurial manor of Ferns. The name Kilbride means 'Bridget's church', but nothing is known of any historical association with this major Celtic saint. Built in 1875 from the proceeds of the will of Matthew Kinch, who specified that the church must be erected within two years, it replaced an earlier church. The oak panelling in the chancel and the carved wooden lectern are dedicated to the memory of members of the Donovan family, proprietors of the demesne since the seventeenth century. One of them, Major C.H.W. Donovan, died in west Africa on active service in 1884 and was buried under a cotton tree. The leaves of the cotton tree are represented on the lectern – designed by a brother of the great Irish artist William Orpen. Like many places in north Wexford, Kilbride was associated with the events of the 1798 Rebellion. Rev. Samuel Haydon, rector of Kilbride, was murdered by the rebels in the streets of Enniscorthy around 28 May, about a month before the famous battle of Vinegar Hill.

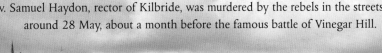

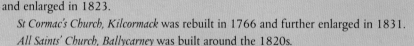

*St Edan's Cathedral, Ferns* is associated with a long monastic prehistory. The monastery was founded by St Maodhóg, which in its anglicised form becomes Edan or Aidan. According to the annals, he died in AD 620 or 625. Ferns owed its prominence in the twelfth century to the patronage of the Ui Cennselaigh kings of Leinster. The most famous member of this ruling family was Dermot MacMurrough, who induced Strongbow and his Anglo-Norman followers to invade Ireland in 1169 as his allies. Dermot founded the Augustinian abbey of St Mary (whose remains are still visible on the south side of the cathedral) between 1160 and 1162, which probably means that the older Celtic foundation was reconstituted as a community of canons regular. The heads of three high crosses and part of the shaft of a fourth, dating from the eighth or ninth centuries, are preserved in the grounds of the present cathedral.

The cathedral was burned by the O'Byrnes of Wicklow in 1575. It was partly reroofed in the seventeenth century. The present building is largely the product of an 1816–17 restoration.

Further improvements were made at the beginning of the twentieth century. These included the addition of a chancel arch and a panelled roof of pitch-pine, and the removal of the chapter stalls from the west end to the chapter house west of the tower. The present church contains some medieval elements in the form of responds of the arcades to the side aisles, and some lancet windows at the east end.

*St Catherine's Church, Toombe* is situated in the village of Camolin. The prebendary of Toombe, Rev. Roger Owen, was more fortunate in his treatment at the hands of the rebels in 1798 than his colleague in Kilbride, but was not unscathed. He was imprisoned and maltreated by them. Although he lived until 1844, he narrowly escaped being killed in the massacre at the bridge in Wexford, which left him 'slightly unhinged', according to his sister. The present church was built between 1772 and 1775 and enlarged in 1823.

*St Cormac's Church, Kilcormack* was rebuilt in 1766 and further enlarged in 1831.

*All Saints' Church, Ballycarney* was built around the 1820s.

St Edan's Cathedral, Ferns
KEN HEMMINGWAY

St Catherine's Church, Toombe
COLIN BOYLE

St Edan's Cathedral, Ferns
KEN HEMMINGWAY

Christ Church, Gorey
KEN HEMMINGWAY

## GOREY, KILNAHUE, LESKINFERE and BALLYCANEW

Gorey and the surrounding area suffered badly in the 1798 Rebellion. It is perhaps surprising that, in spite of the bitter memories engendered on all sides by the rebellion, a minute in the vestry book dated 16 April 1805 records how the vestry offered a reward of 30 guineas for anyone prepared to give information about the smashing of the windows of the Roman Catholic chapel three days previously because 'we hold all such lawless acts in the utmost abhorrence'.

*Christ Church, Gorey* is a very handsome cruciform neo-Gothic building, with north and south transepts and a south aisle, designed by Joseph Welland and completed in 1861. It replaces an earlier church, built in 1819. The glory of the present church undoubtedly is its stained glass. It contains high-quality works by Harry Clarke (1922–3) and Catherine O'Brien (1956).

*St Luke's Church, Leskinfere* was built in 1831.

*St Mogue's Church, Ballycanew* was anciently part of the corps of the treasurer of Ferns.

*St John the Evangelist's Church, Kilnahue* was built in 1813 with the assistance of the Board of First Fruits.

St Luke's Church, Leskinfere
COLIN BOYLE

## KILLANNE, KILLEGNEY, ROSSDROIT, TEMPLESHANBO

*St Anne's Church, Killanne*, built in 1832, has nine finely executed stained-glass windows by Catherine O'Brien, dating from 1934. Each of these focuses on themes from Psalm 23. There are two other windows from the studio of James Powell & Sons, London, dating from 1914.

*Killegney Church*, at Clonroche, was built in 1827, although the chancel was not added until 1906. Killegney means 'the church of Éigneach', an Irish saint of uncertain date associated with Donegal. A motte-and-bailey castle was erected there at the time of the Anglo-Norman invasion in the late twelfth century, probably by Maurice de Prendergast. One of the most interesting rectors of the parish was James Bentley Gordon (1750–1819), who became rector in 1799, only months after the rebellion. Three of his children were taken captive by the rebels, though they eventually survived the ordeal. Two of his sons fought on the loyalist side in the conflict. He was the author of several interesting and wide-ranging books, but is best remembered for his *History of the Rebellion in Ireland in 1798*, first published in 1801. In spite of his close personal association with this momentous event, he attempted to set out an objective account of the rebellion in the belief that actions on all sides had damaged the realm.

*St Peter's Church, Rossdroit* was built in 1805.

*St Colman's Church, Templeshanbo* dates from 1815. According to various hagiographical sources, St Colman was a former king of Connacht who settled near Templeshanbo. The same sources report the customary miracles, such as a capacity to turn water into wine, and the possession of ducks that were miraculously resistant to cooking when stolen.

Killegney Church
SHAY DOYLE

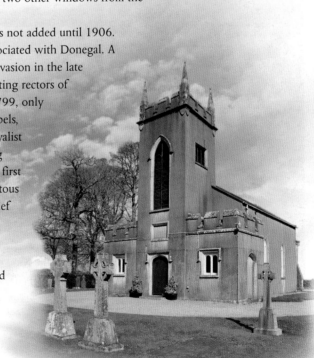

Killegney Church
KEN HEMMINGWAY

## NEW ROSS, OLD ROSS, WHITECHURCH, FETHARD and KILLESK

New Ross was one of the largest and most prosperous ports in medieval Ireland, having been founded by William Marshal, lord of Leinster, who, as a leading member of the Angevin baronage, played a major role in the events leading to *Magna Carta* in the early thirteenth century.

Because of its strategic and economic significance, New Ross has featured in national history. After two days of fighting, the town surrendered to Cromwell on generous terms in October 1649, and the garrison was allowed to leave with its arms and banners. The town was again the scene of bitter fighting in 1798. The defeat of the rebels ensured that the rebellion was largely contained within County Wexford.

*St Mary's Church, New Ross*, one of the largest Norman parish churches in Ireland, is 52 metres long and 42 metres wide across the transepts. Although the chancel and transepts are roofless, they retain their original early thirteenth-century height and proportions. The existing nave is a large, plain nineteenth-century building, replacing the original nave. It is not surprising that New Ross should boast such an imposing parish church.

*St Mary's Church, Old Ross* is situated beside a motte-and-bailey castle (built by Strongbow).

*Whitechurch Church* is close to the John F. Kennedy Arboretum, known as Kennedy Park.

*St Mogue's Church, Fethard* is probably located on a pre-Norman site, as the dedication to an Irish saint suggests. In 1957, Fethard-on-Sea was the scene of an infamous event when local protestants suffered a boycott following a dispute over a mixed marriage. In 1998, Dr Brendan Comisky, Roman Catholic Bishop of Ferns, expressed 'deep sorrow' and asked for forgiveness from the Church of Ireland community.

*All Saints's Church, Killesk* is an attractive neo-Gothic building on the outskirts of the village of Duncannon. It was designed by T.F. Fuller (1835–1925) and begun in 1878.

St Mary's Church, New Ross
SHAY DOYLE

St Peter's Church, Kilscoran
KEN HEMMINGWAY

St Iberius's Church, Wexford
KEN HEMMINGWAY

## WEXFORD, ARDCOLM, KILLURIN, TAGHMON, HORETOWN, KILSCORAN, KILLINICK, MULRANKIN and BANNOW

Wexford was founded by the Vikings in the ninth century and captured by the Anglo-Normans in May 1169.

*St Iberius's Church, Wexford* is named after St Iberius, who, according to the annals, was a pre-Patrician saint credited with the establishment of a monastery on Begerin Island in Wexford Harbour. The present church stands on the site of its medieval predecessor in the main street, having been rebuilt around 1775 by John Roberts of Waterford. The church has an interesting neo-Classical interior. It is broader than it is long, with a handsome sanctuary enclosed by three fine Corinthian columns, attractively decorated in Wedgwood blue. A gallery extends around three sides of the church.

*Ardcolm Church*, Castlebridge was built in 1766.

*Killurin Church* dates from 1785.

*St Munna's Church, Taghmon* is situated on an ancient monastic site, indicated by the remains of a high cross in the churchyard. The monastery is mentioned in the Irish annals for the year AD 777. The present church was built in 1818. The famous hymn writer Henry Francis Lyte was curate of Taghmon between 1815 and 1817. His best-known hymns include 'Abide with Me' and 'Praise My Soul, the King of Heaven'.

*St James's Church, Horetown* was built in 1862.

*St Peter's Church, Kilscoran* was built in 1818.

*St Enoch's Church, Killinick* dates from 1828.

*St Paul's Church, Bannow* was built in 1822.

The remaining church in this union is *St David's Church, Mulrankin*.

St Enoch's Church, Killinick
COLIN BOYLE

348

# DIOCESE OF LEIGHLIN

## ABBEYLEIX, BALLYROAN, BALLINAKILL, KILLERMOGH, AUGHMACART and DURROW

The attractive town of Abbeyleix shows all the signs of landlord improvers – in this case, the de Vesci estate. In 1183, Connor O'More founded the Cistercian abbey of Lex Dei. When the abbey was suppressed in 1552, its lands were granted to the earl of Ormond, passing eventually to the de Vesci family.

*St Michael's and All Angels' Church, Abbeyleix* is situated on the edge of the town. It was first designed and constructed in 1831 by John Semple III (there were five John Semples). St Michael's was essentially rebuilt in 1863 by Sir Thomas Wyatt (1808–80) at the expense of Lord de Vesci, although it retained Semple's imposing tower and spire. The church is well furnished, with good-quality stained glass works whose dates of origin range from the 1890s to the 1940s. These include works from the studios of James Powell & Sons (London) and An Túr Gloine in Dublin, and the largest collection of works in Ireland from the Henry Holiday Studio in London.

St Michael's and All Angels' Church, Abbeyleix

KEN HEMMINGWAY

St Mary's Church, Baltinglass

*Ballyroan Church* dates from *c.* 1800.
*All Saints' Church, Ballinakill* was constructed in 1821.
*Killermogh Church* was built in 1796.
*St Tigernach's Church, Aughmacart* has a fine Hiberno-Romanesque arch. A monastery dedicated to St Tigernach was founded there in the sixth century.
*St Fintan's Church, Durrow* was built around 1795

St John the Baptist's Church, Stratford-on-Slaney

COLIN BOYLE

St Michael's and All Angels' Church, Abbeyleix

## BALTINGLASS, BALLYNURE, STRATFORD-ON-SLANEY and RATHVILLY

*St Mary's Church, Baltinglass* is situated beside the ruins of the Cistercian monastery founded by Dermot MacMurrough, king of Leinster, in 1148. In 1837 the chancel of the abbey was still in use for church services, with the addition of a square tower, constructed in 1815. The present neo-Gothic church was consecrated in 1884. After a competition, it was designed by Richard O'Brien Smyth (1844–1923), an inspector in the land-improvements branch of the Board of Works.

*The Church of the Ascension, Ballynure* (Grangecon) was built *c.* 1814.
*St John the Baptist's Church, Stratford-on-Slaney* was rebuilt in 1904 to replace an earlier building, dating from 1792.
*St Mary's Church, Rathvilly* was built in 1751, with a spire added *c.* 1830.

## CARLOW, URGLIN and STAPLESTOWN

Some time around 1200 John de Clahull, lord of the cantred of Obargy, asked the archbishop of Dublin to institute Thurstin, clerk of Hampton, into the church of St Comgall, Carlow. Whatever the remote origins of this church, it was clearly regarded as parochial at that date, and may therefore be regarded as the original parish church of Carlow, which the Anglo-Normans transposed to the patronage of St Mary. Carlow was acquired by John de Clahull's overlord, William Marshal, lord of Leinster, around 1210, who founded the town around the same date. New parish churches dedicated to St Mary were built in the seventeenth and eighteenth centuries. Jonathan Swift commented: 'Poor town, proud people, high church and low steeple.'

The present *St Mary's Church, Carlow*, although substantially rebuilt between 1829 and 1830, retains much of the Georgian building, including the box pews in the west gallery. The Gothic-style east window was inserted into the Georgian window frame towards the end of the century. The church's most striking feature, however, is the spire (64 metres in height). It was designed by Thomas Cobden (1794–1842), who also oversaw the reconstruction of the south wall and roof. Cobden, who lived for a time in Carlow before moving to London in 1832, also designed the fine Regency Gothic Roman Catholic cathedral in Carlow. The spires of both churches still define the skyline of the town. Among the notable memorials in St Mary's is one dedicated to Sir Richard Morrison, the architect.

*Staplestown Church* dates from 1821. Its tower and spire may also have been designed by Thomas Cobden.
*Rutland Church, Urglin* was built between 1787 and 1820.

St Mary's Church, Carlow

SHAY DOYLE

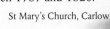

St Mary's Church, Carlow

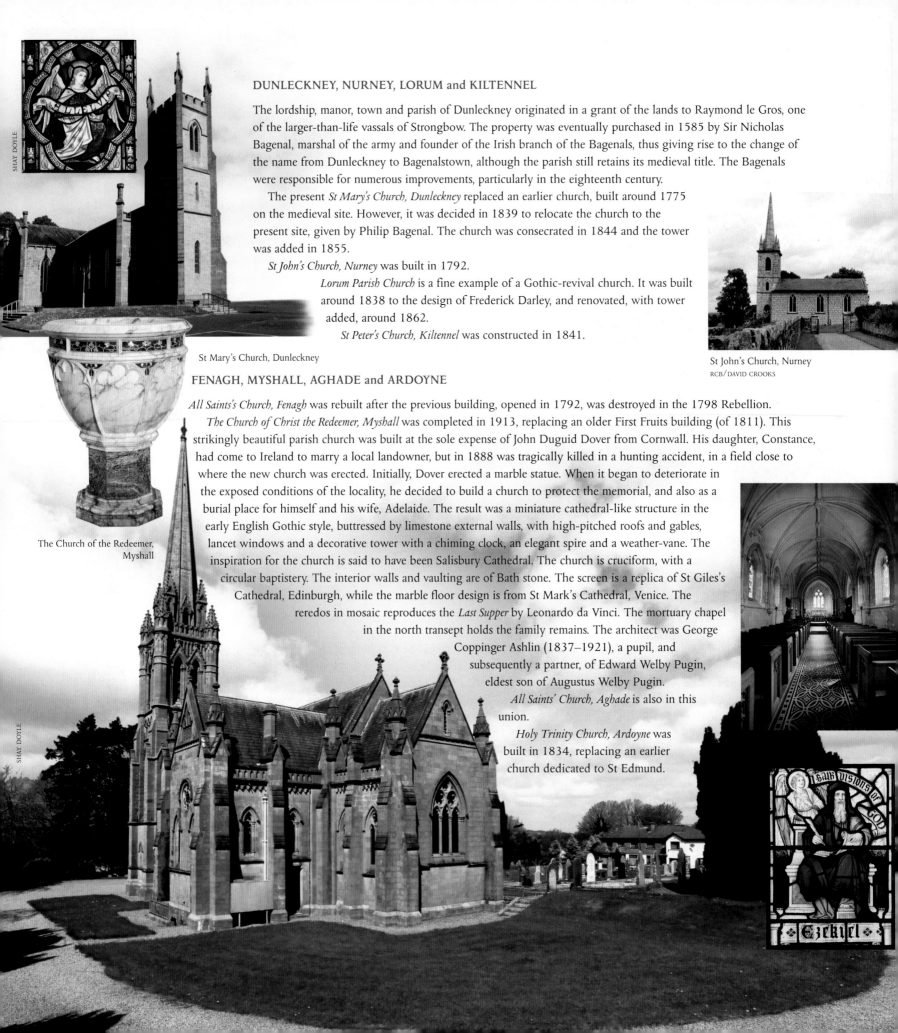

## DUNLECKNEY, NURNEY, LORUM and KILTENNEL

The lordship, manor, town and parish of Dunleckney originated in a grant of the lands to Raymond le Gros, one of the larger-than-life vassals of Strongbow. The property was eventually purchased in 1585 by Sir Nicholas Bagenal, marshal of the army and founder of the Irish branch of the Bagenals, thus giving rise to the change of the name from Dunleckney to Bagenalstown, although the parish still retains its medieval title. The Bagenals were responsible for numerous improvements, particularly in the eighteenth century.

The present *St Mary's Church, Dunleckney* replaced an earlier church, built around 1775 on the medieval site. However, it was decided in 1839 to relocate the church to the present site, given by Philip Bagenal. The church was consecrated in 1844 and the tower was added in 1855.

*St John's Church, Nurney* was built in 1792.

*Lorum Parish Church* is a fine example of a Gothic-revival church. It was built around 1838 to the design of Frederick Darley, and renovated, with tower added, around 1862.

*St Peter's Church, Kiltennel* was constructed in 1841.

St Mary's Church, Dunleckney

St John's Church, Nurney

The Church of the Redeemer,
Myshall

## FENAGH, MYSHALL, AGHADE and ARDOYNE

*All Saints's Church, Fenagh* was rebuilt after the previous building, opened in 1792, was destroyed in the 1798 Rebellion.

*The Church of Christ the Redeemer, Myshall* was completed in 1913, replacing an older First Fruits building (of 1811). This strikingly beautiful parish church was built at the sole expense of John Duguid Dover from Cornwall. His daughter, Constance, had come to Ireland to marry a local landowner, but in 1888 was tragically killed in a hunting accident, in a field close to where the new church was erected. Initially, Dover erected a marble statue. When it began to deteriorate in the exposed conditions of the locality, he decided to build a church to protect the memorial, and also as a burial place for himself and his wife, Adelaide. The result was a miniature cathedral-like structure in the early English Gothic style, buttressed by limestone external walls, with high-pitched roofs and gables, lancet windows and a decorative tower with a chiming clock, an elegant spire and a weather-vane. The inspiration for the church is said to have been Salisbury Cathedral. The church is cruciform, with a circular baptistery. The interior walls and vaulting are of Bath stone. The screen is a replica of St Giles's Cathedral, Edinburgh, while the marble floor design is from St Mark's Cathedral, Venice. The reredos in mosaic reproduces the *Last Supper* by Leonardo da Vinci. The mortuary chapel in the north transept holds the family remains. The architect was George Coppinger Ashlin (1837–1921), a pupil, and subsequently a partner, of Edward Welby Pugin, eldest son of Augustus Welby Pugin.

*All Saints' Church, Aghade* is also in this union.

*Holy Trinity Church, Ardoyne* was built in 1834, replacing an earlier church dedicated to St Edmund.

Good Ground

## KILLESHIN, CLOYDAGH, KILLABAN (CASTLETOWN) and MAYO

There was an early Irish monastery at Killeshin. Its foundation is attributed to various people, but most commonly to St Comgan, *alias* Diermit (*sic*), reputed to have died around AD 570. The present ruins adjacent to the church date from the twelfth century. They comprise the east and west gables and a significant portion of the north elevation. Of particular note is the surviving Romanesque arch, decorated with human, animal, geometric and foliage motifs. The capitals feature human heads with intertwining hair. An inscription on the door in Irish translates as 'a prayer for Diarmait, king of Leinster', a reference to Dermot MacMurrough, who introduced the Anglo-Normans to Ireland.

Killeshin Church
KEN HEMMINGWAY

The present *Killeshin Church* was built in 1826. It was, however, rebuilt in 1846 on a larger scale, because the weight of the vaulted roof was too great for the supporting walls. The spire and west end are all that remain of the earlier building, probably designed by John Semple.

*St John the Evangelist's Church, Cloydagh* dates from 1803.

*Killaban Church (Castletown)* was built in 1801.

*Mayo Church* is dedicated to St John.

SHAY DOYLE

St Peter's Church, Kiltegan

## KILTEGAN, HACKETSTOWN, CLONMORE and MOYNE

*St Peter's Church, Kiltegan*, opened in 1806 and enlarged in 1826, is the principal church in this parish union. It was enlarged again in 1877, with the addition of a sanctuary, clerestory, south aisle and arcade in the French-Gothic style, designed by James Brooks. The church is located near the entrance gate to the Gothic-fantasy Humewood Castle. The east window of the church was commissioned by the Humes.

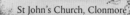

St John's Church, Moyne
COLIN BOYLE

*St John the Baptist's Church, Hacketstown* is also in this union.

*St John the Evangelist's Church, Cloydagh* was built c. 1795.

The present *St John's Church, Clonmore* is a plain building, constructed around 1812. The remains of the old church are adjacent to it.

St Maodhóg of Ferns founded a monastery at Clonmore in the seventh century, as is mentioned from time to time in the annals.

*St John's Church, Moyne* dates from 1816.

St John's Church, Clonmore

# LEIGHLIN, GRANGE SYLVAE (GORESBRIDGE), SHANKILL (PAULSTOWN) and CLONAGOOSE (BORRIS)

*St George's Church, Grange Sylvae (Goresbridge)* was built around 1807 to a design by Francis Johnston. It contains a striking monument to Colonel Arthur Gore, a veteran of the Napoleonic Wars. The church was closed for almost ten years in the 1960s due to its dilapidated state. It was then repaired and reopened, thanks to the efforts of local parishioners.

*St John's Church, Shankill (Paulstown)* was erected in 1811.

*St Moling's Church, Clonagoose* is the private chapel of Borris House, located on a demesne in the attractive village of Borris-in-Idrone, County Carlow, the historic seat of the McMorrough Kavanagh family, who claimed descent from the kings of Leinster. It has been the accustomed place of worship for the local Church of Ireland population since it was licensed for public worship in 1835. This handsome chapel, a good example of the Tudor-revival style of architecture, was designed by Sir Richard Morrison (1767–1849) around 1813. On the west gallery there is an abstract mural, *The Tree of Life*, by the artist Barrie Cook.

St Moling's Church, Clonagoose
KEN HEMMINGWAY

However, the McMorrough Kavanagh Demesne will always be associated with the legendary feats of Arthur McMorrough Kavanagh (1831–89), so named by his father to recall his royal ancestor Art McMorrough. He was born without arms or legs. In spite of these formidable physical limitations, Art became a skilled horseman and traveller. He succeeded to the family estate on the deaths of his elder brothers and proved himself to be model landlord, funding a local railway and redesigning the village. In 1868, he was elected MP for Carlow. He died in London in 1889 and is buried in his beloved Borris.

St Moling's Church, Clonagoose
KEN HEMMINGWAY

*St Laserian's Cathedral, Leighlin*, nestling in the quiet village of Old Leighlin, has not attracted the attention that it deserves. As the dedication suggests, the site has a long history extending back to the early seventh century, when St Laserian is thought to have founded the monastery named after him. Almost all the cathedral's fabric is medieval and it has been fortunate in not having undergone any of the successive restorations in later centuries that so often obscure the original design. Part of the cathedral's charm is its simplicity. Originally cruciform, the south transept has since disappeared. Remarkably, it has no aisles. The long narrow nave belongs to the second half of the thirteenth or early fourteenth century. The crossing is dominated by a fine, square fifteenth-century tower, supported by a splendid ribbed vault. The choir and north transept are probably from the early fourteenth century, with some later remodelling in the early sixteenth century of the east window and the windows on the south side. The cathedral possesses a fine eleventh-century font. The lady chapel was probably built by Bishop Saunders in the 1500s.

Were they to speak, the stones of Leighlin Cathedral would have many curious tales to relate, not least among them being the murder of Bishop Maurice Doran by his archdeacon in 1525. Even in the twentieth century, in 1921, the elderly, retired Dean John Finlay, of whom it was said that he never made an enemy nor lost a friend, was murdered by the IRA at the age of 79. The pulpit is dedicated to his memory.

Recently the cathedral has undergone important improvement and restoration. Discreet solar heating has been installed, together with disability access. Such changes, of course, have been carried out in keeping with best conservation practice. These developments will open up the cathedral for additional cultural, educational and diocesan use.

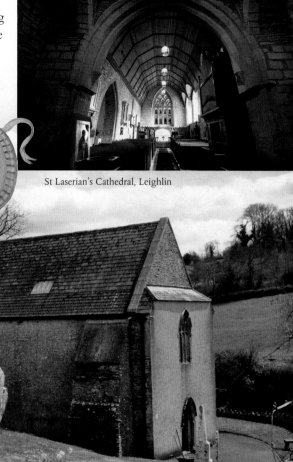

St Laserian's Cathedral, Leighlin

## MARYBOROUGH (PORTLAOISE), DYSERT ENOS and BALLYFIN

The town of Portlaoise had its origin in the centuries-long contest between the government and the regional Irish septs, the O'Mores and the O'Connors, which ended with the establishment of a plantation town in the reign of Queen Mary – hence the name Maryborough. It became the administrative centre of the new county, also called after the queen (Queen's County, now County Laois). In 1929, the town's name was changed to Portlaoise to reflect the nationalist ethos of the new state.

*St Peter's Church, Maryborough*, built in 1803–4, is in the Classical style. The facade and obelisk steeple are attributed to James Gandon (1742–1823).

*Holy Trinity Church, Dysert Enos* is situated at the base of the imposing rock of Dunamase, crowned by the ruins of a once-powerful Anglo-Norman castle going back to the time of Strongbow. It was captured by the O'Mores in the mid-fourteenth century and was the scene of many conflicts thereafter. The church was built in 1845 but, because of the Great Famine, was not opened until 1849.

*St John the Baptist's Church, Ballyfin* was built in 1792. The church was originally under the patronage of the Coote family.

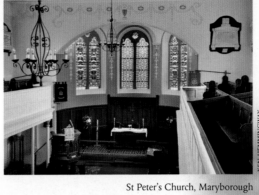

353

KEN HEMMINGWAY

St Peter's Church, Maryborough

SHAY DOYLE

## STRADBALLY, BALLINTUBBERT, CURRACLONE, TIMOGUE and LEGGACURRAN

*St Patrick's Church, Stradbally* was built in 1764 and renovated around 1880. Stradbally was granted to Francis Cosby in 1592. The family and demesne are still *in situ*. The Cosby estate hosts the famous Annual Steam Rally, which is a very popular attraction, in addition to the annual arts and music festival Electric Picnic, which in 2010 was voted the best medium-sized European festival of its kind. This festival takes place in August.

*St Brigid's Church, Ballintubbert* is surrounded by a medieval graveyard, in the corner of which is a well. Near the church is the glebe house, where the British poet laureate Cecil Day Lewis was born, the son of the rector, Rev. Frank Day Lewis.

*St Peter's Church, Curraclone*, built in 1804, has a superb Celtic-Twilight reredos.

St Mogue's Church, Timogue

*St Mogue's Church, Timogue*. Timogue means 'house of Maodhóg', the patron saint of Ferns, who died around AD 620. The special interest of this small, very plain church, built in 1736, is its early eighteenth-century liturgical layout – the three-decker arrangement of the pulpit, boxed lectern and clerk's desk, located behind the altar, all railed off in the form a simple chancel-cum-sanctuary situated at the east end of the church. Similar practical arrangements of liturgical furnishings were common at the time the church was built, but most of them were swept away by the tides of liturgical change in the following century. St Mogue's has preserved its box pews, giving the church a distinctive character.

*The Church of the Resurrection, Luggacurran*, built in 1963, is one of a small handful of Church of Ireland churches to have been erected in the Irish Republic in the twentieth century.

## TULLOW, SHILLELAGH, AGHOLD and MULLINACUFF

*St Columba's Church, Tullow* is modest in size for a town church. The dedication to St Columba suggests that a church or monastic community of some sort existed in Tullow before the arrival of the Anglo-Normans. Two former church buildings are known to have stood on the site before the construction of the present church in 1831. The builder is unknown, but the handsome tower closely resembles that of Carlow Cathedral, which Thomas Cobden designed. On the north wall of the nave there is a fine Classical memorial to Lieutenant-General Clement Nevill, who carried colours for King William at the battle of the Boyne.

St Columba's Church, Tullow

*Shillelagh Church* was initially built in the Gothic style in 1834 on a picturesque site in County Wicklow, donated by Lord Fitzwilliam, but was subsequently enlarged by the addition of two transepts and a chancel in 1888. In its first phase there was a three-decker pulpit, but when the chancel was added it was removed to accommodate changing liturgical tastes. So extensive was the remodelling that only the font was retained after 1888.

*St Michael's Church, Aghold* was built in 1815.

*Mullinacuff Church* dates from 1844.

St Columba's Church, Tullow

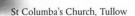

St Peter's Church, Maryborough

# The United Dioceses of Cork, Cloyne and Ross

A potential pitfall of an illustrated history (unless it sets out intentionally to inform the present) is that it may give little sense of either contemporary scene or context. An understanding of history is vital even if, at times, there is an exasperating and wearying sense of our human inability not to repeat the mistakes of the past. A church with a rich inheritance and historic responsibility has to be careful not to wallow in that past to the exclusion of contemporary ministry and future planning. Today and tomorrow are key.

The United Dioceses of Cork, Cloyne and Ross encompass the most southerly parts of the island of Ireland. The Dioceses embrace a logical and coherent area – Ireland's largest county: County Cork as well as Ardmore, a tiny fraction of County Waterford. This alignment with a civic area with one principal city (with its own strong sense of place and identity) is important to the work of the Church in this region. It gives it strength and opens up possibilities.

In 2011, the population of the area was 481,295. Of those, 13,899 in Cork City and County designated themselves as members of the Church of Ireland. Indeed, there were 12,108 Church of Ireland members in Cork County in 2011, the highest of any county in the Republic of Ireland and accounting for 9.4 per cent of all Church of Ireland members.

Therein lies a contemporary challenge. Today, according to the parochial and diocesan figures, only 7,799 are on our records. Our own census of 2011 showed that there are 3,716 households in the Diocese. Of the individuals, 2,417 are under the age of 30; 2,893 are aged between 31 and 60 years; and 2,128 are 61 years or older: a healthy equilibrium in three parts. In the same census 36% of the parishes indicated that they are growing; 50% were much the same size as five years previously and only 14% saw a decline in population. All that said, the current economic and social realities, as elsewhere, present particular challenges.

Archbishop George Simms described this place as 'the delectable Diocese.' And so it is in many ways. The Diocese has a strong sense of family, which is not unrelated to its sense of identifiable place. There are 76 churches or chapels, gathered, either into one of the 22 parochial units or part of a small number of non-parochial ministries. Of the 22 parishes, 14 are in the Diocese of Cork, 5 in the Diocese of Cloyne and 3 in the Diocese of Ross. In addition there are ministries based at Cork University Hospital/Cork University Maternity Hospital (the largest hospital in the State), University College Cork, Ashton Comprehensive School, Bandon Grammar School, Kingston College, Saint Luke's Home Education Centre, as well as a fulltime youth officer and part-time development officer working with young people in schools.

To these ministries are to be added 22 primary schools and 3 second-level schools, 3 housing complexes, an internationally renowned 130-bed care home for the elderly and dementia sufferers with its brand new education centre, a voluntary hospital and a range of other charities, all under the aegis of the bishop, or associated, in particular ways, with the Diocese. Exceptional also is the fact that this small Diocese has, in recent years, produced eleven bishops for the Church of Ireland (priests from the Diocese or who served in it).

A short introduction of this kind falls short in that it cannot adequately convey the energy, faithfulness, innovation, commitment and foresight of this very small corner of the Anglican Communion. It is indeed a delectable place, but over the centuries and today, its remarkable people endeavour to be faithful to the call of Jesus to follow him.

PAUL CORK, CLOYNE AND ROSS

The river Funshion flows under Glanworth Bridge, the oldest bridge in the county.
SCENIC IRELAND

MICHAEL O'NEILL

ST FIN BARRE'S CATHEDRAL

St Fin Barre's Cathedral
SCENIC IRELAND

## St Fin Barre's Cathedral, Cork

Old St Fin Barre's
RCB ARCHIVE

St Fin Barre's Cathedral is one of the most important buildings in the city of Cork. It was built on the site of a seventh-century monastic foundation. The monastery was situated on high ground on the south bank of the River Lee and a succession of church buildings ensured that Christian worship continued there over the centuries. Settlements around the monastery eventually grew into the city of Cork.

By the 1860s St Fin Barre's, a blend of medieval and eighteenth-century buildings, was deemed 'inadequate to the dignity of a cathedral'. A competition to design a new cathedral was held, and won by the English architect William Burges. He was an avid enthusiast of thirteenth-century French Gothic architecture and designed every aspect of the cathedral, including the sculpture, stained glass, woodwork and mosaics. These combined symbolic and decorative functions to produce a harmonious overall design.

Burges insisted on quality: in 1877, he wrote that 'good art is far too rare and far too precious ever to be cheap'. Although he died in 1881, Burges's carefully drawn plans ensured that the work was completed to his design.

Most of the cathedral was built between 1865 and 1879, but work on it continued for many years afterwards. The cathedral was consecrated in 1870 by Bishop John Gregg, whose enthusiasm for the project was essential to its success. He inspired hundreds of donations, including substantial funds from William Crawford of Beamish and Crawford Brewery and Francis Wise of the North Mall Distillery. The new cathedral was constructed just as the Church of Ireland was being disestablished.

Built of grey Cork limestone, the three spires of St Fin Barre's Cathedral are one of the landmarks of the city. The north tower contains a ring of twelve bells that regularly sound out across Cork. The cathedral has a long tradition of music, with the earliest record of a choir dating back to 1328. The organ was first located at the west-end gallery, but was moved to a pit in the north transept in 1889. It was originally built by William Hill of London in 1870 and most recently rebuilt in 2013. Today, St Fin Barre's continues as a living community of liturgy and prayer, with daily worship and special services. As the mother church of the dioceses, it often hosts diocesan services and other events.

AISLING O'CALLAGHAN

# The United Dioceses of Cork, Cloyne and Ross

ALICIA ST LEGER

The united dioceses of Cork, Cloyne and Ross are situated almost entirely within the county of Cork. To the east, a portion of the diocese of Cloyne extends into County Waterford, while in the north-west an area of County Cork belongs to the dioceses of Ardfert and Aghadoe. Otherwise, the diocesan boundaries coincide with the county borders, giving the dioceses of Cork, Cloyne and Ross a unity that contributes much to their distinctive character.

The diocese of Cork comprises an area in the centre and west of the county – including the city of Cork, where St Fin Barre's Cathedral occupies the site of the city's seventh-century monastic foundation. The diocese extends just north of the city and west to the coast. The diocese of Cloyne occupies the eastern and northern part of the county, with its cathedral (St Colman's) in the town of Cloyne. The smallest diocese is Ross, which hugs the south coast and has its cathedral (St Fachtna's) in the town of Rosscarbery. Ross Diocese originally included part of the Beara Peninsula but, thanks to parish reorganisation in 2001, this portion is now part of the diocese of Cork.

## Development of the Dioceses

Harry Clarke stained glass detail in St Barrahane's Church, Castletownsend
DIOCESE OF CORK

The three dioceses have been united since 1835, providing an element of stability that has assisted in their development and administration. The diocese of Cork originally grew out of the monastery that was established in the seventh century in what later became Cork city. Created during the structural reorganisation of the Irish church at the Synod of Ráth Breasail in 1111, the diocese of Cork initially extended from Cork to Mizen Head and from the River Blackwater to the ocean. This territory was later reduced by the emergence of other dioceses.

Mizen Head
SCENIC IRELAND

Twelfth century Romanesque doorway at St Fachtna's Cathedral, Rosscarbery, the smallest cathedral in Ireland

The diocese of Ross was created by the Synod of Kells in 1152 and was based on territory then controlled by the O'Driscolls. In 1583, it was united with the diocese of Cork. The then-bishop of Ross, William Lyon, had been appointed in 1582. In 1583, he also became bishop of Cork and Cloyne. The diocese of Ross has been united with Cork since that date.

COLIN BOYLE

The relationship between the diocese of Cloyne and the dioceses of Cork and Ross is more complex. Cloyne was created after the Synod of Ráth Breasail, taking lands formerly held by the dioceses of Emly, Cork and Lismore, and was recognised at the Synod of Kells some 40 years later. It was an independent diocese until 1429, when it was united with the diocese of Cork. It remained so until 1638. Following the episcopate of George Synge, Cloyne was again united with Cork and Ross for a short period from 1661 until 1678. In 1679, a bishop was appointed for Cloyne alone, and the diocese remained separate until 1835, when it rejoined Cork and Ross. Since that date Cloyne has been part of the united dioceses of Cork, Cloyne and Ross.

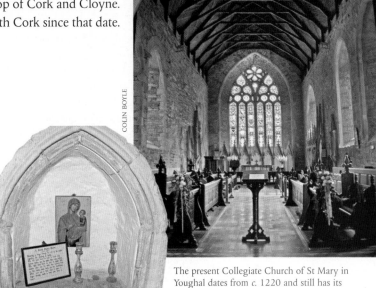

The present Collegiate Church of St Mary in Youghal dates from *c.* 1220 and still has its original oak roof timbers..

The pointed, moulded piscina in Youghal dates from *c.* 1220. The left hand drain is used to wash vessels before use, the water then runs outside. The right hand drain is used to wash holy vessels after use, the water then contains wine, so this drain runs back into the foundations.

## Cork City

The close correlation of the diocesan boundaries with those of the county of Cork has strengthened a sense of family in the united dioceses. This has been helped by the preeminence of the city of Cork in terms of size and geographical location. With just one major city in the dioceses, in which the bishop resides, Cork is a natural focus for certain diocesan and civic occasions. The result is that the representative role of the bishop in civic affairs is larger than in other dioceses. The bishop lives in the elegant Bishop's Palace (1782) opposite St Fin Barre's Cathedral. Although the role of the city is very significant in the dioceses, the strength of the county is equally important. The strong role of the Church of Ireland population in County Cork is reflected in the historic spread of churches and the strength of many parishes.

A richly illustrated seventeenth-century Irish crucifixion scene found on a stone in Galwey Chapel of St Multose, Kinsale. The sun and moon sit above Christ's outstretched arms, with Mary on his left and St John on his right. The two thieves bound to their crosses are carved in perspective.
ST MULTOSE CHURCH

## Seventeenth and Eighteenth Centuries

Over the centuries many people, clerical and lay, have contributed to the development of the united dioceses of Cork, Cloyne and Ross. The seventeenth and eighteenth centuries can be characterised by several figures in particular.

Cork city, the River Lee and St Fin Barre's Cathedral
SCENIC IRELAND

## Bishop Dive Downes (1653–1709)

Dive Downes, the son of a clergyman, was born in Thornby, Northamptonshire in 1653. He studied at Trinity College, Dublin, where he proved a keen scholar, obtaining four degrees between 1671 and 1692. Ordained a priest in 1678, he held positions in Dublin before becoming bishop of Cork and Ross in 1699. He lived during the turbulent struggles in Ireland between the forces of James II and William III. His arrival in the dioceses was in the aftermath of the 1690 siege of Cork, amidst fear and unrest in the region.

Bishop Downes was determined to assess his dioceses and between 1699 and 1706 he travelled throughout the county, examining and recording the state of the parishes. This involved not only detailed work, but also much arduous travel. His meticulous record provides a wonderful glimpse into each of the localities that he visited. Downes described the condition of church buildings, lands and other church properties and the state of the Church of Ireland population, and often made observations on the quality of the land and other local matters. He found many of the churches to be in poor state of repair and the clergy often ill equipped to serve their congregations. He gathered information that allowed him and his successors to improve conditions in the dioceses. His records are a very valuable source for historians and others examining this important period in Irish history.

Bishop Downes was married four times: to Sarah Dowdall, Anne Carlton, Elizabeth Townsend (*née* Becher) and Catherine FitzGerald, and had three daughters and one son. This learned and hardworking bishop died in Dublin in November 1709.

When Bishop Downes visited Kilmoe in June 1700 he found the existing Church of St Brendan at Crookhaven in ruins. The present Church at Crookhaven was built in 1717 by Bishop Peter Browne, who was Bishop of Cork from 1710–35. It was rebuilt in about 1840. The Church was dedicated to St Brendan, the name of the old Church of Kilmoe. In early days St Brendan's was sometimes called 'The Bishop's Church', and the Bishop's Arms are engraved on the outside of the West wall of the Church. Marconi erected his first wireless mast at Crookhaven, on the site of the present Marconi House. Later the mast was erected on Brow Head and Marconi sent his first wireless message from Brow Head to Cornwall. From 1616–42 there was a flourishing pilchard industry, started by Lord Boyle, Earl of Cork. It supplied the French market and it gave considerable local employment.

Robert Traill
JUNE TRAILL

Rev. Dr Robert Traill, rector of Schull parish, died in April from famine fever, or typhoid, which he caught as a result of his work to help the starving in his area. His gravestone inscription at Schull tells how 'with his Blessed Master' he 'went about doing good till at length in the full sacrifice of his superhuman efforts in relieving the prevailing distress in the Famine years of 1846 and 1847, interred to his rest April 1847.'

J.M. Synge was his grandson.

St Brendan's Church, Crookhaven
COLIN BOYLE

## Bishop George Berkeley (1685–1753)

George Berkeley was born and raised in County Kilkenny, attending Kilkenny College before studying at Trinity College, Dublin. Ordained in 1710, he became dean of Derry in 1724. In 1734, he was appointed bishop of Cloyne, a position he held until his death in 1753.

Berkeley was a keen scholar and soon built up a reputation as a philosopher. A highly spiritual man, Berkeley was also very practical. On his appointment to Cloyne he devoted himself to the care and welfare of those in his diocese. He promoted self-sufficiency, urging both rich and poor to work to improve living conditions. In 1753, while in Oxford to supervise his son's education, Bishop Berkeley died. He was buried in Christ Church Cathedral, Oxford. Two of his children were buried in the north transept of St Colman's Cathedral, Cloyne. It was there also that an elaborate memorial tomb to Bishop Berkeley was unveiled in 1890. Created by the sculptor Bruce Joy, the alabaster effigy commemorates a man who was loved and respected in the diocese of Cloyne. Berkeley's philosophical ideas continue to be widely influential. His legacy also survives in Yale University, where Berkeley College commemorates the bishop's endowment of land and books, and in the University of Berkeley in California.

BELFAST CATHEDRAL ARCHIVE

The monument to George Berkeley in Cloyne Cathedral

COLIN BOYLE

## The Nineteenth Century

The nineteenth century produced various other figures who made a notable impact on the dioceses of Cork, Cloyne and Ross.

### The Gregg Family

Bishop John Gregg, 1862–78

Various members of the Gregg family were prominent in the dioceses. The first was John Gregg (1798–1878), who was born in Cappa, County Clare and educated in Ennis and at Trinity College, Dublin. He was ordained a priest in 1827 and worked in Kildare and Dublin. In 1862, he was elected bishop of Cork, Cloyne and Ross, and during his time in the dioceses was noted for his oratorical skills. His enthusiastic support was vital for the building of St Fin Barre's Cathedral. He laid the foundation stone in 1865 and saw the western towers finished shortly before his death in 1878. His son Robert Samuel Gregg was born in Kilsallaghan, County Dublin in 1834. He graduated from Trinity College, Dublin, and was ordained a priest in 1858. He served as curate of Rathcooney (Cork), then as rector of Christ Church, Belfast. He became vicar of St Fin Barre's Cathedral, in charge of Holy Trinity Church, Frankfield, for three years before becoming rector of Carrigrohane in 1865. He became dean of Cork in 1875 and Bishop of Ossory, Ferns and Leighlin in 1875. In 1878, he succeeded his father as bishop of Cork, Cloyne and Ross. Robert Samuel Gregg was an able administrator and his financial skills contributed much at the General Synod in the years after disestablishment. He continued his father's enthusiastic support of the creation of St Fin Barre's Cathedral. In 1893, he became archbishop of Armagh, but died in January 1896. His nephew, John Allen Fitzgerald Gregg, was archbishop of Armagh from 1939 to 1959.

Robert Samuel Gregg's sister, Frances Fitzgerald Gregg, also made an important contribution to the Church of Ireland in Cork. She was active in charitable works and in 1872 founded a hospital in the city, which has been known as St Luke's Home since 1967. In 1994, the home moved to new premises in Mahon, Cork.

Bishop Robert Samuel Gregg, 1878–94
BELFAST CATHEDRAL ARCHIVE

John Fitzgerald Gregg
ARMAGH CATHEDRAL

President Higgins opened the new education centre built on the grounds of St Luke's Home, June 2012. He stated: 'This wonderful new space will allow care givers the opportunity to enhance their skills in caring for older people and will improve the quality, consistency and relevance of education to individuals and institutions committed to the care of older people.
DIOCESE OF CORK

## The Twentieth Century

The united dioceses have been fortunate in that many of their men and women have been actively involved in the local and national affairs of the Church. Until the early twentieth century, the landed families played a significant role in the life of the Church and, indeed, provided many of the clergy who worked in the dioceses and further afield. The First World War had a huge impact on many families. In 1922 a memorial was unveiled in St Fin Barre's Cathedral to honour the 385 men from the dioceses who lost their lives in the war. The disturbed political period from 1919 until the mid-1920s had a particularly significant impact on the dioceses, since the county was one of the main centres of fighting and intimidation. During the worst years, many members of

This ancient entrance was said to have belonged to the Monastery of St Mary of the Isle, a short distance north of the cathedral of St Fin Barre. Left to right: Robert Walker, Contractor of the new building (St Fin Barre) Richard Caulfield, Rev. Frederick Dobbin, resident preacher of the Cathedral, and Charles Hewitt, MD.

QUEEN'S UNIVERSITY BELFAST

## Richard Caulfield (1823–87)

Richard Caulfield was born in Cork city and was educated at Bandon Endowed School. He studied at Trinity College, Dublin. Although originally intending to enter the ministry of the Church of Ireland, Caulfield chose instead to focus on his love of antiquarian research. He became librarian at the Royal Cork Institution and Queen's College, Cork.

He published many articles and books, drawing on sources in Ireland, Britain and Belgium. Amongst his most important works were his transcriptions of the council books of the corporations of Cork, Youghal and Kinsale, published between 1876 and 1879. These and other transcriptions became even more important following the later loss of many original sources.

As a member of St Fin Barre's Cathedral's building committee, he chronicled the replacement of the modest eighteenth-century cathedral with William Burges's striking new structure. In 1864, he published a *Life of St Fin Barre* and, in 1881, wrote the *Handbook of the Cathedral Church of St Fin Barre, Cork*. The following year he produced the *Annals of the Cathedral of Saint Colman, Cloyne*, having published the pipe roll of Cloyne in 1859. Richard Caulfield made a huge contribution to the study of Cork's past and, in particular, to the history of the Church of Ireland there.

## Charles Webster, 1866–1946

Charles Webster was born in Bandon and educated at the Endowed School before studying at Trinity College, Dublin. Webster spent all of his ordained life in the dioceses of Cork, Cloyne and Ross. He displayed a keen interest in the history of the Church of Ireland in Cork. In 1909, he produced his invaluable illustrated study, *The Church Plate of the Diocese of Cork, Cloyne and Ross*. Webster's detailed *The Diocese of Cork*, published in 1920, was followed by an important work, *The Diocese of Ross* (1936). He investigated many aspects of parish history, publishing many articles, including 'The Town of Passage West and the Parish of Marmullane', 'The Cathedral Church of St Fachtna, Ross' and 'The Diocese of Ross and Its Ancient Churches'. Webster was elected as a member of the Royal Irish Academy in 1929.

## Sam Maguire, 1877–1927

The famous Gaelic Athletic Association Cup given to the All-Ireland Senior Champions of Gaelic football was commissioned in honour of Sam Maguire, who actively supported the game especially in the London area where he worked in the Post Office. He joined the London Hibernian Gaelic football team and also became a member of Irish Republican Brotherhood. Sam Maguire was born in the townland of Mallabracka, near the town of Dunmanway in West Cork where the Maguires farmed 200 acres of land and were members of the Church of Ireland. Sam Maguire is buried in the churchyard of St Mary's Church, Dunmanway.

"Taxation without Representation is Tyranny."

**MUNSTER WOMEN'S FRANCHISE LEAGUE.**

**MEMBERSHIP CARD.**

President:—MISS EDITH Œ. SOMERVILLE.

Subscriptions to be sent to the Hon. Secretary—
MISS DAY.
Myrtle Hill House,
Cork.

## Edith Somerville, 1858–1949

Edith Somerville was born into a prominent land owning family at Castletownsend, Co. Cork. Togther with her cousin Violet Martin (pseudonym Martin Ross) she published five novels and three volumes of the 'Irish RM Stories'. She was a strong supporter of the suffragette movement and actively campaigned for women's rights in Ireland and England. In 1910, she became the first president of the Munster Women's Franchise League.

## John Leonard Barry Deane, 1924–2012

A notable figure of the past century, J.L.B. Deane was born in Bandon and educated in Northern Ireland and London. He graduated from Trinity College, Dublin in 1947 and trained to become a barrister. Despite this, he never worked in paid employment and devoted his life to voluntary work.

He made an enormous contribution to the Church of Ireland, following a long tradition of lay leadership in the dioceses of Cork, Cloyne and Ross. At a local level, he was a member of the select vestry of Bandon Union, was parochial treasurer for many years and took an active interest in Bandon Grammar School. At diocesan level, he was a member of the Diocesan Synod for over 60 years, serving as honorary secretary of the synod and of the diocesan board of education. He served on many committees and was a perceptive member of the diocesan board of patronage.

John Barry Deane
DIOCESE OF CORK

J.L.B. Deane was well known in Church of Ireland circles throughout Ireland. For 50 years he was a member of the General Synod, being lay honorary secretary for 23 of those years (1970–94). He was an active member of the Representative Church Body. In 1988, he acted as consultant to the bishops at the Lambeth Conference and subsequently as a representative on the Anglican Consultative Council. In 1997, he was appointed as a lay canon of St Patrick's Cathedral, Armagh in recognition of his distinguished service to the Church of Ireland.

the Church of Ireland (both lay and clergy) left the county. The political climate of the new regime and fears for the future meant that some never returned. By the mid-twentieth century, the traditional strength of the landed families had greatly declined. However, the tenant farmers, who were particularly strong in west Cork, tended to remain on their lands. Although affected by emigration and suffering many difficulties during the War of Independence, they and their descendants remain an important part of the Church of Ireland community.

Change also occurred in the city parishes from the early twentieth century onwards. There was a gradual decline in the working-class and lower-middle-class Church of Ireland community. This was partly because of political unrest and emigration, but it also reflected a sustained movement out to middle-class suburbs such as Douglas. By the mid-twentieth century, city churches saw declining numbers and over the following half century many were closed. By the early twenty-first century, only St Fin Barre's Cathedral and St Anne's Church, Shandon remained in the city centre. Similarly, city centre Church of Ireland schools underwent a process of closure and amalgamation. This phenomena is not unique to Cork, but reflects changes in wider society.

The mid 1960s and 1970s were a time of great change in the educational system. Under the leadership of Bishop Gordon Perdue (1957–78), Cork Grammar School and Rochelle School amalgamated to form the new Ashton Comprehensive School in Cork City. Lay people chaired the new school boards of management. During this time too, parochial groups were reorganised into more viable units. Bishop Samuel Poyntz (1978–88) was key

to breaking down barriers to ecumenical progress. Bishop Roy Warke (1988–98), oversaw the difficult, often painful, task of the closure of a number of churches. Meanwhile he continued the work of ecumenical and civic outreach in Cork.

## The Twenty First Century

Confirmation of eight young members of the church

Bishop Paul Colton (elected bishop in January 1999 at the age of 38) became one of the youngest bishops for some time, and returned to his home city. Perhaps appropriately, therefore this diocese was the first in Ireland to have a website, and the first to engage with Twitter and Facebook. In addition, the internet was harnessed as a tool for diocesan administration.

There have been a number of key focuses for the diocese in recent times. These include programmes to introduce the new Book of Common Prayer and the new hymnal, the extension of St Luke's Home and the building of St Luke's Home Education Centre. Under the auspices of the Hard Gospel Programme, there has been an initiative to look at the contentious and painful history of the diocese during the War of Independence and the Civil War.

A particular emphasis has been placed on equipping the clergy for mutual support in, and the changing requirements of, ministry. New forms of lay ministry have been encouraged, including the introduction of trained lay pastoral workers. There is now a full-time youth worker, and also whole-time chaplains at University College Cork and Cork University Hospital, Cork University Maternity Hospital, the largest hospital in the state. More change lies ahead. In spite of the economic challenges and changes in society, the diocese and its people look forward to the future, under God, as a time for confidence.

Interfaith dialogue

Celebration of Lay Ministry in St Fin Barre's
Cathedral, Cork

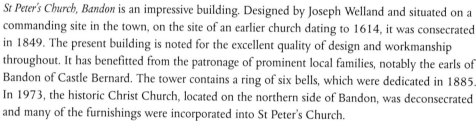
St Mattias's Church, Ballydehob

## BALLYDEHOB and AGHADOWN

*St Matthias's Church, Ballydehob* was originally built as a chapel of ease to Schull Church and became a separate parish in 1870. The present building dates to 1829, when its erection was assisted by the Board of First Fruits. It was later extended, particularly in the 1860s under Rev. Robert Noble. The original 1829 building now forms the centre of a larger structure, situated on a hill on the edge of the village of Ballydehob.

St Matthew's Church, Aghadown

*St Matthew's Church, Aghadown* was designed by Cork architect Henry Hill. It was built in 1873 on a site donated by John H. Becher, beside the main road between Skibbereen and Ballydehob. The Schull and Skibbereen Railway ran along the front boundary of the churchyard from 1886 until 1947. The present building replaced an earlier church located on the banks of the River Ilen to the south.

## BANDON, RATHCLAREN, INNISHANNON, BALLINADEE AND BRINNY

*St Peter's Church, Bandon* is an impressive building. Designed by Joseph Welland and situated on a commanding site in the town, on the site of an earlier church dating to 1614, it was consecrated in 1849. The present building is noted for the excellent quality of design and workmanship throughout. It has benefitted from the patronage of prominent local families, notably the earls of Bandon of Castle Bernard. The tower contains a ring of six bells, which were dedicated in 1885. In 1973, the historic Christ Church, located on the northern side of Bandon, was deconsecrated and many of the furnishings were incorporated into St Peter's Church.

*Holy Trinity Church, Rathclaren* dates from around 1650, with later additions and modifications. Significant work was carried out on the building in 1835, with the help of a grant from the Ecclesiastical Commissioners, while a large tower was added in the later nineteenth century. A peal of ten tubular bells was installed in the tower in 1896 in memory of members of the Sealy family. This historic building is unusual in having a lychgate entrance.

Christ Church, Innishannon

St Peter's Church, Bandon

*Christ Church, Innishannon* was built between 1854 and 1856 on an elevated site on the village's main street. It replaced an earlier church, St Mary's, nearby. Christ Church was designed by Joseph Welland and the interior was embellished by improvements in later years.

*Ballinadee Church* dates back to 1759 and is prominently located in the centre of the village. Various alterations have been made to the building, including the addition of a tower and north transept in the nineteenth century.

*Brinny Church* has its origins in a structure erected in 1737. That church was substantially rebuilt in 1813, with the assistance of a loan from the Board of First Fruits. Further changes were made in the 1880s and 1890s, when the interior was remodelled and a new and distinctive tower was added.

Holy Trinity Church, Rathclaren

## CARRIGALINE and MONKSTOWN

*St Mary's Church, Carrigaline* was built in 1824 on the site of an earlier church. It was designed by brothers James and George Richard Pain and has elegant detail, both outside and inside. A north transept was added in 1835. Amongst the memorials in the churchyard are two fine mausolea to members of the Newenham family of nearby Coolmore House.

*St John the Evangelist's Church, Monkstown* was built in 1832, on a site provided by Gerard and Daniel Callaghan, tenants of the earl of Longford and viscount de Vesci. The church was designed in early English style by Cork architect William Hill. The coats of arms of those who subscribed to the cost of the church (£950) were incorporated into the stained glass of the west window. The church is an impressive feature of the town, situated on a height overlooking the harbour.

St Mary's Church, Carrigaline

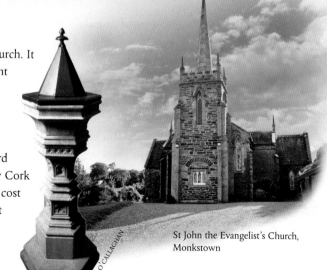

St John the Evangelist's Church, Monkstown

## CARRIGROHANE, GARRYCLOYNE (BLARNEY) and INNISCARRA

*St Peter's Church, Carrigrohane* was built on the site of an earlier church. The main body of the building was designed by Joseph Welland and constructed in 1854. The church was expanded in 1866–7 by the addition of a south aisle and vestry designed by William Burges, who was then working on St Fin Barre's Cathedral. In 1897, the old spire was replaced by a distinctive cut-stone spire designed by W.H. Hill. There is a high standard of craftsmanship in this church, which is situated in the western suburbs of Cork city.

The *Church of the Resurrection, Blarney* is in the parish of Garrycloyne. It is unusual in being of Classical design and was erected about 1776 on an elevated site overlooking the square in the village. The interior was restored and modernised in the 1990s, when it received its present name.

*St Senan's Church, Inniscarra* was built in 1819 and replaced a nearby seventeenth-century church. In 1893, a chancel was added to the building. The church is in a scenic rural setting.

St Peter's Church, Carrigrohane

e Church of the
surrection, Blarney

St Senan's Church, Inniscarra

## CORK

### CORK UNIVERSITY HOSPITAL

The *Chapel of Christ the Healer, Cork University Hospital* was consecrated and officially opened in May 1980. It serves as an oasis of prayer and healing for patients, staff and visitors in the large, busy hospital. The chapel, which usually seats 12–15 people, was refurbished and rededicated in December 2012.

### ST ANNE'S, SHANDON

*St Anne's Church, Shandon* is one of the key landmarks of Cork city. It was built in 1722 on the site of an earlier church, St Mary's. That church had been destroyed during the 1690 Williamite siege of Cork and rebuilt in 1693 on Shandon Street. Population growth led to the construction of St Anne's, with its distinctive colouring: red sandstone on the north and east elevations and limestone on the other two sides. The tower contains a famous ring of eight bells, installed in 1752. The fish weather vane commemorates the important salmon industry on the River Lee. A clock was installed in the tower in 1847, with dials on each side. In the past, discrepancies in the time shown on each clock face led to a local nickname – 'the four-faced liar'.

St Anne's Church, Shandon

### ST LUKE'S HOME, MAHON

The chapel at *St Luke's Home, Mahon* serves the spiritual needs of residents, staff and visitors. Originally called the Home for Protestant Incurables, St Luke's Home was first opened on Victoria Road, Cork in 1872. By 1879, the home had moved to Military Hill. It remained there until 1994, when a new facility was constructed at Mahon. From 1994, the home no longer catered exclusively for Protestants. The Church of Ireland bishop of Cork, Cloyne and Ross is president of the home and its directors are drawn from the Church of Ireland, Presbyterian and Methodist churches, but the home welcomes those of every faith and no faith. The chapel is in regular use for services held by different denominations.

Holy Trinity Church, Frankfield

## DOUGLAS, FRANKFIELD, BLACKROCK and MARMULLANE

*St Luke's Church, Douglas* has its origins in a 1786 building constructed as a chapel of ease to Carrigaline. By 1875, population growth resulted in Douglas becoming a separate parish. In the same year, the church was substantially rebuilt to the design of Cork engineer Osborne Cadwallader Edwards. Such was the demand for space that the nave was lengthened in 1885, while a tower and spire were added around this time to the design of William Henry Hill. Many renowned Corkonians are interred in the large churchyard, including businessman Sir John Arnott and antiquarian Dr Richard Caulfield.

St Luke's Church, Douglas

*Holy Trinity Church, Frankfield* is a trustee church which has shared ministry with Douglas Parish since 1920. It was designed by Cork architects Thomas and Kearns Deane and built in the Cork suburb of Frankfield. Consecrated in 1839, it was funded by Samuel Lane of Frankfield House. The church was built and furnished to a very high standard, costing £5,000. In 1865, the English architect William Burges designed a three-light east window for the modified sanctuary in the church.

*St Mary's Church, Marmullane* (Passage West) dates from 1684. The building was repaired and enlarged over the years, particularly in 1808, 1838–9 and 1855–6. The church contains box pews and richly decorated ceiling timbers. Lieutenant Richard Roberts, captain of the *Sirius* in 1838, when it was the first ship to cross the Atlantic entirely under steam power, is commemorated in an impressive family monument in the churchyard.

*St Michael's Church, Blackrock* was consecrated in 1828 as a chapel of ease to St Fin Barre's Cathedral. In 1836, the spire was badly damaged by lightning. St Michael's became a separate parish in 1873, serving the growing suburbs of the Blackrock area. Notable features include a monument to William Beamish by the famous sculptor John Hogan and a plaque to the mathematician George Boole, who is buried in the churchyard.

St Michael's Church, Blackrock

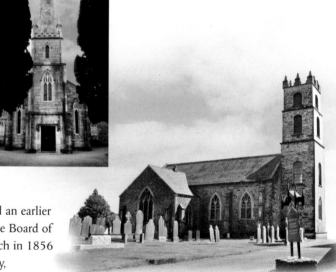

## FANLOBBUS (DUNMANWAY), DRIMOLEAGUE, DRINAGH and COOLKELURE

*St Mary's Church, Dunmanway* was consecrated in 1822 and replaced an earlier church on the same site. It was built with the aid of a loan from the Board of First Fruits. Joseph Welland designed a north transept for the church in 1856 and further improvements were made in the late nineteenth century, including the addition of a chancel.

*St Matthew's Church, Drimoleague* (Dromdaleague) was constructed in 1858, replacing an eighteenth-century building. Designed by Joseph Welland, the church was built on a new site near the village of Drimoleague.

St Mary's Church, Dunmanway

St Matthew's Church, Drimoleague

*Christ Church, Drinagh* replaced an earlier church constructed in 1819 with the assistance of a grant from the Board of First Fruits. This church was demolished, with the exception of the tower, and the stone was used to construct a new church in 1896. The 1896 church, designed by W.H. Hill, was built on a new site nearer to the rectory and school.

*St Edmund's Church, Coolkelure* was built in 1865 and designed by the Cork architect Henry Hill. It replaced a schoolhouse at Carrigskully, which had been licensed for divine worship in 1843, when a mission district was established. The mission was a success and, with the support of Bishop John Gregg and local landowner Colonel E.A. Shuldham, St Edmund's Church was constructed. The church is well proportioned and set in picturesque countryside.

St Edmund's Church, Coolkelure

## KILMOCOMOGUE (BANTRY), CASTLETOWNBERE AND DURRUS

The impressive *St Brendan's Church, Bantry* was designed by the English architect Henry Edward Kendall and built in 1828. Over the years it has had close links with Bantry House and improvements in the 1860s were mainly funded by the earl of Bantry. The church was rededicated to St Brendan the Navigator in the year 2000.

*St Peter's Church, Killaconenagh* (Castletownbere) was built in 1841 to cater for the growing population in the area, many of whom were connected with the naval base on Bere Island and the copper mines at Allihies. Damaged in an arson attack in 2002, the church is no longer in regular use.

*St James' Church, Durrus* was built in 1792 with the aid of a loan from the Board of First Fruits. Located on the site of an earlier church, poor construction led to a partial collapse of the structure; it was rebuilt in 1799 at the expense of the rector, Rev. Henry Jones. In 1832, the building was enlarged with the addition of the tower. Cork architect William Atkins designed a new south aisle and robing room in 1867, while a vestry was added in 1940. This church is situated in a scenic location at the top of Dunmanus Bay.

St James' Church, Durrus
RCB ARCHIVE

St Brendan's Church, Crookhaven

## KILMOE (SCHULL, TEAMPOL-NA-MBOCHT AND CROOKHAVEN)

*Holy Trinity Church, Schull* was designed by Joseph Welland and built in the early 1850s. The gable-fronted church replaced an earlier church on the same site. In 1889 the Flight and Robson (London) organ from the old St Fin Barre's Cathedral in Cork was installed in Schull Church in memory of Rev. John Triphook, rector there for 34 years.

The name of *Teampol na mBocht* ('the church of the poor') tells much about its origins. During the Great Famine of the 1840s, the rector of Kilmoe, Rev. William Allen Fisher, set up soup kitchens and distributed aid. Funds donated to him were used to build the church in 1847, providing much-needed employment in the Toormore and Altar areas. In order to maximise work, no horses were used in the construction of this church.

Teampol na mBocht

The *Church of St Brendan the Navigator, Crookhaven*, built in a scenic location beside the sea, dates to 1717. In that year Bishop Peter Browne of Cork built a small church on which the bishop's arms were engraved. The church was rebuilt in about 1840, but the engraved arms were retained. The simple building is in regular use only during the summer months.

Holy Trinity Church, Schull

## KINNEIGH, KILMEEN, DESERTSERGES AND MURRAGH

*St Bartholomew's Church, Kinneigh* is located on a historic site. After the Vikings destroyed a seventh-century monastery nearby, a new monastery and round tower were constructed on the present site. The round tower in the churchyard is unusual in having a hexagonal base. The present church was built in 1856, replacing a 1794 structure nearby. It is a fine Romanesque building and was designed by Joseph Welland.

*Christ Church, Kilmeen* was built on the site of an older church in a pastoral setting. Consecrated in 1811, it was enlarged in 1865 by the addition of a north aisle, porch and robing room.

*St Mary's Church, Desertserges* was built in 1805 at a cost of just over £553. It was enlarged in 1865 by the construction of a south transept and a new chancel with polygonal apse.

*St Patrick's Church, Murragh* was built at Farranthomas in 1810. An earlier church beside the river had been undermined and washed away. The 1810 building was built with the aid of a loan from the Board of First Fruits.

St Bartholomew's Church, Kinneigh

St Brendan's Church, Bantry
SCENIC IRELAND

ST MULTOSE'S CHURCH, KINSALE

St Multose's Church, Kinsale

## KINSALE, BALLYMARTLE and TEMPLETRINE

*St Multose's Church, Kinsale* is an important centre for worship in the busy town of Kinsale.

*Christ Church, Ballymartle* was constructed in the mid-nineteenth century, replacing an earlier building. In 1869 a polygonal chancel was added, to the design of Henry and Arthur Hill. The church was closely associated with members of the Meade family.

*Templetrine Church*, near Ballinspittle, dates to 1821, when it was constructed with the assistance of a grant from the Board of First Fruits. This small church, with a crenellated square tower, stands on an elevated site.

Bishop Meade 1894–1912
BELFAST CATHEDRAL ARCHIVE

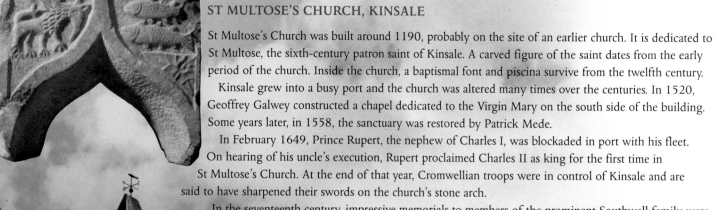

## ST MULTOSE'S CHURCH, KINSALE

St Multose's Church was built around 1190, probably on the site of an earlier church. It is dedicated to St Multose, the sixth-century patron saint of Kinsale. A carved figure of the saint dates from the early period of the church. Inside the church, a baptismal font and piscina survive from the twelfth century.

Kinsale grew into a busy port and the church was altered many times over the centuries. In 1520, Geoffrey Galwey constructed a chapel dedicated to the Virgin Mary on the south side of the building. Some years later, in 1558, the sanctuary was restored by Patrick Mede.

In February 1649, Prince Rupert, the nephew of Charles I, was blockaded in port with his fleet. On hearing of his uncle's execution, Rupert proclaimed Charles II as king for the first time in St Multose's Church. At the end of that year, Cromwellian troops were in control of Kinsale and are said to have sharpened their swords on the church's stone arch.

In the seventeenth century, impressive memorials to members of the prominent Southwell family were erected in the north transept. The arms of King William III were placed in the church after the capture of Kinsale in 1690. There were several changes to the church in the eighteenth century, including the removal of the chancel arch, the construction of a gallery in the west end and the addition of another storey to the original church tower.

In 1835, the outer walls of the side aisles and north transept were raised so that one roof covered the entire structure. Some years later the floor level was raised and the east window was altered. These major changes were followed in the late nineteenth century by the insertion of new floors and woodwork, including a new pulpit.

In 1951 the roof over the chancel was restored to its original height. The church contains some notable twentieth-century stained glass, including windows by Catherine O'Brien of An Túr Gloine, Dublin, and Gordon Webster of Glasgow.

St Multose's Church is part of Kinsale Union of Parishes, with churches at Ballymartle and Templetrine.

St Mark's Church, Kilbonane

St Andrew's Church, Kilmurry

## MOVIDDY (KILBONANE (AHERLA), KILMURRY AND TEMPLEMARTIN)

*St Mark's Church, Kilbonane* is located at the western end of the village of Aherla. The first church on the site was built in 1834 for £150, part of which was contributed by the clergyman. The present building was designed by the Cork architect William Henry Hill and consecrated in June 1901. Some of the cut limestone used in the structure came from the demolished church at Aglish.

*St Andrew's Church, Kilmurry*, an attractive, small church, was built in 1847 to the design of Joseph Welland. It benefitted from the patronage of the Warren family of nearby Warren's Court and in the late nineteenth century the interior was remodelled.

*St Martin's Church, Templemartin* dates to around 1797 and is probably on an early Christian site. It was constructed with the aid of funds from the Board of First Fruits. The impressive tower at the west end is much older and has a stone inscription indicating that it was reconstructed in 1718.

St Martin's Church, Templemartin

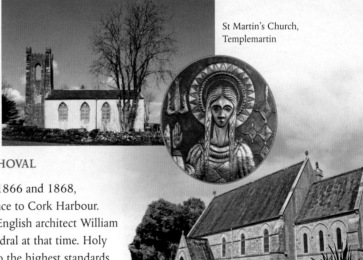

## TEMPLEBREEDY (CROSSHAVEN) AND NOHOVAL

*Holy Trinity Church, Crosshaven* was built between 1866 and 1868, replacing an earlier church overlooking the entrance to Cork Harbour. The new church was a creation of the renowned English architect William Burges, who was working on St Fin Barre's Cathedral at that time. Holy Trinity Church is beautifully designed and built to the highest standards.

*Nohoval Church* was built around 1744 on a prominent and historic site in the village. The building was remodelled in about 1810 and a tower was later added to the structure.

Nohoval Church

Holy Trinity Church, Crosshaven

## THE DIOCESE OF CLOYNE

### CLOYNE, CORKBEG, MIDLETON and GURRANEKENNEFEAKE

*St Colman's Cathedral, Cloyne* dates from around 1250, but has its origins in a sixth-century monastic foundation.

*St Michael and All Angels' Church, Corkbeg* was consecrated in 1881, with the tower being added later. The ruins of an old church are nearby. The 1881 church was designed by William Atkins and closely associated with the Penrose Fitzgerald family. It is a distinctive building, constructed to the highest standards. The interior is notable for its striking use of colour and texture, with imaginative use of bricks, tiles, stained glass and other features.

Holy Trinity Church, East Ferry

*St John the Baptist's Church, Midleton* stands on the site of a twelfth-century Cistercian abbey. There was a succession of churches on the site before the present building was constructed in 1823. The elegant structure was designed by James and George Richard Pain and funded by a loan from the Board of First Fruits. Originally very plain inside, a carved oak screen was erected in 1898.

*Holy Trinity Church, East Ferry* is in the parish of Gurranekennefeake. Designed by William Atkins and built between 1865 and 1867, it is beautifully sited beside the harbour. The use of limestone, red sandstone, brickwork and other materials have created a distinctive, colourful appearance both inside and outside.

St John the Baptist's Church, Midleton

## ST COLMAN'S CATHEDRAL, CLOYNE

The cathedral in Cloyne owes its origins to a monastery founded on the site in the sixth century by St Colman. A succession of churches followed, with the present structure dating back to around 1250. An early building in the churchyard, known as the Fire House, may have been an oratory or may have been used by an order of holy women to keep a fire continually burning. Nearby is a round tower dating from the tenth or eleventh century. It was used by the monastic community as a bell tower, a place of refuge and an observation post. The tower was struck by lightning in 1749 and the top was damaged. A discovery of 1885 shows the early importance of the site: an early twelfth-century decorated gilt-bronze cross, possibly from the cover of a book shrine, was found near the cathedral. It is now in the National Museum of Ireland.

RCB ARCHIVE

The cruciform building has seen many changes over the centuries. There is evidence that there was once a tower at the intersection of the transepts. During the 1641 Rebellion, the cathedral was attacked; repairs were made during the following year. Extensive renovations were carried out in the eighteenth and nineteenth centuries. In 1705, the choir was enlarged and the chapter house repaired. In 1706, the battlements on the walls of the nave were removed and a new roof put in place. Further improvements followed and work during the mid-1770s saw the removal of a 'great arch' at the choir entrance. New windows were placed in the choir around 1856, while in the 1890s there were many changes in that section of the building. They included the installation of a new pine ceiling and new choir stalls, the removal of the gallery on the west wall, and the consequent relocation of the organ.

Amongst the important monuments in the cathedral are the seventeenth-century Fitzgerald tomb and memorials to Bishops William Bennett (bishop 1794–1820) and John Brinkley (bishop 1826–35). The latter was a noted astronomer and scientist. In 1890, a fine monument to Bishop George Berkeley (bishop 1734–53) was unveiled.

St Colman's Cathedral is part of Cloyne Union of Parishes, with churches at Midleton, Corkbeg and East Ferry. The historic cathedral is an important centre in the diocese of Cloyne, carrying on a tradition of Christian worship over 14 centuries.

St Colman's Cathedral, Cloyne

St Marys and All Saints' Church, Rathcooney

## COBH (RUSHBROOKE), GLANMIRE (RATHCOONEY) and LITTLE ISLAND

*Christ Church, Rushbrooke* was designed by Cork architect Henry Hill. It was built in the 1860s to cater for the growing population on the western side of Queenstown (now Cobh). The spire is a landmark of the area.

*St Mary and All Saints' Church, Rathcooney.* Constructed in 1784, this elegant church with its tall spire is a prominent feature in the village of Glanmire. Sarah Curran, fiancée of United Irishman Robert Emmet (who was executed in 1803), married Captain Henry Sturgeon in this church in 1805. The church was extended in the late nineteenth century, when a chancel was built and the interior substantially improved.

*St Lappan's Church, Little Island* was built between 1864 and 1866 with the assistance of a bequest from Miss Hester Bury. Designed by William J. Welland and William Gillespie, the building reveals a high quality of craftsmanship in its construction. It is an attractive limestone church with a prominent spire.

RCB ARCHIVE

Christ Church, Rushbrooke

St Lappan's Church, Little Island

RCB ARCHIVE

St George's Church, Brigown

## FERMOY, BALLYHOOLY, KNOCKMOURNE, ARDNAGEEHY (GLENVILLE) and BRIGOWN (MITCHELSTOWN)

*Christ Church, Fermoy* is on a prominent site in the town, which grew quickly from the 1790s with the establishment of major military barracks nearby. John Anderson, who developed the town and barracks, was also important in the building of Christ Church. Designed by Cork architect Abraham Hargrave the Elder, the church was consecrated in 1809. Its main entrance is very tall, so that colours carried on military parades could be brought in to the church without dipping. The original spire was removed after some years, but a new one was erected in 1858. In the late nineteenth century many improvements were made, including the addition of south and north transepts.

Christ Church, Fermoy

 *Christ Church, Ballyhooly* was built in 1881 on part of the Convamore estate of the earls of Listowel. It replaced an earlier (1774) church and was constructed using cut stone from Bridgetown Abbey in nearby Castletownroche. Christ Church was designed by William Henry Hill and is on a fine site overlooking the River Blackwater.

Christ Church, Ballyhooley

*St Luke's Church, Knockmourne* was built around 1814 and incorporates an earlier tower. A loan from the Board of First Fruits helped to fund the church, which is particularly well designed and well built. Alterations were made to the building in 1859.

 *St Mary's Church, Glenville* is in the parish of Ardnageehy. It was built around 1798, with the assistance of the Board of First Fruits. The church was later extended by the addition of a vestry and chancel.

 *St George's Church, Brigown* is in Mitchelstown. The church was constructed around 1803 and rebuilt in 1830 to a design by architect George Richard Pain. It was funded by the Board of First Fruits and the earl of Kingston. In 1883, a chancel was added to the building. The church, with its elegant spire, faces a tree-lined street that ends in King's Square and the chapel of Kingston College.

 *Kingston College Chapel, Mitchelstown.* Kingston College owes its origins to James, fourth Baron Kingston, who died in 1761. His will established the charity to provide accommodation for retired people. Until 1993, these were exclusively members of the Church of Ireland. Two ranges of houses were constructed, linked by the chapel, which forms the centrepiece of the northern half of King's Square. John Morrison was the architect at the college from 1771 until 1776, when he was replaced by Oliver Grace. The attractive, small chapel was extended in the late nineteenth century by the addition of a chancel.

St James's Church, Mallow

## MALLOW, DONERAILE and CASTLETOWNROCHE

St Mary's Church, Doneraile

Kingston College Chapel Mitchelstown

The construction of *St James's Church, Mallow* began in 1818, and the church was consecrated in 1824. It was built with the aid of a loan from the Board of First Fruits. Amongst later alterations was the enlargement of the chancel in 1903 to a design by William Henry Hill. The ruins of an older church, St Anne's, are nearby.

 *St Mary's Church, Doneraile*, located on the northern outskirts of the town, dates from 1633. The church was altered in 1726 and again in 1815–16, when a loan was procured from the Board of First Fruits. There were close links between the church and the St Leger family at nearby Doneraile Court. Interestingly, the church tower originally had a steeple. In 1752, the sport of steeplechasing had its origins in a horse race between the church in Buttevant and the steeple of St Mary's Church in Doneraile. St Mary's steeple blew down in the 1820s. Since 1890 the church has had a ring of six bells, cast by John Taylor & Co. of Loughborough in England.

 *St Mary's Church, Castletownroche*, situated on a hill overlooking the town, has a distinctive tower and spire. It was built in 1825, on the site of an older church, to the design of James and George Richard Pain.

St Mary's Church, Castletownroche

## COLLEGIATE CHURCH OF ST MARY, YOUGHAL

The present Collegiate Church of St Mary in Youghal dates to around 1220. It contains traces of an eleventh-century church that was badly damaged in 1192, possibly in storms. The church served the growing port town of Youghal and was under the patronage of the Fitzgeralds, later earls of Desmond. In the fourteenth century, it was one of the richest benefices in the diocese of Cloyne. At that time the church was altered by additions to the chancel and the raising of the roof over the aisles, allowing larger windows in the side walls. In 1464, the founding of Our Lady's College by Thomas Fitzgerald, earl of Desmond, led to St Mary's becoming a collegiate church and to the creation of the present chancel with its impressive east window.

The church was damaged during the Desmond Rebellion of 1579. In 1606, Sir Richard Boyle, first earl of Cork, purchased the south transept, repaired it and in 1620 built an elaborate monument depicting himself surrounded by members of his family. Oliver Cromwell spent part of the winter of 1649–50 at Youghal, staying in the college beside the church. One of his officers, Lieutenant-General Michael Jones, died in December 1649; Cromwell gave an address at his burial in the south transept of the Collegiate Church of St Mary.

In 1684, a ceremonial sword rest was placed in the church for the sword of the mayor of Youghal. The church was altered in the 1720s with the removal of the rood screen. There were further changes in the building in the late eighteenth and early nineteenth centuries. The arrival of Rev. Pierce Drew as rector in 1847 led to a period of major restoration. The chancel, unroofed for three centuries, was restored and the windows reglazed. An organ was purchased in 1861 and other improvements were made. By the end of the nineteenth century the church had a new lectern, choir stalls and choir flooring. The church contains significant monuments and tombs from different periods and still has its original oak roof timbers. Today the church remains a centre for worship in the Youghal Union of Parishes, with other churches at Ardmore and Castlemartyr.

The Boyle Monument
SCENIC IRELAND

St Mary's Collegiate Church, Youghal

St Paul's Church, Ardmore

### ABBEYSTREWRY (SKIBBEREEN), TULLAGH (BALTIMORE), CASTLEHAVEN (CASTLETOWNSHEND) and CAHERAGH

*Abbeystrewry Church* stands on a central site in Skibbereen town. In 1827, the first church was built on the present site, replacing an earlier structure beside the river. The 1827 building cost nearly £1,200 and was partly funded by a loan from the Board of First Fruits. A larger structure, designed by William Henry Hill, was completed in 1890. It incorporated part of the old church as transepts and retained the original tower, which has had a ring of six bells since 2002. The craftsmanship in the church is of a very high quality.

Abbeystrewey Church

### YOUGHAL, ARDMORE and CASTLEMARTYR

*St Paul's Church, Ardmore* was built in 1838 on a new site in the village and replaced a much older church near the round tower. The writer Molly Keane, who died in 1996, is buried in the graveyard surrounding the church.

*St Anne's Church, Castlemartyr* is an elegant building set just off the main street of the town. Built in 1731, it has round-headed windows and a tower. The interior has impressive timber panelling, plasterwork and a gallery.

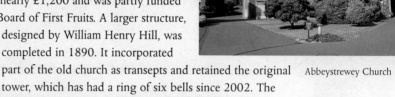

St Matthew's Church, Baltimore
RCB ARCHIVE

*St Matthew's Church, Baltimore* is in the parish of Tullagh. The site for the church was donated by Lord John Carbery and the building was consecrated in 1819. Built with the aid of a loan from the Board of First Fruits, the church has a prominent tower.

*St Barrahane's Church, Castletownshend* is in the parish of Castlehaven, where ruins of an early church can also be found. In 1761, a church was built on the present elevated site and it was replaced by a new building in 1826. Designed by James Pain, the attractive building has a square tower. It is reached by 52 steps, one for every Sunday in the year. The church has close associations with local families, including the Townshends, Somervilles and Coghills. There are three stained-glass windows by Harry Clarke. The renowned authors Edith Somerville and Violet Martin (Martin Ross) are interred in the churchyard.

*St Mary's Church, Caheragh* was built in 1829 with the help of a grant from the Board of First Fruits. It was improved in the late nineteenth century and has a fine organ made in 1870 by J. Seymour Murphy of Cork.

St Barrahane's Church, Castletownsend

St Mary's Church, Caheragh

RCB ARCHIVE

St Anne's Church, Castlemartyr

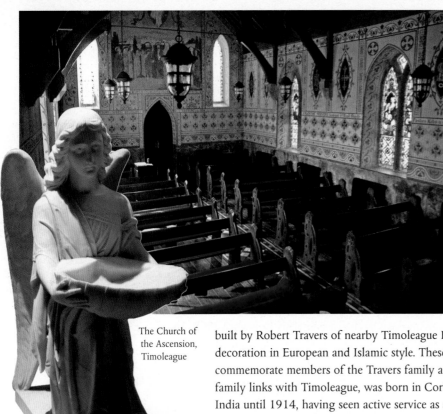

## KILGARIFFE, KILMALOODA, TIMOLEAGUE and COURTMACSHERRY

The ruins of the pre-Reformation *Kilgarriffe Church* are about three kilometres north-west of Clonakilty. The present church, erected in 1818, is the second on the elevated site in the town. It was built with the help of a loan from the Board of First Fruits.

*All Saints' Church, Kilmalooda*, a fine Gothic-revival building, was constructed near Ballinascarthy in 1857–8 to a design by the London architect James Piers St Aubyn. It was erected by William Bence-Jones of Lisselane as a memorial to his two young daughters, Alice and Laura, who both died in December 1851.

The *Church of the Ascension, Timoleague* was built on the site of an earlier church and consecrated in 1811. The Board of First Fruits provided a loan for the construction of the simple rectangular nave with a tower at the west end. In 1862–3, a new chancel and vestry were added, while further improvements were carried out in the 1880s. In 1890, a south transept was built by Robert Travers of nearby Timoleague House. A remarkable feature of this church is the elaborate interior mosaic decoration in European and Islamic style. These richly detailed mosaics were put in place between 1918 and 1925 to commemorate members of the Travers family and Surgeon-General Alymer Martin Crofts (1854–1915). Crofts, who had family links with Timoleague, was born in Cork and joined the Indian Medical Service as a surgeon in 1877. He remained in India until 1914, having seen active service as a military surgeon on the North-West Frontier. He was tutor, mentor and lifelong friend of the Maharaja Madho Rao Scindia of the princely state of Gwalior, south of Delhi. Crofts died in 1915 and, in his memory, the Maharaja financed the completion of the mosaics at Timoleague.

*St John the Evangelist's Church, Courtmacsherry* was originally built as a school under the auspices of the Leslie family in about 1830. In the late nineteenth century, it was converted into a church and is now mainly used during the summer months.

The Church of
the Ascension,
Timoleague

The Church of
the Ascension,
Timoleague

Leap Church

## ROSS, KILMACABEA (LEAP), MYROSS (UNION HALL), KILFAUGHNABEG (GLANDORE) and CASTLEVENTRY

The present *St Fachtna's Cathedral, Rosscarbery* was completed around 1612, replacing an earlier building.

*Leap Church*, in the parish of Kilmacabea, was built in 1827 and has a simple nave and square-plan tower. The Board of First Fruits provided funding for the church, which stands in the centre of the village.

*Myross Church* is located in the coastal village of Union Hall. The church dates to 1827 and was funded through a grant from the Board of First Fruits.

*Christ Church, Glandore* is in the parish of Kilfaughnabeg, in a striking location on a ledge overlooking the harbour. It was completed in 1861 to the design of Joseph Welland. The church, in early English style, has a distinctive bell tower. It provides services for both the local population and holidaymakers during the summer months.

*Holy Trinity Church, Castleventry* was built in 1824 with the aid of a grant from the Board of First Fruits. It was consecrated in 1861 and during the 1870s various improvements were carried out.

Christ Church, Glandore

Christ Church, Glandore

## ST FACHTNA'S CATHEDRAL, ROSS

A monastery was founded in Rosscarbery in the sixth century by St Fachtna. The first cathedral was built in the twelfth century, but the earliest description of a building on the site dates to 1517. The cathedral then was a cruciform, cut-stone structure, with a separate tower containing a bell.

During the episcopacy of Bishop William Lyons (1582–1617), a new cathedral was constructed. It was completed by about 1612, but badly damaged during the 1641 Rebellion. Following the violence of the mid-seventeenth century, the cathedral was gradually rebuilt. In 1696, a new steeple was erected, and further improvements were carried out in the eighteenth century. The steeple was taken down in 1785 and a new octagonal one built in 1806. This was damaged by storms in 1886 and 1923.

By the mid-nineteenth century the cathedral had two galleries, one of which was for Lord Carbery, whose seat was at nearby Castle Freke. Increasing parishioner numbers had led to an extension on the north side and the relocation of the organ. A dividing wall created a large narthex at the west end.

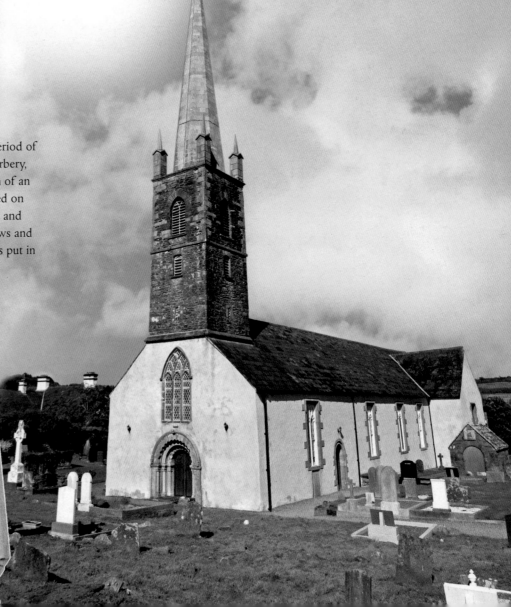

The arrival of Isaac Morgan Reeves as dean of Ross in 1876 led to a period of change and refurbishment at the cathedral. During his 29 years at Rosscarbery, Reeves's alterations included the removal of the galleries, the construction of an elaborate timber ceiling and the insertion of a new western doorway based on Cormac's Chapel at Cashel, County Tipperary. A new pulpit, lectern, font and bishop's throne were installed, as were chapter stalls, stained-glass windows and communion rails. Mosaics were laid in the sanctuary and a new organ was put in place. A peal of five bells was installed in 1897.

In 1927, the closure of Rathbarry Church led to the removal of the Carbery monument to St Fachtna's Cathedral, where it joined the existing large statue of John Evans Freke, sixth Baron Carbery (1765–1845).

A major restoration of the cathedral between 2002 and 2005 included the rebuilding of the organ. The bells were also restored and, in 2012, were augmented by an additional bell. St Fachtna's Cathedral is part of Ross Union of Parishes, with churches at Castleventry, Glandore, Leap and Union Hall. The cathedral is an important focus for parish and diocesan activity in the south-west of the dioceses.

# The United Dioceses of Limerick and Killaloe

The United Dioceses of Limerick and Killaloe include eight of the historic dioceses of the Church of Ireland. Stretching south from part of County Galway, to Valentia Island the dioceses include some of Ireland's most beautiful scenery and favourite tourist locations. There are sixteen parish groupings and over sixty churches that are used regularly for worship. We are largely a rural community and many of our members are involved in farming.

We are conscious of our heritage. St Mary's Cathedral, Limerick and St Flannan's Cathedral, Killaloe are at the heart of our diocesan community life. If walls could speak these cathedrals would tell a fascinating story of life down the years from the twelfth century. Kilfenora Cathedral is an ancient pilgrimage centre and is still used today. Clonfert Cathedral is the burial site of St Brendan the navigator, and is world famous for its elaborately carved door. These treasures belong to the our common history stretching back to Celtic Christian times and it is our intention to find ways of sharing these treasures with others as an inspiration for our contemporary Christian faith today.

Our dioceses also look to the future and has eleven Primary Schools under the bishop's patronage. These schools reflect the Church of Ireland ethos and we are delighted that this is appreciated not only by members of our Church but by families from other Christian denominations and faith communities.

The Church of Ireland family enjoys excellent relations with its neighbours who belong to other Christian denominations. Indeed without the support of the local community, many of our churches would not be open for worship today. We are increasingly aware of those of other faiths who have come to live among us so in recent years we have taken initiatives to be involved in inter-faith dialogue.

As a diocese we also have relationships beyond Ireland. We are conscious that we are members of the Anglican Communion worldwide and have a special relationship with the Anglican Church in Swaziland and the Diocese of Saldanha Bay, South Africa. Closer to home we have a companion relationship with the Evangelical Church of Anhalt in Eastern Germany. We are also committed to eradicating poverty throughout the world through our partnership with Christian Aid Ireland and the Bishops' Appeal for World Development.

As a community we have a lot to contribute at home and abroad. We wish to be known as a caring community, caring not just for members of our own denomination, but for all who are in need. A priority is to extend our excellent relationships with our Roman Catholic neighbours and find further opportunities to serve our local communities together.

In essence we are a community drawn together through the love of God in Christ Jesus. Our worship is one expression of our Love for God, but that would be incomplete if we didn't give equal priority to loving our neighbours as ourselves. We have been entrusted with the Good News of God's love for his world. We will find our meaning and purpose as a Church of Ireland community in finding ways in which God's love can be given practical expression though the life of our community.

The Cliffs of Moher
SCENIC IRELAND

TREVOR LIMERICK AND KILLALOE

# St Mary's Cathedral Limerick

PHOTOGRAPHS BY JOHN JONES

St Mary's Cathedral, Limerick has as many personalities in its spirit as it has pews within its walls. Dónal Mór O'Brien, king of Munster and prolific church-builder, constructed it in the twelfth century on the site of his royal residence. His kinsman, Murrough 'of the burnings' O'Brien, was buried in the O'Brien Chapel in 1674; his body was later removed and thrown into the Shannon, such was the local hatred for his policy of burning churches. Donal O'Brien, bishop of Limerick, erected the original high altar in the thirteenth century, while his kinsman Terence O'Brien, bishop of Emly, heard his own death sentence pronounced from the same altar.

South elevation of the cathedral. The stepped battlements of the corner turrets of the tower and th[e] aisles lend the building a defensi[ve] air which is immediately negated by the elaborate fenestration. (Michael O'Neill)

Peter Barley, organist at the cathedral

William Carey presided in the cathedral as first post-Reformation bishop in 1551. Cromwell's son-in-law, Henry Ireton, stabled his horse in the building. Patrick Sarsfield used the cathedral to give thanks for his victory at Ballyneety, while his opponent William of Orange gave a grant for repairs to damage done during the siege of Limerick. Florence Nightingale subscribed to the erection of the east window in 1860. In 1989, Jeremiah Newman, Roman Catholic bishop of Limerick, preached in the cathedral. The archbishop of Canterbury preached there in 1994.

Limerick Cathedral from the south. Blaymires view 1733. The exterior elevation has changed very little since the 1730s. (Michael O'Neill)

Just as various people have walked through its door, an imaginative mixture of styles has influenced the design and decoration of St Mary's. The original cruciform layout was simple. Now, the underlying plan is difficult to discern because the building received accretions in the medieval period: the transepts and north and south aisles were extended to contain a tower-house and various side chapels.

As the great Romanesque west door (possibly part of the founder's palace) opens, it casts light upon a treasure-trove of history. The stark nature of the interior is striking. Square twelfth-century nave piers rise to support massive cushion capitals, while round-headed clerestory windows break the considerable wall thickness. Wood, glass, stone, metal, art, music, light and darkness all unite to make St Mary's unique. The nave's barrel-vaulted ceiling is of local Cratloe oak. The consistory court was once a great medieval hall, while six of the original peal of bells were presented by the city's mayor in 1673. The credence table dates from the thirteenth century. Of the side chapels, each has its own distinguishing feature: among them are a pre-Reformation stone altar weighing over three tons, a lepers' squint, and cannonballs from the siege of Limerick. Unique in Ireland are the fifteenth-century chapter stalls with carved misericords.

In 2013, the building was undergoing extensive renovation work, but continues its role as a serene place of worship and a welcoming venue for visitors.

Hymn writer John Bell plays in St Mary's Cathedral.
TREVOR WILLIAMS

# The United Dioceses of Limerick and Killaloe

ADRIAN HEWSON

On the island's south-west Atlantic seaboard, the Church of Ireland's united dioceses of Limerick, Ardfert, Aghadoe, Killaloe, Kilfenora, Clonfert, Kilmacduagh and Emly stretch into eight counties and three provinces, and cover an area larger than Northern Ireland. Included within their boundaries are, in Munster, Counties Kerry, Clare and Limerick and portions of County Tipperary. The Leinster portion includes part of south-west Offaly and one church in County Laois while, in Connacht, east Galway and a stretch of County Roscommon bring the united dioceses to their northernmost extremities.

The Shannon, Ireland's longest river, has its estuary at Limerick and has shaped the economic life of the area for centuries. The diocesan landscape is contrasting and attractive. The fertile pastoral land of the Golden Vale in the east contrasts strikingly with the limestone expanse of the Burren, west of the Shannon. The lakes of Killarney, the Ring of Kerry, the Cliffs of Moher and Lough Derg have all made an impact on local tourism. Limerick city with its university is the principal settlement, followed by Tralee, Nenagh and Ennis. Other prominent towns include Ballinasloe, Birr, Killarney, Rathkeale and Roscrea.

The eight dioceses have been in their present amalgam since 1977. Limerick and Ardfert were united with Killaloe and Clonfert in 1976, while Emly was severed from Cashel and added the following year. Ardfert had been united to Limerick in 1661 while Killaloe and Clonfert had been united in 1836.

## St Patrick and his Predecessors

Some pockets of Christianity existed in the area before the arrival of St Patrick. These included an area close to Killorglin in Kerry and Seir Kieran, in the north of Killaloe Diocese, on the Ossory border. History tells us that Patrick's apostle St Dioma had already founded a church at Kildimo before Patrick reached the Limerick area. History also tells us that, while visiting the area, Patrick baptised its local king, banished a snake

Mountshannon Lake
JOHN JONES

Stained glass from St Patrick's
Church, Kenmare
JOHN JONES

to its eternal rest in Lough Gur, and, while walking in its hilly border country, imparted his blessing upon County Kerry. *En route* north from Cashel he passed through east Killaloe, and the areas around Lorrha, Nenagh and Roscrea all claim to have received his blessing.

## The Golden Age

Ireland's response to Patrick's teaching brought the island into its golden age of monasticism. One of its most celebrated centres of learning was at Clonard on the Boyne. While studying there, 12 men became so renowned for their piety and scholarship that they were called the 'Apostles of Erin'. Eight of these learned men made a major impact upon monasticism across the united dioceses. They included Brendan the Navigator of Ardfert and Clonfert, and Brendan of Birr. Others who founded monasteries at that time included Nessan of Mungret and Munchin (sometimes described as 'the patron of Limerick').

Because they were mainly constructed of wood, nothing of the early inland monasteries remains. In coastal regions, however, climatic conditions meant that monasteries were often built from stone. Skellig Michael's beehive huts off the Kerry coast are wonderful examples of the monastic buildings that still survive. The united dioceses boast rich evidence of the work of the monasteries – Lorrha's *Stowe Missal*, Roscrea's *Book of Dimma* and Birr's *Macregol Gospels* are amongst Ireland's earliest literary treasures, while the Ardagh Chalice is treasured as an example of early monastic handiwork.

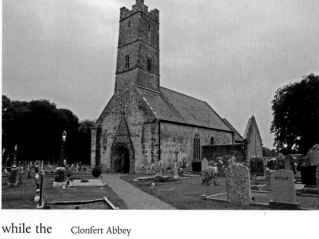

Clonfert Abbey
COLIN BOYLE

The menace of Viking raids restricted monastic growth in the ninth century and the region suffered greatly. Clonfert was burnt six times and the Munster monasteries were almost annihilated. However, despite the strife they engendered, many Vikings settled in the area and became part of the local church's life and history. Olaf Tryggvason, king of Norway, was baptised at Skellig Michael.

## Twelfth-Century Reform

Supremacy over the Vikings increased monastic prestige to the extent that it was in competition with the traditional diocesan structure. The Synod of Ráth Breasail, held in 1111 near Templemore, close to the Cashel–Killaloe diocesan border, regenerated the structure. Eight dioceses emerged in this territory: Limerick, Killaloe, Clonfert, Emly, Kilmacduagh, Ratass (Kerry), Roscrea and Scattery Island. Adjustments were made at the Synod of Kells in 1152, with Kilfenora being allowed diocesan status, while Ardfert replaced Ratass. Scattery and Roscrea were suppressed by the end of the century. Aghadoe was not named, and it is now believed that it never

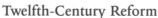

The cross with Kilfenora Cathedral
in the background

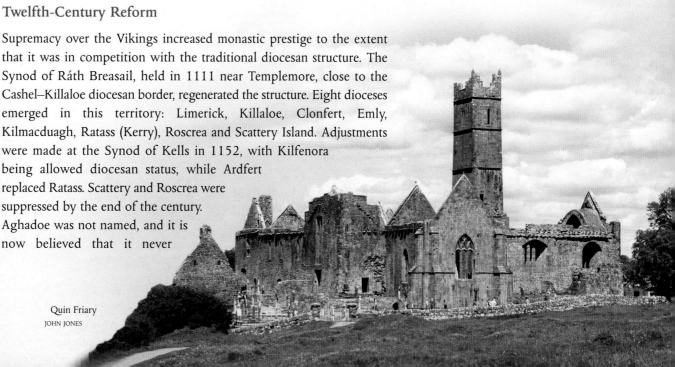

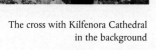

Quin Friary
JOHN JONES

Romanesque arch at Mona Incha
JOHN JONES

existed as a diocese, but was rather a deanery within Ardfert. Cathedrals were built; Kilfenora and Roscrea also created commemorative high crosses.

The Cistercian order arrived in Ireland in 1142. They founded monasteries in places such as Monasteranenagh, County Limerick, and Corcomroe, County Clare. The twelfth century also saw the arrival of the Augustinian canons to Clontuskert and Clare Abbey, while the following centuries saw them establish houses at Adare, Rathkeale and elsewhere.

The Norman conquest continued reform, which included the introduction of the 'tithe'. The Norman/European influence brought more religious orders to local areas. Franciscan foundations included houses at Adare and Kilconnell, while the Dominicans came to Kilmallock and Portumna.

Cross at Mona Incha
JOHN JONES

## Post-Reformation Times

The 150 years following the Reformation were to witness turmoil on the island. The plantations found their response in the 1641 Rebellion, which was answered in turn by Cromwellian invasion. The restoration of the monarchy in 1660 was followed by the Williamite-Jacobite Wars, culminating in the penal laws. Each event influenced diocesan life. Askeaton, Killarney, Shanid and Glin developed as plantation towns, but churches in Limerick and Emly suffered during the 1641 Rebellion. 'Old St Patrick's' in Limerick and Ardfert Cathedral were totally destroyed. St Mary's Cathedral in Limerick suffered at Cromwellian hands, but the restoration of the monarchy brought better times. Vacant sees were filled, with diocesan clerics benefitting. New bishops were appointed to Limerick and Killaloe. However, following the Jacobite defeat at the Boyne, the fighting spread to Aughrim. During the final onslaught at Limerick the cathedral suffered again.

George Webb, Bishop of Limerick, 1634–42
BELFAST CATHEDRAL

Edward Parry, bishop of Killaloe, 1646–50
BELFAST CATHEDRAL

### BISHOP JOHN JEBB

John Jebb, bishop of Limerick, 1823–33, was a Fellow of the Royal Society and a leader in the pre-Tractarian Anglican Church. He was also a noted public speaker, preacher and author. Close friends included William Wilberforce and Robert Southey. His prolific published works were influential, not least with the new Episcopal Church of the USA.

A statue to Jebb stands in St Mary's Cathedral, Limerick

From the mid-sixteenth century, groups of French Calvinists called Huguenots, who had been evicted from their homeland, were settling in Ireland. Some identified with the Established Church. Huguenot military prowess also helped to determine the outcome at Aughrim and Limerick.

Clare Abbey
JOHN JONES

## The Eighteenth Century

The short reign of Queen Anne brought two developments that had lasting influence on diocesan life and landscape. Thanks to the Board of First Fruits, rectangular churches with square pinnacle towers began to be erected in abundance, Ahascragh and Rathkeale being random examples. A social initiative of the reign saw the arrival of Lutheran exiled Palatines from the German Rhineland into Limerick Diocese, mainly Rathkeale and Kilfinane. The newcomers settled into the agricultural and parochial communities.

Resentment at the Norman-introduced tithe disturbed the peace at the end of the seventeenth century and into the eighteenth. This escalated in the 1820s under the Rockite movement, who added agrarian problems to their tithe grievance. Athlacca and Killeedy churches fell victim to their armed attacks and were destroyed in 1822.

The Hon. Ludlow Tonson, bishop of Killaloe, 1839–62
In 1848 on the death of his elder brother he became Baron Riversdale
BELFAST CATHEDRAL

Charles M. Warburton,
bishop of Limerick 1806
BELFAST CATHEDRAL

## The Nineteenth Century

The nineteenth century saw an island with two attitudes – those who supported Westminster rule and those who sought independence. Both groups contained many members of the Established Church, and both attitudes are well reflected in the nineteenth-century life of the united dioceses.

The church population had amongst its benefactors earls and lords, knights, judges, administrators and politicians. Their financial contributions often kept rural churches solvent, while the staff of the 'big house' helped to keep pews filled. Memorial tablets around the dioceses testify to this, as do memorials to the fallen in remote, colonial wars. High-ranking colonial officials also hailed from the united dioceses.

Many people from the united dioceses involved themselves in nineteenth-century independence movements. William J. MacNevin, a distinguished member of the United Irishmen, came from Aughrim. Roscrea parishioner Henry Howley was injured in one of the smaller risings of 1798 but survived to make weapons for the Emmet Rising of 1803 – for which he was executed. The rector of Ettagh in Offaly in 1873 was nephew to Young Ireland party leader Thomas Davis.

### The Great Hunger

Blighted potato stalks, mass graves and coffin ships symbolically recall the atrocity of the Famine. Some people of means helped; others did not, and those who did not later suffered the consequences of their lack of charity. Within the united dioceses two prominent relief workers, both medical doctors, are still affectionately remembered for their efforts. Kenmare remembers George Mahony Mayberry, JP, MD, for his attention to the sick and dying of the surrounding districts. Thomas Harrison, known as the 'Ballinasloe Famine Doctor', cared for the sick and dying in his local area.

### Disestablishment

As parishes in rural areas like Clare and Kerry came to terms with numerical losses due to famine deaths and emigration, the Church of Ireland as a whole was having to become self-reliant with disestablishment in 1869–70. Generally, disestablishment was greeted with resigned acceptance. In an 1873 pamphlet, the rector of Ennis and noted historian Canon Philip Dwyer lamented that in future years the peoples of Kilmanaheen and Kilfieragh amongst others would be unable to provide a living for a resident rector.

THE GREAT FAMINE
1845 — 1849
AT LEAST A MILLION PEOPLE
DIED OF STARVATION IN IRELAND
DURING THE FAMINE YEARS
OVER A MILLION MORE EMIGRATED
MOSTLY TO THE UNITED STATES
THE POPULATION OF THE COUNTRY
WAS GREATLY REDUCED
THE CENCUS OF 1911
SHOWED A POPULATION OF LESS THAN
5 MILLION COMPARED WITH
8 MILLION BEFORE THE FAMINE
REMEMBER OUR FORGOTTEN
PREDECESSORS

A Famine memorial in the graveyard at St Mary's Church, Askeaton
JOHN JONES

## William Smith O'Brien

William Smith O'Brien was a member of the Church of Ireland and also one of the great Gaelic families of Munster. The O'Briens, who became the hereditary Barons of Inchiquin, accepted the changes of the Reformation and supported the crown. By the nineteenth century they still retained their large estates in Co. Clare.

O'Brien was born in 1803. He became a Conservative Member of Parliament in the 1830s but in the 1840s, partly as a result of the Famine, he became an advanced Nationalist. He supported the Young Ireland movement and was involved in the 1849 Rising against the government. He was found guilty of treason and exiled to Van Diemen's Land (Tasmania). In 1856, he was pardoned and returned to Ireland. A statue to his honour erected in 1870 stands in O'Connell Street, Dublin.

## Lady Gregory

384

Lady Augusta Gregory (1852–1932), was born a member of the prominent landowning family of Persse in Co. Galway and married Sir William Gregory, a member of another such family at Coole Park, Gort, Co. Galway. She collected local folklore from which she published a number of books. She wrote plays and edited works of translation from the Irish. She became a key figure in the Irish Literary Renaissance of the early twentieth century. Many involved in this movement, such as W.B. Yeats, J.M. Synge and Sean O'Casey, stayed at Coole Park. She was a co-founder of the Abbey Theatre. George Bernard Shaw described her as 'the greatest living Irishwoman'. Her Gort estate was sold to the ministry of lands in 1927 and the house was later demolished.

The installation of Very Rev. Sandra Pragnell, first female Dean of St Mary's, Limerick, in its 800-year history, 24 October 2012
HERBERT KNOWLES

Overall, however, the Irish Church Act provided a new independent lease of life and people rose to the challenge.

### Twentieth century

Different people have differing views on the position of a peripheral Church of Ireland diocese in the twentieth century. Some see it as a time of diminishment, but others see it as a time when one door closes and another opens. While the early twentieth century saw decline, the years approaching the new millennium offered opportunities to experience church life at international level and to allow other groups of people to share in ministry.

The tranquil opening years of the century were soon overshadowed by the 1914 call to war. Diocesan men and women engaged in conflict from the south Pacific to the North Sea and from Gallipoli to the Somme. By 1918 memorials had appeared in almost every diocesan church to the fallen. Every parish had its roll of honour. World War II, despite national neutrality, also claimed diocesan casualties, and Ballyseedy, Ballingarry and Rathkeale are among the churches with individual memorials.

As Europe smouldered, Ireland experienced its internal quest for independence, followed by civil war. The Church of Ireland had people on both sides of the conflict. Despite encouragement, few people from the united dioceses have involved themselves in national public life. A notable exception, however, was the McGillycuddy of the Reeks, a senator of the Irish Free State from 1928 until 1943.

Sadly, church buildings were not always safe during troubled times in the emerging state. Ahascragh was maliciously destroyed by fire in July 1922 and, after almost 13 years to the day, Kilmallock suffered the same fate. Some three decades later Clonfert Cathedral was internally vandalised.

The 1910 *Church of Ireland Directory* lists 141 stipendiary clergy serving in the area that covers the present united dioceses, with 181 churches in use. The 2010 *Directory* lists 18 stipendiary clergy covering the 64 churches in use. There are many reasons for the century's decline – World War I casualties, often the loss of sons and heirs; changes in political administration caused by emigration of estates landlords and staff; the closure of military barracks; the *Ne Temere* decree of 1907; dire economic circumstances and the decline in rural agriculture, often leading to the loss of entire families to the New World; the lure of city lights for employment and better educational prospects; the materialistic age; and later marriage ages in rural areas. The later twentieth century saw a decline in clerical manpower and rural peripheral dioceses were the first to be affected.

The Church's immediate response was church closure and amalgamation of parishes, eventually leading to the amalgamation of dioceses in 1976–7. In September 1976, E.W. Owen became the first bishop of Limerick and Killaloe. Closure, demolition of churches of non-architectural value and sale of rectories escalated in the 1970s.

The consecration of Bishop Trevor Williams, 2008

Solutions came in the subsequent years. The offices of parish and diocesan readers were utilised. June 1991 was an historic time for the dioceses, seeing candidates ordained to the diaconate of the auxiliary ministry in St Mary's Cathedral and the first ordination of a woman in the united dioceses. Diocesan synods merged in 1990. A new church was built in Killorglin and other churches were renovated, often aided by FÁS schemes. On 11 July 2008, Trevor R. Williams was consecrated in Christ Church Cathedral as fifth bishop of the by then 32-year-old united dioceses.

### Ecumenism and International Relations

Often, in sensitive areas like inter-church relations, only the sensational and negative are highlighted, but in rural dioceses farmers work together, oblivious to denominational barriers, and in urban areas Methodist and Presbyterian children sit in the classroom with their Church of Ireland peers. Thus, just the liturgical aspect of the late twentieth century's ecumenism was new. Difficulties have increasingly been dealt with in a spirit of patience and charity, as called for by H.R. McAdoo, bishop of Ossory, in his capacity as co-chairman of the Anglican-Roman Catholic International Commission in 1965.

Gurteen Agricultural College, a Methodist foundation, was opened in Lockeen Parish in Offaly in 1947. Now a multi-denominational college, it welcomed Church of Ireland students from the beginning. Relationships between the Church of Ireland, Methodists and Presbyterians were further consolidated when Christ Church, Shannon was opened in 1961. Christ Church operated under an arrangement where the three churches shared the venue for worship and was the only church of its kind in Ireland at that time. The diocese has within its bounds Glenstal Abbey and its Benedictine community, with its annual ecumenical conference. The Oak House Ecumenical Retreat Centre was established near Loughrea in 1994.

With encouragement from the Second Vatican Council, ecumenical relationships graduated to episcopal level, with both the Roman Catholic and Church of Ireland bishops of Killaloe attending the Ennis carol services in 1969. In 1989–90, the bishops of Limerick exchanged pulpits. In 1998, the bishops of Killaloe jointly produced a pamphlet on guidelines for inter-church marriages within the diocese. In 2008,

50th Ecumenical Conference at Glenstal Abbey, 2013

Signing of the Companion Relationship between the Dioceses of Limerick and Killaloe and the Evangelische Landeskirche Anhalts, the Protestant Church of Anhalt, Eastern Germany, Bishop Trevor and Rev. Jürgen Dittrich

Dom Mark-Ephrem Nolan was preacher at the consecration of Trevor R. Williams as bishop of Limerick and Killaloe.

Ecumenism has also developed strongly at parochial level. Local school boards have Church of Ireland representation, and in Kyle, County Laois, the *gaelscoil* is the only one in Ireland with both bishops (Killaloe) as joint patrons. Patronal walks and Good Friday pageants in the dioceses are ecumenical. Fund-raising efforts (especially for church renovation) are given whole hearted community support, from Valentia Island to Portumna, and all blessings of industrial or community enterprises are ecumenical.

While clergy and people played strong roles at local level, two diocesan clergy had pivotal roles in ecumenism in its early years. In 1973, Ralph Baxter, rector of Shannon, was appointed secretary to the World Council of Churches, while pride of place must go to Charles M. Gray-Stack, dean of Ardfert, a born ecumenist, who was a representative at the Second Vatican Council.

In the closing years of the twentieth century, some diocesan personnel were granted an opportunity to experience the Church at work overseas. In the early 1980s, clergy visited Kenya and there have been return visits by Kenyan bishops, including Manasses Kuria, primate of Kenya. In 1988, links with the American Episcopal Church were strengthened when the diocese began a companion relationship with the diocese of Southwest Florida. The second companion relationship was a three-way exchange with Quebec and New Hampshire. The most recent international link is also three-way, with the South African diocese of Saldanha Bay and German Lutheran Church in Harzegerode, diocese of Anhalt.

## New Millennium

The year 2011 marked the 900th anniversary of Ráth Breasail and the formation of the dioceses – places chosen for their Christian qualities, monastic heritage and tradition of service to others and spreading the Gospel message. Those same qualities apply today to the united dioceses of Limerick, Ardfert, Aghadoe, Killaloe, Clonfert, Kilfenora, Kilmacduagh and Emly.

Boat building at The Men's Shed, Kenmare, a new social outlet for men in the area

Diocesan Gathering to Go Event, worship, workshops and fellowship in Villiers School, Limerick, 29 September 2013. The final hymn was a real celebration.

# THE DIOCESE OF LIMERICK

## ADARE, KILMALLOCK, KILPEACON, CROOM

This west-Limerick grouping forms part of the fertile Golden Vale. It centres on the tourist village of Adare, and is an area of immense interest to the scholar of medieval monasticism. Trinitarians, Franciscans, Augustinians, Dominicans and Knights Hospitallers have all had an influence on this parochial plain, which also provided a home for German Palatine settlers. For centuries Adare Manor was residence to the earls of Dunraven. The area was also home to the Maigue poets.

The group is an imaginative collaboration of parishes, each retaining its own character. The small villages reveal the great social diversity that is becoming a hallmark of the area. Congregations are small, reflecting the local Church of Ireland population, but the churches provide points of focus for the community. On Sundays there is one service in each church. There is Sunday school in Adare, Kilpeacon and Kilmallock during term time and there is an active ministry to the national school in Adare. An ambitious building project delivered a modern new school, with the official opening in December 2008.

St Peter's and St Paul's Church, Kilmallock

*St Nicholas' Church, Adare* has its origins in the fourteenth-century Augustinian 'Black Abbey'. At dissolution, the abbey was ruined and Church of Ireland worship was held in the earl of Desmond's chapel of ease, but with the arrival of the Palatines a larger building was needed and, in 1808, it was resolved to restore the abbey. Caroline, dowager countess of Dunraven, was the main benefactor. The *Pietà* is considered to be sixteenth-century Flemish, while a simple wooden cross stands as a World War I memorial to Maurice Fitzgerald, who died in Belgium. Stone sedilia and a piscina add to the medieval atmosphere. Retaining the original monastery layout, the parochial complex includes the refectory and the cloisters, with the Dunraven family mausoleum located alongside.

St Beacon's Church, Kilpeacon

*St Peter and St Paul's Church, Kilmallock* was built in 1938, replacing an earlier church maliciously burnt down in 1935. The new church was designed by Frederick G. Hicks, using his characteristic red brick. It has among its stained glass the east window of Bruree Church, which was transferred there at the wish of President Éamon de Valera.

*St Beacon's Church, Kilpeacon.* Kilpeacon derives its name from St Beacon (d. 689), who established a church here. It began its ecclesiastical life in 1690 as a chapel of ease (built by Sir William King) and graduated to church status. Destroyed by the Whiteboys in 1762, the church was immediately rebuilt, with the chancel added in 1867. It was renovated again in 1890. The east window is a memorial to local historian John Westropp, while an ornate marble memorial remembers the founder of the church. Further memorials recognise the Furnells, a noted County Limerick banking family.

*Croom Church* stands on the western bank of the River Maigue and is a small neat edifice with a square tower. It is surrounded by a large graveyard. Amongst the headstones is one remembering Seán Ó Tuama, an eighteenth-century Maigue poet.

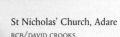

St Nicholas' Church, Adare
RCB/DAVID CROOKS

## LIMERICK, CITY PARISH: ST MARY'S CATHEDRAL, ST MICHAEL'S, ABINGTON

Limerick's Viking and Christian heritage have contributed to its development as Ireland's fourth city. This once-compact urban church grouping has in recent times extended eastwards to include Emly Diocese.

Knowledge of one fact about Abington is necessary: in a corner of the parish the game of rugby was introduced to Ireland by Sir Charles Barrington, a parishioner. It is said there are three cathedrals in Limerick – St Mary's, St John's and Thomond Park (home of Munster rugby). St Mary's Cathedral constantly distinguishes itself in the area of music, as an acoustically superior venue. St Michael's Church Hall is always a hive of activity. Students from St Michael's National School visit the church every week for assembly. Each church community within Limerick City Parish reflects a different style of being, but all are welcoming and outwardly focused.

Stained glass in
St Michael's Church,
Pery Square, Limerick
JOHN JONES

*St Michael's Church, Pery Square* was consecrated in 1844 and built on land given by the earl of Limerick. Spacious and designed in the Tudor Gothic style, St Michael's originally had three galleries. By the close of the nineteenth century the galleries had been removed and a chancel and east window added, while in 1909 the Norwegian-pine vaulted roof was erected. In 1994, the building was reroofed in time for the 150th anniversary celebrations, at which the primate of all Ireland was preacher. Amongst the features of interest is the east window, an eighteenth-century copy of the tracery in St Mary's Church, Oxford. Many memorials recognise clergy and parishioners, with military tablets ranging from India in 1869 to Crete in 1941.

St Michael's Church, Pery Square, Limerick
JOHN JONES

*Abington* is the only Emly diocesan church now in use. The history of this church, once described as a 'mini-cathedral', is also a history of local ecumenism. In 1821, its rector, Dr Jebb, together with the Roman Catholic parish priest, condemned agrarian violence. In 1841, Caleb Powell, MP and Abington parishioner, championed Daniel O'Connell. In the early 1960s, the annual ecumenical conference began at Glenstal Abbey. The present church was built in 1870. It is built in the English Gothic style, with red-brick exterior and an ornately painted interior. Today the church enjoys close links with the Benedictine community of nearby Glenstal.

JOHN JONES

Abington

Abington

## RATHKEALE, ASKEATON, KILCORNAN, KILNAUGHTIN

Flanked by the southern shore of the Shannon estuary, this extensive grouping stretches south to the Mullaghareirk Mountains and winds its way westwards from Pallaskenry through Foynes and Glin to the mouth of the River Shannon and the Kerry coast.

Today the parochial group is a small and scattered community, supported by a part-time priest-in-charge. There is one Church of Ireland-managed national school at Rathkeale, which is attended by children from throughout the area. Church of Ireland parishioners are active members of community choirs, local farming organisations and retirement associations. This has led to considerable support for the parishes from the wider community.

*Holy Trinity Church, Rathkeale*, a garrison church, was built in 1825 of local stone. It replaced an older building, which may have been the place of worship of Sir Walter Raleigh. Of particular interest are two stained-glass windows by artist Catherine O'Brien and a memorial to Colonel Julius Correeguer Del Mege KLG, who died in Tehran in 1877, and his nephew Midshipman Claude, who was killed in action in the North Sea in 1914, aged just 16.

Holy Trinity Church, Rathkeale
RCB/DAVID CROOKS

St Mary's Church, Askeaton
JOHN JONES

*St Mary's Church, Askeaton*, built in 1827, rectangular in shape and of simple design, is surrounded by an ancient graveyard containing the grave of poet Aubrey de Vere. Internally, members of the Hewson family of Castle Hewson are remembered. Nineteenth-century tablets also remember the Langford family of Kilcosgriff Castle.

*Kilcornan Church*, while not having a formal dedication, makes amends for this by having four different names: Kilcornan, Pallaskenry, Castletown and Castletown Waller. Built in 1831, it is rectangular in shape, with crenellated tower and two vestries. Memorial tablets to the Waller family adorn the church.

*St Brendan's Church, Tarbert*, parochially named Kilnaughtin, is located in Ardfert Diocese. Cruciform in layout, with a tower, the church was erected in 1814, renovated in 1988 and rededicated in the name of St Brendan. The church has pews procured from the building it replaced; the east window, lectern and bronze cross all originated in Listowel Church (now closed).

## THE DIOCESES OF ARDFERT AND AGHADOE

### KENMARE, SNEEM, WATERVILLE, VALENTIA ISLAND

This peninsular church grouping winds its way along the Ring of Kerry and incorporates Valentia, the only island church now in use in the united dioceses. South of Valentia are the remote, monastic Skelligs.

This parochial group seeks to provide a service pattern that offers a varied range of worship styles and is closely linked with local community activity, such as the Kenmare Orchestra.

The Church of the Transfiguration, Sneem
DIOCESE OF LIMERICK

There are also a number of concerts through the year, with visiting choirs and music groups from Germany, Switzerland and America.

*St Patrick's, Kenmare*, consecrated in 1858, has a series of lofty arches separating the north aisle from the nave. A communion table and prayer desk from the now-closed Kilgarvan Church are in use there. A wall tablet remembers the service of the local famine doctor. A former curate, Rev. William Spotswood Green, was also a mountaineer, his achievements including the first successful ascent of New Zealand's Mount Cook.

St Patrick's, Kenmare
JOHN JONES

*The Church of the Transfiguration, Sneem* acquired its name when, upon completion of a 1960s renovation, the rector remarked, 'It's totally transfigured!' Erected *c.* 1810, it has an imaginative style. Within the church is an icon of the Transfiguration presented to former rector Dean Charles Gray-Stack by the nuns of the Lebanese Eastern Church in 1972. Interred in the churchyard is Gobnait Ní Bhruadair, alias the Hon. Albinia Brodrick, aristocrat turned republican, who was also the church organist.

*St Michael and All Angels' Church, Waterville*, parochially known as Dromod, was consecrated in 1866, and supports a pointed belfry and weather vane. In 1966 Bishop Wyse-Jackson presented a baptistry cross to the church, its wood coming from a tree from Napoleon's garden in St Helena.

*St John the Baptist Church, Valentia*, located at Knightstown, was built in 1815 and rebuilt in 1860. Over the years island weather and migration factors have taken their toll, and today there is just one parishioner. However, the maintenance of the church is greatly supported by the local community. The sanctuary panelling and mosaic flooring are laid in gratitude for the 1918 Allied victory.

Musicians playing at a Christmas Carol Service
at St John the Baptist Church, Valentia

Incorporating part of the Ring of Kerry and positioned between Dingle Bay and the McGillycuddy Reeks, this grouping is globally renowned as a tourist centre.

Kilcolman union has a vibrant Sunday school and St Michael's has a professional organist. It hosts a number of projects and groups, a prayer garden amongst them, and enjoys good relations with other groups and churches in the area. There is a parish national school with an enrolment in the mid-thirties. Parish and school have a very good relationship, with the school providing the backbone for monthly holy-day services in St Carthage's. The school is involved in many extra-curricular activities and has won two Green Flags.

St Michael's, Killorglin
JOHN JONES

*St Michael's, Killorglin* is a church with a history in the future. It was opened in 1996, replacing St James's Church, which had fallen into poor condition. The church was consecrated on 20 September 1997 in the presence of the primate of all Ireland. Designed unusually in 'Celtic cruciform' style by Peter O'Farrelly and built of good-quality ragstone, the octagonal worship area has a high conical roof and is screened off from the rectangular area of the building, which is a community centre. Internally, the stained-glass windows, procured from the now-closed Knockane Church, honour the McGillycuddy family, after whom the Reeks are named.

St Michael's, Killorglin
JOHN JONES

*St Carthage's, Kiltallagh*, Castlemaine has its origins in the monastery of St Carthage. Some 14 centuries later, to commemorate Carthage's feast day, the dean of Lismore Cathedral (where the saint is buried) presented Kiltallagh Church with a stone from the cathedral. The stone is now within the wall of the church porch. Rebuilt in 1816, simplicity is the hallmark of this church. Buried in the churchyard is the mother of the Hon. Raymond West, judge of the high court of Bombay.

St Carthage's, Kiltallagh

## KILLARNEY and MUCKROSS

Famed for its scenery, this Kerry parish of jaunting cars is legendary. Although regular parishioners are few, the church in Killarney has a worldwide ministry, while the chapel of ease at Muckross doubles as a youth venture centre.

St Mary's has an eclectic but faithful congregation whose main mission focus is the tourist. A series of concerts is provided during the summer, plus guided tours of the building.

*St Mary's, Killarney* sees the church's ministry to tourists at its best. The church offers a Kerry *fáilte* to worshipping tourists and acts as a venue for international choral recitals. In the early nineteenth-century a disgruntled parishioner described the church as 'half ruined [with] few worshippers who sat under a dreary, inoffensive vicar'. In fact, it was not half-ruined but half-built – a project which had begun in 1797 but wasn't completed until 1812. Today the cruciform church, rebuilt again in 1871, is enhanced by an elaborately painted clock tower. The many stained-glass windows reveal the influence of the pre-Raphaelite school of art, and the great west-wall window was given by Jane, countess of Bantry, and commemorates her brother Rt Hon. Henry Arthur Herbert, MP and chief secretary for Ireland 1857–8.

St Mary's, Killarney
JOHN JONES

Close to Killarney is *Muckross House*, once home to the Herbert family. The house, situated in 26,000 acres at Killarney National Park, is now owned by the state. Dedicated to the Holy Trinity, the nineteenth-century chapel of ease there was erected by the Herbert family. Its unusual tin reredos serves as a memorial to the founder.

Also within parochial boundaries is the elevated cathedral site of the diocese of Aghadoe.

St Mary's, Killarney
JOHN JONES

St John's Church,
Tralee
JOHN JONES

This Kerry church grouping extends
westwards from Tralee across the Conor
Pass and along the Dingle Peninsula to
Ireland's most westerly point, Slea Head.
Within parochial boundaries is the ruined
medieval cathedral site of Ardfert.

The parish covers a wide range of
settings, ranging from the urban environment
of Tralee town to the rural communities of
Ballymacelligott and Kilgobbin (Camp). Each of the
churches represents different strands within the Church of Ireland
tradition. In Dingle, there is much involvement in culture and the arts.
Dingle Church is regularly used for art exhibitions and concerts of traditional
and folk music (including the television series Other Voices).
The Dingle Peninsula is particularly rich in early Christian Celtic spirituality, with such iconic
sites as Mount Brandon and Gallarus Oratory with its monastic beehive huts.
A lot of what happens in this group of parishes is underpinned by a sense of ecumenism. Much of
the church's involvement in the community is in conjunction with the area's Roman Catholic parishes.

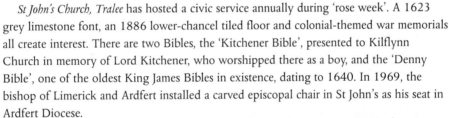

St John's Church, Tralee

JOHN JONES

*St John's Church, Tralee* has hosted a civic service annually during 'rose week'. A 1623
grey limestone font, an 1886 lower-chancel tiled floor and colonial-themed war memorials
all create interest. There are two Bibles, the 'Kitchener Bible', presented to Kilflynn
Church in memory of Lord Kitchener, who worshipped there as a boy, and the 'Denny
Bible', one of the oldest King James Bibles in existence, dating to 1640. In 1969, the
bishop of Limerick and Ardfert installed a carved episcopal chair in St John's as his seat in
Ardfert Diocese.

*Ballyseedy Church* was built of local sandstone *c.* 1845, and almost all the stained-glass
windows are memorials to the Blennerhassett family of the adjacent Ballyseedy Castle.
Three exquisite brass chandeliers hang from the ceiling.

Ballyseedy Church

RCB/DAVID CROOKS

*Ballymacelligott Church* was built in 1824
on the site of the former parish church. The
church is of the nave-and-chancel style.
The oldest memorial remembers Richard
Chute, killed in action in Afghanistan in
1880, while the communion table is a
World War I memorial.

Killiney Church

St James's Church, Dingle

Kilgobbin Church

Kilgobbin Church

DAVID CROOKS

*St James's Church, Dingle* is an 1808
restoration of a medieval church built
by Spaniards, who had a major influence on the town. In 1837, the building was
enlarged. Further restoration took place in the 1970s.

*Killiney Church*, shaded by mountains and overlooking the sea, is located near
Castlegregory. Built in 1810, it is dedicated to St Brendan. Two eighth- or ninth-
century stone crosses in the churchyard suggest the presence of Christianity in the
area since earlier times.

*Kilgobbin Church* near Camp village was erected in 1820 on the site of the
original church of St Gobban. It is built of pink sandstone and has a crenellated
tower. Its stained-glass east window, dedicated in 1980, was procured from
Kilshannig Church in Cork and is the work of a French artist.

## THE DIOCESE OF KILLALOE

St Brendan's Church, Birr
JOHN JOHNSTON

### BIRR, LORRHA, DORRHA, LOCKEEN

This compact grouping stretches westwards from the Slieve Bloom foothills to the shores of Lough Derg. Birr, Lorrha and Dorrha are all monastic in origin, but Birr's development has also been influenced by Birr Castle, home to the earls of Rosse. Located within Lockeen Parish is Gurteen Agricultural College, while St Brendan's Church, Birr hosted the annual Adelaide Hospital service until 1997.

In recent years, the Birr Group of Parishes have focused on playing their role as members of the wider Christian community. Ecumenical relations are excellent, with much parish involvement in joint services with Roman Catholics and Methodists. The Birr Choral Society leads the music at these and many other gatherings. St Brendan's Market, held every Friday, brings together people from across the community, selling produce and making donations from their profits to the parish and local charities.

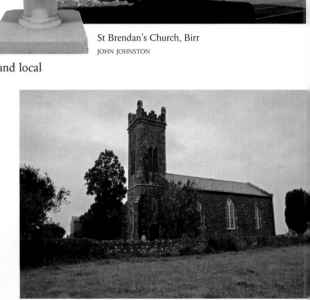

St Brendan's Church, Birr
JOHN JOHNSTON

Another major focus is the connection with Oxmantown School, which celebrated its 150th anniversary in 2010. Children in the school are drawn from a number of local parishes and denominations, but play their part in special services, including the traditional pageant on Christmas Eve in Lockeen Church.

*St Brendan's Church, Birr* was consecrated in 1816 on a site donated by the second earl of Rosse (who had donated a similar site for Birr's Roman Catholic church more than a decade before Catholic emancipation). The church was consecrated in 1816, but the location formerly housed the sixth-century monastery of Brendan the Elder, where the ninth-century *Macregol Gospels* were produced, and a medieval parish church. Architecturally, the influence of Birr Castle is notable. St Brendan's communion silver includes one of the Church of Ireland's oldest pieces of silver. On new year's day 1961, HRH Princess Margaret and the earl of Snowdon attended morning prayer while guests at Birr Castle.

Dorrha Church
COLIN BOYLE

*St Ruadhan's Church, Lorrha* has its roots in Ruadhan's Celtic monastery, dating to AD 550. A pre-sixth-century vellum manuscript known as the *Stowe Missal* was one of the monastery's treasured possessions. The present nineteenth-century building is incorporated into the remains of a twelfth-century stone church. Of interest within is a stained-glass window painted in 1918 by Michael Healy.

*Dorrha Church* near Rathcabbin village was built in 1832, replacing a twelfth-century church, the altar stone from which was gifted to the new Roman Catholic church at Rathcabbin.

*Lockeen Church*, built in 1822 and restored in 1910, includes amongst its communion silver a chalice dated 1636. The church has had associations with Gurteen Agricultural College since it opened in 1947.

Birr Castle
JOHN JOHNSTON

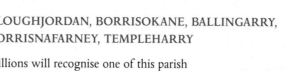

## CLOUGHJORDAN, BORRISOKANE, BALLINGARRY, BORRISNAFARNEY, TEMPLEHARRY



Millions will recognise one of this parish grouping's small villages. On the afternoon of 23 May 2011, the US president walked down its Main Street towards his ancestral home. This church group slopes westward from the Offaly village to the north-Tipperary shore of Lough Derg.

St Kieran's Church, Cloughjordan
JOHN JONES

The Cloughjordan and Borrisokane Group of Parishes is largely a rural farming community. Ecumenical relations are excellent and are tangibly expressed in shared activities throughout the year. It is a young parish with a thriving five-teacher school based in Cloughjordan and active Sunday schools in Borrisokane and Cloughjordan. Ireland's first eco-village development in Cloughjordan has brought increased diversity and with that new vitality to the area. The rector is well supported by a team of parish readers.

*St Kieran's Church, Cloughjordan,* a building in the later English style, was consecrated in 1837. Its central location on the village green meant that it replaced rural Modreeny as the 'mother church' of the parish. Major renovations were carried out in 1969 and again in 1992, when the east window from Modreeny, a World War I memorial, was incorporated into the north wall. The carved lectern and cross are the work of local liturgical artist Fergus Costello, who used local bog oak in their construction.

Borrisokane Church
COLIN BOYLE

*Borrisokane Church,* rectangular in shape, with a small gallery, was built in 1812 and, after major restoration work, rededicated in 1993. The east window from nearby Ardcroney Church, (by then closed) was incorporated into the refurbishment. Memorials adorn the church, many dedicated to the prominent local Stoney family.

*Ballingarry Church* in the shadow of Knockshegowna was built in 1856, replacing an older church. Its unusual conical spire is a local landmark. Internally, memorials acknowledge parishioners who lost their lives in both world wars.

*Borrisnafarney Church* was erected in 1825 under the patronage of T. Ryder Pepper Esq. and served the local Loughton estate. Loughton was owned by Lord Bloomfield, whose memorial in the church recalls his career as governor of Jamaica and private secretary to England's prince regent, later George IV. The Bloomfield vault is in the church grounds.

*Templeharry Church* has been in the international limelight in recent years as the church of President Barack Obama's ancestors. The church was built in 1814. Two brass bookrests commemorate Major John R. French, Second Battalion, Leinster Regiment, who was awarded the DSO in 1918. Also noteworthy is the unusual east window, which features St Elizabeth of Hungary.

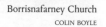

Borrisnafarney Church
COLIN BOYLE

Templeharry Church
JOHN JONES

## ENNIS, KILNASOOLAGH, KILFIERAGH, KILFARBOY (SPANISH POINT), KILFENORA CATHEDRAL

394

This Co. Clare group extends from the Shannon and Limerick city suburbs across the Burren to the Atlantic coast. An area of contrast, it includes monastic Scattery Island and Shannon Airport. There is a monthly service in St Columba's, Ennis aimed particularly at young families. Top organist Nigel Bridge brings an extra dimension to worship. Hospitality at services, not least in festival times, is a key form of witness in the churches of Ennis, Kilnasoolagh and Spanish Point. Cultural events allow use of parish buildings for the wider community and a current parochial project involves exploring the rich local heritage of Celtic Christianity.

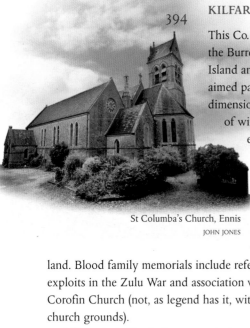

St Columba's Church, Ennis
JOHN JONES

*St Columba's Church, Ennis*, a neo-Gothic Victorian building, was designed in 1871 by Frances Bindon, who had family links with the Bloods, donors of the town-centre land. Blood family memorials include reference to General Sir Bindon, famous for his exploits in the Zulu War and association with Winston Churchill. He is buried in Corofin Church (not, as legend has it, with his horse in a pyramid mausoleum in the church grounds).

*Kilnasoolagh Church.* An ecumenical ceremony to mark 750 years of worship on this ancient site took place in 2006. The present building was constructed in 1815; the spire was destroyed by lightning in November 1991. In their efforts to repair the damage, parishioners experienced the generous support of the neighbouring Roman Catholic congregation. Memorials commemorate key families such as the Inchiquin O'Briens. A large baroque monument depicts Sir Donough O'Brien reclining on a mattress with three cherubs.

St Columba's Church, Ennis
JOHN JONES

*St James's Church, Kilfieragh* has its roots in an ecumenical story. In 1824, a new Roman Catholic church was being built and newspapers hoped that there would soon be a Church of Ireland church for tourists in the seaside town. In 1829, the parish priest offered to subscribe to the building. On a site donated by the marquis of Conyngham, the church opened in 1841. A gallery was later added and the church was often overcrowded. Sadly, today there is only a summer ministry confined to a back chapel.

*Christchurch, Kilfarboy* replaced a nearby Miltown Malbay church, which was destroyed by fire in 1922. It was consecrated in 1927. In 1987, Patrick Hillery, president of Ireland and a native of the area, read a lesson at the diamond jubilee service. Spanish Point is the centre for the holiday chaplaincy serving Clare's coast.

*St Fachan's Cathedral, Kilfenora* has an unusual belfry, prompting one critic to remark that 'it defies every order of architecture'. Built *c.* 1190 of the nave-and-chancel design, the chancel is roofless but the nave in good repair, having been restored by the state in 2004. The cathedral is the burial place of a king of Thomond. The most impressive cross, the 'Doorty Cross', dates to 1152, and the font dates to 1200.

Also of note in this church grouping have been two other churches, *Christ Church, Shannon*, shared with Methodists and Presbyterians but destroyed by fire in 2010, and in Bunratty Folk Park, the rebuilt *Church of Ardcroney* in Borrisokane Group.

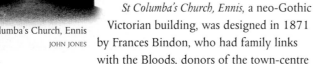

The Doorty Cross

St Fachan's Cathedral, Kilfenora
JOHN JONES

## KILLALOE CATHEDRAL, TUAMGRANEY, MOUNTSHANNON, CASTLECONNELL, KILTENANLEA

Stretching from Lough Derg's Clare shore southwards along the Shannon into Limerick city's hinterland, this grouping breathes history.

In this group of five churches, worship is the first priority, with offices being said regularly and holy days being fully observed. There is also a varied Sunday liturgical life. The parish sees its buildings as resources for the whole community and all are used regularly for concerts, exhibitions and other events. In keeping with this, the parish is pro-active ecumenically and has initiated a variety of interdenominational events.

St Flannan's Cathedral, Killaloe
JOHN JONES

*St Flannan's Cathedral, Killaloe* is dedicated to seventh-century Flannan, a member of the Dalcassian tribe and the O'Brien family. Tradition suggests that his relative Brian Boru built a great church in this area, which is now lost to history. Around 1185, Dónal Mór O'Brien, king of Munster, erected a cathedral at Killaloe, but this too was quickly lost. Historians date the present building, constructed by Dónal Mór's successor Murtagh O'Brien, to between 1194 and 1225. Successive centuries have added their own improvements. The building is of brown and yellow sandstone, cruciform in layout, with a tower. The sanctuary contains an altar presented by the earl of Rosse and made from an oak tree from Birr Castle. Also of interest are a stone inscribed in both runic and ogham (presumably by a Viking upon conversion), a twelfth-century doorway, possibly that of Dónal Mór's lost cathedral, and a twelfth-century crystalline limestone high cross brought from Kilfenora. The cathedral's visitors have included Presidents Éamon de Valera in 1966 and Patrick Hillery in 1985, although the first head of state to pay respects to this hallowed place was Magnus, eleventh-century king of Norway.

Twelfth-century doorway, St Flannan's Cathedral, Killaloe
JOHN JONES

High cross from Kilfenora Cathedral
JOHN JONES

Christmas morning, Killaloe Cathedral
TREVOR WILLIAMS

St Cronan's, Tuamgraney
COLIN BOYLE

JOHN JONES

*St Cronan's, Tuamgraney* is the oldest church in continuous use in the British Isles. It was built in AD 930 and used for worship by Brian Boru. The *Annals of Innisfallen* are attributed to this site, founded by St Cronan in the sixth century. Of interest is the modern beaten-copper cross, made at Glenstal. Part of the church now also serves as an east-Clare heritage centre, opened in 1991 by President Mary Robinson.

*St Caimin's, Mountshannon* has its origins in Lough Derg's monastic island at Iniscealtra, where there has been a Christian presence since AD 520. Built in 1789, a tower was added to the present church in 1831. Owing to its proximity to the Shannon, St Caimin's has attracted many visitors, including, in 1988, the president of Italy.

*All Saints, Castleconnell*, parochially known as Stradbally, was built in 1809 and replaced a medieval church. It was enlarged in 1830. The building acquired international fame in 1988 when a service was held there in celebration of Australia's bicentenary, it being the burial place of Australia's first governor.

*St Senan's, Clonlara*, parochially known as Kiltenanlea, was built in 1782. It was enlarged, with a square tower of locally quarried limestone added in 1830, while the chancel and transepts were erected in 1891, gift of Lady Massy. Within the building, wall tablets commemorate many interesting people, including Royal Navy Lieutenant Lancelot Montgomery, who was associated with HMS *Good Hope*, which sank in the south Pacific in 1914.

St Caimin's, Mountshannon

St Caimin's, Mountshannon

## NENAGH, TEMPLEDERRY, KILLODIERNAN

This north-Tipperary parochial grouping slopes gently westwards from the Silvermines Mountains to the shores of Lough Derg. It serves the county town of Nenagh, the tourist village of Puckane and the picturesque Templederry area.

During the first decade of the twenty-first century, the three churches in the Nenagh union were all completely reroofed, rewired and redecorated. Templederry Church serves a small rural community of about ten families, nearly all involved in farming. Killodiernan Church serves many who live around the southern shores of Lough Derg, comprising retired people, farmers, people in the equine industry and those who commute to Limerick and elsewhere. Many ecumenical services take place in St Mary's. The union has vibrant choirs and music plays an important part in worship.

ST MARY'S CHURCH, NENAGH

Finale of the Children's workshop on Good Friday at St Mary's, Nenagh

It took almost five years to complete *St Mary's Church, Nenagh*. Adorned with spire and gallery, it finally opened its doors in 1860. The local paper's description of its interior when opened is still relevant – the chancel flooring is 'laid of encaustic tiling of very neat pattern'. The *Book of Kells* is the inspiration for the designs of the nine panels on the reredos, the work having been executed by Anne Towers, wife of a former rector.

St Mary's Church, Nenagh
JOHN JONES

COLIN BOYLE

Kilodiernan Church

*Templederry Church* was built in 1828. Its interior is greatly influenced by the local Otway family of Otway Castle. Internally, eight wall memorials and the east window remember the family, and family members are buried in the church vault.

*Killodiernan Church*, built in 1811, is unusual, with its tiny gallery. Because of its proximity to Lough Derg and parochial interest in sailing, the church hosts a regatta service every August.

Kilodiernan Church
JOHN JONES

## ROSCREA, KYLE, BOURNEY, CORBALLY

Straddling the north-Tipperary, Offaly and Laois borders, this group of parishes is home to the source of the Nore and Suir, two of the three 'sister rivers' that act as parochial, county and diocesan borders.

Today the Roscrea Group of Parishes strives to continue the strong monastic values that have undergirded the area for over 1,400 years. It aims to build up excellent ecumenical relations through worship, friendship, and outreach to those in need locally and globally.

*St Cronan's Church, Roscrea* was erected in 1812 on the site of Cronan's seventh-century monastery, where a pocket-gospel manuscript, the *Book of Dimma*, was written. For a short while in the twelfth century, Roscrea held diocesan status and a cathedral was built. When it was demolished, its stones were used to erect parts of the present church. Two ornate World War I memorials, the pulpit and prayer desk, were both carved by William Orpen.

St Cronan's Church, Roscrea
GWNN WALLACE

*Kyle Church* is the burial place of St Molua. Originally built as a chapel of ease for Roscrea, the building also served as a school until 1960.

*Bourney Church*, dedicated to St Burchin, was built in 1780, destroyed by accidental fire in 1942 and reopened in 1945 (minus its gallery). In 1985 and again in 2004 the church was redecorated. It is unique in its simplicity of style.

*Christchurch, Corbally* was originally a mill. In 1829, it was converted into a place of worship and a school was opened in the basement. However, the floor collapsed during Christmas Day worship in 1843 and the entire congregation fell into the basement. Miraculously, there were no casualties, and a major fund-raising programme was launched for renovation work, with Adelaide, dowager queen of England among the subscribers.

Christchurch, Corbally
JOHN JONES

### SHINRONE, KINNITTY, DUNKERRIN, AGHANCON

What have a Young Irelander, a prolific poet, a healer of paralytics and the founder of the Plymouth Brethren all got in common? All had personal links with this south-Offaly parochial valley.

*St Mary's, Shinrone*, erected in 1819, is large and rectangular in shape. The church's amplification system was presented by the Roman Catholic parish of Shinrone in memory of Very Rev. C.B. Champ, rector 1975–86. Among the Christmas decorations is a Christmas tree suspended downwards from the ceiling.

*Kinnity Church* is dedicated to sixth-century St Finian 'the Crooked', who founded a monastery there and who had a reputation for healing paralytics. Located in the porch is a ninth-century grave slab, possibly a memorial to an early abbot. In the church grounds stands a vault where members of the Bernard family are interred, over 30 feet tall and resembling an Egyptian pyramid.

*Dunkerrin Church*, with bell tower built in 1818, was spiritual home to the Rolleston family of Ffranckfort Castle, whose kinsman was T.W. Rolleston, Anglo-Irish poet. A series of stone arches enhances the boundary wall. Erected in 1757, they later provided a seat for Major James Rolleston, who liked to meditate there, clad in light blue socks and knickerbockers.

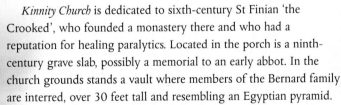

Kinnity Church

St Mary's, Shinrone

JOHN JONES

COLIN BOYLE

*Aghancon Church*, which featured in 1984's *All Things Bright and Beautiful*, was built in 1787 under the guidance of John Darby of Leap Castle. Among the Darby family was Rev. J. Darby, who founded the Plymouth Brethren. Of particular beauty within this church is a series of stained-glass windows that came from neighbouring Ettagh Church, which closed in 1975. A one-time rector of Ettagh was Rev. John Davis, nephew to Young Irelander Thomas Davis.

## THE DIOCESE OF CLONFERT

### BALLINASLOE, AUGHRIM, AHASCRAGH, WOODLAWN, CLONTUSKERT, ARDRAHAN

This east-Galway church grouping in the basin of the River Suck touches Galway Bay. It comprises a major part of Clonfert Diocese and the entire diocese of Kilmacduagh. Serving Ballinasloe, Aughrim, Gort and Loughrea, this church grouping is one of the most extensive in the united dioceses.

Aughrim Union consists of four churches, with parishioners residing in the counties of Roscommon, Tipperary, Galway and Clare – a vast area. The rector has the support of two diocesan and eight parish readers to assist with monthly service. The combined population of the extended parish is about 200 parishioners, 108 families, including 52 children of school age or lower. Ardrahan is a growing congregation at present and a

Holy Trinity Church, Aughrim
JOHN JONES

thriving Sunday school is held during Sunday worship. A healing ministry is very active throughout the union and many parishioners are very much involved in various social activities and organisations.

*St John's Church, Ballinasloe*, like the mythical phoenix, arose from its own ashes. Built in 1818, the church was destroyed by fire in 1899. Over a number of years the stately edifice was fully restored under the guidance of the rector, Dr Philip Graydon Tibbs. The brass lectern was the gift of the earl of Clancarty in 1881. The church tower was chosen as a suitable site for the town clock in 1901.

*Holy Trinity Church, Aughrim* was consecrated on Trinity Sunday, 1819, and its third jubilee in 1969 was marked by a great service of rededication and thanksgiving. Internally, of interest is a stained-glass Huguenot cross, the gift of a former rector, Very Rev. C.B. Champ, to commemorate the role of the Huguenots in the battle of Aughrim.

*St Catherine's Church, Ahascragh*, the most northerly church in the united dioceses, was built in 1813, destroyed by fire in 1922 but rebuilt and reconsecrated in 1926. Large and cruciform, the interior is enhanced by three prominent stone arches. Particularly striking are three large, colourful mosaics erected on the west wall.

*Woodlawn Church* was built in 1874 as a chapel of ease by the second Baron Ashtown, and the influence of the Trench-Ashtown family is evident throughout the church.

*St Matthew's Church, Clontuskert* in the townland of Glan was built in 1818. Its stained-glass east window was erected in 1908, while a memorial tablet remembers Bedela James Cooke, who died in 1917 aged 97.

*Ardrahan Church* in its elevated position, with its landmark tower and clock, was built in 1809. The east window was erected by the fifth Lord Clanmorris as a memorial, while the organ was presented by Bangor Parish in 1887. The church abounds with memorials to the Taylors of Castle Taylor, the Clanmorris family and other local landlord families.

JOHN JONES

Ardrahan Church

## CLONFERT CATHEDRAL, BANAGHER, EYRECOURT, PORTUMNA

The River Shannon separates the east-Galway portion of this parochial unit from its sister church at Banagher in west Offaly, and the power of the mighty river can be seen in the story of the churches.

The congregations of the Clonfert Group of Parishes have in recent times come up with ingenious ways of raising funds, maintaining property and bringing people together. Eyrecourt Parish had a school, which the Galway Library Board converted into a public library. It is now a fine facility for the people of Eyrecourt, and still available for parish use. Portumna Parish has been able to make the church building itself available to local community groups for art exhibitions, musical evenings and craft shows. The Portumna congregation also initiated a novel fund-raising venture when they purchased a flock of sheep. Distributed among the farmers in the congregation, the sheep were then sold, making a profit for the congregation.

Medieval stone carving *c.* 1500

For many years the Heritage Council provided funding that allowed the most vulnerable parts of Clonfert Cathedral to be preserved. With careful conservation, the cathedral should be a centre of worship and spirituality for many centuries to come.

*Clonfert Cathedral* has its origins in the voyage of Brendan the Navigator, who is reputedly buried close

Clonfert Cathedral

to its Hiberno-Romanesque west gable. Built *c.* 1164, various alterations have added to the splendour of the cathedral throughout the centuries. In 1986, the bishop of Limerick and Killaloe undertook a sponsored walk to raise renovation funds. A fifteenth-century mermaid is carved on the south chancel arch. Adjoining the cathedral is an ancient sacristy with a wattle roof. The now-ruined bishop's palace nearby was once the home of Sir Oswald Mosley, founder of British Fascism.

*St Paul's Church, Banagher* was built in 1829 in an English style of architecture with both tower and spire. Its earlier notable parishioners included a governor of Cuba, the novelist Anthony Trollope and Sir William Wilde, father of Oscar Wilde. Located in the churchyard is the tombstone of Rev. A.B. Nicholls, husband to novelist Charlotte Brontë.

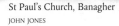

St Paul's Church, Banagher
JOHN JONES

*Eyrecourt Church* was built in 1867 by four members of local families, all called John. Consequently the building was dedicated to St John the Baptist. It is an impressive Victorian Anglo-Gothic building of red brick. Memorials recognise the service of the Eyre family and their military exploits.

*Christ Church, Portumna* was built in 1832 in the Gothic Revival style with a tall, graceful spire. In 1974, part of the spire was destroyed by a winter storm, but restored within two years, the repair work being carried out by Ireland's first woman steeplejack. The site for the church was donated by local landlord the earl of Clanrickard.

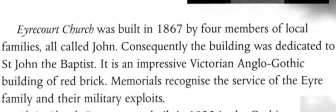

Christ Church, Portumna

Eyrecourt Church

# ACKNOWLEDGEMENTS

'Justice'
Stained glass, St Carthage's Cathedral,
Lismore
Studio of Morris & Co.
KEN HEMMINGWAY

Teamwork is the means by which different people can work collectively to produce uncommon results. This book is a fine example and a large number of people have worked most effectively to ensure the quality of its production.

We are indebted to those who have provided individual contributions to the text and enabled this publication to speak so eloquently about the Church of Ireland:

We are truly grateful to our main photographers, Colin Boyle, Canon David Crooks, Shay Doyle, Dermott Dunbar, Rev. Gordon Gray, Ken Hemmingway, Chris Hill (Scenic Ireland), Very Rev. John Jones, Dr David Lawrence and Alastair Smeaton.

We also express our thanks for visual contributions from: Michael Burke, Jarlath Canney, Lesley-Anne Carey, Jonathan Cherry, Aonghus Dwane, Keith Drury, Ian Elliott, Lady Farnham, Paul Harron, Alf Harvey, Jessica Priddy, John Johnston, Herbert Knowles, Lucy McGonigle, Gary McMurray, Annette McGrath, Gary McMurray, Janet Maxwell, Right Rev. Harold Miller, Aisling O'Callaghan, Michael O'Neill, Miruna Popescu, Helen Roseveare, David Scott, Herbie Sharman, Alan Synnott, Dolly Temple, Gwen Wallace, Richard Watson, Trevor Williams.

A word of thanks goes to Geoffrey Kelly (Diocese of Derry & Raphoe), Glenn Moore (Diocese of Clogher), Annette McGrath (Diocese of Down & Dromore), Karen Bushby (Diocese of Connor), Maud Cunningham (Diocese of Kilmore), Heather Sherlock (Diocese of Tuam), Sylvia Heggie (Diocese of Dublin), Archdeacon Raymond Hoey (Diocese of Armagh), Paul Gilmore (St Anne's Cathedral, Belfast), Karen Seaman & Alison Jones (Diocese of Meath), Herbie Sharman (Diocese of Cashel) and Archdeacon Robin Bantry-White (Diocese of Cork), for their help in gathering information and promoting the book in their respective dioceses. Further thanks go to Michael O'Neill for his work on the cathedral histories, Tony Merrick, Tom Duncan and to Anthony Malcomson for access to his collection of prints and paintings.

Finally, *The Church of Ireland, An Illustrated History* could not have been prepared and published without the practical support of the Representative Church Body represented by their Archivist, Dr Raymond Refaussé, Janet Maxwell, Head of Communications of the Church of Ireland, and Dr Paul Harron, Press Officer of the Church of Ireland. A special word of thanks to Professor Brian Walker, for his editorial and pictorial contribution, invaluable advice and encouragement.

A wide range of sources has been consulted in the research for this book. The following were of special importance. Samuel Lewis, *A topographical dictionary of Ireland*, 2 vols (London, S. Lewis, 1837). *Dictionary of Irish biography*, 9 vols (Cambridge, Cambridge University Press, 2009). Alan Acheson, *A history of the Church of Ireland* (Dublin, Columba Press, 1997). The Ulster Historical Foundation series of lists of clergy of the Church of Ireland (Belfast, Ulster Historical Foundation, 1993–present).

Published by Booklink
www.booklink.ie
Publishing trademark of Cadolux Ltd
Publisher: Dr Claude Costecalde
Picture editor: Wendy Dunbar
Editor: Alicia McAuley
Proof reader: Michael Faulkner
Designed by Wendy Dunbar

ISBN 978-1-906886-56-1
Printed in Slovenia